THE SIMMS LETTERS

WILLIAM GILMORE SIMMS
"This portrait was painted in 1844, when I was 38 years old, by William West, the
American (Kentucky) painter — an artist of great merit."
(From the original painting in the possession of Mary C. Simms Oliphant)

The Letters
of
William Gilmore Simms

Collected and Edited

by

MARY C. SIMMS OLIPHANT
ALFRED TAYLOR ODELL
T. C. DUNCAN EAVES

Introduction by DONALD DAVIDSON

Biographical Sketch by ALEXANDER S. SALLEY

VIDEO VOLANS

In five volumes

VOLUME II—1845–1849

Edited by

MARY C. SIMMS OLIPHANT
T. C. DUNCAN EAVES

UNIVERSITY OF SOUTH CAROLINA PRESS
COLUMBIA
1953

PREFACE

Following the death of Dr. Alfred Taylor Odell the previous year, in 1949 we became co-editors of the letters of William Gilmore Simms. Dr. Odell, who with Mary C. Simms Oliphant, one of the present editors, originated the project in 1937, died while the first volume was in process of being made ready for publication. He thus did not live to see the fruition of his work on the project or to carry on the editing of Simms' letters, of which all but about two hundred of some fifteen hundred included in this edition had been collected at the time of his death. We completed the first volume and saw it through the press, and have edited this volume and undertaken the editing of those to follow.

The original plan for the publication of Simms' letters provided for the inclusion of all of his personal letters which could be located by the editors, and also of the various series of public letters written by him as correspondent or editor of newspapers— such as the series addressed to the *City Gazette* (Charleston) in 1831. This plan, which was carried out in Volume I, had to be modified. So many previously unlocated personal letters were discovered through a new and extensive survey made in 1950 of college, university, public, and private libraries that there is not sufficient space for the inclusion of the public letters in the four remaining volumes planned by the University of South Carolina Press. With regret, we have been compelled to omit them, though we have indicated their existence in footnotes and drawn upon them freely for the valuable information they supply about Simms and his times. The letters appearing in this and the following volumes are, therefore, with several obvious exceptions, Simms' personal letters, of which only a few have ever before been published.

Except as indicated below, the texts of Simms' letters are printed verbatim—misspellings, variations in spelling, and faulty punctuation being retained. We have, however, silently omitted Simms' repetitions of words when he turned from one page to another. Occasionally we have substituted a word Simms obviously meant to write for one erroneously written, though in these cases the original word is given in a footnote. Whenever possible we have supplied conjectural readings of mutilated letters as well as Simms' inadvertent omissions of words necessary to the sense; such conjectural readings are enclosed in brackets. Lack of space has made it impossible for us to indicate in footnotes unimportant words struck through by Simms when he changed his mind as to how he would express his thoughts.

In annotating Simms' letters our aim has been not only to throw light on the matter of the letters themselves, but also to illuminate the events in Simms' life and career not revealed in his surviving letters, and to show through quotations from letters of his contemporaries and through reviews of his works what opinions were held during his lifetime of the man and of the writer. We have drawn upon Simms' surviving literary estate, under seal in the South Caroliniana Library—scrapbooks, published and unpublished manuscripts, notebooks, and miscellaneous material. We have collected photostats or microfilms of all letters written to Simms which have been accessible to us and have used them when they supply information about Simms or are germane to his letters. We have examined almost all American and many British and Continental periodicals published during the period. All essays, reviews, tales, and poems published therein which can be identified conclusively as Simms' have been noted or listed in footnotes to appropriate passages of the letters. Most of the reviews of Simms' publications and articles or comments about him found in these periodicals have likewise been referred to and frequently quoted in part. In addition, the files of all extant Charleston, South Carolina, newspapers and parts of the files of many other newspapers, both Southern and Northern, have been similarly examined and quoted from or referred to in footnotes. Since Simms' contributions to newspapers were extensive and rarely signed, we have not attempted the impossible task of identifying and listing all of them, but instead have contented ourselves with noting those he specifically mentions in letters and those which we consider important for the study of Simms. In the process of this work we have identified a large number of Simms' pseudonyms, and have thus been able to put on record a considerable body of Simms material invaluable in any later biographical appraisal. Our effort has been to make Simms' letters themselves, with their annotations, portray Simms' life and career so completely that he becomes, in a sense, his own biographer as well as a clear commentator on the American literary, social, economic, and political scenes of his day.

Certain editorial devices have been adopted to make the contents of the letters clearer to the general reader and more useful to the scholar. Identifications and explanations necessary for each individual letter are made in footnotes in the customary manner. When fuller information on related matters is found elsewhere in the letters, cross-references are made to those letters, by date. When the information is in another note, reference is made both by the number of the note and the date of the letter where the note appears. A reference to "introductory sketch" is to one of the short biographies included in "Simms' Circle" or "The Family Circle," pages xc-cl of Volume I. The reader may also be led to these biographies and to the shorter footnote sketches of people less important to Simms by consulting the index of this and succeeding volumes. In the index the parenthetical page reference immediately following a person's name indicates the pages in the *Letters* where the most complete identification of that person can be found.

Certain apparent inconsistencies of style in footnoting are intentional. A "see" reference enclosed by parentheses indicates that the reference deals *only* with the matter immediately preceding the parentheses—perhaps only the name of a person, perhaps the contents of an entire sentence. A "see" reference which stands alone as an independent sentence indicates that the reference deals with *all* the preceding information of the footnote. In making reference to published books, in order to make as clear as possible the particular imprint concerned, we have given bibliographical data exactly as they appear on the title pages. Thus, in one footnote, "Carey and Hart" and "Carey & Hart" may be given. The inconsistency is that of the publisher, not that of the editors of Simms' letters.

Again we want to express our appreciation for the aid and encouragement we have received from the University of South Carolina, the University of Arkansas, Furman University, the University South Caroliniana Society, the South Caroliniana Library, and the University of South Carolina Press, as well as for the help from our friends and relatives who are mentioned with deep appreciation in the preface to the first volume of this work, all of whom continue to assist us wholeheartedly. Especially must we express our gratitude to Mr. Alexander S. Salley, State Historian Emeritus of South Carolina, who continues to serve as a court of appeal on complex historical problems; to Professor Hyder Edward Rollins, of Harvard University, who has been our adviser in the planning and in the editorial technique of these volumes and who also graciously continues to help us illuminate obscure passages in Simms' letters; and to Mrs. Edwin O'Kelly, of the University of Arkansas, who aids us in the enormous tasks of deciphering Simms' handwriting and of preparing the manuscript for the press. A considerable number of additional friends have also come to our aid on specific problems in the annotation of Simms' letters. Of these we must particularly thank Mrs. John S. Reynolds, of Columbia, South Carolina; Mrs. Lilla M. Hawes, Director of the Georgia Historical Society; Miss Geraldine Beard, of the New-York Historical Society Library; Mr. Dan Manville Hartley, of Barnwell, South Carolina; Professor Ben Drew Kimpel, of the University of Arkansas; Professor Thomas Mabry Cranfill, of the University of Texas; Mr. John C. Guilds, of Duke University; Miss Martha Venable Davis, of Greenville, South Carolina; Mr. James Henry Hammond, of Columbia, South Carolina; Miss Alice Benson Adams, of Furman University Library; Professors Granville T. Pryor and Allen Morris, of The Citadel; Mr. Marvin A. Miller, Director of Libraries at the University of Arkansas, and Mr. Joseph C. Borden, Miss Delia Mattison, Miss Georgia H. Clark, and Miss Rhoda Burgess, of his staff; Mr. Henry M. Fuller, Reference Librarian of the Yale University Library; Miss Emma Swift, of the Rochester Public Library; Mrs. Marie B. Owen, Director of the Department of Archives and History, State of Alabama; Mr. William T. O'Rourke, Librarian of the Buffalo Public Library; Miss Beatrice Henderson, Reference Librarian of the Syracuse University Library; Miss Mary C. Brown, of the Norfolk Public Library; Miss Elizabeth C. Litsinger, of the Enoch Pratt Free Library; Miss Irene Hester, of the Greensboro Public Library; Miss Virginia Rugheimer, Director of the Charleston Library Society, and Miss Emma Bull, of her staff; Judge Henry C. Hammond, of Augusta, Georgia; Miss Leslie Witherspoon, of York, South Carolina; Miss Vera Schulmeister, Reference Librarian of the Louisiana State University Library; Miss Sarah D. Jones, Reference Librarian of the University of Pennsylvania Library; and Mr. Milton C. Russell, of the Virginia State Library.

Mary C. Simms Oliphant
T. C. Duncan Eaves

August 22, 1952

CONTENTS

PAGE

ILLUSTRATIONS

DEPOSITORIES OR OWNERS OF MANUSCRIPTS

AAH	Alabama State Department of Archives and History
ASS	Alexander S. Salley, Columbia, South Carolina
BPL	Boston Public Library
BU	Brown University
CWB	Clifton Waller Barrett, New York City
ClC	Clemson College
D	Duke University
HEH	Henry E. Huntington Library
HKH	Helen Kohn Hennig, Columbia, South Carolina
LC:GFH	Correspondence of George Frederick Holmes, Library of Congress
LC:H	The Papers of James H. Hammond, Library of Congress
LC:S	William Gilmore Simms Collection, Library of Congress
LC:Sc	The Papers of Henry R. Schoolcraft, Library of Congress
MHS	Massachusetts Historical Society
NCU	University of North Carolina
NCU:EG	Elliott-Gonzales Papers, Southern Historical Collection, University of North Carolina
NCU:M	William Porcher Miles Papers, Southern Historical Collection, University of North Carolina
NYHS	New-York Historical Society
NYPL:B	Berg Collection, New York Public Library
NYPL:BG	Bryant-Godwin Collection, New York Public Library
NYPL:D	Duyckinck Collection, New York Public Library
NYPL:GR	Goddard-Roslyn Collection (Microfilm), New York Public Library
NYPL:S	William Gilmore Simms Collection, New York Public Library
PHS	Historical Society of Pennsylvania
PI	Peabody Institute
SCL	South Caroliniana Library, University of South Carolina
W:T	Tucker Papers, Colonial Williamsburg
Y	Yale University

LIST OF LETTERS

In the following list of letters for this volume of the letters of William Gilmore Simms the address as Simms wrote it follows the name of the addressee. Under the name of the addressee is the postmark, followed by the price of sending the letter. If no address is given, the cover has not survived; if no postmark is given, the cover lacks one. Depositories or owners of the manuscripts of Simms' letters are indicated in the last column. If we have not located the original of a letter, that space is left blank and the source of our text is given in a footnote to that letter.

1845

No.	Date	Addressee	Owner or Depository
225.	January 1	ARMISTEAD BURT	D
226.	January 6	JAMES LAWSON | New York *Postmark:* Washington City D. C. | Jan 14 | I E Holmes MC	SCL
227.	January 15	JAMES LAWSON | New-York *Postmark:* Free A Burt	SCL
228.	January 18	GEORGE FREDERICK HOLMES | Orangeburg | S. C. *Postmark:* Midway S C | Jay 20 | 10	LC:S
229.	January 19	EVERT AUGUSTUS DUYCKINCK | New York— | Care of | H. G. Langley Esq. | Publisher— *Postmark:* Free A. Burt	NYPL:D
230. *c.*	January 19	JAMES LAWSON | New-York— *Postmark:* Midway S C | Jay 20 | 25	SCL
231.	January 26	ARMISTEAD BURT | Washington | D. C. *Postmark:* Midway S C | Jany 27	D
232.	February 11	JAMES LAWSON | New York.	SCL
233.	February 11	EVERT AUGUSTUS DUYCKINCK | New York *Postmark:* Washington City D. C. | Feb 17 | Free A. Burt	NYPL:D
234.	February 12	JAMES MUNROE AND COMPANY | (Publishers) | Boston | Mass. *Postmark:* Washington City D. C. | Feb 19 | Free A. Burt	NYHS
235.	February 12	D. APPLETON AND COMPANY | (Publishers) | New York *Postmark:* Washington City D. C. | Feb 19 | Free A. Burt	D

No.	Date	Addressee	Owner or Depository
252.	May 20	JAMES HENRY HAMMOND | Silverton, | So. Carolina *Postmark:* Midway S C | May 21 | 10	LC:H
253.	June 6	EVERT AUGUSTUS DUYCKINCK | (Care of H. G. Langley,) | Publisher, Astor House) | New York | Politeness | Mr. Head.	NYPL:D
254.	June 7	JAMES LAWSON | New York | Politeness | Mr. Head	SCL
255.	June 8	EVERT AUGUSTUS DUYCKINCK | (Care of H. G. Langley) | New York. | Politeness | Mr. Head.	NYPL:D
256.	June 16	EDWIN DeLEON	HKH
257.	June 16	JAMES LAWSON | New York. | Politeness | Mr Allen.	SCL
258.	June 17	GILBERT ALLEN?	ASS
259. c.	June 18	JAMES HENRY HAMMOND | Silverton, | So Carolina	LC:H
260.	June 25	EVERT AUGUSTUS DUYCKINCK | (Care of Wiley & Putnam) | New York. *Postmark:* Charleston S. C. | Jun 26 | 25	NYPL:D
261.	June 27	JAMES LAWSON | New York. *Postmark:* Charleston S. C. | Jun 28 | 25	SCL
262.	July 2	JAMES LAWSON | New York. *Postmark:* Charleston S. C. | Jul 2 | 10	SCL
263.	July 5	JAMES LAWSON | New York. | By Miss Simms	SCL
264.	July 10	JAMES HENRY HAMMOND | Silverton, | South Carolina *Postmark:* Charleston S. C. | Jul 11 | 5	LC:H
265.	July 15	EVERT AUGUSTUS DUYCKINCK	NYPL:D
266. c.	July 20	JAMES LAWSON | New York *Postmark:* Charleston S. C. | Jul 21 | 20	SCL
267. c.	July 31	EVERT AUGUSTUS DUYCKINCK | New York *Postmark:* Charleston S. C. | Aug 1 | 10	NYPL:D
268.	August 5	JAMES LAWSON | New York *Postmark:* Charleston S. C. | Aug 5 | 20	SCL
269.	August 7	EVERT AUGUSTUS DUYCKINCK | New York *Postmark:* Charleston S. C. | Aug 7 | 10	NYPL:D
270.	August 8	EVERT AUGUSTUS DUYCKINCK | New York *Postmark:* Charleston S. C. | Aug 8 | 10	NYPL:D
271.	August 11	JAMES LAWSON | New York *Postmark:* Charleston S. C. | Aug 11 | 10	SCL
272.	August 15	EDWIN DeLEON	HKH

No.	Date	Addressee	Owner or Depository
311.	June 29	EVERT AUGUSTUS DUYCKINCK | New York.	NYPL:D
		Postmark: U. S. City Despatch Post | Jun 29 | 4 Oclock | U. S. City Despatch Post | Jun 30 | 9 Oclock	
312.	July 2	EVERT AUGUSTUS DUYCKINCK | 20 Clinton Place | New York	NYPL:D
		Postmark: 6 P M | 5	
313.	July 8	JAMES MUNROE AND COMPANY	BPL
314.	July	MARGARET FULLER | Brooklyn, | N. Y.	NYPL:B
315.	July 20	ALFRED BILLINGS STREET | Albany, | N. Y.	SCL
		Postmark: New-York | 22 Jul | 5 cts	
316.	July 30	EDGAR ALLAN POE	BPL
317.	July 31	ALFRED BILLINGS STREET | Albany, | N. Y.	SCL
		Postmark: New-York | 1 Aug | 5 cts	
318.	August 8	JAMES LAWSON	SCL
319.	August 9	EVERT AUGUSTUS DUYCKINCK | (Care of Wiley & Putnam | Publishers) | New York.	NYPL:D
		Postmark: Charleston S. C. | Aug 8 | 10	
320. *c.*	August 22	JAMES LAWSON | New York	SCL
		Postmark: Charleston S. C. | Aug 23 | 10	
321.	August 26	ALFRED BILLINGS STREET | Albany, | N. Y.	D
		Postmark: Charleston S. C. | Aug 27 | 10	
322.	September 14	JAMES LAWSON | New York.	SCL
		Postmark: Charleston S. C. | Sep 14 | 10	
323.	September 14	EVERT AUGUSTUS DUYCKINCK | New York	NYPL:D
		Postmark: Charleston S. C. | Sep 14 | 10	
324.	September 22	JAMES LAWSON | New York	SCL
		Postmark: Charleston S. C. | Sep 23 | 10	
325.	October 1	JAMES LAWSON | New-York	SCL
		Postmark: Charleston S. C. | Oct 2 | 10	
326. *c.*	October 1	EVERT AUGUSTUS DUYCKINCK | New York City	NYPL:D
		Postmark: Charleston S. C. | Oct 2 | 10	
327.	October 9	JAMES LAWSON | New York	SCL
		Postmark: Charleston S. C. | Oct 11 | 10	
328.	October 15	JOHN BEVERLY CHRISTIAN | Rector Board Visitors | William & Mary's College | Williamsburg | Va.	LC:GFH
		Postmark: Charleston S. C. | Oct 16 | 10	

No.	Date	Addressee	Owner or Depository
329.	October 19	BENJAMIN FRANKLIN PERRY | Greenville, | So Carolina. *Postmark:* Charleston S. C. | Oct 20 | 5	AAH
330.	October 21	RUFUS WILMOT GRISWOLD	BPL
331.	October 23	JAMES LAWSON | New York *Postmark:* Charleston S. C. | Oct 24 | 10	SCL
332.	October 24	EVERT AUGUSTUS DUYCKINCK | New York *Postmark:* Charleston S. C. | Oct 24 | 10	NYPL:D
333.	October 30	BENJAMIN FRANKLIN PERRY | Greenville C. H. | South Carolina *Postmark:* Midway S C | Nov 2 | Undercgd | 5 5/10	AAH
334. *c.*November 3		EVERT AUGUSTUS DUYCKINCK | New-York *Postmark:* Midway S C | Nov 4 | 20	NYPL:D
335. *c.*November 6		JAMES LAWSON	SCL
336.	November 17	JAMES HENRY HAMMOND | Silverton, | So. Caro. *Postmark:* Midway S C | Nov 19 | 10	LC:H
337. *c.*November 19		JAMES HENRY HAMMOND	LC:H
338.	November 19	JAMES LAWSON	SCL
339.	November 21	JAMES LAWSON	SCL
340.	November 24	JAMES HENRY HAMMOND | Silverton, | Barnwell Dist. | South Carolina *Postmark:* Columbia S. C. | Nov 24 | 10	LC:H
341.	November 27	JAMES HENRY HAMMOND	LC:H
342.	December 3	JAMES HENRY HAMMOND | Silverton, | S. Carolina *Postmark:* Charleston S. C. | Dec 3 | 5	LC:H
343.	December 6	RUFUS WILMOT GRISWOLD	CWB
344.	December 10	EVERT AUGUSTUS DUYCKINCK	NYPL:D
345.	December 11	JAMES HENRY HAMMOND	LC:H
346.	December 12	JAMES LAWSON	SCL
347.	December 18	JAMES HENRY HAMMOND	LC:H
348.	December 21	RUFUS WILMOT GRISWOLD	BPL
349.	Christmas Day	JAMES HENRY HAMMOND | Silverton, | So. Carolina. *Postmark:* Midway S. C. | Dec 26 | 10	LC:H

1847

No.	Date	Addressee	Owner or Depository
350.	January 2	JAMES LAWSON	SCL
351.	January 2	JAMES HENRY HAMMOND | Silverton | S. C. *Postmark:* Midway | Jan 3 | 5	LC:H
352.	January 7	JAMES HENRY HAMMOND	LC:H

No.	Date	Addressee	Owner or Depository
353.	January 15	ALFRED BILLINGS STREET | Albany | N. Y. *Postmark:* Midway S C | Jany 16 | 10	D
354.	January 25	JAMES HENRY HAMMOND | Silverton, | So. Carolina. *Postmark:* Midway S C | Jan 26 | 5	LC:H
355.	January 26	JAMES LAWSON | New York. *Postmark:* Midway S C | Jay 26 | 10	SCL
356.	February 2	EVERT AUGUSTUS DUYCKINCK	NYPL:D
357.	February 10	JOHN CALDWELL CALHOUN | (Senate U. S.) | Washington | D. C. *Postmark:* Midway S C | feby 12	ClC
358.	February 15	JAMES LAWSON	SCL
359. *c.*	February 20	JAMES LAWSON | New York *Postmark:* Midway S C | Feby 21 [?] | 10	SCL
360.	February 25	EVERT AUGUSTUS DUYCKINCK | New York *Postmark:* Midway S C | Mch 1 | 10	NYPL:D
361.	March 2	JAMES LAWSON | New York *Postmark:* Midway S C | Mrch 5 | 10	SCL
362.	March 2	JAMES HENRY HAMMOND | Silverton, | So Caro *Postmark:* Midway S C | Mrch 5 | 10	LC:H
363.	March 4	JAMES LAWSON | New York. | Politeness of— | Mr. T Addison Richards.	SCL
364.	March 10	BENJAMIN FRANKLIN PERRY | Greenville | Co. House, | S. C. *Postmark:* Midway | Mch 11 | 5	AAH
365.	March 18	GEORGE FREDERICK HOLMES | (Richmond College) | Richmond | Va. *Postmark:* Midway S. C | Mrch 20 | 10	LC:S
366.	March 25	EVERT AUGUSTUS DUYCKINCK | New York *Postmark:* Midway S C | Mch 26 | 10	NYPL:D
367.	March 29	JAMES HENRY HAMMOND | Silverton, | So. Caro. *Postmark:* Midway S C | Mch 30 | 10	LC:H
368.	April 2	JAMES HENRY HAMMOND | Silverton | S. C. *Postmark:* Midway S C | Apl 5 | 5	LC:H
369. *c.*	April 4	JAMES HENRY HAMMOND	LC:H
370.	April 19	JAMES LAWSON | New York *Postmark:* Midway S C | Apl 20 | 10	SCL
371. *c.*	April 20	JAMES LAWSON | New York. *Postmark:* Midway S C | Apl 21 | 20	SCL
372. *c.*	April 22	JAMES LAWSON | New-York. *Postmark:* Midway S C | Apl 23 | 30	SCL

No.	Date	Addressee	Owner or Depository
398.	August 5	CAREY AND HART	CWB
399.	August 9	CAREY AND HART	NYPL:B
400.	August 21	JAMES HENRY HAMMOND | (of South Carolina) | New York	LC:H
		Postmark: Spartanburg C H S. C. | Aug 24 | 10	
401.	September 5	JAMES LAWSON | (56 Merchants Exchange) | New York	SCL
		Postmark: Spartanburg C H S. C. | Sep 7 | 10	
402.	September 6	JAMES LAWSON | Merchants Exchange | New York	SCL
		Postmark: Spartanburg C H S. C. | Sep 7 | 10	
403. *c.*September 6		CAREY AND HART | (Publishers) | Philadelphia	NYHS
		Postmark: Spartanburg C H S. C. | Sep 7 | 10	
404.	September 23	JAMES LAWSON | New-York	SCL
		Postmark: Spartanburg C H S C | Sep 23 | 10	
405.	October 19	ROBERT TAYLOR CONRAD | (Graham's Mage) | Philadelphia	NYPL:S
		Postmark: Charleston S. C. | Oct 19 | 30	
406.	October 20	JAMES HENRY HAMMOND	LC:H
407.	October 20	JAMES LAWSON | New York.	SCL
		Postmark: Charleston S. C. | Oct 22 | 10	
408.	October 26	JAMES LAWSON	SCL
409.	October 26	CAREY AND HART | Philadelphia	MHS
		Postmark: Charleston S. C. | Oct 27 | 10	
410.	November 3	JAMES LAWSON | (Insurance Broker) | New York	SCL
		Postmark: Midway S C | Nov 5 | 10	
411.	November 7	JAMES HENRY HAMMOND | Silverton, | So. Carolina	LC:H
		Postmark: Midway S C | Nov 8 | 5	
412.	Nov. 16 or 17	JAMES LAWSON | New-York.	SCL
		Postmark: Midway | 18 Nov 1847 | 10	
413.	November 22	JAMES HENRY HAMMOND | Silverton, | So. Carolina	LC:H
		Postmark: Midway S C | Nov 24 | 5	
414. *c.*November 30		JAMES LAWSON | New York	SCL
		Postmark: Midway S C | Dem 1st | 10	
415.	November 30	JAMES HENRY HAMMOND	LC:H
416.	December 13	CAREY AND HART	Y
417.	December 14	CAREY AND HART | (Publishers) | Philadelphia	NYHS
		Postmark: Midway S C | Dec 16 | 10	
418.	December 24	JAMES HENRY HAMMOND | Silverton | South Carolina	LC:H
		Postmark: Midway S C | Dec 27 | 5	

1848

No.	Date	Addressee	Owner or Depository
419. c.	January 2	JAMES HENRY HAMMOND	LC:H
420.	January 7	JAMES LAWSON | New York	SCL
		Postmark: Midway S C | Jay 11 | 10	
421.	February 11	EVERT AUGUSTUS DUYCKINCK | New-York	NYPL:D
		Postmark: Midway S C | feby 14 | 10	
422.	February 12	JAMES HENRY HAMMOND | Silverton, | S. C.	LC:H
		Postmark: Midway S C | feby 14 | 5	
423.	February 19	JAMES LAWSON | New York.	SCL
		Postmark: Midway S C | feby 20 | 10	
424.	March 23	JAMES LAWSON | New York.	SCL
		Postmark: Midway S C | Mch 29 | 10	
425.	April 15	JAMES LAWSON	SCL
426.	April 30	JAMES LAWSON	SCL
427.	May 20	JAMES HENRY HAMMOND	LC:H
428.	June 14	JAMES LAWSON | New York	SCL
		Postmark: Charleston S C | Jun 14 | 10	
429.	June 15	JAMES HENRY HAMMOND | Silverton, P. O. | South Carolina	LC:H
		Postmark: Charleston S C | Jun 14 | 5	
430.	July 1	CAREY AND HART	NYHS
431.	July 12	JAMES LAWSON	SCL
432.	July?	CAROLINE GILMAN	NYPL:B
433.	July 20	CAREY AND HART | (Publishers) | Philadelphia	NYHS
		Postmark: Charleston S. C. | Jul 21 | 10	
434.	July 20	JAMES HENRY HAMMOND	LC:H
435.	July 29	JAMES HENRY HAMMOND	LC:H
436.	August 2	JAMES LAWSON	SCL
437.	August 7	JAMES LAWSON | New York	SCL
		Postmark: Charleston S. C. | Aug 7 | 10	
438.	August 10	JAMES HENRY HAMMOND	LC:H
439.	August 22	WILLIAM CULLEN BRYANT	NYPL:BG
440.	August 22	EVERT AUGUSTUS DUYCKINCK | New York | Favored by | Master Robt. Boggs.	NYPL:D
441.	August 27	JAMES LAWSON | (82 Wall Street) | New York	SCL
		Postmark: Charleston S. C. | Aug 29 | 20	
442.	August 29	JAMES HENRY HAMMOND	LC:H
443.	September 12	JAMES LAWSON	SCL
444.	September 14	JAMES HENRY HAMMOND	LC:H
445.	October 17	JAMES LAWSON | (136 Twelfth Street) | New York	SCL
		Postmark: Charleston S. C. | Oct 17 | 10	

No.	Date	Addressee	Owner or Depository
473.	March 7	WILLIAM ELLIOTT | Beaufort | Charleston | So Carolina | Care of J. H. Ladron & Co *Postmark:* Paid	NCU :EG
474.	March 15	GEORGE FREDERICK HOLMES | (Presidt. University Mississippi | Oxford | Mi. | Ford | Wythe Court House | Wythe Coy | Sweet Springs | Virga. *Postmark:* Midway S C | Mch 17 | Oxford Mi. | Mar 27 | Wytheville Va. | May 10 | 5 10/15	LC :S
475.	March 15	NATHANIEL BEVERLEY TUCKER | Williamsburg, | Virginia *Postmark:* Charleston S. C. | Mar 23 [?] | 10	W :T
476.	March 17	JOHN PENDLETON KENNEDY	PI
477.	April 5	NATHANIEL BEVERLEY TUCKER | Williamsburg, | Va. *Postmark:* Midway S C | Apr 8 | 10	W :T
478.	April 12	CAREY AND HART | (Publishers) | Philadelphia *Postmark:* Midway S C | Apl 19 | 10	NYHS
479.	April 23	MARCUS CLAUDIUS MARCELLUS HAMMOND	SCL
480.	April 23	NATHANIEL BEVERLEY TUCKER | Williamsburg, | (Va.)	W :T
481.	April 27	BENJAMIN FRANKLIN PERRY | Greenville C. H. | S. C. *Postmark:* Midway S C | May 1 | 5	AAH
482.	May 5	WILLIAM CULLEN BRYANT | New York. *Postmark:* Midway S C | May 7 | 10	NYPL :GR
483.	May 6	NATHANIEL BEVERLEY TUCKER | Williamsburg, | Va. *Postmark:* Midway S C | May 7 | 10	W :T
484. *c.*	May 6	JAMES LAWSON | New-York. *Postmark:* Midway S C | My 7 | 10	SCL
485.	May 8	LEWIS REEVE GIBBES | Charleston, | S. C.	SCL
486.	May 9	CHARLES L. WHELER	
487.	May 9	WILLIAM BROWN HODGSON | 19 Brevoort Place | New York *Postmark:* Midway S C | My 11 | 10	NYHS
488.	May 13	NATHANIEL BEVERLEY TUCKER	W :T
489.	May 29	NATHANIEL BEVERLEY TUCKER | Williamsburg, | Va. *Postmark:* Charleston S. C. | May 29 | 10	W :T
490.	June 1	NATHANIEL BEVERLEY TUCKER | Williamsburg, | Va. *Postmark:* Charleston S. C. | Jun 3 | 10	W :T

No.	Date	Addressee	Owner or Depository
491.	June	MARCUS CLAUDIUS MARCELLUS HAMMOND	SCL
492.	July?	ROBERT WILSON GIBBES	NYPL:S
493.	July 3	JAMES LAWSON	SCL
494. *c.*	July 9	JOSEPH LEMUEL CHESTER	BU
495.	July 13	NATHANIEL BEVERLEY TUCKER | Williamsburg, | Va. *Postmark:* Charleston S. C. | Jul 15 | 10	W:T
496.	July 14	WILLIAM PORCHER MILES	NCU:M
497.	July 14	NATHANIEL BEVERLEY TUCKER | Williamsburg, | Va. *Postmark:* Charleston S. C. | Jul 16 | 10	W:T
498.	July 27	NATHANIEL BEVERLEY TUCKER | Williamsburg | Va. *Postmark:* Charleston S. C. | Jul 27 | 10 | Paid	W:T
499.	July 31	JAMES HENRY HAMMOND	LC:H
500.	August 16	NATHANIEL BEVERLEY TUCKER | Williamsburg, | Va. *Postmark:* Charleston S. C. | Aug 17 | 10| Paid	W:T
501.	September 3	EVERT AUGUSTUS DUYCKINCK | (Literary World) | New York | Favored by | Mr. J. Russell	NYPL:D
502.	September 5	JAMES HENRY HAMMOND	LC:H
503.	September 5	JAMES LAWSON	SCL
504.	September 5	MARCUS CLAUDIUS MARCELLUS HAMMOND	SCL
505.	September 6	WILLIAM GOWANS | (Publisher) | 178 Fulton Street | New York *Postmark:* Charleston S. C. | Sep 6 | 10	CWB
506.	September 6	NATHANIEL BEVERLEY TUCKER | Warrenton Springs | Virginia | Should Mr. Tucker have left | Warrenton Springs, the P. M. | is requested to forward this | letter to his address at | [Williams] burg, Va. | for'd | Charlottesville | Williamsburg *Postmark:* Charleston S. C. | Sep 6 | Charlottesville Va. | Sep 28	W:T
507.	September 19	EVERT AUGUSTUS DUYCKINCK	NYPL:D
508.	September 27	EVERT AUGUSTUS DUYCKINCK	NYPL:D
509.	October 15	SARAH JOSEPHA BUELL HALE	HEH
510.	October 17	JAMES HENRY HAMMOND	LC:H
511. *c.*	November 1	MARCUS CLAUDIUS MARCELLUS HAMMOND	D
512.	November 2	JOHN PENDLETON KENNEDY	PI
513.	November 24	JAMES LAWSON	SCL
514.	November 28	FRANCIS PEYRE PORCHER	CIC

ABBREVIATIONS AND SHORT TITLES

American [Whig] Review
　American Review: A Whig Journal of Politics, Literature, Art and Science (1845-1847) ; *American Review: A Whig Journal, Devoted to Politics and Literature* (1848—April, 1950)

Dem. Rev.
　United States Magazine, and Democratic Review

Godey's
　Godey's Magazine and Lady's Book (1844-1848) ; *Godey's Lady's Book* (1848-1850)

Graham's
　Graham's American Monthly Magazine of Literature and Art

Knick.
　Knickerbocker, or New-York Monthly Magazine

S. L. J.
　Southern Literary Journal and Monthly Magazine

S. L. M.
　Southern Literary Messenger: Devoted to Every Department of Literature and the Fine Arts (1844-1845, 1848-1850) ; *Southern and Western Literary Messenger and Review: Devoted to Every Department of Literature and the Fine Arts* (1846-1847)

S. Q. R.
　Southern Quarterly Review

Southern and Western
　Southern and Western Monthly Magazine and Review

THE LETTERS
of
WILLIAM GILMORE SIMMS
1845-1849

1845

225 : To ARMISTEAD BURT [1]

Woodlands, Jany. 1. 1845

Hon. A. Burt

dear Sir

A Happy New Year to you and better prospects. I did not mean to give you any trouble in suggesting my desire for a copy of the new map of Texas, but, under the impression that there were copies for extra distribution, I simply put my wishes before you that you might address for my use a commodity which I really could make some use of, in literary perhaps, if not in political respects. While my hand is thus in for troubling you, I would like to procure copies of the following documents of past Sessions — viz. Rep. No. 587, 27th Congress, 2d. Session — Document, No. 70 of 25th Congress, 3d. Session — Rept. No. 587, 27th Congress, 2d. Session [2] — Report, No 449, 27th Congress, 2d. Session & the Report of Mr. Pratt of New York, from the Committee on Public Buildings made the 7th. March 1844. These, or as many of them as can be procured, and all others indeed, which relate to the Smithsonian Bequest, [3] or to Literary & Scientific purposes, which may be furnished the Two Houses, I shall be obliged to you to send me. Documents on Exploration, on Indian affairs or Territorial matters, all lie very much in my way, and a good speech whether for or against our views and wishes will prove acceptable to me. If you have beside you a Message of Tyler for the present Congress in pamphlet form, let me have it. I have it in a newspaper, but I usually have these matters bound up in volumes as they accumulate. I trust that you

---

[1] See introductory sketch. Burt, of Abbeville, S. C., was a member of Congress (1843-1853).

[2] Thus.

[3] After a ten years' debate the Smithsonian Bequest was accepted by the government and the institution was founded by act of Congress on Aug. 10, 1846, largely through the efforts of John Quincy Adams.

will forgive the trouble that I thus propose to give you, and will
take for granted that should it ever occur that I am able to serve
you in similar manner, it will give me great pleasure to respond
to your wishes. — I foresee a long and ardent struggle on the
subject of Texas. I take for granted that Texas will finally form
a part, in political aspects of the great Southern Section of the
country, as she is now in geographical respects; but whether, as
things go, *she* should desire it, is a point of very questionable
propriety and doubt. I am very sure that if South Carolina were
in her position, I should be the last man in the world to desire to
bring her into a conjunction in which she was to meet with
nothing but warfare. I should prefer the struggle against open
foes & poverty, for independence over all other considerations.
Nor, upon reflection should it be desirable for us, with our present views and interests to involve that country, which is probably
destined to be our dernier resort, in meshes from which we are
anxious to extricate ourselves. It may be that Texas is yet
destined to be our background, upon which we may be compelled
to retire for the better waging of the war with those who now
so seriously threaten our institutions. She is particularly interesting to Carolinians in this point of view, and though I have been
very earnest in insisting upon the Annexation, simply with an
eye to our increased political strength, & to the balance of power
in our Confederacy, yet looking to possible results, in regard to
this Confederacy, I am growing more & more doubtful, whether
the first policy of Carolina & the States South of her, will not
be over all things to preserve her independence, to insist upon it,
and to keep her from a connexion which is growing imminently
more and more dangerous to ourselves. But, this is too large
a topic for a hasty letter, and I have much other matter to unfold.
— What is said in the prints about Benton & Missouri [4] on the
score of the abolition of slavery in that state, may be very true
of him — it is like him — but is scarcely so probable of her. I
see few reasons to suppose that the Missourians are prepared for
such a movement. It may be so nevertheless. I am here very much
out of the world in the way of information. — I do not know

---

[4] Though a Southerner and a slaveholder, Thomas Hart Benton (1782-1858),
United States Senator from Missouri (1821-1851), had openly declared in 1844
that he would not introduce slavery into Texas lands where it was not known.
Southern papers accused Benton and Missouri of abolition sentiments. By 1849
Benton had reached the point of proclaiming his personal opposition to the
institution of slavery.

that it will be at all difficult to explain to you the reason for the defeat of the various resolutions which related to the rescision of the 25th. Rule of your House, in ours. The time was late, the members impatient and most of them regarded the resolutions of Mr. Pickens as mere *brutum fulmen*.[5] Their miserable phraseology, the *crude, jejune* character of their expression, was an objection with others. Indeed, as they were phrased, without regard to their obvious intent, we could not have passed them. They were not decent English, as you will see by a correction of them which I send you herewith. There were other reasons which concurred with these. These resolutions said no more than previous resolutions of our house had said. They seemed to us to be mere swagger, and were supposed by many to be intended simply to bolster up a local popularity which had recieved a shock in consequence of the character of the previous resolutions — those which were subsequently passed, — and which were mere wind & fury, signifying nothing. A good many of our young men are impatient of the idea of being chained to the cars of new popular leaders. They are not disposed to disturb the ascendancy of Mr. Calhoun,[6] but they are resolute against any new usurpation, and these measures both originating with Pickens, so wholly differing in temper, & both so really inexpressive, while they did not ad-

[5] During this session of the legislature Francis Wilkinson Pickens (see note 120, Dec. 30, 1842) introduced two sets of resolutions in the South Carolina Senate, both of which were passed, the first after slight amendment. The first (on Nov. 26) relates to Federal policy (the annexation of Texas and the tariff) ; the second (on Dec. 16) is as follows :

"*Resolved,* unanimously, That this Senate considers the recent movement in the House of Representatives in Congress, in relation to the reception of petitions to abolish slavery in any portion of this confederacy, as calculated to endanger the peace of our State; as a *flagrant outrage* upon our rights, and a decided step towards the subversion of our institutions, and the dissolution of this Union.

"*Resolved,* unanimously, That on this subject we admit no legislative power in Congress, and that such legislation will be in fact a dissolution of the Federal Compact.

"*Resolved,* unanimously, That if there should be legislation on this subject, by Congress, that the Governor of this State is hereby requested to call the Legislature together, in order to decide upon the mode and manner in which we shall preserve and defend our ancient rights and liberties."

Both sets of resolutions were sent to the House. Simms, John A. Stuart, and John Bauskett submitted resolutions on the same subject as the second (the "substitute" Simms mentions later in this letter). A number of other resolutions dealing with the same subject were likewise introduced by various other members of the House. Pickens' first set of resolutions was passed by the House; his second and the other similar resolutions originating in the House were indefinitely postponed. See *Senate Journal,* pp. 20, 25-26, 95-96, and *House Journal,* pp. 36, 63, 94, 136, 143-144, 154-156, 161-164.

[6] John Caldwell Calhoun. See introductory sketch.

vance the State one jot, were yet supposed to be designed for his advancement. You will precieve that all the *real* action was *concieved in the House.* It was in the House that the Southern Convention was urged,[7] a measure which was certainly one step toward action on our part, whether responded to or not, on the part of the Sister States. In the House was originated and carried through the decisive movement with regard to Mr. Hoar's expulsion;[8] and could we have had time and a committee to reconcile the differing views, and amalgamate the objects of the several sets of resolutions, you would have seen that there might have been gained much more than we have now. I must also warn you that a majority of the House came to it pacifically disposed, many districts pledged to the peace, & most of them persuaded that the Tariff issue is one upon which you cannot get a rally of strength in the Southern States. Had we not insisted upon the Abolition issue in debate we should have got nothing. That is the matter upon which if we hope to gain anything the true conflict must take place. That will unite every body at home, and, if any thing will unite them, the whole people of the South. Only, we must make up the issue on this ground at the earliest day possible. If, with this view before us, you still ask why the resolutions of the Senate [9] which spoke to this point were rejected, I refer you in addition to what has been already suggested, to the singular uncertainty of the case presented. Here, then, we are required to believe that the rescision of a rule is fatal to us, when not more than six years ago our politicians taught us that the very establishment of that rule was fatal to us, — and on this very ground H. L. Pinckney was superseded by Legaré.[10]

---

[7] On Nov. 28, 1844, a resolution had been introduced by Simeon Fair (*House Journal*, p. 35) : *"Therefore be it Resolved,* That the wisest and safest mode of redressing the acknowledged grievances of the Southern States of this Confederacy, will be for them to assemble in Convention, and devise the proper measures for their common relief. . . ."* The resolution provides that South Carolina send representatives to the legislatures of the slaveholding states to present her views.

[8] Samuel Hoar (1778-1856) was an agent sent to Charleston by the State of Massachusetts for the purpose of collecting and transmitting information regarding Negro citizens of Massachusetts imprisoned in Charleston. The resolution of expulsion, passed in the South Carolina House on Dec. 5, 1844, declares that "the emissary sent by the State of Massachusetts to the State of South Carolina, with the avowed purpose of interfering with her institutions and disturbing her peace," should be expelled. Simms voted in the affirmative. See *House Journal*, pp. 64-65.

[9] See note 5, above.

[10] The first of the "gag resolutions" declaring that Congress ought not to receive petitions in regard to abolition was introduced in 1836 by Henry Laurens

— The fact is, my dear sir, our leaders have been blundering too frequently not to make the people very doubtful of them, and not to make it incumbent on young Carolina, to take a little of the business into their own hands. A good many of our House are equally unwilling to be led by *Bluffton* or *Edgefield*.[11] You understand the allusion. — Many, among them myself, are almost glad that the 25th. Rule is rescinded, since it deprives abolition of one of its principal means of excitement — and enables us to join issue upon the real merits of the question — not to speak of the removal of the pretext on the part of those who insist on the right of petition without any reference to the subject matter of memorial. — You will possibly have observed that I voted with the minority, as to the final disposition of the Resolutions. As the subject was brought in, I was for expressing ourselves decidedly and *grammatically,* & furnished a substitute for the resolutions of the Senate, substantially saying all, & more than, they intended to say. But believing that we had shown the temper of the State, by our *action* in the case of Hoar, much more decidedly than we should do by a thousand resolutions, I was really indifferent to the matter, except in one particular. My fear was that by giving the go-by to the resolutions altogether, we should be inducing a false impression as to our opinions, which might dispirit our friends, and encourage the confidence of our enemies. I regarded both sets of the Senate Resolutions as really meaning very little, — as being full of bluster, and thunder, but, closely examined, without any bolt that had not been shot before — Rockets that had been thrown up & burnt out, and which really stunk in the nostrils of true manliness. In short, the House was not willing to be used by any men — was heartily sick of un-

---

Pinckney (1794-1863), of South Carolina. Pinckney's colleagues considered that the resolutions conceded constitutional power over slavery in the District of Columbia and that he was, therefore, a traitor to the South. This action led to his retirement from the House in 1837. He was succeeded by Hugh Swinton Legaré (1797-1843), who, though an opponent of Nullification, was "safe" on the slavery question. See Laura A. White, *Robert Barnwell Rhett: Father of Secession* (New York: The Century Company, [1931]), pp. 36-37.

11 Upon the arrival in South Carolina from Washington of Robert Barnwell Rhett (see introductory sketch of the Rhetts), member of Congress from South Carolina (1837-1849), his friends arranged a dinner at Bluffton, St. Luke's Parish. Here on July 31, 1844, Rhett launched "the Bluffton Movement" for a state convention and separate action on the tariff. According to Laura A. White (*Robert Barnwell Rhett: Father of Secession,* p. 74) Rhett "appealed especially to the boldness of youth, and young men responded. Opponents jeered at 'the Bluffton boys' and the title was promptly adopted as a badge of honor." The reference to Edgefield is to the influence of Francis Wilkinson Pickens.

meaning vapor, — suspected the patriotism of those with whom the action originated, — and was *& is,* for taking the lead as much out of their hands as possible — has heard the cry of wolf too long, and suspects half the time that it is nothing but a pole cat, — smells it in fact, and believes not in the clamor of the ass though he dons the skin of a much nobler animal. From this crude & hasty scrawl, written under indisposition, you will be able to collect the various causes for the defeat of the resolutions as well of myself as of the Senate. The nature of this letter makes portions of it wholly confidential, but of this you need no intimation. Very faithfully

Yours &c.

W. Gilmore Simms

P. S. I should not forget to hint to you, that in the election for electors Mr Pickens is reported to have run behind Elmore [12] some 30 votes, and one report is that he was *tyed* by Col. Trotti [13] on 3 several ballots. It is very certain that he ran considerably behind the ticket, as reported by the Committee. This, you will remember was between the 1st & last set of resolutions, and, in the meantime the House had shown a singular degree of independence with regard to the first (which the Senate had passed almost instantly & unanimously) and had moved in the business of Hoar to action, while the Senate was preparing resolutions. There is another matter. It was concieved that by referring the abolition petitions to the Committee on the district, a majority of whom were slaveholders & Southern men, the House had given us a full guarantee that the action would be such as we should not have occasion to quarrel with, particularly, indeed, when we remember that this was the practice nearly 50 years ago. — It is thought among us that we should not waste our strength and lose our temper upon the outposts and feint-parties of the enemy. We gain nothing by routing them, and lose much when we fail to do so, — besides diverting attention from the main issue.

---

[12] Franklin Harper Elmore. See note 121, Dec. 30, 1842.

[13] Samuel Wilds Trotti. See note 124, Dec. 19, 1841. An error was made in this earlier note on Trotti: his wife, Maria, was the sister rather than the daughter of John Hugh Means (1812-1862), later governor of South Carolina (1850-1852).

226: To James Lawson [14]

Woodlands, Jan. 6. [1845][15]

My dear Lawson

The compliments of the season, a long life and all the joys of life to you & yours. I have been looking for a scrawl from you for the last two months. Your last was about the 15th. Nov. I wrote you twice, I think, before going to Columbia, and at least once while there. And now I write rather to remind you of my existence and whereabouts, than because I have any thing worth saying. My wife, like yours, has been meditating for something like a month, as to the material of a Letter for the latter personage. I suppose it will be forthcoming before long. Her letter will contain (I suppose) certain instructions for the preparation of hominy, as I have just got from the mill and have had put up a barrel of the corn ground as we usually employ it, which I shall send to the city this week to be shipped to your address by the first conveyance. As sent you, the corn grist contains a certain proportion of husk, which is to be washed off each morning when you proceed to boil, and a certain proportion of a coarse flour; with the latter we usually make a coarse bread generally given to servants; though commonly eaten among our poor white people. But I leave farther details on this subject to my wife who will probably contrive to make them intelligible to yours. — My legislative duties were rather fatiguing than exciting. As a new member, I had too much to learn of the routine and ordinary modes of doing business to take a very active part in the play. Yet circumstances compelled me to do so. I was placed on the Committee on Federal Relations, and what with an insolent proceeding on the part of Massachusetts, and the constant provo-

---

[14] See introductory sketch of the Lawsons.

[15] Dated by Simms' reference to himself "as a new member" of the legislature. In his absorption in his role as legislator Simms neglected to inform Lawson that a dramatization of *The Yemassee* was being presented in Charleston on this date. The *Southern Patriot* of Jan. 6 announces: "Tonight 'The Yemassee' which has been dramatized from Simms' celebrated novel of that name will be performed for the first time before a Charleston audience. It has been very successfully played at the North and when we consider that the author is a very worthy and talented son of South Carolina, of whom the State may justly be proud, we trust that a full attendance will testify that we are not unmindful of *native* genius, nor of this effort, to render it popular." On Aug. 17, 1835, a dramatization of *The Yemassee* had been performed at the Bowery Theatre, New York City (see George C. D. Odell, *Annals of the New York Stage* [New York: Columbia University Press, 1927-1949], IV, 70-71).

cation of some unruly blood among us, I was compelled to take a more active part in the actual business than I had contemplated on taking my seat. In consequence, I was several times on my feet & made several speeches two or three on our federal relations, one in behalf of an appropriation for a Geological Survey of the State, another for an appropriation to establish a seperate Professorship of Greek in the College, and one or two more on local, or district topics.[16] One of the papers of Columbia, just re-

---

[16] For the action of the Committee on Federal Relations, see note 8, Jan. 1, 1845. For these other bills, see *House Journal,* pp. 33, 79, 95, 133, 149. On Nov. 29, 1844, Simms submitted the following resolutions on "Governor Hammond's Message No. 1, as relates to the Tariff, to Texas, and the Abolitionists" (*House Journal,* pp. 41-42) :

1. *Resolved,* That while we look with hope to the action of the administration about to come into power in the Federal Government, and see no reason to distrust the propriety of that support which the people of South-Carolina have accorded to render it successful, we are yet reminded by the experience of the past, of the necessity of maintaining our own strict watch over those vital interests upon which the fortunes and the safety of the South depend.

2. *Resolved,* That our sense of the deep injury inflicted upon us by the operations of the present odious tariff of protection, is in no respect lessened, and that we enjoin our Representatives in Congress to continue their unceasing warfare upon this principle, and the practice under it, until the agricultural labor and interests of the South shall be rendered permanently secure against its injustice.

3. *Resolved,* That the acquisition of the territory of Texas is vastly important to the welfare of the whole Union — to its safety from foreign arms — to its commercial enterprize — to its general industry — and to the South, vitally necessary for the proper growth and expansion of our people.

4. *Resolved,* That we cannot submit to the insulting declaration, that, while all other portions of the Union may extend themselves on either hand, and draw into their folds new States and capacious territories, the slave-holding States shall remain stationary — circumscribed in boundary — fettered and enfeebled by position, until gradually environed by communities hostile to their institutions, and no ways scrupulous in the expression of their hostilities.

5. *Resolved,* That as the interests involved in these previous considerations are, in the opinion of this House, equally important to all the slave-holding States of this Confederacy, it becomes us to invite their co-operation with us in grave and circumspect deliberation upon them : To this co-operation and consultation, therefore, be it further resolved, that the Executive of the State of South-Carolina be requested, by communication to the Governors of the several States aforesaid, to meet us, by their Delegates, in Asheville, North-Carolina, on the fourth day of March, one thousand, eight hundred and forty-six.

6. *Resolved,* finally, That South-Carolina is now, as before, warmly united in her desire and determination to preserve inflexibly the spirit and the letter of the Federal Constitution — the integrity of the Union — the rights of the individual States — and her own people from oppression; and that, while she hails the success of the Democratic party as full of happy augury, she will relax none of that jealous vigilance by which only can happy auguries be converted into certainties, and a gallant people be rendered secure in the possession of their liberties.

On unfavorable report of the Committee of the Whole House these resolutions were tabled and continued indefinitely on Dec. 18, the last day of the session (see *House Journal,* pp. 156, 168). This is one of the "lost" measures to which Simms refers.

cieved, contains an extract from a paper of the interior in relation
to one of my speeches, which I cut out and send you. You are
not to suppose that I think the writer right. On the contrary,
my speech did not satisfy me. I felt so new to the business and
so nervous, that when I sat down, I became conscious that I had
omitted several of the strongest points which I arose to make.
The feeling wore off somewhat before the session is over, and
after two or three, I feel that I should speak with great readiness
and with little or no difficulty. The paragraph sent you, is by a
member of the Senate — a very estimable and intelligent lawyer
— one of my admirers you see — Major Perry of Greenville.[17]
— The new magazine is nearly through the press.[18] The first
no. will probably be inferior as it was prepared just as I was
preparing for Columbia & while I was there fagging day & night
in law & politics. — I have been looking to hear from you or
B & S.[19] How have Helen & the Castle done.[20] They tell me they

---

[17] This clipping, which still accompanies this letter, is probably from the
South-Carolinian, of which no issues for this period are known to be extant.
It consists of a quotation from the Greenville *Mountaineer* of Dec. 13, 1844, in
which Benjamin Franklin Perry (see introductory sketch) says: "William
Gilmore Simms, the Poet and Novelist, next obtained the floor. I had never
heard a speech from a Poet, and felt some anxiety for my friend Simms. As
a talker he is unrivalled. . . . I think he is one of the most interesting men
in conversation I ever heard. As a writer and poet, he ranks with the most
distinguished our country has ever produced. Whilst speaking his voice under-
went such a change that I should not have recognized it. Poets can be em-
barrassed on a new field; but his speech was one which would not detract from
his high reputation. He spoke fluently, and with great ease. He was in favor
of a Southern Convention. In old times he, too, was a Union man . . . and
I am sure he still is. His conclusion was very beautiful: South Carolina had
given him birth . . . cradled him in his infancy . . . she had a right to demand
of him his life, his talents and his exertions . . . and in death, he desired only
to be received into her bosom."

[18] *Southern and Western Magazine and Review* (Jan.-Dec., 1845), bearing
the sub-title of *Simms's Monthly Magazine.* See letter to Lawson of Nov. 27,
1844.

[19] Burgess, Stringer and Co., publishers of New York City.

[20] *Helen Halsey: or, the Swamp State of Conelachita. A Tale of the Borders*
(New York: Burgess, Stringer & Co., 1845), dedicated to Randell Hunt, of
Louisiana, and *Castle Dismal: or, the Bachelor's Christmas. A Domestic Legend*
(New York: Burgess, Stringer & Co., 1844), dedicated to Richard Henry Wilde
(see introductory sketch). The *Southern Patriot* of Jan. 2 reports that "Helen
Halsey . . . this most attractive and thrilling romance by our talented townsman
is just received, price only 25 cents. . . ." The same issue contains a long notice
of Simms' *The Geography of South Carolina: Being a Companion to the History
of That State* (Charleston: Babcock & Co., 1843) and a brief notice of *The
Charleston Book: A Miscellany in Prose and Verse* (Charleston: Samuel Hart,
Sen., 1845), a volume edited by Simms. Of this last the reviewer comments:
"This elegant work reflects the highest credit upon the intellectual talent of
our City, none can examine it without being surprised that here in the very
midst, such a rich literary column, could be raised in commemoration of the

have sold well in Carolina. Let me know as they advance in Count Julian that I may bestir myself with the conclusion. By the way, suppose B & S. offer to Winchester $150 in copies for his plates & the M.S.[21] That is 300 copies, and to enable them to do this, I am willing that they should print that number in addition to the 5000. I could wish, if they have done well with the two Tales [22] that they should immediately publish the volume of Tales [23] if you can persuade them to it at the same price, say $50 and the plates for 6000 copies. — But I am at the bottom of my sheet. I hear nothing of Mathews.[24] Say to him & Duyckinck [25] that I will write them soon. My best respects to Lady Lyde,[26] and a kiss for the children.

Yours,

W. G. S.

227: To JAMES LAWSON

Woodlands, Jan 15. [1845][27]

My dear Lawson

I enclose to your care a letter for Mr. Richards which you will deliver if you see him often, if not, drop into the post office.

---

mental Jewells intrusted to our keeping. The very beautiful manner in which it is got up, entitles its enterprising publisher to the many thanks of his fellow Citizens."

[21] *Count Julian; or, the Last Days of the Goth* had been started by Simms as early as 1839. Part of the manuscript, entrusted to a friend, was lost for two years and, when discovered, passed through the hands of various publishers, among whom were J. Winchester and Burgess, Stringer and Co. It was finally published in 1845 by William Taylor, New York. It bears a dedication to John Pendleton Kennedy (see introductory sketch).

[22] *Helen Halsey* and *Castle Dismal*.

[23] This collection of tales had been planned by Simms as early as June 12, 1843, when he discussed the subject in a letter to Lawson. It was finally published as *The Wigwam and the Cabin,* First and Second Series (New York: Wiley and Putnam, 1845). Though both series bear the same date, the second was not issued until 1846.

[24] Cornelius Mathews. See introductory sketch.

[25] Evert Augustus Duyckinck. See introductory sketch.

[26] Mrs. James Lawson.

[27] Dated by Simms' reference to the publication of the January number of the *Southern and Western. Godey's,* XXX (March, 1845), 144, comments: "W. Gilmore Simms, Esq., has commenced his '*Southern and Western Monthly Magazine and Review,*' in very handsome style. We are pleased with every feature of this new literary enterprize. The papers are, of course, all original, and all brought up to a standard of literary excellence, such as the editor's high reputation for ability and taste requires. The topics discussed in this number are fresh, and handled in a piquant style; and the whole affair has a stamp of nationality which we decidedly approve." Of the *Southern and Western,*

I suppose he has made your acquaintance.[28] The first number of the New Magazine will appear today. I have ordered that it should be sent to you, Duyckinck, Mathews & Headley,[29] — the Ev'ng Post [30] &c. It is scarcely a fair specimen, as my legislative duties greatly interfered with its preparation. You will find it fair, however, in comparison with such of our contemporaries as I have seen for January. As for my legislative career, about which your last letter (recd. yesterday) inquires, — I can say no more than I have said already in a previous letter which no doubt has reached you by this time. My friends say I sustained myself, which, when we reflect that something was expected, is saying much. I covered my last through Holmes [31] or Burt in Washington, and you may write through either of them. My wife wrote a long letter to yours a few days ago, and I have just seen delivered to our factor in Charleston a barrel of grist for your hominy which will be shipped by the first vessel. We have just killed a portion of our hogs for the year, some fifty head, and will send you a few hams as soon as cured. We brag somewhat, you must know, on the strength of our Woodland bacon. I write by this day's mail to Burgess & Stringer touching on various topics. The novellettes [32] have both sold well in Carolina & continue to sell. The Booksellers in Charleston have been compelled to order fresh supplies several times. Marion also sells well here. I percieve that the Mirror has had a fling at it, and that that miserable creature Clarke, copies the fling, under the pretext of dissenting from it.[33] How has the Post noticed all

---

Godey's, XXX (June, 1846), 281, again says: "The name of its editor . . . is a guarantee of its excellence, and, we hope, will insure it success. The April No. is rich in historical articles, and the 'editorial bureau' shows an example of clear and impartial criticism, which should command the attention of every writer."

[28] For Thomas Addison Richards, see letter to Lawson of Oct. 31, 1844, and introductory sketch of the Richards family.

[29] Joel Tyler Headley. See introductory sketch.

[30] At this time the New York *Evening Post* was edited by William Cullen Bryant (see introductory sketch).

[31] Isaac E. Holmes (1796-1867) was a member of Congress from South Carolina (1839-1851).

[32] *Helen Halsey* and *Castle Dismal.*

[33] Lewis Gaylord Clark (see introductory sketch of the Clark brothers) had reviewed Simms' *The Life of Francis Marion* (New York: Henry G. Langley, 1844) in *Knick.,* XXIV (Dec., 1844), 570-571. In the course of his review he says (p. 570): "Mr. Willis remarks, in a notice of the 'Life of Marion' in the 'Evening Mirror' daily journal [Nov. 16, 1844], that 'Mr. Simms' style, always heavy, is especially so in his attempts at historical writing;' and he cites an involved and clumsy passage in illustration of the historian's manner; but we do not altogether coincide with this opinion. We confess that we like Mr.

these Books, and how have you liked them, — or have you read
them? I truly rejoice to hear of your dividends, and fervently
hope that you may go on prospering as you deserve. I shall forgive your occasional delays to answer, whenever you can plead
so good an excuse as business — but, I very well know you plead
it too often. Where are your Sunday afternoons & nights &c. Why,
man, a letter such as we need, is despatched in ten minutes. — I
am glad that you like my portrait. I would not take it from West
till it is wanted by the publisher, since the picture must gain by
his additional touches.[34] He is evidently one of those artists who
improves by elaboration. — And so my cranberries & buckwheat
which I wanted for Christmas Cheer & the New Year have been
ready a month! We have been ready for them all that time. As
for our wife and her sweetmeats, say to her that it is only because she has grown sour that she needs so much urging. I beg
that you will not kiss her again until they are sent. She is a sad
woman, & in these respects, very much like my own. — Did
Forrest return you the MS. of the tragedy before leaving, and
did he give you any opinion upon it.[35] — I am glad to hear that
McCracken promises to write for the Magazine.[36] I will thank
you to call upon him & specially solicit him in my behalf. I like
his manliness and independence of character, & only regret that

---

Simms as a historian much better than as a romancer; and we heartily share
the gratification which has been generally expressed, that his pen has sought
a new field. His style in the narration of actual events is less wordy and
diffuse. . . ." A balance to Clark's comments is found in a lengthy review of the
work in the *American [Whig] Review*, I (Jan., 1845), 104-108. Here the anonymous writer says (p. 108): "The style employed in the biography is among the
best examples of descriptive narrative we have seen for some time. It is a style
not easy to hit, requiring, at times, great simplicity and terseness of language;
at times, an equal degree of richness and fluency; and always a clearness which
shall not give the reader a moment's doubt as to the writer's meaning. The work
is certainly full of interest, and we believe it will add materially to Mr. Simms'
reputation as a writer."

[34] On the back of the West portrait, designed to be engraved for *Godey's*
(see letters to Lawson of *c.* Nov. 15, 1844, and April 7, 1845) and now in the
possession of Mary C. Simms Oliphant, is the notation made by Simms: "This
portrait was painted in 1844, when I was 38 years old, by William West, the
American (Kentucky) painter — an artist of great merit. He painted the most
successful portrait of Lord Byron & published a report of his conversations
with his Lordship." It is reproduced as the frontispiece to this volume.

[35] Simms' tragedy "Don Carlos," written for Edwin Forrest (see introductory
sketch), was never published and probably never completed. Approximately one
and one-half acts survive in MS. in the Charles Carroll Simms Collection, South
Caroliniana Library. Simms was at work on the play as early as July 27, 1840,
when he mentions it in a letter to Lawson.

[36] J. L. H. McCracken (see note 147, Nov. 19, 1844) contributed a review of
Robert Chambers' *Vestiges of the Natural History of Creation* (see note 220,
June 7, 1845).

you did not put him in nomination for Congress in place of that nameless skunk, Eli Moore.[37] Let me know McCracken's Christian name, (I believe J. L.) and address & the Magazine shall be sent him. — I hear nothing from Mathews. Is he offended at any thing. I see a paper of his in the last Democratic.[38] It seems only a beginning. Duyckinck & Headley have both articles in our No 1.[39] I saw the notice of D. in the News.[40] He has shown himself very considerate & friendly, & is a man of correct taste & excellent talent. See B & S. about Julian &c. My wife begs me to say that she will be glad to have the Song in print. Mr. Roach who has quite a talent for music likes it as well as herself.[41] To play it for him was one of her first performances when she got home. Gilmore[42] is the fattest turbulentest rogue you ever saw. We cannot keep him in the house. He too remembers Jimmy Lawson.[43] My wife and her father and Augusta[44] send their best love to Madame and yourself, and mine you will take for granted without special assurances.

Ever yours as Ever

W. G. S.

J. L.

---

[37] Ely Moore (1798-1860) was educated as a doctor but abandoned his practice to become a printer. He was the first president of the General Trades' Union of New York. In 1834 he was elected to Congress with Tammany's support, serving until the expiration of his second term in 1839.

[38] "The Ghost of New York," *Dem. Rev.*, XVI (Jan., 1845), 10-13.

[39] To the Jan. issue of the *Southern and Western* Duyckinck contributed "Time's Wallet. I. The Hystorie of Hamblet"; Headley contributed "An Incident of Waterloo." See notes 58 and 60, Jan. 19, 1845.

[40] It is impossible to tell which of Duyckinck's many notices in the New York *Morning News* and *New York Weekly News* Simms here refers to. For his notices of *The Life of Francis Marion, Castle Dismal,* and *Helen Halsey,* see note 62, Jan. 19, 1845. For his notice of "The Hermytte of Drowsiehedde," see note 283, Aug. 7, 1845. A moderately long notice of *The Charleston Book* "rapidly passing through the press" appears in the *Morning News* of Sept. 20, 1844, a short review of the volume in the issue of Nov. 14, 1844.

[41] "Clydesdale, Farewell!" (see letter to Lawson of *c.* Jan. 19). In the "Editor's Table" of the *Knick.*, XXV (May, 1845), 469, is the following comment: " 'Clydesdale Farewell,' is the title of a very sweet Scottish ballad, the poetry and music by Mr. James Lawson. Mr. Jas. L. Hewitt is the publisher." Both Mrs. Simms and her father, Nash Roach, sang in the choir of St. Paul's, Charleston.

[42] Simms' first son by his second wife, born March 16, 1843.

[43] James Lawson, Jr. (b. 1842). Simms, his wife, Gilmore, and a nurse had visited the Lawsons in 1844 (see letters to Lawson of Aug. 12 and Oct. 29, 1844).

[44] Simms' only child by his first wife, born Nov. 11, 1827.

228: To George Frederick Holmes [45]

Woodlands, Jan. 18. [1845][46]

My dear Holmes

I got your last letter just as I was on the eve of leaving home for the city, & in my care of it have mislaid it, effectually (for the present) out of my own reach. Some of the things you give, *en passant,* and, I suppose, as samples of what may be done, might be very effectually wrought into our mosaic; but subsequent reflection has satisfied me of the utter impracticability of doing a series such as was contemplated in my previous Letter, unless by one hand and with the whole of his time at his disposal.[47] I should be loth to undertake anything which should too decidedly show by what it had been provoked and stimulated, and the cursed variety of my tasks, will utterly prevent me from that deliberate and discursive play of thought and fancy, which such a plan calls for — a seeming freedom from all direction, yet an earnest keeping in view of the object — an avoidance of intentness, and a continual rising into matters of foreign illustration — so much diversity of aim, yet such happy adherence always to the desultory and the indirect. The scheme is too comprehensive and for this reason, if for no other must be abandoned, at least, by myself. There are other reasons. My memory is not sufficiently ready in illustration. My causality has ripen'd at the expense of my comparison.[48] I have the one large, the other inferior. Besides, I lack reading in some degree, except in two or three provinces, am little of a linguist, and become too earnest in my subject, suddenly to permit of its abandonment. There is yet another reason why the scheme should not be attempted rashly. In Black-

---

[45] See introductory sketch.

[46] Dated by Simms' reference to the publication of the first number of the *Southern and Western* (Jan., 1845).

[47] On Dec. 30, 1844, Simms had suggested to Holmes a department for the *Southern and Western* to be modeled on *Noctes Ambrosianae* of *Blackwood's.* Holmes replied on Jan. 7: "Much care and attention would undoubtedly be requisite to produce any thing of a like nature which might successfully follow the 'Noctes Ambrosianae' of Blackwood, but I think that it might be done, and I should be exceedingly gratified to see it well done. You must enlist General Jamison in the project. I am highly flattered by the honourable post you designate for me, and by the complimentary terms in which you pronounce my installation. I fear, however, I shall break down, but if you can lick into decent shape the crude lumps I may send you, I may be able to supply what you want." (Original in the Simms Collection, Library of Congress.)

[48] In "Mesmerides in a Stage-Coach; or, Passes en Passant," *Godey's,* XXXI (Sept., 1845), 111-119, Simms also speaks (p. 111) of "my *causality,* which in my case is a rather large development."

wood, his interlocutors were men of note, distinguished men, some of them with world wide reputations. The Opium Eater, The Shepherd, and Wilson himself, were such. Now, however, meritorious our merry companions may be, known to ourselves, we should only provoke the laugh against us, by recalling to recollection the great names which occur in the Scheme which we propose to emulate. All things considered therefore, I think it well to forego the experiment on the scale as originally suggested. But to a certain extent it may be adopted. Either of us may adopt it as contributors. You may have your "feast of the Ancients" — your "Literary Soirees" in which, through certain parties quaintly or merrily described, rare maskers, you may throw out your wit, learning and philosophy. I think to do something of the kind myself, but, mark me, anonymously. I recommend the anonymous to you also. — Well, our first no. is issued, and I suppose has reached you by this time. I ordered it for you. It has been quite hurried, as you know, but I trust you will like it. The articles are mostly too long. They should never exceed 8 pages & 6 would be better. — I am not so sure that you have not somewhat erred in your notice of Mrs. H. Gray [49] — not that she does not deserve all that you have said, but that you have too much confined yourself to her mistakes in learning. You do not consider the history itself. I have her book on the Sepulchres of Ancient Etruria,[50] — a showy volume which, if you have not read, I will cheerfully put into your hands for review. I have read nothing but her introduction which does not lack interest & has some spirit. It may however have many mistakes. Tell Jamison I am looking for his article on Simcoe.[51] When he is done it & with the book, let him send both of them directly down (by the first opportunity to B & J.)[52] I propose to review the volume at some length myself for Whitaker.[53] I

[49] "Mrs. Gray's History of Etruria," *S. Q. R.,* VIII (Jan., 1845), 211-219. A second notice is included in Holmes' "Ante-Roman Races of Italy," *ibid.,* VIII (April, 1845), 261-299.

[50] Elizabeth Caroline Johnstone ("Mrs. Hamilton") Gray, *Tour to the Sepulchres of Etruria, in 1839* (2nd. ed.; London: J. Hatchard and Son, 1841). Simms later read this volume, apparently with some care, for in notes appended to *The City of the Silent* (Charleston: Walker & James, 1850) he quotes from it at length.

[51] David Flavel Jamison (see introductory sketch) reviewed *Simcoe's Military Journal* (New York: Bartlett & Welford, 1844) in "American Partisan Warfare," *Southern and Western,* I (Feb., 1845), 128-134.

[52] Burges and James, Charleston, publisher of the *Southern and Western.*

[53] Simms did not review *Simcoe's Military Journal* for the *Southern Quarterly Review,* edited by Daniel K. Whitaker during 1842-1847.

have not room in my own journal for all that I would say.[54] I
do not care about the notice of Anthon's Homer, & only thought
that if you had the book, it might please you to write one.[55]
I have it myself. Withdraw your order therefore & let them send
you something of more value. I trust that your friends who are
in the way of it keep their eyes upon your Chair in the College.
If I knew in what way & with whom to serve you, I should
cheerfully lend a hand. Keep such as can work for you busy.
Tend the lady and the love passages. — I hope that all goes merry
as the marriage bell.[56]

Yours very truly &c.

W. Gilmore Simms

229: To Evert Augustus Duyckinck

Woodlands, 19 Jan. [1845][57]

My dear Duyckinck

There has been a Letter of yours lying on my table for a
grievous long time, but you are just one of those men, to whom
I shall never care to make excuses. I take for granted you are
not of the class whose morbid apprehensions of neglect keep in
continual hot water with themselves & friends; but assume for
you a generous readiness to anticipate the excuse and account
for the failure in your own thoughts, of those from whom returns
might be expected. I need not surely say to you that with hands
so full as mine, with laws, legislature & literature, speech &
magazine making, — I confidently counted on the indulgence of

---

[54] Simms' own contributions in the Jan. issue of the *Southern and Western*
include "Americanism in Literature" (pp. 1-14), "Tzelica, A Tradition of the
French Broad" (pp. 15-16), "Geoffrey Rudel; the Pilgrim of Love" (pp. 26-
33), "Weems, the Historian" (pp. 35-47), "The Tax Payer" (p. 47), "Billows"
(p. 66), and "Editorial Bureau" (pp. 67-72). All are unsigned. He was probably
the author also of two unsigned poems: "The Last Flower of Summer" (pp.
34-35) and "Love" (p. 60). The New York *Morning News* of Feb. 3 reprints
a notice from the Charleston *Mercury*: "We have received the first number of
the new Monthly. . . . We . . . know of no man whose personal responsibility
has a higher promise of truth, courage and honesty, than Mr. Simms. . . . His
first article — 'Americanism in Literature,' is good — very good."

[55] For Simms' earlier remarks about this proposed notice of Charles Anthon's
The First Three Books of Homer's Iliad (New York: Harper & Brothers,
1845), see letter to Holmes of Dec. 30, 1844.

[56] Holmes desired a professorship at the South Carolina College. The reference to "the lady" is to Eliza Lavallette Floyd, Holmes' future wife (see note
109, Feb. 25, 1845).

[57] Dated by Simms' reference to the first number of the *Southern and Western*
(Jan., 1845).

my friendly correspondents, and gave myself up wholly to the absolute businesses before me.—

Our Mag. is under way, & the first no. is I suppose already in your hands. I put you, Mathews, Lawson, Headley, Bryant & others on the Free List the first day, and if not recieved, (as is possible at the first beginning) let me know *instanter* and the remedy shall be applied. You will see that our contents are got up hurriedly & perhaps do me little credit. We shall do better as we get on. Headley's paper is clever,[58] and Mrs. Ellet's [59] I have not read. They tell me that is clever also. Your 'Wallet',[60] promises well, and I trust you will keep it filled. It came too late for both nos. & I could only get in one (as I was resolved to do) by leaving out a story of my own. I will thank you to let me have the 3d & 4th. as soon as possible. My critical table was small, not because of want of matter but want of room. Let me have your opinion of the whole, for I look considerably to your judgment in such matters.[61] — I do not know whether in any of my letters, I have thanked you for the kind notices which you have made at different periods of my late labors. I feel that you have written in a genial spirit, & am not sure that where you have found fault you have not been perfectly justified in doing so. I am a very rash writer, — too rapid, regarding much too little, the niceties of the art. I will thank you to let me know how

---

[58] "An Incident of Waterloo," *Southern and Western,* I (Jan., 1845), 54-60. In answer to an unlocated letter from Simms, Headley wrote on Feb. 21, 1845: "I am glad my article pleased you though the very favour it has recd here vexes me. A mere narrative or description that I write at a single sitting & which costs me no labour is read & praised while an article which is the result of thought & investigation is scarcely read. But such is the taste of the *'people'* & who can correct it?

"Your first no. was praised by every body & I am inclined to believe the very rudeness which you think you see in it after all gave lightness & *motion* to the whole magazine. There is an offhand *extempore* way of making up a magazine which has its merits as well as faults. Have you got the right form for a monthly? I don't like your plain blue cover — it looks too much like a catechism. Mr. Duyckinck informed me that you sent me a copy but I did not receive it & was indebted to him for a look at my article. I was astonished at the correctness of the compositor or proof reader or both in following the copy so close when my chirography is so detestable. I did not observe a single mistake." (Original in the New-York Historical Society Library.)

[59] Elizabeth Fries Ellet, "A Daguerreotyped Incident at Rockaway," *Southern and Western,* I (Jan., 1845), 48-54. See introductory sketch of the Ellets.

[60] "Time's Wallet. I. The Hystorie of Hamblet," *Southern and Western,* I (Jan., 1845), 61-66.

[61] Duyckinck published frequent notices of the *Southern and Western* in the New York *Morning News* and the *New York Weekly News.* See notes 54, Jan. 18, 1845; 88, Feb. 11, 1845; 130, March 15, 1845; 156, April 7, 1845; 200, June 6, 1845; 220, June 7, 1845; and 242, June 25, 1845.

Marion sells & the two novelettes.[62] Here, in Carolina, I am told that they not only have sold well, but continue to do so, and here the favorable opinions of many of our best men, console me for those of a different character uttered by one or two of your city papers. Talking of city papers, I should like to recieve

---

[62] Before publication, *The Life of Francis Marion* was noticed (probably by Duyckinck) in the New York *Morning News* of Sept. 7 and Sept. 14, 1844. It received a long, favorable review on Oct. 10. The reviewer comments: "He [Simms] is scrupulously faithful to historical documents, while by his skill in grouping, and advantages of style as a novelist, he imparts to their scanty, meagre facts, much of the fulness and interest of actual life. The facts that would have been, handled in the usual style of the biographers of American generals, a dull collection of hard names, an undigested record of petty skirmishes happening every where in some confined labyrinth of geography, an entirely unreadable book, here assume the happiest method and arrangement." From another notice in the issue of Oct. 19 we learn that "so spontaneous and unusual has been the demand for this new production, that . . . the publisher had to put a second edition to press before even a copy of the *first* had been issued to the public." The writer continues: "As a historiographer, Mr. Simms has presented unequivocal evidence of eminent ability, both in the work to which we refer, and by his 'History of South Carolina,' which has passed through several editions; and, as we hear, it is his design, immediately on his return to the South, to devote himself more to works of a historical character than to those of his hitherto favorite department of fictitious and poetical literature, we are the more gratified at the success of this, his first essay of the kind. The following, we believe, are the forthcoming works which are in contemplation for the coming season: a Life of Sumter, — a Life of Paul Jones . . . a revised edition of Capt. Smith's History of Virginia, a work long out of print, but one of authority and value." On Nov. 2 excerpts were printed from notices of *Marion* in the *Democratic Review* and in the *American* [*Whig*] *Review* and from a review of Simms' works from a London publication.

Duyckinck published a long, favorable review of *Castle Dismal* in the *Morning News* of Nov. 9 (reprinted in the *Weekly News* of the same date), discussed by Simms in his letter to Duyckinck of *c.* Nov. 15, 1844. Duyckinck comments: "If it be any merit in a ghost-story to arrest the reader's attention at the first moment of perusal, and hold it fixed page after page, chapter after chapter, through one hour, two hours to the fitting time of midnight till candle and story go out together, then is Castle Dismal one of the best ghost stories we ever read. The story is well told by Mr. Simms, an adept in this species of narrative. We question whether there is anywhere a better manager in the construction of a tale, who can take such simple unexaggerated material and make so much of it. . . . Simms still relies upon character and passion and literally takes the reader by storm by the downright force and reality of his action. We suspect Mr. Simms and Mr. Cooper[,] the foremost American novelists, stand upon the same broad platform. They are both inattentive to the minor (though not always unimportant) graces of style, and neither have much facility in conversational trifling in their dialogue or felicity in their humorous passages. But when it comes to a matter of earnestness, when there is something to be said or done, of moment, they are both in the thick of the *melée,* on land or shore. They are both energetic, earnest writers, fond of speculation, though Mr. Simms has the advantage of a more philosophic turn of mind as an essayist. If Mr. Simms were writing of the newspaper press, for instance, he would give both sides of the question."

Helen Halsey is reviewed in the *Morning News* of Nov. 29. The review is largely a recapitulation of the plot of the novelette.

that of Harry Franco [63] from the first & will order the Mag. to be sent in return as soon as I know its name. I have written to Langley touching a seeing of some of yr publishers on the score of new books for our journal, and in regard to a certain collection of valuable Letters which I should like to publish, — Letters of distinguished men during the revolution.[64] Will you cooperate with him in this matter. Has Mathews committed suicide or not. Not a word of or from him. Is his Ghost of New York a beginning? [65] It looks so. Present my wife to Mrs D. & self to both of you.

W. G. S.

230: To JAMES LAWSON

[*c.* January 19, 1845][66]

My dear Lawson

The Bbl contains the grist for hominy. I trust that it will reach you safely & that my wifes instructions will enable yours to make use of it. It is decidedly one of the most wholesome & strengthening things for children, seasoned with a little salt & butter and eaten as a bread stuff. — I wish you to call on Mr. Doyle, of the Ladies Companion & get from him the article I left in his hands.[67] That work is now reported entirely dead, and the article may avail for my new Magazine. If you get it cover it to me carefully, addressed to the care of Saml. Hart Sen [68] — Charleston, & get Burgess & Stringer to send it in one of his parcels. I have written to them. By the time this reaches you you will probably have recd. the 1st. No. of the Mag. Write me soon how it pleases you, and see how it likes our friends Duyckinck

---

[63] Charles F. Briggs (1804-1877), frequently called "Harry Franco" from his novel of the same name, edited the *Broadway Journal* from Jan. 4 through Feb. 22, 1845; Briggs, Poe, and Henry C. Watson (1816-1875) from March 1 through June 28; Poe and Watson from July 12 through Oct. 18; and Poe from Oct. 25 through the last issue of Jan. 3, 1846.

[64] Simms' letter to Henry G. Langley, publisher of *Marion* and of the *Democratic Review*, has not been located. For the project here mentioned, see note 95, Feb. 11, 1845.

[65] See note 38, Jan. 15, 1845.

[66] This letter is postmarked Midway, S. C., Jan. 20. The year is established by Simms' reference to the first number of the *Southern and Western* (Jan., 1845).

[67] We have been unable to identify either Doyle or the article. Presumably Doyle was one of the editors of the *Ladies' Companion* when it ceased publication with the issue of Oct., 1844.

[68] Bookseller and publisher.

& Mathews. Say to the former that I should like a third & fourth no. of 'Times Wallet' as soon as possible. — I am out of breath, hauling Gilmore in his wagon about the green. I wish your lad were with him. God Bless you all.

Yours &c.

W. G. Simms

You may write to Scotland that the glories of Clydesdale are chaunted on the banks of the Edisto — a Scottish valley honored upon Indian water. My wife is even now singing to a delighted audience your Clydesdale Farewel,[69] and they all *affect* to admire it — I suppose for no other reasons than that they know how much we esteem the author. It surely cannot be because of the merits of the piece. It *is curious to observe that persons who seem to combine in some degree the gifts of poetry and music have rarely, if ever, been even tolerably successful in either.* What is your opinion on this subject?

231 : To Armistead Burt

Woodlands, Jan 26 [1845][70]

My dear Sir

I do not desire office for its own sake, but circumstances have never allowed me to travel out of the limits of our own country. Literature has only sufficed to enable me to live like a Gentleman at home, and, after reaching the tolerably mature term of thirty eight years, which I am now, I feel that I may, without over-stepping the bounds of modesty, declare my desire to see a little of the outer world. I should like to go to Europe, but it will please me to travel in other regions. I have no particular prefer-ences — after the civilized portions of the old world — for any special region. Of my capacities you all know probably quite as much as I do myself. My studies have been various, my experience not inconsiderable. Though never a commercial man, I am con-sidered a practical one, am a working one, and was born & reared in Charleston, a commercial city. My friends may safely promise

---

[69] See note 41, Jan. 15, 1845. "Clydesdale, Farewell!" is included in Lawson's *Poems: Gleanings from Spare Hours of a Business Life* (New York: John F. Trow, Printer, 1857), pp. 97-98.

[70] Dated by Simms' discussion of his desire for a foreign appointment under Polk. Simms frequently refers to the subject in his letters of this period. See, for example, letter to Lawson of Feb. 11.

that I will faithfully discharge the duties confided to me, as far
as my abilities will allow. I can read a little french, and have some
slight inkling, which a little time would enable me to improve into
an acquisition, of Italian & Spanish. It must be for my friends
to determine not only what will suit me best, but what I am most
good for. I am, I fancy, rather a prudent man than otherwise,
can understand the wink or nod of a minister, — certainly quite
as well as — Mr Shannon![71] — and in all respects, I am patient
to acquire & progress, and cool enough to see my position fairly.
I can keep cool & remain firm, and say 'No!' to the Dons without putting them or myself into a passion. — I have been friendly
to the election of Polk and Dallas,[72] not because I loved them or
cared for them, but because I regarded them as a choice of evils
& am totally opposed to South Carolina throwing away her vote.
However, I have taken no part in their election, except to talk a
little by the wayside, to stump it once or twice in favor of Texas,
and to aid as a Member of our Legislature in electing the Electors,
knowing very well for whom they were to vote. And this is all!
Nay, there is more, I am the author of a very popular Texan
Song [73] which you may have heard our friend Stewart,[74] when
fairly fuddled, singing in the streets & taverns of Columbia. I
have also a very Texan drama,[75] unpublished in my desk, which

---

[71] Wilson Shannon (1802-1877) was appointed United States minister to
Mexico on April 9, 1844. He was recalled in March, 1845.

[72] George Mifflin Dallas (1792-1864) was a rival of Van Buren for leadership of the Democratic Party in Pennsylvania before he became vice-president
under Polk.

[73] In the Charleston *Mercury* for Oct. 11, 1844, under the caption "Simms'
Last and Best," is the following comment on "The Texian Hunter's Bride,"
later published as "The Texian Hunter" in *Areytos: or, Songs of the South*
(Charleston: John Russell, 1846), pp. 21-22: "We recommend to the friends
of Annexation generally, without distinction of parties (liberal men we are)
the following flower-gem from Mr. Simms's varied cabinet of rich and rare.
Let our sweetest daughters of Love and minstrelsy get it by *heart* and fling
rose fling dours [sic] upon it by giving it the voice and utterance of bird-like
tongues and ruby lips — till all out [sic] Southern air trembles into melodious
kisses. Go it my hearties! Go it while you're young! Without ironing [sic],
Dear Simms, this is a hit on the bull's eye — aye on the very pupil of Phoebus!"
The song follows this effusion.

[74] John A. Stuart (1800-1852), editor of the Charleston *Mercury* from 1831
until early in 1845, was a member of the State House of Representatives at
this time. He served with Simms on the Committee on Federal Relations.
Simms again misspells his name *Stewart* in his letter to Hammond of *c.* Feb.
25, 1849.

[75] *Michael Bonham: or, the Fall of Bexar. A Tale of Texas* (Richmond:
Jno. R. Thompson, 1852). It was first published in *S. L. M.,* XVIII (Feb.-
June, 1852), 89-96, 145-149, 234-240, 296-304, 342-349. The play was later
performed at the New Charleston Theatre on March 26, 27, and 28, 1855 (see
W. Stanley Hoole, *The Ante-Bellum Charleston Theatre* [University of Ala-
bama, 1946], p. 183).

will make a rumpus, be sure, if ever it reaches light upon the stage. You may answer for it that I am a genuine Southron, well hated by New England, hostile to the Tariff, Abolition &c, not to speak of a hundred other Yankee abominations. Whether these are qualities to recommend me to Mr Polk, I know not. That they secure me the affections of all genuine Southrons I am very sure. — As a traveller in foreigns, I should perhaps be doing the country a service apart from the performance of official duties. I should be a close observer of what is curious in the traditions, the antiquities & the manners of a people; of these I should make due record, & future elaborate use in fiction or in history. I have never sought for office in my life & would not now that my friends should take any undue pains to force my pretensions. I would not have them do for me, ("crooking the pregnant hinges of the knee," even though 'thrift should follow fawning,")[76] what I would not do for myself. As for the pecuniary value of the berth, I care for it only so far as it will enable me with my little family to maintain the attitude of a Southern Gentleman in a foreign land. And now, you have the whole, and see the extent of my cravings. I shall write to my old friend, Judge Huger,[77] on the subject, and you will suffer our friend Holmes[78] to read this letter. In your & their hands, I leave the matter wholly to be urged or set aside at your discretion. Thanks for your kind consideration, which I shall remember always while I am,

> Yours,
>
> W. Gilmore Simms

232: To James Lawson
(Confidential)

Woodlands, Feb. 11. 1845

My dear Lawson

The South Carolina Delegation in Congress, with other friends, are prepared to present my name to Mr. Polk, and unanimously to urge my pretensions upon him for a foreign appointment. There have been some communications made me on the subject, and

---

[76] *Hamlet,* III, ii, 66-67.

[77] Daniel Elliott Huger (1779-1854), of Charleston, served on the South Carolina bench (1819-1830) and in the United States Senate (1842-1845).

[78] Isaac E. Holmes.

whether there be any prospect of success or not, I am assured that this will not be doubtful if it is to depend at all on the earnestness or warmth of those who are acting for me. The question then occurs, what will suit me. This question rather depends on what I am fit for, and on this head you may help me to a conclusion. My youth, and absence from all connection hitherto in political affairs, will render it out of the question that I should aim at a controlling position abroad in any of those governments, such as France & Great Britain, with which our intercourse is large & likely to be complicated. Still, my own desires, my tastes and pursuits, would make it very important to me that I should be in a literary & an European neighbourhood. In other words, I should greatly prefer a position in Great Britain. Now, as my modesty takes for granted that I cannot be the Ambassador, the question follows how will it suit me to become Secretary of Legation or Consul in that country. And here are the points in which you may help to remove certain of my doubts. Though unambitious of the highest position, I am yet unwilling to sink into one which is merely subordinate, and my impressions of that of a Secretary of Legation, are, that it is that of a very inferior agent, — a mere instrument, without trust or dignity of position. On this subject pray give me your notions and knowledge. The pay too, is, I believe, very inconsiderable. The next office is that of Consul. This office is one of usefulness & influence, but with dignity beyond that of mere commercial agent. Its attraction lies in its pay. Now, to me the pay would really be of little concern, assuming that my leading wish is gratified, and that the compensation is adequate to my wants and appetites, estimating these moderately as you well may. Some of these Consulates in G. B. are I believe profitable. Write me what you know of these, of their duties, of their rewards, & how they would suit me, and whether I would suit them. Say what you know of France, and add all that you can learn touching the Consulate in the Island of Cuba (Havana). I know not, my dear fellow, whether I should not be willing to go as Res. Min. to Constantinople, or as Min. Plen. to Mexico. If the pay is adequate & the labor small, the post of Chargé at Naples, would not be disagreeable in a final resort. I wish you to give me a frank and long letter, as full of detail as you can, in relation to these objects. And pray let it be as soon as possible, as my friends are anxious to know what will suit me best. We must decide on what we want before the inauguration. — You owe me sundry letters. Has Mr. Richards [79] presented himself to you? Pray ask Wetmore [80] if he has recieved from me by any hands, a map on rollers of South Carolina. Have you yet seen Judge Meek [81] of Alabama? I gave him letters to you. He is a fine fellow. Ask Burgess & Stringer to send a copy of Helen & the Castle to B. B. Minor [82] (S. L. M.) and request Duyckinck to ask Langley or Saunders [83] to send him a copy of Marion. Neither of these has he recieved. I got yesterday a Bill of Lading of the sweetmeats &c. Present us affectionately to Madame L. and say that when they reach us, we shall have a flare up in her honor. Has the New Mag. yet reached you. What says Stringer about our various projects, and how have the two books [84] turned out. They still continue to sell here in Carolina. I hear nothing of Mathews, & suppose he is offended by the Review.[85] But he should be grateful rather. The Broadway Journal is spirited, but aims to be piquant at the expense of justice. This is a too frequent error of the mere satirist. I wish you would urge B & S. about the Count Julian & the suggestions in the case of the plates of Winchester. If we only had that small roll of M.S. I could finish the affair in three days. We propose sending you some of our new hams as soon as they are cured. I shall pay off my last heavy debt ($1000) in a few days & shall then feel more comfortable than I have done for many a day.

W. G. S.

233: To Evert Augustus Duyckinck

Woodlands, Feb 11. 1845

Evert A Duyckinck Esq.
My dear Duyckinck.

We shall soon be in want of No 3 of Time's Wallet. I am not sure but that I hinted this in a previous Letter. I have but just returned from a visit to the City where I spent a few days

---

[79] Thomas Addison Richards.

[80] Prosper M. Wetmore. See introductory sketch.

[81] Alexander Beaufort Meek. See introductory sketch.

[82] Benjamin Blake Minor. See note 102, Oct. 13, 1843.

[83] At this time Frederick Saunders (see note 137, Nov. 18, 1844) was employed by Langley. See letter to Duyckinck of June 25, 1845.

[84] *Helen Halsey* and *Castle Dismal*.

[85] "Writings of Cornelius Mathews," *S. Q. R.,* VI (Oct., 1844), 307-342.

and saw that your No 2 was in print.[86] Your suggested alteration
came too late for the correction of the first sentence. The matter
was printed before your Letter was recieved & before I reached
the City. I did not read the proof. It was only on my return to
Woodlands that I recieved your Letter. I am glad that my first
number likes you even moderately.[87] That, and perhaps the two
following, will have been prepared under many disadvantages. In
truth the work is quite too small for my purposes and does not
give me sufficient room for my own utterance. I have to cramp
myself to give variety to the reader. For this reason No 2 will
contain 80 instead of 72 pages. The contents of No 2 are, thus
far — 1. Our Agricultural Condition. 2 The Forest Ranger,
(a Song [)]. 3 Those Old Lunes; or Which is the Madman.
4. Wooing: By a Bashful Gentleman. 5. Time's Wallet — The
Pleasant Commodie of Patient Grissel. 6. Gleams: By Adrian
Beaufain. 7. Sensibility: By James W. Simmons. 8 Song. "Gone
are the sweet hopes. 9. Ambition (a Scrap) 10. The Epochs
& Events of American History as suited to the purposes of Art.
11. Stanzas 12 American Partisan Warfare (*Review of Simcoe
by General Jamison*) (entre nous) 13. Poetry. 14 Cotton & To-
bacco Parallels. &c. Then follows rather a long table Editorial,
probably 12 or 14 pages.[88] I am afraid there is nothing promising
in this Bill of Fare. The articles are all too long. Two of them
are purely local, but they should interest a Northern politician.
The third number will be better. There will be something more
of Weems hereafter,[89] and I have several plots in my head which

[86] "Time's Wallet. II. The Pleasant Commodie of Patient Grissil," *Southern
and Western,* I (Feb., 1845), 100-106. Number III of "Time's Wallet" did not
appear in the *Southern and Western.*

[87] For Duyckinck's notices of the *Southern and Western,* see notes 54, Jan.
18, 1845; 88, Feb. 11, 1845; 130, March 15, 1845; 156, April 7, 1845; 200, June
6, 1845; 220, June 7, 1845; and 242, June 25, 1845.

[88] All articles listed appeared; editorial comments ran to ten pages. Simms'
own contributions include "Our Agricultural Condition" (pp. 73-84), "The
Forest Ranger" (p. 84), "Those Old Lunes! or, Which Is the Madman?" (pp.
85-99), "Wooing; by a Bashful Gentleman" (p. 99), "Gleams" (p. 106), "Song.
— 'Gone Are the Sweet Hopes'" (p. 108), "Ambition" (p. 108), "The Epochs
and Events of American History, as Suited to the Purposes of Art in Fiction"
(pp. 109-127), "Stanzas" (p. 127), "At Parting" (p. 134), and "Editorial
Bureau" (pp. 143-152). All are unsigned except "Gleams" and "Stanzas"
(both signed "Adrian Beaufain"). Simms is probably the author also of two
additional unsigned poems: "Song. — Ah! Turning O'er the Classic Page" (p.
134) and "Friendly Sympathy — From the Latin" (p. 142). The New York
Morning News devotes its notice of March 7 to Simms' "Epochs and Events."

[89] Simms' "Weems, the Historian" had appeared in the Jan. issue of the
Southern and Western (see note 54, Jan. 18, 1845). No further article on
Weems was published in the *Southern and Western,* though Richard Yeadon's

with leisure I can make interesting. I have recieved Nos 3 & 4.
of Briggs' Journal. Pray get him to send me Nos 1 & 2. He is
piquant and pleasant. The danger to which he is liable, is that of
being too much pleased with the character of the satirist to remember always the demands of justice. This is the danger to
which smart men are subject, who have been praised for saying
clever things. They become malicious & unjust. Warn him against
this. Some of his things are very good. His hit at Willis & Morris
is capital.⁹⁰ They are hit off agreeable to their deserts. He is
sensible too where he does not aim to be smart. His paragraph
on the Southern Review & the article on Mathews does not state
the case fairly. But he is one of the professional humorists who
do not relish my doctrines. I am not responsible for the John Ox,
or the Sans potato.⁹¹ The latter is Carlyle's, the former is old &
new. But is not the Broadway Journal poorly got up for a Broadway Journal. Should it not have been very elegant. — I notice

---

"The Marion Family" (see note 188, May 12, 1845) contains much about Weems
and his inaccuracies concerning Marion.

⁹⁰ In the second article in a series on "American Prose Writers," published
in the *Broadway Journal,* I (Jan. 18, 1845), 37-38, Nathaniel Parker Willis
(see introductory sketch) is discussed (p. 37) : "In his poetry, and in the *matter*
of his prose, . . . [Willis] has, beyond doubt, innumerable merits : — still, they
are merits which he shares with other writers . . . his *prose style,* however, is
not only a genus *per se,* but it is his own property 'in fee simple impartite,' and
no man living has ever yet set foot upon it except himself. . . . In the style
of Mr. Willis we easily detect this idiosyncrasy. . . . It is Fancy." In an account
of "General Morris's Complimentary Concert," *ibid.,* I (Jan. 25, 1845), 60,
Briggs writes : "This generous testimony to Mr. Morris as a man and worthy
citizen, fully equalled, in its results, the expectations of the friendly projectors.
We are told that he netted some two thousand dollars. He was called out between
the parts, and responded to the call in a few words neatly turned ; — he would
have said more, but his heart rose to his throat, and his honeyed words were
distilled into tears, and he retired."

For George Pope Morris, see introductory sketch.

⁹¹ In a review of the *Southern Quarterly Review, ibid.,* I (Jan. 25, 1845),
61-62, Briggs writes : "Any literary publication that narrows itself down to so
small a compass as South Carolina prejudices must, of course, be exceedingly
narrow in its moral dimensions. . . . The longest article in the Review is devoted
to the writings of Cornelius Mathews. While the reviewer complains in no
moderate terms of the hardships of American authors, arising from lack of
sympathy among their own countrymen, he does not, himself, appear to be
aware that there are any other writers beside the subject of his paper and
Judge Longstreet. . . . The article is written in a very grave and solemn tone,
but it contains two witticisms, though they are of a rather ponderous character ;
he calls the English John Ox, and the Irish Sans Potato. Without quarrelling
with him for emasculating the national emblem of the English, we must object
to the new name for the Irish — it should be Sans-everything-but-Potato, if
sans anything."

your article on the Benefit to Morris & the Pitches to Halleck.[92] All this is miserable trickery — humbug — I suppose got up in both cases by the parties themselves or their immediate creatures. I do not now see the Mirror so that I must look to you to report its specialties. I had a glimpse of a slender assault upon me, which the Knickerbocker took care to place before my eyes.[93]— I am afraid that Mathews takes my article to heart, and is silent accordingly. I am sorry that he published the chapter in the Dem. Rev. which does not explain itself. He should have furnished more or none. When his work is ready for publication send me a brief review of it.[94] — I will thank you to see Wiley & Putnam, Appleton &c. or get our friend Saunders to see them and request that our magazine should recieve their new publications. We circulate something like 1500 copies already, & the prospect is good of a large increase. You may add to this that our *ipse dixit* is of no small moment in making up the opinion of the Southern Country. Of course while I shall be genial & indulgent, I shall always endeavour to be just. Let them address their publications to me, personally, "Care of Saml. Hart Sen. Charleston." I have something more to write you, but that hereafter. It is now dark &c. God bless you —

W. G. Simms

How would O'Sullivan like a series of papers made up of brief biographies of distinguished men of the Revolution in the South, interspersed with their original Letters. I have MSS. of Henry Laurens, of John Laurens, of John Rutledge, Gen. Gates, Gen. Heath, Arthur Lee, Patrick Henry &c. With a few brief biographical sentences, these letters might be introduced very happily & would form a series of papers equally valuable & interesting.[95]

---

[92] The New York *Evening Mirror* of Jan. 21 contains a long account of George Pope Morris' benefit concert of the previous evening. Perhaps this is the article Simms here has in mind. We are unable to clarify the "pitches to [Fitz-Greene] Halleck" (see introductory sketch).

[93] See note 33, Jan. 15, 1845.

[94] Mathews' "chapter" in the *Democratic* is "The Ghost of New York" (see note 38, Jan. 15, 1845). At this time he was at work on *Big Abel and the Little Manhattan* (New York: Wiley and Putnam, 1845).

[95] Simms had earlier written to Langley, publisher of the *Democratic Review,* concerning this collection (see letter to Duyckinck of Jan. 19, 1845). Though John L. O'Sullivan, editor of the journal, consented (see note 167, April 10, 1845), Simms did not carry out this project for the *Democratic Review.* Later, in 1847, he did write a sketch of John Rutledge containing selections from his letters, and this was published in the *American [Whig] Review* (see note 120, April 19, 1847).

—I shall be glad to see Mr. Fraser.[96] My article on Horne appears in the forthcoming No. of the Review. It was too long for the last, & will make two numbers.[97] I know nothing of Miss —— who writes in the Tribune.[98] Send me some of her things. Have you seen Judge Meek?

Yours again,

W. G. S.

234: To JAMES MUNROE AND COMPANY

Mess'rs James Munroe & Co
Boston, Mass.   Charleston, S. C. Feb. 12. [1845][99]

Gentln.

Suffer me to invite your attention to the within projêt. My purpose is to secure for criticism, within its pages, early copies of your future and recent publications. Our circulation is already large, & promises to become yet more so. Of our modes & standards of criticism (which are equally just and indulgent) you will have a sufficient sample in the number of the work (for January) which I have ordered to be sent you. You will there find, among other literary notices, a favorable critique of the 'Notes on Cuba' by Wurdemann.[100] Address me, to the care of Babcock & Co, S. Hart Sen. W. H. Barrett, or McCarter & Allen,[101] Charleston.

With due respect,
Yr obt Servt

W. Gilmore Simms

---

96 Probably Robert F. Fraser, of New York, at one time corresponding secretary of the American Art-Union while Prosper M. Wetmore was president.

97 Simms' review of *A New Spirit of the Age,* ed. Richard H. Horne (New York: Harper & Brothers, 1844), was published in *S. Q. R.,* VII (April, 1845), 312-349. A second part, entitled "Modern Prose Fiction," was finally published, *ibid.,* XV (April, 1849), 41-83.

98 Undoubtedly Simms has in mind Margaret Fuller (1810-1850), who at this time was writing for Greeley's paper.

99 This letter is written on the prospectus of the *Southern and Western.*

100 Dr. J. G. F. Wurdemann's *Notes on Cuba* (Boston: J. Munroe and Company, 1844) is reviewed in I (Jan., 1845), 70-71.

101 Booksellers and publishers.

235: To D. Appleton and Company

Charleston, S. C. Feb. 12. [1845][102]

Mess'rs D. Appleton & Co

Gentlemen

I take leave to invite your attention to the within prospectus. My purpose is to obtain copies of your publications, as they appear, for the purpose of examination & review. Our standards of criticism shall be just but indulgent. Our circulation is already large, with a prospect of becoming yet more so. That you may the better judge of our modes of criticism, I have ordered that our periodical, as already issued may be sent you. Address to me, care of McCarter & Allen, or Babcock & Co, or Saml. Hart, Sen, Charleston.

Very respectfully,
Yr obt Servt

W Gilmore Simms

236: To Benjamin Franklin Perry

Woodlands, Feb 13. 1845

B. F. Perry, Esq.

My dear Perry.

It was my hope to have seen you on your late visit to Charleston, of which Yeadon [103] gave me some assurances, but I was compelled to hurry out of town, and when I returned to it you had just taken your departure. It would have given me great pleasure to have hob-a-nob'd with you over his madeira, and to have discussed the pleasant world and wines of which we were a part. I may have this pleasure next summer if I succeed in doing what I desire — arranging for a trip to the back country. It is probable that you are in reciept of the first number of my Magazine, and I trust that its contents like you. We were somewhat hurried in their preparation, but they are respectable, and with a little time we shall do better. I need not say that I desire you would resume your labors for its pages. You can surely gather up an interesting additional series of revolutionary events, or these failing, the subjects for literary manufacture, in your parts,

---

[102] This letter is written on the prospectus of the *Southern and Western*.
[103] Richard Yeadon. See introductory sketch.

are sufficiently extensive.[104] My own notion is that we should write as much as possible about home — gather up our own gems & jewels — look about us and within us — what we are, what we have been & what we may be. It is from the use of such materials that author and country alike grow famous. Thus far, for yourself. And now, — it would give me great pleasure if Waddy Thompson could be persuaded to give us a series of sketches about Mexico, its people, its President, its leading men generally.[105] Now that Santa Anna is *hors de combat* his history becomes peculiarly interesting. Thompson who is a sensible man, not wanting in imagination, should be able, I should suppose, to prepare a series equally thoughtful and picturesque which would be creditable to his name in a new department. Can he not be persuaded to it. If you thought it better, I should, though personally unknown to him, write to him myself; but I think it likely that you can do more for our object than any body beside. Broach it to him, *mon ami,* if you second my notions, & let me have the result as soon as possible. — There is a matter which concerns myself, upon which I communicate *sub rosa.* — I have some friends, in Washington & Tennessee, who are disposed to present my name to the new President as one for whom they would like to procure a foreign appointment. The movement is with my approbation. The difficulty is in finding out what is available which would suit me. Will it be in your way to sound Thompson as to the nature of [the] situation while in Mexico — how he relished that city & country and in how far it was agreeable & desirable to himself. To these questions, cautiously urged, he might yield sufficient answer, without suspecting their object. Perhaps, too, his old experiences in Congress might enable him to give some information as to the eligibility of appointments to Italy — the Sicilies for example, — Rome &c. I am in very ample ignorance of the advantages or disadvantages of almost every berth which might be found available. — I am very far from sanguine in my expectations. I have been no clamorer for Mr. Polk, have thrown up no hat, and simply took him for my man, as an alternative. I have no doubt that he is a worthy man, but very far from a great one. Still his

---

[104] No article carrying Perry's signature or initials was published in the *Southern and Western.* Possibly he is the author of "Naming of Places in the Carolinas" and of the two "Revolutionary Incidents" bearing the subtitles of "Charles Davant" and "Israel Andress and Martin Angel," II (Dec., 1845), 367-376, 378-381.

[105] No article in the *Southern and Western* can be ascribed to Thompson (see introductory sketch).

choice of ministers & friends may be judicious, & I may be one
of them! — And now to close, — do nothing & say nothing in
these matters which shall not be perfectly agreeable to yourself.
You are, as I would have all whom I esteem, perfectly at liberty. —
Yet no, — you must work for the Magazine, *pro bono publico*.
It is a cheap work, and will be purely native. Be sure of that. Let
your Editor do his duty, & set some of your young men to work
to beat up subscribers. Present me very respectfully — my wife
joins me — to Mrs. P. & the family of Mrs. McCall.[106]

Yours faithfully

W. Gilmore Simms

237 : To Samuel Henry Dickson [107]

Woodlands, Feb. 18. 1845

Professor S. Henry Dickson.

My dear Professor.

In cancelling the Bond which you hold of mine,[108] and which
I am at length enabled to do after a long and to me humiliating
delay, I am constrained, from a sense of duty, and from a deep
consideration of the many kindnesses I have enjoyed at your
hands, during a period in which your friendship was not the least
of my solaces and comforts, to express my fervent and sincere
regret that, by an inadvertence, — which none regretted more
promptly or entirely than myself, — I should have lost that regard
which I so much valued, and which had served me in so many
important and substantial respects. I have now no reference to the
pecuniary obligation which I hasten to discharge, for that, I am
proud to say, I might have incurred, at their own solicitation, to
several other friends; but I now refer to that warm interest in
my career and fortunes, shown to me when these were very doubtful, which was more to me than any wealth, as it served to compensate for more deficiencies than even money could supply. You
were among those, few but strong, who gave their undeviating
countenance to me in my early struggles — who expressed an
encouraging faith in my claims, and contributed, by the frank

---

[106] Mrs. Perry's mother, Mrs. Hext McCall.

[107] See introductory sketch. The rift between Simms and Dickson (indicated
by this letter) was shortly closed (see letter to Duyckinck of May 15, 1846).

[108] The debt of $1000 mentioned in the letter to Lawson of Feb. 11.

expression of their opinions, to assert and to secure their acknowledgment. These things I cannot forget; and it becomes me
to seize the occasion presented by an otherwise purely business
communication, to say, at least, that nothing can eradicate from
my memory the impression of former kindnesses, and to repeat
my deep regret that an unconsidered reflection should have been
of such a nature, as to leave me open to the misrepresentations
of the malicious, or the misconceptions of those whom I should
always delight to honor. I thank you, my dear Professor, — deeply
and sincerely, for the pecuniary assistance which I recieved at
your hands, — and in cancelling my obligation, which I do
through those of our friend Yeadon, you will permit me to say
that your prosperity, happiness and health, will always be subjects
of affectionate sympathy, to the heart of

W. Gilmore Simms

238: To George Frederick Holmes

Woodlands, Feb. 25. [1845][109]

Geo. Fred. Holmes Esq.

My dear Holmes.

My Congratulations on your marriage are not the less friendly
or sincere for coming late. You have commenced a new career,
& must remember the philosophy of Caliban —
    "Ca! Ca! Ho Caliban —
    Have a new master, be a new man!" [110]
You were never, I believe, a positively wicked person; only
a sinner by the way, as occasion offered. Evil lay in your way,
as rebellion in that of Falstaff, and you did nothing more than
find it. It will be easy for you therefore to turn over a new leaf,
— to sink into the easy chair of matrimony, and deliver yourself
up to the pleasant dreams which come with that condition. It
will not be hard with you to renounce the old paths of misde-
meanor — to give up the accustomed haunts, and to say to the
ancient companion, of no matter what sex, — "Get thee behind
me!" — I trust, however, that you will not be indiscriminate in
this renunciation, and turn in like manner from those who would

---

[109] Dated by Holmes' marriage (between Jan. 19 and Feb. 25, 1845) to
Eliza Lavallette Floyd, daughter of John Floyd, later governor of Virginia
(1849-1852).
[110] See *The Tempest*, II, ii, 193-194.

have counselled you, equally wisely and well, — would have plucked you as a brand from the burning, gathered you as a hen gathereth her chickens, and made a man of you after the most approved fashion. Among this class I certainly count myself. You will not have forgotten, — and I look for it to establish my claim to the confidence & regard of your wife — that I was one of the first to counsel you to come among us Benedictines.[111] Said I not to you, — 'Holmes take a wife!' — and this not once nor twice, nor thrice, but many times, whenever it so happened that we met. Let me add now that in marrying you have equally proved my wisdom & your own. Mine, by doing as I bade you, and your own by choosing — so report hath it — a wife among a thousand. Why man, they speak of Madame H. as a sort of prodigy — a thing of excellences — such a wife as might have won a smile from Cato, — the Senior Roman, I mean — forgetful of his own edicts & the calls of the Senate House. Commend me to her, I pray you, with my most respectful compliments, and heartiest good wishes.

I have just got back from a visit to the city. — I went down the day of the night when you were to be married — regretting very much that I could not attend your nuptials, as I had to escort a lady visitor, who had resolved to go down on that day. I wrote to this effect to Col. Lewis, at Lewisville,[112] to which place, — uncertain of your absolute whereabouts, I address this Letter. The magazine gets on very well. You have seen the first number, & by this time, the second. It is not exactly what I wish, but will improve with time. I was rather disappointed in not hearing from you, but could readily concieve how the delights of a new condition — and such a condition, — should put pen, ink & paper out of your head. But do not let yourself be wholly enervated by Love. Be a man, old fellow — don't yield yourself with[out] a struggle. Call up your spirits. Get your Greeks & Trojans, your Romans & Tyrrhenians — about you; and say to the Tempter, "Avaunt! See you not that I have begun a new article! &c.["]"[113] Yours with best wishes for your health & happiness.

In haste

W. Gilmore Simms

---

[111] An allusion to Benedick in *Much Ado About Nothing*.
[112] William L. Lewis, of St. Matthew's (formerly Lewisville), S. C.
[113] No article in the *Southern and Western* can be ascribed to Holmes.

239: To Benjamin Franklin Perry

Woodlands, Feb 27. [1845][114]

My dear Perry

Will you say to Gen. Thompson that his proposed series suits me exactly. I am disposed to think that the most interesting things we could have from Mexico are those which relate to the moral and intellectual stature of that region. To begin with Santa Anna would be particularly right, just now, while the public mind is in anxiety as regards his fate — while his life hangs in suspense, a feather at the mercy of the popular breath, or the equally capricious wits of those who depend for their own position so entirely upon the popular breath. I could wish that his article on Santa Anna could be prepared as soon as possible, in order that its interest may be felt in all its freshness, and before the fate of that remarkable man should be finally determined. But, of course, we must not hurry the General. Say to him — from me that it will give me great pleasure to recieve and find an early place for all his communications. It will be equally agreeable to me to make his acquaintance in *pro. per.* which if I visit you at Greenville I should hope to do this summer. And while I am in this vein, giving you commissions of this sort, let me request you when next you meet our old friend Mr Poinsett,[115] to say to him that I left for him, a few weeks ago, with J. B. Campbell[116] of Charleston, a diploma from the Maryland Historical Society, which I trust, and take for granted, he will recieve duly. If you can persuade him also to send us some papers, say upon the recent Etruscan discoveries,[117] you will add to your kindnesses. — My prospect of going abroad, is up to this period, nothing better than a hope. Our S. C. delegation are pleased to

---

114 Dated by Simms' discussion of Thompson's proposed series of articles about Mexico. See letter to Perry of Feb. 13.

115 Joel Roberts Poinsett. See introductory sketch.

116 James Butler Campbell (1808-1883), a graduate of Brown University, came to South Carolina in 1826. For several years he taught school on Edisto Island while studying law under Hugh S. Legaré. He began the practice of law in Charleston in 1831, was several times elected to the South Carolina House of Representatives, and in 1866 was elected to the United States Senate, but was denied the seat. In 1877 he was elected to the South Carolina Senate to fill out the term of a Negro who had resigned. He was the sixth president of the New England Society of Charleston.

117 Poinsett's "Etruscan Remains" was published in the *Southern Literary Journal*, II (April, 1836), 81-89, and in *The Charleston Book*, pp. 105-122. The latter also contains his "Literature and the Fine Arts," pp. 306-310. No article which can be identified as Poinsett's appears in the *Southern and Western*.

urge my pretensions, and I fancy that they will find sympathy & support from others of the South. But I am no partisan, and have taken so little part in politics of any kind, that it is scarcely possible to commend me in the ordinary way to Mr. Polk's attention. It is only as a Literary man, one of the few whom the South asserts, that I can possibly hope to find any favor. And a claim like this is not often potential with a Western President. — I have just written to the publishers to know why the Magazine has not been sent you, & to instruct them to see that the neglect is not continued. — I shall look for your contributions with anxiety, particularly that which relates to the Cunninghams. [118] There are several topics of this class about which you could write easily and successfully. — I trust that you are able to find all the localities in the Giant's Coffin,[119] and that you have happened upon old persons who could remember all the parties in the story. This, by the way, is usually a very easy matter. I have been surprised at the facility with which old persons pick up as recollections what were never facts. They need nothing but a clue and a sign, & the rest is certain. You obtain a witness who will swear through thick & thin. — Oates [120] has some good old books — some of which he sells cheaply, but others of which he has large prices for. I have, I am afraid, done some thing towards giving him exaggerated notions of their value. I have bought largely from him, & perhaps too freely expressed my opinions in favor of his stock, and he now charges inordinately for some of his unimportant works. All that I have bought from him are good, & you have no doubt got something equally rare & valuable. — Would I could have seen you in Charleston.

---

[118] No article about the Cunninghams, Loyalists in the American Revolution (see note 212, Oct. 30, 1846), was published in the *Southern and Western.* Simms had earlier asked Perry to prepare such an article for the *Magnolia* (see letter to Perry of March 15, 1843). While the family's name during its recorded history has often been spelled *Cuningham* by some of its members, the spelling given by Simms and also by Simms' contemporaries of the family has been used in this work.

[119] Simms' story of Greenville, S. C., entitled "The Giant's Coffin, or the Feud of Holt and Houston. A Tale of Reedy River," was published in *The Gift, A Christmas, New Year, and Birthday Present, 1845* (Philadelphia : Carey & Hart, 1845), pp. 169-211. It was republished in *The Wigwam and the Cabin,* Second Series, pp. 1-43. In reviewing *The Gift* Duyckinck remarks in the New York *Morning News* of Sept. 20, 1844, that "for the bone and muscle of a story commend us to Simms' Giant's Coffin full of facts, incidents and character, without pause or hindrance, with a denouement in the intense melodramatic vein, worthy of the title."

[120] George Oates, bookseller of King Street, Charleston.

Yeadon tells me there was a pleasant day at his house, and was pleased to regret my absence. Present us, Madame & myself to Mrs. P. and hold me

Very faithfully
Yours

W. Gilmore Simms

240: To JAMES LAWSON

Woodlands. Feb 27. [1845][121]

My dear Lawson

We recieved the creature comforts some few days ago, the buckwheat, the sweetmeats, pickles and cranberries, all in good order, and such a smacking and licking of lips you never heard before. Mr. Roach pronounced very favorably upon the peaches of Lady Lide, and all parties have been luxuriating in her artistical combinations. We wish her invariable success for the next thousand years, in similar preparations for her great grandchildren, of whom, by this time, I have no doubt she begins to make prolific calculations. — Your letter & the paper relating to Forrest,[122] came today. Our hams are now in the smoke house, and will probably be in fit condition for packing in ten days more. We are truly glad that our grist reached you in safety and has proved good, — but, says Mr. Roach, "I am very sure that they have not yet the art of cooking it rightly." I wish, my dear fellow, that our productions were something more worthy of your table. — I thank you for the suggestions in your Letter. My friends in Congress are the whole South Carolina delegation, & some others, I have reason to believe, in the West & South West. I do not flatter myself much with the idea that they can be very successful, and I only seek to know what are the offices that might suit me, without being beyond my claims. I may add, what I hear from every quarter of the South, that there is scarce any appointment that could be made from the South which would command more general approbation in that quarter than my own. Still, as you suggest, I put no faith in Presidents or Princes. Your opinions very generally coincide with my own, and I have intimated to my friends that my first choice would be the Court of the Two

---

[121] Dated by Simms' discussion of his desire for a diplomatic post. See letter to Lawson of Feb. 11.
[122] See note 127, below.

Sicilies at Naples; next that of Sardinia at Turin, and thirdly the Kingdom of Portugal. I am not so satisfied to take the post of a secretary, as I am not of a temper to hold the subordinate position. But I shall write to my friends to say, that *pour le dernier resort,* they may book me if the thing can be done, as Secretary of Legation at London. This, by the way, is of course, a strictly confidential matter, which, *I communicate to you only of all New York!* Your wife, I think, can keep a secret — *one of mine at least,* and I make sure that when you tell it to her, you will mention my earnest wish in this respect. The thing is so completely in embryo, and may be so completely defeated that such caution is only prudent & necessary. — I congratulate you from the bottom of my heart on your becoming a Landholder,[123] and on your progress towards the gratification of your proper desires. Only do not go too rapidly — not too deeply in debt if you can help it. My wife read over this part of your Letter with great delight and rejoices quite as much as myself at your improving pecuniary condition. *None* of your friends takes half the interest in your permanance & general success that we do. May you soon be in possession of your castle, with no mortgage upon it & no notes in Bank. You are at liberty to see Winchester & to suffer him to go on, giving you the $200 or good paper for it at sixty days. As soon as he sends me the proof of what he has, I will finish the story.[124] I have a chapter done, in my possession, which I will forward, and the assurance from you that the note is with you, and a knowledge of the previous portions, not yet printed, which he has and which he may proceed to print as soon as he makes the arrangement, — will prompt me to go to work & to finish the story in a week after the last proofs are recieved. This I cannot do, unless I rewrite and reinvent all that portion which he retains. You will also get from Stringer the printed volumes & retain them for me. I do not care to urge the work upon him, altho he was pledged for it. I wrote to him about some publications (Nos.) which I wished him to send me. Remind him of them. — Confound your fat man! — Do look among your papers for a second vol. of my M.S.S. — foolscap size, — like that which contained "the Biloxi"[125] poem. Write also to

---

[123] Lawson had purchased property and was building a mansion at 136 West 12th Street, New York City.
[124] *Count Julian.*
[125] "The Last Song of the Biloxi" (later called "The Last Fields of the Biloxi"). See note 239, June 25, 1845.

your musical friend to whom you *unwisely* entrusted my songs
(in M.S.) of which I had no copies. I want them music or no
music! *Your* Songs will live doubtless. — Of this even Gen.
Morris will give you the most ample assurance when — you become a millionaire! [126] You say nothing of him & his benefit.
The Broadway Journal is lively and piquant. I am sorry for
Forrest's sake that the English Theatre in Paris proved a failure.
I had no expectations from it. I suppose the Letter in the Post
is Forrest's.[127] Whenever you get an opportunity by private hand,
send me the M.S. tragedy and M.S. poems [128] — if you can find
them. Wife sends her love, and Augusta to yours. Mr. Roach
joins me in saying that we are faithfully &c.

Yrs

W. G. S.

241: To EVERT AUGUSTUS DUYCKINCK

Woodlands, 15th. March 1845

My dear D.

I left Charleston this morning early but have heard nothing of
your friend Mr. Fraser. Your letter, dated the 10th. I find awaiting me at the plantation. I trust you gave Mr. F. instructions
to find his way up to us. If his object be to waste time, a week

---

[126] This is a gibe at George Pope Morris' tendency to praise authors of
wealth.

[127] On Feb. 21, 1845, the New York *Evening Post* printed a letter dated
Paris, Jan. 29, 1845, in which the writer (here identified by Simms as Forrest)
comments: "Among other novelties, Mr. [John] Mitchell [1806-1874], a London
bookseller, has made the experiment of introducing English tragedy upon the
French stage. Mr. Macready, Miss Helen Faucit and Mr. Graham were the
principal actors, and after performing twelve nights to indifferent houses, the
manager was compelled to close abruptly at a loss of a considerable sum of
money. Edwin Forrest, the tragedian, arrived in Paris a night or two before
the termination of the English performances, and much disappointment was
felt among his countrymen and others here, who were anxious to see him
perform for a few nights, that the manager had already determined upon re-
linquishing the theatre. It is understood, however, that a project is now in
contemplation to secure another English company, for the sole purpose of introducing Mr. Forrest to a Parisian audience. . . ." William Rounseville Alger
remarks (*Life of Edwin Forrest, the American Tragedian* [Philadelphia: J. B.
Lippincott & Co., 1877], I, 398) that Forrest wanted to appear in Mitchell's
company and that announcements of his plans to appear were made in the
American and Paris presses, but that Mitchell refused to discuss the matter
with him.

[128] The MS. tragedy is "Don Carlos"; the MS. poems are the volume planned,
but never published, entitled "The Mocking Bird" or "The Mock Bird." See
letters to Lawson of April 22, 1844, and June 7, 1845.

or two with us in the country would not be amiss. We are not
in Charleston (the family) during winter & spring, only in
summer & autumn. My daughter has been down for a month
attending balls & parties,[129] and I run down every two weeks
or so, to show myself & pick up matters and see to business. But
our town house is always closed during this period. I shall be
pleased to see Mr. F. and will give him welcome whenever we
encounter. I quite regret that No. 3 of the Wallet did not come
to hand, as I should like to have carried on the Nos. regularly.
Our March no. is through my hands.[130] Our papers are quite too
long for our pages, and it so happens that the subjects taken up
seem to require it. We shall amend as we advance — perhaps —
in this as other respects. In our April no. there is an attack on
the North American — based on its circular.[131] It is rather too
long. I see your Mr. Briggs does not like us.[132] I mortally of-

---

[129] January and February then, as now, constituted the society season in
Charleston. During these months the St. Cecilia and other formal balls took
place.
[130] Simms' own contributions to the March issue of the *Southern and Western*
include "Literature and Art Among the Indians" (pp. 153-164), "Fragment"
(p. 164), "The Lonely Islet" (p. 165), "The Last Feast of the Lucumo; or the
Picture of the 'Grotta Del Tifone'" (pp. 166-181), "Fame" (p. 181), "The
Epochs and Events of American History, as Suited to the Purposes of Art in
Fiction" (pp. 182-191), "Song — 'Such, Oh! Beauty!'" (p. 191), "The City
Hermit. I. A Life Within the Limits" (pp. 197-202), and "Editorial Bureau"
(pp. 220-224). "The Lonely Islet" is signed "Adrian Beaufain," "Fame" is
signed "G.," and "The City Hermit" is signed "The City Hermit." The rest
are unsigned. Simms is also the probable author of "Consciousness" (p. 191)
and "Halsted's Richard III" (pp. 203-208). Duyckinck reviewed the number in
the New York *Morning News* of March 29, commenting: "The fruits of the
editor's leisure after the adjournment of the State Legislature (of which he is
a member) begin to be apparent in the number and variety of the articles
from his pen. There are at least four, though anonymous, distinctly traceable in
the present number . . . 'Literature and Art among the Indians' . . . 'Benedict
Arnold as a Subject for Fictitious Story' ['The Epochs and Events . . .'] . . .
and 'The City Hermit.'"
[131] "A Passage with 'The Veteran Quarterly,'" *Southern and Western,* I
(May, 1845), 297-311. The article is signed "M," but the bound copy of the
Southern and Western from Simms' library has the "M" changed to "W. G. S."
in Simms' handwriting.
[132] The *Broadway Journal,* I (Feb. 1, 1845), 77, carries the following notice:
"Simms' Monthly Magazine has just made its appearance from the Charleston
press. It professes to be a Southern and Western Review, and the first article
in it is called 'Americanism in Literature,' which is chiefly remarkable for
containing nothing in relation to that subject. There are papers by Mr. Headley
and Evert A. Duyckinck, and a few slight notices of books by the editor. Mr.
Simms complains of the great amount of money which the South expends for
Northern productions in art and literature, and of the small amount which the
North pays for Southern works of a like class. Probably not without good
reason; and if he were earnest in his desire to produce a Southern magazine,
he should, in his initial number at least, have filled his columns with the product
of southern pens. The best things in the present number come from the north."
The *Knick.,* XXV (March, 1845), 281, reprints part of this derogatory comment.

fended his *amour propre,* — as I fear — not only in my paper
touching Mathews, — but in a conversation had in his presence
at Mathews' office, in which, having no cue, I spoke rather freely
— not once suspecting him of being a professed humourist —
one of your crack men in that department. You know my notion
upon humour generally, and American humour, so called, in
particular. These naturally annoyed him, and I suspect, he is not
of a forgiving nature. But *Sessa* — let it pass. Your paper on
Jones is a good & *kind* one.[133] He has his kinks, but he has his
merits also. I am glad that you think and speak well of Poe,[134]
which Mathews was not disposed to do though I tried to open
his eyes to the singular merits of that person. Poe is no friend
of mine, as I believe. He began by a very savage attack on one
of my novels — the Partisan.[135] I cannot say that he was much

---

[133] "Sketches of American Prose Writers. William A. Jones," *Broadway
Journal,* I (Jan. 11, 1845), 26-28, signed "D.," is reprinted in the *New York
Weekly News* of Jan. 18, 1845.

[134] In a review of *Graham's* for Feb. the *New York Weekly News* of Feb. 1,
1845, comments of Poe: "Whenever his name is mentioned it has been with the
comment that he is a remarkable man, a man of genius. Few knew precisely
what he had written, his name was not on Library catalogues or any of his
books on the shelves. His influence has been felt while the man was unknown.
Lowell's article removes the anonymous and exhibits the author of some of the
most peculiar and characteristic productions in our literature. Metaphysical
acuteness of perception, resting on imagination, might be no unapt description
of the powers developed in the creation of tales so remarkable for touching the
extreme of mystery and the most faithful literalness of daily life, and criticisms,
profoundly constructed and original in the mind of the critic, and calling forth
the same faculties as the production of the best books themselves." Undoubtedly
this is the comment Simms here has in mind. "The Purloined Letter" and
"The Raven" had been published in the New York *Morning News* of Jan. 21
and Feb. 3, 1845, respectively. Poe's *Tales* was later reviewed on June 28,
1845, and in the issue of July 24, 1845, Duyckinck published a complimentary
notice of the *Broadway Journal* in which he praises Poe as an editor.

[135] In his review, published in *S. L. M.,* II (Jan., 1836), 117-121, Poe opens
with a listing of some of Simms' earlier works and then passes to a burlesque of
Simms' brief dedication of *The Partisan* to Richard Yeadon. The major portion
of the review consists of an analysis of *The Partisan,* in which Poe expresses
the following opinion of the work: "There is very little plot or connexion in
the book before us; and Mr. Simms has evidently aimed at neither. . . . Of
the numerous personages who figure in the book, some are really excellent —
some horrible. The historical characters are, without exception, well drawn. . . .
The fictitious existences in 'The Partisan' will not bear examination. Singleton
is about as much of a non-entity as most other heroes of our acquaintance. His
uncle is no better. . . . Porgy . . . is a most insufferable bore. . . . Mr. Simms'
English is bad — shockingly bad. . . . Instances of bad taste — villainously bad
taste — occur frequently in the book. Of these the most reprehensible are to be
found in a love for that mere *physique* of the horrible which has obtained for
some Parisian novelists the title of the 'French convulsives.' . . . In spite, however, of its manifest and manifold blunders and impertinences, 'The Partisan'
is no ordinary work. Its historical details are replete with interest. The concluding scenes are well drawn. Some passages descriptive of swamp scenery are

out in his estimate. In some respects, as a story for example, —
& in certain matters of taste & style, that was one of the very
worst of the books I have ever written. Poe's critique, however,
paid little heed to what was really good in the thing, and he did
injustice to other portions which were not quite so good. Besides,
he was rude & offensive & personal, in the manner of the thing,
which he should not have been, in the case of anybody, — still
less in mine. My deportment had not justified it. He knew, or
might have known, that I was none of that miserable gang about
town, who beg in the literary highways. I had no clique, mingled
with none, begged no praise from anybody, and made no conditions with the herd. He must have known what I was personally
— might have known — & being just should not have been rude.
What should we think of an executioner who mocks the carcass
after he has taken off the head. I tell you all this to satisfy you
of my sense of verities. I do not puff the man when I say I
consider him a remarkable one. He has more real imaginative
power than 99 in the 100 of our poets & tale writers. His style
is clear & correct, his conceptions bold & fanciful, his fancies
vivid, and his taste generally good. His bolder effects are impaired by his fondness for *detail* & this hurts his criticism which
is too frequently given to the analysis of the inferior points of
style, making him somewhat regardless of the more noble features
of the work. But, I repeat, he is a man of remarkable power,
to whom I shall strive one day to do that justice which a great
portion of our public seems desirous to withhold. This may be
owing to the fact that he is something of an Ishmaelite. He seems
too much the subject of his moods — not sufficiently so of principle. I suspect he frequently says bitter things through a wanton
consciousness of power. This is an unhappy immorality which
all good men resent, and the blow, however, well dealt, is thus
apt to recoil upon him who gives it. His private life, I am told,
has been irregular, but this, I take it, is owing to his poverty,
which, I also learn, has been extreme. Is it any better now? —
I should like to hear something more of the plan of W & P. Will
they want any thing from me? Why not a collection of "Tales
of the South" — selected carefully & closely revised, making a

---

exquisite. Mr. Simms has evidently the eye of a painter. Perhaps, in sober
truth, he would succeed better in sketching a landscape than he has done in
writing a novel."

handsome volume.[136] — Pray get them to send me Miss Fuller's book,[137] — and tell Jay [138] or Wetmore to send me the Report or Essay of Broadhead.[139] Send me also Poe's Lecture.[140] As for Lawson, don't leave any thing for him to do for — aside from his business, to which he is punctually devoted — he is the most remiss rascal in the world. When you write *me,* address to Midway — when to the publishers, write to Charleston.

In haste. God bless you &c

W. G. S.

242 : To James Henry Hammond [141]

Woodlands March 26. [1845][142]

My dear Hammond

I was in hopes to have met you up at Ashley's, thinking it possible that you might have gone out of your den to have given welcome to your Successor.[143] As his Excellency did me the grace to appoint me (!) one of his aids, — an honor of which I did not avail myself, I deemed it but right to show myself when he came into the district, and say to him that the doors of my castle

---

[136] Wiley and Putnam published these tales as *The Wigwam and the Cabin.*

[137] Margaret Fuller's *Summer on the Lakes, in 1843* (Boston: C. C. Little and J. Brown; New York: C. S. Francis and Company, 1844) was responsible for Horace Greeley's offering her a position.

[138] John Jay (1817-1894), lawyer, author, diplomat, grandson of Chief Justice John Jay, and an active member of the New-York Historical Society. For Simms' earlier remarks about Jay, see letter to Tefft of Oct. 27, 1843.

[139] John Romeyn Brodhead (1814-1873) procured a collection of historical documents in Europe, returned with them to New York in the summer of 1844, and delivered an address before the New-York Historical Society on Nov. 20, 1844, embodying a statement of some of the results of his researches. Brodhead's published *Report* is reviewed by Simms in "Documents of American History in Europe," *Southern and Western,* II (Aug., 1845), 138-139.

[140] The New York *Evening Mirror* of Feb. 27, 1845, reports that Poe will lecture on "Poets and Poetry of America" on Feb. 28. The lecture was not published.

[141] See introductory sketch of the Hammonds.

[142] Dated by Simms' discussion of his hope for a diplomatic appointment by Polk.

[143] On April 1, Hammond replied: "I felt the propriety of going to Ashley's [between Barnwell and Blackville] to meet Aiken & thought I would. But when the time came I was not 'i' th' humour.' Ever since you saw me I have been caged up here dividing my time between business, books, cursing & fiddling, & have had several most infernal attacks of dyspepsia in the meantime, during which I was ultimately as savage as a wolf & as melancholy as a toad." (Original in the Hammond Papers, Library of Congress.) William Aiken, who succeeded Hammond as governor in 1844, was for a number of years Simms' neighbor on Charleston Neck, which at that time was all of the city north of Calhoun Street.

would be thrown open at his approach. — I have meditated writing you ever since I left Columbia, but the cursed drudgery of the Magazine, and the pressure of one or two tasks of Biography,[144] which I was ass enough to take upon my shoulders, at the very moment when good sense would have counselled a temporary retreat at least from all labors, — have kept me incapable of any asides, whether for politics, love or friendship. I have trudged between Charleston and home half a dozen times since December, and shall leave for the city tomorrow (Saturday) to return the day following. These necessities harrass me inconcievably, and, almost for the first time in my life, I am disposed to shirk my correspondence. — News, I have none — positively none that will be news to you. I don't know that I intimated to you in any way that some friends (political) have had it [in] mind, with my consent, to present my name to our new *Master,* for a foreign appointment — one of those pleasant berths in Italy or elswhere, where the salary is decent, and the duties nominal. The project, though suggested by friends in the West, was entertained warmly by certain of our Congressional delegation until the formation of the Cabinet, the *Cast* of which was such as to determine them against offering the name of any Carolinian for any office in the gift of the new man. My expectations were not large; but the disappointment is some! It would have been the most fortunate thing for me, just at this juncture, in a literary point of view to have stolen off to Europe, reposing on my oars for awhile, and preparing for the elaboration of other and more important tasks. I had a grand Carolina poem in my head, a tragedy, and something more, which God knows, may now never see the light. I am now to stay at home a spell longer, perhaps only to do mischief — for I am one of those persons — something like yourself — who must be doing something. — The story goes that you are quite dissatisfied with marl, and have taken to plaistering your land with mud & soil from neighboring bottoms. Speaking of you the other day in a small party of *rather* public persons, it was intimated that you would probably be willing to go to the Senate in the (assumed) approaching vacancy. On this subject I could only say (and do say to you) that in case you

---

144 At this time Simms was working on his *Life of Captain John Smith. The Founder of Virginia* (New York: Geo. F. Cooledge & Brothers, n. d.). Though copyrighted 1846, the volume was not published until March, 1847 (see note 4, Jan. 2, 1847).

desire the office I should [suppo]rt you for it as a matter of course,[145] [ye]t as you are aware already, I would not counsel the movement *now*. A few years would ripen the fruit which might not now fall at your touch. There be some six Richmonds in the field,[146] A. Patterson, Rhett, Pickens, Davie, Richardson & McWillie.[147] — One of the party (above) said that you did not care a straw about office, but had taken up what Byron calls the "Gentlemanly Vice," of money making [148] — that you had set into making an immense fortune — He was pleased to add — "he will do it too." [149] I wish I could get the secret from you. — Enough for this present writing, much of which is *entre nous,* as a matter of course. Let me hear from you & hold me very truly yours &c

W. G. Simms

---

[145] On April 1 Hammond replied: "First, let me beg of you should you ever hear my name mentioned again in connection with the Senate, to say anything you can say to impress the fact that I neither am nor if I can help it (& I presume that will not be difficult) *ever will be* a candidate for that or any other office. I detest office & what is called & is *public* life. I want peace, quiet & retirement now & *forever*. I would give a great deal if I could persuade my friends & my enemies of this fact. The kind solicitude of the former, & the malicious annoyances of the latter are very disturbing to my tranquillity. No one will ever believe that at my time of life any one can be in earnest about retiring. But few have suffered as I have in wearing their honors. I imagine that Hercules would have been glad to pull off the Shirt of Nessus the moment he got it on. He did not feel worse than I have whenever I have been engaged in office. The sublime of courage is political endurance I know, & I have aimed to achieve it — but my success has been dearly won & I want the aid of seclusion to enable me to hold out." (Original in the Hammond Papers, Library of Congress.)

[146] *Richard III,* V, iv, 11.

[147] Angus Patterson (1790-1854) came, in 1807, from North Carolina to Colleton District, where he taught school. About 1809 he accepted a post as tutor in the family of Johnson Hagood in Barnwell, studied law in Hagood's library, and was admitted to the bar in 1813. He was a member of the House (1818-1822) and he was elected to the State Senate in 1822. In 1838 he was elected president of the Senate, a post he held until the failure of his health in 1850. He married Hannah, daughter of Simms' neighbor Francis Trotti, of Briarwood Plantation. They lived at Pine Forest Plantation, near Barnwell.

For Robert Barnwell Rhett, see introductory sketch.

For Francis W. Pickens, see notes 120, Dec. 30, 1842, and 5, Jan. 1, 1845.

Frederick W. Davie, of Tivoli Plantation, Chester District, was a son of the Revolutionary general William Davie.

John Peter Richardson was governor of South Carolina, 1842-1844.

William McWillie (1795-1869) of Kershaw District served in the South Carolina House (1836-1838) and Senate (1838-1840). In 1845 he moved to Mississippi, where he was elected a member of Congress in 1849 and governor of the State in 1858.

[148] *Don Juan,* Canto I, Stanza 216.

[149] In his reply of April 1 Hammond says: "As to making money by planting it is absurd to think of. I have given up the idea. For 4 years past I have made merely a support. I don't plant for much more & am putting all my surplus on my land in various improvements. I think it the safest investment for the benefit of my children." (Original in the Hammond Papers, Library of Congress.)

243 : To CHARLES S. PALMER [150]

Woodlands, S. C. April 2, 1845

Charles S. Palmer Esq.

Dear Sir

I very much regret that it is not in my power to comply with your request for an autograph of Marion. There are but two letters of his, in my possession, and these belong to persons who would part with them on no consideration. They are of no interest seperate from his autograph, and are not of a character which would make it desirable to engrave and frame them — are wretchedly written, on mean paper, and legibly marked with the vicissitudes of time and war. The handwriting of Marion was very bad — the style feeble & involved, — and his signature distinguished by nothing more than a flourish, outre and boyish, — such as was common to our crude writers and farmer soldiers of the period — a distinguishing mark, indeed, as if the purpose were to prevent forgery. In the case of Marion, his flourish was quite as sinuous & bewildering as his marches.

Very respectfully, Sir, Yr &c

W. Gilmore Simms

244 : To JAMES LAWSON

Woodland[s]. April 7, 1845

My dear Lawson

Godey has just written me to say that periodicals are no longer what they were — that he has already $8000 invested in plates engraved already & to be used, and that the portrait must be laid by for the present.[151] He writes also that he wrote to Adams & Co to call upon you for it. Of course, you will not now give it up, and if you have done so, you will instantly recal it. You will be so good as to settle with West and take the portrait into

---

[150] Possibly the Charles S. Palmer who wrote a biographical sketch of his great-grandfather, Gen. Joseph Palmer (1716-1788), for the *New Englander,* III (1845), 1-23. The letter is addressed to Palmer, care of Wiley and Putnam.
[151] Simms was a frequent contributor to *Godey's Magazine and Lady's Book,* at this time edited by Mrs. Sarah J. Hale, Morton McMichael, and Louis Antoine Godey (see introductory sketch). In 1845, however, he contributed only one tale, "Mesmerides in a Stage-Coach; or, Passes en Passant," XXXI (Sept.), 111-119. For Simms' earlier remarks about the proposed engraving of the West portrait, see letter to Lawson of Jan. 15, 1845.

your own keeping, until such time as I am able to redeem it
from you. When this will be I cannot say, though I hope before
the year is out. You must let me know what I owe you. There
is the Bill of our friend Bokee.[152] The tailor, you will remember,
I paid before leaving. I suppose you can settle with Bokee when
you please. I am just now in one of my fits of despondency. I
find them always most oppressive in the Spring. The attack this
year is far more severe than usual, and afflicts me with all kinds
of oppressive reflections. My resources are so small, and the future
so doubtful, that there is good reason for them. Really, there is
something very wretched in the condition & prospects of American Literature, or I am one of the most luckless of our tribe. In
other respects, my hopes are destined to denial. I am not sure
but I wrote to you touching my disappointment in the matter
of the foreign mission. I have been sacrificed by some silly so-
phistications of my own friends. Our delegation in Congress
were pledged to me unanimously to present my claims to the
President. But they took in dudgeon the ejection of Calhoun from
the Cabinet,[153] and resolved to make no application in behalf of
Carolina. But for this I had every reason to hope for success.
I had been written to by a gentleman of the West, suggesting
the thing. He offered, through certain close friends of Mr. Polk,
to urge my claims. My reply to him was, it will look better &,
I should prefer that mine, if presented at all, should be by our
own delegation. And, *voila* the end. It was said by my Western
friend that as the late administration had been distinguishing the
literary men of the North, Irving, Everett, Walsh, Wheaton,
Fay, Bancroft, &c,[154] — that the present, would perhaps like to
distinguish, in similar manner, the only professional author of
the South. And there was something in it. But — enough. The
disappointment dulls me, and coming with other things, the
Season, want of money, and the gross prostration of our literature, leaves me, measurably *hors de combat.* 'Now could I drink

---

[152] John Jacob Bockee (see introductory sketch) was at this time a dealer
in woolens at 62 Maiden Lane, New York City.

[153] John C. Calhoun had been secretary of state in Tyler's cabinet. Instead
of reappointing him to this office, Polk offered Calhoun the legation at the
Court of St. James's, which honor he declined (see letter to Hammond of April
10, 1845).

[154] During Tyler's administration Washington Irving was appointed minister
to Spain, Edward Everett minister to the Court of St. James's, and Robert
Walsh consul-general in Paris. Henry Wheaton was continued as envoy extraordinary and minister plenipotentiary to Prussia, Theodore S. Fay as secretary
to the legation in Berlin, and George Bancroft as collector of the Port of Boston.

black blood.' [155] — And you, selfish average broker that you are, offer me no consolation, and write me a letter once in three months! I am out of place, out of money, out of hope, out of spirits, and — almost — out of friends. Truth is, my dear L. I was never so dull, and dispirited. My nature is elastic in great degree, but this drudgery, this drawing of water in a sieve, is too exhausting, and I begin to sicken. I am no longer doing myself justice. I want repose — encouragement — but repose above all. But, I will not distress you. I am *doing* the Life of Smith, but slowly. The compensation is wretched, and there is nothing in the subject to excite and interest me. My Magazine does not employ much of my time. Indeed nothing just now does, but weary & vexing thoughts. Do you get the Magazine & do you read it. There are some songs in it, — if no music.[156] Have you got my songs from your musical friend? Have you seen B. & Stringer. Do get them to send me all the numbers of "Oneota" after the first.[157] I wrote to them of this & other things. What of Winchester? Don't go out of your way to him, but if he will give you the $200 or a good endorser at 60 days, — close with him, as at first for 6000 copies. Get the printed sheets of Count Julian from B & S. and do not suffer them out of your hands. Winchester has some of the MS. and I have more & will write

---

[155] ". . . now could I drink hot blood." *Hamlet,* III, ii, 408.

[156] Simms' own contributions to the April issue of the *Southern and Western* include "Daniel Boon; the First Hunter of Kentucky" (pp. 225-242), the first part of "Oakatibbe; or the Choctaw Sampson" (pp. 244-255), "Clarice" (pp. 255-256), "Epigram. From the Spanish" (p. 256), "The Epochs and Events of American History, as Suited to the Purposes of Art" (pp. 257-261), "Song — Oh! The South, the Sunny South" (pp. 261-262), "The Unknown Masque. A Sketch of the Crescent City" (pp. 262-269), and "Editorial Bureau" (pp. 285-296). All are unsigned except "Clarice" (signed "Adrian Beaufain") and "The Unknown Masque" (signed "E —"). Probably the unsigned "Lost, Broken, Faded, Dead Within an Hour" (p. 284) is also by Simms. In his notice of the number in the *New York Weekly News* of May 3 Duyckinck comments: "This Magazine is always satisfactory. Its Editor has many strings to his bow. When tired of criticism he becomes an Essayist, and the Essay before it can weary the author, (not the reader) is laid aside for the sterling tale of adventure which gives place to the Biography, or Chapter of History. Mr. Simms, too can tell his tale either in verse or prose. It is the most natural and desirable thing in the world, that such a writer should have his own magazine, if only to relieve his study and his mind of the masses of valuable matter which from time to time accumulate."

[157] Henry Rowe Schoolcraft's *Onéota, or, the Red Race of America* was first published in eight numbers by Burgess, Stringer, and Co., New York, in 1844-1845. An edition in one volume was issued by Wiley and Putnam, New York and London, in 1845.

the rest as soon as needed. If you can write me any thing pleasant and encouraging do so. My love to Lady Lyde & the children.

                    Yours Ever &c
                    W. G. S.

245: To Armistead Burt

                    Woodlands, April 9 [1845][158]

Hon. A. Burt.
My dear Sir

Can you give me any hints or facts regarding the life and political career of McDuffie. I am about to prepare a memoir, to accompany his portrait in the Democratic Review — for which the Editor writes hurriedly — and am compelled to look around me, and beat up for information at all hands. Let me know all that you yourself know, and if you have any of his speeches, from which extracts might be made, send them to me. Name any individuals, of whom, in particular, information may be procured in regard to the personal history & political career of this distinguished man. I wish to do the thing thoroughly, and as well as it is within my ability to do.

                    Hurriedly, —
                    but, Very truly Yours &c.
                    W. Gilmore Simms

246: To James Henry Hammond

                    Woodlands April 10. [1845][159]

My dear Hammond.

I wish you would send me your Speculations on Slavery for the Magazine.[160] This will be a means to rid you of your friends

---

[158] On April 2, 1845, Duyckinck had asked Simms to prepare a memoir of George McDuffie for the *Democratic Review* (see Simms' reply to Duyckinck of April 10). The engraving of McDuffie, unaccompanied by the memoir, was published in XVI (May, 1845). This letter, therefore, is dated 1845. Though Simms as a young man was in violent opposition politically to McDuffie, he admired him greatly. McDuffie had attended Moses Waddel's school and the South Carolina College with Mrs. Simms' uncle Andrew Govan.

[159] The date of the postmark on the cover of this letter is *April 9*; but since it is written by hand and, therefore, may be erroneous, Simms' possibly erroneous date of *April 10* has been retained. The year is established by Simms' discussion of his failure to obtain a diplomatic appointment under Polk.

[160] Hammond's "Speculations on Slavery" did not appear in the *Southern and Western*. Two letters on the subject, addressed to Thomas Clarkson and

and the subject together. I am anxious that you should proceed in the elaboration of a topic which you have already handled so well. Your letter to the Free Church has properly acquired you laurels which were you not the most insufferably concieted person in the world you would be proud and pleased to wear.[161] Publish your essay in the Mag. and I will send it to France, where its translation may effect some good in the present doubtful condition of public opinion, and of Statesmen in that country. I am half minded to send them my review of Miss Martineau,[162] and a copy of Judge Harper's paper on the same subject.[163] Let me entreat you to comply with my wishes, letting your other friends believe as they please on the subject of their influence with you. Good is to be done in this way, to which our people of the South are quite too indifferent. Besides, you give by this means an exercise to your mind, which it will need, and which is the best preventive of dyspepsia. — You are mistaken in supposing that I had any eye to a foreign mission when I consented to go to the Leg. The former subject was broached to me last December for the first time — I had never thought of it myself before — by a friend in Tennessee, who claimed to have some influence

---

dated Jan. 28 and March 24, 1845, were published in the *Southern Patriot* (Charleston), June 17, 18, 20, 21, 24, 25, and 26, 1845. Apparently these had earlier appeared in the *South-Carolinian* (see letter to Hammond of May 20, 1845), though we have been unable to locate copies of the issues containing them. The South-Carolinian Press also issued the letters as a pamphlet entitled *Two Letters on Slavery in the United States, Addressed to Thomas Clarkson, Esq.* (Columbia: Allen, McCarter, & Co., 1845). Later in the same year, under the title of *Gov. Hammond's Letters on Southern Slavery: Addressed to Thomas Clarkson, the English Abolitionist,* they were reprinted in Charleston for free distribution (see letter to Hammond of *c.* June 18, 1845). They are included in *Selections from the Letters and Speeches of the Hon. James H. Hammond, of South Carolina* (New York: John F. Trow & Co., 1866), pp. 114-198. The *Broadway Journal,* II (July 26, 1845), 141, characterizes the letters as "a nervously written pamphlet, the design of which is to show that slavery is an inevitable condition of human society."

[161] In the fall of 1843 John L. Brown, of Fairfield District, S. C., was convicted of aiding a slave to escape. Judge John Belton O'Neall sentenced him to be hanged. The sentence occasioned a flood of protests; and to one of these from a church in Glasgow, Scotland, Hammond replied in his *Letter . . . to the Free Church of Glasgow, on the Subject of Slavery,* dated June 21, 1844, and published as a pamphlet by A. H. Pemberton, of Columbia, editor and publisher of the *South-Carolinian.* The sentence of Brown was later remitted entirely. Hammond's letter is reprinted in *Selections from the Letters and Speeches of the Hon. James H. Hammond, of South Carolina,* pp. 105-113.

[162] *Slavery in America, Being a Brief Review of Miss Martineau on That Subject.* See note 39, Aug. 30, 1837.

[163] William Harper (1790-1847) was chancellor of South Carolina (1828-1830) and the author of *Memoir on Slavery* (Charleston: J. S. Burges, 1838), one of the most famous pro-slavery treatises.

with those who were influential with the President, and he
volunteered to move in the business. My answer was, "Since you
have put the thing into my head, I prefer that the suggestion of
my name should come from my own State." He bowed, and there
ended. How my own State has served me you know. I really
think, putting my own views & wishes out of the question, that
our delegates are a little too fastidious. They virtually say, because we cannot have all our rights, we will fling away those that
we may secure, which is no wisdom. These appointments, to
share, are rights which we claim in common with the rest. They
are not favours. We might as well say, when our *quota of arms*
is proffered we will none of them, unless you modify the Tariff.
But, I must grin and not grumble. If the Mission to England is
offered you, take it by all means, and — publish your novel in
London! There is an anticlimax for you that should reconcile
you to the laurels accorded in the controversy with the Rev.
Tho. Brown.[164] — Let me task you a little more seriously. I
have been applied to for a paper on McDuffie, the Man, the
Speaker, the Statesman, for the Democratic Review, where his
portrait is to appear in one of the forthcoming numbers. I wish
you would compile for me, and thus save me some considerable
groping, a *catalogue* of his career, — his various progresses, —
the steps of his ascent — his particular successes — what you
think of his endowments — his character &c. Point me to his
best speeches, and send me such of them as you have, and refer
me to such persons as will inform me of his birth, education,
and other matters, as above. I will make a similar application to
other friends. Of course, I know a good deal generally speaking
of the subject, but I wish to have the thing correct in its details,
and I shall take particular pains to do it well. Help me as much
as you can, and as soon as you can, and who knows but I may
some day be required to take your life in like manner. — Looking again at your letter, I note what you say, *particularly,* touching your reasons for not publishing. There is only one of them
worth a copper, and that is worth just 25000 coppers — but it
has force only to prevent your giving your MS. to *my* Magazine.
We can't afford to pay you $250 for it. This, if you are wise
you will take — if you are generous, you will refuse, preferring

---

[164] Thomas Brown, D. D., was the moderator of the Free Church of Glasgow. Hammond's *Letter . . . to the Free Church . . .* is addressed to him. There
is no record of Hammond's novel having been written.

the work to appear in my Journal, to any pecuniary advantages.
— Calhoun was offered the appt. to St. James, and declined it.
He was then asked to designate the Carolinian, true to the South
& worthy of the trust, to whom it should be given. Who do you
suppose he named in the first instance? — James Hamilton,[165] —
and Elmore next. Hamilton he might have known was out of
the question. They speak of something more than six Richmonds
in the field for the Senate — A. Patterson, Davie, Pickens, Rhett,
I. E. Holmes, McWillie, John P. Richardson, Judge O'Neall and
some two or three more.[166] How gratifying it is to know that
Sparta has so many men better than ourselves. The Georgia
members of Congress, say that some of ours are too proud to
know them, never cooperate with them, repulse, repel them, and
altogether play such a high head party that it is scarcely reasonable to hope for their sympathies in any condition of things. Let
me hear from you soon.

Yours &c

W. G. Simms

J. H. Hammond, Esq.

247: To Evert Augustus Duyckinck

Woodlands, April 10. 1845

My dear Sir

I congratulate the public no less than yourself, on your acces-
sion to the literary *fauteuil* of the Dem. Review. Your circumspect & good judgment, excellent taste & various reading, as well
among the ancients as the moderns, will enable you to furnish
materiel to that work of a character which it has seemed very
much to need. I could have wished, had it been in my power, to
have *bought you up* for the South & West. Mon. But, it is per-

---

[165] James Hamilton (1786-1857) was a member of Congress (1822-1829)
and governor of South Carolina (1830-1832). He was an active nullifier, president of the Nullification Convention, and the originator of the "Nullification
Clubs" in South Carolina. Upon the death of Calhoun in 1850 Hamilton was
offered his seat in the United States Senate, but he declined.

[166] Patterson, Davie, Pickens, Rhett, McWillie, and Richardson, as candidates
for the Senate, are discussed in Simms' letter to Hammond of March 26. John
Belton O'Neall (1793-1863) was a strong Unionist during the nullification
crisis. In 1835, as associate justice of the court of appeals, he rendered a decision declaring the test oath unconstitutional. So unpopular was this decision
that the court of appeals was abolished. Judge O'Neall was then transferred
to the court of law appeals, where he served until 1859, when he was made
chief justice of South Carolina. For I. E. Holmes. see note 31. Jan. 15. 1845.

haps better as it is, for you at least. I shall look at the articles
carefully which you indicate in the April no. I shall, as leisure
serves, prepare the series of "Men of the Revolution."[167] Touching the Article on McDuffie: You give me too little time. The
material for it is very much scattered. To make the article a
valuable one, I must consult his contemporaries — himself —
look into old discussions and documents, and weigh, more in
detail, than I have yet done, the several elements of his mind &
eloquence. I will do this article as soon as I can, and shall proceed
this very day to institute the necessary inquiries. But it will be
impossible to get it ready in less than a month. It will call for
a large correspondence, at the outset, which will delay the thing
much more than the simple putting of the facts & thoughts together.[168] — I leave it to you to make a bargain with Mr. Wiley
for the Tales. They will probably make two volumes. Consult
with Lawson, and what is agreed upon between you will satisfy
me. The copyright must be in me. If the style of printing cor-
responds, or nearly so, with the usual size of my books, 12 mo.
you may make the stereotype plates an element of the contract.
This was the mode of proceeding in the publication of Castle
Dismal and Helen Halsey. The publishers had the right to five
thousand copies (if struck off within the year) for which the
plates of each became mine with a hundred dollars in cash. This
would assure about $400 for the two — possibly a fraction more.
This, of course, is *entre nous*. You may form some idea of the
wretched wrong done to the native author when I tell you that,
prior to the era of cheap publications, I have recieved for one
story in an annual, which cost me some three or four sittings,
$200. Let me know the style of the series — the number of pages,
size of page &c. — Base your estimates upon a single volume that
there may be no difficulty in the want of matter. I cannot now call
to mind all the stories, but I recollect six — viz —

---

[167] See note 95, Feb. 11, 1845. On April 2, 1845, Duyckinck had written to
Simms: "I have mentioned your proposed series of 'Letters of Men of the
Revolution' to O'Sullivan and he consents. The MSS will be welcome." (Orig-
inal in the Columbia University Library.)

[168] In his letter to Simms of April 2 (cited note 167, above) Duyckinck had
written: "The May number of the Review is to have a portrait of Senator
McDuffie and the Review wants an article on the *man* from you — one to do
justice to a leading Southern Statesman. The latter should be here not later
than the 20th inst." For Simms' inquiries about McDuffie, see letters to Burt
of April 9 and April 23, to Hammond of April 10 and May 10, and to Calhoun
of April 20.

1 Murder Will Out —
2 The Last Wager —
3 The Two Camps — —
4 The Lazy Crow —
5 The Arm Chair of Tustenuggee —
6 The Giant's Coffin &.

There are some others. There is a tale recently published in Graham's Magazine, the title of which he presumed to alter, which illustrates the country and may well belong to such a collection. In Graham it is called the Boatman's Revenge, which is in wretched taste. There will be a better title. — These are all Tales of the South. Shall we give this title. How would you like "The Cabin & the Wigwam["] — or "The Wigwam: or Tales of the South.["][169] — There is in my collection another class of Tales, not domestic, and some of them of an imaginative character. One of them was published by Godey and called "The Passage of a Night" or "The Benefactress." Another was called "Annihilation" & published in the Magnolia.[170] These, both of them, to my poor thinking possess considerable proofs of power. If Wiley's plan succeeds, and he will pay decently, I will prepare him an original Romance of Florida, in one volume, the scheme of which is in my head.[171] Give me some notion of what he can do. I would prepare the work for $500. and have it ready for Christmas. Again — as another subject for you to brood upon, will your series contemplate verse. I have been sketching out the plan of a vol. which I should wish to illustrate with my portrait, and

---

[169] The seven tales here mentioned were published as part of *The Wigwam and the Cabin* (see note 23, Jan. 6, 1845). For " 'Murder Will Out,' " "The Last Wager," "The Lazy Crow," "The Arm-Chair of Tustenuggee," and "The Boatman's Revenge," see letter to Lawson of June 12, 1843; for "The Two Camps," see note 69, July 7, 1843; for "The Giant's Coffin," see note 119, Feb. 27, 1845. In a review of *Graham's* in the *New York Weekly News* of Feb. 22, 1845, Duyckinck writes that " 'The Boatman's Revenge' . . . is a tale of nerve and interest, with the scene laid in that happy time for fiction in which the Southern novelist delights — the breaking out of the American Revolution. . . . It is a graphic, energetic story, with no loitering or trifling by the way."

[170] For "The Passage of a Night; or, the Benefactress," see note 43, Feb. 24, 1841. The tale was later republished as "The Bride of Hate; or, the Passage of a Night" in *Southward Ho!*, pp. 182-217. For "Annihilation," see note 115, Oct. 16, 1843. It was later republished as "The Wager of Battle. A Tale of the Feudal Ages" in *Graham's*, XXXIV (Feb., 1849), 99-109, and again in *Southward Ho!*, pp. 352-379.

[171] This romance was not published as part of Wiley and Putnam's "Library of American Books": it later appeared as *The Lily and the Totem, or, the Huguenots in Florida. A Series of Sketches, Picturesque and Historical, of the Colonies of Coligni, in North America. 1562-1570* (New York: Baker and Scribner, 1850), dedicated to James H. Hammond.

a few delicate etchings. In verse — viz. a series of "Legends, Tales & Traditions of the South." This collection would comprise, among other things, the poem which you may have seen, "The Last Lay of the Biloxi," "Pocahontas", "The Story of God's Judgment," ["]Hunter of Calawassee" &c.[172] But a truce to these enterprises. I am rejoiced that you are in a position to do yourself justice & serve the cause of a national and honorable literature. I only wish I could be with you. If things grow better with me, I shall spend my summers wholly at the North, give up my Magazine which I only aim to establish *pro bono publico* — and leave political life altogether. We could form a pleasant knot in Gotham, & I am very sure, if I were there, I should contrive to bring together a goodly set of good fellows. I am just in rec'pt of a long unsatisfactory letter from Mathews, who is as secretive & mysterious as ever. Do tell Lawson this. As for the latter — , — but I will say nothing of him. Would you have me swear? I wrote them both within the last two days, and in a very serious state of ill humour. The truth is I have had some disappointments.

Yours &c

W. G. Simms

248: To John Caldwell Calhoun

Woodlands, April 20, 1845

Hon. John C. Calhoun.

Dear Sir

I trust that the nature of this communication will excuse me for trespassing on your time and attention. I have been solicited by the Editor of the Democratic Review, to prepare a brief biography of Mr. McDuffie to accompany an engraved portrait of that Gentleman which is to appear in a forthcoming number of that work. Esteeming Mr. McD. as one of the greatest men that our country has produced, I am desirous of bestowing the utmost

---

[172] For the poems here mentioned, see note 239, June 25, 1845. The proposed collection (exclusive of "Pocahontas") appeared as part of *Poems Descriptive Dramatic, Legendary and Contemplative,* 2 vols. (New York: Redfield, 1853). The first volume has as its frontispiece the engraving by W. J. Alais of H. B. Bounetheau's sketch of Simms (reproduced as the frontispiece to *The Letters of William Gilmore Simms, 1830-1844*). Simms remarks of Bounetheau in the *Southern Patriot* (Charleston) of Oct. 23, 1845: "Mr. Bounetheau is a painter of great felicity of touch and a very exquisite — perhaps, a too fastidious taste."

care upon the article, and to present no facts, and urge no opinions, without first securing for them, the sanction of those best informed in the one and best prepared to determine upon the other. To you, Sir, I turn, therefore, in order that I should be equally prepared in both respects. I should like to know what, in particular, are the chief characteristics of Mr. McD's mind, what have been his best achievements, what were the several steps in his mental and political career, — what were his best passages of arms in debate — what is his manner — what his peculiarities, whether of taste, temper, thought, action or expression. — Of course, I should be sorry to confess, that, on most of these points, I had not formed some general notions of my own; but I wish to have my own views fortified, or to be enabled, from good authorities to review and adjust them. All such matters as are suitable for such an article as that I propose to prepare — all matters which may be honorable to Mr. McD. or necessary to the subject — the training of his mind, its first *public* beginnings — its various successes, and a fair examination of his political ethics — all of which, I assume to be in your power to impart — I should be most happy to recieve at your hands. In particular, as furnishing material least likely to be exceptionable and most likely to be attractive, I should be glad, if you could dwell upon his best forensic and public displays — sufficiently indicate the opposing parties to give interest to the contest, — and sum up the general merits of the issue. For a work like the one mentioned — the Democratic Review — I should, of course, avoid all matter likely to provoke discussion. My purpose is simply to satisfy a reasonable curiosity in regard to the *mind* of our subject, and to do him honor in making this attempt.

With profound respect, Sir, I am,
Very faithfully
Your obt and obliged Servant. &c

W. Gilmore Simms

249: To Armistead Burt

Woodlands, April 23. [1845][173]

Hon. Armistead Burt.

Dear Sir.

I thank you for your letter which is very interesting and very satisfactory. Do not think me troublesome if I seek from you some farther information. The two articles on the Tariff in the South. Review which I assume to be Mr. McD's, are the tenth in the fourth number of that work, and the eighth in the seventh number.[174] Let me hear from you if my assumption be right. Will you also give me a description of the personal appearance of Mr. McD. whom I have never seen except at a distance. I have never had the honor of his acquaintance, & have heard him speak but in two instances & then under unfavorable circumstances. I should also be informed where & what family remains to him. [Have] you any knowledge of the passage at arms with Mr. Randolph,[175] and can you procure any information or opinion on that with Tristram Burgess.[176] Would it be proper, think you, to make any allusion to the affair with Col. Cumming,[177] and what can you give me on that point. Of course, I shall be

---

[173] Dated by Simms' letter to Burt of April 9, in which he requests information concerning McDuffie for a memoir to be published in the *Democratic Review*.

[174] Article X of No. IV is entitled "The Tariff" (II [Nov., 1828], 582-619). Simms erred in writing *seventh*: he meant *ninth*. Article VIII of No. IX is entitled "The American System" (VI [Aug., 1830], 206-254).

[175] During the course of a debate in the United States House of Representatives in February, 1822, John Randolph of Roanoke assailed McDuffie, "expecting to annihilate the young South Carolinian with a few sentences of his vitriolic satire." When McDuffie replied in like strain, Randolph became so incensed that he "retorted angrily and with none of his customary sarcasm." McDuffie then "poured forth a torrent of vituperation of withering pungency, in the midst of which Randolph rose and left the chamber in a rage determined to send a challenge to McDuffie. Of this, however, he thought better, when his anger had cooled." See Edwin L. Green, *George McDuffie* (Columbia, S. C.: The State Company, 1936), pp. 26-27.

[176] On March 12, 1828, as Chairman of the Ways and Means Committee of the United States House of Representatives, McDuffie made an exhaustive report on the tariff. The three members of the committee opposed to McDuffie's views were accidentally absent from the meeting, and on account of their absence Tristram Burges, Representative from Rhode Island, "made a violent attack on McDuffie, so personal in nature that he had to be called to order several times by the chair and finally directed to take his seat. McDuffie retained an even temper, explained the absence of the three members of the committee as a pure accident, and disclaimed any originality in his arguments 'which had been the property of the whole world for the last half century.'" See *ibid.*, pp. 86-87.

[177] For the quarrel between McDuffie and Col. William Cumming (1790-1863), which resulted in a series of meetings on the field, see *ibid.*, pp. 28-36.

[scr]upulous to say nothing which should annoy anybody, and still less to detract from the high and well deserved reputation of our subject. You are not to suppose from the minuteness and earnestness of these queries, that I expect to make much of an article. But I wish, in what I do, to steer clear of error, and this, I have long since discovered, is only to be done, by obtaining full knowledge of what you would write about. Write me therefore, frankly and freely, and give me all the information that you can, — trusting to my discretion to make the proper use of it.

Yours very truly &c,

W. Gilmore Simms

P.S. If you have any anecdotes [which] are good, and would illustrate [forci]bly the career of McD. put them down. Can any thing be said, and what, in [regard] to the supposed assistance rendered [by] Mr. Calhoun to him in the early years of the latter? [178]

250: To JAMES HENRY HAMMOND

Woodlands, 10th. May. [1845][179]

My dear Hammond.

I thank you very sincerely for your excellent and full letter, a portion of which furnished your responses to my queries touching McDuffie. As yet I have done nothing towards the article, and the plate is published, — the Editor relying on me to do the thing as soon as possible hereafter. I am kept waiting on one or two persons to whom I have looked for facts & opinions. With your letter, however, and two others which I have from Calhoun & Burt, I could get on very well; but I wish to write from a full mind, and above all, seek to fortify myself as much as possible, so that I may not only speak clearly but with confidence. Have you in your collection & can you spare me, McD.'s speech on the Removal of the Deposites, and that on Int. Improvements in 1823.[180] If you have anything, and to spare, provide me and take

---

[178] For the assistance McDuffie received from the Calhouns during his early years, see *ibid.*, pp. 8-11.

[179] Dated by Simms' reference to the engraving of McDuffie, published in the *Dem. Rev.*, XVI (May, 1845).

[180] *Speech of Mr. M'Duffie, on the Subject of the Removal of the Deposites, December 19, 1833* ([Washington, 1833?]) and *Speech of Mr. McDuffie, on Internal Improvements* . . . (Columbia, [S. C.] : Printed by D. & J. M. Faust,

my thanks — if such a formality be a consideration with you. —
I shall look with real anxiety for your Letter on Slavery, and
seriously think that you distrust yourself (!) too much in relucting at its publication until secure by the judgment of friends.
Your mind and temperament are of that order that they require
only that you should address your *will* to the task, and endow
it with the necessary degree of painstaking to enable you to
succeed triumphantly in it. Of course, the compliment here is
to that acute good sense which you have, and which would effectually prevent you from attempting a labor for which your intellectual man was not perfectly prepared. *Your ambition only
suffers you to work in the sight of the public.*[181] Out of its sight
you grow indifferent, and sink somewhat into the sluggard, unless moved by that other fiend which beset the latter days of
Byron, and divided his thoughts with the gin bottle. Your love
of approbation is a larger development than you will allow, or
perhaps believe yourself; and it is, in your case, a right development. Seriously you are unfortunate in being a too wealthy man.
Your dissuasives to proper exertion, are too potent, to a certain
degree, for your own fame. You will work out of your cloud
yet, and perhaps more brightly for your temporary obscuration.
Of course, I did not think it possible that you should recieve
any appointment from Polk. My meaning was, simply, *that you
should avail yourself of any opportunity to place yourself in the
sight of the nation, without appearing too conspicuous at home.*
Such a policy would, if kept in view, cover contingencies which it
is not easy to conjecture beforehand. — I am very sorry that
I cannot lay hands on a single copy of my review of Martineau,
except in a volume of bound pamphlets. I distributed a number

---

1824). Hammond replied on May 19: ". . . I have neither of the speeches you
desire. I do not preserve speeches for they possess little permanent value &
most good ones are ultimately collected. They are both of them however to be
found I presume in Gales & Seatons Register of Debates, which ought to be in
the Charleston Library." (Original in the Hammond Papers, Library of
Congress.)

　181 In his reply to Simms of May 19 Hammond defends himself: "And in
this you do me great injustice. You are a close questioner of character & a
practiced anatomist of the heart. But with me you are at work on the skeleton
of what I was, the skin I have shed off — & long ago. For 15 years of the very
prime of life & spring tide of ambition I have had office but 2 years & 3 months,
when I might have had it probably the whole period. If I will work only before
the public, I can only say you must think I have worked devilish little. *Three
fourths of my works are unacknowledged,* not worth acknowledging it is true,
but that don't affect the question of my disposition to work without public
reward." (Original in the Hammond Papers, Library of Congress.)

in the district when I was in nomination three years ago. Trotti possibly, or Aldrich[182] has one which may be procured. — I have been absent on a visit to St. Paul's.[183] They are surveying the contemplated route of the Canal from Edisto to the Ashley.[184] My absence & urgent employments have delayed this answer. I have found some marl of inferior quality in the Edisto at our landing.[185] — Write me soon and ever encouragingly. I have never been so prostrate — so utterly dispirited and dull — in all my life as now. If I could have got a respite, — such as that foreign appointment could have afforded, it would have materially served me. My mind, indeed, needs repose, absence, relief of all kinds.[186] I am & have been, for many years, drawing water in a sieve.

Very truly yours &c

W. Gilmore Simms

---

[182] Alfred Proctor Aldrich. See introductory sketch.

[183] St. Paul's Parish, north of St. John's, in Charleston District.

[184] Simms as a legislator was active in the matter of this canal. The *Southern Patriot* (Charleston) of Dec. 13, 1845, reports that the measure for chartering the Edisto and Ashley Canal Company was carried by a large vote, but that the success of Simms and others in the fight for the canal was fruitless in that the Senate had adjourned and the bill was not matured.

[185] Dead River Landing.

[186] On May 19 Hammond replied: "I can fully understand your desire for repose, & as fully concur in the absolute necessity of it to all men, & a large share of it too. . . . I have long seen your want & have told you of it heretofore. It is more & more apparent to me. I do not mean by this to say that you are falling off. On the contrary my estimate of your abilities has been ever on the rise. You exhibit to my judgement constantly, deeper thought, keener observation, more extended information. . . . I know it is only a notion of yours writing for money. But if you were compelled to support yourself by your pen, you would be justified, with your abilities, to imitate the old masters, & live on crusts, that you may have abundant leisure to think thoroughly, & write composedly. To penetrate again and again the inmost recesses of your subject, explore every turn & nook until it is as familiar as your daily food, & then to draw it in bold outline adding only *essential* detail, & to paint with strong, broad, harmonious, & concentrated colour. There is no other way to produce a great work. And you ought to be put to death at once if you do not set about producing one." (Original in the Hammond Papers, Library of Congress.)

251: To Richard Yeadon [187]

Woodlands, May 12 [1845][188]

My dear Yeadon:

You might with perfect safety have used my selected motto from The Merry Wives of Windsor. In my English editions of Shakespeare, the language of Pistol is precisely as I wrote it. In my American editions it is as you copied it. The character of Pistol's usual phraseology and the purport of what he means to say, incline me to prefer the English as the true reading. [']You have read her will, — her wish — the secret desires of her mind — She wills all that you intimated — She is secretly the lecher you describe etc.' [189] A play upon words is suggested by the use of the one in question, and Shakespeare was not the author to lose any such opportunity. Then, while the American editions make sense of the sentence, and what is esteemed very good common sense too, it does not make the sense of Pistol, nor the sense of Shakespeare, — that occult two-fold signification which was in both their minds.

In one of my English copies, there is a note explanation of the passage, though it is not quite satisfactory to me. That the reading as I gave it is the correct one, or at least the received one among the best authorities, I have the proof in Ayscoph's valuable Dictionary of Shakespeare,[190] where the quotation is written as I made it. I care very little for our American editions, and still less for the American editions of Shakespeare. They are generally mere pretenses — cunning Yankees, who have no relish for any poetry beyond that of Wm. P. (?),[191] and have precious

---

[187] We have been unable to locate the original of this letter, printed in the *News and Courier* (Charleston) of March 28, 1937. At that time it was in "a local library" at Pinopolis, S. C.

[188] Yeadon's nine articles entitled "The Marion Family" were published in the *Southern and Western* from Feb. through Oct., 1845 (I, 209-219, 270-284, 347-356, 412-426; II, 50-58, 121-127, 200-204, 265-276, 333-341). Since these have mottoes such as the one Simms here mentions, this letter has been dated 1845. Additional evidence of the date is the similarity of the concluding portion of this letter with that written to Hammond on May 10.

[189] Act I, Scene iii: "He hath studied her well, and translated her will — out of honesty into English." Some editions have "well" instead of "will."

[190] Samuel Ayscough's *An Index to the Remarkable Passages and Words Made Use Of by Shakespeare* forms the third and last volume of J. Stockdale's edition of *Shakespeare's Dramatic Works* (London, 1790).

[191] The correct reading is most likely "Mr. P." — *i. e.,* James Gates Percival (1795-1856). Simms had reviewed Percival's poetry in the Jan., 1844, issue of *Orion* (see note 174, Dec. 13, 1843).

little knowledge of the peculiarities of the Old English. In town I have two copies of Shakespeare which I will examine when I get there. I hope to do so in two weeks at most. Enough, however, I trust is shown you to satisfy you that you might have used the quotation with perfect safety as your epigraph. I will communicate with Mr. Headley [192] what you say touching the correspondence. Pray do not delay our publishers with your next number. You kept us back more than a week the last.

I am and have been for the last two weeks under a cloud like your own. I have been suffering from bodily and mental prostration (?). The Spring usually fills me with infirmities — this season more than usual, and the profitless life I am pursuing — the hopeless drudgery — drawing water in a sieve, drives me into despondency. I have never felt so depressed as now. I want a respite — leisure, escape, hope, sympathy — and see nothing before me but constraint and inferior toils, and profitless burdens, and waning powers. Really, mon ami, I am borrowing your winter cloak. But — I need not thrust it back upon you.

So God bless you and yours.

W. Gilmore Simms.

252: To James Henry Hammond

Woodlands May 20 [1845][193]

My dear Hammond

Your verses to Caroline will have an early place. They are as smoothly turned as if you had frequently practiced at the lathe. But stick to the prose and do more of it.[194] You were right in

---

[192] The *News and Courier* misprints *Heavley*.

[193] Dated by Simms' reference to his being on the committee to examine the Bank of the State of South Carolina at Charleston. He had been appointed to this committee on Dec. 5, 1844. See *House Journal*, p. 70.

[194] On June 3 Hammond replied: "Now in my opinion my verses are devilish good poetry — Ah — I see — you are a poet & like all poets a jealous dog. You are afraid of a rival in me & therefore you wish pitilessly to strangle my muse in its infancy. But you shall not. It is almost dry enough here for me to invoke her aid again — but don't think you can get my *gems* for your magazine any more. When I write for you it shall be prose — prosing prose — you shall be sick of prose — Perhaps you are already. But I have no malice in me at this moment so I will stop." (Original in the Hammond Papers, Library of Congress.) Hammond's verses to Caroline were not published in the *Southern and Western*.

giving your letters to Pemberton.[195] I have no doubt they will do you credit, and maintain the reputation which you have everywhere got by the first. As for the reluctance to publish that which you have deliberately written, and which is wholly without its use unless put in circulation, that, permit me to say, is one of your little affectations which do not become you. You are too much of a genuine man to indulge in such pettinesses. You see I deal with you frankly as a friend should do. While in this frank mood let me beg that you will forbear giving me any title other than those which are in ordinary use. The courtesy of well meaning but misjudging friends have conferred upon me distinctions which, as I have but little pretension to any legitimate claim in these respects, I feel great reluctance to appropriate. To a stranger, I should be loth to say this, for I would not give pain to those by whom I have been thus most unwisely distinguished; but to you, to whom I may speak in safety, I repeat the wish that I may neither be called Dr. nor Col.[196] I am no military man, and have long since learned to smile, at your parade soldiers, of whom when the season of action comes, we seldom hear anything. I confess too it always seems to me to degrade the man to dress him up like a monkey or a peacock. If men must fight, let them go into battle as Cromwell's fire-eaters did in plain buff coats, resolute apart from the guns & trumpets, the glitter & the gewgaws. — I have as little claim to be a Dr. of Laws as any literary man in the country. Never was education so worthless as mine, — i. e. in a classical point of view. I am very little of the linguist, am versed in no sciences, cannot play with chemistry as you do, and exult in agriculture. In brief, my dear fellow, if I were called upon to say in what respect my knowledge was thorough, I should be at great loss to happen upon one element.[197] I have

---

195 A. H. Pemberton, of Columbia, was the publisher of Hammond's *Letter . . . to the Free Church* (see note 161, April 10, 1845). The letters here mentioned are those on slavery addressed to Thomas Clarkson, which first appeared in the *South-Carolinian* (Columbia), edited and published by Pemberton (see note 160, April 10, 1845).

196 Simms had received the degree of Doctor of Laws from the University of Alabama in Dec., 1842. He had also served as colonel on Governor Hammond's staff. Hammond likewise asserted he despised titles. In his reply to Simms, dated June 3, he writes: "As to titles — I have a dozen — from Capt. to Gov. & Hon. You can revenge yourself. I despise them all as cordially as you do yours — & like the fox who lost his tail I am glad to see others in the same fix & delight to tease them." (Original in the Hammond Papers, Library of Congress.)

197 Hammond replied on June 3: "The man who knows *where* information is to be found is well educated. He who has learned to think deserves a diploma. A good memory & well crammed are convenient adjuncts, but not essentials.

a smattering of this & that, picked up, heaven knows how. Of my reputation & how it has grown, you know as much as myself. All that I can claim is this, that what I am I am in *spite of friends,* of fortune, and all the usual aids of the ambitious. I have worked in the face of fortune and many foes. I have never known what was cordial sympathy, in any of my pursuits among men. I have been an exile from my birth, and have learned nothing but to drudge with little hope, and to think and feel and act for myself. Through painful necessities I have come to the acquisition of an Independent Mind. — You will say that I have egotism enough at least. That is one of the evil consequences of my isolation. It is perhaps inseperable from independence. But, here ends. You mistook a hint (probably) which I gave in a previous letter, & hence what I have said about these titles. I must submit to be called Dr. & Col. by that silly class of persons who attach much importance to these things. To you I may safely declare myself & I do so. — There. — I owe you no letter. — But I write in pain, suffering from a swollen testicle! — I think it likely I shall leave for the city on the 29th. inst. — I am on that cursed com'tee for the examination of the Bank concerns. Can you give me any hints.

Yours &c

Simms

253: To Evert Augustus Duyckinck

Charleston, June 6 [1845][198]

My dear Sir

It is now a very long time since I had the pleasure of hearing from you, though I sometimes get glimpses of what you are doing. Your writings in the Democratic Review do you credit, though, if I should object at all, it is to the something too cursory manner in which you develope your subjects.[199] Your taste as a

---

It is a pocketfull of small change that may help you . . . but it is not the treasury that tunnels mountains or throws suspension bridges over arms of the sea. Our lots are not very different. A devoted father at much sacrifice forced on me an education — as it is called — which gave me a nominal advantage. For the rest I have fought every inch too — & *fought alone."* (Original in the Hammond Papers, Library of Congress.)

[198] Dated by Simms' reference to Duyckinck's notice of his article on the *North American Review.* See note 200, below.

[199] Duyckinck's "On Writing for the Magazines" had appeared in XVI (May, 1845), 455-460.

critic goes on improving, & a little more of the organ of con-
centrativeness would make you a keen and earnest critic, as you
are now an adroit and graceful one. It gave me pleasure to infer
from a notice in the News that our paper on the North American
Review, met your notions of its deserts.[200] There was some forbearance manifested in that article. To have said all that might
have been said, might have been imputed to personal rather than
to patriotic considerations. — Did you recieve a letter from me in
reply to one of yours touching a volume of Tales for the Library
of Wiley & Putnam.[201] My purpose in that letter was to give
you *carte blanche* in any arrangement which you might think
proper to make on my behalf with these Gentlemen. I should like
to prepare for them two separate miscellanies, one consisting of
"Tales of the South" purely —border narratives illustrative of
our region, and another of a more imaginative character. Of the
latter, two volumes were published by me, through Geo. Adlard,
entitled "Carl Werner & other Tales." [202] These were put forth
at a most unfortunate season, during the money pressure, and
just as the public mind had been made eager & selfish in consequence of the Cheap Literature passion. I made nothing by the
venture. Adlard had no facilities, and books of Tales at $2. when
similar collections were selling at 12 or 25/100 were not to be

---

[200] In the *New York Weekly News* of May 24 Duyckinck comments of
Simms' "A Passage with 'The Veteran Quarterly,'" published in *Southern and
Western*, I (May, 1845), 297-311: "The article is a long one, exceedingly well
written, evidently from a practised hand, and well calculated, by its sturdy
force and momentum, to disturb even the thrice-drugged conservative North
American." Simms' other contributions to the May issue include the conclusion
of a tale, "Oakatibbe; or the Choctaw Sampson" (pp. 318-329); a critical
review, "Poems of Alfred B. Street" (pp. 330-342); the "Editorial Bureau"
(pp. 357-368); and at least two poems, "For an Infant's Grave" (p. 311) and
"May in the South" (p. 312). All are unsigned except the first, signed "M.,"
and the last, signed "Delta." Probably all the other unsigned poems in this
issue are also by Simms. In his notice (cited above) Duyckinck calls "Oakatibbe" "one of the very best of his Indian tales. It is skilfully wrought, and
highly dramatic, with a moral interest in the light the story throws upon the
capabilities of the Indian for civilization. . . ." Of "Poems of Alfred B. Street"
Duyckinck is likewise enthusiastic: ". . . the poems of Alfred B. Street are
reviewed in this Southern Review at great length, with evident pains-taking
and sympathy, without any lack of due critical discrimination. The South has
never been wanting in magnanimity and generosity towards the literature of
the North. . . there is no periodical of the kind in the country better worthy of
support for the substance and variety of its contents, and none that surpass the
force and *originality* of its views."

[201] See letter of April 10. The volume of tales was published as *The Wigwam
and the Cabin*.

[202] *Carl Werner, An Imaginative Story; with Other Tales of Imagination*,
2 vols. (New York: George Adlard, 1838). See letter to Lawson of Jan. 3,
1839.

thought of. A selection from these tales, with others not yet collected, would form a neat vol. for 37 or 50 and would, I think, sell. I am willing that you should propose these two volumes to W & P. on terms the most favorable to them. — Will you procure & send me No 16 of Arcturus.[203] Mathews undertook to send it me once & sent me 18. I wish to complete & bind the set. Am I to congratulate Mathews on becoming a millionaire? The papers say so. I should be glad, also, if you can procure for me from Dr. Henry, Mr. Cogswell or the publishers Nos 13-14 and 18 of the N. Y. Review, and all (if any have been published) after 18.[204] I would have employed before this, the 3d. No. of Times Wallet (The Three Wise Men of Gotham) had it not been stowed away in my city Library in such a mass that the printers could not have found it. I have it before me now, and it will probably appear in our July issue.[205] I trust you will find it convenient to continue these papers. I should like, if possible, to become a subscriber, from the beginning, to that Shakspeare Society which is now busy in publishing old plays. Will you see W & P. or Bartlett & Welford [206] on this subject & see if the thing can be done. If so, the money shall be forthcoming on the reciept of the publications. I have been busy in trying to procure materials

---

[203] *Arcturus, A Journal of Books and Opinion* (New York), edited by Duyckinck and Mathews, ran from Dec., 1840, through May, 1842.

[204] The Rev. Caleb Sprague Henry (1804-1884) was the founder of the *New York Review* in 1837. He held the position of editor or co-editor from March, 1837, through the issue of July, 1840, when Joseph Green Cogswell (1786-1871) became sole proprietor. Cogswell served as editor of the magazine until it was discontinued with the April number of 1842. George Dearborn was the publisher of the *Review* through the issue of July, 1838; thereafter Alexander V. Blake was the publisher.

[205] The third number of "Time's Wallet" was not published in the *Southern and Western*. Simms' own contributions to this issue include "Egeria" (pp. 8-9), "The Epochs and Events of American History, as Suited to the Purposes of Art" (pp. 10-16), "The Case of Major Andre.— Miss Seward and Her Writings" (pp. 33-42), "Editorial Bureau" (pp. 61-72), and "The Late Edward L. Carey" (p. 72). All are unsigned except "Egeria" (signed "Adrian Beaufain"). Probably the other unsigned contributions in this issue are likewise by Simms.

[206] Bartlett and Welford, New York, handled American subscriptions for the Shakespeare Society and Percy Society publications (see Simms' "Old English Literature," *Southern and Western,* II [Sept., 1845], 209-213). The *Broadway Journal,* I (Jan. 25, 1845), 60, comments: "Bartlett & Welford's shop, in the Astor House, is another seductive place for the lover of rarities in the shape of books. Some of the finest illustrated works ever published, may be here inspected free of charge, and purchased at prices greatly below their first cost. These gentlemen are among the few instances of traders in literature, who know something of the articles they deal in. The senior partner is a good scholar, and an accomplished ethnologist. Besides the fine collection of old books to be found here, may be seen all the late French and English publications that have any thing to recommend them in the shape of illustrations."

for the paper on George McDuffie — a matter which is less easy
than it might be thought. I have succeeded, however, to some
extent having had a correspondence with numerous Gentlemen on
the subject. I wait but an answer from Judge Longstreet[207] to
set about the article. He is, as I suppose you are aware, in a very
critical condition from paralysis. It is scarcely possible that he
can long maintain himself as his frame has been a wreck for
many years. This letter will probably be taken on, by Mr.
Head,[208] a Charleston Bookseller, who will be pleased to bring
any communication bearing my address. He is chiefly engaged
in the Cheap Literature business, of which he has learned to
speak somewhat contemptuously. How does the experiment of
W & P. succeed. I am not so sure that Headlong Hall will be
among the selling Books.[209] It strikes me that Beckfords writings
would prove a suitable set for this library — a selling set. I
know and have his Vathek & his Letters on Italy. But there are
other works — His visit to the Count of Alcobaga &c — all
written in a piquant and charming style.[210] — The magazine of
Tecumseh Colton does not reach me — not one has been recieved.[211] The Broadway Journal has not been recieved for two
months. Is there any good reason for this. How does Poe get
on with the Longfellows.[212] He is more than half right. — I am
in reciept of Lord's poems, which I have not yet examined.[213]
I see that he has talent, and suspect that he has pretensions.
Mathews intimated that he had one or more vols. in preparation,
but, I suppose, that his money acquisitions will effectually expel
literature from his thoughts. — It is barely possible that I shall
look in upon you at the close of the summer, — i.e. if, at that

[207] Augustus Baldwin Longstreet. See introductory sketch.

[208] Amos Head.

[209] Thomas Love Peacock's *Headlong Hall* and *Nightmare Abbey* had recently
been published by Wiley and Putnam as Nos. 7 and 8 of their "Library of
Choice Reading."

[210] We have been unable to discover editions published by Wiley and Putnam
of William Beckford's *Vathek* or *Italy; with Sketches of Spain and Portugal* or
Recollections of an Excursion to the Monasteries of Alcobaça and Batalha.

[211] George Hooker Colton (1818-1847), author of *Tecumseh,* was editor of
the *American [Whig] Review.* Though dated Jan., 1845, the first issue had
appeared in Oct., 1844.

[212] Poe had accused Longfellow of plagiarism in a review of *The Waif*
(Cambridge: John Owen, 1845), published in the New York *Evening Mirror*
of Jan. 13 and 14, 1845. This instigated protests and further accusations. See
in particular Poe's articles in the *Broadway Journal,* I (March 8, March 15,
March 22, and March 29, 1845), 147-150, 161-163, 178-182, 194-198.

[213] Simms' review of William W. Lord's *Poems* (New York: Appleton &
Co., 1845) was published in *Southern and Western,* II (Aug., 1845), 133-137.

period, I shall have any surplus fund to go upon. Lawson writes urgently but it will not be easy to leave home this summer. — The magazine will task me considerably, and I have the misfortune to be one of a Committee appointed by the Legislature to examine into the condition of the Bank of the State, a tedious & uninteresting job which will consume a full month of my time. You see how much of the drudgery of the magazine falls to my share. Of course, writing as I do, I can do no justice to the public and but little to myself. I long to shake it off, and to begin again independently. My mind is full of earnest and original projects, which, of course, I cannot touch, with the toils of a miscellany to encounter. — Write me a long letter, with all the literary details you can accumulate. How will the new post-office law affect us.[214] This, by the way, is double only as I send by private hand. I have usually been remorseful in regard to my correspondents. Present me to Mrs. D., to your brother,[215] to Headley, Mathews &c. Mrs. S. begs to be remembered in Ninth St. Very truly, but dully, — (at the close of a day of drudgery)

Yours &c

W. G. Simms

P. S. Saw you the last South. Quarterly with the art. on Orion's Spirit of Age. A second part is due, but not forthcoming in the next.[216]

254: To JAMES LAWSON

Charleston, June 7. [1845][217]

My dear Lawson

An opportunity by private hand enables me to indulge a natural desire of writing you, and of saving you the cost of a letter at the same time. I got your solitary letter, for the last six months, some six or eight days ago, and would have answered it *instanter*

---

214 By an act of March 3, 1845, the postage charge was reduced to five cents for a single letter (which was defined as one under one-half ounce in weight) for distances less than 300 miles. For distances over 300 miles the rate was fixed at ten cents.

215 George Long Duyckinck (1823-1863).

216 See note 97, Feb. 11, 1845. Richard H. Horne was also the author of *Orion, an Epic Poem in Three Books* (London: J. Miller, 1843).

217 Dated by Simms' reference to the contents of the June issue of the *Southern and Western.* On the envelope of this letter Simms wrote "Politeness Mr. [Amos] Head."

but for the sickness of our little boy.[218] He is now fortunately better, but for some days my wife was in great anxiety. He has infantile remittent with chills. We are in the city where we expect to stay all the summer. It is very doubtful whether I can go north at all. If I do so, it will be very late in the season. I have before me six months of absolute drudgery, public & private. — Political, personal and magazinical. I am very sorry that the potatoes proved a failure. I was very much afraid of them on account of the lateness of the season. It vexed me more that they should spoil the hams. We will act wiser and do better next time. — I have just heard from Mr. William Taylor, a publisher in the Astor House, who has bought from Winchester the plates of Ct. Julian & wishes to obtain the privilege of publishing. I refer him to you. Let him have an edition of 5 or 6000 copies for $200, — or do as you please & what you please. I suppose Winchester will be ready to give up the MS. now that he has parted with the plates. Perhaps Taylor already has it. Will you see to it at once. I have some additional sheets already written and some more to write, all of which I will promptly prepare as soon as the other proofs are sent me. These can easily be sent by mail. It will occasion some, but not material delay. It is certain that I must correct the portion which he shall print from MS. The sheets already in type you will procure from Burgess & Stringer, if you have not already done so, and keep them carefully in your possession until the work is out of press. I have no other security. I think B & S. have not treated me well, and apprehend they are under the malign influence of that wretched cur and scoundrel, Mr. L. G. Clark, of the Knickerbocker. I have various reasons for thinking so. They were contractors for Ct. Julian & as honorable men, were quite as much bound as if the deed had been on record. But *n'importe*. I wrote to them, & to you to get from them, certain numbers of "Oneota" &c, which are not to be procured here. To this no answer from either. I also reminded you to recover from your musical friend, the MS. Songs which you lent him, & of some of which I have no copies. Of some of these, I thought highly. I mentioned also that I had not yet recieved the MS. of that volume of verse which contained my poem to the Mock Bird.[219] This is in your hands or in those of some of our friends. Pray seek after it. The article by Mc-

---

[218] Gilmore.
[219] See letter to Lawson of Feb. 27, 1845.

Cracken forms the leader in our June issue, and is a good one —
well written & in good taste & style.[220] Return him my acknowl-
edgements. It will give me great pleasure to recieve other papers.
There was some delay in its reaching me. I wish you would get
Burges & Stringer to send me half a dozen copies more of Helen
Halsey & C. Dismal. Pray inquire into the sales of these works.
They still continue to sell in the South. Touching the picture,
I trust you will take it into possession & adjust the money matter
with West.[221] It may be some time before I am able to adjust
with you, for, just now, my expenses are greater than usual &
my reciepts smaller. I have had a letter from Duyckinck suggesting one or more volumes of Tales for Wiley & Putnam's Library.
I have referred him to you to make the arrangement. I may say
to you that I would not have you stickle about the terms. Let
him have the matter pretty much his own way. I have never
labored much after money, and these tales have served their
turn. One collection might well be called, ["]Tales of the Cabin
& the Wigwam." — or "The Wigwam & the Cabin" — comprising the stories written for the "Gift" &c. The other volume would
be of things purely imaginative. — I rejoice to learn that your
compy has arranged itself to your liking. I could have wished,
however, to have seen you in a more conspicuous situation. But
you know best. If the pecuniary returns satisfy you the distinction, in the business world, is probably of very small importance.
I am glad that Wetmore is in an office which suits him, and the
returns of which are somewhat commensurate with the claims
of family. What do you hear of Forrest. By last advices he seems
to have been triumphing over his opponents. I sincerely hope that
Mathews may get the million. It will make him a better fellow,
I doubt not, and I fancy it will improve his verses in the sight
of the critics. I am very sure that such a Godsend would do a
great deal for me & mine and you & yours. Is there any such

[220] J. L. H. McCracken's article is a review of Robert Chambers' *Vestiges
of the Natural History of Creation* (New York: Wiley & Putnam, 1845),
Southern and Western, I, 369-378. Simms' own contributions to this issue in-
clude "Accabee—A Ballad" (pp. 378-379), "Leonilla" (pp. 384-385), "The
Epochs and Events of American History, as Suited to the Purposes of Art in
Fiction" (pp. 385-392), "The Snake of the Cabin" (pp. 393-411), "Fast and
Loose" (p. 411), "Isabel" (p. 426), and "Editorial Bureau" (pp. 429-440). All
are unsigned except "Leonilla" (signed "Adrian Beaufain") and "Isabel" (signed
"Childe Hazard"). Probably the other unsigned contributions in this issue are
also by Simms. This issue is noticed in the New York *Morning News* of July 12.

[221] William West's portrait of Simms. See letters to Lawson of Jan. 15 and
April 7, 1845.

luck for us. My wife sends love to yours. With your permission
I do the same, giving a loving kiss into the bargain. You will
please bestow it. Augusta joins me in the act. Kiss the children
all round on our account. We sometimes talk to Gilmore of
Jemmy & his horse Neddy, & the little fellow opens great eyes
of intelligence as he stops to listen. Pray let me hear from you
soon. You should not, so repeatedly & cruelly tax the indulgence
of your friends.

Yours Ever as Ever

W. Gilmore Simms.

P. S. It is barely possible that I shall look in upon you at the
close of the summer. It depends on the turn of a dye and that
silver. Say to your wife that she must not be alarmed, thinking it
my spook, if I open the closet suddenly when she is at her jam
and biscuit. I have fed fat on her peach & quince this winter &
long to see the place where they grow. Once more a kiss for
the little woman whose kindness I cannot sufficiently acknowledge.
I have just refused a seat in the carriage of a friend, who goes
on a two months trip to Tennessee. If the time is to be consumed
in travel, I should rather it should be to a quarter where I have
so much to love & to admire.

255 : To EVERT AUGUSTUS DUYCKINCK

June 8. 1845

My dear Duyckinck

I wrote you a long &, I take it, a very dull Letter, yesterday,
but forgot one little item which it is in your way to attend to.
I am in reciept of Wiley & Putnam's Library to the 7th. No.
inclusive, but have failed to recieve any thereafter, though I percieve that they have been for some time in our city. It has been
suggested that the nos. missing were lost in the Brig Moon. This
may be or not. But you can easily ascertain whether they were
sent. I could wish also that you would inquire whether it is by
design or inadvertence that I do not recieve the Whig Magazine
of Mr. Colton. Not a number has reached me, though our journal
has been regularly sent. For the last two months the Broadway
Journal has failed me also. I do not wish you to urge any solicitations that these may be sent, as sufficient has already been done
in this respect; but simply to see if the omission is an inad-

vertence. Poe's writings are always interesting to me, and if a
fair exchange will procure them, I shall cheerfully keep the B. J.
on our Exchange List. — Let me hear from you at length touching the Bulls & Bears of Literature among you.

Yours &c

W. G. Simms.

P. S. Who, by the way, has been guilty of that most unblushing
piece of dishonesty, the paper on Genl. Morris in the Graham
Magazine.[222] It is evidently by one of more ability than moral.
The damnable discredit cast upon men of letters by such bare-
faced performances, is not the least of the evils which in this
country arrest & retard the progress of our Literature. People
are apt to disparage the profession when the professor is a knave
& an imposter. — As for the letter of Mr. Willis on this subject
— but — why a word. It is melancholy to witness the self-reg-
istered abasement of real talent — its facile descent — and that
it should grin & look exulting the while, is still more wretched
& deplorable. I am coming more & more to the conclusion that
it is necessary for one's own respect, to cast aside all consideration of contemporary opinion. Certainly, as a general rule, this
would be wrong, but God help us, *now,* and *here,* there is no other
way to keep the whiteness of one's soul, — to keep one's skirts
free from taint & pollution.

P. S. Did I tell you that A. B. Meek of Ala. has obtained a situation at Washington under Govt. He has in preparation a History
of Alabama, & a poem in three Cantos, entitled 'The Red Eagle
— A Tale of the Muscoghee,' — founded upon events in the
progress of the War of 1812-15. He will probably visit N. Y.
when ready to publish.[223] I have counselled him to this, and
furnished him with Letters to you & others. — Will you not see

---

[222] "Our Contributors.—No. XVIII. Gen. George P. Morris," XXVI (April,
1845), 145-150. The article closes with a letter by Nathaniel Parker Willis
(see introductory sketch), in which he calls Morris "the best known poet of
the country by acclamation, not by criticism."

[223] Meek supported Polk for the presidency and obtained an appointment in
the Federal Treasury Department. As far back as May 24, 1843, he had written
to John Tomlin (see Meek's letter in Tomlin's "Autobiography of a Monomaniac," *Holden's Dollar Magazine,* III [May, 1849], 278-279) that he had
composed 800 pages of his history of Alabama (never published—MS. now
in the State of Alabama Department of Archives and History) and had almost
completed *The Red Eagle.* Meek dedicated this last to Simms when it was
published by D. Appleton and Co., New York, in 1855.

Lawson touching my Miscellaneous Tales — and have you, or Mathews or Lawson, got, that vol. of M.S. verse, which among other things contains my lines to a Mockg. Bird. — I think Longfellow's "Waif" a poor compilation. I had almost said a dishonest one.[224] His own verses are quite tasteful & pretty.

256: To Edwin DeLeon [225]

Charleston, June 16. [1845][226]

E. DeLeon Esq.

dear Sir

I am rejoiced to find that you have driven your stakes in one of the most pleasant places of the South. Savannah is rich in clever fellows, fellows clever in the two fold sense of Anglo-Norman speech. I trust that you will find the soil as genial professionally, as, I am sure, it will prove personally. — Your sketch has been recieved & given out to the printers. It comes late, & a great portion of the Mage. for the month is made up; but if possible it shall appear in July. It will afford me pleasure to recieve your contributions more frequently. In haste, but very truly

&c Yours.

W. Gilmore Simms

257: To James Lawson

Charleston, Monday Night
June 16. [1845][227]

My dear Lawson.

I have just seen Mr. Allen,[228] and learned from him, very unexpectedly, that he will depart tomorrow for the North. I avail myself of the opportunity to add a few more last words to previous letters, sent on within a few days by Mr. Head, the Book-

---

[224] So did Poe. See note 212, June 6, 1845.

[225] See note 86, July 8, 1844.

[226] Dated by the publication of "Scenes in a Life," *Southern and Western,* II (July, 1845), 43-50. This contribution, dated from Savannah, Ga., and signed "Q.," is undoubtedly the sketch Simms mentions in this letter.

[227] Dated by Simms' discussion of Augusta's proposed trip to the North. See letter to Hammond of July 10, 1845.

[228] Probably Gilbert Allen. See note 231, June 17, 1845.

seller. What I have to say will, I know, occasion some distress to you. It is that Augusta's health is declining.. She is a mere skeleton and without appetite; troubled with cough & phlegm, though not, in this respect, to any extent. When you learn that all her mother's family with herself, perished of consumption, you will see that I have some reason to feel uneasy. At present, beyond the lassitude and lack of appetite from which she suffers, there is no occasion for alarm; if there were, I should not scruple at once to send her to your care & climate for the summer. It may be that I shall bring her on myself toward the close of the season. This will be if her health seems to require it. Whether I shall come myself, in the absence of this necessity is very problematical. I shall try to do so; but if I do, it will be only late in the season — say, about the middle of September. I assure you that I look forward to the prospect with real hope & anxiety as nothing would give me more pleasure than to find myself snug for a few weeks around your pleasant table. Your wife and self both know that this is no blarney. — I wish you could spare time to attend to such of the commissions in previous letters as relate to M.S.S. — Do get me the songs back from your musical friend, & make inquiries of Mathews & Duyckinck for that volume of MS. which contains the poem to the Mocking Bird. Ask Duyckinck when he writes again to say whether Mess'rs. Wiley & Putnam design a series of poetry in their Library. Tell him also that a selection from the numerous writing of Sir Egerton Brydges,[229] might form a couple of pleasing & successful volumes. I enclose you a Letter, (unsealed) which you will read & act upon, if the party to whom it is addressed is findable in your city. He (Mr. Richards) *owes* me the picture.[230] If you obtain it, please place it under the hands of your wife, say that I kiss her hands, and beg that it may find a place on her walls. God bless you & a kiss for all.

Yours &c.

W. G. Simms.

---

[229] Sir Samuel Egerton Brydges (1762-1837), author of novels, poems, and essays.

[230] This letter to Thomas Addison Richards has not been located.

258: To GILBERT ALLEN? [231]

[June 17, 1845][232]

J. L. Allen Esq
My dear Sir

I send you a small packet of specimen from the lands on Edisto which I hope will not encumber you to take with you for an analysis at your leisure. — I also cover you a Letter for our friend Lawson. — My wife & daughter send love for Mrs. A., and we all join to implore for you a prosperous progress and a safe return. — I sincerely hope that your trip will work beneficial results in your own case.

Very faithfully
Yrs &c

W. Gilmore Simms
June 17

259: To JAMES HENRY HAMMOND

[c. June 18, 1845][233]

dear Hammond

Will you suffer our publishers to put forth an edition of your Letters to Clarkson in pamphlet form. A number of Gentlemen

---

[231] Though the MS. has "J. L. Allen" in the salutation to this letter, it is probable that Simms erred and wrote the initials of Joseph L. Allen, his Barnwell friend, rather than those of Gilbert Allen, a friend of both Simms and Lawson, as this Allen certainly was (see Simms' letters to Lawson of June 16 and June 27, 1845; *c.* Aug. 22, 1846; and Nov. 16 or 17, 1847). No J. L. Allen is listed in the New York City *Directories* from 1836 through 1849, though Gilbert Allen, the former president of the Washington Marine Insurance Co., while Lawson was vice-president, is listed consistently during those years, after 1842 as a commercial merchant. For Simms' earlier remarks about the Gilbert Allens, see letters to Lawson of July 20, 1837; May 29 and Aug. 16, 1841; and June 29, 1843. Another possible Allen is Horatio (1802-1890), a civil engineer who moved from the North to Charleston, S. C., in 1829 to accept the position of chief engineer of the South Carolina Railroad Co. to construct its railroad from Charleston to Hamburg, S. C. In 1835 he left South Carolina, traveled abroad for three years with his wife, the former Mary Moncrief Simons, daughter of the Rev. James Dewar Simons of Charleston and a connection of Mrs. Simms, and then settled in New York City. He died at his residence, Homewood, near South Orange, N. J.

[232] Dated by Simms' reference to his letter to Lawson of June 16.

[233] On June 17, 1845, the *Southern Patriot* commenced publication of "Gov. Hammond's Letter on Southern Slavery. — No. 1," reprinted from the *South-Carolinian* (see note 160, April 10, 1845). On June 21 the *Southern Patriot* announced: "Gov. Hammond's Letters on Slavery, in pamphlet form, have been published this day, and will be ready for gratuitous distribution. . . ." This letter, therefore, has been dated *c.* June 18.

of this city are desirous of putting forth an edition sufficiently large not only to meet the demand for it, but to diffuse it through regions where it is expected to produce large benefits. No money is expected to be made by it. The object is simply diffusion — an object which is defeated by the price 25/100 cents which Pemberton's pamphlet sells for. I may add that this movement originates with Merchts. of Charleston (Yankees) who are glad of the argts. & will certainly circulate them better abroad than any body else. Do not suffer the good that may come of this diffusion to be defeated by the selfish policy of a publisher. Here they will be printed for gratuitous distribution at a cost of 3 cents each. Let me hear from you at once.

Yours in great haste

W G Simms

260: To EVERT AUGUSTUS DUYCKINCK

Charleston, June 25. 1845.

My dear Sir

I take a sheet of foolscap to write you, for I feel that I have much 'self' to be expended. Your letter gives me pleasure, & I can readily excuse your previous neglect, when it is followed by such ample atonement. I could wish to hear from you more frequently, but can readily understand the duties upon your hands. These duties are something more than belong to the mere engagement with the publisher. You are now in a situation to do a real service to American Literature,[234] by opening certain fountains to the public taste which will equally please & purify. I believe of you, what I am sorry to say, I can believe of few American Critics that you have a hearty love for the art, unimpressed & uninfluenced by petty prejudices of your own, and a still more petty subserviency to cliquism. That you are free from cant is also so much gained to your catholicity. But why pester you with praises. I prefer to show my liking to my friend by simply declaring him such. — I wrote you some few weeks ago, and doubt if you recd. my Letter, as I do not see that you pay any regard to its contents. I had some reference then to the proposed publication "the Wigwam & the Cabin" & to other similar things, some of which I will try to repeat. But first, to glance at your

---

[234] As editor of Wiley and Putnam's "Library of American Books."

Letter of the 19th. just recieved. 1. It would please me to hear in how much you concur with my course of *criticism* in the Magazine. You refer to it without offering a judgment. I confess that, like Mathews, my taste for reading diminishes, — I suppose in obedience to the constant employment of the home faculty. I am so completely surrendered to the making of literature, that I can read little of that of others. It is a duty that makes me understand what is sent me for notices, & I confess little beside. Your habit, on the other hand, of reading more than writing, is probably so far injurious to you as to keep you from perform- ances of your own. There is little pleasure in putting pen to paper. One does it only in compliance with a mood too imperative to be resisted & [in] which pen & pencil immediately [become] sub- servient to thought. The luxury of literature is with you. The care with me. — Yet I love old books too & have groped no little among them. ii. I have just recieved Headley's Book, and the Journal of an African Cruiser, both of which shall be read care- fully. In a previous Letter, I mentioned that I had failed to re- cieve Hazllitt's 'Table Talk,' Part *2*; the 'French in Algiers' & the 'Ancient Moral Tales.' These, it is suggested by the Book- sellers here, may have been lost in the Brig Moon. At all events I have never recd. them, & will thank you to have me provided. The Crescent & the Cross I have and only this day penned a notice of it.[235] I have yet to recieve the 13. 14. 15 & 16 nos. The Tales of Poe have not come to hand,[236] though I have nos. 1 & 3 of the American Series. I have every disposition to do him jus- tice. I could wish that you would make the title to my collection, "The Wigwam & the Cabin" reversing the relative places of the two. I am not sure but that the material will make two num- bers. The stories are probably rather longer than is usual with such things, and I contemplate publishing a few more than you are probably acquainted with. The tale of "Oakatibbee" belongs legitimately to this collection, so does another, entitled "Barnacle

---

[235] Joel Tyler Headley's *Letters from Italy* and Horatio Bridges' *The Journal of an African Cruiser* (ed. Nathaniel Hawthorne) are reviewed in Simms' "Library of American Books," *Southern and Western,* II (Aug., 1845), 128-131. They are mentioned with *The French in Algiers* and *The Ancient Moral Tales, from the Gesta Romanorum* in "Editorial Bureau," *ibid.,* II (Oct., 1845), 287. Hazlitt's *Table Talk* is briefly noted in "Editorial Bureau," *ibid.,* II (Dec., 1845), 425-426, and Eliot Warburton's *The Crescent and the Cross* in "Editorial Bureau," *ibid.,* II (July, 1845), 70-71.

[236] Poe's *Tales* is reviewed by Simms in the "Editorial Bureau" of *ibid.,* II (Dec., 1845), 426-427.

Sam, or the Edisto Raftsman," which the Editor of Graham's
Mag. villainously converted into "The Boatman's Revenge", after
the old school of Raw Head & Bloody Bones. Then there's "The
Snake of the Cabin" in one of the numbers of the Mag., and a
trifle in one of the early numbers called "Those Old Lunes".[237]
If you have read these you can let me know how far you think
they deserve a place in the collection. — I indicated to you, besides, a collection in one vol. of things purely imaginative, some
of which appeared in a couple of vols. published by Adlard, which
did not take because of the sudden rush, at that time, into cheap
literature. My two vols. were $2.00 when Winchester & Harper
were selling Bulwer, James, Sue and others at 12½ cents. I
refer you to two stories entitled Carl Werner & Conrad Weickhoff, and to a third, all in the same collection, called "The Star
Bretheren". *See Lawson for this collection.* To these three tales
add "The Benefactress", "Annihilation", some others, in which,
according to my thinking, I have done much more natively than
in any of my previous labors.[238] I should like also, if your Library
contemplates poetry, to prepare a vol. which might succeed on
acct. of other qualities besides the verse. The interest of a family
of "Tales & Legends of the South" might commend the metrical
matter to many readers. What think you? In making the collection, I refer you to the following tales &c in a collection of
"Southern Passages & Pictures" (also pub. unhappily in that first
dawning of cheap literature which flooded us with asturia of
whity brown paper more wretched than that of the stage) viz.

---

[237] "Oakatibbe; or the Choctaw Sampson" was published in the *Southern
Literary Gazette,* I (Sept., 1828), 142-149; *The Book of My Lady. A Melange*
(Philadelphia: Key and Biddle, 1833), pp. 277-290; *Southern and Western,* I
(April and May, 1845), 244-255, 318-329; and *The Wigwam and the Cabin,*
First Series, pp. 176-208. For "Sergeant Barnacle; or, the Raftsman of the
Edisto," see note 169, April 10, 1845. "The Snake of the Cabin" was published
in *Southern and Western,* I (June, 1845), 393-411, and *The Wigwam and the
Cabin,* First Series, pp. 149-175. "Those Old Lunes! or, Which Is the Madman?"
was published in *Southern and Western,* I (Feb., 1845), 85-99, and *The Wig-
wam and the Cabin,* Second Series, pp. 79-98.

[238] "Carl Werner" and "Conrade Weickhoff" had both appeared in *Carl
Werner, An Imaginative Story; with Other Tales of Imagination,* I, 1-89; II,
3-82. "Conrade Weickhoff" had earlier been published in *The Magnolia for 1837,*
pp. 188-253 (see note 40, June, 1836). "The Star Brethren" had first appeared
as "The Spirit Bridegroom" in *The Book of My Lady,* pp. 291-299; it had
been republished in the *Southern Literary Journal,* III (Nov., 1836), 193-211,
and in *Martin Faber, the Story of a Criminal; and Other Tales* (New York:
Harper and Brothers, 1837), II, 39-89. The title had been changed to "The Star
Brethren" when it was published in *Carl Werner,* I, 155-207. For "The
Passage of a Night; or, the Benefactress" and "Annihilation," see note 170,
April 10, 1845.

1. A Story of God's Judgment. 2. The Hunter of Calawassee. 3. Albert & Rosalie 4 The Tryst of Acayma &c. In addition to these & not contained in this volume are some better things, viz. 1. The Forest Maiden, a tale of Pocahontas. 2. The Last Days of the Biloxi. 3. Balboa &c.[239] These things will all recieve revision prior to publication. A series of neat parlor volumes of verse, might, it seems to me, be made acceptable to the people. I am sorry not to have seen Fraser.[240] Mathews's book [241] I shall look for with some curiosity. I confess the plan, as I gather it from your letter does not strike me as a very eligible one. — I am sorry to say that it will be late before I shall be able to go North. Circumstances of a domestic nature will keep me here until the middle of August, unless the declining health of my daughter compels me to set out sooner. I confess to great anxieties on her account, — and may, if friends offer, send her on to Mrs. Lawson & some friends in N. England, before I go myself. I look daily for letter from Lawson. He is a sad fellow. From Mathews I heard yesterday & shall write him shortly. The Broadway Journal has entirely failed me for the last two months. Can you tell me why? The American Review has not come at all. Still my Mag. is sent to both. Can it be that I am attacked in them; for such has been the practice with some other Editors. Fathom the subject for me. It may be inadvertence. Can't you give me a budget from 'Times Wallet,['] for my August issue.[242] It will facilitate my

---

239 In addition to their several magazine appearances, "The Story of God's Judgment," "The Hunter of Calawassee," "Albert and Rosalie," and "The Tryst of Acayma" were published in *Southern Passages and Pictures* (New York: George Adlard, 1839), pp. 175-188, 99-108, 197-225, and 95-99. All were later included in *Poems Descriptive Dramatic, Legendary and Contemplative,* pp. 261-272, 288-293, 235-260, and 304-306. "The Last Song of the Biloxi" (later called "The Last Fields of the Biloxi") had originally appeared in the *Boston Notion* (see note 33, Feb. 20, 1841) ; it was later included in *Poems Descriptive Dramatic, Legendary and Contemplative,* pp. 273-287. "Pocahontas" was published in *The Missionary Memorial: A Literary and Religious Souvenir* (New York: E. Walker, 1846) — later reissued as *The Evergreen. A Christmas, New Year, and Birthday Gift* (New York: Leavitt & Allen, n. d.) — pp. 199-220; it was later republished in *Southward Ho!,* pp. 110-123. We have been unable to discover where "Balboa" was published.

240 Probably Robert F. Fraser. See note 96, Feb. 11, 1845.

241 *Big Abel and the Little Manhattan.* Duyckinck reviewed this novel for *Southern and Western,* II (Nov., 1845), 314-322.

242 Duyckinck did not contribute to the August issue of the *Southern and Western.* Simms' own contributions include "Bayard, the Chevalier" (pp. 73-85), "The Miniature" (p. 86), "The Epochs and Events of American History, as Suited to the Purposes of Art in Fiction" (pp. 87-94), "Sonnet. — The Portrait" (p. 94), "No More" (p. 106), "Delphi" (p. 118), "The Red Eagle of Muscoghee" (pp. 119-120), "Library of American Books" (pp. 128-131), "Daniel Boone. — James Moseley" (pp. 131-132), and "Editorial Bureau" (pp.

progress somewhat & help me to go north a few days sooner. I wrote you for no 16 of Arcturus, and made some inquiries touching certain Nos. of the N. Y. Review which are necessary to complete my set. I am trying to make up for you a complete set of the S. Quarterly. I see by the 'News' that Saunders has left Langley.[243] Qu? I hear nothing of Langley. Has he anything on the anvil? And what has been the success, thus far, of the Library? The publication of Mr. Putnam in London is only *American* in the Yankee sense of the word.[244] I am not satisfied with it. I have glimpsed at it only, not having a copy. Do you want an item for the "News." I have in preparation a new romance in two vols. entitled "The Cassique, a Tale of Ashley River —" time somewhere about 1685.[245]   W. G. S.

133-144). All are unsigned except "No More" (signed "Adrian Beaufain"). Probably all other unsigned poems in this issue are also by Simms. The New York *Morning News* of Aug. 23 says of this issue: "We have read nearly every article in this number, a temptation to which we are not often subjected in the current magazines. With enough of ornament and light reading, there is something tangible and substantial, as well to fix the attention, or rather light topics are handled in a profitable manner with a sense of reality about them. The opening article, for instance, is a vivid picture of the days of chivalry in a sketch of several passages in the life of the Chevalier Bayard, but without being at all didactic, it is made the vehicle for thought, and enlists youth in a moral disciple, while he only dreams of a pleasant tale. Some thoughtful verses follow. Then a brilliant review (showing evidently the eye of the novelist) of the Huguenot settlements in Florida, one of the papers on the 'Epochs and Events of American History, as suited to the purposes of art in fiction.' . . . The criticism of this magazine is always elaborately executed with original thought and suggestion. The industry of the editor is sustained by his philosophic habits of mind and his liberal studies. In tone and character this Southern Monthly is far in advance of the popular periodical literature of the day." The *Broadway Journal*, II (Aug. 30, 1845), 121, calls the issue "capital" and remarks that "it contains several of the finest kind of Magazine papers, and is as ably edited as any journal of its species in America—if not more ably edited than any."

[243] We have been unable to locate this item in either the New York *Morning News* or the *New York Weekly News*.

[244] George Palmer Putnam (1814-1872) became a partner in the firm of Wiley and Putnam in 1840. In 1841 he established a branch office in London, where in 1845 he published his *American Facts: Notes and Statistics Relative to the Government, Resources, Engagements, Manufactures, Commerce, Religion, Education, Literature, Fine Arts, Manners and Contours of the United States of America,* here mentioned by Simms, in an effort to improve Anglo-American relations. Later, in 1848, Putnam dissolved his partnership with John Wiley.

[245] Frequently a long period elapsed between the first writing and the actual publication of Simms' works. *The Cassique of Kiawah,* here mentioned, did not appear until 1859, when it was brought out by Redfield in New York. It is dedicated to William Porcher Miles (see introductory sketch). The *Dem. Rev.,* XVII (Aug., 1845), 156, contains a notice: "W. Gilmore Simms, Esq., has, we understand, in preparation a new romance in two volumes, to be entitled The Cacique [*sic*], a Tale of Ashley River, the period somewhere about the year 1685."

P. S. If you have not "Carl Werner" and "Southern Passages" I can procure you copies. Meantime, Lawson can provide you.

261: To JAMES LAWSON

Charleston, June 27. [1845][246]

My dear Lawson

Your very acceptable favor of the 21st reached me last night. That you should not have heard from me of late is somewhat surprising, since I wrote you at length by the same person who carried on the Letter to Mr. Taylor. Your answers to this man were proper, and precisely what they should be. I know nothing about him, but conclude, from your Letter, that he is not the man with whom either of us should care to deal. Still, as he has the plates in hand, and as we have had sufficient annoyance about them, it will be just as well to close with him if he comes up to y'r proposals. I wrote you to a like effect. It will be important that he should procure, or you, or some friend, the MS. which Winchester retains, and which can be of no possible use to him. I presume that he will readily yield it to Taylor. At all events make it a *sine qua non* with Taylor, that he procure the unprinted pages before he can possibly get the rest, — for just now, I would rather forego the publication than undertake to rewrite that portion of the matter. Some more of the M.S. is in my hands, and that which remains to be written, is such as I could easily prepare in a week towards the close of the summer. It may be that, with the permission of Lady Lide, I shall do so, then, within the cheerful influence of her smiles & domicile. — Indeed, my dear Lawson, it may be that I shall not be able to delay my visit until the season advances. This, I should, from circumstances prefer to do, but other circumstances may compel me to see you much sooner than will comport with my first arrangements. These were timed with reference to the expected *accouchement* of my wife, who looks for the event sometime in August.[247] I had designed, & still design, if permitted, to forbear the North till that event is fairly over, but since I have reached the city, the health of Augusta, which has been gradually declining for the last two or three months, has become so seriously affected that I am now

---

[246] Dated by Simms' reference to the plates of *Count Julian,* which had been acquired by William Taylor. See letter to Lawson of June 7.

[247] Valeria Govan Simms was born on Aug. 10.

looking out for friends going North by whom to send her. Failing in this quest, and her debility increasing, I shall have to anticipate my previous arrangements, and carry her on myself. Do not be surprised, therefore, if you see me someday stepping into 'Eleventh St' (are you there still) with my poor child under my arm. My plan is to give her a brief rest with you and then send or carry her up to Great Barrington, the climate of which would be less likely to debilitate and oppress her than that of the city. If you had your villa now, on the North River, — but — ! The Allens[248] went on a week ago, but as they went by land, a fatiguing route, and expected to linger on the way, I dared not venture to trust Augusta with them. She is very feeble & thin, & is totally without appetite. She is now in the hands of the physician. You who know what this child was to me, for so many weary years of privation & loneliness, can readily understand my present anxieties. I must not dwell upon them. — I am surprised that McCracken does not recieve the Magazine. I ordered it to be sent him from the beginning, and will see the publishers tomorrow in regard to it. His paper was remarkably well done, — well concieved & well written.[249] I shall be greatly pleased — say to him — to recieve others of a like value. — I am glad the portrait likes you. I will put a Sonnet on the subject in our next Magazine.[250] — Present me devotedly to Miss Sinclair,[251] with the expression of my desire to hear my words wedded to her music. May the union be as immortal as indissoluble. I trust that she will recover the MS. Songs from your Musical Genius. — I do not envy Bryant in his wanderings, but I could wish that, all my flock at ease, I were with him.[252] I rejoice to see that Forrest is making himself felt as he deserves to be. His only error is in any attempt to win favor from the English. No American can hope for this. They must be made to fear us, and, it is through our scorn and our strength, not through our arts conciliatory that a people so bigoted in self will ever do justice to that other, which spring from their loins, & setting up for themselves, are so fast treading on their heels. — I got a

---

[248] Probably the Gilbert Allens. See note 231, June 17, 1845.

[249] A review of Robert Chambers' *Vestiges of the Natural History of Creation*. See note 220, June 7, 1845.

[250] "Sonnet. — The Portrait," *Southern and Western*, II (Aug., 1845), 94.

[251] Margaret Sinclair, sister of Mrs. Edwin Forrest.

[252] On April 22 Bryant had set sail for Europe. He returned in November.

letter from Duyckinck a few days ago. A portion of my copy [253] is in your hands. You got it from Harper & Bro. and kept it with you to dispose of to Burgess & Stringer. It consists of "Murder Will Out", & other things, mostly printed. Pray look it up for I have no other copies. You must see also that B & S. return to you the printed sheets of Count Julian. Request Stringer to send me a few copies of Castle Dismal & Helen Halsey. These still continue to sell in the South, & I am told that more than 500 copies have been disposed of in Charleston alone. — I have recieved but 3 Letters from you since I left you in N. Y. last October. I wish I could cure you of this diabolical infirmity! Do not forget to look up the M.S. of which I wrote you.[254] Ask Stringer how he would like a story with the title "A Dead Shot, or as Good as a Comedy" — a thing of 150 pages to be written.[255] — I have got a great deal of work planned & digested, but the toils of the Mag., of politics, of a too large correspondence, and the cares of Wife & children — these all combine to curb & fetter my performances. Let me hear from you soon. You are one of the few friends of whom I cannot hear too frequently. A kiss from wife and daughter to Lady L. to whom & the children present me affectionately.

Yours as Ever

W. G. S.

262: To JAMES LAWSON

Charleston, July 2. [1845][256]

My dear Lawson.

It is not improbable that I will send Augusta to sea on Saturday next the 5th inst. in the packet ship Charleston. I consign her to you & your wife, — desiring that she may be sent under some friendly charge, to Great Barington, as soon as she has had a sufficient rest in your domicile. Should she improve in New York, she may continue there, and, indeed, await my coming in

---

253 For *The Wigwam and the Cabin.*

254 See letter of June 7, 1845.

255 *As Good as a Comedy: or, the Tennesseean's Story* was not published until 1852, when it was issued in Philadelphia by A. Hart. It is dedicated to Harry Placide (1799-1870), the actor.

256 Dated by the contents of Simms' letters to Lawson of June 16 and to Hammond of July 10, both referring to Augusta's health and to her voyage to the North.

August. But this will depend upon her feeling & your opinion of
the condition of her health. She is now very feeble and ill looking; and nothing but the circumstance of which I wrote you
lately, prevents my keeping her in my own sight until she is
fairly seated in your city & home. But to go with her, return
instanter, & go north again in August to return again in October,
would be equally fatiguing to myself & exhausting to my pockets.
— I was in hopes to have heard from you before taking this
step which seems so precipitate, but in truth, I have been made
so apprehensive about Augusta, and I am urged so strenuously
to send her off, that I dare not delay too long. — Mr. Sherwood,[257] will advise you of opportunities to Barington — perhaps,
Mr. Bryant may — let Augusta advise them both of her presence
in New York as soon after her arrival as convenient. — I have
written you so recently and so frequently, as to have left myself nothing now to say, but bald as this Letter is, the New
Postoffice-Law makes it a tolerably cheap one, — compared at
least with old prices.[258] My wife sends her love. Augusta joins,
with the hope of soon yielding it in *pro. per.* For my part, you
have me as before, — always yours & your wifes, with kisses
for the young ones.

Faithfully &c

W. G. S.

263 : To JAMES LAWSON

Charleston July 5. [1845][259]

My dear Lawson

You will be Augusta's Cashier until I come on in August. She
will need but little money, just to take her to Barington and
back again, and provide her while there with any trifles she may
desire. I would have given her adequate supplies here, but that
she might lose it on the way. She is rather a careless damsel in
these respects. — I have penned a note to your wife, and have
written you so frequently of late as to find myself now with
nothing to speak about. I hope to be with you about the 20th

---

257 For the William Sherwoods, of New York City, see note 15, June 26,
1837.

258 See note 214, June 6, 1845.

259 Dated by Simms' reference to Augusta's visit to the North. See letter to
Lawson of July 2 and letter to Hammond of July 10.

August. — My hands just now are fuller than ever. I have just contracted with the Southern Patriot newspaper of this place to contribute occasional literary paragraphs for which I get some $50.00 per mo.[260] It costs me no labor, and provides me with some additional change for cakes and ale.

Yours truly &c

W. Gilmore Simms

264: To James Henry Hammond

Charleston, July 10. 1845

My dear Hammond

Troubles and anxieties of sundry kinds, to say nothing of the increasing burdensomeness of my daily tasks, have kept me from writing you, as I had willed it, for some time past. I have been compelled to send my daughter to the North in bad health. Her condition has been a subject of great uneasiness to me for the last three months. Her mother, and all her mother's family were consumptives, and she has been yielding to a degree of debility which, increasing day by day, with other unpromising symptoms, has awakened all my apprehensions. Change of climate & scene may restore her, & I fervently hope will. Our little boy has also been quite sick, and has a return of fever this evening. With these occasions, the approaching accouchement of my wife, and some physical discomforts of my own, with the constant drudgery of the press, I have, I assure, need of all my philosophies and of all the indulgence of my friends. Besides, I owe monies, & have lately had some unexpected money disappointments. To these last, you may ascribe my contracting to write for magazines & newspapers, for which I have no affection, and which tend to fritter away & to enfeeble my intellectual man, to my own mortification and to the disappointment of kindly judging friends. I have just made an engagement to write literary paragraphs for the Southern Patriot simply to add a few hundred dollars to my

---

[260] The *Southern Patriot* of June 30 announces: "We are happy to inform our readers and patrons that we have succeeded in making an arrangement with Mr. W. Gilmore Simms, by which we shall secure his correspondence for the *Patriot* and *Transcript*. Notices of new books, of the arts, the progress of American letters, and the character of foreign literature, may be occasionally expected in our columns from his pen." At this time Martin E. Munro was the proprietor of the newspaper, having succeeded Jacob N. Cardozo in April, 1845 (see the *Southern Patriot* of April 10).

annual income.[261] — Pen, ink and paper, are among my sins and sufferings. What I think of your letters, I have said honestly, but briefly, in a paragraph in my Magazine to which I refer you. I cannot now go into details. Let it suffice you that I hold them by very far the best things you have done, — not that they are in better style than your last Message, for I do not think so, & in some instances, a tone of too much levity, seems to me to impair their dignity & weight, — but the whole argument is so widely & well argued, takes in so much ground, covers so many relations, and examines all the points so thoroughly, that your worst enemy will hardly hesitate to acknowledge them to be very masterly performances. You have succeeded by these Letters, in placing yourself in such a position before the eye of our public, that, if you please, you will be able to take the wind out of the sails, — so I fancy — of any of the aspirants for the Senate. You will see that in my magazine notice of the Letters, I intimate what South Carolina should do in your respect. I trust, that, should she take my hint, you will be prepared to second her wishes, and those of your friends.[262] — There is a project of Aldrich's, about which he has written me, — that of a Southern League against the Abolitionists, which it appears to me can be worked up into something of importance. You are well aware that a league for any object among the States of the South, would bring the Government to terms. I believe that such a league, properly urged,

---

[261] On July 14 Hammond replied: "I am sorry that you have taken the Patriot in hand. Damn money. It should never interfere with any thing better. I love to make it to buy money's worth. But I never would give for it, what it could not buy again. There are some things above cash evaluation. Your time is one—my comfort is (in my estimation) another." (Original in the Hammond Papers, Library of Congress.)

[262] Under the heading "Gen. Hammond's Letters on Slavery," *Southern and Western,* II (July, 1845), 71-72, Simms writes: "No case could have been more admirably argued, with a clearer knowledge of the facts, with a better appreciation of their relations, or with a more rigid and circumspect attention to all the collateral portions of the subject. To a cool, clear head, and abundant materials, Gen. Hammond unites the advantages of acute and cogent thinking, and a bold, direct and energetic style. As specimens of political composition merely, these Letters are good models, which may be read with profit by our young statesmen. But our purpose, neither eulogy nor analysis, is rather to speak of the author of these Letters than of the Letters themselves, which are destined to force themselves upon the attention of the public at home and abroad. What we have to say of him, may be comprised in a sentence. It is this: — South-Carolina must not permit to retire from her councils, a man still in his youth, who is capable of doing credit to her talent, and of maintaining her rights: — she must look around her for the suitable station in which to employ abilities which, if they were ever at any time wanted to her strength and securities, are wanted now. Let her think of this!"

is quite as easily attainable, as it certainly is desirable.[263] Your letters will furnish an admirable preliminary to the scheme, and if you will furnish the clues, it appears to me that the *mouvement* might be advanced just now with equal success & rapidity. It will need thorough digestion, and some considerable suggestion, so as not to offend prejudices & fears, but it properly addresses itself to a topic, and fights under a flag, which once lifted will rally the whole South. Look at it closely and promptly. Can you send me some hints touching the Bank. I ask you as its enemy. Walker [264] has furnished some. On this subject I know little & have time for little — none for study. Make[265] the sinking fund clear to me if you can. — I have so little time that I think I shall wholly withdraw from politics. My literary responsibilities deny that I shall do myself justice in any other department, and the hints with which my friends constantly annoy me, of electioneering to be done, worry & vex me not a little. Write me soon and believe me

Very truly &c

W. G. Simms

J. H. Hammond Esq.

---

[263] Hammond replied on July 14: "Aldrich consulted me about his League. It would be a grand thing. But I doubt very much the propriety of organizing it for the estimable purpose of defending slavery. Abroad it would be construed to indicate weakness, fear, & division here when our safety depends on proclaiming ourselves strong, resolute & united. At home such agitation as would be necessary to bring about the league, that is on the stump & at primary assemblies of all sorts might produce the greatest evils among our slaves. Could a convention have been called last winter & responded to, we should have every thing our own way. The union dissolved — the South out — the world at our feet entreating for our staples & our trade . . . . But we failed then & if it was not too late would fail now. So Ca belongs to Calhoun. *He will not agitate* . . . . Elmore will not agitate — Pickens will not agitate & these three men it is said carry the state in their breeches pocket. We must therefore wait on our 'approved good masters.' You & I & Aldrich could do nothing if we wished. For myself I am in a state of perfect syncope politically speaking." (Original in the Hammond Papers, Library of Congress.)

[264] James Murdock Walker (1813-1854), a lawyer of Charleston, served several terms in the legislature and in 1844 was appointed to serve with Simms on the Committee on Federal Relations. He was the author of a number of pamphlets, among them *Argument in the Case of the State vs. the Bank of South Carolina* (Charleston: Printed by W. Riley, 1843).

[265] Simms wrote *making*.

265 : To Evert Augustus Duyckinck

Charleston, July 15. 1845

E. A. Duyckinck Esq

My dear Sir

An opportunity offering, by private hand, I cover to your care a packet and letter for Mr. Jones which I beg you to transfer to him with my compliments. The packet contains the 7 nos of our magazine already issued. His article has not been recieved, but shall have early place as soon as possible when it comes to hand.[266] I enclose you a Letter also, addressed to Langley which you will oblige me by placing in his grasp. I am in reciept of Headley's volume, and of the African Cruiser, but not yet of Poe's publication. The two former I have read with pleasure. Headley's book is very pleasant reading. That of the Cruiser quite readable, though scarcely calculated to make much sensation — I shall in a few days notice both in the Southern Patriot — a newspaper here for which I have contracted to do literary editorials for certain useful sixpences that help me to my cakes and ale. I have already in its columns noticed Wiley & P's library, and shall have more to say anent it hereafter.[267] Touching your American Series, I can well concieve your anxiety. There is this objection to the beginning which may somewhat account to you for any difference in sales between it & the other. There is some lack of freshness in the books. Headley's vol. is still new to the reading of the public in a former edition. Poe's Tales labor under the same disadvantage, and so with mine. — And the African Cruiser, though a sensible & not unpleasing book is yet not a hit. Could your publishers have held out sufficient inducements to our best authors for the production of some half dozen original books to begin with, it would have been attended with better results. But our old colonial doubts of the *genius loci,* are assisted here by the obvious absence of freshness in the specimens. You see even in this, what disadvantage to the American author. He has no motive from the publishers. Suppose W & P. had said to me, give us a small

---

[266] "The Temperance Question," *Southern and Western,* II (Nov., 1845), 305-313. See introductory sketch of William Alfred Jones.

[267] Headley's *Letters from Italy* was reviewed on July 1. On July 26 in a long review of Wiley and Putnam's "Library of American Books," Simms mentions Horatio Bridges' *The Journal of an African Cruiser* (ed. Nathaniel Hawthorne), Poe's *Tales,* and Alexander William Kinglake's *Eōthen. The Journal of an African Cruiser* received a separate review on Aug. 6.

and carefully designed vol. at six months notice, for which, hit
or miss, for an edition of 6000 copies we will give you $500. Or
suppose they were now to say to Bryant, give us your notes in
Europe in a snug volume of 100 pages, and tack to the end of
it your Letters from the South, and here is our check for so much
money, — or to Mr. Cooper, or to Mr. Willis, or to Mr. Poe
&c, do you not think that your start in public favor would be
infinitely more fortunate. Let it be known that books are to be
paid for & well paid for, and there is no puffing so likely to commend them to the gaping multitudes. That was the secret of the
Longman's in the case of Lalla Rookh. 3000 guineas for an unwritten poem was a splendid advertisement to the world, realizing
the best efforts of the author, and the most anxious desires of
the public.[268] But we will talk over these things when I see you.
If the authors of Am. will only work together we may do wonders
yet. But our first step will be to disabuse the public mind of the
influence of English & Yankee authorities. *Every thing depends
on this*: The latter have done more than any thing besides to
play the devil with all that is manly & original in our literature.
They have, curiously enough, fastened our faith to the very
writers who, least of all others, possess a native character. Such
is Longfellow, a man of nice taste, a clever imitator,— simply an
adroit artist. W. Irving is little more than a writer of delicate
taste, a pleasant unobtrusive humour, and agreeable talent. Miss
Sedgwick [269] is a better fellow than either, yet not a woman of
genius. In imaginative endowment, these are all feeble. — Yet,
these are thy Gods, Oh! Israel! But, I trust a better day is at
hand. Another war with G. B. will take us out of our leading
strings. It is through our political & social dependence, in great
degree, that the national mind suffers. Our Statesmen, such as
Mr. Everett, approach the British cap in hand, as if they felt
conscious of provincialism. A little more courage in our politicians, and mark me, the literature of the country rises. With
every struggle with European nations shall we better know ourselves, & rise more into self respect. Self-Esteem will take the
place of vanity, and even a sound drubbing will help our manliness. — My daughter left for N. Y. a week ago. Her health is

---

[268] For details of this agreement, see Howard Mumford Jones, *The Harp
That Once — A Chronicle of the Life of Thomas Moore* (New York: Henry
Holt and Company, 1937), pp. 168-169.
[269] Catherine Maria Sedgwick. See note 38, Aug. 30, 1837.

delicate. I trust she is safe by this time with our friend Lawson, where I hope she will make the acquaintance of Mrs. D. — Let me hear from you, and I will endeavour to turn profitably in my thoughts the various points of your Letters prior to visiting N. Y. which I expect to do on or about the 20th. August.— I had hoped to have written Mathews by this chance, but time is not allowed me. Say to him I do not forget him and still do honor to his manifold virtues. Present me respectfully to Mrs D. & to your Brother & hold me

very truly your &c.

W. Gilmore Simms

266: To JAMES LAWSON

[c. July 20, 1845][270]

My dear Lawson

Augusta will communicate to you what I have written her touching her early removal to Great Barington. The air of Berkshire will be of help to her, while that of New York, at this season of the year, would only debilitate her more. By going up as soon as she can, she will recruit the more readily so as to be able to return in Sept. to the city, and enjoy the *chaperonage* of Lady Lyde, which I know she desires. I take for granted that she will be in reciept of an early invitation from Miss Kellogg,[271] in which event, I look to you to find (with Mr Sherwood's help) an escort for her. If not, and you find that she continues feeble, I must hope that you will be able to take two days holiday and escort her yourself. This will give you a view of the lovely valley of the Housatonic, and of scenes & spots that Bryant's Muse has rendered famous. There is a fine tavern at Barington & that place is now a famous resort for the Boston fashionables, so that you may persuade Madame L. to go for a week on a visit. A cool day should be chosen for Augusta's trip. She should take no medicines.

Yours faithfully &c. with love to all.

W. Gilmore Simms

J. L.

---

[270] Dated by Simms' reference to Augusta's visit to the North. The letter is postmarked Charleston, S. C., July 21.

[271] Nancy Kellogg. See note 11, March 28, 1838.

267: To Evert Augustus Duyckinck

[c. July 31, 1845][272]

My dear Sir

I have but a moment to tell you on this rumpled sheet of paper that I have sent you a set of the Southern Qu. Review — 7 vols. — by the ship H. Allen, — which you will please recieve safely and with my compliments. I believe the numbers are now sent you. If not, let me know & I will procure them. — I have been noticing your issues in the So. Pat.[273] I enclose you one of them. Poe's Book has not yet reached me. I have the other two.

In haste, but truly Yours

W. G. Simms

E. A. Duyckinck Esq.

268: To James Lawson

Charleston, August 5. 1845

My dear Lawson

I suspect that Augusta's discontent at Great Barrington arises rather from her great anxiety to get back to New York and to the more grateful companionship of your wife, than from any substantial reason arising from the coldness of her reception where she is. The considerations by which I am influenced in keeping her where she is — for the present at least — are such as are sufficiently apparent to yourself. Her health is the paramount object, and, in its pursuit we must sacrifice minor considerations of sensibility for which in fact there may be no substantial grounds. If we knew any one with whom we could trust her with safety & propriety, in any similar region, who would recieve compensation, of course, we should prefer to gratify the desires of the child, and satisfy the exactions of our own pride. But this is the difficulty. I can scarcely imagine that there is any real want of hospitality in the ladies at G. B. but they labor under the usual coldness & phlegm of the New England character, and in manner lack that warmth & eagerness which to a Southron & to you New

---

[272] This letter is postmarked Charleston, S. C., Aug. 1. The year is established by Simms' letter to Duyckinck of Aug. 7 in which he states that he had forwarded the collection of the *Southern Quarterly Review* "a week ago by ship."

[273] See note 267, July 15, 1845.

Yorkers are so essential to the deportment of friends. When I come on, we will see into the condition of Augusta's health, and the temperature of N. Y. By that time, I fancy, she will be better reconciled to her position. —When I shall be able to leave home, exactly, I cannot yet say. The *Event* has not yet taken place. I look for it about the 10th.[274] and as soon as it is fairly over, and all things are easy and encouraging, I propose to set out, taking the land route by Washington. I shall linger a day in Richmond, another in Wash. and a third in Phil. i. e. according to present probabilities. —Your losses by the fire, were a subject of exceeding apprehension with me, & I rejoice to hear that you are so well off after the satisfaction of all claims. May you be secure & prosperous hereafter. I trust your Averages continue to come in & to be profitable.[275] The article of Mrs. F. will be welcome.[276] I shall look for it with great interest. — When does Forrest return. I have concieved the idea of altering for the Stage the play of "Locrine" imputed to Shakspeare, and have succeeded in manufacturing a first act, out of portions of the 1 & 2 of the original.[277] I think by using the knife freely that a good acting play may be wrought out of it. Mr. Roach who is a great lover & *reader* of the Drama, thinks otherwise.—I see that Augusta has dubbed you & Lady Lyde, Uncle & Aunt, —very impertinently, I think, unless you have given her some sanction for it. She is of an affectionate disposition whose fortune it has been to know but few relatives, and she attaches herself with wonderful readiness where she is met with kindness. I may remark to you that one of the Ladies with whom she is staying has spent with us two entire winters & springs, and has always found in ours a welcome and a genial home.[278] I reenclose you the Letter of Augusta. If Lady Lyde writes, she might suggest the importance to her health of overlooking every thing for the present, and

---

274 Valeria Govan Simms was born on Aug. 10.

275 Lawson was engaged in marine insurance.

276 Possibly "A Visit to the Giant's Causeway," written "by a Lady of New-York," *Southern and Western,* II (Sept., 1845), 155-164, is by Catherine Sinclair (Mrs. Edwin) Forrest.

277 Simms published this adaptation as "The Death of the British Brutus. A Dramatic Sketch" in *Sartain's Union Magazine of Literature and Art,* VIII (April, 1851), 249-253. He says in a prefatory note: "There is a tragedy ascribed to Shakespeare, entitled Locrine. . . . I once conceived the idea of rewriting this old tragedy, using the subject at my pleasure, and employing such lines from the old drama as best suited my purposes. Of this tragedy, thus designed, I submit the first act to the reader, as unique in itself, and totally independent of what succeeds."

278 Nancy Kellogg. See note 271, c. July 20, 1845.

yielding herself up entirely to the necessity of employing the
mountain air with all its wholesome associations. She should think
just now of nothing more than how to get well and acquire
strength rapidly. Gilmore is now making a famous uproar, and
with his racket overhead, & fingers cramped with some hours
drudgery at the desk, I will make a short finish by assuring you,
wife & little ones, how truly & lovingly I am

Yours & theirs

W. G. S.

Tell your wife that she must not look to hear from mine at
least for a season.—She is in no spirits to take pen in hand, but
she begs to be remembered with the best old time affection. Gilmore knows nothing of politics. In that respect his education has
been neglected. But he says that he will back a horse with Jimmy
any day.

269: To Evert Augustus Duyckinck

Charleston, Aug. 7. [1845][279]

My dear Sir

I have just looked over your last three letters, with the view
to seeing what matters may be reserved for verbal communication between us — in other words, how many topics may be dispensed with, just at this moment, which finds me unusually busy.
You will note the objects of my exclusion, very possibly, by those
which I do consider. — In regard, first, to an article by Mr. Jones,
which on the 1st July, you tell me "today forward through W &
P. an article by Jones on the Temperance question." That article
has never reached me, nor am I in reciept of the number of
'Time's Wallet' of which you speak on the same occasion. The
articles on Fox and Public Opinion, I may not reasonably look
for under a week from now — though I could have wished that
you had forwarded them by mail. Up to this moment Poe's tales
have not been recieved, & I think it not unlikely that as these
latter were published about the time when Jones's article was
mentioned that Mr. Wiley put them into the same packet. Now,
if he can recal by what vessel they were sent & to whose care, I
can direct my inquiries more profitably. I have called on some

---

[279] Dated by the contents of Simms' letter to Duyckinck of Aug. 8. Though
Simms dates this letter *Aug. 8,* it is postmarked *Aug. 7.*

of our Booksellers, twice & thrice, but hear nothing. I am particularly sorry in respect to Jones's article which, I trust for both our sakes, may be soon forthcoming. The first & third of the Am. Series alone have reached me. Of these, you will see what I say in the next Mag. a sheet of which I send you, and all of which is, I suppose, under weigh toward you.[280] Other notices have fallen from me into the columns of the Southern Patriot, but I can just now only lay my hands upon a hurried one upon Headley. I think I have sent most of the papers which contain notices to W & P. Some of these notices were quite long for a newspaper.[281] I should be very well pleased to make an arrangement with them for one or two 50 cent vol. of Literary Miscellanies for the American Series, and fancy I can furnish a taking collection. I have no desire to issue my books anywhere but in New York, which I take to be the true publishing city. There are my papers on Copyright, on the Moral Character of Hamlet, on the material for fiction in American History, on Washington Allston, on the Conquest of Mexico by Cortes &c. and numerous lighter things, such as Philosophy of the Omnibus, Costume, Morals of the Waltz &c.[282] — Did you concieve my purpose in the papers begun in "Orion" — The Hermytte of Drowsiehedde.[283] They were to form a new & fanciful Utopia in which all should not be fancy.

---

[280] William A. Jones' "The Temperance Question" was published in *Southern and Western,* II (Nov., 1845), 305-313; Duyckinck's "The Tyranny of Public Opinion" in *ibid.,* II (Oct., 1845), 217-221; Duyckinck's "Recollections of W. J. Fox, the Unitarian Preacher" in *ibid.,* II (Dec., 1845), 361-366; and Simms' notice of the "Library of American Books" in *ibid.,* II (Aug., 1845), 128-131.

[281] See note 267, July 15, 1845.

[282] For Simms' three letters on copyright, see letter to Holmes of Jan. 26, 1844. For his article on the moral character of Hamlet, see letter to Lawson of Feb. 15, 1844. For his papers on the material for fiction in American history, see letter to the Georgia Historical Society of Nov. 25, 1841. For his article on Washington Allston, see letter to Lawson of Sept. 29, 1843. For his article on the conquest of Mexico, see letter to Lawson of March 8, 1844. "The Philosophy of the Omnibus" had been published in the *American Monthly Magazine* (New York), III (May 1, 1834), 153-159; revised and republished in *Godey's,* XXIII (Sept., 1841), 104-107. "A Thought on Dress" had been published in the *Southern Literary Journal,* N. S., III (April, 1838), 274-277. "The Morals of the Waltz" had appeared in the same journal, N. S., III (March, 1838), 176-181.

[283] See note 83, c. June 30, 1844. In the New York *Morning News* of Sept. 18, 1844, Duyckinck comments: "A series of papers commenced in Orion, 'The Hermytte of Drowsiehedde,' are very pleasant in themselves, and a happy illustration of the variety of Mr. Simms's talents, who introduces us to a Castle of Indolence, and from the most industrious and [v]oluminous of writers shews himself the most luxurious and sympathetic among idlers. The short asthmatic sentences with which the paper opens, are of the very height of the idle man's humor."

That, when finished, would be a vol. by itself. You may discuss
with Wiley the project of this miscellany, to do which, on my
part, I give you ample discretion.[284] I should like, if possible, that
my books could always be put as cheap or cheaper than the English. I would recommend that this experiment be tried with the
Am. Series — the sales of which I then fancy would far exceed
the former. — I trust that your Printers will be prepared to go
on with the 'Tales'[285] as soon as I reach New York. This will
be late in August, and there will be but a month or so between
that & the period of my return, and this I hope to crowd with
business. Mathews's book[286] is a pleasant one to those who will
concieve his plan; but I fear that the great body of readers will
not do this. He is too entirely New York. Not that I object that
he should find his subject & materials there, but that, in his delineations, he assumes so much to be already understood by the reader.
His pictures are not sufficiently ample. His episodes are too few.
He should have contrived an independent one, showing the social
morale of the community in every chapter. A great deal of his
picturesque will be thrown away upon those who know nothing
about the city. — Tell him that I shall try & write him shortly,
but that I have nothing to say to him that I have not said to you,
& that just now, pen & ink sicken me. — I am afraid Langley
is not enough *liberal*. Is that the word? But this *inter nos*. More
when we meet.

Yours truly &c

W. G. Simms

E. A. Duyckinck Esq

Thanks for the Broadway Journals which have come to hand,
all but No 9. of Vol 1. which, if convenient, procure and send
me. In B. J. for May 31 is a poem signed with my name at length
entitled "The Whippoorwill" which is an imposition.[287] I never

---

[284] Wiley and Putnam subsequently published as part of their "Library of
American Books" a collection of Simms' miscellaneous critical articles under
the title of *Views and Reviews in American Literature, History and Fiction*,
First and Second Series, dedicated to Professor E. Geddings, of the Medical
College of South Carolina. Though both series are dated 1845, the first was
issued around May 1, 1846 (see letters to Duyckinck of March 17 and May
15, 1846), the second in July, 1847 (see note 38, Feb. 2, 1847).

[285] *The Wigwam and the Cabin.*

[286] *Big Abel and the Little Manhattan.*

[287] I, 350. Later, on Aug. 30, the *Broadway Journal* states (II, 125): "Some
time ago we published, as the composition of William Gilmore Simms, a little
poem called 'The Whippoorwill.' It belongs to Dr. Bird, of 'Calavar' memory."

wrote it. Will you enquire how it came there? The B. J. (I suppose Mr. Briggs) asserts what is not true, when he says that I put the signature of Mathews to my article on the N. A. Review; and otherwise misrepresents greatly what I did say in a conversation held in his presence touching New England & Southern scholarship.[288] But of this anon. — The Whig Review has not yet reached us — not a number. Yet Mr. Colton must have continued to recieve my magazine. I sent you the S.Q.R. a week ago by ship.

Yrs again

W. G. S.

270: To EVERT AUGUSTUS DUYCKINCK

Charleston, Augt. 8. 1845

My dear Sir

It was only yesterday that I put into the P. O. a Letter making inquiries on the subject of the several MSS from yourself & Mr. Jones, and today they all came to hand in safety through the Post Office. A Letter of yours accompanies them, a portion of which only needs an answer at this moment. This portion relates to the price which W & P. pays for the Tales. Eight cents is small but I am willing to leave it to them and to yourself, satisfied that with your controlling suggestions they will be prepared if things turn out well to do better hereafter. It strikes me that the "Wigwam & the Cabin" will make *two* volumes of 220 pages each — though I am at a loss to know how my matter will run in the peculiar form which the Library adopts. I suppose that the page will not consume more than did that of the "Gift" and at that rate my stories might average 40 or 45 pages. Are you familiar with all of these Stories? Say with

---

On Sept. 27, however, the *Broadway Journal* announces (II, 184) that "Mr. Simms, the novelist, . . . will hereafter contribute." With the exception of the issue of Nov. 15, poems by Simms appear in each issue of the *Broadway Journal* from that of Oct. 4 through that of Dec. 13.

[288] The leading article in the *Broadway Journal* for May 31 is entitled "The North and the South" (I, 337-339), an attack on Simms' "A Passage with 'The Veteran Quarterly'" (see note 200, June 6, 1845). Briggs writes (p. 339): "We once heard a literary Carolinian say very seriously, in a company of learned men at the North, that there were no classical scholars in this country except at the South . . . that there was no such thing as humor at the North."

1. "Murder Will Out."
2. The Two Camps
3. The Gamester of the Mississippi.
4. The Lazy Crow.
5. The Giant's Coffin.
6. The Arm Chair of Tustenuggee.
7. The Edisto Raftsman.
8. Oakatibbee.—
9. The Snake of the Cabin.
10. Those Old Lunes.—

There may be others which will occur to me in looking over my papers.[289] In the collection of 'Carl Werner' there are two Indian Tales which I might employ in an emergency. That collection, I think I told you, failed of circulation from the simple fact that it was an expensive book after the old time prices — say $2.00 just at the moment when the great revolution in cheap literature had begun. I could wish that you would read these two volumes, which, it strikes me, contain as adequate proofs as I have ever shown, of the imaginative & inventive power. — I should like to get the two vols. through the press while in New York, — or even three, — leaving it to W & P. to publish at their leisure. Would they make any attempt to publish in London. I have read Jones's article, which *entre nous* is clumsily & carelessly written, & by no means profound. One passage touching the Methodists, I shall take leave to omit. It is employed only by way of analogy & its omission will not hurt the sense. If I have time & space, I may accompany the paper with some remarks of my own.[290] Your articles I have not read, — preferring as I have so little time just now to enjoy that pleasure when they are in print.[291] What you tell me of Poe distresses me. But, in his circumstances, & for such a man, it is difficult to devise anything,

---

[289] All ten stories listed (see note 169, April 10, 1845, and note 237, June 25, 1845) are included in *The Wigwam and the Cabin.* "The Gamester of the Mississippi" appears as "The Last Wager, or the Gamester of the Mississippi"; "The Edisto Raftsman" as "Sergeant Barnacle; or the Raftsman of the Edisto." In addition to these, *The Wigwam and the Cabin* includes "Jocassée, A Cherokee Legend" (previously published in *Carl Werner,* II, 133-173), "Caloya; or, the Loves of the Driver" (see note 61, Sept. 28, 1840), and "Lucas de Ayllon" (previously published in *Ladies' Companion,* XVII [May, July, and August, 1842], 36-40, 147-152, 184-190).

[290] Simms' remarks on Jones' "The Temperance Question" appear as the last paragraph of his "Editorial Bureau," *Southern and Western,* II (Nov., 1845), 360.

[291] See note 280, Aug. 7, 1845.

— unless it be to control his infirmities with a moral countenance which coerces while it soothes & seems to solicit. This should be the care of the circle in which he moves. — There is a great deal to be done in behalf of our literature. There are immense harvests to be reaped. After all, *mon ami* it is the laborers we want — and of that class who will be content to work *con amore*. Don't you see that such were the Gods of Shakspeare's Olympus. They lived like blackguards, but were not beggars. They triumphed starving, and consecrated rags & excesses and despair by song and story and glorious abstraction. To be great & successful, we must fling *convention* to the dogs, & how many Americans do you know prepared for this.

W. G. S.

A volume of Imaginative Stories — purely such, &, in my poor conceit, singularly original & successful as such, — such, indeed, as have no resemblance in American Literature, unless in the writings of Poe, and partially of Hawthorne — are to be collated out of my materials. I can give you some titles, the articles — some of which — are in your hands.

1 Carl Werner —
2 Conrade Weickhoff —
3 Logoochie —
4 The Star Bretheren —
5 Annihilation —
6 The Benefactress —

These are samples.[292] If you have them by you examine them with reference to my claims as above asserted. But a truce to egotism. At all events, it proves to you my faith in you.

Yours Ever &c

Simms

E. A. D.

---

[292] For these tales, with the exception of "Logoochie," see note 170, April 10, 1845, and note 238, June 25, 1845. "Logoochie" had originally appeared in *The Magnolia for 1836* (see note 2, May 28, 1835). It had been republished in *Carl Werner*, II, 83-129. The collection here proposed was never published.

271: To James Lawson

Charleston, Augt. 11. [1845][293]

My dear Lawson

The trying event is over and so far all promises well doing. My wife presented me last night (Sunday 10th.) with a very fine daughter, at about a quarter to 11. She is thought to be the largest child we have had at birth, is very fat, and they all affirm, more like me than all the preceding children. Of course, this being the case, *she is decidedly the best looking of all.* This last half sentence is written particularly for the benefit of your wife. Gilmore is in finer health and finer appearance now than I have ever seen him, and his mother is doing, in the ordinary phrase, quite as well as can be expected. If these prospects continue, I shall set out from home on or about the 18th. I propose to stop a day in Richmond, one in Washington & one in Philad. But, it is possible that I may only linger in the latter city for that length of time, and be in New York about the 22d. Much will depend upon the travelling weather, and my humours *en passant.* You may be sure I am particularly & most anxious for N. Y. which I have come to look upon as my own city. — I have written to Augusta to say that I hope to visit her in G. B.[294] about the 5th Sept. Then, if it so pleases you, you & Lady Lyde will take a trip up with me, for the first time, to look upon that beautiful region. Shall it not be so, old boy. Shan't we shake off the averages for a few days, and make our wife happy. Kiss the 'gude woman' on my account, and persuade her that she owes it to you, to me, to herself, & the country, to make the excursion. Augusta writes as if she absolutely looked for it. And now, God bless you all. You will understand that my hands & thoughts are full of newly born cares & anxieties to which I must give heed. A kiss all round to 'gude wife & bonny bairns.' There's a snatch of Scotch for you, which you may repeat to Thompson[295] to prove that I am not wholly forgetful of the Land of Bobby Burns &c. — 'Willie brew'd a peck of malt," should be "Jamie

---

[293] Dated by Simms' reference to the birth of Valeria.

[294] Simms describes his visit to Great Barrington, Mass., in one of his letters written as "correspondent" of the *Southern Patriot* (see note 304, Aug. 28, 1845). The issue containing it is that for Sept. 23, 1845.

[295] Alexander Thompson, cousin of James Lawson.

brew'd a peck of malt, — and Corn. (Cornelius, Vulg. Mathews)
& *Willie* cam' to see.' There's my hand on it

Servt &c

W. G. S.

272: To EDWIN DELEON

[August 15, 1845][296]

dear Sir.

I regretted very much not having seen you in Charleston. I
called twice at the pavilion, and once to my regret after your departure. I am on the wing myself, and shall leave for New York
in a very few days. May I hope that the Magazine will be honored
during my absence with your contributions.[297] They will be particularly agreeable to us during that period. —

Yours Very truly &c

W. Gilmore Simms

E. DeLeon, Esq.   Augt. 15
P. S. I congratulate you on the appointment of the Societies at
Columbia College.[298] You will do them justice. Give us something
honorably and fearlessly American.

273: To BRANTZ MAYER [299]

Barnum's Hotel

Hon. Brantz May'r   Augt. 20. [1845][300]
dear Sir.

Passing through your city, it would give me great pleasure to
make your acquaintance in proper person, but that I do not ex-

---

[296] Dated by Simms' reference to his forthcoming trip to New York. See
letter to Lawson of Aug. 11.

[297] No contributions which can be identified as DeLeon's appear in the
Southern and Western for the remainder of the year. For his previous contribution, see note 226, June 16, 1845.

[298] The address was published as *The Position and Duties of Young America.
An Address, Delivered before the Two Literary Societies of the South-
Carolina College, December 1845* (Columbia: A. S. Johnston, 1845). It is
noticed in *S. Q. R.,* IX (Jan., 1846), 283, and in the *Southern Patriot* of Jan.
31, 1846.

[299] Brantz Mayer (1809-1879), lawyer and author, was sent to Mexico in
1841 as secretary of the United States legation. He returned in 1844 and in
the same year published *Mexico as It Was and as It Is.* He was instrumental
in founding the Maryland Historical Society and subsequently became its president (1867-1871). He was the author of several other works on Mexico and
also of a number of books concerned with the history of Maryland.

[300] This letter is arbitrarily dated 1845, probably the only year in which
Simms could have been in Baltimore on Aug. 20.

actly know how to find my way to you. I shall remain here till
sometime tomorrow, and in the meantime should be glad to see
you.

Yours very truly

W. Gilmore Simms
of South Carolina

274: To ABRAHAM HART [301]

[August 28, 1845]

A. Hart Esq.
Dear Sir

Let me burden you on your return to Phila. with the enclosed
Letters, and remind you of the copies of Richard Hurdis and
Border Beagles, two of each if you have them, which I am anxious
to procure. There is also, among the Tales which I am desirous
to bring together into one volume,[302] one entitled "The Lazy
Crow" published in the Gift a few years ago, — perhaps *five*.[303]
Can this volume be spared me? I am now about to write a series
of Letters for the press in Charleston,[304] so that any additional
information of your doings & intentions will help me to a desirable
variety, and may promote the circulation of your books. These, —
such as you design for my notice, you will please send me here,
care of Wiley & Putnam, during my stay in New York.

Yours very truly &c

N. Y. Augt 28.   W Gilmore Simms

275: To HENRY ROWE SCHOOLCRAFT [305]

[*c*. September 26, 1845][306]

dear Sir

I am very anxious to procure the numbers of 'Oneota' after
the first. I have applied for them in vain to my booksellers. May

---

[301] Partner in the firm of Carey and Hart.
[302] *The Wigwam and the Cabin.*
[303] See note 54, June 12, 1843.
[304] This series of twenty-four unsigned letters "From Our Correspondent" was
published in the *Southern Patriot* during September and October. It is omitted
from this edition of Simms' letters because of lack of space.
[305] See introductory sketch.
[306] This letter bears no postmark. On the MS., however, is written "Sept
26, 1845," and the probability is that this date was taken from the postmark
or perhaps noted by Schoolcraft himself.

I beg that you will supply me if it be within your power. The first number I have, and have examined it with great pleasure. I have also, — and have read with exceeding interest your Algic Researches.[307] — Assist me, my dear Sir, to make my collection complete, and I shall be greatly pleased, hereafter, to requite you after the same fashion.

Very truly & respectfully &c.

W. Gilmore Simms
76 Eleventh Street. N. Y.

276: To James Lawson

Sunday Morning, Oct 12. [1845][308]

Instead of going to Church, my dear Lawson, as a good Christian I should, I go to the desk to let you and your dear wife know that we have reached our homes in safety, and under comparatively agreeable circumstances. Our journey was not a particularly fatiguing one, and we find every body well at home. My wife is quite thin and looking not so well as I expected or could wish, but free from suffering or complaint. The winter in the country will probably bring her up. Gilmore is the famousest fattest rogue in the country. Not as tall as Jemmy, he is yet probably twice as stout and has the shoulders of a ploughboy. The baby is remarkably fat and I think remarkably good looking. She will be called Valeria Govan, after an Aunt and friend of my wife. All the rest of our family are in good condition and good spirits. Our crop will be short, like every other in the country, but, much better I believe than most, and better than we were prepared to expect from the Season which has been dreadfully adverse. It was necessary for me at least, that the literary crop should be more encouraging. This I take for granted that you will look to. I would not insist upon the money in advance from Taylor, but only on the publication of each work, — unless he delays it unreasonably. But I would only let him have one

---

[307] *Algic Researches, Comprising Inquiries Respecting the Mental Characteristics of the North American Indians. First Series. Indian Tales and Legends,* 2 vols. (New York: Harper & Brothers, 1839).

[308] Dated by the reference to the naming of Valeria Govan Simms. The name Valeria was for Mrs. Simms' friend Valeria Gough (Mrs. Edward North). Govan was for her great aunt Rachel Govan Carroll, mother of Charles Carroll.

work at a time.[309] See to the Copyright of Julian & prevent its publication, until you get the sheets off by the Steamer. Let a dozen copies be sent me at the earliest; and tell Duyckinck to furnish Taylor with the names of persons to whom I could wish copies sent as I furnished them to W & P. Request him also to see that John Neal of Portland, & Peter Force of Washington [310] are provided with copies of my books as they appear. I will write him at first leisure. I find a mountain of work before me, and shall have to go to it with a rush. The Letters awaiting me here are a sight to see, & the business of the Magazine is greatly behind hand. My wife and Mr Roach are both quite disappointed that Lady Lyde should not be able to decide upon the visit; and we all earnestly hope that she may grow wiser & more amiable in sufficient season to give us the better part of winter and spring with as many children as she pleases. If she does so, I recommend that she come by sea, as quite as safe, much cheaper and far less fatiguing. — In my confusion looking after trunks & tickets, I entirely forgot to pay the coach, another item which you will place to my score. God bless you and your little flock. A kiss to Lyde and the children. Wife & daughter send love. You will soon hear from them directly

Yours faithfully as Ever

W. G. S.

J. L.

277 : To George Frederick Holmes

Charleston, Oct 18. [1845][311]

My dear Sir

Why do I not hear from you, and where do you keep yourself? I am glad to see that you have an offer from the Richmond College, though I know nothing of its claims to your attention.

---

[309] For this proposed republication of the "Border Romances," see note 14, Jan. 7, 1846.

[310] For Neal, see note 170, Dec. 13, 1843. Peter Force (1790-1868), apprenticed as a printer at the age of sixteen, became president of the New York Typographical Society when he was twenty-two years old. In 1815 he moved to Washington, where, in 1823, he established the *National Journal*, which he edited and published until 1830. Force collected a vast amount of material in regard to the history of the English colonies in America. His collection, consisting of 22,000 books and 40,000 pamphlets, was sold to the United States Government in 1867.

[311] Dated by the fact that Holmes became professor of belles lettres at Richmond College in 1845.

I should prefer that you should succeed in So. Ca. but shall rejoice to hear of your success anywhere. —

Yours very truly &c

Geo. Fred Holmes, Esq W. Gilmore Simms

278: To Evert Augustus Duyckinck

Charleston 19. Oct. [1845][312]

My dear Duyckinck

I have just got through reading the proof of your very favorable notice of Big Abel — a notice too favorable for the deserts of book and author. I do not deny their merits. On the contrary. My quarrel with the author is that he studies hard to wrong his talents & to forfeit his friends. A more qualified language in his behalf, would not only be more just, but much more kind. Believe me the almost unqualified and very high eulogy in which you deal in the present case will only provoke hostility, and force the critics into the other extreme. But I will not censure. I propose only a better policy, & this too in behalf of the author, whom (strange to say) both of us are accused of laboring to bolster up in spite of himself. Would we could do so, by setting him in the right track. Your article on 'Tyranny of Public Opinion' is our leader for Oct. and has one or two ugly typographical blunders, but otherwise reads very well.[313] — I am busy on the Nov. (issue) which, as well as the last contains very little of my own.[314] I am now working up my literary notices; shall pre-

---

[312] Dated by Simms' reference to the proof of Duyckinck's review of Mathews' *Big Abel and the Little Manhattan, Southern and Western,* II (Nov., 1845), 314-322.

[313] See note 280, Aug. 7, 1845.

[314] To the Sept. issue of the *Southern and Western* Simms contributed "The Epochs and Events of American History, as Suited to the Purposes of Art in Fiction" (pp. 145-154), "The Child Angel" (p. 165), "The Maiden's First Dream of Love" (pp. 165-166), "Elodie. — A Ballad" (pp. 179-180), "Stanzas" (pp. 191-193), "Bayard, the Chevalier" (pp. 193-200), and "Editorial Bureau" (pp. 205-216). In the Oct. issue only "Editorial Bureau" (pp. 277-288) can definitely be ascribed to Simms. To the Nov. issue he contributed "Kaatskill" (pp. 295-296), "The Huguenot Settlements in Florida" (pp. 324-332), "Come Out to Play" (pp. 341-342), "Hast Thou a Song for a Flower" (p. 342), and "Editorial Bureau" (pp. 343-360). His contributions to the Dec. issue include "Boat Horn on the Congaree by Moonlight" (pp. 376-377), "Wander, Oh! Wander. — A Serenade" (p. 391), "Thou Art Here" (p. 395), "Ask Me Not Whither" (pp. 408-409), "Fireside Aphorisms" (p. 420), and "Editorial Bureau" (pp. 421-432). "The Child Angel" and "Thou Art Here" are signed "Adrian Beaufain," "Kaatskill" is signed "Claude," and "Stanzas" is signed "Il Penseroso." The others are unsigned. Other unsigned poems and articles in these issues are also probably by Simms.

pare the material for Decr. and leave town for the plantation by the 3d. Nov. — remain at the plantation some two weeks in the clear, and then proceed to the Legislature — get home by Christmas, — and with the beginning of the New Year put myself fairly in the harness for 'My Wiley' & others. It is barely possible that I may send you the 'Life of Bayard' by the first of Jany. — to be published, mark me, under a *nom de plume*.[315] This I will follow up by "The Huguenots in Florida," [316] getting ready *ad interim* the material for the 2d. vol. of 'Views & Reviews.' I see that the dirty fellows of the Mirror have been carping at my books & sneering at Poe for affecting them.[317] It is sufficient

---

[315] *The Life of the Chevalier Bayard; "The Good Knight"* (New York: Harper & Brothers, 1847), dedicated to John Izard Middleton, was not published under a *nom de plume*. Two articles by Simms entitled "Bayard, the Chevalier" appeared earlier in *Southern and Western,* II (Aug. and Sept., 1845), 73-85, 193-200.

[316] Published as *The Lily and the Totem; or, the Huguenots in Florida* (see note 171, April 10, 1845). Chapter xiv of this history appeared earlier in *Southern and Western,* II (Nov., 1845), 324-332.

[317] In the *Broadway Journal,* II (Oct. 4, 1845), 190-191, Poe published a review of *The Wigwam and the Cabin,* in which he says: "This is one of the most interesting numbers of the Library yet published — and decidedly the most American of the American books. . . . In a recent number of our Journal [I (Sept. 20, 1845), 168] we spoke of Mr. Simms as 'the best novelist which this country has, upon the whole, produced;' and this is our deliberate opinion. We take into consideration, of course, as well the amount of what he has written, as the talent he has displayed; — he is the Lopez de Vega of American writers of fiction. His merits lie among the major and his defects among the minor morals of literature. His earlier works of length, such as 'The Partisan,' were disfigured by many inaccuracies of style, and especially by the prevalence of the merely repulsive, where the horrible was the object — but in invention, in vigor, in movement, in the power of exciting interest, and in the artistical management of his themes, he has surpassed, we think, any of his countrymen: — that is to say, he has surpassed any of them in the aggregate of these high qualities. His best fictions . . . are 'Martin Faber' . . . 'Beauchampe'; 'Richard Hurdis'; 'Castle Dismal'; 'Helen Halsey'; and 'Murder will Out.' . . . 'Murder Will Out' is the first and the most meritorious of the series now lying before us. We have no hesitation in calling it the best ghost-story we have ever read. It is full of the richest and most vigorous imagination — is forcibly conceived — and detailed throughout with a degree of artistic skill which has had no parallel among American story-tellers since the epoch of Brockden Brown." The New York *Evening Mirror* of Oct. 6 contains an article entitled "Poe-lemical" and signed "*", which takes Poe to task for his assertions: " . . . it is above the power of any single critic — or of all the critics in the country combined, to convince the world that William Gilmore Simms is a better novelist than Cooper, or Brockden Brown. He is certainly less known and read at home and abroad. We doubt if the copy-right of all Mr. Simms's collected works would bring as good a price in America or England, as the 'Norman Leslie' of Fay, or the 'Sketch Book' of Irving." In the *Broadway Journal,* II (Oct. 11, 1845), 216-217, Poe republished the *Evening Mirror's* article with his own characteristic comments. In spite of its attack on Poe's criticism the *Evening Mirror* of Sept. 29 contains a flattering review of *The Wigwam and the Cabin:* "After Mr. Simms' Tales of the wild West, stories of daring adventure, stormy passions, dark deeds, and

to denote the sort of critic with which one has to deal, when we find him not canvassing the merits of an author, but insinuating his want of popularity — his inferior sales &c. As for Fay, — let these people go to H & B. and ascertain how many copies of the Yemassee & Norman Leslie have respectively been sold,[318] including all the editions — ask — but the thing is of a piece with the wretched & base creatures who conduct that print, — which, I suspect seizes upon the suggestion of that other dirty crawling creeping creature, Clarke, in the Knickerbocker to insinuate deficient popularity, when I know, and all the publishers know, and the public — South of the Potomac at least know — that my popularity was perhaps never greater than at this very moment.[319]

startling fortunes, have been eagerly perused by his countrymen, and highly praised in Europe, there seems little left to say on this, their appearance in a new and very attractive dress. The opening novelette, 'Murder will out,' was pronounced by the London critics, the best ghost-story of modern times, so thrilling is its interest, and so natural and striking its development. Others of the stories are perhaps not inferior to this in merit of various kinds. An air of reality pervades them all; and though we may wish that this had permitted the exclusion of certain touches of coarseness, we must allow it to be a great merit, and one which would plead for greater blemishes." Poe revised his review of *The Wigwam and the Cabin* and republished it in *Godey's*, XXXII (Jan., 1846), 41-42. *Godey's* had already published a notice of the volume in XXXI (Dec., 1845), 271: "'*The Wigwam and the Cabin*,' by W. Gilmore Simms, is a collection of stories by the great novelist of the South. These short pieces are among the best of Simms' productions. The necessity for bringing his work within a certain compass appears to prevent the diffuseness in which he is apt to indulge in his novels. They have more nerve and not less beauty and grace than his larger works."

[318] Harper and Brothers, New York, were publishers of *The Yemassee*, 2 vols. (1835) and of *Norman Leslie*, 2 vols. (1835). Theodore S. Fay (1807-1898), author of the latter, was, in 1845, one of the editors of the *Mirror*.

[319] In an unsigned article entitled "American Humor," published in the *Dem. Rev.*, XVII (Sept., 1845), 212-219, William Alfred Jones writes (p. 212): "In a late number of the 'Southern Quarterly Review' . . . in an article on the prose works of Cornelius Mathews, appeared some strictures of a kind so singular and mistaken, as to deserve, as it appears to us, some special notice. The writer of the article, himself at the head of the Southern scribes, a gentleman who, however slightingly we may regard the mass of his romantic and poetical efforts, has still, in several instances, proved himself a sensible critic, both of men and books, though rather a comprehensive and hearty, than a very fine or delicate judge of either; a master of an animated vein of description; as a local and personal historian excellent (in his magazine papers) ; and, altogether, a manly, intelligent, liberal, miscellaneous writer in the departments we have mentioned, and a good specimen of the Southron, to boot, personally and intellectually, has still failed in his discussion of the subject of humor generally, and particularly in the case of American Humor." In a review of this article, which continues with an attempted refutation of Simms' charges of the lack of humor in American literature, the *Knick.*, XXVI (Oct., 1845), 378, comments: "'Mr. Jones' . . . has an article in the last number of our '*Democratic*' . . . which we quite concur with the 'Broadway Journal' [II (Sept. 20, 1845), 169] in characterizing as 'contemptible, both in a moral and literary sense;' and as 'the production of an imitator and a

— I am fortunately prepared to wait my time, and do not suffer my sleep to be disturbed by vexation at the delay in time's revenges. A truce to this. They tell me that the Wigwam is selling here. But, to this hour, though the booksellers have had the books for ten days, no copies for the Editors have been received. Yeadon, whose name was given on my list, had got none up to last night. — I find all thriving at home, — but really miss you all, — Lawson & family, and our old ranges. I suppose I must only console & reassure myself by thinking of you the more. — I have been giving a few words to the series & to yourself today, for my next bureau. Poe also, comes in for a paragraph, (fanciful as he merits) and C. M. for another, referring to your review, but of more guarded commendation, such as he merits also.[320] — Let me hear from you soon, & tell me what progress. In particular, advise me of any splenetics. Shall I remind you that after all the 2 Nos. of Arcturus were forgotten — 16 & 18. — And if you conveniently can, get me 19 of the N. Y. Review. Will you see B & W.[321] and ascertain whether they have yet laid hands on the copy of his Ph. Henslowe, and any other Nos. due me of the Shakspeare & Percy publications. As they seem to be rather careless or indifferent anent this matter, suppose you arrange it so that I shall get them regularly through W & P. & get them to pay my subscription up regularly, so that I may not forfeit. — I have just written to Saunders — will you contrive and see him. I would that you & Lawson could visit me this winter or in the spring, — see how we do things in Carolina. Come, — and you shall help to set the Yule log, and there shall be cakes & ale, and ginger shall be hot in the mouth in spite of your virtue.

God bless you.

W. G. Simms

E. A. Duyckinck Esq

---

quack.' It is quite baseless, moreover; being suggested by an article in a Southern magazine, of small circulation and smaller influence, written by a very voluminous author, now in the decadence of a limited sectional reputation; a writer who, having no shadow of humor of his own, is poorly qualified to judge of the humor, or lack of humor, of any body else. He might with equal fitness and propriety have indited a didactic paper upon the scholarship of the country."

[320] "Editorial Bureau," *Southern and Western,* II (Dec., 1845), 424-428.

[321] Bartlett and Welford.

279: To James Lawson

Charleston 27. Oct. [1845][322]

My dear Lawson.

Will you see Stringer & say to him that I have a collection of Tales of a highly imaginative character, which I propose to make into a volume.[323] He shall have it on the same terms with that of Castle Dismal and Helen Halsey. — Will you also get from him, if you have not already obtained them the certificates of Copyright of the same works. I percieve that a Georgia Editor has been pirating 'Castle Dismal!' [324] Did you see about the Copyright of Count Julian, and about the transmission of the sheets? And what of the other novels? — I withdraw from the Magazine at the close of the present volume, and the work will then be united with the Messenger. Minor has bought out our publishers. I have agreed to do his critical department. — On Saturday next, the first, we set off for the plantation. Present me affectionately to Lady Lyde, and say that we shall look for her this winter. We are all anxious to hear about Christina. Let us hear from you soon. Address me at Woodlands. A kiss all round. In haste & very sleepy.

Yours &c

W. G. Simms

J. L.

280: To Evert Augustus Duyckinck

Charleston, Oct 28. [1845][325]

My dear Duyckinck

I have written you once already since my return home, and may have already expressed to you some of the contents of the

---

[322] Dated by Simms' withdrawal from the editorship of the *Southern and Western*. In his "Editorial Bureau," II (Dec., 1845), 421, he says: "We trust that our friends will continue their contributions to our Magazine hereafter, when it becomes united with the 'Southern Literary Messenger.' Since our last sitting, arrangements have been made between the proprietors of the two Works, by which their mutual fortunes will be shipped in the same argosy. May they float long, with prosperous breezes, the honor and attraction of the South."

[323] This collection of tales was not published. See letter to Duyckinck of Aug. 8, 1845.

[324] We have been unable to locate this pirated edition of *Castle Dismal,* published in a newspaper (see letter to Lawson of Nov. 13).

[325] Dated by Simms' withdrawal from the editorship of the *Southern and Western*. In a letter addressed "To the Patrons of the 'Southern and Western

present, but as I still have something to say which that did not certainly contain, I see no reason to apprehend the risk. In our forthcoming number, I deliberately announced my determination to withdraw from the Editorial Chair, and at the same time, I wrote to Minor, informing him of the fact. He at once came on to negotiate for the work, is now here, and has succeeded in buying it from the publishers, and will publish hereafter simultaneously in Richmond & Charleston. He has engaged me to conduct the critical department. I edit the work here till the close of the year, and will continue to review all the new publications as they come to my address. I have consented to the proposed arrangement as it will still enable me to give to Southern opinion that tone & character which it is so desirable for the independence of the intellectual character of the country that it should possess. — On Saturday the 1st. Nov. I leave town for the plantation. Your letters therefore, from this date, you will please address me at that place (Midway)[.] I have just put up and sent to Hart's Bookstore, to be forwarded to W. & P. a portion of vol 2 of Views & Reviews. It is the complete series on American Literature, copyright, & Lit. property. I have revised it with considerable care. I am now on the 2d. article, being the review of Mrs. Trollope's Manners of the Americans which I am rewriting entirely. This I shall follow up with the paper on Mathews : — which I shall also revise. The next will, I think, be something on the Northmen in America — a subject which I have treated in several articles. These I shall amalgamate. I shall sift for the rest among numerous papers.[326] — I send you by mail a copy in loose sheets

---

Messenger and Review,'" dated Oct. 30, 1845, and published in *S. L. M.,* XI (Dec., 1845), 761-762, Simms writes: "The subscriber, having concluded to withdraw, at the close of the present volume, from the conduct of the above journal, takes pleasure in commending to its patrons that which, in connection with the 'Southern Literary Messenger,' has been based upon it. The works thus blended, and specially addressed to the people of the South and West, will be eminently useful in concentrating and forming public opinion among us, in all those things, particularly, which belong to *Belles Lettres* and the Arts. The increase of strength, in talent and money, which must necessarily result from this union, will secure to us a highly valuable periodical, which, if regarded with proper favor, need be second to none in the country; and I trust, sincerely, that my friends and those of Southern literature, the subscribers and the contributors to the Magazine from which I withdraw, will yield a hearty support to that which will succeed it, and which, I feel very sure, will faithfully and honorably represent their interests."

[326] The articles on American literature, copyright, and literary property were not republished in *Views and Reviews,* Second Series. The volume contains "Domestic Manners of the Americans by Mrs. Trollope," pp. 1-56; "The American Sagas of the Northmen," pp. 57-100; "The Case of Major Andre,"

of my "Sonnets," as pub. in the Messr. comprising some 60 pages
or more.[327] They will not be published, but merely circulated
among the select, the sacred few. I beg that you will read *all*
of these little poems *carefully, to yourself.* They contain, I fancy,
some of my best things, and I am vain to think are the best collection of sonnets ever printed in America. This, *inter nos.* There
are some errors in them which I pencil. Others may escape me. —
I shall send a copy to Mathews, though I fancy, he will scarcely
thank me for it. — And how do the books sell? They tell me
here that mine is doing pretty well. — Have you & Lawson seen
about 'Count Julian.' Pray, if it be ready, get Taylor to send
me a copy per mail, — and some dozen copies, through the publishers in Charleston. I shall be able to send you all the matter
for the Views & Reviews before I go to Columbia, and hope to
begin the Huguenots as soon as I return — say about Christmas.
Do not couple me with any talk about Bayard, as I propose that
we shall put forth that anonymously. What think you. I recommend that W & P. send no more of their publications to the
Savannah Republican. The Editor of that work is a Yankee named
Chapman, who in a late notice speaks contemptuously of & dis-
misses in a single sentence the whole of the American Series.[328]
There is no use in troubling a person with a commodity which he
scorns. Let W & P. address their publications specially to the
"Georgian" of the same city. This advice is to *you.* Make use of
it if you please. Let me hear from you soon, and advise me of
what is going on. Best respects to Mrs D and your brother.

Yours truly &c

W. G. S.

E. A. D.

---

pp. 101-122; "Weems, the Biographer and Historian," pp. 123-141; and "The
Humourous in American and British Literature," pp. 142-184. This last is
concerned with the various writings of Cornelius Mathews.

[327] *Grouped Thoughts and Scattered Fancies* (Richmond, Va.: Printed by
Wm. Macfarlane, Messenger Office, 1845). Under the same title these sonnets
were published as "by a Southron" in *S. L. M.,* X (July, Aug., and Sept.,
1844), 422-424, 483-484, 520-521; XI (Feb., March, July, Aug., and Sept.,
1845), 102-103, 177-178, 441-442, 485-486, 555-557.

[328] Copies of the Savannah *Republican* for this period have been inaccessible
to us. Samuel T. Chapman (1809-1854) was associate editor of the newspaper at
this time. He was succeeded by Edwin DeLeon in April, 1847 (see the *South
Carolinian,* April 21, 1847).

281 : To James Lawson

Woodland[s], Nov. 3. [1845][329]

My dear Lawson

We were just on the eve of quitting the city for the plantation when your welcome letter assuring me of the improvement of all among you came to hand. It gave us great pleasure, I need scarce assure you, to hear of Christina's[330] health, and excited quite a lively sensation, on all hands, to learn that there existed some probability of seeing our Lady Lyde at Woodland[s] this winter. I trust that she will not be able to resist the force of public opinion. We will try to make her happy, and all the little flock that she may bring with her; nor will it lessen our satisfaction a whit to see both of the Jemmies, Jemmy Senr. & Jemmy, Jr., of the party. We have just come in from a long ramble over the fields, Mr. R. my wife, Auga., and myself. We picked up a couple of doves for our wife's breakfast, without hunting them. The day we arrived, a wild cat of decent dimensions, was shot on the place which, you may say to young Jemmy, will be sent him by young Gilmore, that he may see what sport may be had when he gets able to shoulder his gun. The weather is very fine & pleasant, though it begins to cloud as I write, and a smart rain will bring us a heavy frost which as yet we have not had. Our carriage has just arrived from the city bringing us a dozen of sweet oranges, the first we have had from some young trees grown in our garden in town. They are very fine. Once more let me say that we will try to make Lyde & yourself as happy as possible whenever you may think fit to honor us with your presence. My wife has been making sweetmeats & pickles in sufficient quantity, I fancy, and has contrived out of her store to put up a couple of jars of each, which we packed before leaving town and sent to our grocer with instructions to forward you by first vessel. He will probably send you Bill Lading. — Mathews is a mere child & a very simple one. I never neglected him, and was in his office almost daily until his folly drove me away. What other attention did he seek? At your house, having business with Duyckinck, he representing Wiley & Putnam, I drew him aside for the discussion of that business. I had no

---

[329] Dated by Simms' reference to the unbound sheets of *Grouped Thoughts and Scattered Fancies,* printed for private distribution in 1845.

[330] Lawson's eldest daughter, born in 1836.

right, even were I willing, to make it public. You or your wife
might just as well have complained. The thing's ridiculous. He
might as well complain that I went aside to make my toilet, to
change my breeches, or kiss a sweetheart in a corner. — I do
not know that I owe him any thing for my popularity. Was
Marion reviewed by him or any of my friends in the Dem. Rev.
or elswhere?[331] Were Castle Dismal or Helen Halsey? No! Not
even noticed. And Willis and Clarke blackguarding me all the
time! I may claim to have done something toward making him,
since I find my favorable opinions in the Review & elswhere undergoing repetition; and have been censured for them by friends.
Mr. M. forgets himself when he talks this language. He has
behaved, as you say, very like a spoiled child, & must be left
to come to his senses. The regrets I expressed on leaving his
office were not in the nature of an apology, but simply because I
should have played with one so little capable of appreciating my
goodhumored familiarity. His caprice & exacting nature will lose
him his best friends. — Of course, you will apply the funds to
the Portrait & Bockee's,[332] and of what remains send me a keg
of cranberries, and a half barrel of hickory nuts. They will help
to spice our creature comforts when Lady Lyde comes. Let me
know what she likes best, &c. — I sent you by mail, in sheets,
a copy of the 'Sonnets.'[333] — There were none bound or covered,
and I was ready to start when they came. Read them through
carefully. I contend that they are far the best collection of Sonnets and small pieces ever published here. I have a hundred copies
of "Donna Florida."[334] Can Stringer sell them at 12/100 apiece?
He might, giving you 10/100 for the lot. Ask him. Touching
Castle D. & H. H! — Say to him that if he is disposed to issue
a second edition 3000 each, he may do so at 4/100 each. I have
an introduction to C. D. which will improve it I fancy. It is humourous!![335] *Credat judaeus!* Ask Langley if he wants D of D —
frankly. If not, you can negotiate with Taylor making it one of

---

[331] *The Life of Francis Marion* is reviewed in the *Dem. Rev.*, XVI (Jan.,
1845), 103-104.

[332] For William West's portrait of Simms and John Jacob Bockee's bill,
see letters to Lawson of Jan. 15 and April 7, 1845.

[333] *Grouped Thoughts and Scattered Fancies.*

[334] *Donna Florida. A Tale* (Charleston: Burges and James, 1843), dedicated
to James Lawson.

[335] *Castle Dismal and Helen Halsey.* The text of the second edition of *Castle
Dismal* (New-York: Burgess, Stringer & Co., 1845) is identical with that of
the first.

his series.[336] Don't forget the Copyright & get those of C. D. &
H. H. from B & S.[337] — Write me about the Wigwam. I hear
nothing from Duyckinck. How does it get on, and when does
Views & Reviews appear. Don't wait upon any event to write.
That is all pretext. Ten cents postage on a letter from you, *or your*
wife, I will cheerfully accord twice a week, if it pleases you
to write them. A kiss and love to all from all.

Yours &c

W. G. S.

282: TO JAMES LAWSON

Woodlands, Nov. 13. [1845][338]

My dear Lawson.

Your Letter of the 8th came to hand yesterday. The two notices were recieved the day before. The assaults upon Clarke are
not as strong as they should have been. Indignation expresses
itself in more emphatic language. Duyckinck is only too gentle

---

[336] Neither Langley nor Taylor republished *The Damsel of Darien,* 2 vols.
(Philadelphia: Lea and Blanchard, 1839). For Taylor's proposed republication
of the "Border Romances," see note 14, Jan. 7, 1846.

[337] Burgess, Stringer and Co.

[338] Dated by Simms' reference to Duyckinck's attacks on the *Knickerbocker*
in the New York *Evening Mirror* and the New York *Morning News.* In the
Mirror (Nov. 7) he writes: "We regret to see Mr. Clark's frequent attacks
upon some of the best writers of the country in the Knickerbocker. . . . During eight years the Knickerbocker Magazine has published various attacks upon
Mr. Mathews and his writings, with a malignity and pertinacity which once
induced the *Tribune* to call loudly for private reasons which instigated such a
course. It has misrepresented and traduced him in many ways by mistatements
[*sic*], by partial quotations, by hints and inuendoes and all the machinery which
a little mind knows so well to employ for its ends. . . . In the same spirit
were some remarks in the last number on Mr. Simms, one of the most respected
of American authors, the leading author of a large portion of the country, and
deservedly so by the genius and industry of many years spent upon almost
every department of literature, including poetry, the novel, history, criticism,
the quarterly, monthly and daily press; at present, too, sitting in the legislature
of his native state; with, every day some addition to the esteem in which he
is held, as his mind ripens under the discipline of various studies, and his noble,
manly course claims the admiration of the fearless and the good. Mr. Simms
is a man who may stand as a representative of the true American character.
. . . Mr. William A. Jones . . . is also attacked." This article, signed "S. T.,"
is reprinted in the *New York Weekly Mirror,* III (Nov. 15), 96, and in *Godey's,*
XXXII (May, 1846), 240. In the *News* (Nov. 8) Duyckinck also attacks the
Knickerbocker for its treatment of Mathews, adding: "We should not object
to the Knickerbocker's criticism, if it had any to offer, but we do enter our
protest against the tone of depreciation which the magazine has assumed in
repeated instances towards such men as John Neal, Mr. Simms, . . . A. Jones
. . . Mr. Poe, . . . and others."

an enemy. But Clarke is a creature to be kicked or spit upon not argued with or spoken to. Having given him the lie in print, and refused to know or notice him in society, it is scarcely con- sistent with selfesteem that I should make him a subject for remark. D. begs me to do it, and I must try how to express my disgust passingly, as one turns up his nose and makes a wry- face, at something unsavoury by the wayside. Strange that just when I was recieving your Letter telling me that Langleys did not want the Damsel yet, I got their letter asking what had be- come of her. I wrote to them to see you, stating what you had said. Why has Taylor delayed the Count?[339] I see Benjamin has arrived in Baltimore! [340] The Bells were rung—i. e.—the news- papers resounded — on the occasion. If you can by any possibility procure me a copy of that "Nat. Hist." you brag of,[341] do not let it pass. Those Sonnets[342] are some of them [the] most famousest things that I have yet done in verse, & the world will one day say as much. — Say to Langley that I am now busy on the Life of Smith — Captain John — and will be able to send him half a dozen chapters next week. I may get 8 or 10 ready for him before going to the Legislature, which I shall do in ten days more. I take my seat on the 4th. Monday in Nov. If you write me promptly on the receipt of this, I shall recieve it here. Do so! I wish you to urge upon Burgess & Stringer that volume if you can.[343] I have three tales never yet included in any compila- tion, which I propose to put with Conrade Weickhoff & Carl Werner. The whole making a snug volume of 250 pages like Castle Dismal. By putting forth such a vol. they can draw at- tention to new editions of Helen Halsey & C. Dismal, which have not been half distributed. See a Letter & newspapers which I sent them, showing them a Georgia Editor reprinting Castle Dismal, from the original nos. in the Magnolia, not knowing of the vol. or that he was violating Copyright. If B. & S. are will-

---

[339] *Count Julian,* published by William Taylor.

[340] In the fall of 1845, through the influence of Brantz Mayer, Park Ben- jamin moved to Baltimore, where he became an editor for the firm of Taylor, Wilde and Company. On January 3, 1846, he established the *Western Con- tinent,* a weekly modeled on the *New World.* On July 11, 1846, the paper was turned over to other editorial control and Benjamin, who had purchased the interest of Wilde, sold his interest in the firm and returned to New York. See Merle M. Hoover, *Park Benjamin* (New York: Columbia University Press, 1948), pp. 156-157.

[341] Unidentified.

[342] *Grouped Thoughts and Scattered Fancies.*

[343] The never published volume of tales of the imagination.

ing, they can have the work out by Christmas & you can see to the proofs. Let me know before I go to Columbia that I may send you the matter. It is probable that I may take it down with me to the city next week. I shall run there for a day or two. — I rejoice to hear of Christina's improvement. To make it certain you have only to pack off that woman of yours to Woodlands. I have bought a season ticket on the Rail Road, simply on her account, that I may be able to run down at any moment to bring her up. I go to Columbia on the 4th. Monday in Nov. & leave it about the 20th Decr. In that time, I may see Woodlands once, for we cannot leave during the Session. Augusta has just got an invitation to the Commencement Ball, & is all agog to go but whether I shall carry her or not is a question. It comes awkwardly as her mother cannot leave home, and the want of a maternal woman like Lady Lyde to be her chaperon is severely felt. Tell Lady Lyde, she sees at what time I shall be absent from home, but should it suit her to come on during this period, I will start off to the city for a day to bring her up, even though the Black Rod is sent after me. Present me to her respectfully & affectionately with a kiss for her and the children. My wife & Augusta join with me in all the friendly & affectionate parts of this Epistle.

Yours &c

W G Simms

J. L.

283 : To EVERT AUGUSTUS DUYCKINCK

Woodlands Nov. 13. [1845][344]

dear Sir

I have yours of the 6th. now before me & have read your two notices of the Knickerbocker contained in the "Mirror" and the "News." The Knickerbocker for Nov. containing the notice of Mathews is also before me.[345] No doubt you should long ago

---

[344] Dated by Simms' reference to Duyckinck's attacks on the *Knickerbocker*. See note 338, Nov. 13, 1845.

[345] In commenting upon Mathews' *Big Abel and the Little Manhattan* Clark says in *Knick.*, XXVI (Nov., 1845), 451-452: "Mr. Cornelius Mathews . . . sustains . . . the character of an amiable (and harmlessly-egotistical) person in private life. . . . There is no 'plot' to the story. 'Story! God bless you! he has none to tell, Sir.' . . . But such straining after *bizarreries* of expression; such struggles to avoid saying plain things in a plain way; such kaleidoscopic views of nature and artificial objects; such far-fetched and dissimilar similes, the very perfection of catachresis; we 'rather suspect' our readers have seldom encountered."

have silenced or crushed the miserable reptile in question. Had I been living in N. Y. I could not have refrained, long ago, to have scourged him hip & thigh for the scoundrel & puppy that he is. He is of your parish not of mine, and he deserves that you should use the flail without mercy. But you have erred in making his assault upon Mathews the particular text. You should have anticipated that assault, and had you all turned in & hammered him when Poe began the game, you would have timed it rightly. In taking up the cudgels for Mathews, after letting so many equally important occasions, equally full of provocation pass by, you lay yourself open to a charge, which, in your case, & in regard to M. will always lessen the force of what *you* say in N. Y. There you are looked upon, to use your own expressive language in regard to this very subject as "Swallowing him 'whole,[']" and it is only necessary for your antagonist in this issue to dwell quizzically upon the fact or opinion to increase your annoyance, and to lessen the chances of success against him. Mathews should not have been your text for another reason. He is confessedly your *questio vexata* in New York. Wilful in the employment of his talents, rejecting wholesome counsel and quarrelling with those who bestow it, he perversely wars not less upon his own genius than upon public opinion. This, I hold to be unquestionable. I give him credit for large resources, but feel sure that he not only knows not at present how to use them, but is really ignorant in what they consist. At present he fights against himself. This you will say is my *ipse dixit*. But it is not mine alone, and there are numbers, who looking only at the *surface* in his performances, deny him the possession of any thing in reserve. In brief, you will find it less easy to get up the proper sympathy for & with him, in the present instance, than if you had taken up the cudgels with John Neal (another impracticable by the way) or almost anybody else. Now that you are in for it, however, you must not mince the matter. Recollect Polonius's counsel to his son how to bear himself in the fight.[346] You must make all the allies you can, and identify as many cases with that of M. as possible, and speak of Clarke all the truth that you can. It is the truth that will crush and kill him. I shall do a trifle in the Patriot & Mag. but really having given him the lie in print and cut him in society, I feel loth to

---

[346] *Hamlet,* I, iii, 65ff.

soil my fingers with the skunk.[347] — The Mirror was falsely advised in several respects in regard to me & my writings but let it pass.[348] — I sent you by this day's Mail a se[cond] Copy, in sheets, of the Sonnets.[349] Say to Poe that I wanted, before sending him one, to get them covered, which the binder has not done yet. At present I am busy on my Life of Smith for Langleys. — I have sent on two articles for the Second Series of 'Views & Reviews' — (on American Literature, Copyright &c. & another reviewing Mrs. Trollope on the Manners of the Americans[)]. I propose that Mathews shall be third, and I will modify the Review on several points, or rather elaborate more clearly so as to show to some of my readers, what they did not clearly comprehend. Clarke never saw that review at all, but quoted at second hand from Jones.[350] Tell Wiley I have not recieved a copy of the Wigwam, except some four or five which I got while in New York. Let him send me ten or a dozen with his next bundle. Send me a copy of Views & Reviews through mail, if ready, at once — or if ready in the next two weeks, to me in Columbia. I go to the Legislature on the 4th Monday in the month. Time your letter to reach me on the Friday previous, and I will get it here. Let W & P. address to me, personally, all copies of their books sent to the Patriot, as when I do not prepare the notice myself I get it done, & in my absence from the city the printers appropriate the copies which go to the office. In other words, let him send me two copies of all his books & *none* to the paper. Do you get any advices from London that you count upon selling 500 there? I propose, as soon as I return from the Legislature to prepare for you the Huguenots in Florida, and (*anonymously*) the 'Life of Bayard.' These anonymous works will give variety to your Library. But you must keep the secret to yourself — sacredly. This must be wholly *entre nous*. We shall have *sport &*

---

[347] The *Southern Patriot* of Nov. 19 contains the following comment: *"The Knickerbocker Magazine.* — We perceive that some of our Northern contemporaries are beginning to speak of this dishonest and trashy periodical, in the terms which it deserves. But they are slow in waking up. The editor of the 'Knickerbocker' has himself saved them the necessity of a labor which is now almost gratuitous. The total want of character which its matter exhibits, has sufficiently done the work of criticism upon it; and it is only in the contempt and indifference of the public, that the critics begin to see the demerits which, had they done their duty, they should have been the very first to insist upon." Simms failed to publish his "trifle" in the *Southern and Western.*

[348] See note 317, Oct. 19, 1845.

[349] *Grouped Thoughts and Scattered Fancies.*

[350] See note 319, Oct. 19, 1845.

capital out of it. Send me a copy of Poe by mail.[351] By the way get from Noah a copy of his essays.[352] I put up for you before leaving town a bundle of Magnolias — all that I could lay hands on. If I can get others hereafter to complete the set, I shall do so. As for the Southern Quarterly, I am thinking to curse & quit.[353] The Editor is disposed to cheat me out of my wage. Let me hear from you soon & believe me very truly

&c your friend

W. G. Simms

E. A. Duyckinck Esq

284: To James Lawson

Woodlands, Nov. 21. [1845][354]

My dear Lawson.

I am just on the wing for Columbia—Shall set off tomorrow bright and early taking Augusta with me. She *would* go. I wish Lyde were here to go with her, and see something of our fashionable world, displaying her graces in the waltz, which she so much loves, along with some of our Carolina Cavaliers,—whom she ought to love better than she does. I ran down to town a few days ago, and left there to be sent by first vessel, a packet addressed to you containing seven tales, and by yesterdays mail, I sent you the eighth which I had accidentally omitted in the package. These will make two volumes in the style of Castle Dismal, and will readily bring 25 cents each, and will sell promptly at that. If B & S. will do them up handsomely, & put forth a new edition of the others, in uniform style, something may be made

---

[351] *The Raven and Other Poems* (New York: Wiley and Putnam, 1845) is favorably reviewed by Simms in the *Southern Patriot* of March 2, 1846. Earlier, in the *Southern Patriot* of Nov. 10, 1845, Simms published a lengthy and very favorable critique of Poe's work.

[352] Mordecai Manuel Noah, *Gleanings from a Gathered Harvest* (New York: C. Wells, 1845).

[353] Apparently he did. The review of *A New Spirit of the Age* (see note 97, Feb. 11, 1845) is the only article that can be identified as Simms' published during the remainder of Whitaker's editorship. When J. Milton Clapp became editor with the issue of April, 1847, Simms again contributed to the *Southern Quarterly Review*. See note 22, Feb. 19, 1849.

[354] Dated by Simms' reference to the tales of the imagination which he had previously offered to Duyckinck for publication by Wiley and Putnam and which for the past month he has been offering to Burgess, Stringer and Co. through the medium of Lawson. See letter to Duyckinck of Aug. 8 and letters to Lawson of Oct. 27 and Nov. 13.

by both of us. Of course, make the same terms for these, that
you did for the others.[355] — Gilmore is putting up for Jimmy a
number of Woodland productions, upon which the latter may
establish a new menagerie, or museum at least. He has a couple
of wild cats, a raccoon, a possum and a rattlesnake already, all
stuffed & large as life, which will delight the little fellow's eyes.
Tell Jimmy that Gilmore was working all day in the garden like
a horse. He takes to work like his father, with a hearty courage,
as if he loved it. — Tell that lazy woman your wife, that she
does not know how much she cuts from the years of her life in
not going abroad whenever she can. If she can only persuade
herself to give up Broadway for a season it will give her twenty
pounds more of good solid English (or Carolina) rotundity. —
My wife rejoices in the hope which your last letter holds out.
We all hope that she will find the will, knowing very well that
you can find the way. I repeat my readiness to run for her to
Charleston when ever she arrives. *Madame* S. and *M'amselle* S.
send their love with mine, which please present with as many
kisses as you are willing that I should bestow by proxy.

God bless you all.

Yours Ever

W. G. S.

Send me a couple of barrels pippins.

285: To Evert Augustus Duyckinck

Columbia, Nov. 24. [1845][356]

My dear Duyckinck.

I am writing you from my desk in the Hall of Representatives,
amidst the buz and bustle of our opening organization. I do not
see that there is much prospect before us of a busy or a stormy
Session, yet there is no saying how suddenly in a community
so very inflammable as ours, occasions of discussion & disturb-
ance may arise. It is not improbable that a radical change in our
domestic policy will be begun this Session, in the attempt to
introduce manufactures into our State. The applications for

---

[355] *Helen Halsey* and *Castle Dismal.*

[356] Dated by Simms' reference to the quarrel between Duyckinck and Clark.
See letters to Duyckinck and Lawson of Nov. 13.

charters, several of which are contemplated, may provoke a violent resistance among those who, in their excessive obtuseness will confound manufactures with the Tariff. As I am disposed to believe that the one can very well exist without the other, I can reconcile my vote for a charter with my long and deadly hostility to a protective Tariff.[357] It is barely possible that I mistake the feeling of our Legislature, or of a portion of it.—You will have recieved before this, a paper or two containing brief paragraphs in relation to the Knickerbocker. I mentioned yesterday to the Editor of the Carolinian[358] that I would furnish him with a paragraph on the same subject, and of the same character. This you shall recieve in due season. I trust you will keep up the fire, now that you have begun it, from all your auxiliaries. It is necessary that the war once begun should be a war of extermination. Either this, or you just make noise enough to give him notoriety & prolong his existence. You should speak more plainly and show him up as a mere liar & skunk. Do not treat him as a literary man at all, but as the swindler of literary men. Such only is his character. — Send me to my address here, a copy by mail of the Views & Reviews, — and if you begin printing the second vol. let the proofs be sent me here. — I have long had reason to fancy that the Dem. Rev. has not looked favorably or friendlily upon me. It has admitted one or more sneers (*en passant*) such as our friend Jones's, — and has utterly forborne a notice of my Life of Marion, or any of my works for several years — to say nothing of special omissions of my name in all summaries of our novelists &c. Is there any foundation for my

---

[357] Simms supported a bill, introduced on Dec. 10, 1845, to incorporate the Graniteville Manufacturing Company. *See House Journal,* p. 102.

[358] A. H. Pemberton or A. G. Summer. We have been unable to locate copies of the issues of the (Columbia) *South Carolinian* (title hyphenated under Pemberton's editorship) for this period, but sometime in late 1845 or early 1846 Summer succeeded Pemberton as editor and proprietor (see Simms' letter to Duyckinck of Feb. 9, 1846, in which he speaks of "Col. Summer of the 'Carolinian'"). In the issue of Aug. 27, 1846 (the first discoverable issue of that year), Summer and B. R. Carroll are listed as editors and proprietors. On March 3, 1847, Carroll became sole editor and proprietor. He was succeeded by Summer with the issue of May 12, 1847. In Oct., 1848, Summer sold one-third of the paper to A. T. Cavis, and the issue of Oct. 3 gives the publishers as Summer and Cavis, the editor as Summer. With the issue of Jan. 2, 1849, the publishers became Johnston and Cavis, the editor William B. Johnston. The newspaper was a weekly except during the sessions of the legislature, when it became a semi-weekly published on Tuesdays and Fridays.

For Simms' remarks in the *Southern Patriot* about the *Knickerbocker,* see note 347, Nov. 13, 1845.

conjecture of unfriendliness, or is it simply indifference on the part of O'Sullivan?[359] —

But I must stop. I am interrupted and can only say, I write to let you know where I am, and to tell you that I am very faithfully

Yours &c

W. G. S.

Send me an occasional 'News' to this place, Mirror, Broadway Journal, or anything that you think will interest me aside from politics. Present me to all friends in the proper fashion.

286: To Evert Augustus Duyckinck

Columbia, Decr. 12. 1845

My dear Sir

Your Letter of the 2d. reached me several days ago, but I have been so busy as scarcely to be able to read it satisfactorily. Our business here has been very pressing, &, through a premature movement in such of the members (a majority) as come to do nothing but to vote and recieve their pay, our Session is found too short to do our business. Much valuable matter has been thrown overboard, deferred to another Session. In this way, I lose two favorite measures which I had introduced, and had set my heart upon. To write, to read or think, except in the legal and political atmosphere is here impossible and writing to you at my desk during the progress of our general orders, I am compelled to watch closely, and to make frequent pause, through fear of saying to you some thing of our penal laws and domestic economy — matters which, I suspect, would interest you little. Somehow, I have become quite a debater this Session & have found my hands full of business, and heard my voice, perhaps, too frequently for the ears of others.[360] At all events, I have

---

[359] For Jones' remarks on Simms, see note 319, Oct. 19, 1845. *Marion* had been noticed in the *Democratic Review* (see note 331, Nov. 3, 1845).

[360] On Dec. 5 Simms introduced "a Bill to maintain in the freeholder, the integrity of the freehold, by the exemption of real Estate from levy and sale under execution. . . ." It was eventually tabled. On Dec. 10, from the "Minority of the Committee on Federal Relations," he made a "Report on a Resolution of enquiry as to what action, if any, be necessary to be had at the present session of the Legislature, in reference to the late Act of Congress, prescribing the time for holding elections of Electors of President and Vice-President of the United States." Also on Dec. 10 he introduced the following resolution:

not shrunk from my work; though, whether it is well or ill done, be a matter of doubt among my neighbours.—I sent you yesterday a copy of the South Carolinian Newspaper, contg a notice of the Knickerbocker.[361] The Editor goes into the conflict *con amore*, and certainly speaks the truth. You will think so. I am told his Decr. No. is full of provocation, but have not yet seen it.[362] — I have written to B & W.[363] for some of the books. I fancy a taking work may be made out of Haroun.[364] I propose to do it in the vein *orientale*. *Nous verrons*. Are you not too slow in the issue of your American Series? Why not one of the foreign & one of the domestic weekly? You surely will be able to provide the matèriel. I have suggested to G. F. Holmes, a couple of volumes on the Domestic Life of the Romans & the Greeks, — their sports, their suppers, their games, Amphitheatre &c. The topics are likely to be taking ones, & he can treat them properly. What think you? R. H. Wilde, I saw not long ago, and told him I had almost ventured to suggest his Danté to you.[365] He speaks despondingly of the work — probably lacks impulse, and might be driven to the task by an application. Jones's Letter is highly complimentary particularly with regard to Views & Reviews, so I suppose, you have put them into his hands. I am particularly anxious that the collection should succeed, as I am persuaded that the notions may be of great public utility in the infant condition of our Literature.

"Resolved, that our Representatives in Congress be requested to use all proper endeavors, in their Representative capacity to procure the establishment of a Branch Mint in the City of Charleston." This resolution was passed. On Dec. 11 he introduced a resolution to the effect that "during the remainder of the present Session, no member be suffered to speak more than ten minutes, in the first instance, no more than five in the second." This resolution was lost. See *House Journal*, pp. 75, 94, 101, 103, 109, 135.

[361] We have been unable to locate copies of the *South Carolinian* for this period.

[362] The *Knick.*, XXVI, 579-583, continues its attack on Mathews and his defenders. In addition, it says of Simms (p. 587): "We have been wofully berated lately by a correspondent of an evening print, for representing a voluminous southern novelist as experiencing 'the decadence of a limited sectional reputation.' And yet we spoke 'by the book.' Prices, supply and demand, were our *data*. Moreover, the very journal in which appears the communication referred to, did not hesitate to say: 'We doubt if the copy-right of all Mr. Simms's work, (some forty volumes, it is said,) would bring as much money in America or England, as the 'Sketch-Book' of Irving, or the 'Norman Leslie' of Fay.'" See notes 317 and 319, Oct. 19, 1845, and note 338, Nov. 13, 1845.

[363] Bartlett and Welford.

[364] We can find no record of this proposed work having been written.

[365] In the "Editorial Bureau" of *Southern and Western*, II (Aug., 1845), 144, Simms writes glowingly of Richard Henry Wilde's *Life of Dante*, then said to be in preparation for the press. Wilde's unfinished MS. is in the Library of Congress.

— I will thank you to ask W & P. what the publications of the Camden Society are up to this moment, what they will cost, and what is the annual subscription. — Do not speak to any one of the Haroun Alrashid project. It must ripen slowly. It will not be possible for me to do any thing for the Messenger until late in January, and what I shall do then will depend somewhat upon the degree of provocation afforded by the character of current publications. I am pledged for a Review of Hugh Legaré,[366] and another of Curwen's Letters.[367] — Lawson tells me that you think the collection of Imaginative Sketches which I propose to publish, might impair the success of those I put into the Library. But why not take them yourself? I frankly think them quite as good as the other tales & equally unique. Read them & see. Read Conrade Weickhoff, The Benefactress, the Wager of Battle &c.[368] What of Poe & the rest. Write me the details &c. In haste & uproar,

Yours &c

W. G. Simms

287: To EVERT AUGUSTUS DUYCKINCK

Woodlands Decr 22. 1845

dear Duyckinck.

Yours of the 16th has just reached me advising me of one of an earlier date, not yet recieved, addressed me at Columbia.

---

[366] Simms' review of the *Writings of Hugh Swinton Legaré,* 2 vols. (Charleston, S. C.: Burges & James, 1846-1845), appears in XII (April, 1846), 252-254. It is signed "**." During 1845 Simms contributed to the *Messenger* "Grouped Thoughts and Scattered Fancies" (see note 327, Oct. 28, 1845); "The Two Carolinas," XI (March), 138-143; a letter (see note 325, Oct. 28, 1845); and possibly "The Battle of King's Mountain" (signed "***"), XI (Sept.), 552-555. During 1846 he contributed the above mentioned review of Legaré; a series of articles reviewing Curwen's *Journal* (see note 367, below), a review of Street's *Poems* (see note 143, July 20, 1846); "The Eye and the Wing" (see note 23, Jan. 15, 1847); "The Ruins," signed "W. G. S.," XII (Sept.), 531-532; and "Niagara," signed "S.," XII (Nov.), 657-658.

[367] Simms' review of George Atkinson Ward's edition of the *Journal and Letters of the Late Samuel Curwen . . . to Which Are Added . . . Biographic Notices of Many Prominent Loyalists and Other Eminent Men* (New York: Leavitt, Trow & Co., 1845) was published in the form of five articles. The first three, entitled "The Civil Warfare in the Carolinas and Georgia, during the Revolution," appear in *S. L. M.,* XII (May, June, and July, 1846), 257-265, 321-336, 385-400; the fourth and fifth, entitled "Biographical Sketch of the Career of Major William Cunningham, of South Carolina," in *S. L. M.,* XII (Sept. and Oct., 1846), 513-524, 577-586.

[368] See note 292, Aug. 8, 1845.

Of course the tidings of your failure, are the first which I had
of your projected review. I need not tell you how much I regret
this defeat, but the circumstance is one rather to be deplored
than dwelt upon. Do not hurry events. Be patient, and all will
come right. I am very sure that, but for your loyalty to C M.
there would have been no difficulty with J. Wiley.[369] This *entre
nous.* Wait events — wait! I can just now think of no better
counsel. I think you have been rash in one or more respects,
and it is just as well that you should give yourself an opportunity
to recover. You hold a fortunate position at this moment in public
favour, which you must not endanger. Your taste, judgment and
reading are all held in high esteem. Economize what you have
gained. Better, indeed, if you could get some man of straw at
the head of the mage. whom you could move at pleasure without
being seen by others or suspected by himself. Again — go to work
privately, and bring out a vol. carefully planned & penned, under
the shield of the anonymous. Win capital in that way in addition to what you have got. You will value the anonymous some
day as highly as I do. If you attempt the periodical, of course,
you may hold me pledged for regular contributions. Again —
there's a way of managing an obstinate man of prejudices, by
seeming to humor them. Rather than lose your game wholly yield
some of the points. Besides, the experience of a man like J. W.
founded as it is upon *sales,* is not without its value. — I have this
day written to W & P. touching the publication of Views & Reviews. I have thought of doing so for some time past. I looked
to see them out in October. At this rate, the second vol. of Wigwam & Cabin would be out by July, and that of Views & Reviews
by next Christmas, year. By the way have the several articles for
Vol 2 of V & R. been recieved. Write me on this head. I have
been looking for the proof sheets of them. As they are to be
printed deliberately, the printing should be begun early. The sheets
of Vol 2. W & C. reached me at Columbia. I take for granted
that Vol 1. has sold well. In Carolina during the session of legislature, it could not be procured for love or money. Let me hear
on this point. The Decr. Democratic is before me. I percieve that
nearly all of W & P's several series have been noticed in that

---

[369] We have been unable to locate Duyckinck's letter to Simms concerning
the failure of his projected review. Apparently Duyckinck had asked John
Wiley to be the publisher, and he had refused. Simms attributes his refusal
to Duyckinck's close friendship with Cornelius Mathews, whom apparently
Wiley disliked.

work but mine. On this subject I wrote before. It is something curious, but such has been the fate of Castle Dismal, Helen Halsey, Marion & the Wigwam. I cannot help thinking that it seems a designed omission. — I find myself undergoing translation into German through the medium of a German newspaper published in Charleston which has considerable circulation in the South & in Pennsylvania.[370] "Murder will out" "Jocassee" & several other tales now lie before me in their German costume, and the Editor tells me that they are far more popular among the German people, than the tales of all other American writers put together. Here then is fame under one's *nose,* of which he *knows* nothing. I have scarcely yet got to work, after the political excitements of the Session. It was my fortune to take a very active part in the business, and I have not yet subsided into that repose which is so necessary to literature. By the way, I have a vol. of poetry, as unique as possible, about the size of Poe's which I wish published in the Library. It *is by my young friend Adrian Beaufain.*[371] He expects no pay for it, — only some fifty copies — and will give the use of it for five years. It might appear as No. 15 of the Series, or 18 or 20. *It will be the beginning of a new contributor,* and you must urge it strenuously. All that he insists on is that it be sold at 25 cents retail, and as there is no copy money this can be done readily. — Will you see Poe & ask him what became of a little poem that was left with an elderly gentleman at his desk (the Bookkeeper) I believe, just before I left New York. The Poem was a "Ballad by Adrian Beaufain,"[372] with a memorandum for Mr. Poe, by myself. The verse was a peculiar one, and the strain a melancholy one. It has not appeared in print as far as I have seen. Request Poe to send the Broadway Journal to me hereafter at this place, & discontinue it at Charleston, except to the "Patriot." Let me hear from you soon on these several matters & above all see that W & P. send out their American books more frequently. They discourage the American Writer in this way, and dispirit hope and defeat & mock endeavour; and then they point to the failure as ours.

Yours truly &c

W. G. S.

---

[370] We have been unable to locate any information concerning this newspaper.

[371] "Adrian Beaufain" was a favorite pseudonym employed by Simms.

[372] This poem was not published in the *Broadway Journal.*

288: To James Henry Hammond

Woodlands Decr 22. [1845][373]

My dear Hammond.

I have been cudgelling my brains for some time past to ascertain whether you owed me a letter or not; — my conclusions, — prompted by my indolence no doubt, — always inclining me to think that you did. I was assured that I wrote you in August, just before I left for the North; and I knew that I had sent you a batch of sonnets in sheets just before I left for Columbia; — and to neither of these instances of appreciation, could I find that you had made any response. Thus thinking, I had begun to resolve to wait events as the Conservatives have it, and bide the thawing of your humours, when it suddenly struck me that you were a captain of tens & hundreds, and could do mischief to a small person at the polls. This last consideration moves me to unbend. I doff my Ebenezer accordingly and ask—how do you like my sonnets? You might have volunteered a critique without subjecting me to the necessity of soliciting one. And here let me apologize for sending you a copy in sheets, — but this was due to the cursed binder who disappointing me, threw me upon the necessity of supplying all my friends, after the same fashion, or of leaving many of them unsupplied, so long as to seem to have forgotten them. For the *brochure,* let me tell you, is as yet unpublished. Whether it will ever be published is a question. It may be, hereafter, when I make a complete collection of my poetical miscellanies, but, — it's a far cry to Lochawe,[374] — &, in the present condition of our Literature, the motives to publication of a metrical character are very few. — Aldrich & other friends tell me that my reelection will not need much electioneering if any — will not need, indeed, that I should do more than was done last year, — viz a weeks travel with the military. But for this assurance, I had determined not again to trespass upon the favor of Demos; and even now if he prefers to do without me, I should prefer to retire. To you, in common with other friends, I leave that question, and I look to you frankly to say whether my course has met with approbation in your quarter. I am pleased with the assurance in my own neighbourhood that such is the case. — I propose to give myself a week or ten days in the spring, and in

---

[373] Dated by Simms' reference to *Grouped Thoughts and Scattered Fancies.*
[374] A proverbial expression found also in Scott's *Rob Roy,* chapter xxix.

that time to look upon you in your den. "Shall there be no more cakes and ale?" [375] — Talking of cakes & ale, rem[inds] me that Lewis [376] & myself at Columbia, enjoyed some hearty sniggering at your, his & my expense, recalling the eventful scenes of the Orange Encampment. Of his share in the transaction he seems heartily to repent. He says he was just drunk enough all the while to know that he was anything but sober. Let me hear from you. This scrawl is simply meant to break the ice—a phrase which I owe less to the proverb than the present weather.

Yours truly &c

Simms

J. H. Hammond, Esq.

---

[375] See *Twelfth Night,* II, iii, 124ff.
[376] Probably William L. Lewis. See note 112, Feb. 25, 1845.

1846

Woodlands, Jany 1. 1846

Rev. Rufus W. Griswold

Dear Sir

Permit me to congratulate you on the pleasant aspects of the New Year. May it prove to you a prosperous and happy one.— I did not recieve your note, until my return yesterday from the city, and did not hear of your arrival, until I reached it the day before.[2] With the necessity of an immediate return to the plantation, under arrangements, to meet a guest, I found it impossible, in the 24 hours allotted me in Charleston, to do more than send you a verbal message, which, I trust, and take for granted, has already reached you. It was confided to Mr. Hart,[3] and to Mr. Russell,[4] and was to the effect that I should be extremely glad if you could visit me at Woodlands. Let me repeat the request in this place. It is easy reaching me, by Rail Road, in the course of five hours. My post town is Midway, which is but two miles from the plantation. If you will suffer me to know, by mail, a day or two before hand, of your purposed visit, I will send the carriage, and probably come myself, to meet you at the depôt. Such a visit will show you something of our middle country, and I shall rejoice to give you welcome.

Very faithfully &c. Yours

W. Gilmore Simms

P. S. Let me beg that you will contemplate at least a week's stay with me, and come provided accordingly. I can give you a desk and table and any amount of pen ink & paper in my studio. I

---

[1] See introductory sketch.

[2] Griswold arrived in Charleston on Dec. 20, 1845, on the steam packet *Wilmington*. See Joy Bayless, *Rufus Wilmot Griswold* (Nashville, Tennessee: Vanderbilt University Press, 1943), p. 109.

[3] Samuel Hart, Senior, Charleston bookseller and publisher.

[4] John Russell, Charleston bookseller and publisher. See introductory sketch.

take for granted, that, with these implements, an author is pretty much at home anywhere.

290: To James Lawson

Woodlands, Jan 7. [1846]⁵

My dear Lawson.

Take as matter of course my cordial congratulations on the New Year. My little flock unite in wafting a boon of blessings for yours. Present me affectionately to your wife, and kiss her & the young ones (four?) on my account. You may say to her that hope deferred maketh the heart sick.⁶ She is a sad creature, and must certainly design that I shall not look into the arrangements of the house in 12th. Street next summer.⁷ As for not getting an escort, the thing is utterly absurd. There are hundreds of persons coming South at this season, whom you could easily find out, and who would only be too happy to take charge of so fair a burthen. But it is not too late, and I have the plan of *mouvement* in my head. My wife will go to town (Charleston)

---

⁵ Dated by Simms' reference to the forthcoming engagement in Charleston of Mrs. Charles Kean (Ellen Tree). She opened on Feb. 2, 1846, as "Mrs. Haller" in William Dunlap's *The Stranger, or Misanthropy and Repentance* (see Hoole, *The Ante-Bellum Charleston Theatre*, p. 123). Simms had seen the Keans in New York during the previous summer and in a letter dated Sept. 23, 1845, and published in the *Southern Patriot* of Sept. 26, 1845 (see note 304, Aug. 28, 1845), he says of them: ". . . Mr. Forbes promises you a goodly *dramatis personae* this winter. You will have with you the Keans, man and wife, and Mrs. Mowatt. I had the pleasure of seeing the two former in 'As You Like it,' [*sic*] and promise you that you will find no falling off in Ellen Tree. Her 'Rosalind' is quite as admirable and exquisite as ever. The 'Jaques' of Charles Kean is scarcely to my liking. But the part is not a playable one. The contemplative and melancholy Jaques is rather to be listened to than seen; and I suppose Kean only takes the character, as tributary to his wife's performance of 'Rosalind.' I remember Kean some fifteen years ago, as a well-informed, intelligent young man, of good taste, and tolerable person, who made his exits and his entrances becomingly, but who was not destined by nature, nor prepared by art, to sustain the glories of his paternal name. [See Simms' letter to the *City Gazette* of April-May, 1831.] It is impossible for me to say whether he has improved at all since that period, judging only by his 'Jaques.' He has certainly grown considerably stouter, and scarcely appears so gracefully as then. But his wife is inimitable. She is, indeed, an actress, — conscious of every movement, discreet in every gesture, true and intelligent in every simile. She realised admirably the *ars celare artem* of the teacher, and conceals the effort in the guise of a grace which leaves nothing for the spectator to complain of, or to require."

⁶ Proverbs, 13:12.

⁷ Lawson was planning to move from his residence at 76 Eleventh Street to 136 W. Twelfth Street, where he was building a mansion. See letters to Lawson of Feb. 27, 1845, and Feb. 20, 1846. See also the New York City directories for 1845-1846 and 1846-1847.

with me sometime this month, as soon as we hear of the arrival
of Mrs. Kean (Ellen Tree) whom she is anxious to see. Can't
you contrive to get her Ladyship on at the same period when
after a night or two at the Theatre, and a day or two in the city,
I can bring up my two wives and twenty mothers to Woodland[s]. Is not the scheme a refreshing one? Think of & act upon
it. I really regret that she had not been here in season to go with
Augusta to Columbia. I could have ensured her a famous flourish
or two in the Ball Rooms of that fashionable town.—And so you
undertake to answer my letters—you at the office & they at home.
Was ever such an absurdity. The result is that you answer nothing, but go on prattling like Falstaff in the bedclothes.[8] And then
you talk of not being in my debt, opposing one hasty scrawl at
the office, to my three or four copious epistles. Fie upon you.
You must do better hereafter. I sent you the other day several
papers containing reference to my labors in Columbia,—which
were equally continuous & irksome.[9] My Constituents—some of
them at least—say that I must run again.—My answer is,—you
may elect me, but I will not electioneer.—As for the notice
of Clarke, I do not see that he deserved less.[10] He is a dirty rascal.
I see that his Decr. no. repeats his offences.[11] From Street I hear
nothing & have recieved nothing. His book has not reached me.
I made in the Mage. a complimentary notice of his previous
volumes, but he took no notice of that.[12] I suppose he saw it.

---

[8] *The Merry Wives of Windsor*, III, v.

[9] The *Southern Patriot* of Nov. 29, 1845, reports: "Mr. W. Gilmore Simms,
submitted a Resolution instructing the Committee on Federal Relations to
inquire into the subjects of a law of Congress, passed at its last Session, direct-
ing a uniform time for casting the votes for Electors of President and Vice
President of the United States, and to ascertain in what manner our constitution
will be affected by this act. It is thought that it will have for its effect a material and very awkward alteration of our present system; compelling us to
some change in the periods of our annual Session (which now seems impossible) or compelling us to elect our Electors, some nine or ten months before
the time when they will be required to give their votes." The issue of Dec. 8
reports that Simms made a speech in favor of "a bill to abolish the punishment
of death in cases of forgery and counterfeiting" and that the bill was passed
by a "triumphant vote." Perhaps these are the newspaper accounts Simms here
mentions.

[10] See letters to Duyckinck of Nov. 13, Nov. 24, and Dec. 12, 1845, and
letter to Lawson of Nov. 13, 1845.

[11] See note 362, Dec. 12, 1845.

[12] The new volume by Alfred Billings Street (see introductory sketch) is
The Poems of Alfred B. Street (New York: Clark & Austin, 1845). In *Southern and Western,* I (May, 1845), 330-342, Simms published a critique of Street's
The Burning of Schenectady, and Other Poems (Albany: W. C. Little, 1842)
and *Drawings and Tintings* (New York: Burgess, Stringer & Co., 1844)
under the title "Poems of Alfred B. Street." Although he commends Street's

You know that I think well of him. You can inquire if a copy
of his work is sent me.—Regarding Mr. Ogden as a man of
sense, I have no doubt I shall be pleased with his discourse
when it reaches me.[13] I shall be anxious to read it. But why the
d—l did you suffer him to put it into that kennel publication?—
As for Count Julian, you should know as much or more of it
than myself. I have heard but once from Benjamin, who wrote
to say that the copy of R. H. had been lost, begging for another,
and requesting that I would send on at the same time, a written
authority to print the whole *four* works.[14] I wrote an authority
for R. H only, & sent a second copy of that work. Since then
I hear no more of him. I have written him—and Taylor.—Wiley
& Putnam are equally neglectful. The absent are always shoved
aside. Do you hear any thing touching the sale of Wigwam &
Cabin? I see that Hoffman is out with new paper [15] & new
Poems.[16] Remind him of me. I sent the 'Wigwam' to him & put

descriptive ability, Simms is unsparing of his faults. He declares (pp. 330-331):
"He has done his work hastily. His plans have not been well laid,—his foundations not sufficiently sunk for his superstructure. He has given himself no time
to mature his conceptions, to elaborate or complete his designs, to polish and to
prune his verses. . . . The very subject chosen by Mr. Street for his first volume, 'The Burning of Schenectady,' denotes a certain crude condition of the
mind, by which we see our author has rushed, without proper thinking, to his
task."
    [13] James De Peyster Ogden, "Our Knickerbocker Fathers. An Address De-
livered before the St. Nicholas Society on the Evening Preceding Its Last
Annual Festival, Held on the Sixth Ultimo," *Knick.*, XXVII (Jan., 1846),
21-34.
    [14] At this time Park Benjamin was editor of the *Western Continent,* a weekly
published in Baltimore by the firm of Taylor, Wilde and Company (see note
340, Nov. 13, 1845). The firm planned to issue, in addition to books of general
interest, cheap editions of novels and popular works (see Hoover, *Park Benjamin,* pp. 156-157). Apparently Simms had been approached concerning the
republication of the four "Border Romances" then published: *Richard Hurdis,
Border Beagles, Confession,* and *Beauchampe* (see in this connection Simms'
letters to Lawson of Oct. 12 and Nov. 3, 1845). The only file of the *Western
Continent* accessible to us (that in the Enoch Pratt Free Library, Baltimore)
contains none of Simms' novels. The issue of July 11, 1846 (then under the
editorship of William Tappan Thompson), however, lists Simms together with
many other prominent writers whose works are in the future to be published
in the *Western Continent.* The issue of Jan. 2, 1847, contains Simms' "The
Palmetto Regiment." Possibly other contributions appear in issues missing
from the file.
    [15] The first issue of *Hewet's Excelsior and New York Illustrated Times,*
edited by Charles Fenno Hoffman (see introductory sketch), is dated Jan. 1,
1846, though actually it was published somewhat earlier. The periodical ceased
publication in February. See Homer F. Barnes, *Charles Fenno Hoffman* (New
York: Columbia University Press, 1930), pp. 168-170.
    [16] The *Knick.*, XXVII (Jan., 1846), 93, states: "One of the neatest and
prettiest volumes of the season, clad in a beautiful garb of gold-and-blue, is
'*The Vigil of Faith, and other Poems*,' from the well-known pen of Charles
Fenno Hoffman, Esquire, recently put forth by the Brothers Harper. . . . the

his name on the List of W & P.—What of Stringer? If he is
cold on the subject of that vol. there is P & B. They shall have
it on the same terms with W & P. viz 12½ per cent. and the
privilege for five years.[17] I wish you would see Taylor & remind
him that R. H. was to appear on the 1st. Jan. & Border Beagles
in Feb. The other works to follow at monthly intervals.[18]—While
in that neighbourhood, you might see what Langley intends on
the subject of the Damsel.[19] Ask him also if he is in reciept of
6 chaps. of the Life of Capt. Smith.—Say [to P &] B. that Trippings in Authorland, Rambles by Land & Water, & Morris verses,
and Maturin's Montezuma have not reached me though they
have reached Charleston.[20] Remind Stringer also of his promise
to send me his publications.—I wish his "home & Traveller's
Library" & being the Editor of two newspapers, can give him
as much criticism as he wants.[21]—The Creature Comforts came
safely & we are even now enjoying them. Remember me to Bryant
and family, and present me with best regards when you write, to
Forrest & wife. Do you ever see Catharine Sinclair? Is she well
& thriving? Say to Jimmy Jr. that Gilly Jr. hopes to put up his
menagerie shortly. At present it consists of a rattlesnake, with its
tail & rattles, but without its head—a raccoon, and two wild
cats. He waits only to add a 'Possum' to the collection, to enclose the whole to his address.—We are all well—the children
particularly flourishing. I am at the old Drudgery with constant
yearnings to escape, for one year of freedom at least. But—! God

---

present is the *fourth* edition of the work." The volume is reviewed in *Dem.
Rev.*, XVIII (Jan., 1846), 71-72.

[17] Simms is here referring to the never published volume of tales of the
imagination, first offered to Duyckinck for publication in Wiley and Putnam's
"Library of American Books" and then to Burgess, Stringer and Co. (see letter
to Duyckinck of April 10, 1845, and following letters to Duyckinck; see also
letters to Lawson of Oct. 27, Nov. 13, and Nov. 21, 1845). Paine and Burgess,
New York, are now to be offered the volume on the same terms as those proposed to Wiley and Putnam. Simms says in his "Editorial Bureau," *Southern
and Western*, II (Nov., 1845), 356: ". . . there is a publishing house
newly established,—that of Messrs. Paine & Burgess,—who declare their plan
to be not only the publishing of American books, but of American books solely."

[18] See note 14, above.

[19] *The Damsel of Darien.* See letter to Lawson of Nov. 3, 1845.

[20] Paine and Burgess, New York, published these works: Fanny Forester
(pseudonym for Mrs. Emily Judson), *Trippings in Author-Land* (1846); Benjamin M. Norman, *Rambles by Land and Water, or Notes of Travel in Cuba
and Mexico* (1845); George Pope Morris, *The Songs and Ballads of George
P. Morris* (1846); and Edward Maturin, *Montezuma; the Last of the Aztecs,*
2 vols. (1845).

[21] In addition to the *Southern Patriot* (Charleston) and the *South Carolinian* (Columbia) Simms was also writing reviews for the *Southern Literary
Messenger* (see letter to Lawson of Oct. 27, 1845).

bless you & yours. Once more health and happiness from all here, for all with you. I throw my heart, such as it is, after many strange mishaps, into Lady Lyde's lap, as a New Years gift. May she make much of it.

Yours & Hers

W. G. S.

291 : To Evert Augustus Duyckinck

Woodlands, Jany 10. [1846][22]

My dear Duyckinck

I send you two collections of Sonnets, one consisting of twelve, the other of four sonnets, which I will thank you to offer to the Democratic Review for *thirty dollars*.[23] If they cannot afford this, or if you find that you cannot get it from them, you may submit to $20. But not till the last moment. The collection strikes me not only as corresponding in tone & spirit with the Editorial temper of the Review, but as being such a series as will attract some attention. Between us, I look upon the sonnets, all, as being full of vigor & fire, full of political truth and political prophecy,—to say nothing of what is simply morally just, though still original— scattered through them. Of course, this letter is for your private reading only. I speak to you with a degree of frankness in regard to myself, which I show to few. The first twelve should appear in the February number, and will I suppose be in time for it. I do not hear from you. Have you any news. What of Lawson, Mathews & the rest. The Editor of the 'Carolinian' writes to me for a criticism on Big Abel, and I fancy I must send him one.[24] He has lately given a very ugly thrust at Griswold—I know not why. R. W. G. is at Charleston & has written to me. I answered

---

[22] Dated by Simms' reference to his invitation to Griswold to visit Woodlands. See letter to Griswold of Jan. 1.

[23] These collections were published under the following titles: "Progress in America. Or, a Speech in Sonnets, on the Relations between Great Britain and the United States," *Dem. Rev.*, XVIII (Feb., 1846), 91-94, and "The Hostility of England to America. In Four Sonnets," *ibid.*, XVIII (March, 1846), 213-214.

[24] We have been unable to locate copies of the issues of the *South Carolinian* for this period. For an account of the various editors and publishers of this newspaper, see note 358, Nov. 24, 1845.

him promptly, giving him an invitation to visit me at Wood-land[s]. To this, I have no answer yet.

> With cramped fingers, but
> very truly Yours.
>
> W. Gilmore Simms

E.A.D.

P. S. *E. A. D.* If you succeed in disposing of the within, for the sum designated, place the money, or the promise of the Editor, in the hands of Bartlett & Welford, to my credit, & instruct them (in that case but not otherwise) to send me the copy of Hackluyt and of Adair.[25] My usual resources are somewhat unexpectedly cut short for the present year, and I must economize all round, and—sell all the verses I can. Can you find me a market with Colton or anybody else, on moderate terms.

292 : To RUFUS WILMOT GRISWOLD

> [*c.* January 15, 1846] [26]

R. W. Griswold Esq.

Dear Sir.

Above, you have the order which I promised you, & which the variety of my engagements in town caused me to forget.[27] You will find the collection a valuable one in several of the departments, particularly the scientific—in natural history, & I believe, in the arts. I send you by this mail, a copy of the 'Sonnets'.[28] I shall be at home for a couple of weeks.

> Very truly &c
>
> W. Gilmore Simms

---

[25] Simms, of course, is here speaking of Richard Hakluyt's *The Principall Navigations, Voiages, and Discoveries of the English Nation* and James Adair's *The History of the American Indians.*

[26] This letter is postmarked "Jany 16th/1846."

[27] This order cannot be positively identified. Possibly it is a file of the *Southern Quarterly Review.*

[28] *Grouped Thoughts and Scattered Fancies*

293 : To Alfred Billings Street

Woodlands Feb. 1. 1846

Alfred B. Street Esq.

Dear Sir

I had just covered to your address and despatched by mail, a little *brochure* of my own,—a small pamphlet vol. of Sonnets,—[29] when your friendly Letter came to hand. I am glad, from this letter, to discover that your sympathies are in the right place. I had feared, I confess, from your long silence, that something in my hasty criticism might have given offense,[30]—knowing that you properly belong to the tribe,—the *genus irritabile*—of whom the proverb gives us sufficient warning.[31] But I looked over the essay in question, and could not see how any thing there said could have disquieted you, and so I surrendered myself to my philosophies, in waiting events. The result has not disappointed me, and your Letter sets all things right.

I do not see that you owe me any acknowledgements for the notice to which you refer. I certainly meant it to be a kind one, but did not the less determine that it should be a just one. It is true you have not been always accustomed to this sort of treatment,—but as I had occasion, on one occasion to say to one of your New England Editors—'I was a Gentlemen before I became an author',[32] I cannot now persuade myself,—strange as it may seem to the critic herd in America,—to sink the one in the other character. I believe, in treating your writings I dealt quite as freely in censure as in praise, being really anxious to serve your genius & its aims in a proper manner. Mere praise is of very little service at any time, unless to that class of authors, like John Keats, who lack greatly in self esteem. But authorship itself, as a general rule, implies the contrary. The courage & the consciousness of Genius, are quite as much its characteristics, generally, as originality & independence.

---

[29] Simms sent copies of *Grouped Thoughts and Scattered Fancies* to many of his friends. In a letter dated Nov. 27, 1845, Henry C. Lea writes: "I hasten to express to you the pleasure that I have derived from the 'Grouped Thoughts' with which you have favored me. I had read most of them before, as they appeared in the 'Messenger,' & I am much gratified to have them in a collection & permanent form." (Original in the New York Public Library.)

[30] See letter to Lawson of Jan. 7, 1846.

[31] *Genus irritabile vatum.* Horace, *Epistles,* Bk. ii, epis. 2, line 102.

[32] This statement was made to Peabody of Peabody and Company, publisher of the *Knickerbocker* in 1833-1834. For an account of the circumstances provoking the remark, see Trent, pp. 77-80.

I see you despond about your sentiment. But sentiment is quite as much nature as the waters & the woods. Speak *yourself,* and you speak both. Only let yourself alone, in giving your emotions proper utterance. The error of young writers is in asking how they shall please or pacify the critics, as of young lawyers, how they shall meet the requisitions of the elder faculty around them. I would say to both speak to your case, and let the critics go to the devil. If Mr Street is pleased with a scene let him describe it, only not forget in merely describing its actual features to say how these impressed him,—with what associations, analogies &c. This is associating the moral with the physical, as is done by Wordsworth, Bryant &c. Besides, you must not describe by details, since it is the *tout ensemble* that strikes & impresses you & not the constituents. Remember that! Struck by a scene, you proceed to ask how it is compounded, & thus make a survey rather than a picture. But a truce to this.—Your vol. has not yet reached me.[33] I shall be very glad to recieve it.—I regretted very much that I did not see you last summer, & scarcely hoped that our very forgetful friend J. Lawson, would have remembered to convey to you my regrets to this effect.—I trust to be more fortunate next season, when, God willing, I shall again visit New York. Let me hear from you at your convenience & hold me

Very faithfully Yours &c

W. Gilmore Simms.

294: To GEORGE FREDERICK HOLMES

Woodlands, Feb 3. 1846

Geo. Fred Holmes, Esq.

My dear Professor

That you are safely housed is one thing certain, settled, and so far a fact satisfactory, however much may be wanting to your more ambitious desires. Small oaks from little acorns rise, and it will be your policy, & ought to be your pride, to lift the Richmond College into the position which in good energetic hands, it might be made to attain. It is the few working men, who, in all such cases, achieve the good work, in spite of discouragements. Put your own shoulders to the wheel, not thinking of yourself,

---

[33] *The Poems of Alfred B. Street.*

and you will do wonders. And if you have another working man in your faculty, there can be no doubt of your ultimate—nay rapid success. But be prudent—no talking—say as little as you can. Utter no opinions of your neighbors however you may entertain them, but keep a single eye on the Institution with which you are identified. Identify yourself with it. Encourage a sympathy between your boys & yourself—they are the masters of their mothers and fathers. It is the damnable blunder of certain of our Professors of the S. C. College, that they suffer the whole state to see that they care not a straw for anything in the Institution but their salaries. Hence they have no hold on the affections of the State by which they are maintained. Now a salary though necessary to the professor should not be his sole consideration. The higher considerations of duty render it subordinate; and I trust you will find in your boys a family group whom you will learn to love as well as teach. This will be your security & the secret of your success,—and to this I exhort you, speaking to one who, for aught I know, may soon be a father, and who is now required to cast behind him the petty and always inferior concerns of the youthful and the purposeless. — You see, my dear Holmes, I speak to you with the language of seniority. It is as a father, as one who has always toiled and often suffered, that I presume to speak to you in the voice of counsel. You are yet a very young man, and because of a certain vivacity and eagerness of temperament, will need all your prudence and reflection—frequent pause, and just deliberation—to keep from inadvertence. With a wife to maintain, with children to provide for, it is not so easy to recover a false step, a lapse, or an indiscretion. Forethought must prevent the necessity of regret and repentance. Now that you are a man,—and no one is truly such until he becomes husband & father—you must do as St. Paul did, and cast behind you the things of boyhood.[34] Enough after this fashion. Be successful & happy is my farther counsel, and these depend wholly upon the other.—The Southern Quarterly is not out. I see and hear nothing of Whitaker. I cut him in Columbia, but he would not stay out & forced his hand upon me. I treated him with cold civility, bowed & drew off. A controversy with Breckenridge[35]

---

[34] I Corinthians, 13:11.

[35] Robert Jefferson Breckinridge (1800-1871) was one of the ablest and bitterest controversialists of his time. As a minister in Baltimore, he began a crusade against the Catholics, split the Presbyterian Church into "Old School" and "New School," and led a fight for temperance. Breckinridge

will be a gentlemanly one of course & may help to bring you out. Do not think of giving him a rasping. Think only of making out your case.—I saw a few passages of the Homer of Mr. Munford,[36] in N. Y. last summer, and was surprised at their ease & fluency. I did not read more than twenty lines, but they were quite respectable—nothing great or grand, but respectable—and this after Pope & Cowper, to say nothing of Old Chapman and modern Sotheby is saying a good deal. I sent you by mail a few days ago, a copy of my 'Sonnets',[37] a small pamphlet vol. of sixty odd pages, in which please see something better than usual. They are unequal,—but all writings are so. Some of them are domestic & may please your wife, to whom please present me.

Yours faithfully &c

W. Gilmore Simms

295: To JAMES LAWSON

Woodlands, Feb. 3. [1846][38]

My dear Lawson

It has suddenly occurred to us that your long silence, for more than six weeks, may be occasioned by sickness in your little flock, and the anxiety which this thought occasions has made us forget our anger with you. I really trust that nothing is the matter more than your old complaint of fat and laziness. Your last letter represented Christina as quite well again, and we had hoped that by your silence you intended that we should have a surprise, in place of a letter, in the sudden appearance of that woman wife of yours on our coasts. In this last notion and hope we were tolerably content to wait events, but hope deferred too long maketh the heart very sick indeed; and I now, on the eve of a run down to Charleston (where I take my wife tomorrow) scribble you the amount of my fears, anxieties, angers & apprehensions. I have

---

consistently opposed slavery and, while a pastor in Baltimore, fought an effort on the part of Maryland to exclude free negroes.

[36] William Munford's translation of the *Iliad,* 2 vols., was published by C. C. Little and J. Brown, Boston, in 1846.

[37] *Grouped Thoughts and Scattered Fancies.*

[38] Dated by Simms' references to Griswold's visit to Charleston and to sending Street and Bryant copies of *Grouped Thoughts and Scattered Fancies.* Upon the receipt of his copy Bryant wrote in the New York *Evening Post* of May 23, 1846: "A little collection of Simms's Sonnets has been published at Richmond. Among them are some of the best verses of the author. Their tone is manly, and the expression free, bold and vigorous."

nothing else to write about. My head is weary with profitless toils, and my heart is sad with vague expectations. I have become a very grievous discontent, my friend,—dissatisfied with what I am and have, without well knowing what I should wish to be & to possess. All is well in our little family,—yet I am struggling against renewed fits of depression, which impair my energies & baffle my successes.—I am again about to make an effort to leave Carolina. This, for the present, must be wholly between ourselves, or must not go farther than your wife. I feel sure I can confide to her as safely as to you. Some friends are now making inquiries to ascertain whether it is possible to procure for me an appointment abroad.[39] I will have nothing less than a Chargé-des-affaires, unless at one of the two Great Courts of St. James & St *Cloud,* where I would be content with the place of a Sec. of legation. But a minor post is preferable, if independent. I have no idea what success will attend the inquiry. Do not trouble myself about it—and only hope. Our delegation will urge my wishes, whenever there shall be occasion, and there are other friends at work. Whether this comes to any thing or not, will not affect my purpose to visit the North early in the Summer. If your wife will come out in the Spring, I will bring her home early in the Summer, and will be content & pleased, to find a chamber (in that event) in Twelfth Street, in the Lawson Palace. But!—My desire will be to put to press at that time the several things which I shall have been able to prepare *ad interim.* I am now on my Life of Smith and doing little else. But I hope by that time to get ready my Huguenots & possibly something more. But things work greatly against me. Here I am out of the world, and am lost sight of by friends if not by foes. In spite of what is claimed by certain of them, (you know whom) to this day the Dem. Rev. has noticed neither Castle Dismal, nor Helen Halsey, nor Marion, nor Wigwam,[40]—yet both Duyckinck & Mathews are writing for that work into which they always have access. Look at others, and you have the same history. I am almost the only literary man in the country who succeeds without a party, and in

---

[39] In reply to a lost letter from Simms, Hammond wrote on Jan. 22, 1846: "Now as to your foreign longings. You know I have always approved that idea, with the hope it would give you the time & stimulate you to do something worthy of yourself. . . . I don't remember who is Secretary of Legation at Paris. For a literary man that would be the most desirable post." (Original in the Hammond Papers, Library of Congress.)

[40] Simms erred: the *Democratic Review* did review *The Life of Francis Marion.* See note 331, Nov. 3, 1845.

spite of the hostility of party. But I must not grumble. Enough, my friend, that I despond, & am weary. I wish to escape & find respite for awhile. Let me hear from you. You might write me more frequently in these days of cheap postage.[41]—I do not think that Stringer treats us well. It does not matter to him whose books he sells & he has his hands full without troubling mine. Don't you think that the plates of C. D & H. H. in the hands of H & B. coming out with a new edition would sell well? What if you try them or Wm. Taylor? That is, assuming that B & S. give you no satisfaction.[42] You can also see H & B. about an Illustrated work which I propose for next Christmas, to be called "Lays of Apalachia," consisting of 12 or 15 Tales in verse, Illustrative of events in our history in the different States—'Pocahontas' was one, the 'Biloxi' another & so on.[43] I propose them with a portrait of myself & six or eight other pictures. See H & B. or confer with Duyckinck, touching Redfield—or Paine & B.[44] Griswold is here in Charleston—seems disposed to be very civil, and I look to see him at Woodlands. I have just answered a letter from Street, though his book not yet recd. I have just sent him and Bryant a copy of my Sonnets. Present me kindly to Bryant, & when you write to E. F. and wife.[45] My wife joins with me, as well as Augusta, in saluting yours and the children. She dreamed of little Jimmy last night and Gilmore is always talking of him. Tell Jimmy that I would have put up and sent on his menagerie, but that I have been waiting until we could add a possum to the collection—a matter in which our negro boys are slow. But they are sure. I am looking for Mr. Ogden's address [46]—don't forget it.

Yours faithfully &c

W G Simms

---

[41] See note 214, June 6, 1845.

[42] Two editions of *Castle Dismal* (1844 and 1845) and one of *Helen Halsey* (1845) from the press of Burgess, Stringer and Co. are recorded. There is no record of an edition of either being issued by Harper and Brothers or William Taylor. See A. S. Salley, *Catalogue of the Salley Collection of the Works of Wm. Gilmore Simms* (Columbia, S. C.: The State Company, 1943), pp. 67-68.

[43] *Lays of Apalachia* was not published. Section III of Volume I of *Poems Descriptive Dramatic, Legendary and Contemplative,* entitled "Tales and Traditions of the South," is probably the revised *Lays of Apalachia.* For "Pocahontas" and "Biloxi," see note 239, June 25, 1845.

[44] In the 1850's J. S. Redfield, New York, was the publisher of many of Simms' works. For Paine and Burgess, see note 17, Jan. 7, 1846.

[45] Edwin and Catherine Sinclair Forrest.

[46] See note 13, Jan. 7, 1846.

296: To Evert Augustus Duyckinck

Woodlands Feb. 9. 1846

My dear Duyckinck

I thank you for your promptitude in dealing with O'Sullivan,[47] and will thank you still farther to open a negotiation with him for farther contributions in verse. I will agree to send him one or more pieces of verse monthly at *Ten dollars* per month, provided he will publish them regularly.[48] I am trying in this way to amass with reference to certain money deficiencies under which I labor. I propose to make a series of Sonnets agt. the punishment for death & in reply to Wordsworth,[49] & to deal otherwise with practical subjects in the same manner. Say this to O'S.—I will adopt your suggestion touching the order in favor of B & W.[50] anent the London pubr. of Count Julian. I wrote to W & P. in New York long ago, covering my sanction to any engagement which Mr P. might make in London.[51] Am I to understand that Mr. Wiley has not heard from me on the subject? You are right in what you say of our chance before American critics. But the American publisher sets the example. He even employs the Am. Series for puffing the foreign,—see cover & appendix, but never the foreign in puffing the American. The very reverse of this should be the practice. I agree with you as to the propriety of putting forth the two parts of Views & Reviews together, and will thank you to hurry the printing of Vol. 2.[52] Let me have the proofs 10 or 12 pages or more at a time that there may be no delay. Send them through the mail as periodical sheets. I will shortly forward you the residue having addressed myself on the reciept of your Letter to the article on Mathews which I am retouching, revising

---

[47] For the two series of sonnets accepted by John L. O'Sullivan for publication in the *Democratic Review,* see note 23, Jan. 10, 1846.

[48] An agreement was reached: sonnets signed by Simms appear regularly in the *Democratic Review* from June through Dec., 1846. Additional sonnets are in the numbers for May and June, 1847. *Yankee Doodle,* I (Nov. 7, 1846), 54, facetiously comments: "Mr. Simms, after an incredible labor, has produced another sonnet. It will appear in the next number of the Democratic Review."

[49] We can find no record of this series having been written.

[50] Bartlett and Welford.

[51] *Count Julian* was republished in London (see Trent, pp. 124, 341). We have been unable to locate a copy of this edition. For George Palmer Putnam, see note 244, June 25, 1845.

[52] The Second Series of *Views and Reviews* was issued both separately and bound with the First Series. Though both are dated 1845, the first was issued around May 1, 1846, the second in July, 1847. See note 284, Aug. 7, 1845.

&c.[53] This I propose to make the 3d. You have the 1st & 2d. already. What the residue shall be I have not yet decided, as I have several articles from which to choose, & cannot well conjecture the run of the preceding. I propose as soon as I can, to send you the MS. of Huguenots in Florida.[54] Will thank you accordingly to see & order for me at once from B & W. the copy of Hakluyt, upon which I somewhat depend. Hurry them with it & say to them that I do not recieve the publications of the Shakspeare Society — not one since last July or before it — the copy of the work I spoke to them of last summer as being in the country & which your brother had then, not yet having reached me. I will write to them also. — I propose to visit the North this summer at an earlier day than usual as I have to return in September. I shall then endeavour to show to Wiley what I concieve to be the defect & the error in his plans of publication, and how the domestic author suffers. I have some views of the subject for you also. Cheever's books, by the way, are, in my notion, the least likely to attract out of his own parish, of all the collection. His Jungfrau is a most tedious piece of declamation throughout — and that too a commonplace declamation without the slightest particle of freshness. Headley's books are very far superior though less studied & elaborate performances.[55]—Griswold I have seen in Charleston. He preaches there occasionally — appointed to visit me at the plantation but failed to come. I have had some serious talk with him. Between himself & Mathews, Col. Summer of the "Carolinian" has been moved to attack him very savagely & *morally*.[56] I have written to Summer about it & hope to set things

---

[53] Simms' "Writings of Cornelius Mathews" was first published in the *Southern Quarterly Review* (see note 85, Feb. 11, 1845). The revised article was published as "The Humourous in American and British Literature," *Views and Reviews,* Second Series, pp. 142-184.

[54] *The Lily and the Totem, or, the Huguenots in Florida* did not appear as part of Wiley and Putnam's "Library of American Books": it was published in 1850 by Baker and Scribner.

[55] As part of the "Library of American Books" Wiley and Putnam had published George Barrell Cheever's *The Pilgrim in the Shadow of the Jungfrau* and *Wanderings of a Pilgrim in the Shadow of Mont Blanc.* Joel Tyler Headley's *Letters from Italy* and *The Alps and the Rhine* also form part of this "Library."

[56] We have been unable to locate copies of the issues of the *South Carolinian* for this period. Adam Geiselhardt Summer (1818-1866), lawyer, agriculturist, and editor, was admitted to the bar in 1840 and practiced law at Newberry, S. C. Soon afterwards he moved to Columbia and edited the *South Carolinian* (see note 358, Nov. 24, 1845). In 1850 he was elected from Lexington District to the South Carolina House of Representatives. In 1857 he moved to Florida. He served as brigade judge advocate during the Confederate War. Simms was a visitor at Pomaria, his plantation in Newberry District.

in proper train for explanation. The attack of a guest, just marrying into the State [57] is to us excessively awkward. I hear nothing
from Lawson or Mathews. I am about to prepare a notice of Big
Abel for Summer's 'Carolinian', at his request.[58] Has Lawson
really killed himself drinking Whiskey Punch. When does Jones's
Book appear.[59] Is it not something singular that the Dem. Rev.
has noticed none of my books for the last 18 months? [60] And what
of Colton? Does his Rev. continue? I never see it. Will he pay
$10 for a contribution of verse monthly.[61] Where stands your
neighbour the Knickerbocker now? When you write me run up
your score at length — let me know what is stirring in your
goodly city. And do tell me if there have been any assaults upon
the Wigwam & by whom. I should like to get the English notices
when they reach you.[62] They might be reprinted for the benefit of

---

[57] On Aug. 20, 1845, Griswold reluctantly married Charlotte Myers, of
Charleston. The marriage was never consummated, and they were divorced in
1852. See Bayless, *Rufus Wilmot Griswold,* pp. 103-113, 212-227.
   [58] See note 56, above.
   [59] This collection by William Alfred Jones was not published by Wiley and
Putnam: it later appeared as *Literary Studies, a Collection of Miscellaneous
Essays* (New York: E. Walker, 1847).
   [60] Simms erred. See note 40, Feb. 3, 1846.
   [61] No poem which can be attributed to Simms was published in the *American
[Whig] Review* during 1846.
   [62] The *New Monthly Magazine,* LXXV (Dec., 1845), 499, comments:
" 'The Wigwam and the Cabin' First Series . . . contains seven different
spirit-stirring tales, illustrative of border history in the southern states. The
life of the planter, the squatter, the Indian, and the negro, of the bold and
hardy pioneer, and of the vigorous yeoman, are given with a truthfulness that
leaves the namby-pamby imitations, extolled as Cooper-like in this country,
far, far, in the back-ground." The same journal, LXXVI (March, 1846),
377-378, further remarks that "the tales of 'The Wigwam and the Cabin' . . .
are full of profound and startling interest." The *Critic,* N. S., II (Nov. 22,
1845), 605, says that "The tales . . . are . . . written with a flowing pen,
never at a loss for words, and seldom for ideas. . . . The pictures of border
life are very vividly drawn; there is flesh and blood in the personages who
figure in them." Of the Second Series the same journal, N. S., III (Feb. 7,
1846), 149, comments: "They are faithful pictures of American life. . . .
Occasionally we light upon passages of really fine writing, full of eloquence
and poetry, and the descriptions of scenery are often extremely vivid. . . .
'Caloya, or the Loves of the Driver,' is the most original and the most interesting." The *Mirror of Literature, Amusement, and Instruction,* N. S., IX
(May 23, 1846), 334, remarks: "This is a very curious and interesting volume
of tales told with rough vigour, very characteristic of the subject. The first,
'The Giant's Coffin, or the Feud of Holt and Houston,' is a genuine border
narrative with all the terrible features which belong to such tales. 'Sergeant
Barnacle, or the Raftsman of the Edisto,' is perhaps as terrible a story as any
we ever read. It is painful in the extreme. . . . It is like a nightmare, but it
is good. 'Which is the Madman,' 'The Lazy Crow,' and 'Lucas de Ayllon,'
are clever, but 'Caloya, or the Loves of the Driver,' is a gem. We never
read a better told story, though it has faults referred to by the author himself." *Tait's Edinburgh Magazine,* XIII (April, 1846), 267, likewise comments favorably, but the *Spectator.* XIX (Feb. 21, 1846), 186-187, dissents:

American purchasers whom the costive terms of native Editors might discourage & mislead. If W & P. will but take the same pains with native books that are taken with foreign, the domestic author would be better satisfied to place himself in the harness.— Is Lester in New York? And what is he doing? How does his Series go?[63] I am sorry that you decline Adrian Beaufain:[64] I suppose discouraged by Poe's volume.[65] What of him? I am told that the B. J. is stopped fairly, and Excelsior & Heaven knows what besides.[66] What of all. Present me respectfully at home, to Mathews & the rest. Let me hear from you soon. I am kept alive here only by the letters of friends.

Yours Ever &c

Simms.

297: To Evert Augustus Duyckinck

Woodlands, Feb 20. 1846

My dear Duyckinck

I am in receipt of your letter covering that of Jones, and also of his complimentary notice in the Mirror.[67] I note, in the same

---

"The book possesses this peculiarity, that its matter is American; and, if derived from other books, they are not those of Europe. The tales, however, are not equal to some others we have read of a similar kind. The subjects are not pleasing, the treatment, though vigorous, is coarse; and the author leans too much to the physical and the extravagant."

[63] Charles Edwards Lester (1815-1890) was the editor for Paine and Burgess of the "Medici Series of Italian Prose." Simms reviewed the first three translations of this series and noticed the fourth in his *Southern and Western*, II (Nov., 1845), 357-359. In 1846 Paine and Burgess published Lester's *The Artist, the Merchant, and the Statesman, of the Age of the Medici, and of Our Own Times*, which Simms noticed in the above-mentioned review of the "Medici Series" (p. 359) and in the *Southern Patriot* for Jan. 20, 1846. In 1846, also, Baker and Scribner published Lester's *The Artists of America*.

[64] Simms was contemplating a volume (never published) to be entitled *The Poems of Adrian Beaufain*. See letter to Duyckinck of Feb. 20, 1846.

[65] In 1845 Wiley and Putnam published Poe's *The Raven and Other Poems* as No. 8 of their "Library of American Books."

[66] The *Broadway Journal* ceased publication with the issue of Jan. 3, 1846. For *Excelsior*, see note 15, Jan. 17, 1846.

[67] This letter from William Alfred Jones has not been located. He again wrote Simms on April 28: "I recd your brochure [*Grouped Thoughts and Scattered Fancies*]. . . . The Songs of the land are so full of the lyrical spirit of the South and of the Spring, that it seems so discourteous to attempt a criticism, as it would be to analyze the soft airs and delightful verdure of this charming season. . . . Also, glance your eye on Southern and Western Stories ["Tales of the South and West," *Dem. Rev.*, XVIII (June, 1846), 471-476], where I have a brief criticism of the Wigwam & Cabin." (Original in the New York Public Library.) In his notice of *The Wigwam and the Cabin*

Journal, your semi-political article as very judicious, and have read with pleasure your notice of Life in California, — a book which I shall be curious to read.[68] For all of these favors I am grateful. I will write Jones at the first leisure moment. I have just sent him a no. of the Mage. which he expressed a wish for. I have also sent to Mathews & yourself a notice of his 'poem on Man,'[69] though no copy of the work has been sent me. What will Mr. Fuller give for a weekly letter from South Carolina, which shall be of somewhat better staple than such things ordinarily are? He is fortunate in being rid of Morris & Willis — the former certainly, who is quite *passée* and never was good for anything.[70] — I am now busy on the fourth or fifth article for Vol. 2, of Views & Reviews. It is a group from Rev. Hist. — in which Arnold and

---

in the New York *Evening Mirror* of Feb. 5 (reprinted in the *Weekly Mirror*, III [Feb. 14], 304) Jones says: "This second part of Mr. Simms' collected tales, admirably faithful, spirited, and characteristic as they are, is not, however, quite equal to the first in variety and spirit. . . . In even the largest notice which a daily journal could allow to the productions of any modern author, it would be impossible to do full justice to the talents of Mr. Simms, as an author, the essential value of his productions, and his personal character, as one of the best specimens of the genuine Carolinian." Jones then lists "the more striking features of his romantic Muse and the general complexion of his writings. A certain manliness of style in the selection of subjects, and in the bearing of his favorite characters; a purity and precision of language, with general power of style, truly English and without a particle of the affectation of mere fine writing, which would only disturb the conduct of the narration, and really injure the interest of his legends and prose romances; the absence of cant, and a total freedom from the vicious and petty tricks, whether of artistic manner or of a more personal character, that common writers employ to catch attention." Simms is then compared with other writers of fiction: "Simms and Hawthorne, are among the best tale writers not only of this country, but, as we are inclined to think, the foremost among living English writers, in this department. The southron (the best man by far, as to authorship south of New York, and in his walk, unequalled throughout the country) has much skill in the arts of the romances. . . . His serious writing, whether critical or in his fiction, like that of the best writers, is his best. His lighter talent is not perceptible, though he is not wanting in that. The highest order of imagination, that of the poet or dramatist, of the first class, does not, we apprehend, belong to Mr. Simms, but the domestic, more literal, imagination of the novelist of real life, we think is his, in an eminent degree. The imagination of such a writer as Fielding, is of a lower class than that of Mr. Simms' best efforts, which come nearer to the most powerful works of Cooper and Godwin; though for general power, we place Mr. Simms above either."

[68] Duyckinck's review of *Life in California* appears in the New York *Evening Mirror* of Feb. 11 and Feb. 12. The semi-political article may be "Peace and War" (Feb. 12) or "Capital Punishment" (Feb. 10, 11, and 17).

[69] In the *Southern Patriot* of Feb. 16, 1846, Simms writes of Mathews' *Man in the Republic*, published by Paine and Burgess (a reprint of *Poems on Man, in His Various Aspects under the American Republic* [New York: Wiley and Putnam, 1843]?), that "the writer relies rather upon the strength than the smoothness of his verses — rather upon the thought than the sentiment."

[70] Hiram Fuller, George Pope Morris, and Nathaniel Parker Willis edited the New York *Mirror* during 1844-1845. Fuller was sole editor from 1845 to 1857.

André, Washington & Miss Seward, figure, — an art. based on a paper in my Mage. It concludes with notice of a dram. fragment by Calvert on Arnold, and with a Dram. fragmt. of my own on the same subject, — with passing criticism & opinion. I propose, if there be room, to wind up with a notice of the case of Hayne of Carolina executed by Lord Rawdon — and of Gen. Williamson of the same State who played Arnold here after a fashion.[71] I have one or two other suitable articles, all American, for the same vol. should they be necessary to the required pages. I do not know that there will be any use in doing any thing as yet upon the "Huguenots," for your series comes forth with such angelic pauses between that they will scarcely be needed before next Christmas. I think already, I have burdened you with commissions, but there are yet a few, which, at your leisure, it may suit you to attend to. I shall have ready to go to press when I visit N. Y. next summer, a volume entitled "Lays of Apalachia" — being "Legends & traditions in verse ["] — some 15 stories of 15 or 20 pages each like my Pocahontas. For these I wish a publisher.[72] With good engravings, they would make a famous Christmas volume. I propose also a third vol. of Tales, but not of a domestic character; [73] and I have a third vol. of articles, which I call "Miscellanies in Literature and Criticism." [74] It is my desire also, (unless I publish the "Lays of Apalachia" [)], to include these in a complete collection, in one vol. of my poetical writings— with portrait &c. The poems of Adrian Beaufain — too, might tempt some publisher, particularly as an edition may be had for

---

[71] Article III of *Views and Reviews,* Second Series, is entitled "The Case of Major Andre," pp. 101-122. The published version is considerably different from that proposed here: it contains neither Calvert's dramatic fragment nor Simms' own dramatic fragment. It is based on Simms' "The Case of Major Andre. — Miss Seward and Her Writings," *Southern and Western,* II (July, 1845), 33-42. The articles on Hayne and Lord Rawdon and on General Williamson are not included in *Views and Reviews.*

[72] See note 43, Feb. 3, 1846.

[73] The never published volume of tales of the imagination. See note 17, Jan. 7, 1846.

[74] This collection was never published. On Aug. 30, 1845, the *Broadway Journal,* II, 126, had announced (apparently before Wiley and Putnam decided to publish *Views and Reviews*) that "Messrs Burges & James, of Charleston, S. C., . . . propose . . . to issue 'A Selection of Miscellanies in Criticism and Literature, by William Gilmore Simms' — in three handsome volumes duodecimo." Presumably Simms (who was in New York at the time and doubtless gave this information to Poe) originally planned three volumes of articles, but wisely approached Wiley and Putnam with only two. He must also have been considering Burges and James in case Wiley and Putnam refused to publish the work.

fifty copies.[75] Now, if you can, without suffering your variety to
be suspected, manage to negotiate for one or other of these with
one or other of your publishers you will materially oblige me.
Lawson's business is such as does not allow him to leave his office.
There are Paine & Burgess; Gates & Stedman; Redfield &c, who
may be treated with. With Harper & B. Langley &c. I will treat
in all probability for other matters when I come on. — I could
wish to see what the British critics say of our tales.[76] Can you
send me any of them. Any of their favorable notices might be
paraded before our blind public on the publication of the 2d. volume. Had your publishers given us any encouragement, I should
have got up an original thing, anonymous, to make a sensation.
But *cui bono*? Write me also how the stories sell and have sold.
It seems to me that an American vol. might be published weekly
with success. Cheever's books do not strike me favorable.[77] This
inter nos. They are crowded with examples of false eloquence —
a straining after the fine — stately, declamatory, not at all descriptive, and very monotonous. Yet, as they are moral & inoffensive, nobody finds fault. But does he sell? — except to his congregation? If, when I come on, we can get Mr. Wiley to a con-
fabulation, I think I can suggest a new *modus operandi* for a
fresh series, which may do something. Write me soon & all the
news. I get nothing here & am in bad spirits — tired & very
desponding. The world is growing very tedious.

Yours very truly &c

W. Gilmore Simms

E. A. Duyckinck Esq.

298: To James Lawson

Woodlands, Feb. 20. [1846] [78]

My dear Lawson.

    As Christina still seems to continue ill, I will make one more
suggestion: Our Spring will soon be here, and with it are frequent opportunities for securing an escort for ladies. If your wife
will bring her on to us, and stay with us till the last of May, I

---

[75] See note 64, Feb. 9, 1846.
[76] See note 62, Feb. 9, 1846.
[77] See note 55, Feb. 9, 1846.
[78] Dated by Simms' reference to taking Mrs. Simms to Charleston to see
the Keans. See letter to Lawson of Jan. 7.

will myself bring her on in June by any route you think proper, sea or land. It is perfectly safe in Carolina until August and September, and usually safe enough even then. A trip across the water, temporary change of climate, and the genial influences of our Spring months will do wonders for both Lyde & the child. The expense will be only going & coming and that is a trifle. There will be none after her landing in Carolina. Do not suffer any calculations, short of the absolutely unavoidable, to make you hesitate, if it is thought that Christina's health may benefit by the change. — In sending you commissions to execute, you should know I refer them wholly to your leisure. They are none of them of an impatient order. But I have taken your suggestion, and have written to E. A. D. on the subject.[79] He will confer with you. — I rejoice to hear that the 'Palazzo' is so near its finish. I am only afraid that when your wife gets fairly into it she will hardly be willing to know "puir bodies." Whether my folks will ever see her, or it, in their united glories is a question. It is not likely that any of our folks, beside myself, can leave home this summer; I may probably come on early, as I am compelled to return by October on business. I am sorry to tell you that my dullness & low spirits still continue. Constant drudgery, and a conciousness that in Literature we are fighting against all sorts of evil influences, are doing their work upon my moods & mind. I despond now more frequently than usual, and feel a sense of weariness in my progress which I never felt before. My longing is for sleep — a long repose — a calm — respite and relief of a sort equally indescribable, yet present to my desires & imagination. The business of the mission is in *statu quo*; and I am not the man to urge it. I cannot be an office seeker if I would. — Philosophy *has* done much for me & with me — but cannot do all. — Street's book, Ogden's address & the other matters you speak of, do not reach me yet. I suspect they are drowsing on W & P.'s counter.[80] It is surprising how neglectful these booksellers are. I hear nothing from Mathews. I wrote him briefly from Columbia, being hurried & being of opinion that it was his duty to have explicitly regretted his conduct, — and I suppose my

---

[79] See letter to Duyckinck of Feb. 20.

[80] For Ogden's address and Street's book, see letter to Lawson of Jan. 7, 1846. Apparently they were to be sent to Simms in a package from Wiley and Putnam.

brevity piqued him.[81] Well! — Gilmore has been puny — is probably troubled with worms — has been feverish and is still fretful.
The baby is also — slightly ill at ease. Otherwise we are all doing
well. I took my wife to town for a week, some ten days or more
ago, where we saw the Keans with a great deal of pleasure.[82]
She (my wife) is thin, but not complaining. I should like to have
had your wife with her at our little theater. This is Race Week
in Charleston,[83] and were she with us, I should be there. As it is
I am too dull for it, and shall mope here over my desk & papers.
Yet I am doing little or nothing — nothing that I could wish to
do. — I do not think that there is any prospect of war — I never
have thought so. But your Whigs are never satisfied without a
panic, and all the Evils of your Merchants come from their own
imaginings. If they gave themselves no trouble about politics,
politics would scarcely ever trouble them. The truth is Polk knows
what he is after, and the Oregon matter will be settled without
loss to us, and without disturbing John Bull's equanimity. — But,
I am too dull to inflict my torpor upon you. Kiss the wife & children on my account & hold me

Ever truly Yours &c.

Simms.

299: To CAREY AND HART

Woodlands, Feb 27. 1846

Gentn.

Let me bring to your knowledge my friend, Mr. John Russell,
who is on his way to establish a personal and business intercourse
with the publishers. He is about to establish for himself, having
been for several years the chief clerk in the establishment of our
friend Saml. Hart. Mr. R. is an old acquaintance & friend of
mine though not an old man. He begins auspiciously & according
to his deserts, which are worthy of the best friends hopes—with
a cash Capital, and the countenance of many of our best men,

---

[81] At this time Mathews' attitude toward Simms was cool because of Simms'
frank reviews of his work. Also Mathews appears to have felt that he had
received some personal affront from Simms. See letter to Lawson of Nov.
3, 1845.

[82] See note 5, Jan. 7, 1846.

[83] The carnival of the year in Charleston was "Race Week," always held
in February. Business was practically suspended, planters and their wives
flocked to the city, a dinner was given on Wednesday, and a formal dance was
held on Friday.

literary & professional. Perhaps, no person in our State is more highly competent to, or more familiar with, the business than himself. Personally & considerably acquainted with books, he knows something about selling them & is highly popular in the bargain. That this introduction will ripen into a permanent personal & business intercourse between you, is the sincere desire of Yrs

Very truly as Ever

W. Gilmore Simms

Mess'rs Carey & Hart, Phila.

300: To EVERT AUGUSTUS DUYCKINCK

Woodlands, March 17 [1846] [84]

Evert A. Duyckinck Esq.

Dear Sir

I put up for you and left with a friend in Charleston, some two weeks ago, the articles intended for the second Vol. of Views & Reviews, in addition to those sent on a previous occasion. These, the 3d. & 4th. were the paper on the writings of our friend Mathews, and a paper entitled "A Group from Revolutionary History," being the case of Arnold and Andre elaborated from an article which you may remember to have seen in my Magazine. The whole of this paper was not sent, as I did not succeed in copying it out in time for the packet. The residue will be sent by an early opportunity, and I trust that the parts already forwarded & those to be yet despatched will reach you in due season. I could wish that Vol 2. should be put to press as soon as possible. The two volumes might be got in readiness to be issued by the first of May or June. And as the proofs are to be sent me, it will need some time for carrying the work through the press. In sending proofs let me beg that two impressions of each sheet should be always sent, but by different mails, in order that we may have a chance in reserve against failure. I have found this plan the only safe and proper one in reading the proofs of other works. It may be that the 2d. Vol. of Reviews will need a greater number of articles. I hope it may and am prepared to furnish them; but I can only judge of the necessity by seeing how the

---

[84] Dated by Simms' references to the contents of *Views and Reviews,* Second Series. See letters to Duyckinck of Feb. 9 and Feb. 20.

first two articles will run. You will see by the fourth that I have incorporated into the article the rough sketch of a tragedy on the subject of Arnold, which may have the effect of giving a greater life and variety to the volume. Should more matter be necessary I propose to furnish a similar group from History in the Case of Col. Hayne of So. Ca. executed by Lord Rawdon as a spy. These two articles will be wholly new to the public, and for that matter the whole two volumes will be thoroughly new to all the country a very small section excepted. But, it appears to me, properly to carry on the American Series, there should be some special inducement held out to authorship. I wrote recently to W. & P suggesting to them an American Tale of Christmas, for which I have the scheme of a very pretty story.[85] You will probably be consulted in the matter. It is my present purpose to visit New York at a somewhat earlier period this summer than usual. I hope to be there on the 4th. July, when I propose to talk with you at some length with regard to future operations. I have not heard from you for a long season, nor from Lawson for a longer, nor from Mathews for an eternity. Nor do I see that you are over busy. The operations of W & P. do not seem so large or so rapid as formerly. Did you receive a notice of Poe's & Headley's Vols. that I sent you, — and of other things?[86] Where is Poe now & what doing. I percieve that P. Benjamin has come down with a savage assault upon Lester, charging him with downright misrepresentations of Powers the Sculptor.[87] What says our Italian friend[88] to that? I suppose you have looked into Count Julian, which is more than I have done, for the excellent publisher has sent me not a single copy; — not a single copy has been sent to any of our Southern Editors, and the publication has been made a sort of monopoly by one only of the trading book establishments of Charleston.[89] Who are Gates & Stedman, and there are some other

---

[85] "Maize in Milk" (see note 151, Aug. 8, 1846). Simms used Woodlands as a model for the scene of this story.

[86] Simms published a long and favorable review of *The Raven and Other Poems* in the *Southern Patriot* of March 2. *The Alps and the Rhine* is reviewed in the issue of March 5.

[87] Charles Edwards Lester had recently published a biography of Hiram Powers (1805-1873), the sculptor. The *Western Continent,* edited by Park Benjamin, had published a letter from Powers denying the authenticity of the work. Lester's reply, containing letters from Powers, appears in the New York *Evening Mirror* of April 16.

[88] Lester was United States consul at Genoa during 1842-1847.

[89] On March 6, 1846, the following notice appeared in the *Southern Patriot*: "'Count Julian; or the Last Days of the Goth' . . . may be found at Mr. Head's."

new publishers in the hands of Lester, Baker & Scribner, — who
are these. Can't you give me a scribble of odds & ends & *on dits.*
By the way, Griswold lectures tonight in Charleston before a
Mercantile Association.[90] He proposed to visit me not long ago.
I sent the carriage for him, but he failed — *but I hear of him.*
Let me hear from you soon & believe me

very truly &c

W. Gilmore Simms

301: To James Lawson

Woodlands, March 17. [1846] [91]

Dear Lawson

Yesterday was Gilmore's Birthday & having brought up some
fireworks, we had quite a display in honor of the event. I thought
of you and Jimmy Junior, and of the additional pleasure we should
have had with you and him, the girls and your vexatious woman
of a wife with us to enjoy the fun. And then again the suggestion
forced itself upon me that probably some of you were sick or
suffering. There was scarcely any way to account for your long
silence. One fear has disquieted me particularly — that your company has been losing by these terrible disasters on the sea. I certainly hope not, at least to any extent, on your account if none
other. Of course, I do not wish to obtrude myself upon your cares
at a moment when you may have no time to spare, answering idle
questions, — but it will relieve a real anxiety to hear from you
that all is well & happy in your little family, and all prosperous
in your Company. — Here, we have not been so well. I myself
have been & am an invalid — though as you see, I cling to my
daily toils at which I look suddenly to be seized by the mortal
enemy of the race. I take too little exercise and am likely to pay
the penalty for it. I am troubled with Nausea, with vertigo, languor, indigestion, — and worst of all, that general distaste to the
usual subjects of employment and survey which denotes a ma-

---

[90] The *Southern Patriot* of March 18, 1846, comments: "We were one of a
small audience listening to this gentleman last evening, at Temperance Hall,
'On the condition and prospects of Literature and the fine arts in the United
States.' . . . [Griswold] handled his subject ably, and showed that he was
entirely at home upon it."

[91] Dated by Simms' reference to *Areytos: or, Songs of the South* (Charleston: John Russell, 1846) being "in press." For notices of this volume, see note
123, May 15, 1846.

chine entirely & unequally overworked. But I must dree my destiny. I am very weary of it — very discontent with what I am,
and the prospect before me. I do *not see the opening,* and am
impatient of the denial and the drudgery for which there are no
fruits. Well! In God's own time I suppose, — but the waste of
the nervous energy is becoming too great for the supply. Enough,
in this respect. My indispositions have interfered with my labors,
but I have begun a notice of Streets book which has at length
reached me, and I shall pen one also of Mr. Ogden's. By the way
send me another copy of the latter. You may have recieved a brief
notice of the 'address' in a 'Southern Patriot' which I sent you.[92]
I have in press a little vol. of 'Songs of the South' which I will
send you shortly — particularly that you may wed one of them
to *immortal harmonies.* Some of them may persuade Margaret
Sinclair to the full completion of one effort. I have included one
song simply because she made a beginning upon it. — In the
book way I get precious little here. Count Julian is out, but the
publishers have not sent me a single copy, nor one to any Editor
in the State. Have you permitted yourself time to read it, or has
Lady Lyde. I should sooner have her opinion of it than yours, —
though I doubt if it pleases either. One friend, however, tells me
that it is one of my best. This really provoked me to laughter, for
you know what I think of it. But one portion of it really satisfies
me, & that is the delineation of the processes by which the fanati-
cal priest is acted upon. Of the second part of the Wigwam I hope
better things, though I do not look to have justice done to that
collection in this country, — not this season at least.[93] You say
not a word to me about my Sonnets,[94] some of which, but — I
won't say it. And what is likely to be done with the collection of
Tales in your hands.[95] I see that B. & S. announce Castle Dismal
& Helen Halsey anew — are these new editions.[96] And how gets

---

[92] Simms' review of Street's *Poems* was published in the *Southern Patriot*
of April 22. We have been unable to locate either the notice or the review
of Ogden's address (see note 13, Jan. 7, 1846), probably published in issues
missing from the file at the Charleston Library Society.

[93] For American reviews of *The Wigwam and the Cabin,* see notes 317,
Oct. 19, 1845; 67, Feb. 20, 1846; 205, Oct. 24, 1846; and 249, Nov. 19, 1846.
The First Series is also reviewed in the *American [Whig] Review,* II (Nov.,
1845), 545-546; in *S. L. M.,* XI (Nov., 1845), 701; and in the New York
Morning News of Oct. 2, 1845.

[94] *Grouped Thoughts and Scattered Fancies.*

[95] The never published collection of tales of the imagination.

[96] No editions of these works issued in 1846 are recorded. See note 42,
Feb. 3, 1846.

on the Palazzo. I am half afraid that it is this commanding interest
which makes you & your wife forgetful of us. Will you know a
body when you are in 12th. St? Will you give us an obolus *en
passant?* Do let me hear from you & believe me Ever truly

as Ever Yours & Yours

Simms.

302: To Alfred Billings Street

Woodlands, March 17 [1846][97]

Alfred B. Street Esq.

My dear Sir

I got your friendly Letter a few days ago. Your volume had
reached me in safety during the preceding week, — and a very
pretty volume it is. Your publishers deserve credit and I hope
will recieve cash along with it.[98] Could my wishes or efforts avail
you will both recieve them. It was my purpose to have noticed
your volume before I recieved it, and on the simple intimation of
its coming. On examination the resolve was renewed, the more
particularly as I felt that I could do so with safety & propriety.[99]
I percieve that you have attended to some of my suggestions. I
only wish that I had been by you to have counselled others. But
these will be the work of time. That you are willing to amend —
that you are not absolutely sure that you are already perfect is
the fortunate thing in your favor. That being the case, amendment is not only inevitable but easy. As for writing no more, —
and this being your last volume, permit me to say that this is
all out of the question. The power is too decided in your case, the
faculty, the endowment — ever to allow you to give it up, —
and I fancy the taste, the passion for its exercise are already too
much confirmed by practise & experience to suffer you willingly
to do so. Besides, Sir, no conscientious man can honestly forego
the exercise of his endowments. They were given for this purpose, and are to be persevered in honestly & tenaciously, even at

---

[97] Dated by Simms' reference to *Grouped Thoughts and Scattered Fancies.*
See letter to Street of Feb. 1.

[98] *The Poems of Alfred B. Street.* The *Knick.,* XXVII (Jan., 1846), 93,
also comments on the beauty of this volume issued by Clark and Austin:
"[Street's] . . . new and beautifully printed and illustrated volume we have
great pleasure in cordially commending to our readers."

[99] See letter to Street of Feb. 1. 1846.

some sacrifice. Of course, other duties are to be performed. You must not be infidel enough to neglect your family, but this considered the duty of giving employment to the decided mental attributes of the individual, I hold to be as clearly written as any of the recognized laws of God. — And it is in your power to succeed. Hitherto, you have indulged in poetry as an aside. But it is to be made a study, and to be prosecuted as an art. You have caught up your subjects, from external rather than innate suggestions & hence their want of moral & purely descriptive characteristics. Try the former in connection with the latter, as Bryant does, as is done by Wordsworth, by Thompson &c. But study Milton — go through a course of the old blood & bone & sinew dramatists of the Shakspeare period, — and, — but this is not the place, nor did I set out now to counsel. I hope to see you in N. Y. next summer, & to talk with you over this matter. I am glad you like my Sonnets. You see how precious little descriptive they are. But this is my demerit. I am deficient just where you are strong. These things have been growing upon me from boyhood — the fruit of the occasion, the bud & blossom of the hour, the issue of the pregnant impulse, the pleasure or the pain. They form but a third or little more, of a collection, many of which have never been in print. My life has been one of letters wholly. I have written half of my days without knowing it, and things accumulate on my hands without my knowing it. I suppose, though I have published numerous vols. of verse that I have quite as many on hand that the world has never seen. Whether they will ever see them is a question. — It will give me pleasure to hear from you, and as leisure serves, I shall be pleased to say to you what skies we have in Carolina, and what is the promise of our fields. We are just now planting corn & potatoes — our wheat and rye are green beneath our windows. Spring is already before us, full bosomed & affluent, and the voice of the turtle is beginning to be heard in the land.[100] May you soon be happy in her presence & her smiles.

Yours &c

W. Gilmore Simms

---

[100] Song of Solomon, 2:12.

303: To Evert Augustus Duyckinck

Woodlands, March 27. [1846] [101]

My dear Duyckinck.

I have been a little disquieted by two items in the a/c. just re-cieved with W & P. In the first place I am charged with a dozen copies of W & C which I think unusual. H & B.—L & B.—C & H.—J & H. G. L.[102] and other publishers with whom I have dealt never made a charge for copies to the author — certainly not to me, and I generally got from them as many as I wished. — Next: I find myself charged with the copy of Catlin's Indian Portfolio [103] which was loaned me for examination while I was in N.Y. and which, when I was leaving I requested some one of the Gentle-men who attended in the store of W & P. to send for, — which he promised promptly & frankly to do. The vol. was carefully folded up and J. L. had instructions to deliver it, and my present impression is that it was delivered either the day or the night be-fore I left the city. If not, it is still in Lawson's keeping, and if not, it was I am very sure delivered. I think it likely, upon reflec-tion, that Mr. W. or some of his Gentn. will remember my speak-ing on the subject. Will you do me the favor to see to this matter. I have no doubt that Mr. Lawson will remember all about it. It will be a serious matter to pay for the thing I do not want, & have not got, out of the small returns of W & C.—Again, I find the following items

$\left\{\begin{array}{l} 250 \text{ sheets to London} \\ 150 \text{ on hand there 1 Jan.} \\ \overline{} \\ 50 \text{ sold} \end{array}\right.$ .... @ 6 ....$3.00.

Is this good arithmetic. I should state the balance sold at 100—but calculate for yourself. I note also that $1.50 is charged for Copyright. In all the a/cs. which I recieved the charge made for securing Copyright has never been above $1. — but this of $1.50 may be for both parts. You can enquire into this without suffering it to be supposed that I have noted it. It may be that

---

[101] Dated by Simms' reference to the material for *Views and Reviews,* Second Series. See letters to Duyckinck of Feb. 9, Feb. 20, and March 17.

[102] Simms is here referring to Wiley and Putnam, *The Wigwam and the Cabin,* Harper and Brothers, Lea and Blanchard, Carey and Hart, and J. and H. G. Langley.

[103] George Catlin (1796-1872), ethnologist and portrait painter, was the author of *Catlin's North American Portfolio* (New York: J. Ackerman, 1845), the work which Simms here calls "Indian Portfolio."

the fees of the clerk have been increased. Of course there is a fee bill, of which Counsellor Cornelius [104] can give you all the details. And, I would not have you allow Mr. Wiley to suppose that I complain of anything. I fancy that inadvertence, forgetfulness, the haste or the mistake of a clerk, will account for all these matters. — I have just placed in the hands of a book-seller in Charleston, the closing portions of the article, No 4 for second vol. of V & R. on the case of André. — I could wish that this vol. should be put to press at once & that as soon as ready both vols. should be launched together on the doubtful seas of popular favor. My own impressions are favorable to their success. I believe they contain much that is original and much that is interesting. Another article will be ready, should the vol. need it. But this can only be told while the vol. is going through the press. I must insist that you send me the proofsheets, for my scrawl in many parts of the M.S. will be hardly intelligible to the printers. — I perfectly concur in the force & propriety of the reasons which you give for not acting for me with the publishers. I will keep the matter over till I come on. Herman Melville recieved but not yet read.[105] — I feel gladdened to find myself well remembered by such congenial spirits over the good spirits of Jemmy Lawson. If he has got Mathews to the bowl, he will do wonders with him. By the way, I send a notice of Mathews — a very scorcher! — to be published Editorially in the Columbia Carolinian.[106] I have seen enow of the controversy between P B & C. E. L.[107] to satisfy me. By the way, has the Knickerbocker been saying any dirty thing about me lately? I suspect it, as,

---

[104] Cornelius Mathews.

[105] A brief notice of the publication of *Typee: A Peep at Polynesian Life* (New York: Wiley and Putnam, 1846) appears in the *Southern Patriot* of April 9, 1846. Later, in the *Southern Patriot* of April 25, Simms comments: "Typee . . . is a very curious and interesting narrative of savage life, and well deserving perusal. It reminds us of those delightful volumes of our boyhood, the voyages of Cook, Carteret, Byron and Anson, over the plates and pages of which we so loved to linger. The residence at Typee lacks nothing but the plates to be as attractive as either of these voyages. The scenes, the circumstances, are quite as fresh, and the regions of the world in which they occur are still quite as novel and unexplored as the day of their first discovery by the voyagers of Europe. We have every reason to believe that Mr. Melville is a veracious chronicler though it must be confessed he tells a very strange and romantic story."

[106] Copies of the issues of the *South Carolinian* for this period have not been located.

[107] Park Benjamin and Charles Edwards Lester. See Note 87, March 17, 1846.

for the last two months, they have stopped sending it.[108] — Griswold has been delivering a Lecture upon American Literature in Charleston — was exceedingly mortified, I am told, in an exceedingly small audience.[109] — I percieved, looking over the Retrospective, or Censura Lit. that Beckford, author of Vathek published when a young man, — a collection of Imaginative Biographies — of painters — a work stated to be worthy of his reputation. That should be procured, if possible, for your Library.[110]— Your hints with regard to Poe, the Ladies, Billet doux &c quite provoke my curiosity. What is the mischief — who the victims &c. *Entre nous,* I half suspected that mischief would grow out of all those fine critical discriminations &c. It is dangerous to the poetess when the critic teaches her the use of spondees, and trochaics, dactyls, trimeters & dimeters.[111] But, I wait tidings and will hush conjecture. Let me hear from you soon. Have you read Ct. Julian? Present me respectfully at home and to Friends. Say to Jones that I have his essays & Letters & have written to Minor.[112] But I am interrupted by a party of visitors to dinner —

So God bless you &c.

W. G. S.

304: To John Pendleton Kennedy [113]

Woodlands, April 9, 1846

Hon. J. P. Kennedy

My dear Sir

I could have wished to use your name in connection with some more fortunately concieved work than that in which it appears,

---

[108] The *Knick.,* XXVII (March, 1846), 273-274, continues its discussion of Simms' "Writings of Cornelius Mathews" and Jones' criticism of the article (see note 319, Oct. 19, 1845). It is further continued in a review of *Count Julian,* XXVII (April, 1846), 354-359.

[109] See note 90, March 17, 1846.

[110] We can find no record of an edition of William Beckford's *Biographical Memoirs of Extraordinary Painters* being published by Wiley and Putnam.

[111] Undoubtedly Simms is here alluding to gossip of Poe's relations with Mrs. Frances Sargent Osgood and Mrs. Elizabeth F. Ellet. See Bayless, *Rufus Wilmot Griswold,* pp. 139-142.

[112] These are probably essays in manuscript (with accompanying letters to Simms), which William Alfred Jones had asked Simms to read and submit to Benjamin Blake Minor, editor of the *Southern Literary Messenger.* No essays by Jones, however, were published in the *Messenger* during 1846 or 1847.

[113] See introductory sketch. This letter is in reply to Kennedy's of March 18 (reproduced in facsimile in Ernest E. Leisy's edition of *Horse-Shoe Robinson* [New York: American Book Company, (1937)]), thanking Simms for his dedi-

had it not been that I was anxious to guard myself against disappointment, and to be sure of doing that which has long been the object of my desire. In my dedication I have dealt frankly with yourself & the public.[114] Count Julian is very far from satisfying me now that it is written. That it did satisfy me, *when* it was written, I cannot deny. I need not say to you with what doubt & disappointment we are apt to look back, after the lapse of a few years, on what has been the favorite achievement of our youth. Still less need I say to you in what particulars Ct. Julian fails. But an author's writings are always useful — even when abortive as works of art—to those who would study his career & properly analyze his endowments; and I was not absolutely sure that my own progress had been such as to render my present judgments any more valuable than my past. But the value of my tribute to your worth & genius, 'does not, fortunately, depend upon the intrinsic value of the thing proffered. As the honest expression of my thought & feeling, the tribute has an independent value which can lose nothing by the awards of criticism. Still, I trust, that its perusal will give pleasure to yourself and others. Perhaps, it might be well to read it in connection with "Pelayo" — a work of which it is the sequel. This will afford some idea of the inherent difficulties & *improprieties* of my plan.

I am just in receipt of your pamphlet on William Thom [115]— sent to the Editor of the Southern Patriot of Charleston. You are probably not aware that the literary notices in that journal, are most generally written by myself. — It was in its columns

---

cation of *Count Julian.* Kennedy remarks: "I am no better than a laggard in the glorious path where you have become a leader, yet still have enough of the esprit de corps about me to take pleasure in the contemplation of your distinguished career. You may always count upon me as one to vindicate your claim to the high reputation you have earned in the literature of our country; and, if nothing more, you will, at least, find me a good bottle-holder whenever you may have occasion to enter the ring."

[114] In his damning review of *Count Julian* in the *Knick.,* XXVII (April, 1846), 354-359, Clark is particularly caustic in his comments on Simms' dedication to Kennedy (pp. 356-357): "Being not over-well versed in scientific matters, we would not assert, as a friend at our elbow has just affirmed, that 'No one can read one of Mr. Simms' essays, wherein he takes occasion to allude to himself, without thinking that he would become 'a burning and a shining light' if somebody could contrive to set fire to his gas;' yet we may well assume that a better specimen of his peculiar brilliancy in this kind could hardly be found than in the dedication of 'Count Julian' 'to the Hon. John P. Kennedy, of Baltimore, Maryland.'"

[115] Simms reviewed *Some Passages in the Life of William Thom: A Lecture Delivered February 4, 1846, before the Asbury Sabbath School* ([n. p.], 1846) in the *Southern Patriot* of May 23. The *Patriot* prints "Thorn" instead of "Thom."

that I acknowledged the Lecture on Calvert,[116] which you were so good to send me.

Did you get from me a small collection of "Sonnets." [117] It is my conviction that I addressed you a copy, — but I can provide you another should the first have failed you.

Very faithfully
yours &c.

W. Gilmore Simms

305: To James Lawson .

Woodlands, May 15 [1846] [118]

My dear Lawson

In ten days more we proceed to the city, so that if you write me after the reciept of this, you will address me in that quarter. I have thought for some time of scribbling to you, though I fancy you are heartily tired of the unequal game between us, as I subject you thrice or more frequently to the post office levy, to every sheet which I get from you. On the first of May I thought of you, your *little* wife, and *large* palace. I fancied I could see the joy & tribulation (mixed) which naturally come with the toils of moving, and the delights of moving into one's own wigwam. I take for granted you are now in twelfth Street, where I am not sure that your [wife] wants to see me at all. I begin to fear from certain items which have reached me that she has repudiated me as her favorite, & set up that false God, Cornelius Mathews in my place. If so, tell her that my ghost will haunt her for she will assuredly have been the cause of my death. That you are safely and comfortably housed, I suppose to be beyond doubt or question, and I sincerely & fervently hope, my dear Lawson, that your dwelling may long be the abode of peace & happiness. I wish it were in my power to contribute to these results in proportion to your deserts & my desires. — I presume that you have been kept exceedingly busy between your public & private affairs, and do

---

[116] Simms reviewed Kennedy's *Discourse on the Life and Character of George Calvert, the First Lord Baltimore* (Baltimore: J. Murphy, 1845) in the issue of March 10, 1846. In it he speaks of Kennedy as "one of our most accomplished authors and orators."

[117] *Grouped Thoughts and Scattered Fancies.*

[118] Dated by Simms' reference to having sent Lawson a copy of *Areytos.* See letter to Lawson of March 17.

not therefore think that you have entirely cut me from your book
of recollections. I have more than once trembled for your office
this winter, as the newspapers brought us advices of shipwreck
& disaster. That you have escaped totally unscathed, is, I suppose,
impossible, — that you are not seriously hurt, I hope & believe.
That, amid all these cares, to say nothing of averages, you should
have thought of me & mine, I could scarcely imagine without a
most extravagant degree of presumption. But that your wife
should have suffered you to remain so neglectful, I can only account for on the supposition that that Behemoth [119] Cornelius has
won her heart away from me. Pray, give her the benefit of these
conjectures. — It is highly probable that I shall leave Charleston
for the North about the middle of June. It is essential that I get
back early in September. My wife is again *enceinte* and her accouchement will take place in that month.[120] Such is our calculation. I shall go via Washington & Balt. and between these places,
Richmond & Phila. may linger a week or ten days. Whether I
shall be ready before I leave home with all the books I propose
to print during the summer is very questionable. I am still under
a cloud. Man delights not me — nor woman neither.[121] But don't
tell Madame *that.* I am still a discontent longing for — I suppose
— the unreal & the impossible. If I could hear more frequently
from you & other friends, I fancy I should be better, but with
crowds of correspondents, I look with repining for the more
agreeable remembrances of others. — You have been getting up
a sub. for a Bust of Bryant. I take for granted that, if within my
proper means, you assumed my desire to be one of the subs. I
see by the papers that Forrest has been hissing Macready and
arguing for it.[122] I am sorry that he did so. I am willing to believe that M. deserved it all, — but for Forrest's own policy, the
proceeding was a great mistake. Did you get my Areytos? Will

[119] An allusion to Mathews' novel *Behemoth: A Legend of the Mound-
Builders* (New York: J. & H. G. Langley; Boston: Weeks, Jordan & Co.,
1839).

[120] Mary Lawson Simms, named for Mrs. Lawson, was born on Sept. 13.
[121] *Hamlet,* II, ii.

[122] While playing "Othello" in London on Feb. 17, 1845, Forrest was hissed
by his audience. Assuming that this treatment was instigated by his rival,
Macready, he retaliated by hissing Macready when the British actor was playing
"Hamlet" at the Theatre Royal in Edinburgh on March 2, 1846. For this act
of bad taste, Forrest was severely criticized in the English and the American
press. See Alger, *Life of Edwin Forrest,* I, 391-412.

you marry any of them to immortal music? [123] And what of all
my books — the Count, — the Wigwam — the Views — Do
you know that you have not said a word anent either? And what
is Mathews doing? Hints have reached me that Poe had been
dealing in mischief, &c. Duyckinck talks of strange doings, & I
see by one of the papers that it was gravely thought to send P.
to Bedlam.[124] — Tell your wife that Augusta has just returned
from the Encampment Ball, of which I have no doubt she will
give her a flaming description. I leave the task to her. Write me
soon, and write nothing but good news. Present me, my wife &
all to Lady Lyde. Mr. Roach sends his respects. For yourself hold
me as Ever,

very truly yours, —

Simms

A kiss round for the children. Gilmore has a couple of wild cats,
a rattlesnake, a racoon, an opossum & some fox & cat squirrels,
which he means for Jimmy Junior, — but whether you have assigned a chamber for the menagerie in the Palazzo is a question.
If you are willing to give them house room or to recieve them at
all, I will send them. Perhaps it may please you to ship them to
some friend in Scotland. Well stuffed, they will make a show.
Now they are badly stuffed with straw by the negroes. If you
write at once, your answer will reach me here.

---

[123] A reviewer of the volume in *Godey's,* XXXII (June, 1846), 285, remarks:
"Rich in the beautiful imagery of the South, these songs seem to breathe the
soft spirit of the land where the magnolia perfumes the air and the rose is
ever in bloom[.] There is also a vein of patriotic as well as of tender love
running through the compositions—the true, loyal feelings of the American
heart, which will make them favourites with all who love their country. We
have no space to point out particular favourites in this collection; many deserve
to be set to music, if they have not already been so. We particularly like the
song beginning—
   'Quiet is on the earth.'
And another—
   'Come when the evening into silence closes.'
And this—
   'Be at my side when the winds are awaking.' "
Of *Areytos* Poe says in "Marginalia," *Dem. Rev.,* XIX (July, 1846), 31-32:
"I fully agree with Simms (W. Gilmore) that the Provençal troubadour had,
in his melodious vocabulary, no title more appropriate than the Cuban 'Areytos'
for a collection of tender or passionate songs—such as we have here. . . .
Altogether I prefer . . . 'Indian Serenade' to any of Mr. Simms' poems. . . .
Mr. Simms is, beyond doubt, one of our most original writers."

[124] We have not located this particular newspaper report of Poe. For Simms'
earlier remarks on some of his difficulties, see letter to Duyckinck of March 27,
1846.

306: To Evert Augustus Duyckinck

Woodlands, May 15 [1846] [125]

My dear Duyckinck

Professor Dickson, of Charleston, is an excellent essayist, writes in good style and spirit and with considerable grace. He is quite popular in our state, is a frequent lecturer and always a successful one. His subjects are moral, social & semi-scientific. He can make you up a volume with materials of this character which will do credit to the library, and it has been suggested to me to inquire if such a collection would not be desirable.[126] If it would, I should like you to communicate to me as soon as possible after recieving this letter. Professor D. is a man of property, and does not attach much importance to the matter of compensation, but he would nevertheless, insist upon it as a matter of right in his own case, and of duty to others. I suppose it would sufficiently satisfy him to recieve 6/100 on each copy of a 50/100 cent book. At all events, you will oblige me by procuring him a place in the Library, on the most liberal terms. Money, he probably would not take from his publishers. He would seek rather to be paid in his own coin, — by books. Let me hear from you at the earliest moment. — I propose to leave the country for Charleston on the 15th. inst., will probably remain in the city till the 15th. prox., then proceed by slow stages, to New York, halting in Baltimore, Richmond, Baltimore, & Philadelphia, in all a week or ten days. I am busy still on my Life of Smith, which promises to be a volume quite as large, if not larger that Marion, &, I think of superior interest. I hope to get it done before leaving home. It is my wish to run the second vol. of 'Views' through the press in New York—the 'Huguenots' and possibly, a vol. of Tales & one of Poems. But this *entre nous.* These I wish to get out of the way before undertaking some new tasks in other departments. I am curious to hear what you say of Ct. Julian & the 'Views.' The latter, I think, wears a very respectable visage. It has surprised me to hear it said by some devout novel readers of the South that Ct. Julian is a story of superior interest. My fear was

---

125 Dated by Simms' references to *Views and Reviews,* Second Series, *The Lily and the Totem; or, the Huguenots in Florida,* and the never published volumes of tales of the imagination and of lays of Apalachia. See letter to Duyckinck of Feb. 20.

126 Wiley and Putnam did not publish a volume of Samuel Henry Dickson's essays. Later, in 1852, Lea and Blanchard, Philadelphia, published his *Essays on Life, Sleep. Pain . . . .*

that it was in this respect, in chief, that it would fail. But, *De gustibus* &c. From Mathews I got a friendly letter which shows that he has properly come to his senses. To get angry with one's friends is great folly — and I had shown him from the beginning as just and discriminating a regard as any wise man could have wished. Why was Headley's Marshals excluded from the Library? Why are not Jones's essays published? What think *you* of Hall's stories.[127] Waddy Thompson *is* a man of parts, but scarcely of good taste. He belongs to the better class of our upper country gentry — men of worth and substance of whom the low country-men are apt to suppose that there is a lack of real refinement and nice delicacy. I will explain to you these distinctions when we meet. Thompson is a strong man *on the stump* — good at an *ad captandum* — has, in this way, beaten Calhoun in his own precinct.[128] I do not hear from you. Write me soon and if you write on the reciept of this, you may address me here — if not, in Charleston. I hope to be there by the 15th. — My spirits have not been good all this winter. I feel a sad sense of weariness. I lack repose, — or rather, I lack the conflict such as will so consume and exhaust the nervous energies as to keep them from chafing and afflicting me. My blood & spirit are like a keen sword fretting against the sheathe. I can give the rationale of my own condition, I believe, but see not just now how to remedy. It is in change that I must hope; and this change must be radical for the time. It must find me not only a new field, but new *foes* — in other words, new departments of struggle. You will smile if I tell you that as yet, I have never striven openly in those pursuits, in which I hope to find my true successes, but this is sad egotism. Only write to me, since I must have sympathy,—if not—succour.

Yours Ever truly

Simms

---

[127] Joel Tyler Headley's *Napoleon and His Marshals,* 2 vols., was published by Baker and Scribner in 1846; William A. Jones' *Literary Studies, a Collection of Miscellaneous Essays* by E. Walker in 1847; and James Hall's *The Wilderness and the War Path* by Wiley and Putnam in 1846.

[128] In 1838 Thompson defeated by a large majority Calhoun's candidate for Congress, Solicitor Joseph N. Whitner, of Anderson District.

307 : To John Tomlin [129]

Woodlands, May 19. [1846] [130]

My Dear Sir,—

I am just in receipt of your kind notice of Areytos, in your new and pleasing miscellany, the "New Era," and hasten to say how much satisfaction I receive from your continued remembrance of me. There are some little mistakes in your article. "Woodlands" is not on the Ashley but the Edisto, and I cannot longer be considered slender, since, though not corpulent, I now weigh over 160, and am much stouter than in those days of boyhood when it was our pleasure to meet. I might suggest some other trifling alterations in your notice, but, altogether, it is remarkably correct, when we consider how long a time has passed since we have seen each other. It will always give me pleasure to note your doings in the "New Era," or elsewhere. Merie, whenever it is in my power you shall hear of. I sent you, some time ago, a pamphlet of "Sonnets." If they did not reach you let me know, but to prevent failure, I send you another with this. I am now busy on my life of Capt. John Smith, the founder of Virginia, and propose to publish that and a second series of my Views and Reviews this summer at the North, to which place I go in June. In five days more I leave Woodlands on a brief visit to Charleston.

Very truly yours,

W. Gilmore Simms

---

[129] Tomlin (1805-1850), born in South Carolina, was at this time postmaster at Jackson, Tenn. He had been a contributor to Simms' *Magnolia* and *Southern and Western*. Apparently Tomlin was devoted to Simms, for in his letters to Poe he speaks of him always with high praise. On Nov. 22, 1840, he wrote to Poe (James A. Harrison, *The Complete Works of Edgar Allan Poe* [New York, 1902], XVII, 62) : "Some years ago, he [Simms] was my friend and gave me much good advice. The most pleasant walks I have ever taken in the fields of Literature, were made in his company. Since then he has far outstripped me, and I am where he was when he first commenced to ramble among the *genii* of Fiction. . . . When I was a boy, I used to love to hear the Author of 'Mellichampe' talk. He said much to interest one of my years. As I grew older, my reverence for the man increased, until in my own mind, I am persuaded, that I shall 'never look upon his like again.' "

[130] Dated by Simms' references to his "pamphlet of 'Sonnets' " (*Grouped Thoughts and Scattered Fancies*) and to Tomlin's review of *Areytos* in the *New Era* (unlocated, but undoubtedly printed shortly after the publication of the volume). The original of Simms' letter has not been located. Our text is from Tomlin's "The Autobiography of a Monomaniac," *Holden's Dollar Magazine,* III (May, 1849), 277.

308: To James Henry Hammond

Woodlands May 20. [1846] [131]

My dear Hammond.

With this I send you a paper in which you will find briefly expressed my notions on your marl pamphlet. I think you may take for granted that I am sincere in my ordinary expressions of opinion; I have never had motives sufficiently strong at any time to seduce me into flattery; and I trust that my antipathies are sufficiently under the control of my conscientiousness, to forbear the expression of unjust or rancorous sentiments. That you avoid scientific details is only what should be expected in a work of this sort meant to be useful; and unless you entertained leading speculations of an original sort in regard to first principles, of what use the cumbersome topics of a science which your common blockhead finds in Cyclopediaes. Half the orations, tracts, treatises &c of the day are purely encyclopedique and my detestation. Really, the cant of learning is quite as disgusting as that of religion. — That practically as well as scientifically master of your subject, you should express yourself well & clearly, was inevitable from your practice and habitual thinking; — and this too when you make least effort. Habitual thinking — by no means a common practice — is the secret of wonderful propriety & promptness of expression, and where this has been as in your case, associated with so much experience in public & political life, it is equally inevitable that to clearness of utterance, will be united force, elegance & compactness, as well as variety. To sum up all on this subject, let me assure you that your 'marl' pamphlet was just the thing, and while forbearing to trouble & annoy the persons particularly addressed with matters beyond them & totally unnecessary to their purposes, satisfactorily conveyed to others the sufficient impression that you avoided the scientific matter, rather because of the deficiences of your hearers & readers, than your own. — I very much regretted not having seen you when I took the route up the Savannah. It was not until I was within 25 miles of you or less, that I heard positively of your absence. I thought to have gone up again according to an arrangement made with Aldrich sometime this month, but time is not allowed me, and

---

[131] Dated by Simms' reference to his comments in the *Southern Patriot* of May 20, 1846, on Hammond's *Marl. A Letter Addressed to the Agricultural Society of Jefferson County, Georgia* (Augusta: Printed by James McCafferty, 1846).

I am half sorry that I went at all, for it seems some of your neighbours of whom I never heard in my life, have taken offence that I did not seek them out. My labours and present engagements are such that I heartily regret having consented to run again, and if you can provide me with a decent reason to withdraw, you will do me a real favor. I feel that there is no serving two mistresses, and the Muses of Politics & Poetry draw badly together in the same harness. Can't you procure me some appointment, which will enable me to back out. — Well, and how did you relish the St. John's? The country is full of doubts as to your future purpose. It is thought that your visit had some regard to the future &c.[132] — I say nothing of the Mexican War, of which you see enough in the newspapers without seeing anything. I have long thought that progress on our part is inevitable equally from the national necessity and the national temperament, and though you affect to differ, I cordially suspect you of thinking with me. — On Monday next, the 25th. I leave for Charleston, where I will stay a few weeks, moving for New York via Washington, about the middle of June.[133] I am & have been in low spirits. The world goes ill with me, and I am becoming daily more & more impatient of my limits. Send me a scrawl of consolation & direct to me at Charleston (for the present) "care of John Russell, Bookseller."

Yours truly

Simms

Gen. Hammond

---

132 Hammond had just returned from a trip down the St. John's River in Florida. At this time every move of Hammond was thought to have political implications. His popularity had soared throughout the South after the publication of the "Clarkson Letters" (see letters to Hammond of April 10, May 20, and *c*. June 18, 1845). When it became evident that McDuffie would soon retire from the United States Senate because of his health, influential men throughout South Carolina began demanding that Hammond become a candidate for the Senate. Hammond, as usual, was non-committal: his attitude was that if he were drafted, he would be forced to accept, but that he would not seek the office.

133 Simms wrote *about the middle of New York*.

309: To James Lawson

Charleston, June 12. [1846] [134]

dear Lawson

I expect to leave Charleston for the North on Monday next the 15th. provided our baby is recovered from a bowel complaint (teething) which now troubles her. I propose to remain a day or two in Richmond and two or three in Washington, and I write to persuade you, as your wife has never been to Washington, to snatch a chance & meet me there. It will be a pleasant trip to you both & will give you some respite from your daily drudgery. Can't the thing be done? If not, write me *there; as I shall linger, perhaps, in the hope of seeing you.* I should propose to stay a day in Philadelphia also, which might please both of you to do also.

In haste but truly
Yours & hers

W. G. S.

J. L.

P. S. You might help me in my quest at W. — But mum!

310: To John Caldwell Calhoun

New York, June 29. [1846] [135]

Hon. J. C. Calhoun

My dear Sir

Can you give me in half a dozen sentences the particulars in relation to Genl. John Caldwell & his family, which you afforded me in conversation the other day. I am not unconscious of the great & continued draft upon your time and mind, in your position at this moment, and would not trespass upon you for a single instant, — but that I desire to be perfectly at home in the preparation of a paper in relation to Wm. Cunningham on which I am

---

[134] Dated by Simms' discussion of his plan to leave Charleston for the North on June 15 (see letters to Lawson of May 15, to Duyckinck of May 15, and to Hammond of May 20). In 1846 June 15 fell on Monday. The baby mentioned herein is Valeria (see letter to Lawson of Aug. 8).

[135] Dated by Simms' request for material concerning Major (here incorrectly called General) John Caldwell (1746-1781), uncle of John C. Calhoun and William Cunningham's captain, to be used in his review of Ward's edition of the *Journal and Letters of the Late Samuel Curwen,* published during 1846 in the *Southern Literary Messenger* (see note 367, Dec. 12, 1845).

now engaged; — and a single letter sheet will contain all that is
necessary to my objects.

With great respect, I am Sir
very faithfully &c
Yrs

W. Gilmore Simms

311: To EVERT AUGUSTUS DUYCKINCK

New York, Monday Mg.
[June 29, 1846] [136]

My dear Sir

The proposition you make me on behalf of Mr. Wiley is entirely out of the question. I am no publisher, and see no reason to
lose sight of the original understanding on the subject of the publication of Views and Reviews. Permit me to say, also, that I
shall be compelled to look to you as my chief witness in the matter. Though Mr. Wiley may forget the arrangement, I entertain
no fears or doubts that you will not remember thoroughly the
frequent conferences between him & myself to which you were a
party, and in which the matter was very clearly understood. I regard him as bound to me and both of us to the public. I cannot
suffer my credit to be injured by a failure to publish the sequel
of the work begun, and should regard it as certain ruin to the
book if the second vol. were not put forth. It will not be sold till
complete. Let me add, also, that never was vol. put forth with
(seemingly) so little disposition on the part of the publisher to
bring it properly to the view of the public. I think it probable that
it has not been published in a single newspaper. Noticed, it
scarcely can be, by any thoughtful critic, until the whole work is
fairly before him. — It strikes me, I have been quite liberal in giving Mr. W. the privilege of taking the Huguenots or of declining
it. But this privilege is only conceded in the assumption that we
have no trouble on the score of Views & Reviews. Upon his compliance with that engagement, I feel it my duty to insist. I could
wish to respect Mr. W., and that our intercourse should be conducted in future as harmoniously as it began, but I cannot suffer

---

[136] The year is established by Simms' discussion of the delayed publication
of *Views and Reviews,* Second Series, and by his reference to *The Lily and the
Totem; or, the Huguenots in Florida.* The letter is postmarked June 30,
which, in 1846, fell on Tuesday.

myself to be sacrificed. You publishers, it appears to me, are but too apt to regard the Author as a fixture or a movable, — a thing without character or volition to be adjusted or disturbed at pleasure. — This is the common case. I had supposed, & will endeavor still to persuade myself, that Mess'rs W & P. had juster notions of the mutual rights of the parties. At all events, I must not surrender mine. I will probably confer with Sedgwick [137] in a day or two, and have no sort of doubt that he will confirm my conviction of the clearness and justness of my demand, fortified as it is by my own impressions, your evidence, and the unequivocal announcement on the title page of the published volume. But I should prefer that you should prevent this. I will do something to avoid strife — waive the Huguenots, if you please, make the matter in the 2 vol. of the V & R. more fresh & diversified &c. — but not forego its publication according to the original understanding. — Do not suppose I complain of you in this business. My only regret, however, is, that you did not draw up the articles in writing, as I more than once requested you.

> Very respectfully
> yours &c
>
> W. Gilmore Simms

E. A. Duyckinck Esq.

312: To Evert Augustus Duyckinck

> Thursday Morning. [July 2, 1846] [138]

My dear Sir.

I am glad that Mr. Wiley & yourself have adjusted the matter. There was no good reason, our mutual policy considered, that there should be difficulty between us. It is scarcely possible to determine upon what is, or is not, profitable or successful, which shall be put forth at a season like the present; and I have no fears but that the two vols. in question will have a steady sale and a permanent value. They unite some thinking and some romance,

---

[137] Probably Theodore Sedgwick (1811-1859), lawyer and author. See note 124, *c.* Nov. 15, 1844.

[138] This letter has been dated July 2, a Thursday. It is in reply to a lost letter from Duyckinck in answer to Simms' letter of June 29, which certainly would have provoked an immediate answer. As published, *Views and Reviews,* Second Series, is considerably shorter than that proposed by Simms in his letters to Duyckinck of Feb. 20 and March 17, 1846.

with much that is novel & impressive in our history. The volume
which you suggest will be rather a small one; and I presume it
is not meant, by the limits which you give, to say that we shall
imprudently abridge the variety of the work if twenty additional
pages will secure it. I shall accordingly work on this principle. I
will try to look in upon Mr. Wiley tomorrow or Saturday, when
I trust to see you, and when you can arrange at what time the
printer will be ready for the copy. My object will be to get through
with this volume & one which I am printing elswhere,[139] by the
first of August.

Yours hurriedly &c.

W. Gilmore Simms

E. A. Duyckinck Esq.

313: To James Munroe and Company

New York, July 8, 1846

Messr's James Monroe & Co
Boston.

Gentlemen.

I subscribed to "The Dial" through the medium of a Charleston Bookseller, but failed regularly to get the work. The nos. 13
& 14 are still wanting to the completion of my set. Miss Margaret
Fuller tells me that you can supply them.[140] If so, please forward
them to me at this place, and instruct me where I can pay for them
in this city.

Very respectfully
Yr obt servt &c

W. Gilmore Simms

---

[139] Although in 1846 G. Gleason, Boston, published a reprint of *Carl Werner*
under the title of *Matilda: or, the Spectre of the Castle,* Simms probably is
here referring to *The Life of Captain John Smith,* at this time in the hands
of J. and H. G. Langley.

[140] Margaret Fuller had been editor of the *Dial* from the issue of July, 1840,
through that of April, 1842. Nos. 13 and 14 are for July and Oct., 1843.

314: To Margaret Fuller

[July, 1846] [141]

My dear Miss Fuller.

I have recd. from Munro & Co of Boston, a No. 13. of the 'Dial.' No. 14. they tell me is entirely out of print, and not to be had except from contributors & subscribers. My anxiety to complete my set of a work which I have learned to value, alone prompts me to intrude upon your attention, at a moment when I know your time is precious. Can you, among your acquaintance of this city, indicate a person from whom this number may be procured? Of course I am prepared to pay any reasonable charge, if required, beyond the subscription price. May I be permitted to wish you God speed on the voyage before you.

Very faithfully & respectfully

Yr obt serv.

W. Gilmore Simms

315: To Alfred Billings Street

[July 20, 1846] [142]

My dear Sir

I am pleased to see a very excellent picture of you in Graham, with a complimentary notice of your poems. I have had, partially prepared for some time, a critique for the Messenger, but have been too busy hitherto to finish it. I may do so before I return South which will be about the 1st. August. Did I send you an article which I published on you in one of the Charleston papers? [143] If not I may still contrive to do so. I am at present with our excellent friend James Lawson, and shall be happy to hear from you.

Yours truly &c

W. Gilmore Simms.

New York

July 20.

Alfred B. Street Esq.

---

[141] Dated by reference to Simms' letter to James Munroe and Co. of July 8, in which he asks for Nos. 13 and 14 of the *Dial*. Margaret Fuller sailed from Boston to Europe on Aug. 1 on the steamer *Cambria*.

[142] Dated by Simms' references to the picture of Alfred B. Street, published in *Graham's Magazine*, XXIX (Aug., 1846), facing p. 61, and to the notice of Street's poems, published in the same issue, pp. 61-66.

[143] Simms' review, entitled "Street's Poems," was published in *S. L. M.*, XII (Dec., 1846), 711-720. He also favorably reviewed the volume in the *Southern Patriot* of April 22, 1846.

316: To Edgar Allan Poe [144]

New York July 30. 1846

Edgar A. Poe, Esq.

Dear Sir

I recieved your note a week ago, and proceeded at once to answer it, but being in daily expectation of a newspaper from the South, to which, in a Letter, I had communicated a paragraph concerning the matter which you had suggested in a previous letter, I determined to wait until I could enclose it to you. It has been delayed somewhat longer than I had anticipated, and has in part caused my delay to answer you. I now send it you, and trust that it will answer the desired purpose; though I must frankly say that I scarcely see the necessity of noticing the sort of scandal to which you refer.[145] — I note with regret the very desponding character of your last letter. I surely need not tell you how deeply & sincerely I deplore the misfortunes which attend you — the more so as I see no process for your relief and, extrication but

---

[144] Two copies of this letter in Simms' handwriting are extant. We print here the letter as sent to Poe, now in the Boston Public Library. The other (Simms' first draft), now in the South Caroliniana Library, contains additional material (see note 146, below). The letter has been frequently and somewhat inaccurately quoted.

[145] Poe's letter to Simms requesting aid in "The War of the *Literati*" is unlocated. In a literary letter to the *Southern Patriot*, dated July 15 and published in the issue of July 20, Simms writes: "Among the petty excitements common to authorship is that which Mr. Edgar A. Poe is producing by his pencil sketches of the New York Literati in Godey's Ladies Magazine. He has succeeded most happily (if such was his object) in fluttering the pigeons of this dove cote. His sketches, of which we have seen but a few, are given to a delineation as well of the persons as of the performances of his subjects. Some of them are amusing enough. I am not prepared to say how true are his sketches, but they have caused no little rattling among the dry bones of our Grub street. Of Poe, as a writer, we know something. He is undoubtedly a man of very peculiar and very considerable genius—but is irregular and exceedingly mercurial in his temperament. He is fond of mystifying in his stories, and they tell me, practises upon this plan even in his sketches; more solicitous, as they assert, of a striking picture than a likeness. Poe, himself, is a very good looking fellow. I have seen him on two or three occasions, and have enjoyed a good opportunity of examining him carefully. He is probably thirty three or four years old, some five, feet eight inches in height, of rather slender person, with a good eye, and a broad intelligent forehead. He is a man, clearly, of sudden and uneven impulses of great nervous susceptibility, and one whose chief misfortune it is not to have been caught young and trained carefully. The efforts of his mind seem wholly spasmodic. He lacks habitual industry, I take it, which, in the case of the library man who must look to his daily wits for his daily bread, is something of a deficiency. He, also, is in obscurity, somewhere in the country [at Fordham], and sick, according to a report which reached me yesterday [from Poe?], of brain fever." For the series of letters of which this letter forms a part, see note 158, Aug. 9, 1846.

such as must result from your own decision and resolve. No friend
can well help you in the struggle which is before you. Money, no
doubt, can be procured; but this is not altogether what you require. Sympathy may soothe the hurts of Self-Esteem, and make
a man temporarily forgetful of his assailants;—but in what degree will this avail, and for how long, in the protracted warfare
of twenty or thirty years. You are still a very young man, and one
too largely & too variously endowed, not to entertain the conviction—as your friends entertain it—of a long & manful struggle
with, and a final victory over, fortune. But this warfare, the world
requires you to carry on with your own unassisted powers. It is
only in your manly resolution to use these powers, after a legitimate fashion, that it will countenance your claims to its regards
& sympathy; and I need not tell you how rigid & exacting it has
ever been in the case of the poetical genius, or, indeed, the genius
of any order. Suffer me to tell you frankly, taking the privilege of
a true friend, that you are now perhaps in the most perilous period of your career—just in that position — just at that time of
life — when a false step becomes a capital error — when a single
leading mistake is fatal in its consequences. You are no longer a
boy. "At thirty wise or never!" You must subdue your impulses;
&, in particular, let me exhort you to discard all associations with
men, whatever their talents, whom you cannot esteem as men.
Pardon me for presuming thus to counsel one whose great natural
& acquired resources should make him rather the teacher of
others. But I obey a law of my own nature, and it is because of
my sympathies that I speak. Do not suppose yourself abandoned
by the worthy and honorable among your friends. They will be
glad to give you welcome *if you will suffer them.* They will rejoice
— I know their feelings and hear their language — to countenance your return to that community — that moral province in
society — of which, let me say to you, respectfully and regret-
fully,—you have been, according to all reports but too heedlessly
and, perhaps, too scornfully indifferent. Remain in obscurity for
awhile. You have a young wife — I am told a suffering & interesting one, — let me entreat you to cherish her, and to cast away
those pleasures which are not worthy of your mind, and to tram-
ple those temptations underfoot, which degrade your person, and
make it familiar to the mouth of vulgar jest. You may [do] all
this, by a little circumspection. It is still within your power. Your
resources from literature are probably much greater than mine.

I am sure they are quite as great. You can increase them, so that they shall be ample for all your legitimate desires; but you must learn the worldling's lesson of prudence; — a lesson, let me add, which the literary world has but too frequently & unwisely disparaged. It may seem to you very impertinent, — in most cases it is impertinent — that he who gives nothing else, should presume to give counsel. But one gives that which he can most spare, and you must not esteem me indifferent to a condition which I can in no other way assist. I have never been regardless of your genius, even when I knew nothing of your person. It is some years, since I counseled Mr. Godey to obtain the contributions of your pen. He will tell you this.. I hear that you reproach him. But how can you expect a Magazine proprietor to encourage contributions which embroil him with all his neighbours. These broils do you no good—vex your temper, destroy your peace of mind, and hurt your reputation. You have abundant resources upon which to draw even were there no Grub Street in Gotham. Change your tactics & begin a new series of papers with your publisher. — The printed matter which I send you, might [146] be quoted by Godey, and might be ascribed to me.[147] But, surely, I need not say to you that, to a Southern man, the annoyance of being mixed up in a squabble with persons whom he does not know, and does not care to know,—and from whom no Alexandrine process of cutting loose, would be permitted by society — would be an intolerable grievance. I submit to frequent injuries & misrepresentations, content, though annoyed by the slaver, that the viper should amuse himself upon the file, at the expense of his own teeth. As a man, as a writer, I shall always be solicitous of your reputation & success. You have but to resolve on taking & asserting your position, equally in the social & the literary world, and your way is clear, your path is easy, and you will find true friends enough to sympathize in your triumphs. Very Sincerely though Sorrowfully, Yr frd & Servt.

W Gilmore Simms

P. S. If I could I should have been to see you. But I have been & am still drudging in the hands of the printers, kept busily em-

---

[146] In Simms' first draft of this letter the following passage is struck through: "Of the subject of which you wrote me sometime ago, I have thought since, and a paragraph has been sent on to the Southern Patriot of Charleston, in one of my Letters to that journal, which I suppose has been published. It embodies the matter which you wished to have in print and might. . . . "

[147] Simms' defense of Poe is not reprinted in *Godey's*.

ployed night and day. Besides, my arrangements are to hurry back to the South where I have a sick family. A very few days will turn my feet in that direction.

317: To ALFRED BILLINGS STREET

New York, July 31. [1846] [148]

My dear Sir

I will endeavor to procure & send you from Charleston (to which I hasten) a copy of the notice of your Poems which I made in the Southern Patriot of that city. When I reach home I shall seize an early opportunity to review you in the Messenger. Will you advise me of the *standing* of your publishers, and whether they would like a select edition of all my poetical writings with portrait & vignette.[149]

Yours truly, but in haste. (I leave for the South on Monday)

W. Gilmore Simms

A. B. Street Esq.

318: To JAMES LAWSON

Charleston, S. C. Augt. 8. [1846] [150]

My dear Lawson

I reached home yesterday according to calculation, and rather less fatigued than I expected to be. I succeeded in transacting my business, in some degree, with Godey, having arranged to write him a nouvellette descriptive of Southern Life — a sort of tale for Christmas, to occupy two or three numbers of his Book, and thus to complete the year. After that, we are to set a novel in progress, say Jany. 1. to run through the year. The engagement for the latter not positive on either part.[151] I procured from Godey

---

[148] Dated by Simms' reference to his plan to review Street's *Poems* in the *Southern Literary Messenger*. See note 143, July 20, 1846.

[149] Clark and Austin, New York, did not issue a volume of Simms' poetry.

[150] Dated by Simms' reference to the health of Valeria Govan Simms (Aug. 10, 1845-Sept. 20, 1846).

[151] "Maize in Milk. A Christmas Story of the South," a novelette, was published in *Godey's*, XXXIV (Feb., March, April, and May, 1847), 62-67, 146-152, 199-204, 249-258. It was republished in *Marie De Berniere: A Tale of the Crescent City* (Philadelphia: Lippincott, Grambo, and Co., 1853), pp. 320-422. No full-length novel by Simms was published in *Godey's* until 1850, when *Katharine Walton* appeared in eleven installments (see note 191, Oct. 15, 1849). During 1846 and 1847 Simms published several poems in *Godey's*:

a copy of his number for August, which I send you with this. I
spent but the close of Monday in Phila. and left for Balto. next
morning, went down the Chesapeake, left Richmond to the right,
and then continued with due speed home. We got into Charleston
by six oclock Friday M.G. and found all well except Valeria, who
is very thin, puny & fretful. She is still teething. — And how does
our dear little sister Lyde get on without me to scold her and
lecture her about fashions, extravagance and the children? And
how does the venerable Segnior [152] get on without his usual drubbing at Backgammon. We are all losers by the exit, for, you know,
I have nobody whom I dare to scold here, any more than you
have at home. The domestic tyranny is quite as vigilant & jealous
in Charleston as it is in New York, — though you will of course
suffer neither your wife nor mine, to see this passage. Tell her,
I really felt monstrous dull & lonesome, missing you all, until I
had two nights rail car sleep upon it, and such an influence soon
knocks all domestic cares out of a man's head in filling it with
foreign ones. The route, however, by the Chesapeake, is not so
fatiguing. The worst night is that before you get to Wilmington.
Hereafter, when I travel in Summer, I will take the night cars
as far the pleasantest. Leave N. Y. in the afternoon, run from
Phil. next afternoon in the Steamboat for Balt. Then take the
Chesapeake boat, and you have only one night on the Rail Roads
of Virginia. — Your brandy flask served me famously, and suc-
coured an old friend. We flourished it in the face of the multitude
in Car & Boat with the air of folks who knew the *quality* &
strength of their comrade. I had a 'wee drop' to swear by on
reaching home. — In addition to the commissions which I left
with you, let me beg that you will get Robt. Donaldson to procure
for Mr. Roach two of the iron cauldrons, the price of which he
ascertained for me. We wish one of thirty (30) Gallons for
$15.00, and one of the 40 Gals. at $18.00. This money you will
please pay, & draw upon me for it here, or wait a few weeks when
I expect to draw upon Wiley & Putnam & J & H. G. Langley.
Get R. D. to procure also a couple of the hoes for digging potatoes,

---

"The Gift of the Dying," XXXII (May, 1846), 231; "The Ranz des Vaches.
A Paraphrase," XXXII (June, 1846), 272; "Sonnet. To a Friend Departing
for England," XXXIII (Oct., 1846), 180; "Heart Fancies.—A Series of [Five]
Sonnets," XXXIV (March, 1847), 156; "The Quest for Peace" (signed
"Adrian Beaufain"), XXXIV (June, 1847), 277; "Despondency and Self-
Reproach. A Group of [Three] Sonnets," XXXV (Oct., 1847), 168.

[152] Robert Donaldson, father of Mrs. Lawson.

which he described to me, should they not exceed 75/100 or $1.00. These I should like forwarded as soon as possible, and if he has not already shipped the boxes left with you, the whole may be sent together. — If your young man can get any more money out of Starr,[153] it will help to lessen my money obligations to you. I left a memorandum with Lady Lyde touching various matters you were to attend to. Enclosed I cover a note from Gilmore to Kate [154] which you or your wife will read to her. You will find a shilling under the seal, and by making her open it herself, it will occasion some pleasant surprise. I have little or nothing to write about and as you may suppose, write with quite a nervous and spasmodic feeling. Not yet at home — not yet seperate from you all — scarcely able to realize the change, and fancying half the time that I hear your wife's voice upon the stairs. By the way, she must know that if she does not turn in to let Jimmy rough it, Gilly will beat him all hollow. I find upon measuring him that G. is rather the tallest, though being so much stouter than Jimmy he does not look so. In the 'Courier' of this morning, there is a Letter translated from the French of a Parisian physician, on the subject of the cold water practice.[155] Read it. The paper comes to you at the office or I would send it you. Augusta and my wife are both doing well, and send their love to Lady Lyde, yourself & the children. They look confidently for Christina in the winter, and think that you will both be acting very childishly not to suffer her to spend the winter & spring with us. — Well — once more adieu, *mon ami*. Kiss your wife affectionately on my account, if not on your own. I can very well concieve that in the case of a woman so extravagant you will be loth to bestow upon her many marks of affection, for fear of making her more so.

Yours — and God bless you.

W. G. Simms

---

[153] Unidentified.

[154] Catherine Sinclair Lawson.

[155] The Charleston *Courier* of Aug. 8, 1846, contains the letter of the Parisian physician, entitled "Hydrotherapy, or the Treatment of Diseases by Cold Water and Transpiration." It is dated Paris, July 1, 1846, and signed "Gibert, Physician of the Hospital, St. Louis." The translator is given as "Wilber."

319: To Evert Augustus Duyckinck

Charleston 9. Augt. [1846] [156]

My dear Duyckinck.

Still something nervous after my journey, I hasten to say to you that I saw Griswold in Phil. He says that Carey & Hart sent a bundle to my address, care of Wiley & Putnam, nearly four weeks ago, and a clerk of C & H. showed me the reciept from R. R. for it. With that package, which contd. his edition of the British Poets,[157] was a Letter for you. You will please enquire for the Packet & if found, open it and possess yourself of the letter. The book may be sent on to me by W & P. in any of their packages to Charleston. I send you by this a paper contg Letters with sundry small matters & things, in which you may be interested.[158] I shall probably write you next week when Mr. Russell goes on.—I made an engagement with Godey for a novel or rather a novelette to be completed during the present year; — and partly engaged with him for another, to occupy the whole of next year. Of Griswold, & some of his views, I shall write you hereafter. His misfortune is to have a most unhappy New England bias in most literary matters, which needs to be corrected. — Will you do me the favour to ask at W & P's if they were able to find for me No. 40 of Knight's Pict. Shakspeare.[159] You will also do me the favor to keep in mind the 19th. No. of the N. Y. Review. — I will send by Mr. Russell a copy of the So & West. Rev. to Mr. Putnam.

You will note in the Letter of the Patriot something anent Mr. Murdoch.[160] It will give me pleasure to promote his objects should

---

[156] Since the stamped postmark on the cover of this letter is dated Aug. 8, it is probable that Simms erred in his date. The year is established by Simms' references to his contract with Godey and the illness of Valeria (see letter to Lawson of Aug. 8).

[157] *The Poets and Poetry of England, in the Nineteenth Century* (Philadelphia: Carey & Hart, 1844). For Simms' later review of this volume, see note 192, Oct. 21, 1846.

[158] During his visit to New York City and shortly thereafter Simms acted as "correspondent" for the *Southern Patriot* and published therein eighteen unsigned letters, printed during July and September under the heading of "From Our Correspondent" or "From a Correspondent." These are omitted from this edition because of lack of space.

[159] Charles Knight, ed., *The Pictorial Edition of the Works of Shakspere,* 8 vols. (London: C. Knight and Co., [1839]-1843).

[160] In his letter of June 30, published in the *Southern Patriot* of July 9, Simms writes of Cornelius Mathews' *Witchcraft* and its leading actor, James Edward Murdoch (1811-1893): "Of Mr. Cornelius Mathews, the story goes that he is the author of the very successful drama of 'Witchcraft' which has

he come South. I find all my family doing well, except my little girl, who is still puny from teething, very fretful, and frequently feverish.—She will probably keep thus all the Season. — Present me to C. M.[161] and other friends, and don't forget the Mirror's for the last three weeks, and hereafter.

Yours truly tho' hastily
&c &c

W. Gilmore Simms

320: To James Lawson

[*c.* August 22, 1846][162]

Mr dear Lawson.

I had not the least idea that you were so hard run, pecuniarily, or I should have made out without the fifty which I consented to take from you — the more particularly as I had occasions to draw upon your purse subsequently. I cover to you a draft at sight for $35. and two orders upon Langley's & Wiley & Putnam. Perhaps something more can be got out of Starr. Minor writes me that he has a balance still in his hand which he acknowledges — some trifle. At all events you should get the general draft from him. I have drawn upon L. & W & P. prospectively, though the latter house ought to have some cash for me & would probably settle up at once if applied to — at all events up to July 1. — I wish I could send you money enough to extinguish your builders. I am sorry to hear that Christina suffers. Of course you should send her to us, any how, when Mr. Allen [163] comes on. Tell your wife if she still kicks at it I will never forgive her. I am glad you have found a place for them all, and trust they will thrive & enjoy themselves finely. Here, we are all getting on tolerably. The

---

been lately produced in Philadelphia. With some defects of judgment, and with something to learn, Mr. Mathews is yet destined to make a very considerable figure in the original literature of this country. . . . Mr. Murdoch, an actor who has recently taken to the stage, promises to wear with dignity and grace the roles of his new profession. He is expected here [New York City] in the middle of July, and will have a strong voice of welcome from the metropolitan city."

161 Cornelius Mathews.

162 This letter is postmarked Aug. 23. The year is established by Simms' reference to Valeria's health. See letters to Lawson of Aug. 8 and to Duyckinck of Aug. 9.

163 Probably Gilbert Allen. See note 231, June 17, 1845.

baby rather better though still puny, fretful & suffering from occasional dysentery.

Yours truly as Ever

W. G. S.

321: To ALFRED BILLINGS STREET

Charleston Augt. 26 [1846][164]

My dear Sir

I enclose you the trifling notice from the Charleston paper to
which I had reference. The notice in the Messenger will embody
some of this notice, and some of the matter contained in the South
& West. Mage. It would not be easy, reviewing the same material, to change & make original any notice which I should now
write. Your *new* poems may call for a new critique. — I thank
you for your attention to my inquiries. If the question be a fair
one, pray tell me if you derive any thing as yet & what, from
your last vol. I simply wish to govern myself in my own bargains
by the knowledge of your facts. The matter shall be wholly between us. Absent from the publishing ground, I may trouble you
hereafter to negotiate for me with your publishers should they
be in better condition to publish than now.

Yours truly &c

W. Gilmore Simms.

P. S. I am now doing the notice for the Messenger.

322: To JAMES LAWSON

Charleston, Sep 14. 1846

My dear Lawson

My wife was delivered last night of a fine little girl.[165] The
mother is not so well this morning, but I hope will improve as the
day advances. My poor little Valeria is very puny from teething,
and has fever & diarrhœa on her now. I should not be surprised

---

164 Dated by Simms' references to his notice of Street's *Poems* in the
Southern Patriot, to his earlier critique in the *Southern and Western,* and to his
forthcoming review in the *Southern Literary Messenger.* See letters to Street
of Feb. 1, July 20, and July 31.
165 Mary Lawson Simms.

if we lose her. Indeed, I am just now more uneasy about her than ever. The rest of the family is well. — I have just got in from the country, where I have been on a brief tour among my constituents. The canvas for the next election is now in warm progress, and I have been compelled to mount the stump in several instances. I am heartily sick of this task, but am so far in for it, that I must needs go through. I got in only yesterday, & but a few hours before Madame was taken in labor. — I wrote you some time ago covering you a draft for $35, (cash) and two others upon Wiley & Putnam & J & H. G. Langley, — all of which I hope you have recieved. — Let me beg you, *with all despatch,* to see Sherwood & get him to send on the wheat seed *instanter.* By the time we can get it here, the season for planting it will have arrived. Let it be the bearded wheat such as Mr Hopkins procured for us last year.[166] Three Barrels are required; and you will pay him the amount, (which I suppose will hardly exceed $15[)] and if you need it, at the time, I will transmit you the cash at once. Let me entreat you to see to this matter as soon after the reciept of this letter as you can, as not to recieve the wheat shortly will greatly prejudice the growing season. — I have not heard from you for a long time. I sincerely hope that Christina & all are doing well. But let me exhort you & your wife to send Christina out with Mr. Allen. Don't trifle with the health & constitution of the child. If Lady Lyde will come with her & bring the rest, so much the better, — but if not, let her at least not with-ho[ld] the opportunity from Christina. Give [Mad]ame, my affectionate respects, & im[press] this upon her from me. I write [labori]ously, as you see, being up nearly all night & fatigued from travel. Let me hear from you soon & believe me Ever truly

Yours as Ever

W. G. S.

---

[166] William Sherwood, of New York City, had married one of the Kelloggs of Great Barrington, Mass., a friend of Mrs. Simms. Hopkins, who cannot be positively identified, was doubtless a relative of Mrs. Sherwood. For the Sherwoods and Hopkinses, see note 15, June 26, 1837, and note 11, March 28, 1838.

323: To Evert Augustus Duyckinck

Charleston, Sep. 14. 1846

My dear Duyckinck

I do not get a word from you, nor a book from W & P. None of their publications have reached me since I left New York. I see that the 'News' has perished.[167] This is bad news. And what of the sheets of Smith, and what of the proofs of 'Views & Reviews?' I am bothered to understand the delay in the latter case, and almost fear that Wiley has again taken the studs. Pray write to me about all these matters & relieve my anxieties. I have some of these at home of a more serious nature. My wife has just gone through her confinement & added another little girl to my stock. My daughter born last summer [168] is now in a very critical state from teething, and it is with great effort only that I can put pen to paper. I write to you only to get information & not with the hope to furnish any. I forwarded you several papers & have sundry others to send you. I have noticed Mathews & Witchcraft, but hear nothing from him. You may have seen a long letter cut up into three, which I published on the subject of the Drama in general, — it was less an essay, than hints for one. It was in the Patriot, and some things in it might deserve your attention.[169] Will you say to Bartlett & Welford that of the publications of the Shakspeare Society I have never recieved Heywood's Apology for Actors, being among the publications of 1841, nor The Taming of *a* Shrew being one of the publications for 1844. The following is the list of all that I have recieved of this series — viz.— 1. Armin's Nest of Ninnies. 2. Ghost of Richard 3. 3. Chester Plays, Part 1.; 4. Timon. 5. Pride & Lowliness 6. Gosson's School of Abuse. 7. Oberon's Vision. 8. The Alleyn Papers. 9. Nash's Pierce Pen. 10. True Tragedy of Richard 3; 11. & 12 Two nos. of Shakspeare Soc. Papers. 13 Sir Thomas More. 14 Collier's Mem. of Alleyn. 15 Tarlton's Jests. 16 Secd. & Third parts of Henry 6 17 Coventry Mysteries; 18. Revels at Court. 19. North-

---

[167] The New York *Morning News* ran from Aug. 21, 1844, through Sept. 8, 1846; the *New York Weekly News* from Sept. 7, 1844, through Sept. 5, 1846. It was edited by J. L. O'Sullivan and S. J. Tilden. The publisher was J. and H. G. Langley. Duyckinck was the literary editor.

[168] Valeria.

[169] Simms' three letters on the drama, entitled "Thoughts on Theatricals," form part of his series published in the *Southern Patriot* during July and September (see note 158, Aug. 9, 1846). They are printed in the issues for Aug. 19, 20, and 21.

brooke's Treatise. 20. Johnson & Drummond. 21. **Tracts by**
Forde. 22. Heywood's Ed. IV 23. Patient Grissell. 24. MS of
Henry IV. 25. Illustrations of Fairy Myths. 26. Merry Wives of
Windsor. 27. Fair Maid of Exch. 28. Henslowe's Diary. These
are all. If they have other numbers in their collection they are
mine. Will you see them on the subject, and write me in regard
to this & the other matters. As soon as I get over present troubles,
I shall discourse to you more satisfactorily.

Yours faithfully &c.

Simms

E. A. Duyckinck Esq.

324: To James Lawson

Charleston Sep 22, 1846

My dear Lawson

God has again stricken us with his anger, and we are again
mourners. I committed to the grave yesterday our dear little girl
Valeria, who has been suffering more or less all the summer. Her
sufferings ceased on Sunday night. She had reached her four-
teenth and had entered some ten days on the fifteenth month of
her age. Teething, which in all climates is the severe period for
trial with our young, caused all her sufferings. To us, this dispensation is particularly severe, not simply because of the loss of
the one precious little object, but because it seems to show that
our misfortunes of this sort are not lessened in their repetition.
When we reflect that this is the fourth dear child whom we have
been required to surrender to the giver in a comparatively short
space of time, the heart shrinks with terror from what would seem
to be a peculiar and unrelenting destiny. We ask of our secret
terrors where & when this destiny will forego its demands, and
tremble at the probable requisitions which it may still make at
our hands. Were we good Christians, and could we hope that our
virtues, sublimed by our sorrows, would make us what we should
be, we should surely find some consolation in this conviction; but
when I look back and percieve how little, in this respect, our previous losses have done for our hearts, — how stubborn, how cold,
how insensible and unmovable we continue — how full of human
pride, — how easily won by human vanities — we can only weep
as hopelessly over our own hearts, as we weep mournfully over

our children's graves. — God keep you & your dear wife, my friend, from sorrows such as ours, and make you worthy of his favour, without subjecting you so severely to his scourge. Keep us in your thoughts and prayers.

I wrote you on the birth of our little Mary Lawson, and apprised you that we had called the little one after your wife. It is thus that God compels us to thank his bounty even while he makes us feel his severity. If he takes away, he gives. He blesses even while he punishes. The infant is a fine and very hearty one — looking, they tell me, very much like me. The mother is not so well as we could wish. She has been thinner than usual, for some time past, — & is too averse to exercise to be healthy. We shall try & amend it this winter. — Do not forget me in the joy & pride which you naturally feel in the deserved successes of Forrest at the Park.[170] I sympathize with him & yourself as well as I am able to do at this moment. Present me to him affectionately and with my best respects to his wife & Miss Sinclair. I do not despair of doing something yet for Forrest, of which neither he nor I shall be ashamed. — If you have not procured the wheat seed, through Sherwood — if he has neglected it, — I beg that you will see about it without delay, as the season approaches rapidly for planting it. Procure three barrels of the *"bearded*["] wheat seed, new crop, and forward them addressed to me. The money you can draw for or leave over as you think proper. I will try soon and send you an article or two for Colton's Review, for which he promises cash.[171] I have not heard a syllable from Duyckinck since I reached home, nor a proof sheet nor any thing. Is any thing the matter? God bless & keep you all in health and happiness. Give my love and that of my wife and Augusta to Lyde & a kiss for the sweet children.

Yours faithfully

Simms.

---

[170] Forrest opened at the Park Theatre, New York City, on Sept. 14 as "Lear." On succeeding nights he played "Othello," "Hamlet," "Macbeth," "Richelieu," "Spartacus," "Damon," and "Metamora" (see Odell, *Annals of the New York Stage*, V, 249). Although Forrest had met with reverses in London during the previous season and although there were many Americans who had become weary of his display of physical force, he still had an ardent following.

[171] "Structure and Moral of Prose Fiction." See note 173, Oct. 1, 1846.

325 : To James Lawson

Charleston, Oct. 1, 1846

My dear Lawson

My wife has just had prepared for yours, a couple of Southern dishes which we shall send by the Steam Packet Southerner to your address which we trust will reach you in safety, and which we as sincerely trust will not be wanting in 'attraction' for your palates. One of these is a pie made of shrimps, and the other a potato-pone.[172] The first is a dish for the ordinary dinner, the last is usually eaten by way of desert. Our shrimp may remind you of your lobster, but is considered of far greater delicacy. The potato pone is a favorite pudding among our young people, and may please yours. My wife tells me to say that how far they may be well made is out of her power to determine. She could not see to them herself, and Augusta, who has no great experience in such matters, had a chief hand in their preparation. The shrimp pie must be heated pretty warmly before eaten, but the potato pone *may* be eaten cold. Some people prefer it cold, others warm; but by warming it you can try it both ways, a portion being suffered to remain & become cold again. Gilmore has filled up the vacant space in the little box with a few potatoes for Katy & Jimmy—such, he says, as he would give them every day if they would come to see him at Woodlands. I will try & send you on a Barrel of them after I go to the plantation. — I have just prepared an article on the "Structure & Moral of Prose Fiction" which I will endeavour to forward by the Southerner to your address. I have designed it for Colton's American Review, and under an arrangement with him, you will be so good as to offer it to him at $20, though it should bring at least $30. I am not bound specifically by this arrangement, which contemplated another class of writings, — so that if he *will* pay you more than $20 for it, I do not think you would err in taking it. I may send you another for him or for the Democratic in the course of an-

---

[172] Shrimp pie and potato-pone are favorite Charleston delicacies. Shrimp pie is of two basic varieties, made with bread or with rice. The latter was perhaps the Simms version—a quart of fresh tomatoes stewed, a quart of fluffy, dry-cooked rice, two or three pounds of the famous small Bull Bay's shrimp, browned spring onions, baked to a turn with home-cured bacon stripping the top. Potato-pone is a nutty concoction of raw grated sweet potato; softened with boiling water, seasoned with butter, sugar, lemon juice and nutmeg; shaped like a corn pone and browned in an iron skillet.

other week.[173] Enclosed, I send a little poem for Taylor's Illustrated Magazine.[174] Do me the favor to see Taylor, and say to
him that I have not recieved the Septr. or October numbers of
the work, nor any of his publications since I left New York.
You must get him to make me up a collection of what he has
issued since that period, and in particular, his dramatic publications. Young Taylor will do this for you very obligingly. Let
him take my address & send his issues, or let him give them to
you & you can send them through W & P. or H & B. The last
of his Dramatic Library which I recd. from him was No. 20.
(Venice Preserved). Perhaps Duyckinck would see Colton about
the article, but this just as you please. — We hear nothing as
yet about the wheat. If Sherwood has sent it he has sent, or we
have recd., no Bill of Lading, and vessels are arriving constantly,
in short passages, & our planting season is rapidly going. Pray
ask by what vessel the wheat was shipped & when. She may have
gone to the bottom. — We are here in dull condition. My wife
is very lowspirited, and looking worse than I have ever seen. Our
little Mary Lawson thrives finely, is very fat and hearty, and it
is thought very pretty. She should be to satisfy her namesake. I
propose to set off tomorrow on a brief visit to my constituency.
I visited them some three weeks ago. I do not know that this is
necessary but it is proper. My friends tell me that there is no
doubt of my reelection, though I have made few efforts to secure
it, and would have withdrawn if I could. I visited the plantation
at the same time; but the prospect there is very gloomy. The
catterpillar has swept the cotton fields there as everywhere else
throughout the State. Write me soon about the wheat, and hold
me

Ever truly Yours — &c —

W. G. S.

---

[173] No article on this subject was published in either the *American* [*Whig*]
Review or the *Democratic Review* during 1846-1847. Perhaps Simms' "Modern
Prose Fiction," *S. Q. R.*, XV (April, 1849), 41-83, is the article he here
refers to. Simms' only signed contribution to the *American* [*Whig*] *Review*
during 1845-1846 is a poem, "Monna," II (Dec., 1845), 622-623. Nothing
bearing his signature appears in the *Democratic Review* for 1845. For his
contributions during 1846, see note 23, Jan. 10, 1846, and note 48, Feb. 9, 1846.

[174] The *New York Illustrated Magazine* (Sept. 20, 1845-June, 1847) was
published by William Taylor and edited by Lawrence Labree. Simms' poem is
"The Martyr," II (Nov., 1846), 416.

326: To EVERT AUGUSTUS DUYCKINCK

[*c.* October 1, 1846][175]

My dear D.

You will have heard before this of the scourge to which we have been subjected in our little family. I have learned to endure perhaps too stubbornly, but my poor wife suffers at once from actual pain, as from her privation. We hope no benefit to her till we can remove to the plantation, which we shall do about the 1st. Nov. or before, if a heavy frost will justify the transition.— I can scarcely be said to have done anything in a literary way, since I left the North. I have been nursing & anxiously waiting all the while, and I shall probably do no great deal until I leave town. If again returned to the Legislature, I shall really do little before the New Year.— Then, however, God willing, to determined labor.— I thank you for what you have done and are doing towards my little commissions.[176] Do not suffer Langley to evade you. They are exceedingly dilatory in that establishment. I shall look for the sheets of V. & R with some anxiety. Did you note my alterations & explanations in the article on C. M.[177] From him I hear nothing. How came you to publish Hochelaga [178] —perhaps one of the most malignantly hostile of all the English books upon America, and a work of no great ability either. An impertinent & ignorant book! A *good* book on the Jesuit Miss. ought to be acceptable.[179]—I could wish to have a copy of the

---

[175] This letter is postmarked Oct. 2. The year is established by Simms' reference to the death of Valeria on Sept. 20.

[176] See letter of Sept. 14. On Sept. 22 Duyckinck wrote to Simms: "There is always some little eddy in New York but nothing lately of a whirlpool character worth sending you. Putnam got off and with him your package of presentation copies. The sheets of Smith are not yet ready but the Langleys promise them to me by the first in time for the next steamer. They do not publish till afterwards. Views & Reviews is all stereotyped & I will have the sheets forwarded which you have not yet seen. . . . A 'Yankee Doodle', an American Punch is in a state of forwardness—a really creditable thing to appear on the 3d October. . . . Mathews lets off a leader. . . . If you have a hatful of epigrams I will be happy to communicate them." (Original in the Columbia University Library.)

[177] Simms' article on Cornelius Mathews, entitled "The Humourous in American and British Literature," *Views and Reviews,* Second Series, pp. 142-184.

[178] Eliot Warburton, ed., George D. Warburton's *Hochelaga; or England in the New World,* 2 vols. (New York: Wiley & Putnam, 1846).

[179] Simms reviewed William Ingraham Kip's *The Early Jesuit Missions in North America* (New York: Wiley and Putnam, 1846) in the *Southern Patriot* of Nov. 25, 1846.

new ed. of Typee—containing the sequel—and a copy of Foster's work. I thank you for the children's books, which I greatly affect, and of which a good notice has been written.[180] If I can get the papers on the Drama, I will send them you. Some *were* sent. I shall probably weave them into something elaborate for the Messenger or some other vehicle.[181] I have put up for Lawson an article which he will probably get you to hand to Colton, or if Colton should not like it to the Democr. Review. It is some 27 pages foolscap, on the "Structure & Moral of Prose Fiction" — an idealizing of the subject.[182] It should bring $30. but I leave the matter to J. L. who has a good business scent.—I am not sure that any of the persons you mention for 'Yankee Doodle' are wits of the proper order. All persons of talent, true, — but not of that sort, it strikes me, (if Punch is the model) which will answer.[183] But they may have resources which have not been developed. The thing is frequent. Some of my epigrams you have seen — most of them have been published. If any thing strikes me, I will send it you.[184] — Will you ask some of your publishers what have been the works already put by the Camden Society, and what will be the cost of procuring them; also — what the annual subs? But I write languidly — and have nothing to say. I am about to set off on a three day's visit to the country. Do W & P. get the notices I send them frequently. Did Mr. P. get the mag.

---

180 Though Simms had earlier reviewed *Typee* in the *Southern Patriot* of April 9, 1846 (see note 105, March 27, 1846), he apparently did not notice this second edition, published about this time. *The Life and Correspondence of the Rev. John Foster,* ed. Dr. Ryland (New York: Wiley and Putnam, 1846), was reviewed favorably in the *Southern Patriot* of Nov. 23, 1846; the children's books, under the heading of "Juvenile Gift Books," received a favorable notice on Oct. 3, 1846.

181 See note 169, Sept. 14, 1846. We have found no record of these letters on the drama having been revised and published as an article.

182 See letter to Lawson of Oct. 1, 1846.

183 *Yankee Doodle* (Oct. 10, 1846-Oct. 2, 1847) was edited by Cornelius Mathews. His assistants were Richard Grant White and George G. Foster. See note 176, above.

184 Simms' epigrams, under the heading "Wayside Laconics," were published in the *Southern Patriot* of April 22, April 28, May 26, Sept. 6, Sept. 28, Dec. 1, Dec. 18, Dec. 22, Dec. 23, and Dec. 29, 1846; Jan. 8, Jan. 20, Jan. 21, Jan. 23, Feb. 8, Feb. 12, Feb. 13, Feb. 25, March 11, March 12, March 20, March 25, March 27, April 3, April 6, and April 13, 1847. Some of these are signed "Skia," a hitherto unrecognized pseudonym of Simms. The epigrams were later included in *Egeria: or, Voices of Thought and Counsel, for the Woods and Wayside* (Philadelphia: E. H. Butler & Co., 1853).

&c. Present me respectfully at home, to C. M. and other friends.[185]

Yours faithfully &c

W G Simms

E. A. D.

327 : To James Lawson

Charleston, Oct. 9. 1846.

My dear Lawson

In an hour or two I set off for the country to see my constituents, & to remain with them till after the election which takes place on Monday. There is a very strong opposition to me, and my long absence from the plantation affords some specious means to the opposition for operating against me. The cry is that I am a Northern man, that my affinities are with the North &c. The opposition to me is dictated by a selfish desire on the part of certain obscure but vain men in the district who regard me as very much in their way. There is another motive. One of my particular friends is the Commissioner in Equity.[186] His office is desired by another — a man of large family influence, — and as this office is elected by the Legislature, he runs a ticket of persons pledged to his support. Among a people so ignorant as many of our poor farmers are, it is not difficult for cunning men who are also unprincipled, to effect a great deal, and a great many slanders & misrepresentations have been used against me. I have met the enemy with the broadest challenges. Have given them the lie openly in public speeches, and it is possible that I may yet get into some personal issues before the canvas is over. The office is nothing to me, but once in the field, I must keep up the fight on account of my friend, whose office is at stake. Should I be defeated, you may have a visit from me sooner than you expect, or probably —wish? My friends tell me that there is no danger of my defeat, and there is scarcely any name cried but

---

[185] Simms is here speaking of the firm of Wiley and Putnam; the copy of the *Southern and Western Magazine and Review* he had sent by John Russell to George Palmer Putnam (see letter to Duyckinck of Aug. 9, 1846) ; and Cornelius Mathews.

[186] At this time Alfred Proctor Aldrich was running for re-election as commissioner in equity (see letter to Perry of Oct. 19, 1846). His opponent was Winchester Graham, of Barnwell District, admitted to the bar at Columbia in 1843.

mine in the whole district. I am less sanguine, and think it probable, as I am personally so little known, that I shall be run very
closely. *Mais, nous verrons.* — We have recieved from Mr. Hopkins the B. Lading for the wheat, but it has not reached us yet.
I will thank you, as soon as possible, to send me the Bill of what
it cost — including drayage &c. as I am to spare a portion of it
to a neighbour, who is very particular — who will not recieve a
present and is very curious always in knowing exactly what is
to pay. — I shall probably write you again after my return from
the country. Little Mary Lawson is thriving finely though her
mother has very little milk to give her. But her alimentiveness is
good & she eats without effort. Gilmore is all agog to get into the
country. He rides whenever he can get a chance, whether in cart
or carriage or on horseback, with one of the boys. He promises
fine times to Jimmy this winter if he will come on. It would be
a new world, at Woodlands, to your wife & children, if the
former were not so wedded to the pallazzo in 12th Street. Her
kind letter has been recieved and will be answered shortly. My
wife was sensibly affected by it. Remember us all affectionately
to her. Present me to Mr. & Mrs. Forrest, & to Miss Sinclair.
I should like to be at the dinner to F. — I remember him every
now & then in our papers.[187]

Yours in haste.

W. G. S.

---

[187] In the *Southern Patriot* of Oct. 8, 1846, is the following notice: "The
complimentary dinner to Mr. Forrest, the Tragedian, by citizens of New-York
is to take place at the 'N. Y.' Hotel on the 16th inst." For this dinner see
notes 199, Oct. 23, 1846, and 250, Nov. 19, 1846. Earlier, in the *Southern
Patriot* of Aug. 21 (see note 169, Sept. 14, 1846), Simms comments: "Forrest,
let me say, is the creation of the popular theatricals. His bold personations, his
daring reaches, his free, fearless execution, wild and startling transitions, great
physique, and fresh, prompt resources—are due to, and illustrative of, the
influence of the masses. His vigor compensated [*sic*] for his crudenesses—his
courage for his frequent harshness—his genius for his defective tastes,—his
unique entireness for his frequent disregard to details." In the issues of Aug.
31, Sept. 4, and Sept. 25 Simms further comments on Forrest.

328: To John Beverly Christian [188]

Charleston S. C. Oct. 15. [1846][189]

Hon. John B. Christian

Rector, Board Visitors, Williamsburg Va

dear Sir — It may appear presumptious in a stranger to trespass upon your attention, but the desire to serve a worthy Gentleman & friend, as well as to promote the interests of your Institution, prompts me to recommend to the favorable notice of your Board, the claims of Mr. George Frederick Holmes, late of South Carolina, now of your State, who is desirous of filling the Chair of Belles Lettres & Philosophy in William & Mary College. As to the competency of Mr. Holmes for this situation, there is but one opinion among us in Carolina. He is a Gentleman of moral & character, an industrious student of rare industry and of powers of expression & acquisition quite as remarkable. Thoroughly acquainted with the departments which he seeks to fill, he has yet resources within himself of originality which I have no doubt, would enable him to improve the lesson which he teaches, and commend it with novel aspects to the minds of his classes. He is singularly well read in most branches of literature, has digested his reading with success, and is a graceful, free & impressive writer. — While I thus urge the claims of one whom I personally esteem, I feel sure that I commend to your favour, a Gentleman, who, in the chair to which he aspires, would be of great service to your Institution.

I am, Sir, with great respect

Your obt. & obliged Servt

W. Gilmore Simms

---

[188] John Beverly Christian (1796-1856) was born at Cedar Grove, New Kent County, Va. He was educated at the College of William and Mary; settled in Williamsburg, where he practiced law; and served as judge of the general court in Williamsburg (1835-1848). From 1844 to the time of his death he was a member of the Board of Visitors of the College of William and Mary. His sister was the first wife of President John Tyler.

[189] This letter is dated by the fact that George Frederick Holmes was appointed professor of history and political economy at the College of William and Mary in 1846. He entered upon his duties in 1847, but served only a year. His services were terminated by a schism among faculty members which was so disrupting that classes were suspended during the session 1848-1849 to let tempers cool off. At the time of the writing of Simms' letter Holmes was professor of ancient languages at the University of Richmond.

329: To Benjamin Franklin Perry

Charleston, Oct 19. [1846][190]

My dear Perry

To take time by the forelock, let me entreat you not to suffer the claims of my friend, A. P. Aldrich, Esq. the present incumbent of the Commissioner's (Equity) office in Barnwell District, to be anticipated by any other applicant. I am induced thus to request your attention, as we have discovered that an exceedingly secret & insidious attempt is making to wrest him of it, and place it in the hands of one of his neighbours. The conspirators have with great adroitness, and many falsehoods, succeeded in defeating my re-election. We trust to defeat the principal of the party, in reaping the fruits of his treachery & theirs. Aldrich, I need scarce tell you, is not only a most excellent man, with a large family, but is a first rate Commissioner. A most insane cry for rotation in office—as if office was a public cow at whose dugs every body had a right to suck—has helped the opposition. Let me hope for your assistance for my friend, and believe me yours

As faithfully as ever

W. Gilmore Simms

Hon. B. F. Perry.

330: To Rufus Wilmot Griswold

Charleston Oct. 21. [1846][191]

My dear Sir

Your friendly note, — addressed to me in N. Y. but not recd. till long after I had been in Charleston, — accompanying the copy of English Poets, — should have been answered before now but for the severe afflictions & troubles of my family. I have been a nurse, awaiting the most painful dispensations of Providence daily, ever since I reached the South — have lost another dear child, the fourth in almost the same number of years, — and have my wife at present in very feeble condition. But for this I should have noticed your work in our papers. I still propose to

---

[190] Dated by Simms' references to Alfred Proctor Aldrich's campaign for re-election as commissioner in equity and to his own defeat for re-election to the South Carolina House of Representatives. For the results of the latter election, see note 239, Nov. 17, 1846.

[191] Dated by Simms' reference to the death of Valeria on Sept. 20.

do so, and shall send you the notice when it appears.[192] — I thank you for it, not only as a token of your regard, but as it supplies a considerable space in my library. Several of the Poets of the century were unknown to me except by name. For this reason I could have wished that you had been more copious in your extracts from those authors of whom we have no American Editions. — I shall look hopefully for your promised copy of Milton, and shall be pleased to examine editorially its claims to public favor.[193] When you come South, seek me at Woodlands, where your letters, *ad interim,* will find me.

Very truly Yours &c

W. Gilmore Simms

Rev. R. W. Griswold

331 : To James Lawson

Charleston Oct 23. [1846] [194]

dear Lawson

Enclosed is a Letter which I have this moment recieved. I propose to answer it favorably, and to send you an article as soon as I go into the country which I do tomorrow.[195] My wife has already gone, though not to the plantation. I took her up to a healthy precinct, with little Mary Lawson, about a week ago. She (my wife) is very puny & feeble — looks wretchedly, and has broken inconcievably within the past year. Sorrow & frequent breeding are the causes of her prostration. We have had enough, as you know, to overthrow any spirit less stubborn than my own. But mine is not wholly unshaken. The truth is, my dear Lawson, I have become greatly a discontent. Carolina has been a region of tombs for me, and my worldly prosperity is by no means such

---

[192] In his review of *Poets and Poetry of England, in the Nineteenth Century* in the *Southern Patriot* of Nov. 10, 1846, Simms writes that Griswold has "performed it in such a manner as to leave little to be required, and less to be complained of. . . . It is an excellent library book, beautifully printed, and illustrated by seven rich engravings on steel."

[193] Griswold's two-volume edition of *The Prose Works of John Milton* was published by H. Hooker, Philadelphia, in 1845. A second edition was published by Wiley and Putnam in 1847 (see the *Literary World,* II [Sept. 25, 1847], 182). It is probably this second edition that Simms here has in mind.

[194] Dated by Simms' reference to his defeat for re-election to the South Carolina House of Representatives. For the results of this election, see note 239, Nov. 17, 1846.

[195] See note 198, below.

as to make me desire to continue here. Mr. Roach's affairs
do not prosper, and I seriously deliberate upon the propriety
of transferring myself, family or not, to Philadelphia or New
York. There are some reasons why I should think of Phila.,
which I shall communicate hereafter. At present, I must wait
for certain events. I will go to work industriously for the next
six months and get as much matter under weigh as I can make
available next summer at the North. It is possible, however,
that I may come to New York as soon as I have got Bayard[196]
ready for the press. My constituents fortunately have relieved me
from farther service. I intimated the probability & the causes
for this event in a previous letter. [197] Though to me of no sort
of importance, it has yet caused quite a sensation as well out
of the district as in it, proving me to be much more popular
than I ever fancied myself before; — and already have I been
applied to by leading men to consent that I shall go into the
canvas for the next Congressional election when no such difficulties will prevail to my defeat, as have operated upon me in
this. But, I have given them no encouragement. — In sending
you any thing for Mr. Labree you must get the cash for it. I
shall probably send you a Tale in three parts, for each of which
you will demand $20 cash, unless you prefer the $3 per page
arrangement. I suspect that each part will make more than 7
pages. But, this for yourself when you recieve the article.[198]

---

[196] *The Life of the Chevalier Bayard.* See note 315, Oct. 19, 1845.

[197] See letter of Oct. 9.

[198] In a letter dated New York, Oct. 20, 1846, Lawrence Labree, editor of
the *New York Illustrated Magazine,* writes to Simms: "We are now engaging
contributors for our next vol. of the Ill. Mag'n and should be happy to consider
you among the list of the *regulars.* If we can agree upon terms, you might
contribute an article a month. We don't pretend to offer less than $3—a page,
but could you not contribute prose articles for that at present? As we do better
—and I have every reason to believe we shall—you shall be secured a satisfactory price. At any rate, will you contribute an article for our January No.?
Make your price as moderate as you can, and say what you *will* write for
regularly. I should like to have your article in hand as soon as the 5th of
November, prox. as we must have the Magazine out by the last of that month,
for Wiley & Putnam to send off an Edition for London. We intend to make, Sir,
a really elegant and valuable Mag. I should like you to illustrate, in your
articles, incidents of our Southern history, Indian Legends, connected with
the early settlements, or with our *righteous* wars against them—adventures of
our hardy Pioneers, and such other American matter as you may fancy. Your
own taste, however, will be your best guide. Continuous papers I think I will
defer for the present, unless you have a proposition to make." (Original in
the South Caroliniana Library.) Simms' contribution, "The Maroon," was published in III (Jan.-June, 1847), 8-12, 54-59, 112-115, 149-154, 219-224, 291-296.
It was republished in *Marie De Berniere: A Tale of the Crescent City,* pp.
190-319.

— I percieve that you have given a famous dinner to Forrest.[199] I congratulate you, not less than him, on his successes. — And when is he to bring out C. M. — and when is 'Witchcraft' to appear in N. Y.[200] — and what think you of the Doodle? These are questions to puzzle you. Our friends will see by the career of Yankee Doodle, that what I have all along told them of American humour, is true to the syllable. The two first numbers have reached me, and I am not encouraged by them with any hopes. I suppose the leading article in No. 1 to be by C. M.[201] — Eh? — Let me hear from you, and present me & Augusta, — who is all, with the exception of Gilmore & Mary Steele [202] whom I have with me in town, to your dear wife & children. Say to the former that she must not be confounded, to see me some day in December bolting in to dinner at the palace in 12th Street. Well, you are all fixed & flourishing. My regards to Forrest, of whom I have made frequent note,[203] — to Bryant & the rest —

Yours Ever as Ever —

W. G. S.

332: To Evert Augustus Duyckinck

Charleston, Oct 24. [1846][204]

My dear D.

Tomorrow I remove for the plantation where I hope to hear from you soon & frequently. I regret that up to this moment I get none of the sheets of Vol 2. V & R. Pray let me have those of the last forms that I may revise them prior to publication. I

---

[199] A full account of this dinner in honor of Edwin Forrest, held at the New York Hotel, New York City, on Oct. 16, is given in the New York *Evening Post* of Oct. 17. William Cullen Bryant presided. In the *Southern Patriot* of Oct. 8 is an announcement of this dinner, of Oct. 21 a short notice, and of Nov. 7 a long account of Bryant's speech delivered on the occasion.

[200] Cornelius Mathews' *Witchcraft* was not brought to New York until May, 1847. See note 44, Feb. 2, 1847.

[201] "'Yankee Doodle Come to Town,'" I (Oct. 10, 1846), 3-4. Under the heading "Yankee Doodle's Come to Town" Simms writes of this periodical in the *Southern Patriot* of Oct. 19: "Here is the veritable lad before us—rather more striking than comely—rather more flourishing than fine—but still a fellow of imposing points, and of considerable character after his own fashion."

[202] Mary Govan Steele (born on November 6, 1818), whose father (John Andrew Steele) was a first cousin of Mrs. Nash Roach (Eliza Govan) and whose mother (Harriet Roach) was a sister of Nash Roach.

[203] See note 187, Oct. 9, 1846, and note 199, above.

[204] Dated by Simms' reference to *Yankee Doodle*, which ceased publication with the issue of Oct. 2, 1847.

see that the N. A. is down upon me after an expected fashion. A curious contradiction exists between its generalities & its specifications. In summary, I am nothing; but my tales are pronounced upon very highly in comparison with such productions generally, which the critic, however, differing from all authorities, ancient & modern, rates at a low standard. But the thing is not so bad as I had reason to look for at such hands. We shall survive it, I fancy.[205] — And talking of tales reminds me that I have a collection which I hold to be far superior to those of the W & C. of a purely imaginative character.[206] Can we do anything with these in your quarter. Pray advise me of whatever

---

[205] This review of *The Wigwam and the Cabin,* First and Second Series, and *Views and Reviews,* First Series, appears in the *North American Review,* LXIII (Oct., 1846), 357-381. The reviewer remarks (p. 376) that the articles in *Views and Reviews* "contain but little valuable criticism; they unfold no principle of beauty, and illustrate no point in the philosophy of literature and art. They breathe an extravagant nationality, equally at war with good taste and generous progress in liberal culture." Though thus damning *Views and Reviews,* the *North American* accords the tales in *The Wigwam and the Cabin* a place "in the not very high department of literature to which they belong" and then praises them in detail (pp. 359-373) : "Compared with either of these selected representatives [Poe's *Tales* and Headley's *The Alps and the Rhine,* both also recently published as part of Wiley and Putnam's 'Library of American Books'], The Wigwam and the Cabin is a collection of masterly efforts. . . . There is much in them that is characteristic, much that fixes attention and remains in the memory; and something that gives us a real insight into the forms of life and the relations of society, which are the central point around which they turn. . . . The first story in the collection is entitled Grayling, or Murder will out. The incidents are well selected and neatly arranged; and the superstitions and circumstances of fact, which blend curiously together to bring about the conviction of the murderer, are ingeniously managed. The piece called The Two Camps contains vivid descriptions of border life and Indian warfare. . . . The Last Wager is a story in which a more soaring manner is attempted, and therefore the attempt is followed by less success; but there are some vigorously wrought passages, as, for example, the game at cards on the dead body of the poisoned horse. . . . The Arm-Chair of Tustenuggee is a well constructed and amusing story, founded on a not unpoetical legend of Indian superstition. . . . The Snake of the Cabin is a tale of vulgar villany, well told, but not superior in material to criminal reports which may be read daily in the newspapers. One of the best pieces in the collection is the story of Oakatibbé. . . . Besides its merits as a specimen of narrative fiction, it deserves the attention of the philosopher. . . . The Giant's Coffin is a striking but disagreeable tale, which might have been wrought into a greatly superior delineation of fierce passion, had the author possessed a more delicate artistic sense. Sergeant Barnacle is extravagant; but that, too, embodies the materials of a fine piece of narrative and character-drawing. The Old Lunes is an amusing, but rather commonplace story. The Lazy Crow is a capital picture of negro superstition. . . . Caloya, or the Loves of the Driver, is in a more pretending vein. . . . But the plot is feeble and foolish, and the negro driver is simply disgusting. . . . Lucas de Ayllon . . . is well told, and the final catastrophe of De Ayllon . . . shows his powers of description in a very favorable light." *Yankee Doodle,* I (Oct. 24, 1846), 33, facetiously replies to the *North American Review*'s criticism.

[206] The never published volume of tales of the imagination, frequently discussed in connection with *The Wigwam and the Cabin.*

happens in our way & world, as you are aware that I have material actually ready, which I wish to launch whenever circumstances are favorable. Is 'Yankee Doodle' a hit? I fear not. You will soon discover, as I have taught & written, that American humor is a blank. The thing is totally inconsistent with American character; and to prove that Tom, Dick & Harry, have sometimes said & done humourous things, proves nothing for the national ability & susceptibility. I have some squibs which I may send you hereafter, if you think them desirable.[207] But I make no pretensions to wit or humour, — if for no other reason than the single one that my neighbors always insist upon their own & deny mine. I am willing that they should have their own way. — I am going to work hard on my Bayard & my Huguenots. I may make a dash at something in another way. — Talking of Yankee Doodle, did you see a paragraph I put into our paper intimating the probability of Yankee Doodle being an old child's jingle of our British fathers.[208] For this suggestion see Halliwell's Nursery volume in the Percy collection. There, it runs thus —

"Yankee Doodle came to town
Upon a Kentish Poney;
He stuck a feather in his hat,
And called him Macaroni."

The thing may be modern enough, but you will find it at p. 82 of "The Nursery Rhymes of England" — in Percy Society Pub. Was it not to ridicule the militia of N. E. that the British Grenadiers struck up the nursery jingle — the feather in the hat &c — of a militiaman might well provoke the ridicule &c. Let me hear from you soon, and write copiously. Give us all the intelligence. Can't you send me the heroines of Shakspeare after 2.[209] I should like also the Nos. 14, 19, 22 & 22 [210] of the N. Y. Weekly Mirror. My constituents have left me out at the last election greatly to my relief, so that I shall have another month for books & papers &c

Yours faithfully &c

E.A.D. — Esq   W. Gilmore Simms

---

[207] Simms submitted at least one contribution. See his letter to Duyckinck of *c.* Nov. 3, 1846.

[208] Simms' paragraph, which contains the same material as that given here, appears in the *Southern Patriot* of Oct. 2, 1846.

[209] Anna Brownell Jameson's *Characteristics of Women, Moral, Poetical, and Historical* was being published in parts by Wiley and Putnam.

[210] Thus.

Do not give your affections to Yankee Doodle. It cannot live.
It suits neither you nor me, nor Mathews. It has no vitality.
It gives you no room. You will only fritter yourself away upon
it. Look rather to a work of different character. Keep in view
the magazine—an earnest, high-toned, bold, and various mode
of speech & philosophy. This is for yourself. I would not wittingly
discourage our friends who have larger hopes of Y. D. than are
mine.

333: To Benjamin Franklin Perry

Woodlands, Oct 30. 1846

My dear Sir

It would be a long history which would occupy much more than
a letter sheet, to account to you for my defeat for the Legislature.
I should be doing injustice to our people, however, not less than
to myself were I to suffer you to suppose that my claims were
not really felt & acknowledged among them. It will suffice perhaps
were I to say to you that I was run against by all the candidates,
six or seven in number. Two of them were interested, domestically, in the ulterior object of ousting Aldrich in favor of a
relative; [211] and they succeeded in what is termed *logrolling* with
the rest; — and by dint of great & sleepless as well as secret industry, and the supineness & confidence of my friends in some
places, in barely beating me. I refused to treat or to electioneer,
and at my own box, from which I was absent all the time, the
people never turned out to vote — believing me in no sort of
danger. There where I got nearly every vote that was given,
there were but 80 odd votes given, when the box might easily poll
160. I was beaten by 45. My friends supported three of the opposition candidates. But a truce to this. I was not over solicitous,
and would have declined the contest, but for the urgent entreaty
of my friends & neighbours. Our members elect are a very sorry
set, who cannot greatly help your legislation. — I am glad that
you so frankly allude to the Cunningham papers.[212] I certainly,

---

[211] See letters to Perry of Oct. 19, to Lawson of Oct. 9 and Oct. 23, and to
Hammond of Nov. 17.

[212] Simms' review of George Atkinson Ward's edition of the *Journal and
Letters of the Late Samuel Curwen* was published in the *Southern Literary
Messenger* in the form of five articles (see note 367, Dec. 12, 1845). The fourth
and fifth articles, entitled "Biographical Sketch of the Career of Major William
Cunningham, of South Carolina," are concerned with an appendix to the
Journal. This appendix, a sketch of William Cunningham (pp. 638-648), was
written from notes furnished by Ann Pamela Cunningham (1816-1875), the

after reading the biographies in Curwen, never supposed them to come from a Lady. I had heard more than once last year, that Miss Cunningham had been, & still was, engaged in the preparation of a volume on the subject, and it was conjected that these biographies had fallen from her pen; but this was subsequently denied by some one in Columbia last Session, and it was understood, or seemed to be understood, that Mr. Ward had been supplied with material, upon which he had dilated as we have seen. I wrote with this conviction, as, I fancy, must appear from the perusal of my papers. Of Miss Cunningham herself, I had recieved from a lady, an account equally touching & curious, and I should have been anxious, had I been assured that these papers were hers, to have foreborne any thing which might have given pain to a creature so delicately constituted.[213] Besides, it strikes me that you must see that I have treated the cases of Robt. & Patrick Cunningham with great forbearance & respect. I had many extrinsic reasons for this, apart from their own claims. I remembered the connection of Mr. Robt. Cunningham with the Union Party in 1832 &c., and had every motive to consider his claims to my regard & respect, as a worthy & intelligent Gentleman. What you tell me in regard to him is only what I had heard repeatedly before. But more than this. If you refer back to our frequent correspondences, it strikes me you will find my letters entreating you to prepare a defense of the loyalists — such as were *loyal,* — and suggesting that a good case might be made for them, in which, from material in my possession, I offered to assist.[214] But I never dreamed of papers so rash & reprehensible as these, — partic-

---

founder, in 1853, of the Mount Vernon Ladies' Association. Simms blasted the defense of her Tory relative, thereby occasioning difficulties with both the Cunningham family and Ward. Before writing his review, Simms had asked Andrew Pickens Butler (see note 18, March 15, 1843) for his opinion of the defense given for William Cunningham. Butler's reply of Aug. 21, 1845 (original in the South Caroliniana Library), severely criticizes the author for giving a false picture of the indefensible Cunningham, murderer of members of the Butler family. Robert and Patrick Cunningham are discussed by Simms in his second and third articles. (The family name is spelled, both in the past and today, differently by its individual members — sometimes *Cuningham,* and sometimes *Cunningham.* The documents of this period read *Cunningham.*)

[213] Ann Pamela Cunningham had been crippled since early youth as a result of a fall from a horse.

[214] See letter to Perry of March 15, 1843, in which he suggests that Perry get aid from Robert Cunningham, of Laurens District, the son of Patrick, who was the brother of Robert, John, and David and the cousin of William ("Bloody Bill") Cunningham. Perry himself discusses the Cunninghams in "Revolutionary History of South Carolina," *S. Q. R.,* XI (April, 1847), 481-485. He defends the brothers, but like Simms damns "Bloody Bill."

ularly in relation to William Cunningham — about whom tradition furnishes thrice the amount of enormities which I have
placed to his account. As for attempting to justify and defend
such a person, I trust no member of the Cunningham family will
think of it. They are neither responsible for his deeds nor identified with his infamy & name, and any solicitude on the subject
will only incur the danger, in the vulgar mind, of becoming
so. In my papers devoted to his family, I trust & believe I have
approached their memories with a deportment of which they have
no right to complain. I have certainly found fault with them,
but only as a historian should. I certainly esteem the *sentiments,*
and the whole tone of the papers which provoked my critiques
as objectionable in the highest degree; and though I wrote the
latter fully acquitting Miss C. of the biographies (except, probably, as furnishing notes & anecdotes — in which opinion I was
confirmed in a conversation recently with Mr. B. C. Yancey — a
relative)[215] I certainly cannot think that even though written by
a Lady, they should, whether as opinion or history, escape appropriate animadversion. Had I known that they were hers I
certainly should have shown more tenderness in my phraseology,
but as an act of justice, I could not have changed my opinions.
The report which ascribed them to her was subsequently con-
tradicted — Judge O'Neall,[216] was whispered as having a hand
in them, & indeed, the hand seemed quite too masculine to suffer
me to ascribe them to a creature so young & so nervously sensitive
as Miss C. had been described to be. Really, my dear Perry, I
should be sorry to give pain to one so highly endowed, and so
morbidly diseased as I cannot but esteem her now. To her, I
should really be glad to commend myself if any regrets for my
critic temper could soften the asperity of her moods towards me.
— Mr. Cunningham I should be equally sorry to offend, but of
course shall make no communication to him, and shall wait
patiently for his.[217] I have already suggested sufficient reasons,

---

[215] Benjamin Cudworth Yancey, son of Simms' father's lawyer, Benjamin
Cudworth Yancey, and brother of William Lowndes Yancey, the famous seces-
sionist, was a lawyer, admitted to the bar at Charleston in 1841.

[216] John Belton O'Neall. See note 166, April 10, 1845.

[217] On Nov. 9, 1846, John Cunningham, Charleston attorney at law and
solicitor in equity, wrote to Perry: "By tonights mail I send a communication
to Simms, under cover to A. P. Aldrich, a copy of which I enclose you. I
determined upon and prepared it without consultation with, or knowledge of
anyone. I came to the conclusion upon reflection that it was proper—in fact
my feelings too demanded it, and at once I acted. If Simms' reply to the second
question is affirmative and without the 'Amende humble, I shall either challenge

why I should have every motive to treat him with kindness & respect, & I really can concieve of none which should provoke me to do otherwise. — By the way, it is a feeling of blind vindictiveness, that I charge to the writer of the biographies, — and this I think fairly gatherable from their tone & temper, — and not 'motives of cruelty & bloody revenge', — as you phrase it. But, I hope to see you in Columbia during the first week in the session when we shall chat the matter over. — I thank you for your favorable word for Aldrich. I will not be in Charleston at the time you speak of, but the Saturday before the Session will probably be on the road for Columbia. Join me if you can & believe me very truly, though hurriedly,

Yours &c

W. Gilmore Simms

---

or denounce him—the first I think. I have no wish however for a mere personal affair with him, and design no impulsiveness in my course with him. In case his answer be in the negative, would you advise me to publish the correspondence or not?" In the copy of the letter to Simms, mentioned above, Cunningham writes: "As one of the Cunningham family, memoirs of whose ancestry contained in an appendix to 'Curwen's Journal and Letters' under the titles of 'The Cunninghams of South Carolina' and 'Major William Cunningham of South Carolina', were received and criticised in a series of contributions to late numbers of the 'Southern and Western Literary Messenger and Review', and as the brother of Miss A. Pamela Cunningham, who furnished the materials and statements from which these Memoirs were prepared by Mr. Ward, the editor of the above work, I deem it proper to propound to you the two following questions. Are you the author of those two contributions? Were you, when any of them were written and furnished, aware of the fact that Miss A. Pamela Cunningham furnished the materials and statements of the articles referred to? The propriety of the above questions and of a candid and prompt reply to them fully appear from the fact that the writer of those contributions frequently intimates that the author of the articles must have been a South Carolinian, one rendered partial by some tie or interested motive, and other than Mr. Ward; and indirectly as well as directly uses language allusive to such supposed author that is highly offensive. And also that those contributions are generally attributed to you.

"I here disclaim any intention, or the assumption of any right, to seek to make a personal demand upon you *in the character of an historical reviewer* for any criticism upon an historical work, and having reference solely to historical facts and personages. I place this communication upon the ground that a living private person and a lady is made the object and subject of offensive language and insinuations." (Originals in the Perry Collection, State of Alabama Department of Archives and History.) For further developments which almost resulted in personal encounters between Simms and Cunningham and Simms and Ward, see letter to Hammond of January 25, 1847.

334: To EVERT AUGUSTUS DUYCKINCK

[*c*. November 3, 1846]²¹⁸

dear D.

Enclosed is a trifle, which, if you think it of any use, you may employ, just as you deem proper, in the pages of Yankee Doodle or the Mirror, — or wherever else you please. Of course, keep all parties ignorant of its source; for nobody will suspect me of wit or humour. 'Tis *not* my vocation Hal;²¹⁹ — and even if these be the qualities of the trifle (which I don't mean to assume) it would be quite sufficient to cast doubt & discredit on the claim, to have it made as mine. Should you desire more of this sort of stuff, you can have it. I place but small value upon it. I hear nothing from you, but got Dombey & Son²²⁰ (I fancy from your hand) last night, and read it thro' before I slept, with pleasure. What new? And what the prospect of your Mage? I doubt the fate of Yankee Doodle — have no faith in the humour of a single man of all your faculty. But for the world don't tell them that. I could scarcely hope to persuade one of them out his own faith, — at least in his own case.

Write me soon & believe me very truly

Yours as Ever

W. Gilmore Simms

335: To JAMES LAWSON

[*c*. November 6, 1846] ²²¹

My dear Lawson.

Will you see to the above, the cash for which should be forthcoming with promptitude. I have, by this days mail, forwarded the second part of the story,²²² for which I will draw in your favor, as soon as I hear that it has been recieved. It may be as

---

²¹⁸ This letter is postmarked Nov. 4. The year is established by Simms' reference to *Yankee Doodle*, which ceased publication with the issue of Oct. 2, 1847. We have been unable to identify the contribution Simms mentions herein.

²¹⁹ "Why Hal, 'tis my vocation, Hal." *Henry IV*, Part I, I, ii, 116.

²²⁰ Only Wiley and Putnam's first monthly part. See letter to Duyckinck of Feb. 25, 1847.

²²¹ This letter (which lacks an envelope) is dated *c*. Nov. 6, 1846, since Simms' account of the dinner in honor of Edwin Forrest was published in the *Southern Patriot* of Nov. 7. See note 199, Oct. 23, 1846.

²²² "The Maroon." See letter to Lawson of Oct. 23, 1846.

well that you should get the money for one before presenting the
other. The *third* part, I shall send to you, unless I find that the
money for the two preceeding, has been duly paid. This will
give you some little hold upon the publisher, in the event of
his proving dilatory or treacherous. — I do not hear from you,
and feel some anxiety lest some of you should be sick and suffering. We are all now at the plantation, but my wife is very feeble
still — a mere skeleton. She does not nurse the baby,[223] for which,
however, we have procured a nurse. The little thing thrives, and
is said to resemble me very much. Tell your wife this. I fancy
it will please her, — assuming, as I do, that she thinks me not
an ill looking fellow. — Augusta will write shortly, but as I have
consented to take her to Columbia during the session, she is much
more busy in getting her clothes ready than her correspondence.
I got a Phila. paper, containing an account of the Forrest dinner,
of which I have just prepared a notice. I am not sure that the
details were fully given. Have you suffered by the storms, and
how are the averages. Present us affectionately at home, and
repeat to Madame our entreaty that we may see her & the flock
at Woodlands this winter.

Yours truly

W. G. S.

J. L.

336: To JAMES HENRY HAMMOND

Woodlands: Nov. 17. [1846] [224]

My dear Hammond.

The game which Elmore plays in regard to the Senatorial
nomination is undoubtedly well calculated to make us conclude

---

[223] Mary Lawson.
[224] This letter is dated by the discussion of Franklin H. Elmore (see note
121, Dec. 30, 1842), John C. Calhoun, and Ker Boyce (see note 225, below)
in a letter from Hammond to Simms dated Oct. 6, 1846. Hammond writes:
"Boyce is a stalker of Calhoun. Calhoun wants E. [Elmore] in the Senate
to pull ruses & in especial to act the go between with Polk, with whom he
has great influence. . . . A short time ago the Mercury discussed the Bank
editorially, closing with something like this—Perhaps under all the circumstances
one of the most inauspicious omens is the nomination of its President for the
U. S. Senate. Was that nomination made by Col. Elmore's friends or by
enemies. Was it extended in good faith to pave the way to an elevated station
for which it is acknowledged on all hands he is eminently qualified or was it
supposed he might be seduced by a brilliant bait, from a trust so long and
with such unusual consent confided to him, at the moment of its greatest
difficulty & when his experience, ability & hold upon public confidence cannot
be supplied?" (Original in the Hammond Papers, Library of Congress.)

that he seeks it — the very fact that he says nothing publicly to settle doubt as to his wishes, is one that almost says what they are; — and yet he must sacrifice greatly to go to the Senate — his pecuniary interests must suffer, and his position in the Senate must be simply subordinate, wanting as he does in the ultra combativeness of character, such as yours, which is necessary to resist Calhoun. This auxiliary position can do him no good, as his chances for the Presidency are worth ten times over those of Calhoun. Besides, if he hopes to gain a Prest. for the Bank, and a direction, quite as flexible as now, he may do so; but they will not avail him long. It is very clear to me, and I fancy must be to him, that his *ratting* signifies a falling house. It is a measure which is fatal to the Institution. This is so obvious that a strong party is busy now (not Boyce's but in this unconsciously cooperating with him) in urging his election to the Senate, to get him out of the City & the Bank, simply that the latter may perish.[225] This, I happen to know is somewhat the feeling of 'Young Charleston,' & somewhat that of 'Young Carolina.'[226] If E. knows

---

[225] George McDuffie offered his resignation from the United States Senate on Aug. 17, 1846, and Elmore was immediately considered a possible successor. The *Southern Patriot* for Aug. 29 carries an unsigned letter (attributed to State Senator Ker Boyce) suggesting the nomination of Elmore, President of the Bank of the State of South Carolina, to succeed McDuffie. The contingency of Elmore's resignation from the Bank at once aroused a furor of controversy as to its solvency. Boyce (1787-1854), wealthy and prominent Charlestonian, had earlier been a member of the House from the combined parishes of St. Philip's and St. Michael's (the city of Charleston). He was one of the founders of the Graniteville Manufacturing Company, Edgefield District, and the president of the Bank of Charleston for several years.

[226] Both Simms and Hammond allied themselves with the younger politicians of the state, often referred to during this period as "Young Charleston" and "Young Carolina," in opposition to the entrenched party of Calhoun, Elmore, and Boyce. Simms terms this latter group "Hunkers." Though numbering numerous personal friends among this group, he warred constantly against them politically. In a letter written from New York and published in the *Southern Patriot* of Aug. 15, 1846, Simms says that "the old Hunkers, always opposed to any progress which tends to lessen the offices and the spoils, will be more apt to side with Whigism, or even Abolitionism, rather than with those among their own avowed associates, who require them to make a patriotic surrender of their fleshpots." The *Southern Patriot* of Dec. 1, 1846, further comments: "New names are necessary to every political party. When will ancient Hunkerism learn this truth, as old as the days of Aristides? He was voted into banishment, because people were tired of the same name constantly sounded in their ears. The masses get vexed with and jealous of the assumed superiority of one great person. . . . The same old politician keeps in place the same old parasites, and the great majority have nothing to hope at his hands . . . and old Hunkerism must be taught that it can only live and maintain itself, by an annual infusion of *young* blood into the old veins. The old must absorb the young. . . . " On Sept. 9, 1846, the "young men" were urged by the *Southern Patriot* not to "forget to go and register your names at once. Many of you lost your votes at the recent election from your neglect.

this, & resolves to leave, then the Bank is in a worse way than any of us think it, and he, compelled, even against a higher ambition, to seek the Senatorial Chair as you suggest, with reference to money matters. Colcock,[227] as his successor (for that seems to be the scheme) is weakly sacrificing himself, in a doubtful concern, subject to annoyances of which he does not dream, and in gears and a vehicle which he knows not how to draw. He has wealth enough too, to keep him from such folly. But that is his look out, — not E.'s. Black (Comptroller)[228] told me a few days ago that, during the summer, E. told his brother that he would not be a candidate. Gen. Adams,[229] whom I met in the cars a few days after, told me that he had heard from another source that E. had declared his purpose *to run*. Who shall decide? At all events, your friends feel that he is your *worst* customer, and will, I suppose, determine what is to be done in a very short time after reaching Cola. Rhett,[230] most likely, regards his chance as hopeless. Davie,[231] is said to have gone to the Legislature, simply with regard to this object. The hopelessness of Rhett may be one reason of E's running. I take for granted that D. has no possible chance. Pickens[232] & his friends are busy still, as far as I can learn; but it is thought that he alone could not stand against you. This opinion is qualified by *the grave shakes of the head of certain of the Richlandaises.*[233] In Columbia, it is feared, that there will be some clamor against you, though Sid Johnson,[234] with whom I talked the matter over, was of opinion that your especial enemies in that quarter would find it politic & proper to be silent. The fact that Manning[235] calculates to suc-

---

Do not forget it, but perform this duty at once. You may again be called upon to support the cause of Young Charleston."

[227] William Ferguson Colcock (1804-1889), admitted to the bar at Charleston in 1825, was speaker of the South Carolina House of Representatives at this time. He had served in the legislature since 1831 and as speaker since 1841. During 1849-1853 he was a member of Congress, during 1853-1865 collector of the Port of Charleston.

[228] William C. Black was comptroller-general of South Carolina during 1846-1850.

[229] James Hopkins Adams later became governor of South Carolina in 1854. He served for one term only.

[230] Robert Barnwell Rhett. See introductory sketch of the Rhetts.

[231] F. W. Davie, from Chester District, was a member of the South Carolina House of Representatives.

[232] Frances W. Pickens. See note 120, Dec. 30, 1842.

[233] Voters of Richland District.

[234] Algernon Sidney Johnson, city alderman.

[235] John Laurence Manning, son of Richard Irvine Manning (governor of South Carolina, 1824-1826), did not succeed David Johnson (1782-1855) as governor. He served from 1852 to 1854.

ceed Johnson for Govr. is an argument to make his set cautious. You out of the field,[236] I frankly tell you, I prefer Elmore to all the tribe. I not only think him a *wiser,* but a *better* soldier than the rest, and I acknowledge his friendly deportment toward myself at all times inclines me to him after yourself, — though I am clearly of opinion that he blunders inconcievably in this present seeking. I have told Walker [237] to send to you for perusal the paper I had addressed to E. and for which we can scarcely get a publisher now.[238] But what could you expect of the 'Courier', which has always been governed by the narrowest considerations of local & selfish policy. The Mercury, so far as it might dare assert Rhett, would probably oppose Elmore's nomination as earnestly as anybody — but — that has necessities also, of a slavish nature, which make its will & wishes subject. — On Saturday, God willing, I shall go to Columbia for four or five days. I go, at some sacrifice, of time & temper. I have much work to do, making up for lost time, and I am in a sad state of mental depression. My family afflictions rather increase than end. While I had one child dying in my arms, my wife was bringing forth another. From this confinement she has never recovered, & her condition now is such as to alarm us all. I myself am physically a sufferer, with something [like] pleurisy, or a severe attack of rheumatism which looks like it. I have been for two days and nights in great suffering & write now, with several umschlags (as the Germans have it) wet linen swathings around my body. — These have allayed the inflamation, and I am mending tolerably fast. I have had losses in pecuniary matters, & but for the condition of my wife I should be tempted, repudiated as I am here, to clear out, and try my fortune wholly in literature either in the North or Europe. This defeat in Barnwell may hurt me elswhere — my pride at least.[239] It was my boast that I had the sympathies of

---

[236] Hammond had written Simms on Oct. 6: "Between you & me, I firmly believe that a winter at Washington will cost me my life. Possibly not actually kill me outright but do it effectually. I feel bound to risk it if called on. I do not feel bound to seek it. . . . But I belong to So. Ca. If she requires my services in *any line,* she shall have my best." (Original in the Hammond Papers, Library of Congress.)

[237] James M. Walker. See note 264, July 10, 1845.

[238] We are unable to identify this paper.

[239] The vote for the House of Representatives in Barnwell District stood:

James J. Wilson	1,257
Col. John M. Allen	1,154
Dr. Jas. J. Harley	1,143
Major Henry B. Rice	905
W. Gilmore Simms	860

my people — that they believed in me and were grateful for my labors. — I felt my risk in going into the contest, & should never have been beguiled into [it] by any regard to the office merely. Should I incur this risk again & on what foundations? No! you quite mistook my meaning in what I said anent Congress. I spoke only in reply to your suggestions & hinted the claim of Trotti,[240] in order that he might have no further cause of complaint. That he has real claims upon neither of us, I feel very sure, and I am equally sure that he can beat nobody who may please to run whether they hail from Beaufort or Orangeburgh. It will be a question with us in Barnwell. — Rhett out of the field, — whether we shall be overslaughed from below or not. I suppose Ed. Rhett [241] would seek to succeed him, but he is less popular than his brother. There is one man, Ben Allston,[242] who has talent. Whether it could be available or not is the question. I speak now of what is wholly in the future, though as if the question were open to you, and the summing up in regard to them myself is briefly this, that I would consent to run from B. only that she should not be compelled to waive her position, or risk it upon a candidate who could do nothing for himself. I should doubt the possibility of my contending successfully with Rhett. My ancient unionism would be made to operate against me in this district more than any other. The matter was a subject of conversation with Jamison & Aldrich[243] last spring, and the above is what we came to. They said that after you, they looked to me, in the event of any necessity occurring for contesting with a new man from below. I named Trotti, and it was at once agreed that a new man who could take the stump vigorously could beat him here, in all probability, on his own ground. My

James M. Patterson 781
John Plunket 82
The first four were elected, Simms losing his seat by 45 votes. On Oct. 15 Hammond wrote Simms: "I never had cause before to complain of Barnwell. She has generally given a cordial & creditable support to her best men. But to see you & Patterson, the only two men offering who were fit to go to the Legislature left at home & such men sent as she has sent this time not only mortifies me but deeply *disheartens* me. . . . There are several causes to which I attribute your defeat. First you were not personally known to a majority & circumstances had not enabled you to make any display which identified you with the people & made them feel generally that you were a Barnwell man." (Original in the Hammond Papers, Library of Congress.)

    240 Samuel Wilds Trotti. See note 124, Dec. 19, 1841.
    241 Edmund Rhett, of Beaufort, brother of Robert Barnwell Rhett.
    242 We are unable to identify this particular member of the Allston family.
    243 See introductory sketches of David Flavel Jamison and Alfred Proctor Aldrich, friends of both Simms and Hammond.

answer was, — I will only consent to a contest in order that the District should not be overslaughed. Of course this *entre nous.* The contingency may never trouble any of us. — I saw Walker the other day in town. We tried to cover all our points in the conference. Aldrich certainly failed to convey our distinct idea to Jamison. This, if Walker sends it you, you will find embodied (though he thinks too copiously) in my article which Ja'n. would not ignorantly father.[244] He was perhaps right. At all events, nothing now can be done till we get to Columbia. Write me *instanter,* if you can give any hints, to reach me *there,* — where I shall stay five or six days. — I am told that our people are beginning very heartily to repent of their misdoings in the election, — alledging that they were grossly decieved &c.

Yours truly, &c.

W. Gilmore Simms.

How far are you from Aiken or Hamburg?

337: To JAMES HENRY HAMMOND

[c. November 19, 1846][245]

dear Hammond

Among the Letters recently recieved, is one from our veteran mob-raiser of Orangeburg, who shows the old blood as certainly as ever. It may interest you to see what he says *en passant.* I wrote you a few days ago. I propose to go on Saturday to Columbia, and shall remain there something like a week. Write me there, if it be necessary to suggest any thing.

Yours hastily

Simms

J. H. H.

---

[244] See note 238, above.

[245] This letter is written on the third page of a letter to Simms from John Myers Felder (see note 21, March 17, 1843), dated Oct. 22, 1846. Simms' note was written a few days before Nov. 21, the Saturday on which he planned to go to Columbia. Actually he left on Sunday (see letter to Lawson of Nov. 21).

In his letter to Simms, Felder remarks of Hammond: "He ought to be one of our Senators in Congress. But his strictures on the bank of the State of So. Car. is 'imagining the thing to death,' & there is no hope for him till we get more correct notions in regard to breaking the connection of Bank & State. Bank first, state second; Bank master, state slave; Bank head, state tail; &c &c."

338: To JAMES LAWSON

Woodlands, Nov. 19. [1846][246]

My dear Lawson.

I am just in reciept of yours of the 11th. and rejoice to find that you are well, & that your Coy. has suffered little by the storms. I trust that these have nevertheless brought grist to your individual mill. I am sorry that you have had so much trouble with W & P. the more particularly as there is so sorry a pittance to requite you. I am by no means satisfied with their charge of 5 mos. interest. In that payt. they made no advance of more than $10. Their own semi annual statement made a bal. of 80 or 90 dollars in my favor, and I drew for $100. I will look up their statement & see to it. An occasional note to Langley will perhaps, be all that's necessary, until Smith has been published a few weeks, and then it may be well to trouble him. I could wish that you would send the article to Colton at $20 and say from whom it comes, and see if he wants it.[247] I suppose that Duyckinck will take charge of this mission for you. If he does not want it, it may be tendered to the Democratic on the same terms, though they can scarcely pay you cash for it. I have sent *three* parts of the story [248] to Labree, and when I send the fourth, or concluding part, it will be to you. The sooner these publishers get the several articles & publish them, the sooner will there be afforded vacancy for new supplies. Pray say to Mr. Labree that I have not recieved a single number of his mag. since that of September. I want all since, and he may send them by mail. Tell *him* also of Taylor's publications. I want their dramat. series from the close of their second vol. In looking over my papers I found some memoranda which will enable us to approximate our accounts. — Here they are. I add the wheat &c. in round numbers.

Cr. J. L. for advances to W. G. S.	
For Picture to West . .	$100.00
Cash to self—1845 . . .	50.00
,, ,, ,, ,, . . .	20.00
,, ,, ,, ,, . . .	10.00

These are items of which the amounts are known to me, although some of them as the Wheat & Boilers were a fraction less than the round figures put down here. — Here follow

---

[246] Dated by Simms' reference to his dissatisfaction with the account rendered by Wiley and Putnam. See letter to Duyckinck of March 27, 1846.

[247] "Structure and Moral of Prose Fiction." See letters to Lawson of Oct. 1 and to Duyckinck of *c.* Oct. 1, 1846.

[248] "The Maroon." See letter to Lawson of Oct. 23, 1846.

Picture Frame &c" ...   4.25
Washer woman 1.00
3 Bbls. Wheat 16.50
2 veget. Boilers 35.00
                       ————
                    $236.75

items of which I have not the amounts, but which you can readily procure from your papers, or estimate from known prices at the season when you sent them. In the — Cash paid to Bokee, you must not include the tailor's Bill, for which I left the cash with you at our settlement. — Cash paid to Bokee for cloth. — 2Bbls. apples in 1845 ½bbl nuts — Keg Buckwheat — Keg Cranberries — Postage to company in July & Augt. 1846 — These, I think, cover all the items. — and now for the offset.

Cr. W. G. S. payts. to J. L. as follows:
Cash recd. from Taylor & Co. in 1845 ....$150.00
   "   "   "   L. A. Godey dft. 1846 ....   25.00
   "   sent in dft. to J. L. ——— " 35.00
   "   from Wiley & Putnam   " 48.32
                                                       ————
                                                    $258.32

With these particulars you can easily find out how much I still owe you, & I beg that you will, for amongst my present cares is that of providing, as far as I can, for all my creditors. — I enclose you once more the a/c of Wiley & Putnam. To my notion it contains errors against me to the amt. of $30 at least. Thus see the Item "Balance of a/c as per our last statement— $63.48." If I do not err this balance was made by charging me $20 for a copy of Catlin's Indians which I had returned, and charging me with other matters all of which I made the subject of a letter to Duyckinck who wrote me that the thing had been rectified. See him on the subject & let him see them. Let them ascertain how the Bal. of 63.48 is made. *Between us, mon ami, there are few publishers but* — enough. — I only drew after their statement, & after I had shown that their credit should have been nearer $90 than $63 — and how can I be charged int. on whole amt. of five months, drawing in adv. I drew in June, the pub. being made in the autumn of the previous year. — I am, I confess, still greatly troubled — my children dying — my wife an invalid — business unproductive — capital diminishing, and I — feeling that I am not working as I should be, in my proper sphere, in my true employments. We will see what the next two months will bring forth; but if I come to N. Y. I could not again be a trespasser on your kindness, and that of your dear wife — whom

I shall ever love & esteem with yourself — longer than will enable me to fix myself quietly in some snug cheap lodging house. Do not suppose me ungrateful or unfriendly, but only a little jealous of incurring to my friend more obligations than I shall ever be able, or he will ever suffer me to pay. — On Saturday next I take Augusta to Columbia where she will spend the Session. I myself will return home in the space of a week. — I have seen the North American but not the Knickerbocker. The former notice, though unjust, dishonest, and malicious, will probably do me service, since the writer while showing what he really feels, is compelled to make some large acknowledgments in my favor. His unwillingness is manifest, but he is forced to speak. He comes to curse wholly, but he is made to mix blessings even with his curses. I can readily conjecture what would be the language of the Knickerbocker.[249] —How it would echo the ill words, and forbear the residue. — But I don't know that the echo is heard by any body. At all events, I am not much disturbed by it, or either of them. If I have any merits, I have faith in the future to find them out. Once in print, they are not to be suppressed, if they contain any thing vital; and if they do not, why my solicitude should be none at all. — I recieved the Post contg. the notice of the Forrest dinner. I thought Mathews exceedingly unfortunate in alluding to the N. A. on such an occasion.[250] He

---

[249] For the review of *The Wigwam and the Cabin* and *Views and Reviews* in the *North American Review,* see note 205, Oct. 24, 1846. In the "Editor's Table" of the *Knick.,* XXVIII (Nov., 1846), 450-454, is an account of this article. Though containing the usual flippances and sarcasms about Simms' writings, the *Knickerbocker's* account is a fairly accurate recapitulation of the *North American Review's* criticism.

[250] For this dinner in honor of Edwin Forrest, see note 199, Oct. 23, 1846. In the course of the evening Cornelius Mathews made a short speech, a plea for American nationality in literature. One object of attack was the *North American Review:* "No nation . . . has gone so long as this triumphant country of ours, without a drama of its own. . . . I am told by a quarterly journal, published in one of the Eastern states, that this demand for nationality is a false one; that we had better go on, as we began, dependent on the resources of other countries for entertainment, instruction, and the means of intellectual existence. It is very well for that aged imbecility . . . to amuse itself in its dotage with talk like this; but the country is passing—has passed—the low water mark drawn by such doubters, such advisers; and, in the rising tide, all such wretched hindrances will be swept away forever. It is certainly a very agreeable business, in idleness, to watch the caperings and imitative bounds of the street organ-grinder's monkey; hopping on the walk, leaping to his master's back, and allowed now and then, with his feeble paw, to grind out of the old hurdy-gurdy some antique and well-worn ditty.

"This suits well (I can readily understand) the tastes and cheers the heart of that prime organ of the Monkey School in literature, the old North American Review. . . . " See the New York *Evening Post,* Oct. 17, 1846.

should allow the thing to go by default any how — or at all events, use no bad words & show no anger. You probably censure him too much in supposing he meant to convey any such judgment as that you mention upon Forrests genius. If the latter comes to Charleston I will try to run down & see him; but don't know. I am quite too dull for the city. I have sent my Texian drama to Forbes — whether he will play it or not is a question.[251] I have cut it considerably. If I muster time & courage for "Locrine" I may give it him also. [252] If I were in N. Y. or Phila. I could do wonders in the way of work, under constant attrition of neighbour & rival minds. Present us affectionately to Madame, and kiss all the children for us. Tell Jimmy that Gilmore is always on the go — and will show him a hundred things if he comes to Woodland[s].

Love to Lady Lyde & self

W. G. S.

339: To JAMES LAWSON

Woodlands, Nov. 21, 1846

Dear Lawson

I wrote you two days ago & should not now write you, but having folded you up a newspaper which contains something in regard to myself, I thought it just as well to give you a sheet of explanation. You see that I am put in nomination as Lieut. Gov. of the State.[253] This has been done without my privity, and

---

[251] *Michael Bonham* (see note 75, Jan. 26, 1845). William C. Forbes was manager of the Charleston Theatre during 1842-1847. He also had interests in theatres in Savannah and Augusta, Ga.

[252] See letter to Lawson of Aug. 5, 1845.

[253] In the Greenville *Mountaineer* of Nov. 13 Simms is proposed for the office of Lieutenant Governor "as one richly meriting this honorary distinction. He is a Carolinian by birth, and has a reputation in the literary world equalled by no man in the South." The *South Carolinian* (Columbia) of Nov. 18 quotes the *Mountaineer's* nomination, and later, on Nov. 28, prints the following communication, signed "South Carolina": "We have noticed with great pleasure, the announcement of Wm. Gilmore Simms, for the office of Lieutenant Governor of this State. The Election of this gentleman, will be equally honorable to himself, and the State. His name is already connected with the history of South Carolina, as her most successful native author, in the field of Literature. We have heretofore, as a people, conferred upon him no distinctions, nor, have we acknowledged his labors in the cause of Education and Literature at home, and the increase of our reputation abroad, even in mere words. It is due ourselves, that he should receive, as he deserves, this proof that he has 'done the State some service,' and she knows and appreciates it." The *South Carolinian* of Nov. 25 contains the following account of Simms' opponent, William

emanates from the middle & mountain country. I heard of it by the merest accident a few days ago & have not been at all consulted in the business. The truth is, the whole State is indignant at my defeat in the district, a defeat brought about in the perfect confidence of my friends that I stood in no danger. So great was this security in several places that at my own poll where I got 84 out of 87 votes, — if the people had turned out they could give 170, — and I only needed 45 for election. I had every candidate against me, 7 in number, & was defeated by their log-rolling, though every leading man in the district was in my favor. I refused to treat or to electioneer, and the activity of the opposition was in consequence of their anxiety to get for one of their friends, the office of Commissioner in Equity, held by a friend of mine, whom, it was well known that my influence in the Legislature would suffice to reelect.[254] *In* the district the result *now* is one of peculiar mortification — out of it, it is one of indignation; and I am accordingly put in nomination for Lt. Gov. by friends [who] are desirous of relieving the State from the position which seems to have been assumed by the district. Of course there is no telling of the result. My own opinion is that my friends are too late in the field, for two candidates were in nomination some months ago. We shall see when I go to Columbia, which I do tomorrow, whether they have laid their plans with any skill, and have arrived at any certainty. The nomination comes from the most populous region of the State, and the men at the bottom of it are among the most influential. I shall say nothing in the matter until I am approached, and cannot say now upon what I shall then decide. Other friends are eager to run me for Congress next term; and in Charleston two months ago I was solicited to accept the nomination for Congress against Holmes,[255] in which I could have had an easy victory. — By the way, the question is often asked at home — *Could* Mrs. Lawson ever have recieved the little Box we sent by the Palmetto, and *did* the potatoes *keep* through the voyage. You are probably un-

---

A. Cain, signed "Low Country": "This distinguished gentleman having been spoken of as a candidate for Lieut. Governor, his friends respectfully urge in support of his claims his long term of public service, having been for twenty-six years a prominent member of the Legislature of South Carolina—first in the House of Representatives and more recently as a member of the Senate. Mr. Cain is a high toned, dignified Carolina gentleman, and would deserve this compliment in an eminent degree."

[254] See letters to Lawson of Oct. 9 and Oct. 23 and to Perry of Oct. 19 and Oct. 30, 1846.

[255] Isaac E. Holmes.

aware that for nearly three months we got but one letter out of you, — so busy were you at the Forrest dinner. *Your wife* would not have served us after such a fashion. Once more, — *Addio, amico mio.*

Simms.

Ask Duyckinck how the publishing business gets on and if I come north whether he will get up a Mage. Why should I not publish my tales of Imagination now?

340: To James Henry Hammond

Columbia, 24. Nov [1846][256]

My dear Hammond —

I write this from the chamber of our friend Walker, and with him in consultation. We have concluded, after careful *computation* not to risk your name in the struggle. McDuffie *has* resigned, and Elmore *is* a candidate. We are persuaded that he & his friends have been at work effectively for some time. He has satisfied the doubts of *his* friends, & has silenced if he has not satisfied the fears of those who regard the safety of the Bank. He comes into the field, it is understood, as you supposed, with the *certificate* of Mr. Calhoun. In other words, Mr. Calhoun favors his election. That, at least, is asserted. Mr. Colcock is to have his support as President of the Bank, and this is an inducement (strange to say) to the friends of Colcock. We believe — the most of us — that *his* election — Elmore's — is certain; — there are some who *profess* to *regard your claims only,* who doubt. Among these are J. M. Felder, Col. Davie & Mr. Northrop.[257] *We* doubt these as authorities, and have concluded, as we cannot now *count our men,* to peril nothing at the *present,* when it is *now* certain that *all* can be had before very long. The truth is you will soon be

---

256 This letter is dated by Simms' letter to Hammond of Nov. 17, in which he discusses the political campaign in which Walker, McDuffie, Elmore, Calhoun, Aldrich, and Davie figure. In his reply to Simms on Nov. 23 Hammond had written: "By this time you know certainly whether Elmore runs for the Senate. . . . If he is a candidate or in any event, unless there is a strong tide running in favour of me for that office, I trust you & all my friends will say at once I am no candidate. I am myself as friendly to Elmore's election as you are. He is the most suitable of all the candidates. . . . But I don't think any one can beat him." (Original in the Hammond Papers, Library of Congress.)

257 Claudian B. Northrop, admitted to the bar at Charleston in 1834, was at this time a member from St. Philip's and St. Michael's parishes of the South Carolina House of Representatives.

called for. Your strength is not only quite as great as we thought it, under ordinary circumstances, but much warmer than we had reason to suppose. Your friends in the Up Country are firm and increasing, and are already many. We are satisfied that you would even now beat any man in the field *but* Elmore; and an additional reason which prompted us to waive your claim, in the present instance, was that so many of E's friends were yours, but not against himself. We have, we think, established in the minds of his friends a claim on your behalf, by our present resolution. Felder in his hostility to the Bank, is blind to the manifest impropriety of using you simply as a club to break over his enemy's head. Davie is himself anxious for the seat, and will doubtless be a candidate at all hazards. The vote given to him will show nothing more than the strength of those who are absolutely foes to E. under any circumstances. His candidacy (Davie's) is absolutely laughed at. Of the support he will get, I have no idea beyond the single one that he has no possible chance. He may command all the *discontents* & his own & Dessaussure's [258] personal influence. We are not exactly in either category, for, next to yourself the preference of myself, Walker & *id omne* &c., is for Elmore. I may mention that the friends of yours with whom I have consulted are Walker, Jamison, Aldrich, and we have the occasional suggestions and information of others, such as Tradewell [259] &c. These all concur in our decision. It is barely possible that an attempt will be made by Felder to use your name whether we think it right or not. His hostility to the Bank has no measure of prudence & to get his revenges — nay, merely to iterate his wrath, — without any hope of his revenges — he will fling his best friends at the head of his foes, without much caring if they go through the windows. — But I must stop here, for the room fills. God bless you, and approve if you can, of what we have resolved on.[260]

Yours faithfully

W. Gilmore Simms

---

[258] William Ford DeSaussure (1792-1870), born in Charleston, practiced law in Charleston and Columbia. In 1846 he was a member from Richland District of the South Carolina House of Representatives. In 1852 he was appointed and subsequently elected to fill the vacancy in the United States Senate caused by the resignation of Robert Barnwell Rhett and served from May 10, 1852, to March 3, 1853, when he resumed his practice of law in Columbia.

[259] James Tradewell, attorney of Columbia.

[260] On Nov. 27 Hammond wrote to Simms: "Todays mail brought me your letter of Tuesday from Columbia & I hasten to express my entire satisfaction

341: To James Henry Hammond

Columbia, 27 Nov. [1846][261]

My dear Hammond.

I wrote you a few days ago and now have your letter. Our views are confirmed by subsequent events & revelations, although some of your friends are of opinion that you could make a stronger run than we are prepared to think. But we are not willing to hazard you when we cannot make any certain count in the matter. Undoubtedly you are very strong, but your friends will not speak out. Many would vote for you quietly, no doubt, — but they are not willing to give any assurances on the subject. They show no hands. You have numerous direct friends, & many might support you who do not love you; but we are very far from being persuaded that you can be elected, particularly as it is certain, that many who are really disposed to prefer you, are not prepared to resist the influence which Elmore, as President of the Bank, necessarily brings to bear upon them — in some instances (as I believe in that of the Greenville & Spartanburgh delegations) with peculiar force. But it will be impossible to prevent you from recieving a large vote whether you run or not — I form this impression from what is said frequently by individuals. It is additional reason with me for withholding you now, that your strength is certainly & daily increasing, and that already there are those on whom perhaps we have not counted, who regard you as the necessary nucleus for a new formation of party. I do not fancy that your enemies would be so foolish as to stir the consideration of any offensive matter. We have thrown out our determination to combat the claim of individuals to denounce you on the score of a purely private matter the particulars of which are not spread before our judgment, also.[262] This, I think, has

---

with the course you pursued. I feel really grateful to you & all concerned because you have exhibited the thoughtfulness & prudence as well as the zeal of friends. The result is in every respect just what I expected & feel assured must happen. . . . I know Felder well & you judge him properly. And so do you Davie. I concur entirely with you as to supporting Elmore. . . . Elmore will be Mr. Calhoun's evil genius after all. . . . I think he has adroitness enough to hoodwink Mr. C. until it will be *too late.*" (Original in the Hammond Papers, Library of Congress.)

[261] Dated by Simms' letters to Hammond of Nov. 17 and Nov. 24 and by Hammond's to Simms of Oct. 6, Oct. 15, Nov. 21, and Nov. 23, concerning Hammond's campaign for the United States Senate.

[262] On Oct. 6 Hammond, in a portion of a letter marked "Private," wrote to Simms concerning certain gossip, charging him with indiscreet conduct, which played a large part in his political career: "But there is a matter connected

already had its effect. I have not hesitated to say touching the
Senator's election what you yourself said in recent letters — that
is to say — all that is necessary to be said — and this is only
said since our decision has been taken. But I reserve much for
another Letter. I write amidst some bustle, and with many tongues
around me. I trust you feel satisfied that in what we do we aim
to be prudent, and not to expend you unnecessarily. That you
will be *called* for, as you are certainly needed — is now very
clear to me, though I fear I am as sorry a prophet as politician.
Make out this scrawl as you can, only believing me

very truly Yours &c

Simms

342: To JAMES HENRY HAMMOND

Charleston. 3d. Decr. 1846

My dear Hammond

I am here on a painful business — having brought my wife to
town on Monday last, to consult the physicians about her health,
— which still remains unaccountably feeble. We shall probably
leave for the plantation today or tomorrow. I left Columbia on
Saturday last, with the full conviction that Elmore was to be run.
This was the positive assertion of all his friends. In a conversation
with himself on Friday night, he simply said that he had not yet
consented. This I regarded as conclusive that he was to consent.
I told him that your friends, myself among them, would only
forbear coming in conflict with himself. My counsel to our friends
was based upon the opinion that you could beat either Rhett, or
Davie, or Pickens, — who were the only persons likely to take
the field. I think so still, — and think it likely that Walker &

with the Senatorship that I know you have thought of but have not mentioned
directly between Hampton & myself. I don't for a moment suppose that he or
any one whom he could control would renew that matter now & introduce it
here. He must be satisfied to let it die away. I have myself the same objections
to agitating it now that I always had. *I have no right to explain* it, do not
desire it, & *could not be forced to it by anything* coming from *any quarter —
save from him.* Now doubtless some of E's friends might desire to make capital
of it. In that case all I desire to be said for me is that I have no explanation
to make & every man may think what he pleases about it. I am not to be
drawn out by any *third persons.* . . . I will not conceal from you however, my
consciousness that if the State was to elect me Senator, it would put all these
calumnies to rest forever. . . . The good opinion of no man or set of men is
necessary to my happiness. I have too long stood alone. . . ." (Original in
the Hammond Papers, Library of Congress.)

others have put you in nomination. Such is your strength that sundry persons thought that you could beat Elmore himself. It may be so, — but the risk was too great for your friends to take, under the restrictions which you imposed upon them,[263] and the counting of noses was not easy. I have not heard from Columbia since leaving it, except through the newspapers. I trust that you have done so, and that you are in nomination. For my own part, I am satisfied that you can beat Pickens or Rhett, or Butler;[264] — I may decieve myself, but can scarcely think so — I write at this moment with my head ringing with interruptions. I must wait till I get to Barnwell before I can respond to your letter fully. As for the office of Lt. Gov. I have said to my friends — 'If you can elect me, do so, — but do not sacrifice me.' The office is so entirely honorary that I certainly should not seek it. Now, however, it may serve to do away with any false & injurious impression which might extend to other states.

In haste & suffering
Yours truly

Simms

343: To RUFUS WILMOT GRISWOLD[265]

Woodlands, Decr. 6. 1846

dear Sir

I am truly sorry to hear of your infirmities. To a Literary man, the eyes are too precious, not to occasion the greatest apprehension for their slightest annoyances. I sincerely trust that nothing serious threatens yours, and that you will soon be enabled to resume your ordinary routine of labor as actively as ever. Though exceedingly busy, & subject to frequent interruptions of care and business, I seize a moment of respite, though not of

---

[263] See note 256, Nov. 24, 1846.

[264] F. W. Pickens, R. B. Rhett, and A. P. Butler.

[265] This letter is printed in part in *Passages from the Correspondence and Other Papers of Rufus W. Griswold* (Cambridge, Mass.: W. M. Griswold, 1898), pp. 80-86. The original is now in the collection of Mr. Clifton Waller Barrett, of New York City. A copy of most of the letter (made for *Passages*) is in the Boston Public Library. Simms' letter was undoubtedly written in reply to one from Griswold asking for biographical material for his *Prose Writers of America* (Philadelphia: Carey and Hart, 1847). Griswold's half-praising, half-damning sketch of Simms and evaluation of his work appears on pp. 503-505 of this latter work.

ease, to respond to the request which you make, and which I regret I did not answer duly when made some time ago. I can only afford you a few heads out of which you can make what you please. I commenced writing in rhyme at a very early period. At eight or nine years of age, while the events were in progress I rudely versified the achievements of our navy in the last war with Gt Britain. At fifteen I was a scribbler for the first time in the newspapers, and about the same time wrote a narrative poem in four cantos entitled "The Ring" — a tale of Italy. Before I was twenty one I had published two collections of miscellaneous verse, and had written portions of numerous things beside, ballad & epic & drama, some of which I have subsequently turned to account in print.[266] I had discretion enough to suppress most of these things which now it would be scarcely possible for even such an industrious collector as yourself to find. Two other collections followed between my twenty first & twenty fourth years, prepared & published while I was busy in the arduous toils of a newspaper Editor.[267] These were in a more ambitious vein, but are also beyond your reach, and almost of my own. In 1832 I published "Atalantis, a Story of the Sea" — a poem in the dramatic form. This production received the favorable notice of the 'London Metropolitan' then under the control of the poet Campbell. He speaks of it as "a well written poem of a dramatic cast, the versification of which is polished throughout, the characters sufficiently marked, and the machinery really very beautiful." [268] Among the numerous favorable notices of this poem in

---

[266] No portions of "The Ring" appear to have survived. The two volumes published at this time are *Lyrical and Other Poems* (1827) and *Early Lays* (1827). Among Simms' later published volumes which had their inception in this early period are *Pelayo* and its sequel *Count Julian, The Cassique of Accabee,* and *The Cassique of Kiawah.*

[267] During 1828-1829 Simms was editor of the *Southern Literary Gazette,* during 1830-1832 editor of the *City Gazette.* His statement here appears to be erroneous, for *The Vision of Cortes, Cain, and Other Poems* (1829) was published during his editorship of the former (see note 295, below, for a review in the Nov. issue of the *Yankee*), while *The Tri-Color, or the Three Days of Blood in Paris with Some Other Pieces* (1830) was published during his editorship of the latter. There is the possibility, however, that Simms worked in some editorial capacity on the *City Gazette* during 1829.

[268] IX (Jan., 1834), 12. Campbell writes: "We certainly look upon it as a high compliment, that our trans-atlantic brethren should waft across the ocean their poetical effusions for our critical opinion; but this flattery must not bribe us into partiality. As we have much to say in commendation, we will first begin by noticing what we think are blemishes. What has most disappointed us is, that it is so thoroughly English. The construction, the imagery, and, with a very few exceptions, the idioms of language, are altogether founded upon our own scholastic and classical models. This may be considered as high praise on

the United States, it may be sufficient to mention that of the
New England Magazine, then under the conduct of the two
Buckinghams — which says — "The author has shown a great
deal of fancy in the treatment of his subject. There are passages
of great power, particularly in the second part. The descriptions
are almost invariably beautiful & graphic & the language is well
chosen & picturesque. The songs and chorusses are of high merit.
We hope to hear from the author again, for he is capable of
doing excellent service to the Literature of his country." [269] Mr.
Flint, then editing the "Knickerbocker" magazine, said of the
same work — "It is a clear and well got up Arabian Night affair,
a real sea goblin concern, with enough imagination & eloquence,
& beautiful figure, and splendid conception, and wild paintings
of such stuff as dreams are made of, thrown away upon it, to
have woven & embellished a real painting of life & living things,
&c." [270] The error of the poem was in the dramatic form, and
in the redundancy of the descriptive portions. I have lately revised or rewritten it.[271] While I am in for the poetry, I may as
well place in this connection the names of my subsequent publications in verse. These are 1. A volume entitled "Southern Passages
& Pictures" the name of which will probably be found to describe its character. This was succeeded by a poem (incomplete)
entitled "Donna Florida," which has been unjustly assumed to
be an imitation of Don Juan, — and which is *not* distinguished
by any of the grossnesses of that poem. Four Cantos of Donna
Florida left the work still incomplete — the story, with the exception of the last Canto, being pretty well sunk in the digressions.
Here, if you please, you might quote, as a sample, the opening
verses of the 4th. Canto, in which the Muse of the Nation is

---

the other side of the water, but with us, it is only a source of mortification.
It is high time that the Americans created for themselves a national poetry.
As yet, they have not done so; but when they do, we prognosticate for them
a great success. They bring one grand requisition to the undertaking — independence of character. But to return to the book before us. It contains a well-
written poem of a dramatic cast, the versification of which is polished throughout, the characters are sufficiently marked, and the machinery really beautiful.
But it appeals to the imagination only. We admire the glittering vision, but the
bosom remains untouched. We recommend the perusal of this poem earnestly.
It will well repay even the most fastidious for the time that they may bestow
upon it, independently of the regard and courtesy that we ought to show
to an elegant and an interesting stranger, so recently come among us."

[269] See note 10, Jan. 22, 1833. For Joseph Tinker Buckingham and his son,
Edwin, see note 11, Jan. 22, 1833.

[270] II (Oct., 1833), 311-312. For Timothy Flint, see note 20, Dec. 29, 1833.

[271] This was later published by Carey and Hart, Philadelphia. Though the
volume is dated 1848, it was not issued until 1849.

invoked, and the country personified. So also, if you think proper, might be given from the same Canto the conflict between De Laye, a Spanish adventurer, & the Chief of the Seminoles. At all events, you may say of the poem that it is playful & mischievous, and not vicious or wicked. The story is perfectly innocent and the illusions all inoffensive. "Grouped Thoughts & Scattered Fancies" forms the next publication which is a collection of Sonnets. This volume is either imaginative, moral, or contemplative, or all mixed. For a sample or two of each of these characteristics, you might quote "Progress in Denial" at p 42 — "First Love" at 44 — "By the Swannannoa" at 46 — and "Home Service" at 20. To these succeeded "Areytos, or Songs of the South." The object of these poems is not simply to associate the sentiment with a local habitation & a name, but to invest with an atmosphere of fancy, such as distinguished the passion of love in the days of Chivalry, the ordinary utterance of this first emotion of the opening heart. As specimens of this volume, you might quote the song at 15; that on 19 & 20, and that on 74. These will all be found to embody equally the supposed warmth of a Southern temperament with the refining fancies which are assumed to have distinguished the loves of a Sidney & Bayard. But the work which, in my literary career succeeded to the publication of "Atalantis," was "Martin Faber," a gloomy & passionate tale, which, assumed by certain *European* critics as well as American to have been provoked by the British tale "Miserrimus" was in fact expanded from a tale which I published ten years before in a Magazine in Charleston,[272] and which contained all the distinguishing traits and scenes of the subsequent romance. "Martin Faber" belongs to the family of which Godwin's Caleb Williams is the best known model. But those who read the two works will fail to see any imitation on the part of the American author. Of this work, the New York American, then edited by C. F. Hoffman, — says — (I enclose you the paper cont'g this notice.)[273] This will suffice

---

272 "The Confessions of a Murderer," *Pleiades and Southern Literary Gazette*, II (Nov. 7, 1829). No copy is known to be extant.

273 The issue of Sept. 28, 1833, contains the review. Charles Fenno Hoffman (see introductory sketch) says: "Martin Faber we have perused with close attention, and we do not hesitate to say, that since Godwin carried that singular and impressive style, first introduced in modern fiction by our countryman Charles Brockden Brown, to such perfection in Caleb Williams, no work of that school has come under our notice which shows more power than the little tale before us." After quoting a fairly lengthy scene, "so strongly wrought up in the best style of the authors with whom we have compared the author of Martin Faber," Hoffman remarks that "the painter of such a scene has literary

as a sample of the criticism which followed the publication of
M. F. All admitted the power & interest of the work, but some
cavilled at the moral. The hero charges his crimes upon fate —
an ordinary habit with such persons, & this is charged upon
the author. He uses crime for his material, & in his case, as a
young American beginner, the practice, unavoidable for any writer
of fiction that ever lived, was supposed to be criminal. This work
had several bretheren of the same order, which followed at
intervals. Among these may be mentioned "Castle Dismal" a
tale which has been supposed to be particularly original 1 vol —
Confession or the Blind Heart, 2 Vols; Carl Werner, 2 Vols;
Wigwam & Cabin, 2 vols. These publications forming in all some
ten vols, were marked chiefly by the characteristics of passion
& imagination — by the free use in some cases of diablerie and
all the machinery of superstition & by a prevailing presence
of vehement individuality of tone & temper. They constitute,
in all probability, the best specimens of my powers of creating
& combining, to say nothing of a certain intensifying egotism,
which marks all my writings written in the first person. There
are yet other tales belonging to this category, & perhaps not
inferior in merit to any of these, which have appeared in annuals
& magazines, but which I have not yet collected in book form.
Of one of these stories the London Examiner spoke in terms of
the highest commendation, — I will send you the article, which
may interest such of our people as reverence foreign opinion with
implicit trust & confidence, — if I can find it.[274] But, anterior to
the publication of most of these, and soon after the publication
of Martin Faber, I gave my first novel to the public. This was
"Guy Rivers." It was meant to illustrate the border & domestic
history of the South. The first vol. of 'Guy Rivers' was written
some time before the second, & the style betrays the labor and
anxiety of a young author, highly ambitious of his tools but, as
yet unpracticed in the use of them. The difference between those
portions of the work where he forgets himself in the excitement of

----

talents of no common order." Two other passages are then quoted, and Hoffman concludes: "We may seem to have already bestowed too much space upon
a book that purports to be meant only 'for the use of children;' but a writer
of such approved discernment . . . must well know the ill effects of letting
one's own powers lie idle; and will therefore enter into our views, when we
express our unfeigned wish to hear soon again from the author of Martin
Faber."

[274] In Simms' MS. this sentence is a footnote to the preceding. For the
London *Examiner's* comments on "Grayling," see note 1, Jan. 29, 1842.

the story, is apparent at a glance. The work was highly successful, was stereotyped, and soon passed to a second third & fourth edition. Of this work, the critics spoke very indulgently. At the time of its appearance, Mr. Cooper had sole possession of the field. Mr. Paulding had not confirmed the impression made by his Dutchman's Fireside in his subsequent novel of Westward Ho.[275] Guy Rivers rose to instant favor. It was republished in London in three vols. Of the thousand notices of the press, mostly favorable, which it recieved, I refer you to that of Mr. Clark of the Knickerbocker.[276] This Gentn. who, since I pronounced him a liar & refused to know him, has spared no occasion to lie about & disparage me, spoke of G. Rivers as "superior in many respects to the general works of Mr. Cooper." But I send you the notice of this magazine in order that you may compare it with what he has more recently said of me & my writings. Retain the notices I send you so that I may have them when you have done with them. — Belonging to the same family with Guy Rivers, are Richard Hurdis, Border Beagles, Beauchampe, Helen Halsey, — some ten or a dozen volumes, — distinguished by great activity of plot, vehement & passionate personality, and pictures & sketches of border character & border scenery, in which I claim to be equally true & natural. There are running through all these works, a strong penchant to moral and mental analysis — such as led Hoffman, in one of his notices, to suggest that I would do well to devote a work entirely to the business of working out my metaphysical vein.[277] These works were not published consecutively. 'Guy Rivers' made some enemies for me in New England, simply because Jared Bunce, a Yankee Pedlar, was not made the hero of the novel, and was kept simply what he set out to be a Yankee Pedlar. In this humble character, he is yet a good fellow — Humane, intelligent, and stedfast, — and only like all pedlars, cunning. It is not true, as you have thought and taught that I got my rogues from N. E. Guy Rivers himself is a South Carolinian, and he is the monster of the book. By the way, whole pages of Guy Rivers have been stolen by Seatsfield, and have been quoted abroad as superior to what could be done by an

275 James Kirke Paulding's *The Dutchman's Fireside,* 2 vols. (New York: J. & J. Harper, 1831), and *Westward Ho!,* 2 vols. (New York: J. & J. Harper, 1832), were published anonymously.

276 IV (Aug., 1834), 145-149.

277 See Hoffman's review of *The Yemassee,* quoted in note 281, below.

American, even describing his own country.[278] My Jared Bunce, is his Jared Bundell, — so close is the plagiarism. Richard Hurdis was published anonymously and instantly went to a second edition. Border Beagles & Beauchampe were also published anonymously. — But these works, though of the same order, did not follow the publication of Guy Rivers. That work was succeeded by "The Yemassee" the first of my Historical Romances. The success of the Yemassee was even more decided than that of G. R. The New York papers spoke of it in one language of commendation. The Times calls it — "the Romance of the Season, immeasurably the best that has appeared since — indeed we cannot tell since when." [279] The Mercantile says of the reader "his feelings are controlled by a master hand &c" [280] The American (by Hoffman) "This is no common book. The design of the story is bold & original, & the execution is graphic & vigourous." — "The Yemassee displays as much power, fancy & original resource as any

---

[278] In a review of *Life in the New World* (New York: J. Winchester, [1844]) by Seatsfield (Anton Postl) in *S. L. M.*, X (July, 1844), 447, this plagiarism is briefly noted: "There is a story of a Yankee pedler, who hired a negro to let a box fall on his leg, that the pedler might recommend his un-rivalled salve, by instantly curing it. The pretended groans of cuffie and the whole scene are *ridiculous,* not ludicrous. This same pedler is to be found in one of the works of the distinguished Southern Novelist, Mr. Simms. In 'Guy Rivers,' he is called Jared Bunce; in Seatsfield, Jared *Bundell* — scarcely a change of name. Besides, Bunce and Bundell both cheated the good people with their worthless coffee-pots, and, by a strange coincidence, assign the same reason for their worthlessness. (*Life in New World,* part 2, p. 64-5. *Guy Rivers,* vol. 1, 3rd edition, p. 71.)"

[279] April 16, 1835. The reviewer continues: "We have read it with extreme delight; expecting much from the known talent of the author, his intimate knowledge of character, scenery, Indian peculiarities, and the early history of his native State, his power of invention and observant mind, but surprised, and it may well be imagined, how much pleased, to find our warmest expectations far exceeded by the reality of his noble performance. . . . His savages are different, in many respects, from those of any other writer with whom we are acquainted, and, we suspect, more true to the reality. He represents them as more susceptible of the general feelings, passions, weaknesses if you please, of human nature. Certainly he makes of them less monotonous and more interesting characters, and this is a great thing in a novel. . . . We conceive that by this work the reputation of Mr. Simms is permanently established. . . ." In the issue of May 19 the same paper remarks that the first edition of *The Yemassee,* "though unusually large, had been sold within thirty hours from its publication" and that "we have before us now the second edition, published we believe some weeks ago; at least it was put to press immediately after the original publication was exhausted."

[280] *Mercantile Advertiser and New-York Advocate,* April 15, 1835. The reviewer comments: "We confess that we take a warm interest in the literary fame and prosperity of Mr. Simms, not only because he is a man of talent and industry, but also because he sets a good example by drawing his materials from the rich, as yet almost unexplored and inexhaustible sources of his own country and her history. . . . The Yemassee is a fine romance; there is talent in every page of it, and it will not pass away and be forgotten."

work of fiction, by a native writer, that we can call to mind."
&c.[281] The Commercial says, "as a story of Indian warfare &
extinction, there is none in the whole range of American fiction
that is superior to it."[282] The New Yorker (Greeley) "We have
read this new romance with a deeper interest and more unalloyed
gratification than any preceding work of imagination since the
Last Days of Pompeii." [283] The Balt. American says — (I send
the paragraph) [284] But it was reserved for the Evening Post, to

---

[281] April 18, 1835. The review is not wholly enthusiastic. Hoffman remarks
that Simms' "chief defect is a too great indulgence in those metaphysical dis-
quisitions which were so often misplaced in the mouths of his characters in
Guy Rivers. In the present work these are very properly put forth as the views
of the author speaking in his own person, but though often ingenious, and sometimes beautifully written, they do not seem always to grow out of his subject,
and they are often so unskilfully introduced as to delay the action of the story,
and consequently impair the interest of its finest scenes. Mr. Simms has
evidently two distinct complexions to his mind, and we should like to see him
try his hand at a novel of the Godwin and Brockden Brown school, if it were
only to find a new outlet for those kind of speculations which appear to us
out of place in a pure Romance like the Yemassee. It is one thing for a writer
to stamp his peculiar mind and character upon his productions, and it is another thing to send all the coin from his intellectual mint with precisely the
same impress. . . ." Hoffman, however, was greatly impressed with Simms'
abilities, for after remarking that *The Yemassee* "displays as much power, fancy,
and original resource as any work of fiction, by a native writer, that we can call
to mind," he continues: "The author has succeeded admirably in wakening a
noble and extinct race of Indians, to life, in the deep forests of the south; and
the gallant cavaliers who settled his native Carolina, not less than to the plumed
chieftains of a hundred years ago, are made to flit with magical reality before
the mental gaze of the reader. — There is, indeed, a warm tissue of poetry,
pervading the whole work — an atmosphere of fancy, which raises the ideal
creatures of the author's brain, somewhat above actual life, but which makes
them gain in poetic vitality, all that they may lose in truth. The writer has
evidently proposed to himself that master-piece of *unmeasured* poetry, (the only
perfect romance, except Fenelon's *Telemaque,* that ever was written,) Ivanhoe,
— as his model; and we only wish that he had not introduced a single touch
to remind us of the ordinary novel."

[282] The New York *Commercial Advertiser* of April 2, 1835, lists *The
Yemassee* as "in the Press of Harper & Brothers." The novel is reviewed in
the issue of April 18: "'Yemassee' is an honorable evidence of the ease
with which the prominent faults of former productions have been avoided.
It is in all respects an improvement upon 'Guy Rivers' — more carefully written in point of style — more complete in plot, in the harmony of parts, the
unity of action, the adaptation of the character to the incidents, and to each
other — in fine, in all that distinguishes it as a work of art. . . . As a story
of Indian warfare, and extinction, there is none in the whole range of American
fiction, that is superior to it."

[283] April 18, 1835. The notice also reprints chapter xxv of the novel.

[284] April 23, 1835. The reviewer comments: "The reading of a few pages
suffices to get a hold on the attention, which is never for a moment released
until the stirring story is ended. . . . the Yemassee is fresh, and instinct with the
aboriginal spirit. The mind of the natives as it may have supposed to have been
in the period of the first settlement of the Atlantic coast by the Europeans,
and the overwhelming power of civilized man in contact with the uncivilized,
are graphically portrayed . . . while a story is intricately and so skillfully in-
terwoven in the historical narrative as to give scope for the development and
play of various passions."

discern what seems to have escaped all the other critics that the
entire Mythology of the Yemassee, which they took for Gospel
History was of the author's pure invention, elevating his claims
to originality & that of the work to the standards of pure romance.
Hoffman half conjectured this and the Post (Leggett) speaks
only to conjecture. The Post says "The management of the Indian
part of this story is the result either of a long & close study
of Indian history, character & habits, or else is evidence of a
creative power which is seldom equalled." [285] See further the
marked passage as I send it you. — The Yemassee was the first
of a class to which belongs three other works — viz. The Damsel
of Darien, Pelayo, & Count Julian. These three works are all
founded on Spanish story, though the scene of the first is in
our own country & the events belong to modern times. I do
not think that the D of D ever had justice done it, though it recieved high encomiums from certain quarters. The theme was
too stately for the taste of our day which at that time ran on
the rough & tumble. I inclose several notices. Among these is
one of the N. Y. American which may be by Hoffman, though
I know not.[286] — Pelayo & Count Julian, though full of scenes
& passages of which I should never be ashamed, are yet, in design,
not the things that I would make them now. Their history is
given in the preface to the latter work. — These did not follow

---

[285] New York *Evening Post*, April 6, 1835. William Leggett (see introductory sketch) continues: "There is nothing in this portion of the work
which the reader — forgetful that he is perusing a romance — does not readily
conceive as truth, or at least does not so harmoniously accord with his pre-
conceived general ideas of Indian habits and customs as not to disturb the
illusion which the story is calculated to occasion. Yet, when we reflect how
few and imperfect are the accounts of the peculiarities and social or domestic
traits of the early Southern Indians we can scarcely avoid the conclusion that
the number and picturesque details of their manners and customs, as modified
by the affections, by the duties of religion, and by the fierce passions of un-
tutored nature, with which the interesting pages of the Yemassee abound,
are rather creations of the poetick mind of the author, than relicks gathered
on the scanty field of history. If this conjecture is true, to the praise of fertility
of invention must be added that also of consistency and *vraisemblance* in detail,
which if not so high is at least as rare and to the novelist, not less important
merit. . . . We have often met with negroes in American works of fiction,
but never with one in which the distinctive peculiarities of the African race
were better delineated, or with less of exaggeration or burlesque."

[286] October 26, 1839. The reviewer remarks: "Mr. Simms' reputation as a
novelist is already well established, and his tact in drawing upon the legendary
lore of this hemisphere, with the industry and fidelity to history which marks
all his researches, will yet extend his fame as a writer. His style is bold, and
his fancy exuberant. In tropical scenes he revels with luxurious and astonishing
power, and his descriptions of the storms and hurricanes which so frequently
devastate those regions of beauty and fertility, exhibit his powers of contrast
in a striking light."

the Yemassee in direct order. The Partisan, a Tale of the Revolution succeeded the Yemassee — a book which sold better, and was better liked by readers than by critics. Though distinguished by delineations & scenes which satisfy me, the design was feeble, the parts clumsily put together. In truth the printing of the work was begun, before the first fifty pages were written. Wherever the *action* was in progress, the story told, but there were frequent breaks & lapses, which spoiled the effect. The *Knickerbocker* writes — "Of all the efforts of the author — the *gifted* Simms — we esteem this in many respects the best. Nature, effective imagination & fine description are its prominent characteristics &c." [287] The New Yorker — The work is marked by all the better characteristics of the novelist &c.[288] The Southern Literary Messenger, edited by Poe, pronounced a severe, but in many respects, just critique upon the work, but said — "The historical characters are, without exception, well drawn. The portraits of Cornwallis, Gates & Marion, are vivid realities — those of DeKalb and the Claverhouse — like Tarleton positively unsurpassed by any similar delineations within our knowledge." Again, after a protracted criticism as full of detailed objections as a plum pudding is of currants, he says — "The Partisan is no ordinary work. The historical details are replete with interest. The concluding scenes are well drawn. Some passages descriptive of swamp scenery are exquisite." [289]—"Mellichampe" was a continuation of the Partisan & succeeded it. It was, as a whole, a better work, and better written, but possibly had not so many scenes of power. I send you a few of the notices, which are meagre, but all that my family has kept.[290] — 'The Kinsmen, or the Black Riders of the Congaree' — belonging to the same family followed these after some interval. It was, as a story, a better work than either, and an edition (I think) of 2000 or 2500 copies were sold at $2. retail, when Bulwer & James were retailing at 25/100. Ask Lea & Blanchard anent this.[291] — In History and Biography, I have written a History & Geography of South Carolina — 2 vols — a Life of General Marion, and one of John Smith, the Founder

---

[287] See note 4, Jan. 27, 1836.

[288] Brief notices appear in the issues of Dec. 5 and Dec. 12, 1835. Simms quotes from the second.

[289] See note 135, March 15, 1845.

[290] For reviews of *Mellichampe* in the *New York Mirror* and the *Knickerbocker*, see note 8, March 31, 1837.

[291] For reviews of *The Kinsmen* in the *New York Mirror* and the *Ladies' Companion*, see note 37, Feb. 24, 1841.

of Virginia — the last not yet published, but printed. The History
of South Carolina, though limited in circulation to the State, has
already in five years gone to three large editions. The success
of 'Marion' you probably know as well as myself. I have been
guilty of two orations which have been published — one delivered
before the Erosophic Society of the University of Alabama, entitled "The Social Principle, the true Source of National Permanence," — the other, before the citizens of Aiken, S. C., by request
of the Town Council, on the 4th July 1844, entitled, "The Sources
of American Independence." As a writer of criticism, I have
contributed numerously to Periodicals North & South — reviewing Mrs. Trollope in the American Quarterly — Miss Martineau
in the Messenger — Montgomery's Messiah in the Knickerbocker
(under Flint) Prescott's Mexico, Horne's Spirit of the Age,
Allston's & Mathews Writings &c. in the Southern Review,[292]
and an immense variety of the same sort of writing in the Southern Literary Journal, the Magnolia, Western & Southern Review
&c. Of these contributions, the Reviews of Mrs. Trollope, Miss
Martineau have been republished in Pamphlet form, and a selection devoted entirely to American topics, has been made in two
volumes for Wiley & Putnam's Library.[293] I have now gone over
the list of books which I have published & which I care to acknowledge, and may as well recapitulate. Of the Moral Imaginative
you have a large collection of Tales, some of which make an entire volume — viz. Martin Faber 2 Castle Dismal; 3 Carl Werner
&c. 4 Wigwam & Cabin. These make eight volumes. Of the Border
Domestic Novels, you have 1. Guy Rivers; 2. R. Hurdis, 3.
Border Beagles, 4. Beauchampe; 5 Helen Halsey &c 10 vols.
In Historical Romance, you have 1. The Yemassee; 2. Damsel
Darien; 3. Pelayo; 4 Count Julian. — 8 vols. of the Revolutionary
Novels: 1 The Partisan; 2. Mellichampe; 3 The Kinsmen; 6 in
Biography & History, you have the Life of Marion, Life of Smith,
Histy. & Geo. of So. Car. — 4 vols. — In criticism 2 vols. & in
Pamphlets 2. In Poetry there is 1. Atalantis— 100 pages 8vo.

---

[292] Only one of these articles has not hitherto been discussed: the review
of Montgomery's *Messiah,* first published as "John Milton versus Robert
Montgomery. Or a Modest Comparison of the Paradise Lost and Regained,
of the One, with the Messiah, Now Published in the Sacred Annual, of the
Other," *Knick.,* IV (Feb., 1834), 120-134; revised and published as "Montgomery's Messiah" in the *Magnolia,* IV (Jan., 1842), 1-15. A note to the
article in the *Magnolia* states that "this article was in great part written in
1832, when the Messiah was published."

[293] *Views and Reviews,* First and Second Series.

Southern Passages 250 12 mo. Donna Florida 100. Grouped
Thoughts 60. Areytos, 100.— Talking of Poetry, & of the suppressed volumes, let me remark that Jas G. Brooks,—(Florio)
reviewing one of them published when I was 19, opens thus—
"It is with more than ordinary pleasure that we have to pass
judgment on the vol. before us. Mr. Simms is entitled to take
his place among the first of American Poets. The fire of true
genius burns in his song, & its light is pure, warm & brilliant.
We have read his poetry with unqualified pleasure. We like its
very faults, for they are the bold, generous faults of high genius
& lofty feelings." This was published in the "New York Literary
Gazette and American Athenæum.["] The review & extracts
occupied several pages.[294] Of another of these Boyish volumes,
John Neal says in his "Yankee"

> The man who could write this poetry, could, if he would
> wait awhile and take time for it do so much better, that
> instead of speaking highly of what he has done, we are
> resolved to say nothing in its favour: although if he
> had not excited such high expectations by here and there a
> brief passage, a line or two— a thought — or a single word,
> mayhap we should be among the first to say— here we have
> another poet, springing up in the busy solitude of our
> country, among the ten thousand other neglected flower-
> bearers of a similar root and a similar growth, born to per-
> ish— if they do not hold back their strength till the day of
> their maturity.[295]

[294] See the New-York Literary Gazette and American Athenaeum, III (Feb.
3, 1827), 161-164. The quotation is from p. 161. For Brooks, see note 8, Sept.
11, 1830. The review is of Lyrical and Other Poems.

[295] N. S., I (Nov., 1829), 279. The notice (pasted to this letter) is of
The Vision of Cortes, Cain, and Other Poems. Neal (1793-1876), the editor,
also writes in the same journal, II (Jan. 8, 1829), 13-14, of Simms' and James
W. Simmons' Southern Literary Gazette: "These two numbers are all that I
have yet seen of this clever periodical; and I say this now, that the editors —
one of whom I knew abroad [Simmons] — may not charge me with intentional
oversight. . . . The Southern Literary Gazette deserves encouragement. The
prose now and then is rather heavy — the poetry rather so-so-ish, and the
articles rather too long; but sometimes we have superb flashings of eloquence,
great strength, cool judgment, good humor, and beautiful poetry (The Lost
Pleiad [by Simms] for example.) And therefore it is that I should recommend it to the encouragement, not only of the South, but of the North. We
are but one family, whatever others may say; and the more we know of
each other, the better it will be for us all. Our prejudices will disappear, and
our affections flourish with our intimacy." In a notice of Lyrical and Other
Poems and Early Lays he comments in the same journal, II (April 30, 1829),
143: "As to reviewing two volumes of early poetry — by any body on earth
now, that is altogether out of the question; but still, it is fair to say that Mr.

I send you, to close fitly this long detail, a sonnet which was published anonymously, but which is supposed to be by Rev. Mr. S. Bulfinch, on the appearance of Atalantis.

Sonnet,
On reading Atalantis

Simms! thou hast woven a garland, fit to wreathe
    Thy country's brow of glory; — all things fair
    And wonderful are blent together there—
The ffower [*sic*] of spring,—the smooth-lipped shell. There breathe
From forth their mystic twines sweet spirit voices,
    And in the spirit are they heard. The heart
Of one young brother of the lyre rejoices
    In thee and blesses thee; for thy high art
    Hath wakened thought, and made the feelings dart
Up to their birthplace, where in boundless light
Dwell the realities of our visions bright,
    And where *thy* inspirations have a part.
    Go on then in the brightness of thy mind,
And in thy country's praise, thy crown of glory find.

S.

Augusta, Geo.[296]

Of another suppressed work, the Knickerbocker, conducted by Flint, writes thus.

> We admire the spirit in which the book is written. It comes on us in 'this age of calulations' like a sunbeam from the days of Froissart. We like the chivalrous gallantry, the romantic devotion, the generous enthusiasm; all bespeak, not the cold respect of an economizing, calculating generation, but the high, and to us congenial, feeling of some southern and sunny land, where hearts beat with a prouder and a loftier sympathy than in these colder climes.[297]

I gather up & send you along with this, all the odds & ends of criticism, — such as it is — which have been preserved from a bulky mass which my writings have provoked. You may find

---

Simms really does make poetry, and with great apparent ease; though to be sure, his grammar . . . is not always *English* grammar. . . ."
    [296] This clipping (pasted to the letter) is from the *Rose Bud,* I (March 23, 1833), 120.
    [297] This clipping (pasted to the letter) is from a review of *The Book of My Lady* in II (Dec., 1833), 481.

some use in looking over them. This summary has been written *stans pede in uno,* and I have neither the taste nor leisure to run my eye over it after writing. Excuse faults, and try to repair deficiences as you read. Shall we not see you in the South this winter. If you come to Só. Caro. seek me out at Woodlands. Meanwhile, hold me very truly,

Yours &c.

W. Gilmore Simms

344: To Evert Augustus Duyckinck

Woodlands, Dec. 10 [1846] [298]

My dear Duyckinck

I thank you for the Doodles which reach me with tolerable regularity. Martin's *head* of me is very well done.[299] I congratulate the work on his acquisition. What you say of the employment of H. Andy strikes me as singularly just.[300] But it only proves what I have long since asserted on the subject not only of our own claims to humor, but of the convictions — concurring with mine — of the public. Of C. M. the very success of 'Witchcraft' ought to open his eyes to his true *rôle.* I got two notices of that Drama today, for which I fancy, I owe my acknowledgment to you.[301] They certainly speak the language of encouragement very strongly. — I am continuing my drudgery of the desk at home, but scarcely to my satisfaction. My wife's condition disturbs my mood too greatly to leave me free to the utter forgetfulness of self which proper literary work requires. You suggest that I might answer the N. A. in the V. & Reviews, —but I think not.[302] In

---

[298] Dated by Simms' reference to *Yankee Doodle,* which ceased publication with the issue of Oct. 2, 1847.

[299] For Charles Martin's drawing of Simms, published in *Yankee Doodle,* I (Dec. 5, 1846), 106, see illustration facing p. 259 of this volume. Simms writes of Martin in the *Southern Patriot* of Dec. 14: "The graceful and spirited pencil of this gentleman, well known to our citizens is already establishing for Yankee Doodle a new claim on the patronage of the public."

[300] Three chapters of a series entitled "Handy Andy's Post Bag" had been published in *Yankee Doodle,* I (Nov. 21, Nov. 28, and Dec. 5, 1846), 87, 99, 111.

[301] These were probably notices of the performances of Mathews' *Witchcraft* in Cincinnati or St. Louis. Duyckinck later quotes reviews from these cities in an article entitled "The Tragedy of Witchcraft," *Literary World,* I (March 27, 1847), 184.

[302] Simms did not answer the *North American Review*'s attack (see letters to Duyckinck of Oct. 24 and to Lawson of Nov. 19, 1846) in *Views and Reviews,* Second Series.

this case I do not see the need of it & the policy of answering your critic —unless by satire — is always a doubtful one. — By the way, should not V & R. be out soon, — and will you oblige me by asking of Langley what detains Smith. As for the sheets, you should have had them months ago. They were all revised by me before I left New York. —I think it likely that I shall do nothing more, up to the summer, than prepare the life of Bayard and the Huguenots. I propose to bring them on with me. I may get in readiness an Edition of my poetical writings if I can find a publisher. Will you confer with Wiley touching a new Edition of 'Castle Dismal' & Helen Halsey—the plates of which I have. It strikes me that the former work, with its diablerie, illustrated by Martin, would make a hit. Suggest the matter to Wiley. With pictures the book would command 50/100 in the style of Carey & Hart's publications, I hear very infrequently from New York. Even Lawson fails me. Have you any news of any sort. Is there any progress among you? What is there from Great Britain? Refresh me, if you can with a frequent scrawl, and help me to forget the troubles at home that I have no art to combat.—Present me respectfully to Mrs. D. and remind your brother abroad that I have asked after him in his wanderings

Yours truly &c

Simms

P. S. Are you out with the Mirror, and who is the Thersites of that establishment.[303] This *inter nos.*

345: To JAMES HENRY HAMMOND

Woodlands. Decr. 11. 1846

My dear Hammond.

I had hopes to meet you a few days ago at the Court House, having been assured that you were to be present. It was there that I was first advised of the result of the Senatorial election,[304]

---

303 Unidentified.

304 On Dec. 3 the Charleston *Mercury* announced: "In regard to the Senatorial seat to be filled it is pretty generally understood that Col. Elmore has refused to let his name go before the legislature. Among those spoken of are the Hon. R. B. Rhett, Gen. Hammond, and Judge Butler." On Dec. 7 the *Mercury* stated that on the fourth and last ballot Hammond received 65 votes, Butler 84, and the other candidates 15. In regard to his defeat Hammond wrote to Simms on Dec. 8: "From my letters from several distinct quarters I learn

which, when you look at the anxious among the solicitors, and
the anxious lawyers seeking to be solicitors, is perhaps easy to
be accounted for. But, when I left Columbia, it was not supposed
that Butler would run—that he would be so foolish as to risk a
permanency, for an office from which it is not improbable that
in two years he will be ousted. He is not the man to keep in
Calhoun's harness, and if seriously or strongly opposed at the
regular election will be beaten. Elmore could not have beaten you
by a larger vote, and Butler was the only man in the State (in
my opinion) after Elmore, by whom you could have been beaten.
Nor could he have done it relying on his intrinsic strength. The
Judgeship gave him 25 votes, at least. — I cannot say that I
regret that you were run, since my impression is that the contest
results in placing you *rectus in curia*. That I should have urged
your running, had I been in Columbia, is doubtful. I might have
been scared from it by the threats of your enemies, and by my
own conviction that you had some atonement to make. But now
that it is over, I feel that you have gained a point in the game
which is of immense importance to you hereafter. It will not
be possible for Hampton [305] and his friends to commit a second
time the monstrous blunder of which they have been guilty—a
blunder which, while it might have forced upon you the admission
of error, subjected themselves to an exposure than which nothing

---

that I have at least survived the storm. My friends all speak of my gaining
a triumph — but I do not build on that. . . . But I build on this — *my penance
is accomplished*. I have *endured* to the bitter end. My enemies have made their
issue — *done their worst*. . . . When the next charge comes I shall advance.
The ground I took in the statement I gave Aldrich was on the last ditch. . . .
And they saw too the unflinching gallantry with which I was sustained. . . .
To you & all my dear Simms I feel as though I owed a life — a separate
life to each. Such generous & abiding confidence in one who wrapped himself in mystery, while the *nobles* of the land denounced him in such unmeasured
terms is without parallel. It consoles — it compensates me a thousand fold
for all that I have suffered. . . . No man ever had such friends. . . . Nor shall
my friends stand alone, if there is another fight. . . . God bless you." (Original
in the Hammond Papers, Library of Congress.)

[305] Col. Wade Hampton (1791-1858), of Millwood, a plantation near Columbia, was the father of Gen. Wade Hampton (1818-1902) of the Confederate
War. B. F. Perry says of the elder Hampton in his *Reminiscenses of Public
Men, with Speeches and Addresses,* Second Series (Greenville, S. C.: Shannon
& Co., Printers, 1889), p. 110: "In after years, he was solicited time and again
to become a candidate for the Executive chair, but he would never consent
to have his name used for that purpose. He preferred making governors to
being one himself. For more than twenty years he was the great Warwick of
South Carolina, and took an active part in the gubernatorial elections. Seldom
did any one succeed to the chief magistracy of the State without his support."
His son (Gen. Wade Hampton) married as his first wife Margaret, sister of
William C. Preston. For Hammond's difficulties with the family, see note 262,
Nov. 27, 1846.

could be more unhappy. In your case, what the outer world conjectured was no doubt much more ugly than the truth. You had
suffered the worst. Actual revelation could not have done you
greater harm; and such a development must have only injured
those to whom it was of importance that the thing should remain
equivocal. My notion is that you could have lost few votes by it.
Your friends have been encouraged & strengthened. They will
stick to you. They will increase, as they will naturally absorb
all those in the State whom the vast shadows of some two or
three persons have kept from the sunshine of public favor. 'Young
Carolina' will probably make you a rallying point for a new party.
At least, many of those to whom this cry is becoming grateful,
as it promises release from bondage, are, I know, looking to you
as to a centre. I need not exhort you to patience. Perhaps, an
excess of coolness — a something too much of *recoil* and stoicism
— is your foible. I wish you had a little more of the boy in
you — a little more of enthusiasm & faith. It was your misfortune
to have been caught too young—to have been but too little of
the boy. Boyhood is the term for the training—not the crushing
or stifling of the faith. You, I fear, believe too little in your
neighbours. — But you will wait, & you will triumph. I look
around, and see the unavoidable necessity of the young men of
the country turning to you. Where else? What are the public
men? The good are too weak. The strong are too selfish and
not wise. Barnwell,[306] Colcock & a few others of this class, are
worthy fellows but can do nothing. And of another class, Rhett,
Pickens, Davie, — not absolutely weak — nay smart, all of them,
each in his way — yet not one of them with the slightest claim
to wisdom. Elmore has something of this. This is his secret.
He is wise rather than smart. He has that species of social
prudence, which is a minor sort of wisdom, by which he passes
for more than he is worth himself, and persuades others to a
conviction of his necessity to them. I think him equal to all that

---

[306] Robert W. Barnwell (1801-1882) was a member of the State House of
Representatives during 1826-1828, a member of Congress during 1829-1833, and
president of South Carolina College from 1835 to 1841, when he resigned.
He was appointed to the United States Senate to fill the vacancy caused by
the death of Franklin H. Elmore and served from June 4 to Dec. 8, 1850.
He was a delegate to the Nashville Convention and also to the convention of
the seceding states in Montgomery, Ala., where he cast the deciding vote in the
South Carolina delegation, thereby giving the State to Jefferson Davis and
making him President of the Confederacy. During 1861-1865 he was a member
of the Confederate States Senate.

I have named, put together, in the capacity of being useful —
which I hold to be the first essential of a good politician. He
has one faculty which you perhaps do not sufficiently use — that
of persuading others that they are in reality turning the wheel
on whose spokes they only revolve. You have too much will for
this, — yet the art is a useful one. — But none of these men will
answer for the approaching emergency. — I had almost said
crisis. And I see no young ones starting up in the shade. Do
you? — As for myself, I am pretty well tired of a game in which
it is so easy to be beaten.[307] Besides, I am ill at ease at home. My
affairs are in a doubtful way, my prospects gloomy, my wife
in very bad health, and I myself very much dissatisfied with
what I have done & what I am. I have almost come to persuade
myself that my career has deluded nobody but myself, and that
I should regard my recent defeats as a sufficient proof that I
am not the person that I suppose myself & possess but few of
the endowments upon which I had but too easily been satisfied
to count. In my present frame of mind, I should consent to run
for nothing, to hope for nothing, to think of nothing, the gift
of which might depend upon the people from whom alone one
might confidently look for anything. God bless you.

W. Gilmore Simms

J. H. Hammond Esq.

---

[307] W. A. Cain, of Pineville, was elected lieutenant governor by a slight
majority over Simms. On Dec. 18 Hammond attempted to explain the defeat
to Simms: "Yesterday's mail brought me yours of the 11th inst. This election
is a cursed vexatious thing & I feel as if I could cut the throats of the damned
fools in Columbia who can't elevate themselves to a sentiment of delicate
justice, & the infernal malignants who can forgo no chance whatever to glut
their petty spites. The blow I presume came from the salt-water — from those
you have injured by outstripping. You are simply my dear Simms in a run
of bad luck & you are too much of a philosopher to be cast down by it,
or to make any resolves under its sting. The truth however probably lies deeper.
Ours are a very simple sort of people, with all their chivalry & impracticability. With them a spade is a spade & nothing else. You are a Novelist. As
such only are you regarded by even the intelligent of our State. Your histories
& biographies remain as yet under the shadow of your romances & you are
a Novelist. Now our people do not comprehend your political aspirations, nor
believe you really have any. They regard your excursion into politics as a sort
of eccentric movement in search of excitement — having no purposes but momentary pleasure. They do not recognize you as a political character. . . .
But they do not still exactly realize how a man of letters can be a Statesman." (Original in the Hammond Papers, Library of Congress.)

346: To James Lawson

Woodlands, Decr. 12. [1846][308]

dear Lawson

I have just seen announced in a northern paper that Coolidge & Brother of New York have in preparation my Life of Captain Smith. Now I know nothing of this firm. My contract is with Langley & Brother. The Copyright is in my name & the certificate in my hands, and it appears to me that no use can be made of my Copyright or of my contract with Langley, unless with my privity & consent. I must solicit you therefore, to make immediate inquiry into this business & to arrest every publication of the work until you be satisfied. For this, the present Letter will be your sufficient power of attorney, until another of more formal character can be sent you — if required. The Langley's have not honored my drafts in your favor or in favor of Bartlett & Welford. They have not rendered me any account of Marion since July 1845. A couple of weeks ago I got a Letter from them proposing to buy from me the Copyrights of Marion & Smith, and desirous of realizing a present sum of money, I consented that they should have them on the payment of $1300. Cash. I confer upon you the power of selling these two works to them or to Harper & Brothers at that price. Of course, the works are not to be exposed to sale, but it would be well to see H & B. as well as the Langleys immediately. The plates of "Marion" are deposited with H & B. (or were) by J & G. H. L. but H & B. have no authority to publish a copy. No doubt they will buy. If they will, & you find that Langleys are not able to come to the point, negotiate with H & B. and for this my Letter will be your sufficient authority. When you tell me that you want the Copyrights they shall be sent you. But let me entreat you as you value my interests, to see to the matter at once. Perhaps you may have to arrest the publication of Smith by injunction. You can first ascertain if one will lie, and if my contract with Langley's is transferable to other parties who have given me no securities. Never was poor devil so harrassed by publishers as myself. I am cheated and bamboozled on all hands. If necessary for me to come on let me know as soon as you can. — Here we are still under the cloud. My wife remains very feeble, and

---

[308] Dated by the fact that the copyright of *The Life of Captain John Smith*, published by Geo. F. Cooledge and Brother, New York, in 1847, is dated 1846.

at a moment when my resources are at the lowest, my expenses have increased. The management of our planting affairs is such as to dispirit me utterly, and but for the health of my family, I should certainly leave them for the daily drudgery of business in N. Y. or Phil. Here I run to waste, and feel myself a weed. Write me soon and satisfy my doubts about this cursed business. Who is Coolidge & Co. If good men & true, & if they have any lien upon the Langleys, let the latter pay up my drafts, make up our accts today, & then, if you can, negotiate with Coolidge. In July 1845 I got the accts of J & G H. L. A month later they were printing a new Ed. of Marion — so they told me.[309] When I was on last August they had got the plates from H & B. to print another Edition. These two I know of, which are not included in their accts, and how many more are there? My books have been paying their current expenses, while I am harrassed with their neglected drafts, & their transfers of my rights to persons of whom I have no knowledge. — I begin to fear that you love us no longer. I don't know the day when I have heard from you, & you write always impatiently, making a few words cover the sheet, and yawning, no doubt, between every sentence. Tell your wife that I must quarrel with her upon this score. She promised me that you would write me frequently, if only to assure me that we were still what we desire to be always, Yours & hers most truly & affectionately

W. G. S.

A kiss for all round.

347: To James Henry Hammond

Woodlands, Decr. 18. 1846

My dear Hammond

I write simply to say that you must not look for me at Christmas. I have engagements in the neighborhood & tasks, which at that period, will keep me here. But I think it very likely that when I attend the Session of the Free School Commissioners, of which honorable body I have the honor to be Chairman, I shall persuade Aldrich to join me in a visit to you. Before that

---

[309] A. S. Salley, in his *Catalogue of the Salley Collection of the Works of Wm. Gilmore Simms* (Columbia, S. C., 1943), lists the following editions of *The Life of Francis Marion* published by Langley: 1844, 1845, 1846 ("Third Edition"), 1846 ("Fifth Edition").

period I shall probably run over to Orangeburgh to see Jamison
& others. I have a Letter from Jamison just recieved, a portion
of which concerns you. (Perhaps you may think it proper to
write to him or send a message. You owe it him.) He writes—
"Hammond, it is true, was not chosen, but thank God" (—thank
him for the fervency) "that canvas put him on his feet again,
and his opponents are little satisfied with their doubtful victory.
Since the election not one word has been breathed disrespectful
to Hammond, and I feel assured that if it were to be tried again,
the result would be different. . . . I repeat Hammond is now
safe &c." I have simply omitted a few more sentences in the
same vein. — How does Glover [310] stand affected toward you?
I should suppose favorably, and hope so, but wish to know that
I may forbear at the proper season, should we chance to refer
to you on meeting. I don't know but that I drew your attention
in my last to the defeat of those humble claims of my own, which
my friends rather injudiciously assumed were quite too safe. The
Charlestonians [311] — who would generally prefer to elevate a
sweep rather than myself, played their game very adroitly; and
having secured as many pledges as they could before my name
was announced, solicited my philanthropic friends here & there,
for a vote, simply that "poor old Cain should make a decent
show." But, I have some reason to suppose that there were others
busy besides the Charleston delegation, having in fear a certain
contingency. Verb. Sap. — There are many topics which are not
to be discussed in this fashion, and I shall really try to see you
in Jany. Meanwhile, take such a survey of the State as I indicated
in my last. If you are to play a game—which, it appears to me
you must — you should secure as many trumps as you can before
hand. You must look to the rising generation, whom *declining*
statesmen—politicians rather—are quite too apt to set aside. You
are I suppose not more than 40. Either you are to live *out &
openly,* according to the claims of your intellect, or not at all.
The moment you determine to take the shelf, you are a dead
man, as was Nick Biddle,[312] — a man who perished from the
nonuses to which he was doomed, —and whom the Whig Party,

---

[310] Thomas Worth Glover, brother-in-law of David F. Jamison, was for
a long period clerk of the South Carolina House of Representatives. He was
a circuit judge until ousted by the "Radical Government" after the Confederate
War.

[311] The delegation from Charleston.

[312] Nicholas Biddle (1786-1844), president of the Bank of the United States.

had they not been doomed—*Quem Deus* &c. — should & could have made President of the United States. No doubt you can make a good farmer of yourself, but that will be a policy like that of my worthy father-in-law, who puts a young negro to the carpenter's trade, makes an excellent mechanic of him, and then turns him into picking peas. Will you sit down to see P. or R. or D. [313] or who else a' God's name, scuffling for Elijah's Mantle [(]—was it Elijah or Elisha?—look) and can you quietly brood over your marl, and congratulate yourself upon a famous potato yield? Not, mon ami, till you yourself become a potato! Well, and what is the prospect. The next Presidential canvas, it is resolved that J. C. Calhoun is to be run—party or no party. You can judge of his prospects? But, if defeated, will he remain in the Senate — will he remain in public life, — subject to the parallel with J. Q. A.[314] — conscious of the self-reproach of Laberius — "Why lingers thus the veteran on the stage,"[315] — which he must suppose will be that of the people also. *Ad interim* what is the prospect of the two Senators [316] pulling famously together. What is the whole prospect — and where are you, and what will you do, — & but there is no room for other questions.

Yours

W. G. S.

J. H. H.

348: To Rufus Wilmot Griswold

Woodlands 21 Decr. [1846][317]

dear Sir

Can you tell me if a journal or periodical published in Phila. in 1785 called the *Independent Chronicle* is to be seen any where in that City, — and whether the matter which relates to Col. John Laurens of So. Caro. and which occurs in its columns or pages, on the 2d. Decr. 1784, is worthy transcribing, and not

---

[313] Pickens or Rhett or Davie.

[314] John Quincy Adams.

[315] Laberius, the writer of mimes, having offended Caesar, was ordered to appear as an actor, a position ordinarily reserved for a slave.

[316] John C. Calhoun and A. P. Butler. Butler had just defeated Hammond for the United States Senate.

[317] Dated by Simms' reference to his "long epistle." See letter of Dec. 6.

expensively long.[318] — Will you make the inquiry at your first convenience. I sincerely hope that your eyes have undergone improvement. Are you to see South Carolina this season? How gets on your book, — and did my long epistle reach you, and was it satisfactory.

Yours very truly &c.

W. Gilmore Simms

Rev. R. W. Griswold.

349: To James Henry Hammond

Woodlands, Christmas Day. [1846][319]

My dear Hammond

A season of repose and peace to you & yours. To wish you merry would be to wish you vulgar, and with the earnest purposes of life before us, would be consistent with neither of us. But a respite is something, — and a season of peace — repose from all strifes & excitements, to those who are certainly born to them — would be worthy of both of our desires. — The *office* of the Lt. Gov. is such a nullity, that one might well feel a sense of shame at being suspected of mortification when defeated in seeking it. Nay, he should not seek it. If I have any regret at all in the business it is that it should be thought the thing was at all desirable to me. In seeking an office my sole aim would be to be useful. It is the exercise afforded us in making the development of the endowment we possess, that is grateful, and not the empty honor which attends the name. I have no wish for political place except as affording a field in which I may work according to my vocation — and, as I believe — according to my destiny. But no more of egotism. *It is something, perhaps, to have it thought worth while that I should be suppressed as well as yourself.* People will ask 'Why?,' — In both cases, and, I fancy, that neither of us need be dissatisfied to wait for the inevitable self-conclusions that will follow the question. — In my instance you are probably quite correct in assuming that the novelist hurts the politician. To a

---

[318] The brief account of Laurens appears in the *Independent Chronicle: and the Universal Advertiser* (Boston) of Dec. 2, 1784, as a footnote to the first part of an article entitled "Fragment of an Original Letter on the Slavery of the Negroes, Written in the Year 1776, by Thomas Day, Esq; (Lately Published in London)."

[319] Dated by Simms' references to his defeat for lieutenant governor and to Hammond's defeat for the United States Senate.

certain extent it does so undoubtedly. I speculated on this subject
myself in a paper in the Southern Quarterly on Horne's Spirit
of the Age.[320] Still, I do not think the evil of so great activity
as you suppose. I may decieve myself as to the position which I
occupy in the minds of our people, but I believe that the intelligent
give me credit for something more exact & literal — more practical and suited to everyday necessities. The lawyers themselves
are not unconscious of their own deficiencies, whenever they are
required to rise from the subject to the principle which governs
it. Memminger,[321] for example, as shrewd a scoundrel as ever
fenced himself in with dicta, is notoriously incapable of a moral
or philosophical view of a principle. He has not imagination
enough for an argument for which his memory does not furnish
him with all the *data & criteria.* His attempts on the Bible were
most monstrous abortions. His speeches on Duelling, mere balderdash and idiot fury. — Well, — his neighbour lawyers see his
weakness. Of the whole tribe of whom I have any idea, it seems
to me that Judge Harper [322] and—B. F. Hunt!!![323]—(don't be
surprised) are really the only two, whom at a moments warning I
could summon — as answering, in their craft, to the definition of
Genius. I put McDuffie & Calhoun & yourself out of the question
—since my notion is that, with less profundity you must each of
you have been better *Lawyers.* But whither do I wander? — To
return, I flatter myself that our folk are beginning to know me—
quite as much as a politician as they do as a novelist. — Perhaps
not so favorably, for I have done nothing — had no chance; —
but where we have not, it appears to me, that their estimate of
my claims has sensibly risen. — You are right, I think, in charging something in my late defeat, to the salt water. *Not all,* however. No doubt, they would always go against me, *having a
pretext.* Here they had one. Most of them, through the activity
of Yates, Northrop [324] & others, were pledged to Cain before my
friends in the up-country had announced me. True, no such pledge

---

[320] See note 97, Feb. 11, 1845.

[321] Christopher Gustavus Memminger. See note 129, Dec. 19, 1841.

[322] William Harper. See note 163, April 10, 1845.

[323] Benjamin Faneuil Hunt (1792-1854), a native of Waterford, Mass., was
a lawyer and advocate of Charleston. He was a member of the South Carolina
House of Representatives for many years.

[324] Jeremiah D. Yates was a member of the South Carolina House of
Representatives from 1844 to 1846, elected from the combined parishes of St.
Philip's and St. Michael's. Claudian B. Northrop was also a member from the
same election district.

is obligatory among men of sense, — for the pledge implies that
the condition of the field is fully known when made; — but the
argument, though obvious enough, they were not disposed to
make. Our friend Jim Walker, I believe, was the only one who
insisted upon his liberty & used it. But they were active also, and
there were other motives governing them, I fancy, having reference to the succession. Do you not see why the office of Lt Gov.
has usually been conferred upon men of straw? This must always
be the case, where, as now, the successor is fixed upon for the
Gubernatorial Chair, even before the just elected has taken his
seat. The Lt. Gov. succeeding by the contingency and making a
respectable figure in the seat, would most probably be continued
in it. You will probably have seen & suspected this. — In Charleston, I believe, that, *with the great body of the people,* I should
be something of a favorite. I do not decieve myself with the
notion that I have a dozen persons there, in the professions, who
would not openly destroy me if they dared. But they are very
civil. Some of the very persons who were most active for Cain
were full of regrets to me & to my known friends, and several
suggestions of the *quid* were thrown out to me, should I be pleased
to refuse myself to those who nominated me. — To strip for the
field as you counsel would be, just now, *to take cold only.* Positively there is no field at present. One of my reasons for favoring
the giving the elections to the people of Electors was to make a
field where we should secure fair play & ask no favor. Do you
suppose that if your election had been confided to the people of
S. C. you would not have beaten Elmore, Butler, Pickens, &
Rhett out of sight? I am sure you would. But we are under an
oligarchy. The Legislature is such. We have our thirty tyrants,
and I am becoming everyday more & more satisfied of the baneful
hostility of the Bank to our political Independence.[325] The loss
of the money would be an evil; but it operates more evilly through
its moral & social agencies. I found that this influence, in a way
that I do not yet see, turned against you several up-country votes,
which, had the *purse*onal influences been wanting, must have
been yours. That Boyce & Aiken [326] should have power — that

[325] Through Elmore, politicians of the Rhett faction easily borrowed from
the Bank of the State of South Carolina.

[326] William Aiken (1806-1887), of Charleston, was a member of the State
House of Representatives during 1838-1842, State senator during 1842-1844,
governor of South Carolina during 1844-1846, and a member of Congress during
1851-1857. Aiken and Simms at one time lived within one door of each other
on King Street. David Duncan Wallace in *The History of South Carolina*

McDonald [327] should have power — that Elmore should be assumed to be the strongest man in the State — is wholly due to the money influence, and that influence brought to bear directly upon the necessities & against the Independence & safety of the citizens. This influence, though lessening, is still enough to decide the Legislature, and is, I believe, addressed, not so much against the candidate as against the individual. The office may be a very small one, having no political weight or tendency; but it is important to keep from power those who are not of the faction, — or who, without going against it, exhibit a lack of sympathy with its objects & desires. What can an honest man, whatever his endowments, do with such a body, *unless some great & commanding political issue is to be made up.* Such an issue would afford us an opportunity, and we might venture to strip for the contest. But till then, the mind of the General Assembly, like that of the people, in the absence of the same sort of excitement, is in a state of sluggish apathy, and may be wrought upon by any industrious worker, who, having a selfish purpose at heart, is willing to labor with individuals, finding a fitting argument for each. Whether a period will ever occur for either of us, which will enable our friends to insist upon our claims in our several places, is a question. But the chances are that our sluggish fortunes are destined to undergo alteration. Domestically, I have already indicated, in previous letters, some of the events which may be anticipated. I take for granted that Calhoun & Butler will hardly draw together to mutual satisfaction. Butler, I take it, not only possesses independence, but lacks prudence, of character; and Calhoun knows better how to deal with rivals and opponents than folks give him credit for. But, whatever may happen between these two — assuming that all goes on well between them — still, the resolution to run Calhoun at all hazards for the presidency, will put him on the shelf forever. I am disposed to think that his pretended friends run him for this very purpose. They flatter him with the idea that Virginia will nominate him. Perhaps she will; but in all probability, Virginia herself will be Anti-Demo-

---

(New York: The American Historical Society, Inc., 1934), II, 488-490, says: "The race for the Governorship in 1844 was exceedingly bitter. Whitemarsh B. Seabrook, the wealthy Edisto Island planter and a Blufftonite, wrote Calhoun that his defeat by the wealthy William Aiken was brought about by corrupting legislators through banking accommodations backed up by Ker Boyce and the Charleston money power."

[327] Alexander McDonald was at this time a director of the Bank of the State of South Carolina.

cratic at the next election. Alabama seconds the nomination of Va. & is followed by Louisiana, Mississippi, Florida & Carolina; — and all these conceded, still the hope is to bring the election into the House. Are you prepared to believe that his chances are much bettered by this. His friends say so, — and he, naturally enough, believes it. But whether made Prest. or not, he is removed from So. Ca., and the mantle falls upon — Who? It is this mantle which is in the eye of the Rhetts, Pickens, Elmore &c. Will they recieve it? Can they wear it? No! For very good reasons — the best of which is that — they are neither of them, J. C. C. — who is certainly a very remarkable man, and, in certain respects, quite a tactician. If defeated, he is laid on the shelf for he is no longer young & vigorous, and he himself, I fancy, as well as all others, will hardly think of his playing the game of J Q Adams & emerging in his dotage. But, have I not prattled of this before? What then, assuming his retiracy, are you to do with Butler? — Who put with him? — You see that Rhett & Pickens are afraid to run — that Elmore, though sure of election, yet felt that, not to be elected by a very triumphant majority would be — with his assured popularity before all eyes, — a sort of Pyrrhus victory, which would leave him undone — and his friends & self soon saw that his majority could not be great. Who was feared? You only! Well! And why? Because of the universal impression of your great mental superiority! Well! And are the issues now approaching such as are calculated to make our people less solicitous of the employment of their ablest men. With the war in Mexico, — destined perhaps for long continuance — with the increase of taxation & a terrible struggle & not the last — with the manufacturers to be resumed upon the Tariff, — and another seven years conflict with the Free States on the subject of the acquisition of the Californian & other Mexican territory, by which alone are we to be compensated for the loss. If, with a cloud upon you, — with many active enemies among the strongest monied men & politicians in the State — in a time of no struggle and no anticipated difficulty, this Legislature so much the creature of your opponents, — are yet disposed so strongly to insist upon your claims — what must be the case when the crisis comes, — when the inefficiency of our public men is forced painfully upon the popular sense, and when imbecility, instead of seeking office, skulks timidly from all responsibility. That time seems to me to be approaching, and you have only to wait for it. A time when the South will need its best men, and when it will busily look them up. Whether I should then be pleased to serve with you — under you if you please, or if our people please — at home or abroad, must, I take it, be left to our friends. It will not do for me to urge my own claims — my own fitness — in the teeth of two notices to quit, — [one] so immediately after the other.[328] I think you will find that, if the business I am on is adequate to the employment of all my abilities, I shall be easily able to concentrate myself upon it. But my previous labours for several years have been in great degree those of the *amateur,* while, from peculiar circumstances, I have been subjected to many absolute necessities requiring me to work. In the first place, I am an author without living in the city of publication — an anomaly which is not to be found in other countries, or even in our own in the case of other individuals. This abridges my profits, while it increases my necessities & tasks. You will see the difficulties of this point without my dwelling upon them — that I am here & thus arises from the almost impossible of my condition. My wife is an invalid—breeding every year — is an only child — her father advanced in life — unwilling that she should leave home even for a week's visit, — and I too have learned to be a nurse — to rise at midnight & kindle light & fire — to warm the infant's tea, and subdue myself to something of the drudge. To leave my family, when such a relation subsists between us, is not easy — to separate my wife from her father in his situation would be scarce humane — and with a good capital, as well mine as his — I am compelled to see it gradually diminishing, since it is not well administered — certainly not profitably. This will explain to you the language of my difficulty in previous letters. I sincerely thank you for your frank & liberal tender.[329] Fortunately, I have no

---

[328] Simms is referring to his two defeats this year, that for the South Carolina House of Representatives and that for lieutenant governor of South Carolina.

[329] In a letter dated Dec. 18 Hammond had urged Simms to permit him to help him: "I think the occasion will excuse me for expressing to you an opinion not now formed, but long entertained, that you have abilities capable of *any thing*. The wide range of your powers, is the greatest failing of your intellect. Consummate efforts in any line are neither appreciated or rewarded here, & you have therefore indulged yourself too much in wantonly sporting through all. I have in other words often rebuked you for this. I don't think you want the power, but the will to concentrate — without an immediate & active stimulant. Such a mind as yours, should content its possessor to die while he lives, that he might live when he died. The immortality you might achieve would be worthy of the finite sacrifice. You know I speak sincerely, & I trust you will again bear with me, when I exhort you to make choice of one walk in

need to expect such favors from my friends — hope never to have
— but should such a necessity arise I know none to whom I
would more boldly apply than yourself. I use but little money —
owe but little — and earn by my pen all that I use. No[w] — Did
I ever send you, or did you ever see a vol. of Poems of mine,
entitled 'Southern Passages & Pictures'? If not I will send you
a copy. In this vol. I have *expressed myself* more fully than in
most of my books, & much of the matter, though written at desultory periods, and years ago — is such as I am by no means
ashamed of now. — I think it likely I shall get up to visit you
towards the last of January. Tomorrow, I go with my daughter
to Orangeburg, where I shall see Jamison &c. — I shall write to
Aldrich to join me if possible, on my route to Silver Bluff.[330]

Yours very truly &c

Simms

Gen. Hammond.

---

literature or politics if you prefer it — & devote your whole energies to some
mighty work that will do to throw upon the waters — that can stem the rapid
current of oblivion. I have perhaps made too light of the pecuniary troubles
you have heretofore alluded to. I have been under the impression that they
were somewhat fanciful — such as should not *weigh* upon a mind like yours. I
may be wrong. How can I aid you? You are not one of those who think that
because a man is somewhat wealthier than some others, that he has an ex-
haustless purse & needs only to will to do. I have use for all I have & do use
it. Yet — tho perhaps I should not say it — I often assist my friends, & there
are few for whom I would do what I can so cheerfully as I would for you.
Come up here & let us talk over the evils of the world — damn it & lay our
plans to get our feet upon its neck — I have a great deal to talk to you about
on my own account." (Original in the Hammond Papers, Library of Congress.)

[330] Silver Bluff, located on the Savannah River, was Hammond's plantation.
Many historians consider it the spot where De Soto crossed the Savannah
while on his way to the Mississippi River, and where he captured an Indian
Queen, whom he employed as a hostage.

1847

350: To James Lawson

Woodlands. Jany 2. 1847.

God bless you & keep you & yours! The opening of a new year, suggests naturally this prayer. My wife is a little better—seems slightly, but very slowly to improve, and is still very feeble. Her infirmity is no more definite than this. She labors under a protracted & astonishing debility. This it is which keeps us uneasy.— We are all well. Gilmore & little Mary Lawson both have whooping cough; but it is of a very mild kind, and they are both exceedingly hearty. The latter particularly so. She is, I fancy, the prettiest of our children, & — let your wife hear this— she is said to resemble me very greatly. We are all greatly distressed at the failure of the pie & pone.[1] My wife is monstrous vexed & worried that all her attempts to indoctrinate yours in the merits of S. C. dishes should have proved abortive. — I have no doubt that your version of our accounts is right. There may be a mistake in the item of Godey's. My memoranda may have contained the charge without the credit — see to that point.[2] I have not my papers here, but in town. It matters not much either way. Enclosed, I send you another order for Twenty five on Labree, which you will collect as soon as possible after due. You do not tell me whether Langleys have or not failed — whether they have transferred Marion as well as Smith to Cooledge &c.[3] I have, as you know, a contract with the Langley's for Marion as well as Smith. This gives them the exclusive right of publishing that work till 1850. Now, how, without their consent to sell the copyright, —

---

[1] See letters to Lawson of Oct. 1 and Nov. 21, 1846.

[2] In his letter of Nov. 19, 1846, Simms had credited himself with having paid Lawson $25 through a draft on Godey.

[3] See letter to Lawson of Dec. 12, 1846. The failure of J. and H. G. Langley and the transference of the rights to *The Life of Francis Marion* and *The Life of Captain John Smith* to George F. Cooledge and Brother become of considerable concern to Simms throughout the early months of 1847. See letters to Lawson of Jan. 26, Feb. 15, and c. Feb. 20.

unless subject to their temporary privilege? This is a difficulty which, I suppose, could be easily overcome as the Langley's have not settled up & cannot give security for their payments. I have had no acct. from them since that of July 1. 1845, and know that they have published several editions since that period. I drew on them while in N. Y. for $70 or thereabouts in favor of Bartlett & Welford — pray see if this be paid, and let B & W. secure themselves (if not paid) as well as they can. I have written them to compel payt. — I have read the letter of Cooledge & Bro. It seems fairly meant enough, but is wrong in its premises. The life of Smith is far more rich in material than ever Putnam's can be; and old Put, though good subject enough for a clever biographical sketch, was yet no great shakes of a hero.[4] He will attract to a certain extent. Smith was the great hero of modern discovery — English discovery I mean, & a superior character in that respect to Raleigh. — Marion has a proverbial reputation, & my book has gone to ten editions, though that of old Weems had been in the market & extensively popular for more than 30 years.[5] It is worth quite as much as Smith and both books will find readers to a regular amount annually, for fifty years to come. In the hands of judicious publishers this cannot but be the case. You are authorized to sell them the Life of Smith for what they offer $500 and on the terms of payt. which they suggest. For Marion you will demand $600. I have no doubt that Harper & Brothers will readily take the two works for $1200. And unless C. & B. come to your terms promptly, I should like you to see them. It is not improbable that Langley has been proposing for C & B. He offered $900. — To enable you to act efficiently & decisively, I accord you full discretion, and will consent, should

---

[4] Israel Putnam (1718-1790), general in the American Revolution, was the subject of a biography by William Cutter (1801-1867). The first three volumes of Cooledge's "Illustrated Library," containing Simms' *Life of Francis Marion* and *Life of Captain John Smith* and Cutter's *Life of Israel Putnam,* are advertised in the *Literary World,* I (March 13, 1847), 124. Earlier, on Feb. 6, the *Literary World* (I, 18) announced that "Geo. F. Cooledge & Brother, N. Y., have nearly ready 'The Life of Captain John Smith,'" but it was not until late March that the volume actually was published. The *Literary World* for March 27 (I, 185) carries the following note: "George F. Cooledge and Brother, have now ready the 'Life of John Smith, the Founder of Virginia,' by W. Gilmore Simms, illustrated by numerous engravings." Cutter's *Life of Israel Putnam* appeared somewhat later. It is reviewed in the *Literary World,* I (May 1, 1847), 294-296.

[5] "Parson" M. L. Weems' *Life of Francis Marion* was first published in 1809. Simms' critique of Weems' historical work, entitled "Weems, the Historian," was published in *Southern and Western,* I (Jan., 1845), 35-47.

you be able to effect nothing better, to your taking $1000 for the two works, — but you must see that the Langley's have satisfied Bartlett & Welford, & they must honor the draft made in your favor. The matter touching the percentage can be left over. If I am to deal farther in this sort of business, we had better deal with H. & B. with whom I recommend you to have an early conference. — I was beaten for Lt. Gov. by one vote, & this with 9/10ths of the Legislature in my favor. The case was this. I was nominated in a county paper which was published *weekly,*[6] and before it was known that I was announced, my friends in the Low Country had become pledge[d] to my opponent who was a very worthy old Gentleman, who worked himself & operated through a very early & active correspondence. I took no step in the matter, and was not within a hundred miles of the Capital for two weeks before the election! Nobody doubts but that I am one of the most popular men, at this moment, in the regards of the Legislature & people; and I have had applications numerously, before & since the election, to permit my friends to use my name for other offices. I have thus far declined. The office of Lt. Gov. was chiefly an office of honor & compliment. — On the subject of coming North hereafter, I will write to Lady Lyde next week and put myself, I trust, *rectus in curia.* Don't let her scold me, however and don't think of it yourself. I suppose we know each other thoroughly. I hear nothing from Duyckinck & Mathews— nor do you tell me much about them, or Yankee Doodle. I have been idling away my time famously— go to work next Monday upon Bayard. I have 3 parts of my story (concluding it) for Labree, which I will send you one by one, drawing for the pay on each occasion.[7] There are 6 in all, three of which he has. My love & Augustas & wifes, to Madame L. and the little ones. Augusta will write shortly. A New Year's kiss, on my account to Lady Lyde — if she will recieve it *from you. I* would much rather deliver it myself.

Yours &c

W. G. S.

---

[6] See note 253, Nov. 21, 1846.

[7] See letter to Lawson of Oct. 23, 1846, for "The Maroon," the serial written for the *New York Illustrated Magazine,* edited by Lawrence Labree.

351: To James Henry Hammond

Woodlands. Jany 2. 1847.

dear Hammond

The result of my recent visit to Orangeburgh is a partial arrangement between Jamison, Aldrich & myself to visit you sometime in this month, say between the 3rd & 4th Mondays in Jany.[8] J. & A. have served you very faithfully & are anxious to see you & arrange the plan of a future campaign. Our idea is that you are to be used the very next Senatorial vacancy and that you can be used with success. I have suggested that nothing could better help the common cause than an Independent newspaper. I counselled the plan of one. The difficulty is in getting the proper conductors. Jamison suggests as one of them, your old friend Pemberton.[9] He alleges as an offset against the deficiencies & infirmities of P. that he is faithful & fearless, and will take his political clues cheerfully from you. We are all agreed to subscribe according to our resources, — which, by the way, are quite small in my case, as, in addition to my other items of ill luck, I have just recieved tidings of the failure of one of my publishers, who has left some of my drafts unpaid, and has probably lost me the labor of nearly two years.[10] "The fates make war against

---

[8] In a letter to Hammond of Jan. 5, 1847, A. P. Aldrich refers to an unlocated letter from Simms: "Simms informed me by letter that he & Jamison intended to be at my house on the third Saturday before the third Monday in this month and invade you the day after just in time to get your dinner." (Original in the Hammond Papers, Library of Congress.) After this visit D. F. Jamison wrote to G. F. Holmes on Jan. 28: "By the bye, I have wiped out all the old scores against Simms, and we are now as thick as thieves. He spent his Christmas with us—and a merry Christmas it was—and leaving the author at his brick library at 'Woodlands' or elsewhere, he brought the man alone with him—and we had a healthy man, a simple-hearted, downright, clever fellow, for a week or more, with us. To compensate for years of puritanical affectation, and eschewing of the devil and all his works, we frolicked throughout the holidays—had pleasant dancing parties every night for a week, to the great horror of Hanscombe Legaré [Presbyterian minister], who on the successive Sundays anathematized all fiddles, triangles, and tamarinds, (I believe that is the way to spell a certain instrument of music), that were ever invented and denounced all skipping turns or dancing as inventions of the evil one. But as every man, woman, and child of his congregation or audience were implicated more or less in the offence, his logic was unheeded, and his discourses were more amusing than edifying." (Copy in Holmes' "Letter Book," Duke University Library.)

[9] A. H. Pemberton was the publisher of Hammond's "Letters on Slavery." See letters to Hammond of April 10 and May 20, 1845.

[10] Simms was not certain of the failure of J. and H. G. Langley. See letter to Lawson of the same date.

us!"[11] — I have written to Walker on the subject of the paper,
& to suggest to him to look out for a proper subject for the
business department.[12] — At Orangeburgh, I learned all the details in the events at Columbia. It does not appear that we have
any reason to be dissatisfied at the prospect. Glover who is a cool
& shrewd fellow concurs with Jamison. I saw Felder frequently
— another shrewd fellow where his own interests are concerned.
He professes to be with us, and is certainly with you, — since
your strongly avowed hostility to the Bank, sanctions his own,
and flatters his vanity by an idea of coincidence & sympathy.
'Great wits jump together' [13]—you know. He talks big and something at random, but though he seldom takes the bull by the horns,
he seldom fails to have hold on him somewhere. He speaks of a
caucus during the summer. But we are silent. The truth is, though
our friends in Orangeburgh are scarcely disposed to think it, —
he is somewhat in the keeping of Pickens. They correspond and
he avows P. to be a great man with a good heart &c. "You" says
he to me "dislike Pickens." "Not so," I say. "I would have no
objection to P. if he would be content to stay where he is put;
but I see no necessity, when the purple falls from present shoulders, for any more Kings in Israel." "He doesn't want to be
King," says F. "Very good!—*and I have no objection to his being
Governor after Johnson!*" "Eh!" says F. And I say no more,
but call for another mug of his persimmon beer. I suppose what
I have said will work in him quite as actively as his beer has done
in me. But though P. might be useful to us, there could be no
faith between us, and we should only share, by a connection, the
odium which has fastened upon him by his hostility to Mr. Calhoun. But of these things you will have a more perfect judgment
when we meet. F. is to be heard with patience & good nature,
smiled on as occasion serves, and to be encouraged to work, when
there are no pastries of our own in the oven. — It might be well
to run over in your mind your acquaintance—seeking for such
persons as might fairly be entrusted with the conduct of a political journal. Such an organ is absolutely necessary. Call it "Young
Carolina" & use that party which is destined to grow, for it has
a truth to build on.[14] We can furnish clues to Pemberton or any

[11] *Aeneid,* IV, 440.
[12] Simms' letter to James M. Walker has not been located.
[13] "Great wits agree." A proverb.
[14] See note 226, Nov. 17, 1846. No newspaper with this title was established.

other editor, until he has got well along in harness. We can write
his political editorials. Do you see how Elmore laid himself open
in that correspondence with the London Bankers — that inviting
of them to an opinion the key note of which is suggested by
adroit & improper issues?[15] Well, — these might all be reviewed
and all the kindred topics in the newspaper. I suppose Felder sent
you what he calls his skeleton of a speech.[16] Some of his phrases
might be well employed to round a paragraph.

Yours &c.

W. G. S.

352: To JAMES HENRY HAMMOND

Woodlands. 7th Jan. 1847

dear Hammond

I think it very probable that we, — Jamison, Aldrich & myself,
will leave Barnwell C. H. for your den, either on the 17th or the
24th of the present month. We propose to let nobody guess our
route; and to start off at early gray. In a letter which you have
probably recieved before this, I mentioned my visit to Orangeburgh, and gave you some idea of the social & political atmosphere
in that quarter. I deemed it proper to urge upon Jamison to go
with me to see you, — having several reasons for it. He could
tell you much of the game in Columbia which would reach you
from no better quarter— to afford you in person an opportunity
of showing him that you *felt his fidelity*. I value J. very highly
as a true man, — single hearted & tenacious of his position. Making our start from the C. H. we shall come in our own establishments, but hereafter, I may, for greater rapidity, convenience &
secrecy, use the Rail Road & your wagon for my purposes. I
fancy that the party of *four* will not interfere except partially
with our conferences, and you will so manage it that we may talk
poetry together, at least.— What is it you now mumble about
"your health"? Do you know I look upon health as something of a

---

[15] Letters from Elmore's correspondence with Baring Brothers and Co. of
London, Hambro and Son of London, Edward Everett, and George McDuffie
concerning the Bank of the State of South Carolina are printed in the Charleston *Mercury* of Dec. 30 and Dec. 31, 1846.

[16] See note 245, *c.* Nov. 19, 1846.

humbug. All your complaining is sheer repletion— resulting from
the consciousness of wealth, health, strength and general ability to
be mischievous. You are in the case of Jeshurun, waxing fat, and
kicking accordingly.[17] We shall give you such a rouse when we
come that you will never again dream of suffering. Your rheu-
matics and dyspepsia will no longer afford you material by which
to extort your neighbours' sympathies, — and with the necessity
of stirring a little in the political cauldron, you will soon find other
occasions for growling.—We at least shall not quarrel greatly
whether the power be in the hands of Demos or the Assembly.[18] I
care not much about it — secure as I am that, if the proper men
can be brought to act in the business, its exercise will be legitimate
no matter in whose hands it keeps. You are not wholly right, nor
am I wholly wrong. I don't know but I somewhat incline to yr.
opinion. At least, I am willing to waive the subject, particularly
when there is so much more obnoxious game. —

To organize—to bring together the good & true—to enable
the middle districts so to unite as to always determine the balance— to find out how those young men think & feel who are now
coming forward & who have resources to make themselves felt—
how to give the right direction to them—how to break ground
against the log-rolling system—how to show to the people that
they are governed by their debtors everywhere—how to make
the independent men of the Legislature revolt at the manner in
which they are managed—to show them the wirepullers &c.—how
to establish a paper, and by whom—to prepare the gradual development through its columns, of our facts & philosophies. In what
way to act upon the Bank, yet give no exercise of power to the
sharks of bankers who, in Charleston, are only hostile to it because, in the business of sharking, its connection with the State
gives it certain advantages. These, and many more, are points
which I could wish you to turn in your mind before I see you. Do
you know Orr of Anderson?[19] He is a correspondent & friend of

---

[17] Deuteronomy, 32:15.

[18] Hammond was a staunch opponent of all popular elections; Simms consistently favored elections by the people rather than by the legislature.

[19] For James Lawrence Orr, at this time a member (from Pendleton) of the
South Carolina House of Representatives, see introductory sketch. Simms and
Orr served together in the House during 1844-1846.

mine—on general terms. He supported you. Jamison thinks he is
to be cultivated — and he is popular at home.[20]

Goodnight.

W. G. S.

353 : ALFRED BILLINGS STREET

Woodlands Jany. 15. 1847

My dear Sir.

Let me give you at the beginning the blessings of the Season,
may the present and all the future years of your life, long &
vigorous, be equally prosperous & pleasant. I thank you for your
letter. Its friendly tone & generous sympathies are equally grateful & encouraging. It should have been answered before, but for
my frequent absences from home, and the constant interruptions
of company, which must be always looked for on our Southern
plantations at this season of proverbial festivity. I would that we
could have had you, Lawson & a few others of your & our friends
to have given you a taste of our quality at Christmas time. I trust
that this is a pleasure in store for us at other returns of the
Season. — That I was not elected Lt. Gov. of S. C. was wholly
owing to the confidence of my friends, who knowing my strength
in the Legislature persisted in running me without taking the
usual precautions, though it was known that our opponent—a
Senator and very worthy Gentleman— had been, with his friends,
electioneering & securing pledges, fully a month before I had been
put in nomination. I was beaten by *one* vote, having 7/10th of
the Legislature in my favor.[21] The office was not one which I
sought. It was one rather of honor & distinction than of much

---

[20] In his reply of Jan. 11, an answer to both this letter and that of Jan. 2,
Hammond remarks: "I trust you will all be in no hurry to return. We shall
not talk of half we want to discuss unless we exhaust ourselves three or four
times over. Jamison & I can talk two days incessantly about planting. Then
two more for poetry &c with you—two de omnibus rebus with Aldrich & then
about the affairs public & private for at least four more. I want you to make
a survey of this locality & immortalize Silver Bluff in a romance.

"As to the extensive political projects you suggest, we must digest all of them.
Your outline is a grand one but the filling up is no small matter. Revolutions
are the work of time. But things are I think tending favourably. The Bank is
tottering. I dread her recuperative powers, & wish there were some strong
arms to give her blows thick & heavy. . . . As it is their whole influence is
centred in Columbia where Preston rules omnipotent. . . . " (Original in the
Hammond Papers, Library of Congress.)

[21] See letter to Lawson of Jan. 2, 1847.

responsibility, and I never spoke of the subject except when spoken to, and studiously avoided the Capital when the canvas was in progress. Had it been an office of greater trust, I should have been elected undoubtedly. As it is, I have rather gained than lost by the proceeding, as the result has mortified my oversanguine friends into a determination to make the *amende* to me at the earliest opportunity. I have every reason to believe that I have in high degree the sympathies & confidence of our people.— In asking after the returns of your vol. I had certainly no desire to pry into the affair between you & your publishers, but rather to give you my hint that you might always expect to yield to them the Lion's Share. Your answer is only what I expected. I can hardly believe, however, that Mr. Willis has made any such sacrifice of his copyrights as they tell you.[22] I, however, have never expected to realize money by versemaking in our day & in America. And yet I regard poetry as my forte, particularly in the narrative & dramatic forms. All my desire is to put myself on record. It was with such views & wishes that I mentioned my desire that you should confer with yr publishers in regard to my collection. Whenever it shall be in your way to do so, I beg that you will remind them of your former suggestion. I propose a collection of all my choicest things in verse, & will designate a few of their heads that you may speak advisedly. My volume would open with "Atalantis" which I have entirely rewritten. 1. Atalantis; 2. Southern Passages & Pictures; 3. Lays & Legends of Apalachia; 4. Areytos; 5. Grouped Thoughts & Scattered Fancies. — These works are all probably known to you. They have all undergone revision and the Songs and Sonnets will be more numerous than they were in the original publication. The collection would be very various. There are numerous tales & traditions. The descriptive portions have been highly successful, and much has been said of the passionate. To the South & West the vol. would appeal greatly, not merely because of its source, but because of the locale of so much of its material. With a portrait (—which, as none has ever yet been published of me, might be an attraction with many—) and a vignette illustrative of a portion of the volume, I think it might command a large circulation, to say nothing of

---

[22] Street's reply to Simms' letter of Aug. 26, 1846, has not been located. Apparently it contained a discussion of his and Nathaniel P. Willis' arrangements with the publishing firm of Clark and Austin, New York City.

those readers to whom my prose writings have given pleasure.[23]
When you happen to be in N. Y. or to write to your publishers,
you may draw their notice to the matter. *If, however, they are
in Mr. Willis's keeping, they will* probably give no heed to what
you may urge. *He* has for some years shown himself hostile to
me.—You acknowledge my notice in the Charleston paper. Have
you seen the Review in the Messenger?[24] I trust that you find
that equally considerate of your claims with the other. I trust
that in both I have shown myself equally friendly and just. My
wife improves slowly—she is still something of an invalid. She
begs to thank you for your kind remembrance.

Yours very truly

W. Gilmore Simms

354: To JAMES HENRY HAMMOND

Woodlands, January 25. 1847.

My dear Hammond

I had no idea, when leaving you, of writing you quite so soon
after reaching home, but none of us can well foresee the occasions which compel us to think of our friends. I shall probably
need your services, and certainly need your counsel. You have
probably recieved your number of the Southern Literary Messenger for the present month. Let me beg you to address your
attention to an article, by the Editor of "Curwen's Memoirs" — a
work which I reviewed in several successive numbers of the same
periodical.[25] This article, to which I cannot refer you more spe-

---

[23] For the publication of the second edition of *Atalantis* (Philadelphia: Carey
and Hart, 1848), see note 328, Dec. 14, 1847. Though the volume contains
other poems by Simms (notably the group called "The Eye and the Wing,"
which had originally appeared in *S. L. M.*, XII [Oct. and Nov., 1846], 627-629;
XIII [Jan. and Feb., 1847], 28-29, 113-114), it was not until 1853 that a collected edition of Simms' poems was published in two volumes by Redfield,
New York.

[24] For Simms' reviews of Street's *Poems* in the *Southern Patriot* and in the
Southern Literary Messenger, see letters to Street of July and Aug., 1846.

[25] For Simms' review of George Atkinson Ward's edition of Curwen's
Journal and the resulting difficulties with the Cunninghams, see note 367, Dec.
12, 1845, and letter to Perry of Oct. 30, 1846. In *S. L. M.*, XIII (Jan., 1847),
48-51, Ward published a sarcastic reply, attacking Simms for inaccuracy, inconsistency, and inability to distinguish "the characteristic difference between a
biography and a general history; between a private journal and an historical
disquisition." Of Simms' remarks about Robert Cunningham, Ward says that
he "has evidently either wantonly or ignorantly confounded neutrality with

JAMES HENRY HAMMOND

". . . my most confidential friend for near twenty five years.
Never were thoughts more intimate than his & mine. We had
few or no secrets from each other — we took few steps in life
without mutual consultation. . . . there was something kindred
in our intellectual nature."

(From a photograph in the possession of Mr. John Shaw Billings,
Redcliffe Plantation, South Carolina)

Literary Temperatures.

OUTH of Mason & Dixon's Line the temperature of the literary and moral atmosphere undergoes quite as great a transition as that of sky and air. A round, rattling hail-storm at the North, which dashes in church-windows by the phalanx, and knocks down young children and ripe grass exposed to its fury, grows genial as the clangor of its icy wings fades faint in the Southern horizon; and melting to b r i g h t tears of penitence for all the harsh mischief it has done, it stoops in tender dalliance with the spiced air slumbering amid cane and orange blossoms. Then, as it rises, sleepy with odorous kisses, the very thunder grows musical, like the laughter of its dream.— [YANKEE DOODLE quotes this paragraph from *Guy Rivers*.

But sunshine and thunder, orange-blossoms and cane-juice, new whiskey and corn dodgers, although their influence is quite as marked upon authors as hail-storms, is not always of the same subduing and mollifying character. It is certainly true—and YANKEE DOODLE records the fact to the disgrace of the North—that literary men and editors at the South seldom indulge in the scurrility, envious malignity and persevering misrepresentation which, too often here, form the weapons with which men who write, propel their crazy vehicles along the crowded and dusty avenues to fame and distinction. One reason, perhaps, for this may be the explosive nature of the great Southern staple, and the habit which prevails among editors in Southern cities, of settling their difficulties over the boll. As a general thing, our authors, both at the North and South, possess a great deal more spirit than their books, and are far more extensively read. This, however, is not their fault; and to extend as far as possible the circle of their readers and admirers, YANKEE DOODLE is glad to see a growing disposition among them to read and admire each other. This ought to be faithfully performed—as our obligations to the dead, however painful, are too sacred to be neglected.

CARICATURE OF SIMMS
"Martin's *head* of me is very well done."
(From *Yankee Doodle*, I [Dec. 5, 1846], 106)

cifically (as it so happens that my copy has not reached me, and what I know of it comes from a hasty glance at one that I saw at Aldrich's) contains much that is abusive and offensive to myself, and which may or may not have been intended to provoke hostilities. At first reading, knowing how little the people of the North are inclined to final issues, it struck me as doubtful whether the writer meant anything more than to be insolent in security, —but as I have turned the matter over in my thought, it strikes me, from a recollection of the offensive language, that he has really contemplated battle *à outrance,* and I conclude, at all events, that he must be tried. Now, as I am very little experienced in such matters, I am anxious that you should examine the article, and say what step I should take—say, in brief, whether the matter is sufficiently equivocal to admit of any preliminary inquiry, or whether it does not call for a direct challenge. — The Editor of the Book in question is a Mr. George Atkinson Ward, whom I have no reason to suppose other than a Gentleman. That he has had no right to speak as he has done (unless his purpose be a quarrel) is unquestionable. I do not think, in anything I wrote, that I gave occasion for any personalities. My reviews were stringent, certainly, but altogether within the limits of historical & literary criticism. But nothing need be said on this point. We cannot prescribe the bounds for our neighbour and must only accommodate him when nothing better can be done.—The difficulty before me is the distance which lies between us—the fact that my friends in New York, are not persons practiced in such matters, and might be very reluctant, with the dread of the State Prison in their eyes, and hard labor for seven years or for life, to risk themselves in the business. There are two persons whom I think I may call upon in the initial proceedings—one I trust, certainly, and to him I propose to confide such a communication as you may counsel me to send. I am very sure that I could procure his conveyance of a note of inquiry, but my doubt is whether the provocation be such as would not make such a missive ridiculous and idle. Another little difficulty occurs to me, which might

---

independence," and continues with accusing Simms of a "perversity or confusion of ideas," of possessing a "hodge-podge . . . intellect." Toward the close of the article, Ward remarks that he regrets "that we quoted him [Simms] as an historian at all" and quotes passages from *Views and Reviews,* First Series, to demonstrate that Simms' ideas of history are wholly those of a writer of romance. Ward followed with a similar attack in *S. L. M.,* XIII (July, 1847), 422-428.

make it desirable, when the final issues are made up, that the
affair should not take place until May—if it be in the power of
a challenging party, pleading particular necessities, to prescribe
the time at all. My domestic relations will render it very inconvenient to go North until that period, and I am under obligations
to the publishers (Harper & Brothers) for a work which I must
carry with me when I go — upon which they have already made
me a considerable advance.[26] It would, perhaps, be equally disagreeable for you to leave home before the opening of summer,—
and I frankly declare the hope, that, if we are to fight, you will
attend me on the occasion. Now, then, you have the whole matter.
I need not refer you to the especial provocations in this article.
Indeed, I cannot, except from memory, until I get the number of
the work in question, for which I have written. I propose, when
I recieve it, to answer the article quietly in the Messenger, and
in such a manner as to prevent suspicion. But your counsel on
the whole matter will be useful & I beg you will not withhold it.
Let me hear from you as soon as possible.[27] — Did I think to say

---

[26] The Life of the Chevalier Bayard. See note 315, Oct. 19, 1845.

[27] Before seeing the article, Hammond wrote to Simms on Jan. 28: "I
cannot but think that your sensitiveness has got the better of you. You have
taken fire when it was only intended to make you 'take water.'

"You were very severe on the 'Cunningham Family' & it strikes me that
this answer does not probably come from the North, but from much nearer
home. The Cunninghams here are extremely sensitive and always on the qui
vive for insults on their ancestry. . . Are men to write history or canvass
historical characters with pistols at their breasts? Is an example to be set
requiring such writers to answer with their lives to the insolent descendants
of daring villians, when they venture to paint them in their true colors in
history or historic criticism? . . . Stick to your historic position—answer facts
& arguments—pass personalities by, as foreign to the controversy—as allowable
to the 'galled jade'—but unworthy of you & your purposes."

Later, on Feb. 1, Hammond again wrote: "I found & read the obnoxious
article in the Messenger. I give up my conjecture. It was written by a Yankee.
But my dear fellow you certainly had gunpowder put in your liquor at
Aldrich's. After scrupulously weighing every impression in the piece, I am
decidedly of opinion that you would not only have no justification for calling
the author out, but that you have not even the right to demand an explanation.
You must have rested on the words 'lie direct' & the aforesaid gunpowder
(or liquor) prevented you from discovering—which it requires some exercise of
mind to do—that the writer only aimed to say that the June article did in one
particular give the 'lie direct' to the May article—& all in fun—tho' not very
successful in it. He speaks of your 'fictitious imputations'—but that is nothing,
& his disparagement of you as an historian, tho' pretty sharp cannot be made
a ground of quarrel—or rather of fight. Both the attempts to shew your
inconsistency are failures I think & so will all think whose opinions you would
value—tho' certain malignants may regard them as hits. And among them I
will reckon the Editor of the Messenger whom I advise you to cut. His comment.
on your Rudolph article is captious, ill-natured & more offensive in my opinion

to you that in *yours 'M.S.'* you spell *"draught"* — drink, beverage &c, as if it were an order for cash upon your banker — *"draft".*[28] Would you believe it, I have been purring over this trifling matter daily since I left you. We had a horrible cold drive of it, both days, between Silver Bluff & Woodlands,[29] and I have been chilly & uncomfortable ever since, with a violent headache which lasted me a whole day in spite of my panacea.

Present me to Mrs. H. & hold me faithfully yours &c.

W. G. S.

355: To James Lawson

Woodlands. Jany 26. [1847][30]

dear Lawson

I am truly sorry to hear of your accidents. You walk quite too fast for a man with one limb so feeble & uncertain. You are also, as I have repeatedly told you, a very incautious person. You would suffer terribly were you to fracture the bone — more so than most other persons. From such an evil, the fates guard you! — My wife is certainly better. She thinks so herself and we think so; but she is a mere skeleton, and recovers her strength very slowly, — but beware of writing of her condition when you write to me, for she *will* read your letters as your wife probably will read mine; and one that you sent me, some time ago, in answer to one of mine in which I expressed my fears & anxieties, it disquieted me very much to find in her hands. She wrote Lady Lyde yesterday. That *I* have not written her arises from several causes, one of which was that I have not often been in the mood. I have been sick & suffering, — have been besides involved in the affairs of other persons, been dealing with poli-

---

than any thing from Curwen's Editor." (Originals in the Hammond Papers, Library of Congress.)

Advised by Hammond, Simms satisfied himself with only a brief reply, signed "Philo," published in *S. L. M.,* XIII (April, 1847), 250-251. See letter to Hammond of March 2, 1847.

[28] We are unable to identify this manuscript, which Simms evidently read during his visit to Silver Bluff.

[29] Silver Bluff, Hammond's estate on the Savannah River, was about fifty miles from Woodlands.

[30] Dated by Simms' references to his visit to Hammond and to his transactions with the publishers George F. Cooledge and Brother and J. and H. G. Langley. See letters to Hammond of Jan. 7 and Jan. 25, 1847, and letter to Lawson of Jan. 2, 1847.

ticians, and otherwise drawing water in a sieve. I have just reached home, after an absence of a week, on a visit to General Hammond & other friends, our chief object being affairs of State &c. *But this to you only!* When I write to her, I wish to be free from cares and disquietings, so that I may only dilate in the language of affection. You must not suffer her to be angry with, or to complain of me. That I should think of going elswhere than to Twelfth St. arose only from the fear that I should too much tax a friendship which I had always found quite too precious to lose. As I grow older, I find myself growing more & more jealous of the affections of those I love. I have had so few friends all my life, that I feel the necessity more & more daily, as life grows shorter, of doing nothing which shall lessen their sympathies or render them cold to my regards. If she says anything saucily to you, at any time, in relation to me, I beg that you will stop her mouth with kisses one of which you will place to my account. The note of Cooledge & Bro. seems to speak as if an agreement had been made about the publication on account. But it might be well to prevent this, and compel their purchase. Still, I leave all to you. Do you hear any thing of Langley, & what of Marion. He writes me nothing. I forwarded to Labree, a few days ago, the *fourth* part of a story, for each part of which I require $20. There are two other parts which I shall send to you. The six parts will be $120 — the drafts in your favor are $50. When I send you these parts, I will send you two other drafts for the balance.[31] Colton says he will publish my article in April, and will then pay.[32] I should be glad to see Forrest, but it will not be possible for me to do so. The mountain cannot go to Mahomet this

---

[31] In reply to an unlocated letter from Simms, Lawrence Labree had written on Dec. 31, 1846: "Excuse my silence and inattention. Your letter of 21st inst. came to hand two days ago, and your directions to Mr. Taylor I saw put in train, and your name for the Magazine put on the books—I thought it had been placed there before. It will henceforth be mailed regularly.

" 'The Maroon' was commenced in the Jan. No. as you will see—I like it much. Please send on soon the concluding part—the *fourth*.

"I hope you will like our Magazine—but we must keep on improving. 'Rome was not' &c—what a musty proverb. A great improvement remains yet to be made in our plates. I hope to have ere long the best Magazine in the country. . . . " (Original in the New York Public Library.)

[32] The only identifiable article by Simms in the *American* [*Whig*] *Review* for 1847 is a biographical sketch of John Rutledge (see note 120, April 19, 1847). Since it was unwritten at this time (see letter to Lawson of April 19, 1847, and following letters to Lawson), it is certainly not the one planned for publication in April.

time. I will send a notice, however, to one or other of the papers.[33] When you will see me is a question which I cannot just now answer. It is possible not before May. — What has become of Mathews & Duyckinck. I have written them but hear nothing. I do not even see Yankee Doodle now. By the way, do you know any thing of a Mr. George Atkinson Ward, a Gentleman, I believe, of your city. Is he a Gentleman or not, & what is he? Pray make the inquiry for me at an early day, and let me hear. I have a special reason for the inquiry which I will make known to you hereafter. Do not suffer it to be suspected that the inquiry comes from me. Perhaps Wetmore can tell you all about him. — It rejoices me to hear that you are all well & keep so. We have had a mild form of Whooping Cough on the plantation, both Gilmore & Mary Lawson being sufferers; but they are both nearly free of it, and both quite flourishing. Say to Lady Lyde that I will try soon & put myself in the proper mood for writing her. When my fancy warms to the temperature of my heart she shall hear from me.

Yours truly

W. G. S.

356: To EVERT AUGUSTUS DUYCKINCK

Woodlands, Feb 2. [1847] [34]

My dear Sir

I look with some anxiety for the issue of your initial publication. I am not sure that you have got the most taking title, but I believe that you can make a good paper under any title. That you will make a sound one, I trust and confidently believe. As for my

---

[33] Forrest's engagement in Charleston lasted from Jan. 25 through Feb. 6 (see Hoole, *The Ante-Bellum Charleston Theatre,* p. 125). For Simms' notice of Forrest, see letter to Lawson of Feb. 15, 1847.

[34] Dated by the appearance of the first issue of the *Literary World* on Feb. 6, 1847. A weekly published by Osgood and Co., the *Literary World* remained under the editorship of Duyckinck until the issue of May 1, 1847, when the publishers announced (I, 293) that his "connexion with this Journal ceased with the last number." The issue of May 8 reports (I, 315) that Charles Fenno Hoffman "commences his duties [as editor] with the present number." Hoffman continued as editor until the issue of Oct. 7, 1848, when the periodical, which had been purchased by Duyckinck and his brother George, was taken over by them as joint publishers and editors. The last number of the *Literary World* is dated Dec. 31, 1853.

contributions, I cannot at this moment promise you much.[35] What with the sickness & suffering in my family, which unhappily still continue, and some larger connexion with domestic politics and politicians than usual, I have somehow so dawdled away the time, that I find myself greatly in arrear to the publishers. My life of Bayard which should have been in the hands of H & B. before Christmas is only half done and cannot be ready for a month or two, and I have one or two elaborate periodical essays to cogitate which must be done in the same space of time.[36] Besides, I must see somewhat the style, manner & design of your journal before I begin. I must note equally your lines & limits. But I nothing doubt that you shall hear from me long before you need me. — I have a letter from Putnam (in Eng.) who reminds me of the Sheets of Smith, which he says have not been recieved & for which he thinks he can do something. Will you see Lawson promptly on this subject if the matter has not already been attended to & send them off by the first steamer. Give Putnam *carte blanche* in the matter so that there may be no delay in giving the London publisher the start of the American. I will thank you to hint to Putnam about asking for an account of sales from the publishers of Count Julian in London.[37] The penny apiece small as it be, is quite as agreeable in my hands as in theirs. Sometime ago I returned to Lawson the a/c of W & P. on account of certain errors which I supposed them to have left uncorrected. I hear nothing from him or them on that subject. Do you know what came of it. And, by the way, while my inquisitive cap is on, what of 'Views & Reviews.' When is it to be published. Let me recommend to you, if any notice is made of it by you, to intimate gently to the simple public, that in the article on the uses of history, I am speaking in the character of the artist especially & not of the historian — that I am not disparaging the history which is known, but [am] suggesting the free use which the imaginative mind may make of that which is unknown, fragmentary & in ruins — the *debris* of history, and not the perfect

---

[35] If Simms contributed prose articles to the *Literary World* in 1847, we are unable to identify them. For his poetic contributions, see note 84, March 25, 1847.

[36] Possibly Simms is here referring to his sketch of John Rutledge. See letter to Lawson of April 19, 1847, and following letters to Lawson.

[37] For George Palmer Putnam, see note 244, June 25, 1845; for the London edition of *Count Julian*, note 51, Feb. 9, 1846. We have been unable to locate a copy of the London edition of *The Life of Captain John Smith*.

fabric. In such a notice, it would be well to extract the several pictures of the Huguenot Massacre, — the progress & death of De Soto, the rescue of Smith by Pocahontas, and the treachery of Arnold. These, I think will tell with the unsuspecting public. Occasional passages from the article on Boone, that on the Conquest of Mexico, that on Mrs. Trollope, and you might quote entire the passage relating to the fate of Bjorn Asbrandson. The gross misinterpretation of the work which has been made by certain parties, may be corrected in this manner better than in any other.[38] As I do not see the Knickerbocker, you will be so good as to say whether it contains any thing in the last few months relating to myself of more than common import. Lawson alluded faintly to some assault upon me & would scarcely have done so had it not been more than usually malignant.[39]—

---

[38] It was not until late July that *Views and Reviews,* Second Series, was finally published. The *Literary World* for July 31 (I, 624) contains Wiley and Putnam's advertisement of the volume in which it is described as *"just ready."* By this time Duyckinck was no longer editor of the *Literary World.* Simms' reference to "the gross misinterpretation" of *Views and Reviews,* First Series, is to George Atkinson Ward's comments in the *Southern Literary Messenger.* See letter to Hammond of Jan. 25, 1847.

[39] The most recent attack on Simms had appeared in Nov., 1846. See note 249, Nov. 19, 1846. In reviewing Griswold's *Prose Writers of America* in April, 1847, however, the *Knick.,* XXIX, 365, remarks of Simms: ". . . Mr. Griswold observes, that in the writings of Mr. Simms, our attention is sometimes engrossed by actions, 'but,' he adds, 'we feel no sympathy for the actors. He gives us too much of ruffianism. The coarseness and villany of many of his characters have no attraction in works of the imagination. If true to nature, which may be doubted, it is not true to nature as we love to contemplate it, and it serves no good purpose in literature. Mr. Simms does not discriminate between what is irredeemably base and revolting, and what by the hand of art may be made subservient to the exhibition of beauty.' This is almost the very language of the Knickerbocker." In Dec., 1847, the same periodical again borrowed an attack on Simms for its pages (XXX, 556) : "The *'Boston Morning Post,'* one of the liveliest and pleasantest journals of the country, thus 'hits the nail on the head' in a notice of Mr. Simms' pen-and-ink *'Views and Reviews of American Literature*[']*:* 'If we understand Mr. Simms and his colleagues,' ('Puffer-Hopkins'-Mathews and the rest.) [']it is necessary that our writers should choose American subjects, in order that their productions, however good, should constitute a real "American literature;" and that they should fill their books with a certain mysterious "American spirit," very difficult to describe and exceedingly hard to imagine. Hence Shakspeare's "Romeo and Juliet" is scarcely English literature, because its subject and its spirit are Italian. At least, this is all we can make of the argument of Mr. Simms and his brethren. It is a pity that some one of these gentlemen should not *produce a work* which would serve to show what this singular "American literature" really is. One look at such a *model* would be more convincing than the perusal of scores of essays.' It was thought for some time that we could have no 'American literature' unless our writers infused a large proportion of Indian character into all their works; so that we came to have aboriginal ingredients in all our indigenous intellectual food; Indian bread, Indian hoe-cake, Indian Johnny-cake, Indian Hasty-pudding, (*very* hasty, much of it,) and Indian baked-pudding, by 'half-baked' authorlings, until the public became utterly surfeited with these 'made-dishes.' "

I hear nothing from Mathews. Pray remind that young Gentleman that I have the care of a large & suffering family upon my
hands & he must not expect that I should equal him in the frequency of my scrawls. Is Yankee Doodle defunct? I see the
'Mirror' still hammers at you & Cornelius, and occasionally
honors me with a bolt, which is always soon shot.[40] What is the
eternal firm of Morris & Willis doing? I do not see their paper.[41]
Is the Democratic stopped? I must really beg that you will report
progress to me more frequently than you have done for some
time past. I get your letters by angel carriers 'whose visits,'[42] as
you know &c. I fancy that the Library scarcely does much at
this moment. It has probably reached its limit. The book of Taylor [43] is chiefly interesting from the way in which the journey is
made. Does it sell? Doubtful! Too much books of travel and
nothing new in any. What of Murdoch & Witchcraft? [44] I am
afraid that Godwin's Goethe will tire the public by the number
of volumes.[45] The two recieved scarcely begin his career. Where
is it to end? Something of every thing in your next. The plans
& books in embryo, how authordom flourishes—what new things,
and good things are forthcoming—and what is become of Poe,
and Lester and all the ineffables. Do you note my papers in the
magazines,[46] — and by the way what of the Langleys—are they
bankrupt or what, — and pray tell me how I am to protect my

40 We have not located these particular remarks.

41 At this time George Pope Morris and Nathaniel P. Willis were publishers
and editors of the *Home Journal,* a weekly published in New York City. The
first issue had appeared on Feb. 14, 1846, under the title of the *National Press:
A Home Journal.* With the issue of Nov. 21, 1846, the name was changed
to the *Home Journal.*

42 Possibly Simms has in mind the line from Thomas Campbell's *The
Pleasures of Hope,* Part II, line 377: "Like angel-visits, few and far between."
This idea, however, is common.

43 Bayard Taylor's *Views A-Foot* (New York: Wiley and Putnam, 1846)
is No. XXIII of the "Library of American Books."

44 In 1846 James E. Murdoch presented Mathews' *Witchcraft* in Philadelphia,
Cincinnati, and St. Louis, where it met with considerable success (see notes
301, Dec. 10, 1846, and 79, March 25, 1847). On May 17, 1847, he presented
the play at the Bowery Theatre, New York City, where it was a failure.

45 Parke Godwin's edition of Goethe's *Autobiography* was issued by Wiley
and Putnam in four parts during 1846-1847 as Nos. LXXV, LXXVI, XCVIII,
and XCIX in their "Library of Choice Reading." The four parts were translated respectively by Godwin, John Henry Hopkins, Jr., Charles A. Dana, and
John S. Dwight.

46 Simms' recent contributions to periodicals include "The Maroon," "Maize
in Milk," "Michael Ney, Otherwise, Michael Rudolph," the review of Ward's
edition of Curwen's *Journal,* and the review of Street's *Poems.*

interest in regard to Marion, the right of which they have (under certain conditions) until 1850. Enough.

Write me soon & believe me truly yours &c

W. G. S.

357 : To John Caldwell Calhoun

Woodlands, Feb 10. 1847

My dear Sir

I can well concieve that, just at this juncture, your time is very much employed, and I beg you therefore to choose your own leisure in according me an answer to the subject of this Letter. During the last session there was submitted in your body a resolution voting a bust or statue to Mr. John Rutledge of South Carolina. I should like to be put in possession of the report upon this matter, & to be informed of the course which the proposition took, and whether anything was done in it.[47] — We are all looking very anxiously to your course on the subject of our Mexican relations. That the South desires the territory we have gained — that the public mind everywhere is fully resolved that we shall keep it — I have little question; but the point with us is to make the conditions preliminary, by which our domestic institutions will be made secure. I think the popular greed will put down the abolitionist faction at the North, if once satisfied that the acquisition of territory cannot be made unless the South is pacified. How far the South, by a temporary coalition with the opponents of Government, can succeed in withholding supplies &c. is a question. But I prattle something too idly, and write thus only to let

---

[47] In his biographical sketch of John Rutledge (see note 120, April 19, 1847) Simms writes (*American [Whig] Review*, VI [Aug., 1847], 125) : "At a late session of Congress, it was, on motion of Mr. [James Diament] Westcott [Jr., of Florida] that the Senate of the United States directed the Committee on the Judiciary to report a Bill for a bust of Mr. John Rutledge, of South Carolina. On the 17th July, 1846, a Bill was accordingly reported for this purpose, from the Committee. It passed to a second reading, but was not again recurred to during the session, and now remains in abeyance, to be called up at some future opportunity." The bill for the erection of a bust of Rutledge was finally passed in 1857, and the bust (by Alexander Galt, of Virginia) was placed on a bracket attached to one of the columns of the Supreme Court Room sometime before 1860 (see *Arts and Artists of the Capitol of the United States of America* [(Washington, D. C.) : Government Printing Office, 1927], pp. 161, 174, 357).

you see the direction which our minds take in my obscure neighbourhood. I am, Sir,

With great respect
Your obt Servt &c

W. Gilmore Simms

Hon. Jno C. Calhoun.

358: To James Lawson

Woodlands. Feb 15 [1847] [48]

My dear Lawson

Enclosed I send you the fifth part of the story which I am furnishing Mr. Labree for his Magazine. There will yet be another part which I will also send you. With these in hand, you can, I suppose, easily succeed in extracting the money for them—at least the greater part of it. The six numbers at $20 each will be $120. I forget just now for what amount I gave you the two preceding drafts, but I think, $25 each. I send you another for a like amount, which you can probably insist upon when you deliver the article. Should the two preceding drafts both be paid, it may be just as well to let him have the fifth part without reserve and wait upon him a while for the draft. But this as you think proper. — I have recieved a long letter from Cooledge & Bro. from which I do not understand that they have bought from you or in any way acquired the right to publish. How is it? I should prefer to sell as I wish a sum of money about $500 this summer, and see no other way of getting it. I do not see that my contract with Langley's can be transferred to them without my consent — do not see in fact what is to prevent me from selling the privilege elsewhere, as well of that work as of Marion. I can get no account from Langley's — have got nothing in the shape of account sales since July 1845 — now nearly 2 years, — and I fear my drafts remain unhonored as well to Bartlett & Welford as to you. Is it possible for you to make an inquiry of B & W. I gave them a dft on J & H. G. Langley for something less than a hundred dollars, which was accepted but not paid at maturity. They wrote

---

[48] Dated by Simms' references to the fifth part of "The Maroon," the serial written for Lawrence Labree's *New York Illustrated Magazine,* and to the transactions with the publishers George F. Cooledge and Brother and J. and H. G. Langley. See letter to Lawson of Jan. 2, 1847, and following letters to Lawson.

me (B & W.) & I told them to get it as they could, but not to subject me to loss if they could help it. In other words to collect the money while the Langleys could yet be made available for a small sum. I hear nothing from them since. — If Cooledge & Co do not promptly buy Smith at $500 — if they delay a month raise your demand to $600. *The book will take — it reads well.* The Harpers ought to give $12 or 1500 for that & Marion. Give me your opinion as to the right of Langley's to transfer my contracts with them to other parties — they having violated all the conditions repeatedly. — I am busy now on Bayard which I may get ready by March. If so, & circumstances allow I may visit N. Y. towards the first April; — and this, with the object of returning to Carolina in midsummer. It is probable that I shall take my family into the backcountry for the improvement of my wife's health.[49] Seriously, I am greatly concerned at her condition. An invalid for months & reduced to a mere skeleton, she was just beginning to improve a little in strength and appetite, but very slowly, when she was seized with an epidemical cold or influenza which has fastened upon her head, and has been distressing her for a week past with intense pains, soreness in her head & bones, and a troublesome cough. My life is past in constant drudgery & unremitted anxieties, & I feel myself growing old with fearful rapidity. I wish you would write a little more frequently than you do, for I look to the continued affections of yourself & wife, as my greatest consolations out of my immediate family precincts. I trust they may always continue so. In writing to me, beware of making any allusion to what I have written you in regard to my wife's health; for she always looks to read your & your wife's letters. — Tell Lady Lyde, not to despair of me, but that I do not wish to write to her till I can feel myself in that happy mood when I can hope to address her ears without paining or dulling them. — I should have liked greatly to have gone to see Forrest, and should have asked him & Mrs. F. to visit us as before, though we have so repeatedly asked in vain; — but the sickness of my wife who has been in her chamber for two weeks, was conclusive against it. I enclose you one of the notices, however, which I wrote of him.[50] Tell your wife that Gilmore

---

[49] Simms took his family to Spartanburg and Glenn's Springs (now Glenn Springs), S. C., in the summer of 1847, leaving Charleston on Aug. 11 and returning about the middle of October.

[50] This notice (from the *Southern Patriot* of Jan. 27) is still preserved with this letter.

& little Mary Lawson are both thriving finely — the latter in particular. She looks like me, — with deep blue eyes, light but thick hair & fine clear complexion. God bless you all.

Yours

W. G. S.

359: To JAMES LAWSON

[c. February 20, 1847] [51]

dear Lawson.

You will note the contents of within.[52] Let Cooledge & Bro give you their notes one payable on first June for five Hundred, the other first August for five hundred more, and the copyrights are theirs. The transfer of copyright to be made on the liquidation of the two notes. Should they not comply at once with the arrange- ment — should a month's delay supervene, raise the amount to $1100. Two months should bring it to $1200. The copyrights are worth thrice the money. As for Langley, it is nonsense to talk of copies on hand. They are for sale & he or his assignees own

---

[51] The year is established by Simms' enclosure (see note 52, below) ; the month and day by an unfinished letter to Lawson dated "Woodlands, Feb. 20," which accompanies this letter. In this unfinished letter Simms writes: "Dear Lawson/Since writing you a couple of days ago I have a Letter from Mess'rs Langley touching the treaty with Cooledge & Co. They state that [end of letter]."

[52] Simms enclosed a letter dated "New York Feby 8, 1847," and signed "J. & H. G. Langley": "Mess. Cooledge have requested us to write you on the subject of their proposition for the purchase of Marion & Smith.

"Mr Lawson names $1000. cash and the Mess. C offer the same amount at 6 months. Now as the difference is only the interest $35. (for the risk is nothing as the Copyrights can be retained as Collateral) we have thought it for the interest of all to advance our opinion. They are anxious to close the matter up; as it is in an unsettled state, and also, because the spring season is advancing & the books would be somewhat effected if matters remained unsettled. Please write on the subject.

"A word as to the above gentlemen—they are considered as one of the safest—and most enterprising firms in the trade. You can ascertain from Mc-Carter & Allen of Charleston.

"We shall certainly make out your statement in the course of the week. We regret the situation of matters connected with ourselves but will explain in our next. To give you an idea of the a/c—now—it stands a balance due us, if Six hundred are allowed that are *now on hand* and the draft of Bartlett & Welford is paid by us, you will owe us about $20.00. So you see we are not much in your debt after all.

"The delay in sending the a/c here originated from the absence of our binder (out of this City) from whom we designed obtaining a statement of the number bound, to accompany our a/c, so that the impression you had when in New York may be removed." (Original in the South Caroliniana Library, University of South Carolina.)

them. Whether he sells or not it is the same thing. He pays me for the copies that he holds. He pays me for every edition printed — for which he should give me credit when printed. But for my necessities I should not sell these copyrights at all. — My wife is a little better in the last two days. Love to yours & a kiss all round

Yours truly

W. G. S.

360: To Evert Augustus Duyckinck

Woodlands, Feb. 25. [1847][53]

My dear Sir

I was in the city a few days ago, where I learned that Mr. John Russell, whom I took the liberty to designate as your agent, has already procured you some ten or a dozen subscribers, though as yet he has recd. but a single copy of your work. Mr. R. is a worthy and intelligent person upon whom you can rely. Send him your issues promply. I have penned one or two brief notices of the 'World' in our newspaper. Might I suggest, you would make it a little less didactic—infuse a larger dash of playfulness and passion—and be a little less bookish. What you do is well done, but variety must not be forgotten. — The South. Quarterly Review has just fallen into tolerably good hands, — nay, as the times go, into very good hands. Its present editor is Mr. J. M. Clapp, late Editor of the Charleston Mercury.[54] He is a gentle-

---

[53] Dated by Simms' reference to his notices of the *Literary World*. Though the first issue of the periodical had appeared on Feb. 6, a copy had not reached Simms when, on Feb. 8, the *Southern Patriot* carried a short notice, in which he says: "From a personal knowledge of the editor, and of the contributors which he has called to his assistance we have no hesitation in declaring the conviction that the Literary World will furnish one of the ablest and most honest publications of its class, yet put forth in America." A note in the *Southern Patriot* of Feb. 9 announces that the first issue of the *Literary World* has arrived in Charleston.

[54] The Charleston *Mercury* of Feb. 1 contains a notice signed by Clapp: "The Mercury passes this day into the hands of Mr. J. E. Carew, who will henceforth be its recognized proprietor and editor." Clapp succeeded Daniel K. Whitaker as editor of the *Southern Quarterly Review,* his first number being that for April, 1847. On Feb. 17, 1846, Clapp had written to Simms: "For the promise of your good will and your assistance, I heartily thank you, and hope it will not be long before you will put something on the stocks. I am very well convinced of the importance of a more intimate knowledge than I have of the country into which I have ventured and that you could give me many valuable hints—but at present I am fettered here." (Original in the New York Public Library.)

[man] of talents and classical attainments, whose style is very easy, graceful, and sometimes playful, who is acute and frequently admirably satirical & witty. If he will work much himself, he will make the work a good one. I shall probably write frequently for it myself, if I continue to write at all, but I don't know but that I shall after the present year retire from the literary arena, upon potatoes & politics.[55] I send every now & then to you & W & P. a batch of newspapers in which something is said about you or them. Recently I sent to you & to Mr. Jones a notice of him, with which, I trust, he is not dissatisfied.[56] I could wish

---

[55] The earliest identifiable article by Simms published during Clapp's editorship is a review of Fannie Kemble Butler's *A Year of Consolation* (New York: Wiley & Putnam, 1847), XII (July, 1847), 191-236. The same issue contains (pp. 271-272) a highly complimentary review of Simms' *Life of Captain John Smith*, praising both the biography and the character of Simms: "We take up a new book from the pen of Mr. Simms, not only with the confidence, warranted by the character of his past performances, that there is good in it, but with a grateful feeling towards the author for the manly perseverance that has so strongly marked his literary career. He has met many difficulties,—far more than usually beset the path of the author, and he has surmounted them all, with a patience of labor and a firmness of will, that are of themselves as certainly the evidences of superiority as they are the means of success. It should be added too, that his reputation is the simple result of what he has done. It is no gift of a literary cotery, whose members combine on the principle of mutual insurance, and make reputations for themselves by echoing and re-echoing each others praises from so many invisible coverts along the world's highways, that the unsuspicious public is made to believe it hears the noise of a mighty fame. There is a high-toned pride of character in Mr. Simms, that has kept him far above such artifices. He would not accept reputation thus stolen,—the goods of success thus swindled from the public. Hence he has not only had no aid of a cotery to manufacture fame and ability for him, but being not of them, he has been treated as an enemy,—a free trader, and of course a foe to the true art and mystery of regularly initiated book-making and author-making. He may well be proud of his success amid such difficulties, and we too are proud not only of what he has done, but of the unsullied manhood which he has guarded as a possession better than fame, through his whole career. . . .

"We might point out some blemishes in the author's execution of his work [*The Life of Captain John Smith*], but they are trifling at any rate, and we have followed the current of his narrative with so much pleasure and sympathy, and felt at the conclusion of it that he had so well effected his object of bringing fully into light all the impressive and noble lineaments of his hero, that we have no disposition to speck our praise with petty censures. His Life of Captain Smith will address itself to every generous heart, and if it does not increase the reputation of the author, it will prove that he knows well how to preserve what he has so worthily won."

[56] William A. Jones' two-volume collection of essays, *Literary Studies*, published by E. Walker in 1847, is reviewed in the *Southern Patriot* of Feb. 16. Simms writes: "It is a rare thing to find a volume of full fledged essays issuing from the American press. . . . We have the pleasure to know Mr. Jones personally, and his mind is one which . . . has borne, and is capable of bearing, excellent fruits. . . . " The *Literary World*, I (April 3, 1847), 206, comments on the "liberal sympathy" of the *Southern Patriot* and quotes at length from Simms' review.

that you would have supplied to me certain breaks in my series, vols, which have never come to hand. For example, I have never recd. Mrs. Jameson's Memoirs & Essays, nor the *first* part of Carlyle's Revolution nor the second part of Typee, nor Head's Book, nor Mrs. Kirkland's Spencer, nor the *second* and after parts of Dombey — only the first.[57] — If you can put me up these odds & ends you will oblige me as nothing offends my organ of order so consumedly as broken setts in my Liby. — I have nearly finished my Life of the Chevalier Bayard which goes to Harper & Brothers. — I think to get ready to bring on with me my Huguenots in Florida, and may visit N. Y. in April next. When are we to have V & R? How would you like a volume of sketches of the South, — its scenery & traditions entitled "Slopes & Summits of the South?"[58] I have the materials for such a vol. But, on this head, mum. If I prepare it, it shall be anonymous. Do you note my "Maize in Milk" in Godey's. — It is simply descriptive. —How do you succeed? And Jones — does his book sell. What is there new in the prospect, — what new on the anvil. Are there any new lights, burning and about to shine, and what fate attends the old ones. How fares our venerable Behemoth, Cornelius the Centurion,[59] who I verily believe has cut me utterly for some offence, real or fancied. Or is he busy heaving with unutterable things. Well, — I must wait on him. — I suppose Lawson has let you know the condition of my wife. It has been such for the last two months as daily to make me anxious, and she is still a sufferer, though, showing signs of improvement. It is probable that her case will not enable me to remain at the North this summer. My notion is to go early, say in April & return about the 1st. June or thereabouts so as to take her & our children during the summer to the mountains. We should prefer the North, but as we have a colored nurse, your vexatious abolitionists forbid that we should cross the Potomac. Present me to Mrs. D. with

---

[57] These books, all published by Wiley and Putnam, are as follows: Anna Brownell Jameson, *Memoirs and Essays Illustrative of Art, Literature and Social Morals* (1846) ; Thomas Carlyle, *History of the French Revolution* (1846), 3 Parts: Herman Melville, *Typee* (1846), 2nd ed; Sir Francis Bond Head, *Bubbles from the Brunnen of Nassau* (1845) ; Mrs. Caroline M. Kirkland, *Spencer and the Faery Queen* (1847) ; Charles Dickens, *Dombey and Son* (1847).

[58] This idea is doubtless the germ of *Southward Ho! A Spell of Sunshine* (New York: Redfield, 1854).

[59] Cornelius Mathews.

respectful remembrance, and say to your brother in Europe that I do not forget to ask how he fares & whither he wends.[60]

Success & health from Yours &c

W. Gilmore Simms

361: To JAMES LAWSON

Woodlands. March 2. [1847][61]

dear Lawson

I take for granted, and trust, that the within paper will suffice to satisfy the Mess'rs Cooledge, who might convince themselves by a single question addressed to Harper & Brothers, or almost any body who knows me in New York, that what I agree upon I will certainly adhere to. I am in possession of no means where I am of executing a more formal instrument, and shall scarcely visit the city again until I take it *en route* for the North. This I expect to do late in April or early in May, when I will bring with me the Certificates of Copyright, and endorse them properly. If these Gentlemen hold off on the plea that the authority is informal, then you will give them to understand that our treaty is at an end. I am quite indifferent to selling these works at the price mentioned as I am very sure much more might be got for them with a little delay. The terms that they name are such as I agreed upon with them—always provided that you were satisfied of their soundness. In a day or two I will send you the sixth part of my story for Labree which it may be well to keep *until called for*. He may be rich, but—we are poor and terribly in want of our sixpences. The notes are to be made payable, for five hundred each, on the 1st. June & 1st August, of this year. I shall probably need the money in July. I hope to see you in May, but our present plan is to take my wife into our mountain country in August. She & the family can't visit the North on account of the slave by whom the child is nursed — so much for your Abolitionists & the friendly relations of a Sister State. But if I

---

[60] George Long Duyckinck.

[61] Dated by Simms' references to his transactions with the publishing firm of George F. Cooledge and Brother and to the completion of the sixth part of "The Maroon" (see letter to Lawson of Dec. 12, 1846, and following letters to Lawson). The enclosure, missing from the letter, was probably a contract with Cooledge for the publication of *The Life of Francis Marion* and *The Life of Captain John Smith* (see in this connection Langley's letter to Simms quoted in note 52, *c*. Feb. 20, 1847).

can get on in May, I will linger with you through that month
& a part of June. My wife is improving, though I have been
to the city within ten days to get counsel from our physician. —
Little Mary Lawson is thriving famously, and Gilmore is, I take
it, quite as big as Dandy Jim [62] of Twelfth Street. — We have
Mr. T. Addison Richards now with us. He came a few days
ago & is on his way North. If I were through my 'Life of Bayard', I should go on with him. Mr. R. is an amiable young man,
who paints a good landscape, and who is modest and intelligent.
I could wish you to know him better. He will probably visit
you in N. Y. & I would like to persuade my fair cousin, Lady
Lyde, to smile upon him as well as Cornelius and sometimes ask
him to sip his tea with her. I send her my own & the loves of
our family, in which you must share. A smack for the children.

God bless you &c.

W. G. S.

J. L.

Examine the within paper and deliver it or not.

362 : To James Henry Hammond

Woodlands. March 2. [1847] [63]
My dear Hammond.

All your letters have been recieved & in due season; but since
I wrote you I have been greatly troubled & greatly anxious about

---

[62] "Dandy Jim, from Carolina: A Popular Negro Melody as Sung by B.
Williams" appeared as a stage song of the Negro minstrel type in 1843.
According to an introductory note by S. Foster Damon to this song (No. 34)
in *Series of Old American Songs. Reproduced in Facsimile from Original or
Early Editions in the Harris Collection of American Poetry and Plays, Brown
University* (Providence, R. I.: Brown University Library, 1936), "Barney
Williams" was the stage name of an Irish singer, Bernard O'Flaherty (1824-
1876). The song was written by J. Richard ("Dan" or "Ole Bull") Myers
(1808-1874) and Silas S. Steele for John Hidges (1821-1891), known as "Cool
White," the organizer of the "Virginia Serenaders" in 1843.
The "Dandy Jim" of this letter is James Lawson, Jr.
[63] Dated by Simms' discussion of Ward's attack on him in the *Southern
Literary Messenger* (see letter to Hammond of Jan. 25, 1847). Having received
no reply from Simms to his letters of Jan. 28 and Feb. 1 (see note 27, Jan.
25, 1847), Hammond again wrote to Simms on Feb. 23, stating that he
feared his letters had gone astray. He continues: "If it were not that in
spite of all your 'bonhomme', you are a veritable son of the 'genus irritable
vatum' I should be at some loss to account for your rage. The Curwen Editor
. . . utterly failed to exhibit any inconsistencies in your views & statements,
& his effort to be-little you is supremely ridiculous. . . . But my dear fellow
—cut the whole set of magazines & all the curs that follow them. Make a

the condition of my wife, who never having quite recovered from
her confinement five months ago, was seized not long since, at
a perilous moment in her progress, by an epidemical influenza,
which not only threw her back, but threatened to fasten upon
her lungs, and kept her in a state of continual & extreme suffering
—so as to compel me to visit the city a second time this winter,
to consult the physician. It is only within a few days that she
has shown decided symptoms of improvement. The reciept of
your first two letters decided me, at all events, to wait and see
what would be said by Mr. Ward in his second paper which he
promises. It will be easy perhaps, to gather from that what he
designed by the first. I am not so sure that you are right in your
conclusion and did not percieve the new reading which you give
to the equivocal passage. As for seeking a fight unnecessarily,
I am as far from it as any man. I rather prefer to risk nothing
of a life which my self-esteem prompts me to fancy was designed
for something better, and of which a great deal yet remains to
be developed; but my natural reluctance to avoid such issues as
the one in question, as naturally compels me to distrust my own
judgment when the question is, *should* I seek them; and the
same reason makes me now hesitate somewhat to decide as you
counsel. I assure you my real desire is to escape if I can from
any such necessity, and this is the true object of my inquiry. As
for the substance of the man's article, the tone of which he has
contrived to make equally brutal & impertinent, there is, as you
rightly percieve nothing in it. The dolt seems to be incapable of
seeing what is apparent to all beside, or is so much the more
a fool as to castrate even sentences in order that a fragment may
be found to fortify his assertions. Had he gone to the second
sentence any where in his quotations, he would have seen that
there was neither contradiction nor inconsistency in anything I
said. — His sneers at my writings are merely silly. They have
not disquieted me in the least & the offensive matter did not
enrage me—it simply forced upon me the question, — which I
put to you—and that question was based upon the supposed conventional necessity for asking it. Since writing you, a friend in
New York advises me that Mr. Ward is supposed to be beyond
the period in life when such demands are proper to be made, —

---

swoop far far above them & strike for immortality. . . . " (Original in the
Hammond Papers, Library of Congress.)
    Simms' letter is defective, and the material in brackets has been supplied by
the editors.

being on the road from 50 to 60.[64] It might be, therefore, that
a call would only make the caller ridiculous. But, we have resolved to wait. You're right with regard to Mr. Minor from whom
I shall certainly shake myself wholly free before long.[65] His note
was really caused by an unexpected draft of mine which took
from him certain monies which he was calculating to use in another fashion. That he has to *pay me* is very vexatious to him.
That an Editor should be such a fool as to sneer at the correspondents whose articles he publishes, is surely the perfection
of folly. Now, the truth is the article in question is quite a good
magazine paper, full of animation, somewhat novel & a case,
though I say it myself, rather ingeniously argued. Such are the
very kinds of articles for a periodical. But this booby of a fellow
knows nothing. He has written to me somewhat apologetically,
but I have only answered him by sending him two brief papers,
one in relation to the offense given him by the imputation of
"being premature," and one containing a few extracts from my

---

[64] Simms' "friend in New York" is undoubtedly Lawson, to whom he had
written on Jan. 26 for information concerning Ward.

[65] In *S. L. M.*, XIII (Jan., 1847), 17-23, Simms published "Michael Ney,
Otherwise, Michael Rudolph," an unsigned article presenting the evidence for
the legend that Marshal Ney was in reality Michael Rudolph, a native of
Maryland and officer in the American Revolution. In his letter to Simms of
Feb. 1 Hammond called Simms' attention to an impertinent editorial note
printed at the close of the article (see note 27, Jan. 25, 1847). Having referred
to Simms' comments that the *Messenger* had made a "somewhat premature
remark" concerning the tradition of Ney and Rudolph (in a review of Joel
Tyler Headley's *Napoleon and His Marshals* in *S. L. M.*, XII [July, 1846],
455-456, and in a brief letter to the editor published in *S. L. M.*, XII [Nov.,
1846], 700) and that he regrets that his "own more deliberate research should
have been forestalled by a premature publication," Minor continues: "We
respectfully suggest that we do not see the appropriateness of these observa-
tions; nor how our publication was the least premature, except to the immature
purposes of the above writer, whose 'more deliberate research' was unknown
to us, and might have been still prosecuted in silence, despite of St. Leger, our
'correspondent,' and ourselves. He shows that the interesting tradition referred
to has been long known, and yet regrets that it was not reserved for him to
startle the Public with its annunciation. . . . " Simms' reply to Minor's note,
a paper signed "Satilla" and entitled "Ney and Rudolph," was published in *S.
L. M.*, XIII (April, 1847), 214-215. In it he apologizes for giving "some offence"
to the editor, protests his innocence of any design to offend, but still insists
that "if the original note in the Messenger, which prompted the article on Ney
and Rudolph, was not premature, it was *im*mature,—and this last, perhaps,
had been the more proper word." Simms continues: "It was not my purpose
to contend for the tradition which I furnished. . . . My object was simply to
give the narrative fair play—to let your readers see it. . . . I did not myself
argue in its behalf, except as a lawyer. . . . My faith in its truth is exceedingly
moderate. . . . " At the conclusion of the paper Simms gives a brief account
of a more recent legend that Ney escaped and came to America. Of this he
comments: " . . . of such stuff as this, even thus crude and improbable, do the
the [*sic*] poet and the romancer weave some of their most enduring fictions."

Views & Reviews which Mr. Ward has so dishonestly garbled.[66] —Your thoughts on the subject of Calhoun & Butler, are just such as suggest themselves to me.[67] Writing to the former a few weeks ago to inquire as to the fate of a certain resolution of the Senate last session decreeing a bust to Mr. Jno. Rutledge, I took occasion to say to him that we should only vote men & monies now to the war upon certain preliminaries being complied with — namely, the substitution of such a resolution for Wilmot's as would guarantee the rights of the South, and which, forced upon the administration by a "balance of power party" could be made the only condition for securing the appropriations. Of course what I said was general, merely to show that it would not suffice that the resolution of Wilmot should be dropped, for the Wilmots committed a great blunder to start it so soon; but that some guarantees should be exacted which should, however imperfectly, secure to us our share of the spoils & the permanence of our position.[68] There is no doubt that he was moved wholly by a conviction that the Presidency was not to be reached through the Polkites — and he still holds to the idea, I doubt not, that a large portion of the Whigs, despairing of their own candidate will rally upon him, and thus assist in the formation of a third or Independent party — a thing which is wild & impossible, but

---

[66] For the paper replying to Minor, see note 65, above. Simms' reply to Ward, signed "Philo" and entitled "Views and Reviews in American History, Literature and Fiction," was published in *S. L. M.*, XIII (April, 1847), 250-251. At the beginning of the article Simms states: "Our purpose is by no means to give you a review of this volume, but simply to request the attention of your readers to an allusion which is made to it, by an anonymous writer in your January number, by which its contents are misrepresented in some measure, and from which its character may be misunderstood." The remainder of the article consists of a discussion of these misrepresentations and an explanation and defence of Simms' ideas.

[67] In his letter to Simms of Feb. 23, Hammond had written of Calhoun and Butler: "And so Calhoun has split off from the administration also. Do you remember my predictions two years ago when this same man set his hooks at me for *doubting* Polk, that they would all have to wheel to the right about in six months & we should be called on to denounce Polk through all our Borders. . . . The truth is Mr. C. will follow any set of men no longer than he thinks they are following & aiming to promote him. He will quit any Party who has another man in view for the Presidency . . . he is evidently full of malice toward Polk—& no man can be more malignant than he can. His onslaught on poor [Thomas] Ritchie [see note 91, March 29, 1847] indicates an unhinged temper. It was silly as well as malicious. . . . It does not become you & I—the rejected—to speak above a whisper. Let us be still over what So. Ca & her leaders will do. We have no responsibility. Our views it might be said were raised from disappointment. . . . But if I mistake not Calhoun has cut his throat this time & has made poor Butler cut his in spite of all his affected independence." (Original in the Hammond Papers, Library of Congress.)

[68] See letter to Calhoun of Feb. 10, 1847.

still entertained by these who are otherwise hopeless. An approaching election will always dissipate third parties in this country. Butler has made a sufficient judge of himself in reporting his speeches. That he should become a mere follower of Mr. Calhoun only shows that [he] would defer to the power which the latter wields at home, — and he gains nothing among his own friends by the exercise of a policy which is at the expense of his independence. While in town, I went to Walker, and had a talk with him. Were he a stronger man *in will,* he might do something there. Charleston can be easily revolutionized by a man of courage & popular talents. It struck me that a public meeting might be held at the C. H. at which you might come forward and introduce certain resolutions in relation to our federal affairs, by which your friends would see that you are ready to answer to their call; but subsequent reflection convinces me that the policy is as you suggest, to lie low & keep dark and wait events. Our movement now would only retard the fate of others & incur some of its danger for ourselves. I am sure that you will be called for, and are needed greatly now. I was told by one in Charleston the other day, [who] was not greatly your friend, that one of the members who voted for Butler had declared to him frankly that could he have forseen the progress of events at Washington, he would sooner have voted for you than for any other person. This conviction is growing, and I hear from several quarters that no further attempt will be made to connect the private affair with your public career.[69] Still, it may be well to prepare, and [hold in] readiness the narrative elaborated with [*one or two words missing*] which I have counselled. In reading the le[tter] or Dessaussure[70] (which I [recieved)] I note the vague manner in which he speaks of the result of the elections last session, as if he desired to convey the impression that he voted for you & supported you with his friends. But from what I learned, and what I believe, he did no such thing, & the treachery of his friends, with Davie at their head, probably carried the day against you. His class is going out in snuff. A few days—yet awhile — and manhood becomes necessary to the whole people. If you go to Charleston, which I am disposed to think will be

---

[69] Hammond had opposed A. P. Butler in the election of 1846, but had been defeated largely because of an indiscretion he had committed. See letter to Hammond of Nov. 27, 1846, and following letters to Hammond.

[70] William F. DeSaussure, member from Richland District of the South Carolina House of Representatives.

advisable in summer, I have no doubt that something might be done toward showing Young Charleston how they may recover their independence. — Who is it that calls upon Barnwell Rhett, from Barnwell C. H. to rescue & became the saviour of the State [71]

Yours faithfully

Simms.

363 : To James Lawson

[March 4, 1847]

dear Lawson

I enclose & send you by the hands of Mr. Richards, the Sixth and Last part of "the Maroon" for Mr. Labree's Magazine. Below you have a statement of the account & an order for the balance. You can say to Mr. Labree that I will send him something farther very shortly or bring it myself in Season for his July issue.[72] Love to all

Yours Ever &c

Lawrence Labree Esq.   W. G. S.

To W. Gilmore Simms

To 6 nos. of the Maroon @ $20 each $120.00
    By Drft to Mr. J. Lawson . . . .$ 25.
       ,,   ,,   ,,   ,, ...   25.
       ,,   ,,   ,,   ,, ...   25.   75.00

                             Bal. Due $45.00

Lawrence Labree Esq. Ed Illd. Mage.

Dear Sir—Please pay above balance of forty Five dollars to Mr. James Lawson & oblige Yr. obt. Serv.

March 4. 1847.   W. Gilmore Simms

---

[71] In the Charleston *Mercury* of March 1 is a letter addressed to Robert Barnwell Rhett, dated from Barnwell Court House, Feb. 13, 1847, and signed "Lang Syne": "It has been our custom in times past to look to you for the signal of danger. . . . You should at once retire from the present arena of labors, and if the 'temple of our liberties' is destined to fall you should be present and perish with your fellow citizens 'amid its ruins'. . . . If the doctrines of State Rights and secession, formerly advocated by the party here, was ever correct, *now is the time* to give an example to us, and mankind abroad, of their propriety and force." The author of this letter is Joseph Allen (see letter to Hammond of April 2, 1847).

[72] The *New York Illustrated Magazine* ceased publication with the issue for June, 1847.

364: To Benjamin Franklin Perry

Woodlands. March 10. [1847][73]

My dear Colonel.

I am anxious to find some healthy summering spot in your mountain country to which I can take my family during the months of August, September and a portion of October. My wife is an invalid, and we are of opinion that, during that period, the clear dry mountain air, either in our own State or in Georgia, will be of great service in restoring her health. Our family will consist of myself, my wife, my daughter and two young children, one an infant with a nurse (a negro slave). We will accordingly require three apartments. Our object would be to compass health, economy & a convenient, comfortable, neat place of abode, with some private family, either in or near a village, or in a country residence contiguous to a settlement and not far from the great route of travel. Cleanliness, without regard to variety or delicacy in the fare, would be the desideratum. Plain food would satisfy us such as the family is accustomed to into which we should enter. My wife, though wanting health would yet not be such an invalid as would give trouble. Our infant (since the birth of which she has been feeble) is now about five months old. In August she would be ten. Our boy is now four years old, and not a very troublesome fellow. My eldest daughter is grown and rather good natured than otherwise; and I am neither quarrelsome, nor troublesome in my intercourse with either sex. It would be my object to look about me while in your country, picking up traditions and taking notes for future printings. If, with a knowledge of my objects and myself, you can, in as short a period as possible, ascertain for me whether I can procure for my family such accommodations as I describe, in your neighbourhood, you will certainly oblige me very much & do me a great service. I would wish you to keep in mind that I am not wealthy — as, indeed, it would scarcely seem proper for an author to be — and that I should desire above all things to procure as economical an abode as possible. The terms therefore is something of a consideration with us. I trust that you will be able to let me know something in relation to the subject, without putting yourself to too great inconvenience or trouble. I expect

---

[73] Dated by Simms' references to Ward's reply to his review of Curwen's *Journal.* See letter to Hammond of Jan. 25, 1847, and following letters to Hammond. For Simms' earlier difficulties with John Cunningham, see letter to Perry of Oct. 30, 1846.

to go North early in May in order to put to press a Life of the
Chevalier Bayard which I have in hand at this moment and hope
to finish shortly; and returning in July, I propose to seat myself
down in some one of our mountain abodes for two months more
while I prepare a mountain story, of some size, if I can possibly
feel myself in the mood, and find the necessary materials. I should
look to you in particular to help me to some of the raw material.
— I met young Cunningham in Charleston a few weeks ago, and
had an interesting & frank conversation with him. He seems to
regard the matter of the Curwen biographies rationally, and to
regret their publication. — You have probably seen the idle and
indecent paper which Mr. Ward has put forth in reply in the
January number of the Messenger. There, he seeks, by declamation and flings at my writings to do away with my facts & arguments. He has garbled almost every quotation which he has made
from my writings, and in the occasional *suppressio veri* has shown
himself eminently capable of the *suggestio falsi*. I wait till he
concludes before I respond to him. There is a portion of his language which, if you have read the paper, seems to be intended
as a personal indignity. I should like your opinion as to the mode
with which this point should be treated. My own opinion was that
he should be called upon, but a consultation with certain friends
who are supposed to be *au fait* in such matters advise against
it. Let me know what you think and your answer shall be wholly
between us. Of course, all these latter things are *entre nous.*
Present my wife & self respectfully to Mrs. Perry, and, with a
hope that I may soon hear from you, believe me very truly &
faithfully

Yours

W. Gilmore Simms

365 : To George Frederick Holmes

Woodlands. March 18. [1847] [74]

My dear Holmes

I have been for some time anxious to hear how you get on
& to say to you that, though silent for a long while, I have still
had a lively interest in your fortunes. I should have written to

---

[74] Dated by Simms' references to the birth of Mary Lawson Simms and the
death of Valeria Govan Simms in Sept., 1846.

you before this, but for the variety and pressure of my labors, and the constant and distressing infirmities and afflictions of my family. My wife has been an invalid all the winter, more or less seriously threatened by diseases of the worst character. This misfortune, and its influence upon the mind, of a literary man particularly, you can now fully appreciate as a married man and a father. I should not forget to tell you that the incipient cause of my wife's sufferings was her last confinement. She brought me a fine girl in September last, and has been sick ever since. You may be aware also that about the very same time I lost a dear little child more than a year old. I mention all these things to you by way of accounting for my not writing you before, taking for granted, as I do, that I am in debt to you a letter. — I was quite sorry that the prospect of your success in the So. Ca. College was so slender that your friends concluded not to present your name to the Trustees. They acted prudently, and with a just regard to your feelings. Unfortunately, the public prejudice had been so greatly aroused against strangers from other states, in consequence of previous selections unhappily made, that any appeal to this feeling would have been successful against any candidate whatever might be his merits. Yours were every where & fully acknowledged, and but for this, your election, it strikes me, would have been effected without difficulty. Let me assure you that your friends are exceedingly mortified that they were compelled to forego your claims by a regard to extrinsic matters. I trust that there will be a time hereafter — meanwhile, I sincerely hope that your present situation is a tolerably agreeable one. I think I wrote you on a previous occasion, entreating you to keep your mind in patience, & to wait without complaint or restiveness.[75] You are yet a very young man, and must expect to endure yet for some time before you fully triumph. — I do not see or hear from you in the literary way, though I believe you have written for the So. Quarterly. Mr. Whittakers having contrived to evade payment of what he owed me, on my ceasing to write for him, ceased to send me his Journal, so that for more than a year its contents have been sealed from my eyes. It is now in better

---

[75] Simms had long interested himself in trying to secure for Holmes a position on the faculty of the South Carolina College (see letter to Holmes of Nov. 6, 1844). In 1847 Holmes was on the faculty of Richmond College, though he had received an appointment as professor of history and political economy at the College of William and Mary for the coming academic year of 1847-1848 (see note 189, Oct. 15, 1846). Simms' earlier letter to Holmes, here mentioned, is that of Feb. 3, 1846.

hands, and I have promised Clapp to write for it.[76] I trust you will do the same. — By this time, my Life of Capt. John Smith has been published. I have for some time been engaged upon a Life of the Chevalier Bayard which I have at length nearly completed. Whether I shall attempt to get any thing else ready before I go North, is questionable. It is highly probable that I shall pass through Richmond early in May, on my way to N. Y. when I should greatly like to see you. You do not write for the Messenger. I have done & still do so, though Mr. Minor has certainly taken a strange mode of showing me that he likes my contributions.[77] — I go this early to the North, in order to return South in July; as I then propose to take my wife to the mountains for the benefit of her health. Is there any convenient & healthy village in Virginia where one may take his family for a couple of months and keep them dog cheap? — I beg that you will present me respectfully to Mrs. Holmes, and kiss the little one on my account. Let me hear from you soon.— I have just consented to deliver the anniversary oration next Nov. before the Literary Society of Oglethorpe University, Geo.[78] —

Yours very truly

W. Gilmore Simms

G. F. Holmes, Esq.

366: To EVERT AUGUSTUS DUYCKINCK

Woodlands March 25 [1847][79]

dear Sir

Your 'World' improves decidedly. If you could put forth weekly a story, sketch or essay, and just one small original poem, it

---

[76] For Simms' contribution to the July issue of the *Southern Quarterly Review*, see note 55, Feb. 25, 1847.

[77] See letter to Hammond of March 2, 1847.

[78] Simms' oration, "Self-Development," was delivered on Nov. 10. See note 258, Oct. 20, 1847.

[79] Dated by the review of Rufus W. Griswold's *Prose Writers of America; with a Survey of the History, Condition, and Prospects of American Literature* (Philadelphia: Carey and Hart, 1847) in the *Literary World*, I (March 20, 1847), 149-151. In commenting on Griswold's remarks about the South, Duyckinck writes: "Mr. Griswold takes the South as representative of the men of wealth, and says 'we have, in the Southern States of this republic, a large class, with ample fortunes, leisure, and quiet; but they have done comparatively nothing in the fields of intellectual exertion, except when startled into spasmodic activity by conflicts of interest with the North.' We need go no further than Mr. Griswold's own book for a refutation of this. Without look-

would add to its variety & claims. Your last number containing
a notice of Griswold's Prose Writers gives me the first knowledge I have obtained in print of that work, which has not yet
reached me. From the delay, I should think it doubtful, whether
it was intended to send me one. I note what you say of Mathews.
I had thought that Griswold & himself were rather intimate &
did not concieve, at all events, that there should be anything half
so savage & offensive in his essay as the samples which you quote.
In regard to Mathews Griswold, &c. I must reserve myself till
I see you. Of the former you are aware of my opinions. You
know that I regard him as wilfully going wrong, and fighting
against his stars — as having endowments which he will not
permit himself to show & perversely assuming his *forte* to be one
thing, when every characteristic of his mind proclaims it to be
another. He will not submit to counsel and must go through the
painful ordeal always in reserve for such persons. He is still
sufficiently young to make his case a hopeful one. — It will be
some time I fancy before I shall be able to do any thing for
the South. Quarterly. The Editor & Publisher have been at me,
and I have half promised them a political article & one on the

---

ing beyond his list, which might be enlarged, we find from the South, born
under the shadow of Southern institutions, Jefferson, Madison, Marshall, Calhoun, Audubon, Washington Allston, Legaré, W. Gilmore Simms, William
Wirt, Richard Henry Wilde, Kennedy, Bird, Edgar A. Poe—one-fifth nearly
of the numerical force of the whole volume." Of Griswold's treatment of
Mathews, Duyckinck says: "Of the coarse and illiberal treatment of Mr.
Mathews we offer no refutation. It is, with the exception of the paper on Miss
Fuller and one or two other instances, a departure from the method of the
whole book, and indicates an unworthy purpose. It is an attempt to *degrade*
the author, which must react in his favor. We are told that one of his books
'is low, and base, and as untrue as it is revolting,'—that the style of Mr.
Mathews 'indicates a mind accustomed to the contemplation of vulgar depravity.'
'Some writers are said to advance on stilts; our author may be said to proceed
differently, strainingly jerking through mire.' The rest is one of Mr. Griswold's
diatribes on nationality, which are plastered over the whole volume. Whatever
errors of taste there may be in Mr. Mathews's works, there is not a line base
or immoral. That they have gone abroad and been highly praised in influential
journals, as Tait's and Douglas Jerrold's magazines, the Athenaeum, and the
Westminster Review, is true, and no cavil of Mr. Griswold's will reverse the
judgment." In a later issue of the *Literary World,* I (March 27, 1847), 183,
Duyckinck further comments on Griswold's treatment of Mathews: "Mr. G.
tells us that the drama of Witchcraft so highly spoken of in the paper on
American Literature [Margaret Fuller's *Papers on Literature and Art*] met
with a 'quick damnation in the theatre.' . . . We know something of the
history of Witchcraft; its 'quick damnation' is a mere matter of invention. It
was acted at Philadelphia, on its first presentation to the public, for four
successive nights. Mr. Murdoch afterwards carried his manuscript play to
Cincinnati, where it was received with unbounded applause."

'Phases of Poetry';[80] but I am too much absorbed by present tasks. I wish to get my Bayard, & if possible my Huguenots, ready before leaving for N. Y. My present calculation is to do so & come on early in May, — so that I may accomplish the printing before the close of June. My duties will require me at home in July when I propose to take my family to the mountains for the summer. My wife's health still keeps feeble, though she exhibits improvement. — It is not improbable that I shall then commence a Correspondence with you from the South, and describe our mountain scenery & pick up for you some of our mountain traditions.[81] I can show you some samples when I come on. — Are W & P. disposed to take the 'Huguenots' now? You can ascertain for me. It is a long time since I have recd. any of their books. I sent you a mem. of things which never reached me, but I did not mean that you should say a word on the subject unless the omission to send me was the result of inadvertence.[82] Have you read Smith?[83] I send you a sonnet — (*anonymous*) Yours &c.

W. G. S.

Attica.[84]

Methinks, that now we breathe a purer air,
 And lovelier looks the climate. The blue sky

---

[80] No articles on these subjects were published by Simms in the *Southern Quarterly Review* for 1847.

[81] This series of letters was not written for the *Literary World*. Simms' scrapbooks in the Charles Carroll Simms Collection, South Caroliniana Library, contain voluminous notes taken on this trip.

[82] See letter to Duyckinck of Feb. 25, 1847.

[83] In the *Literary World*, I (March 27, 1847), 185, *The Life of Captain John Smith* is advertised as "now ready." A long complimentary review of the biography, probably written by Duyckinck, was published in the same periodical, I (April 10, 1847), 221-223. The reviewer comments (p. 222): "It is a highly agreeable, instructive popular history, related with a fund of good humor, which proceeds from a love of the subject, and an instinctive knowledge of the man, from a sympathy with his chivalry and energy. In other respects, too, Mr. Simms is peculiarly qualified for this narrative. The novelist cuts down into an admirable historian, and long familiarity with the effective treatment of deeds of adventure, intimacy with the details and spirit of Indian life, a genuine Americanism which kindles with enthusiasm at every footprint of his hero on Virginian soil, would naturally claim this task for the author of 'The Yemassee.' "

[84] This sonnet, signed "Linus," was published in the *Literary World*, I (April 17, 1847), 252. Later it was included in *The Cassique of Accabee* (New York: Harper & Brothers, 1849), p. 111. In line 7 the printed version has *Euboea*. Other poems by Simms were published in the *Literary World* for 1847 under the pseudonym of "Pierre Vidal": " 'Zephyrs That Wait on My Lady.' A Southern Areyto," I (May 29), 398; "Proper Understanding," I (June 5), 421; "Ballad" ("Hark! the trumpet's note through all our valleys . . . "), I (June 12), 448; "Madrigal" ("Not to that grove . . . "), I (June 26), 495.

Might well persuade us of a happier sphere
  Than aught our northern countries may supply; —
Look for your history now! — Beneath our Eye,
  Lies Attica, — there, bounded by the sea,
  There, by Æubea; — yet, how boundless she
In sole dominion; — with a realm outspread
  Wherever Genius breathes, or memory broods,
  O'er the past works of genius! — In our woods
We felt the mighty aspects, which still shed
An atmosphere of Empire, far & near; —
And though o'erthrown the altars of her God,
From the vast ruins still, he sends his spells ab[road.]

Linus

Do not suffer *any one* to suspect the source of the preceding.

367: To JAMES HENRY HAMMOND

Woodlands, March 29. [1847][85]

My dear Hammond

I wrote you not long ago, but really did not hope while writing, to do justice either to our topics or ourselves; for while I scribbled at my desk, I was companioned in my library by a young artist who was paying me a week's visit and then on his way to the North, who kept me in talk at odd intervals while I wrote, and left me very doubtful what I had said at the close of every sentence.[86] That I had delayed answering you before was due to circumstances which I endeavoured to explain in that Letter, for all of yours had been seasonably recieved and were particularly satisfactory. In the Curwen business my anxiety was not to suffer myself to be trifled with, and to arrest the attempt on the threshold, if you should think it proper to do so. Your views are confirmed by those of Perry of Greenville to whom I also submitted the question at the same time. — He even goes to say that the thing of Ward is not worth answering. At all events, my conclusion is, from what you advise, to suffer him to exhaust himself

---

[85] Dated by Simms' reference to Ward's attack on him in the *Southern Literary Messenger*. See letter to Hammond of Jan. 25, 1847, and following letters to Hammond. See also letter to Perry of March 10, 1847.

[86] T. Addison Richards was visiting at Woodlands on March 2. See letters to Hammond and Lawson of that date.

fairly before I look after the slain & wounded. As for the Messenger, I shall be quit with it very soon. Here, again, your counsel confirmed my own impressions. The note to the article on Ney was offensive and very impertinent as nothing could have been more innocently thought and said than my comment on the prematureness of his publication. The miserable creature revenged himself in this fashion because of a draft of mine which came upon him unseasonably and the payment of which he could not well escape.[87] But did you ever know such an ass of an Editor as to disparage his own correspondents, on the very page on which he gives place to their communications. I shall have done with him, and really desire to cut the magazines wholly. They fritter away the mind, exhaust the energies & consume one's most valuable time; but they yield me a few Hundred per annum and I am not in the situation to discard this resource without incurring responsibilities which would lessen my independence. A knowledge of the peculiar condition of American Literature would explain to you how a magazine will pay when a volume might not. It was with the wish to break off from these connections, and not because of any ambitious hankerings that I desired a foreign mission.[88] — But talking of foreign missions reminds me of politics. When the Wilmot Proviso was under consideration in the house I wrote to Calhoun, on the subject, making that & the Mexican War, tributary to certain inquiries which I had occasion to put, touching the action of the Senate, during the previous session on the subject of a bust which it was proposed to decree to John Rutledge. I had some letters of J. R. which had never been published & which I proposed to weave into an article for one of the periodicals.[89] I told Mr C. that while I was for sustaining the War and even for acquiring territories, I thought the South ought tenaciously to insist on certain preliminary securities — in other words that the action on the Wilmot Proviso should satisfy us — before we voted any more men & money. The Proviso I regarded as a *brutum fulmen* — offensive rather than dangerous — for all abolition could not keep our people with their slaves from any *contiguous Southern* territory. They might enact what they pleased, we should take & keep what we could get. Once in, it would be in no power under the sun to

[87] For Simms' difficulties with Minor, see note 65, March 2, 1847.
[88] See letters to Burt, Lawson, Perry, and Hammond of January—April, 1845.
[89] See letter to Calhoun of Feb. 10, 1847. For Simms' article on John Rutledge, published in the *American [Whig] Review*, see note 120, April 19, 1847.

dispossess us. Oregon was a different matter, but as in the case of Texas, so, beyond the Rio Grande, what we once acquired would enure to the South & to the South exclusively, and though I did not say this, I thought that it might ultimately help us to a sufficiently large republic of our own &c. I threw out the hint that the Anglo Norman race would never forgive the public man who should fling away territory. His resolutions followed some ten days after I had written — perhaps not so long. Then came his speech.[90] To his views as to the war in Mexico, I did not so much disagree, except that my plan would be to make the boundary to be maintained include all the regions we have taken. As for going back to the Rio Grande, I cannot persuade myself to that, as I should be convinced that we should only have to do the work over again. As for five thousand men holding this region or even with the Rio Grande for a boundary, the thing is absurd, and I regard the regular army under the peace establishment as quite too small by at least ten thousand men. On the whole, however, so far as regards the Mexican War, its continuance, and the desire to press forward into the interior, I do not know but that Mr. C's opinions may be adopted with but little reservation. His generalizations are just and we should differ only on the details which I have mentioned. But you are right in all the rest. It appears to me that Mr. C's anxiety to justify his vote against the declaration has led him into farther errors, and as you remark with just emphasis, that we should break with a free trade administration unless in a case of paramount importance seems to be perfectly monstrous and unintelligible. As for the expulsion of old Ritchie could anything have been more weak & childish.[91] But you will have seen the proceedings & the speech in Charleston.[92] In that speech there is certainly an ingenious

[90] Calhoun presented his resolution on the slave question to the Senate on Feb. 19. Speeches were made by him in the Senate on Feb. 20 and Feb. 24. On March 9 he delivered a speech at a meeting of the citizens of Charleston.

[91] Thomas Ritchie (1778-1854), editor of the Washington *Union*, a national administration newspaper established at Polk's request, was excluded from the floor of the Senate because of an article published in his newspaper, entitled "Another Mexican Victory," which attacked Calhoun for defeating the Ten Regiment Bill for increasing the army in the war with Mexico. For this expulsion Calhoun and his henchmen were bitterly attacked in the Democratic press, not only in Virginia, but throughout the South. See Joseph G. Rayback, "The Presidential Aspirations of John C. Calhoun, 1844-1848," *Journal of Southern History*, XIV (Aug., 1948), 339-340.

[92] The *Southern Patriot* of March 10 prints in full Calhoun's speech of the previous evening at a meeting of the citizens of Charleston, presided over by Henry Bailey. Calhoun says: "The main cause or motive, then, of this crusade

argument to show that we have been wholly wrong hitherto — that instead of the Presidential Election being nothing as Mr. Calhoun's friends have always insisted, it is really every thing, and this with the farther reason that it is the only way to break down abolition. Well, we should not deny all this, if we could concede the premises to Mr. C.[93] If he will persuade the South to a united action — If he can get Benton, Bagby, Soule, Lewis, Colquitt, Hunter, McDowell, Ritchie,[94] and, indeed, all the leading Democrats north & south of us, but within the tabooed region of Mason's & Dickson's, — there can be no doubt that Northern Democracy will yield to the stronger force which the South can bring against abolition into the field. But if Mr. C. can persuade the South to this, he will persuade them into making him President. What chance is there that they will recognize him as the Peter the Hermit whose preaching will make them take up the Cross against Democracy? To my thinking none; and, indeed, we see already the beginning of the end. It strikes me that when Colquitt & Speight[95] draw off from him, the game's up. Ingenious as the argument of the Charleston speech may be considered, I

---

against our domestic institution, is to be traced to the all-absorbing interest, which both parties take, in carrying the electors, especially the Presidential . . . should party machinery for President making prove strong enough to force the slave holding States to join in a convention to nominate and support a candidate who will be acceptable to the Abolitionists, they will have committeed the most suicidal act that a people ever perpetrated. . . . I hold it safer, and in every way preferable to leave the election where the Constitution has placed it; to the Electoral College to choose; and if that fails to make a choice, to the House of Representatives, voting by States, to elect the President from the three candidates, having the highest votes."

[93] On March 21 Hammond had written to Simms: "It is not only confusing, but fatiguing to follow his [Calhoun's] windings nowadays & it is not a little mortifying to see So Carolina so manifestly moved from her position by his mere nod, without any pretense of a principle involved. It was weak of him to split off from Polk upon mere expediency, in time of war. . . . I have been opposed to the war from the first & have thought I myself could see mismanagement in its conduct, but the almost unanimous opinion of the people *pushed the administration* into it & it was manifestly occasioned by the annexation of Texas. Mr. Calhoun cannot falsify these facts with all his ingenuity & it is folly to attempt to do it . . . no party can possibly be formed on such issues as Mr. Calhoun has made. . . . I have today read his Charleston speech. Its object *palpably* is to unite the Southern vote on himself for the Presidency." (Original in the Hammond Papers, Library of Congress.)

[94] Thomas Hart Benton (1782-1858), United States senator from Missouri; Arthur Pendleton Bagby (1794-1858), United States senator from Alabama; Pierre Soulé (1801-1870), United States senator from Louisiana; Dixon Hall Lewis (1802-1848), United States senator from Alabama; Walter Terry Colquitt (1799-1855), United States senator from Georgia; Robert M. T. Hunter (1809-1887), United States senator from Virginia; James McDowell (1796-1851), member of Congress from Virginia. For Ritchie, see note 91, above.

[95] Jesse Speight (1795-1847) was United States senator from Mississippi.

NASH ROACH

For him, "an affection which has steadily advanced with my just appreciation of his integrity and gentleness of character."

— From the dedication to *The Wigwam and the Cabin*.

(From a photograph in the possession of Mary C. Simms Oliphant)

TURTLE COVE.

**The foregoing picture is from nature, and
represents a scene in the swamp at "Woodlands,"
the beautiful country-seat of Mr. Simms. He
himself, has given us a word-picture of the scene,
even more characteristic than that of the graver.
We quote from his *"Southern Passages and Pictures."*

" 'Tis a wild spot, and hath a gloomy look ;
The bird sings never merrily in the trees,
And the young leaves seem blighted. A rank
    growth
Spreads poisonously round, with power to taint,
With blistering dews, the thoughtless hand that
    dares
To penetrate the covert. Cypresses
Crowd on the dark, wet earth ; and stretched at
    length,
The cayman—a fit dweller in such a home
Slumbers, half buried in the sedgy grass,
Beside the green ooze where he shelters him.
A whooping crane erects his skeleton form,
And shrieks in flights. Two summer-ducks aroused
To apprehension, as they hear his cry,
Dash up from the lagoon, with marvellous haste,
Following his guidance. Meetly taught by these,
And startled by our rapid, near approach,
The steel-jawed monster, from his grassy bed,
Crawls slowly to his slimy, green abode,
Which straight receives him. You behold him
    now,
His ridgy back uprising as he speeds,
In silence, to the centre of the stream,
Whence his head peers alone."

THE SWAMP AT WOODLANDS

"Mr. [Thomas Addison] Richards . . . has painted several pictures of Southern
scenery, and one upon the river swamp at my residence at Woodlands, which might
make a vignette at once novel & attractive."
(From the *Southern Literary Gazette*, N. S., I [Jan. 31, 1852], 54)

am not sure that it will have that effect upon the *party* elswhere which is necessary to the adoption of his views. Party is the obvious organization by which the timid cover their halting patriotism, & the selfish their individual aims. It is not easy to do evil, or to suffer the imputation of evil, when with the multitude; and the South, just at this period, is the last region in the world to do any thing for patriotism, or even for the common safety. We are cursed with too much talent which is trained from its cradle to the business of party, and to look for its food & proper element to Washington. It is not quite so much the case throughout the [South] as in Charleston where self-esteem and profligacy have kept admirable & even pace together, — where of the men who now swear by Calhoun, nine in ten hate him & loathe his supremacy. When I was there last I had a conversation with our friend Walker, who only needs equal force of talent to make his character tell in that community, and who, with you there to back him, might be brought to do something. I suggested him to take a part in the public meeting which I felt sure would be called — to anticipate the proceedings, if possible, of the Old Hunkers,[96] and by getting *their* cards in his hands, secure some of the points in the game. Perhaps, he was right in the opinion that he would only be contributing to make capital for Boyce & others. Though an honorable fellow & a smart one, he has not weight enough in that community, and is farther kept down by that incubus self-esteem [which] demoralizes all the natives of that rotten borough. But if you were there, with your *will* & *strength,* I am convinced that Charleston might be revolutionized. There are hundreds of fine fellows there, who are restive, and who only lack a leader. You note the transfer of the Mercury to Carew.[97] He professes the best of feelings for you & all of us, but this is mere gammon. The truth is Carew is or will be soon

---

[96] See note 226, Nov. 17, 1846.

[97] See note 54, Feb. 25, 1847. The *South Carolinian* (Columbia) of Feb. 3 gives the following account of the *Mercury*: "Since its establishment, . . . [the *Mercury*] has had the good fortune to be edited by several of the most talented writers of the Southern Country. First, under the scholarly and elegant conduct of the Hon. H. L. Pinckney; next illuminated by the brilliant though eccentric conversations of J. A. Stuart; then with the elegant fluency of J. M. Clapp; the course of the Mercury has been such as to require a successor to the chair of these gentlemen, of no ordinary or commonplace requirements. Nor have we any doubts that such a successor will be found in our friend, J. E. Carew, into whose editorial charge and proprietorship the Mercury has just passed."

a needy man. I am satisfied that some of his Editorials already proceed from Elmore's hand. Dukes [98] from prudential considerations declines doing anything *at present*. He will watch events. He is with us. But to return. Since Mr. Calhoun has reached Fort Hill, he has answered my Letter.[99] The contents are so purely public that I freely send it you instead of making a summary of them. You will see that he is even more earnest in this brief compass & makes a stronger case against the South in the present condition of affairs, than he did in his speech in Charleston. I have no doubt that he calculated sanguinely on the prospect of carrying the next Presidential Election into the House, and possibly has hopes of Virginia and North Carolina. [You] may judge better than myself of his hopes & calculations. Certainly, nobody more really desires that Mr. C. should be President of the United States than we do. But in good sooth, he does not seem disposed to play for the high stake a bit more sagaciously today than twenty years ago. Is there not in his mental constitution a singular deficiency. Does he not acquire his great metaphysical powers at the loss of others by which he fails duly to appreciate the nature of the very animal to whom he most appeals. — Dessaussure's course at the Butler meeting in Columbia is quite a commentary on the oblique tenor of a part of his Letter to you.[100] Do you suppose that D. really thought me anxious for such an office as Lt. Gov? — Let me have Calhoun's letter as soon as you have read it. — I am working hard — expect to go North by the last of April.

Yours truly

W. G. S.

---

[98] At this time William C. Dukes was a director of the Bank of the State of South Carolina.

[99] Fort Hill, Calhoun's estate in South Carolina, is now the site of Clemson College. Apparently Calhoun's letter to Simms, which we have been unable to locate, was in reply to Simms' letter of Feb. 10, 1847.

[100] The Charleston *Mercury* of March 18 gives an account of this meeting held in Columbia on March 15 "to welcome Hon. A. P. Butler, one of our senators in the Congress, on his return from Washington." William F. DeSaussure introduced Butler in glowing terms: "We shall find in you a worthy successor of the able and patriotic McDuffie, and, the high minded Huger, and that the destinies of the State have been safely confided to your hands."

368: To James Henry Hammond

Woodlands. April 2. 1847

dear Hammond

I wrote you but a couple of days ago, and again some 8 or 10 days ago, but as you lose your letters & mine frequently miscarry, I will simply acknowledge yours of the 26th ult. & say that its topics have quite as much interested & made me anxious as yourself.[101] I discussed them at large but two days gone with young Ayer (Lewis Malone Ayer Jr.) who spent a day & night with me, and who is one of those persons who believes that Mr. Calhoun is immaculate. He is also disposed to believe in you *where you do not come in conflict with Mr. C.,* and I have told him that as he desires very much to see & know you, that you will gladly recieve & entertain him if he will call & see you. He is ambitious of distinction; is now a Major of Battalion, will run for the Legislature next session, and is rather, I fancy, tenacious of his own *expressed* opinions, than of Mr. C's infallibility. He will not be unwilling to be enlightened, perhaps, if appearances are preserved, & he is not called upon for any committal which might endanger his hopes or affect his self esteem. I have counselled him to lie close, keep dark & wait his time— that he need not declare himself with regard to Mr. C or in relation to present events at all, and that before he can come fairly into public life that of Mr. Calhoun may probably be so determined as to make it a matter of no moment what he thinks. He will probably according to my suggestion pop in upon you some time this month. He is Aldrich's brother-in-law,[102] & by the way, I may as well say to you that I have suggested to Aldrich as a subject of proper seeking with himself, the office of Solicitor whenever Edwards makes way for him.[103] In a few years he

---

[101] We have been unable to locate Simms' letter to Hammond of "some 8 or 10 days ago" or Hammond's to Simms of March 26.

[102] Lewis Malone Ayer (1821-1895), of Runnymede Plantation, Barnwell District, son of Hartwell Ayer, was a distinguished student at the University of Virginia. Later he studied law at Harvard. At his own expense he led a company to Kansas in 1856, but soon returned to South Carolina. Ayer defeated D. F. Jamison for a seat in the Confederate House of Representatives, and when Robert Barnwell Rhett launched his attack on Jefferson Davis, he, as champion of the President, defeated Rhett in his home district. His sister Martha was the wife of Alfred Proctor Aldrich.

[103] John D. Edwards, born about 1797, was a nephew of Chancellor DeSaussure. After graduation from the South Carolina College, where he had been a classmate of Hugh Swinton Legaré, Edwards practiced law in Walterboro and Barnwell. In 1836 he succeeded Franklin Elmore as solicitor of the

will be ripe for it. — I told Ayer pretty much what you have said, that the move of Mr. C. was evidently influenced wholly by rabid anxiety for the Presidency, and that at all events, such would be the conviction everywhere out of S. C. — that, granting all he alleges, the question naturally recurs, — what more can you get than the Democratic Party has given you — a Slave Holder for the President, Free trade, a full recognition of State Right Doctrines, — in brief all that So. Ca. has ever demanded. Now, let the Wilmots proviso as they please, what more could we desire? The scheme of Mr. C. is impracticable, as, not seeing with his eyes, the South will never engage in the organization which he counsels. If they did, in what could they increase our securities, unless by secession *en masse* from the Union. As long as we remain in it, there will always be a sufficient number of Wilmots & Preston Kings [104] to throw into Congress some such firebrand as the present which will *gratefully* furnish capital to such as desire a pretext to secede from an alliance by which they have failed to gain what they have sought. But what is the measure proposed now by Mr. C. but a Southern Convention which we old Union men preached to him 20 years ago, & which I brought up again in the Res. on yr message? [105] And to think that we, who have been taught for 20 years by Mr. C. & his followers, that the President's Election was of no importance to us, are now to be taught that it is of the last importance in regard to which tariff, free trade, Int. Impr. & all things must give place! But what is to be done? You see where S. C. is destined to be hurried. The Mercury declares her course, or rather in declaring Mr. C's. silences every other man in the State.[106] If anything could be done, why, — but what hope. Were you to speak aloud, it

southern circuit of South Carolina. He held this position until 1848, when he was superceded by M. L. Bonham of Edgefield, later governor of South Carolina during the Confederate War.

[104] Preston King (1806-1865), member of Congress from New York (1843-1846), had advised Wilmot to introduce his Proviso. King did not seek re-election to the Thirtieth Congress, but he was elected in 1848 and again in 1850.

[105] See note 16, Jan. 1, 1845.

[106] In replying to an attack on Calhoun made in the *Federal Union* (Milledgeville, Ga.), the Charleston *Mercury* of March 26 devotes a full column to Calhoun's views. Of the *Federal Union*'s claim that Calhoun's course was governed by his presidential aspirations, the *Mercury* says: "Truth and justice, sooner or later, will vindicate the wisdom, firmness and patriotism of Mr. Calhoun's course. . . . Nor is it just to impute, even by innuendo or inference, that Mr. Calhoun interrupted the 'harmony and energy' of the party, while engaged in a war that demanded it; or that he chose such a moment, and 'censured the president, condemned the war, and allied himself to the Opposition. . . . ' "

would organize against you all those who now, not caring for Mr. C. would yet be glad to find a topic upon which to distract your friends & impair your future influence. There is no way to break ground, that I can see, and even if the opportunity did offer there is no sort of reason why you should peril anything of your present position or future prospects by making a demonstration in a matter so perfectly personal to Mr. C. as the temporary position of S. C. I look upon it as written that for the next two years at least, she must be where she has really been for 20 — nowhere — fighting like Ishmael — battling the air, — losing position, dignity & all the advantages that might accrue from our connection with the Federal Union. I concur with you in the fervent wish that Mr. C. should be made President, not only because he is worthy of the seat & would make one of the very best that we have had, but in order that there might be a resurrection of that independence among our people which can never be the case as long as his ambition remains ungratified. His shadow falls heavily upon our young men, and darkens all their pathways; and regarding his career I have often fancied that I discovered the true key to the reason for the vote of ostracism given by the countrymen who found fault with Aristides for being proverbially called the just. In one way or another, the established names of a country are apt to become its tyrants. Nothing would more delight me than to see Mr. C. raised to the Presidential Chair tomorrow, but has he not always committed suicide. Do you not know that his doctrine of the State veto arose wholly from Jackson's recognition of Van Buren as the heir apparent, and what caprices have marked his course since in regard to Whig & Democrat, Van Buren & now Polk. — I sent you his letter to me which you will return as soon as read. It is one which I shall find it difficult to answer. It assumes so much. That I can support him cheerfully for the Presidency gives no sanction for the assumption that I concur in the propriety of his course & my opinions were they be given freely would only startle and offend him. Had he ever been pleased to have regarded me as a personal friend, I should then be justified in speaking frankly, but his tone, however kind and conciliatory warrants no such openness, and nothing remains but to deal in such generalities as will forbear the tabooed regions while concurring with his own. To us, as individuals, it really matters nothing how the cat jumps. The catastrophe is none of ours. It cannot be said that we are selfish in being silent, since our public repudiation by the Legislature, would seem to deny us properly to speak. We can do what all are doing. Declare ourselves firmly against the Wilmot assumption, and follow Virginia when she pleases to move. But this is what we have all along been doing. The Wilmot provisos are in fact the tubs which selfish politicians throw to the abolition whale at home. Nobody even doubts that the South, with its slaves, would possess itself of all *Contiguous* territory suited to its purposes, in spite of all the enactments of the Congress from now to doomsday. The proviso was rather offensive than dangerous. At all events, the question again occurs, how will it strengthen our cause to quarrel with the Democratic Party, they giving us a slave holder for the President, & adopting all our principles? — I expect to be at the Court House at the next meeting of the Commissioners of Free Schools of which I am Chairman. I will write to Aldrich to let you know when that is, for really I do not know. Try & meet me there.[107] It is our only chance for the present, as I propose to go North immediately after, say the first of May, in order to return in July for the back country. My wife is better & improving. Thank you for the reciept &c. — Once more, it seems to me that your proper policy is to say as little as possible. The game is a sure one if no present hazards are incurred.

Yours truly but hurriedly

W. G. S.

P. S. House full of company now. My head is completely muddled. The Rudolph paper causes quite a sensation.[108] I suspect that the Ed. of Curwen will say no more. Suppose you send me the Hamburg paper to which you allude.[109] I can readily understand your annoyance. A self-willed chuckle-headed friend is the worst of social & political grievances. Did you see Allen's appeal to Rhett?[110]

Taylor is an admirable soldier but as you say he has not followed up his victories. If the Mexicans at the battle of Resaca de la Palma could cross the Rio Grande in retreat, he could just as well have crossed in pursuit. But the reason is that he is no

---

[107] The meeting took place on Monday, April 26.
[108] See note 65, March 2, 1847.
[109] Apparently this is an allusion to the contents of Hammond's letter of March 26, which we have been unable to locate.
[110] See note 71, March 2, 1847.

longer a young man. No man over 45 ought to be sent at the head of an invading army. This was fatal to Wm. Hull.[111] The energies necessary to enterprise fail ordinarily at 45. All the successful invading generals were *young* men, of your age or mine, from 30 to 45, — need I remind you of Scipio, Pompey, Sylla, Alexander, and lastly Napoleon, who, in the Hundred Days was no longer the Napoleon of Marengo &c, or he never would have lost the game at Waterloo. Old generals are great at obstinate defense; and, when over 50, (unless very extraordinary men as Old Jackson) ought to be put in defense of fortresses only. They would keep such places.

369: To James Henry Hammond

[*c.* April 4, 1847][112]

dear Hammond.

While the fit is on me, and fresh from the reading of your Letter and that of Judge Tucker,[113] I concluded to shape you another hurried scrawl, though it is but a day or two since I sent you a full satisfaction (so far as number & quantity are concerned) for all past favors. I am really gratified to discover that with so little acquaintance with the political world, I should so happily jump to your conclusions. It was but yesterday that, speaking with some friends & in my family, of Taylor's victory at Buena Vista, and the conquest of Vera Cruz, I remarked that they were quite as fatal to Mr. Calhoun as to the Mexicans. The analysis made by Judge Tucker of this remarkable man is singularly just, and strengthens me in my precious convictions. I remarked to young Ayer, of whom I wrote you recently, that I had no doubts of Mr. Calhoun's honesty but that he was the victim of such a passionate idea of the Presidency (which I considered his right in the Carlyle sense) that his philosophy & all his principles readily yielded to the leading object of his soul, and his ingenuity enabled him to make a plausible case out of all his inconsistencies. I mentioned the remarkable contradiction be-

---

[111] William Hull (1753-1825), American general who surrendered Detroit to the British on Aug. 16, 1812.

[112] April 4 is the probable date of this letter, written after that of April 2 and "fresh from the reading" of Hammond's letter of April 1. No envelope survives. Dated April, 1847, this letter is printed in A. T. Odell, "Letters of William Gilmore Simms to James H. Hammond, 1847-1850," *Furman Bulletin* XXVI (May, 1943), 3-6.

[113] Nathaniel Beverley Tucker. See introductory sketch.

tween the constant & scornful denunciation of the Presidential
Chair, for the last 20 years by him & his followers, as an object
of interest and importance, and the sudden change to a policy
by which we are instructed (The Tariff & Int. Imp. being no
longer available as pretexts) that the Presidency is the question
— the interest paramount to all others. His scheme, as propounded
at the Charleston meeting, means, if anything, that the South
should organize a party for itself, all other interests merging in
that of Slavery, to the exclusion & defiance of the North, unless
where individuals from that region choose to lose themselves in
ours — a proposition which at once forces a corresponding organization upon the North — a result which leaves us in rather
worse condition than before. Any man with one idea so deeply
fixed as to become with him a passion, must necessarily be demented, wherever that idea becomes the object of consideration.
I had this opinion of Mr. Calhoun in 1830, when but a boy myself, & new to politics, & the world. It appears to me that he
has been impaling himself on this passion ever since I have been
able to watch his course. You think it over with him now. But,
hardly, until the result of the next election is fairly known. I
think I wrote to you six months ago that this game was to be
tried, that of bringing the election into the House, and it strikes
me that I got the assurance to this effect from one of the immediate satellities of Mr. Rhett.[114] There is no doubt that certain
of those to whom Mr. C. unwisely looks for counsel, have taught
him to hope for the nomination of Virginia, and the support of
Alabama, Mississippi, Louisiana & S. C. to say nothing of other
states, where strong factions were to be found. My own opinion
is that they who counsel him thus, know better, and that their
purpose is to beguile him to defeat, satisfied that, in no other
way can he be laid upon the shelf. To dispose of him is now
the leading object with all those who aim to control the State.
They swear by his power, while it lasts, incapable of disturbing
it, but they hate him for this very necessity. I suppose that, if
he embarks in the next conflict, it will be the closing act in his
public career. He has no such hope & no such fortune as Taylor.
Perhaps, it is quite as well that he should have his own way. —
Carew may be a very honest person, but my fears spring from
his notorious need. We know the cost of such a paper as his

---

[114] We have been unable to locate this letter. Simms here refers to Robert
Barnwell Rhett.

& in his hands it never can be made to pay expenses. He must go to the Banks and be enslaved & bought up like all [*two words missing*] Charleston politicians. I suppose you are right in the notion that he does not exactly know our politics, and Aldrich was no doubt loose in his definition. I concur with you in regard to Charleston generally. I recognize fully her feebleness & shame, and my wish to regenerate her was not so much that she might do for us, as that I might lose some of the mortification which distressed me as I reflected upon the morals of an ancient homestead. It was not that she might serve us, as that we might succour her. Still, her vote in the Legislature is something, and her weight more — a weight rather felt than acknowledged.[115] — I do go to the North but expect to set off on or about the first week in May, as it is necessary that I should return early so as to take my wife into the back country. I think something may be done in getting a publisher for Judge Tucker.[116] I am willing to contribute what I can, of influence, in procuring one.

---

[115] In reply to Simms' letter of March 29 Hammond had written on April 1: "I perceive you take precisely the same view of the Charleston Speech that I do. It is indeed but a development of his true motives for splitting off from the administration which *every man* must have seen clearly from the first, since there has never been a doubt about them perceptible to me. And does it not seem that he must be actually demented to attempt such a game as this— thus to tamper with the great interests of the country & above all with the vital question of the South for the vile purpose of throwing himself into the House as one of the three highest Presidential Candidates. There is but one way to look at it, so as to avoid regarding Mr. C. as a second Cataline & that is to consider that he honestly & earnestly believes that his election to the Presidency is so essential to the prosperity and even the existence of the Republic. . . .

"His pitiful movement against Ritchie has destroyed utterly his prospects in Virginia. The late proceedings at Richmond shew that & the enclosed letter [from Nathaniel Beverley Tucker] confirms the fact. The recent victories in Mexico have prostrated him on the ground he assumed in reference to the War. Unfortunate *silly* man to place himself in a position in which his country's victories are fatal to him, & his hopes of success were dependent on the defeat of her arms!—Alas how are the mighty fallen. I ought not to question Carew's friendly feelings towards me since he voted for me throughout in the late election. . . . I do not approve of all I have seen in his paper. I am inclined to agree with you that he belongs to Elmore, but I should be sorry that you or I should do him injustice by thinking he did not mean what he said. What you say of Walker is true. He is a sterling fellow by no means deficient in talent, but not strong enough to revolutionize Charleston. That I think would be an Augean task. . . . If I mistake not the old Hunkers have burnt their fingers this time & will not again receive Mr. Calhoun as a 'Conquering Hero' without waiting for news from Mexico and the South generally." (Original in the Hammond Papers, Library of Congress.)

[116] In his letter of April 1 Hammond had expressed a desire to aid Nathaniel Beverley Tucker in the publication of his works on government: "I think it would be a great thing to have his political works published. . . . I am ready to contribute $500 to the publication of the Judge's views of our govt." (Original in the Hammond Papers, Library of Congress.)

I esteem the Judge very greatly as a sound man, an able thinker and a charming writer. My first knowledge of him was derived from his excellent & thoughtful novel of George Balcombe.[117] But you must not think to publish writings. Collections won't do. His works must be classed & put forth separately. I would recommend that his lectures on Gov. & politics be made to form a volume to themselves & be recommended as a Text Book to the Schools & Colleges of the Country, by such men as McDuffie, yourself, Preston, and as many leading politicians South & West as you can find. These, alone, will prompt a publisher, such as the Harpers, to try the experiment.[118] There is nothing in this business to derogate from the dignity of an author, though I am of opinion that in good hands, the thing may be done without it. If you & he say so, I can initiate the steps in May & June, and leave you to perfect the work when you come on. But say nothing of more works than the one. Do not alarm publishers & public [by a collection or] a mass at all. Mass meetings [may be] reasonable enough, but masses of manuscripts are the terror of timid publishers, and all the American publishers are timid, as they must be in a country where there are no recognized standards to which the common mind everywhere can turn, and of which they may be sure before they buy the objects which they propose to rate. If I knew something more of the Judge's materials, I could then better devise a scheme of publication: Suppose you ask him to class for you his writings, say what are the titles of the works political & what the nature of his several performances. Get the title at length of each as he would publish it, and a description of its externals, i. e. of its bulk in type & M.S. I shall really be pleased to serve him & think that, with some effort & management the thing may be done without calling for any money from himself & friends, and only by yielding half the copyright. To show readiness to yield the whole, would be to present such an estimate of the value to a publisher as might frighten him at once from the prey. Again, it would be well to ascertain whether the works have or not been offered to a publisher already, & to

---

117 *George Balcombe* was published anonymously in two volumes by Harper and Brothers, New York, in 1836.

118 This plan was not consummated. Earlier, in 1845, Carey and Hart, Philadelphia, had published Tucker's *A Series of Lectures on the Science of Government; Intended to Prepare the Student for the Study of the Constitution of the United States.* For George McDuffie and William Campbell Preston, see introductory sketches.

whom. — I do not exactly see what the proposed leadership of a party involves, nor how it can be tendered from any one quarter. I have been of the opinion, for some time, that it will come to you, not from one but from many quarters. Judge T. really only indicates the want of resource in his own state, of which I have long felt aware. The want is similar in ours. Apart from yourself & Elmore, I really see few persons, as I have said to you before, to whom the South can turn; & it is to Virginia & So. Ca., the two maternal States of the South, that they must turn, still from all the States of the South. Can't you meet me at the Ct. House? [119]

Yours truly &c.

Simms

370: To JAMES LAWSON

Woodlands 19th. April [1847][120]

dear Lawson.

In a few days I shall probably send to your care an elaborate biographical Sketch of John Rutledge of South Carolina, with a

---

[119] In a letter to Hammond of April 13, A. P. Aldrich refers to an unlocated letter from Simms: "Simms has written me word that he will be at my house on the Saturday before the 4 Monday in April, that is the 24th. He is anxious that we should all have a good sociable talk together, and so am I— Can't you arrange your plantation affairs as to take a day or two holyday and meet us? . . . Rhett will speak here and is anxious to have a good meeting, on sale day in May. . . . " Unable to meet Aldrich and Simms in Barnwell, Hammond wrote to Simms on April 19 in regard to political matters discussed in this letter of *c*. April 4: "Your political speculations run in precisely the same line with mine & you have expressed my own views more clearly than I could have done myself. Recent events in Mexico have proved the shortsightedness of Mr. Calhoun & it will be amusing to see where he will catch to save himself & prove his 'consistency.' These victories have destroyed him as a Prophet & I fear as an aspirant. It seems now about certain that Taylor will be our next President. . . .
"As to organizing a plan-holding party in special reference to the Presidential Election as suggested by Mr. Calhoun it is utterly abominable. It would be the most fatal in the long list of blunders the South has committed. It proves that Mr. Calhoun's desperate ambition for the Presidency has not only prostrated his judgment, but *sapped* his *patriotism*, that he should propose. What a position we slave-holders would occupy before the world to make a final rally & catch at such a straw. And missing it, as we surely would, where should we be? Sunk forever. . . . We must place our rights on the Constitution & not just for security on the occupant of the Presidential Chair." (Originals in the Hammond Papers, Library of Congress.)
[120] Dated by Simms' reference to his "A Sketch of the Life and Public Services of John Rutledge of South Carolina, with Extracts from His Unpublished Correspondence," *American [Whig] Review*, VI (Aug. and Sept., 1847), 125-137, 277-291. See letters to Hammond of March 29 and to Lawson of *c*. April 20, *c*. April 22, and April 23, 1847.

review of his public services, & extracts from his unpublished correspondence. This I wish you to offer to Mr. Colton on his usual terms to favorite contributors, & on condition that he will not delay the publication after it shall have been recieved. The article will probably make two good papers in his review. Mr. John Rutledge is the Statesman in regard to whom the Senate of the U. S. now has a bill pending for the purpose of honoring his memory with a bust. He was a very great man, the Patrick Henry of S. C. as an orator. — I am done with Bayard, and hope to get in readiness to start north some time in the first week in May. I shall remain a few days in Charleston, a day or two in Balt., two or three days in Phil, and expect to reach N. Y. somewhere in the middle of the month. I wrote under cover to your lordship an affectionate scribble to that heartless woman your wife; but she deigns no more return for my civilities than for my affections. Has that sly lawyer & politician—Cornelius P. Hopkins, been employing 'Witchcraft' upon her. Has he weaned her from us entirely. Are you aware that he has again cut me, and has foreborne to answer my last letters.[121] What can be in the wind now? I have just penned a complimentary notice of Wetmore & the Art Union of which he is made President. It will appear in the Patriot & when it does I will send you a copy.[122] 'Auld Lang Syne' prompted the paragraph, for with all his neglect of me, I still think of Wetmore as a man of worth and a Gentleman. He has probably made some mistakes with regard to me which time will correct. I am too unostentatious a personage for him. But he will find that he has not the most power who makes the most show, nor he the least influence who does not trouble himself to exercise or boast of it. Enough. You shall have the paragraph, the more particularly as I fancy you have thought hardly of me for not *seeking* Wetmore more than I have done. But this was impossible. — Your Songs of the people, I have read with pleasure; some of them have pleased me, but others not at all.[123] Your Ballad, if I do not greatly mistake, you read to

---

121 Simms here is alluding to Cornelius Mathews, author of *The Career of Puffer Hopkins* and *Witchcraft*.

122 In his notice in the *Southern Patriot* of May 7 Simms characterizes Wetmore as "a writer of fine talents, and a most accomplished gentleman."

123 Under the general heading of "Poems for the People," Lawson published a series of poems in the *Dem. Rev.*, XX (Jan., Feb., March, April, and June, 1847), 55, 153, 232, 328-329, and 544: "Song," "The Knighting of Robert Burns," "Our Flag," "Albert Merle.—A Ballad," and "Signs—False Signs." None is signed, but in the index the author of the first, "Song," is given as "D.

me at Armitages 12 years ago, under a different title & in a cruder state. You have certainly done much toward its improvement. I remember it was the subject of a long discussion between us as to the *essentialities* of this sort of composition, and it was to illustrate some of my views in regard to it that I wrote, my "Story of God's Judgment," which appears in the "Southern Passages" &c.[124] But why call these things Songs for the people? Who are the people? — Why for them only, & whom do you exclude. I look upon this special apostrophizing the people as a wretched sort of cant which you should not fall into. Write for all who will read whether Princes or people. In fact you wrote for yourself & without thinking of others. — Can't you let us hear from you before I leave home? You or your wife or both might certainly do the liberal and fill me a sheet or two. Indeed you must as I shall not see you perhaps before the 15th. prox. and shall leave home about the 2d. or 3d. — My wife improves but is still meagre & feeble. Little Mary Lawson is fat & hearty & full of life & laughter — a blue eyed sandy haired lassie that might pass for a Scotch girl even in the opinion of Margaret Sinclair. Do not forget to present me to her, Mrs. F. & Forrest.

Love to your wife. For yourself hold me Ever as Ever Yrs. &c.

Simms

J. L.

Drysdale," apparently one of Lawson's pseudonyms. For Simms' further criticisms of these poems, see letter to Lawson of April 23, 1847.

[124] Perhaps the ideas Lawson expresses in his note to "Albert Merle.—A Ballad," *Dem. Rev.*, XX (April, 1847), 328, had earlier found expression at the home of Benjamin Armitage, 30 Vesey Street, New York City (see the *New-York . . . City Directory*, 1835-1836), where Lawson stayed before his marriage and where Simms also stayed during his visits to New York at that time. In his note Lawson, after a few statements concerning the substance of his poem, writes: "In this age of mock sentimental rhymes, and sweet, unmeaning verse, ballads are very unfashionable—unless, indeed, they are very old: few read them, and fewer still appreciate their nicest and rarest qualities. Directness of narration; simplicity of thought, in a style natural and innovate, are the chief merits of a ballad. Now-a-days, they are too often regarded as 'see-saw-Margery-Daw' sort of things, only fit for the nursery. Let children-of-a-larger growth, who deride them, forget but for a moment their too much sophisticated notions, then, our word on't, they will not idly condemn a style of verse that once delighted and instructed nations." Simms' "The Story of God's Judgment" appears in *Southern Passages and Pictures*, pp. 175-188.

371: To James Lawson

[c. April 20, 1847][125]

dear Lawson

Here is the first instalment of the article which I advised you of as intended for Mr. Colton of the Whig Review. Pray let him know that if he publishes it he must do so promptly. If he does not wish it, let it be sent to the Democratic Review where it ought to be acceptable. Mr. Colton & the Democratic both give $2. per page. At all events you will please require from them as much pay as they give to any body. By another mail you will recieve the second instalment. The articles will no doubt attract much attention in the South.

Yours truly &c.

Simms

372: To James Lawson

[c. April 22, 1847][126]

My dear Lawson.

I enclose you the conclusion of the first part of the paper on Mr. John Rutledge of South Carolina, of which the first ten pages were sent two mails ago. This you will convey with the preceding portion as soon as possible, to Mr. Colton of the Whig Review. Of the terms, I spoke in my previous letter. You may mention that the second part of the article will be about the same length with the first part./ It is of a kind to suit his pages particularly, but should he not wish it, or seem unwilling to give it an early place, you will please tender it to the Democratic. In this negotiation, it is probable that Mr. Duyckinck will be willing to assist you. Of course the article is too long for his Journal.[127]
— On Monday next, I have to attend the Board of Free School Commissioners of which I am Chairman, at Barnwell Court House, and on the ensuing Monday, the first in May, I think

125 This letter is postmarked April 21. The year is established by Simms' reference to "the first instalment of the article . . . for Mr. Colton of the Whig Review" ("A Sketch of the Life and Public Services of John Rutledge of South Carolina"). See letters to Lawson of April 19, c. April 22, and April 23.

126 This letter is postmarked April 23. The year is established by Simms' reference to his sketch of John Rutledge. See letters to Lawson of April 19, c. April 20, and April 23.

127 The Literary World.

it likely I shall set off for Charleston, whence, after a delay of
a few days, I will proceed North. The conclusion of the article
on Rutledge, I will bring with me. It is already written, but not
copied or corrected.

Yours truly &c

Simms.

373 : To James Lawson

[April 23, 1847][128]

dear Lawson.

The following is included among sundry notices of periodicals
which I sent to the Patriot a few days ago. It is horribly sprinkled
with errors, but you know the habitual slovenliness of a daily
newspaper. I would have said more, but these notices are necessarily brief.

2. The *Democratic Review,* for April, opens with a portrait of Hon. Ellis Lewis, a stout Democrat and a Judge
in Pennsylvania. The contents of the present number are
fair and various; but there is a lack of tone and spirit, without the power of which a periodical lacks authority, and
without the latter, attraction. A series of Ballad Poems, "for
the people," forms a new feature of this Review. Some of
these poems are impressive from their very simplicity.
We doubt, however, whether a good imitation of the old
English ballad, does not require that higher form of simplicity which we call quaitness [*sic*] and which, in its day,
was really a refinement. "The letters from Jerusalem" also
constitute a new attraction in the Democratic, as they relate
to the period and the events in our Saviour's Mission.[129]

I have just recieved an exceedingly curt letter — I mean in respect to length rather than style, though something in that strikes
me as ungenial. Well! — But say nothing. I am afraid he [130] is
predestinately wilful. — I don't know that I mentioned to you in

---

[128] Dated by Simms' statement that "tomorrow (Saturday) the 24 I go to
the Court House, and on the first Monday in May I propose to set off for
Charleston." See letter to Lawson of *c.* April 22.

[129] This review, cut from a copy of the *Southern Patriot* of April 22, is
pasted to the letter. For Simms' earlier comments about Lawson's poems in the
Democratic Review, see letter to Lawson of April 19, 1847.

[130] Probably Cornelius Mathews, whose negligence in writing Simms had
interpreted as a "cut." See letter to Lawson of April 19.

any previous letter, that I had been tutored this winter in a new
game (to me) which I like very much & which, God willing and
your wife permitting, I propose to teach to both her & you — provided you have been ignorant before. This is "Cribbage". My
wife & myself hammer at it almost daily & we both like it, perhaps
as much as backgammon. — I wrote you two or three scribbles
within the last two weeks, in two of which I covered you articles
for the Whig Review. This is probably the last Letter with which
I shall trouble you before I reach Phila. Tomorrow (Saturday)
the 24 I go to the Court House, and on the first Monday in May
I propose to set off for Charleston. The last of the same week
will probably find me in Phila., where I think it likely I shall
linger a few days, and whence I may write you. — *But of this
delay say nothing unless to your wife.* I shall hope to see Forrest
when in N. Y. as I am anxious to talk with him dramatically.
I should like to get ample material for an article on the drama. —
Did Wetmore write the article in defence of the Mexican War
in the Democratic.[131] Unless that Review is better edited, &
secures a greater number of good contributors, its days are
numbered. It lacks life and character. The South. Lit. Mess. is
also destined to perish. The Editor has been playing a very
childish game with me of which I shall tell you when we meet.
Have you seen Griswold's book — Prose Writers? It has just
reached me, but I have not yet examined it with care, except
so far as to discover that I am no great personage in his eyes.[132]
Well again! I must wait, I suppose.

How does your friend & mine, Labree, come on. Has he dis-
gorged? I hope so, for I shall need all the money I can raise.
Did you get a copy for yourself, of the John Smith, from the
publishers? I trust you did. I am sure the book will take. It has

---

[131] "The Mexican War—Its Origin and Conduct," XX (April, 1847), 291-
299.

[132] The *Southern Patriot* of April 29 contains a notice of Griswold's *Prose
Writers of America.* Simms writes: "To say that it is imperfect, incomplete,
and defective in many respects, is to speak with safety only; to designate any
individual who could have succeeded better, would, at the same time, be very
difficult. . . . Mr. Griswold is clearly not without his partialities, nor is he
superior altogether to antipathies of taste and association. . . . It is in consideration of what he has done, that we are indulgent to our editor in regard to what
still remains for him to do. The prejudices of his New England birth hang
about him, and render it necessary, before he sneers at the few performances
of the South, that he should not exclude from notice what its sons have done,
quite worthy to rank with much, if not most of the material of the present
volume. . . . We are yet constrained to pronounce this volume a highly useful
and interesting one. . . . "

life, spirit, energy and these are the essentials. But no more.
God bless you & yours, & Believe me Ever

As Ever Yours

W. G. S.

374: To WILLIAM HENRY CARPENTER [133]

Woodlands S. C. April 24. [1847] [134]
dear Sir,

You should have come home with me. Letters afford but a
sorry substitute for conversation; and the topics broached between
us, & such as are likely to come up, could be discussed through
no other medium. — You do me but justice in supposing that
I take an interest in your fortunes & labors. Your ballads caught
my eye long ago & led me to inquire after you; and I rejoice to
hear that you meditate collecting them for the public. [135] Not
that I suppose such things can be profitable, in America at least,
and at this early day in our Literature; but they will assuredly
give *you* position, as a writer of exquisite taste, and as an artist
who has studied successfully the happiest forms of expression in
the language. We have had few or no ballad writers in America.
Mr. Longfellow, whose friends insist upon his pretensions in
this respect, lacks utterly that muscle, that bone, sinew & nervous
energy which, with a delightful quaintness constituted the peculiar
characteristic of the English ballad, — a better model, in my
opinion than that of the Spaniard, — though something less romantic. The volume of Pendleton Cooke is full of the true vein,
and is an excellent contribution to our literature. [136] With less
of the artist than Longfellow, he has a far more active & native
fancy, and is better imbued with the spirit of our old time litera-

---

[133] William Henry Carpenter (1813-1899), of Baltimore, novelist, historian,
and editor, was one of the chief contributors to the *Baltimore Literary Monument* (Oct., 1838—Oct., 1839), edited by T. S. Arthur and John N. McJilton,
and with Arthur he edited histories of Connecticut, New Jersey, New York,
Ohio, Pennsylvania, and Vermont. He was also the author of histories of
Tennessee and Massachusetts. Of his novels, *Claiborne* (see note 137, below)
is the best known.

[134] Dated by Simms' reference to his projected trip to New York with a
stopover in Baltimore "during the first week in May." See letter to Lawson
of April 19, 1847.

[135] We have been unable to discover whether such a volume was published.
[136] *Froissart Ballads, and Other Poems* (Philadelphia: Carey and Hart,
1847).

ture. His original ballads have all the characteristics of Froissart, and of the Ballad mongers of his day. If you could send your volume forth as a Christmas Gift, with three of four handsome illustrations, it would be more likely to fire attention and compel the public regard. These adventitious helps are not to be rejected by the author particularly where the obstacles are so great to his simply obtaining a hearing. Your novel of Claiborne & nouvellette of John the Bold have been duly recieved.[137] The latter I had the pleasure of happening upon & reading some time ago; and I then remarked it as a skilful subjection of a difficult passage of history to the purpose of art. I have now read Claiborne, and with a good deal of pleasure. My opinion is that the scheme of the story has been less malleable in your hands than that of John the Bold. In the latter there are fewer impediments to the progress of the story. But if less perfect on the score of compactness, Claiborne exhibits a greater variety of resource & power. Indeed, something of your deficiencies has arisen from the crowded state of your possessions. You have too many persons to manage. You cannot group them into consistent & condensed action. You bring forward too prominently persons who do not help on the action, and several of the early scenes which delay the reader have no obvious connection with the catastrophes. Something of your mistakes has arisen from the *first*. The subject is a difficult one, chosen by patriotism rather than by your judgment. When the action fairly begins you succeed admirably. The latter days & adventures of Rugly are well told. The quarrel between Claiborne & Ingle, brings out the former very happily, & he would have furnished you with a proper hero had he only done anything. But his rebellion seems to have been a madness from the first conducted by some thing less dignified than insanity to its close. But my space allows me no more on this subject, unless to say that your descriptions are good, and your style a little too good for dialogue. In other words, the adoption of the quaint old phraseology — stately & grave, such as suited the mouth of Sydney, was scarcely suitable to the period of which you write and quite unsuited to any but the Cavaliers & Gentry. I shall be happy to recieve any of your future publications. I thank you for your suggestions in the way of topics for my own pen. On this head

---

[137] Carpenter's *Claiborne, the Rebel* was published by E. Ferrett and Co., Philadelphia, in 1845. In the New York *Evening Post* of April 29, 1846, *John the Bold, or the White Hoods* is advertised as published by William Taylor and Co.

I will gladly talk with you when we meet. This may be very shortly, since I hope to be in Baltimore, on my way north, during the first week in May. I shall spend a day in your city & should be glad to meet you. I go to the Exchange.

Yours very truly &c,

Simms.

375: To James Henry Hammond

Woodlands. May 1. [1847] [138]

My dear Hammond

I am really quite sorry that you could not meet me at the village. There was so much to be said and letter writing is such an inadequate substitute for speech. There is no reason, however, why we should not meet in N. Y. I shall go to Charleston on Monday & leave in the Wilmington boat on Tuesday or Wednesday, remain in Phil. & Balt. a few days, then proceed to N. Y. where I shall probably continue till the middle of July. Enquire for me at Harper & Brothers, or Bartlett & Welford's or Wiley & Putnam's. But in the meantime write me to that city, and let me know whether I may hope to see you there or not. Our interviews there would then be untrammelled and *unsuspected*. Some of our friends, I fancy, have been *sounded*. Aldrich tells me that Elmore charged upon us hostilities — was apprised of the contemplated paper, and either had heard or had assumed that the principle by which we were bound together was hostility to him.[139] I am very sure that all of us have been very forbearing and very friendly to him. I don't know any arrangement that would better please me than to put him & yourself in the Senate together. I confess to a really friendly feeling for Elmore, and don't know, indeed, but that this feeling has somewhat modified that hostility to the Bank which has been growing upon me regularly from the moment when you first drew my regards to the subject. I told E. myself that I should be opposed to a Charter, that I looked on the Bank as unconstitutional, and my only

---

[138] Dated by Simms' references to his projected trip to New York and to the plan to publish Tucker's writings. See letter to Hammond of *c.* April 4, 1847. This letter is printed in Odell, "Letters of William Gilmore Simms to James H. Hammond, 1847-1850," pp. 6-9.

[139] See letter to Hammond of Jan. 2, 1847, and following letters to Hammond.

question was that of expediency — in other words how shall we avoid doing mischief.[140] Perhaps, I should have arrived at my conclusions without your aid, if I had not, after my repudiation 20 years ago as a Union man, dismissed as much as possible from my mind the consideration of subjects over which it appeared to me I was destined to have no control. It was then that I first appreciated Mr. Calhoun's powers for evil as well as good.[141] It was then that I first became conscious of the intense passion for the Presidency that has ever since warped his better mind, and baffled his own purposes, realizing for him the description of that vaulting ambition, which Shakspeare tells us, "falls on t'other side." [142] You, perhaps, will not agree with me, but my notion is that, but for the fact that Jackson showed him that V. B. was the heir apparent & said to him in the language of Othello to M. Cassio, "never more be officer of mine" [143] — you never would have heard *from him* of the doctrines of the veto. He has been *nullifying ever since,* and precisely under the same provocation. I have no doubt that Taylor will be elected by acclamation, if nothing untoward should happen. His fortune has been very curious. Chosen, with an *inferior force*—he himself but a Col. to tempt the Mexicans to a commencement of hostilities, he was used in the first instance as a foil to Scott. His successes were fatal to Scott and dangerous to the administration. Scott being no longer to be feared, it was necessary that he should be used against Taylor, and a brilliant affair against San Juan de Ulúa & the Villa Rica was to obscure the impression of Taylor's victories. But the affair of San Juan, though of great & necessary importance, was anything but a brilliant one, and Scott's subsequent penetration of the country, even to the halls of Monte-

---

[140] In reply to this letter, Hammond wrote to Simms on May 15: "There is no quieting the suspicions of intriguing men like Elmore. They always see a thousand times more than is meant or thought of. Hence the impossibility of cordial & confidential operation with them. I like Elmore personally & always have. . . . Yet I could never risk myself wholly on him because he does not believe in *good faith* & cannot conceive of disinterestedness. . . . To organize a clique simply to oppose certain men *whatever they may do,* is perfectly abhorrent to my feelings. . . . " (Original in the Hammond Papers, Library of Congress.)

[141] On May 15 Hammond remarked: "As to Mr. C. our views even of the past do not differ so much as you suppose. Young & blinded as I was in 1830 by party zeal & admiration of him, my present views of his character date also from that period . . . . his ambition has got the better of his patriotism." (Original in the Hammond Papers, Library of Congress.)

[142] *Macbeth,* I, vii, 27-28.

[143] *Othello,* II, iii, 249.

zuma will avail nothing against the man, who, at the very moment when Scott & the administration together had withdrawn from [him] all his regular & favorite troops, leaving him in front of a very subtle & powerful foe, achieves his greatest victory. There is a fate in it which works against the administration — against the existing organization of parties, and for a new organization— in other *words, for us.* Scott will not be permitted to bring the war to a close. This was the reason for putting Benton forward. Scott & Taylor were to win the victories, compel the subjection of the Mexicans, and Benton, at the moment of their humiliation was to interpose and make a Brilliant Bentonion treaty in which the New England and Middle States were to be benefitted by peculiar commercial & trading facilities, and the West by lands, all of which were to be bought, if necessary, out of the common purse. Benton's vanity, as a military man, probably defeated the scheme. He was not content simply to be a civilian, and, except as Lt. Gen. he could not have controlled the military operations which were as necessary to his self-esteem as his negotiations were supposed to be to his hopes. So far, fate favors Taylor. We should not hesitate to support him. He is our instrument no less than Fate's. He will assist in breaking down the System, and in laying a host of selfish greybeards upon the shelf forever. I confess to you that I greatly regret that such is to be the fate of Mr. Calhoun. He would have made a first rate President, with a bold foreign policy which is what we want. Our foreign policy, derived from Washington's time & notions, has always been feeble & purposeless. Jackson did more for it than all the Presidents. As for Taylor's Whiggism, that's all in my eye. The Whigs don't believe him. Besides, what are the substantials? He is a Southron — a slaveholder — a man who has good sense, and if he does not write his own despatches himself has very judiciously chosen the person who does. As was said of Queen Elizabeth, a fool never chooses wise counsellors.[144] He could not if he would forego the free trade policy. He might as a western man, recognize the new definition of the Mississippi valley — might approve of large appropriations for national roads, bridges & ferries. But of the subject of the inland sea something may be said. Some time ago, more than five or six years, I thought I saw in the erection of the town of Natchez into a port of entry, the sur-

---

[144] We have been unable to locate where this proverb was used in connection with Queen Elizabeth.

render of the Mississippi, to this point at least, to the care of the General Govt. The discovery of Atlantic steam navigation may give Silver Bluff & Augusta new privileges at the expense of Savannah, and change the political relations between these regions & the Gov. at Washington. Eh? *Quien Sabe?* But to return. Nothing could be more fatal in the suggestions of Mr. Calhoun, than that the South should take him at his word & organize a party on the slavery question. This would at once force the North to do the same, & then, according to Mr. C's own showing where would we be, with the free States gnawing with such cupidity. As for the idea that there is a considerable body at the North with us on the question of Slavery, this is the absurdest of all. There is not a man, woman or child, who is not against us. The farmers and mechanics are everywhere so — it is only the commercial men engaged in Southern trade who are willing to avoid the subject, but even their opinions are most certainly against us. Force them to take sides in any organization upon the subject & they side against us to a man, however reluctantly. The truth is, the organization of the Democratic party is truly valuable *to us only as a mask for them.* Under this cover they find an excuse for their inactivity on the slavery question. Deprive them of this excuse, and they are as rabid against us as any of the rest. — But if not democrats, we certainly are not *whigs.* But if I mistake not the signs of the times, this is to be the *parole* with Mr. Calhoun's followers. The occasion for the first decisive demonstration will probably be made on the advent of Mr. Webster. *Nous Verrons.* Now, it is better that Taylor should be elected by acclamation than by the Whigs & the Calhoun wing in alliance. Such an alliance would only bind us in subjection for at least two years to a Whig dynasty. But I don't know that we have any need to talk on this subject. We can do nothing and prevent nothing. Will Elmore commit himself in this business? I think not. It will be the process by which to cut Mr. Calhoun off very effectually from any future but that at Fort Hill, but will E. commit such suicide? The close of Taylor's term of four years, will give signal for requisition for new men, and who has sown so heedfully or so judiciously with regard to this very exigency as Elmore? — I tire you, however, and will postpone this topic to your wiser consideration & our better leisure. — I suspect that Judge Tucker's volume is only printed by Carey & Hart, and not *published* in the usual business sense of the word, except among the immediate pupils of the Professor.[145] I have never seen them. You have done right in representing me as willing to do what I can in procuring new editions of his writings. You may repeat the assurance authoritatively, and if the Judge will write me in New York, and find means to send me in that city, the copy of anything he particularly desires to put into print, I will serve him with as much diligence as I would yourself. Let me repeat the counsel, however, which I have already given. Let all these writings be *classed,* and such as are of a sort to permit of this mode of publication, ought to be put forth anonymously. "George Balcombe" by the Judge, was thus published, but his secret was badly kept. I knew it before the work was out of the press. — I don't exactly recollect what I told you touching certain books. Very probably my suggestion was that you should possess yourself by subscribing (they can be got in no other way) to the several *serials* of ancient English literature now in course of publication in England, under the titles of the Camden Society Publications, the Shakspeare Society & the Percy Society. The subscription is £1. *per ann.* to each. $6.50 will probably cover the expense of each year, and the publication runs back five or six years. Say $100.00 for all, already published, & then 3.12. for the annual subs. to the three. There is a copy of Shakspeare in N. Y. (or was) for $20 or $25. which was unique, being one of the best folio editions & containing all the *imputed* plays viz. Locrine. The London Prodigal, Sir Thomas Cromwell, Widow of Watling Street, Sir John Oldcastle &c. which Shakspeare was at one time supposed to have written & which he may have written when a boy. In some of them he certainly had a hand. If you come on to N. Y. I can easily show you these things, or can have them procured & sent you if you desire it. — The letter of W. C. P. does not surprise me.[146] I never did give him the credit of

---

[145] See note 118, *c*. April 4, 1847.

[146] On April 19 Hammond had written to Simms: "I have lately recd a letter from Wm C. Preston—not directly but almost the same thing—wholly disclaiming any connection with the late movement in the Legislature against me—denouncing it as a 'pitiful revenge'—declaring that his counsel was warmly against it, but was rejected. What does all this mean?—Don't speak of it at present. I *am not sure hc tells the truth*—tho' I am sure he said what I have stated." Later, on May 15, Hammond wrote: "I have a second edition of Preston's conversation from the same press. It seems he declared that my course since the rupture with H. was 'wholly unexceptionable'—'indicated the highest sort of courage' and would 'cover a multitude of sins.' This is just what I wished to arrive at. If he, hearing only the statements of my enemies, inclines to think I have made sacrifices enough to atone for my offences, I am encouraged to think that all disinterested persons would be of the same opinion if the

prompting the Columbia movement, for the simple reason that I always thought him too old a stager to commit so rank a folly. Whatever his errors & faults, *he is in position,* and would not be so blind as to peril himself where he could gain nothing in any event and might lose much in your triumph. Perhaps his letter (which I assume to have been intended for your eye) indicates something of the political wind at home. It is certain that *your strength* is acknowledged and fully understood. Whether he tells the truth or not, his letter *being intended for your eye,* indicates a strong *desire that you should suppose he told the truth.* This in other words, exhibits a consciousness that you are able to exert a local influence, to do mischief, to make yourself felt by an enemy who provokes beyond his limit. One thing strikes me as a matter for your consideration. You are disposed, naturally enough, to acquit the tender gender of all participation in this crusade against you. It may be so, yet the report is that H. is engaged to J. M., and these alliances breed strange antipathies as well as sympathies.[147] Besides, duty requires that they should denounce and hate you, if they would be consistent with themselves. It is highly probable that *disappointed* that you should be the first to show signs of relucting & repenting they feel equally the goadings of mortified self-esteem as well as passion. But— God bless and make a good man of you.

Yours &c

W.G.S.

376: To JAMES LAWSON

Philadelphia, Sunday Mg. [May 8, 1847][148]

dear Lawson

I simply write to let you know how near you I am, and to say that I shall most probably be with you on Wednesday next —

---

whole truth were known. I had myself concluded you know that I had made full concession & made up my mind to make no more should another attack come off. . . . I trust I could believe he [Preston] thinks it practicable to close —if not heal—the breach between H. & myself. I am ready." (Originals in the Hammond Papers, Library of Congress.)

147 A political alliance between Col. Wade Hampton and John Laurence Manning (a member of the South Carolina Senate in 1847 and later governor in 1852-1854). The reference is not to a marital alliance, as the words seem to imply.

148 The year is established by the fact that in 1847 Simms started for the North the first week in May. The letter is postmarked May 9, which in 1847 fell on Monday. The envelope bears the stamp of the Jones Hotel.

possibly on Tuesday, if I can get through my business in season
& see the friends that I propose to see. I left Charleston on Thursday afternoon & got here before day this morning. What a seven
hours sleep I have had since. It is now twelve o'clock and I have
just despatched breakfast; but my nerves are scarcely in good
order even for a scribble like this. Tell your wife that I was sad-
dled with another man's woman, on leaving Charleston, who was
old, ugly, had two children & twenty trunks, boxes, bundles,
baskets &c, to take charge of, and I am so thoroughly worn out
with the charge (which, thank heaven is at an end) that I have
an oath in heaven never again to take charge of any woman
unless she be handsome & young & willing to pay for every thing
I do for her *en route,* in just such coin as I most fancy at the
moment. But, I can't write. God bless you all.

W. G. S.

377 : To Rufus Wilmot Griswold

[*c.* May 18, 1847][149]

dear Sir

I have done a portion of the paper on Greene, and will have
all ready in a few days. How shall I send it to you? Will you
do me the favor to see Judge Conrad [150] and say to him what day
you will leave for N. Y. and that you will bring on with you
any packet which he may be disposed to send. Pray, let me beg,
that you will also burden yourself with the books that Mr.
Baird [151] was so good as to promise to put up for me. Should
there be any *new American subject,* which would suit me particularly to review for the South. Quarterly, bring it on for me.
It is possible that Mr. Hart [152] or Mr. Baird may have some M.S.
or packet for my address. I mentioned to H & B. that you were

---

[149] Dated by Simms' letter to Griswold of May 29, in which he says: "I
wrote to you more than ten days ago to apprise you that the article on Greene
was in progress. . . ." For Simms' article on Nathanael Greene and his other
contributions to Griswold's *Washington and the Generals of the American
Revolution,* see letter to Carey & Hart of Aug. 9, 1847.

[150] Robert Taylor Conrad. See introductory sketch.

[151] Henry Carey Baird (1825-1912), grandson of Mathew Carey, entered
his family's firm of Carey and Hart in 1841. When the firm was dissolved
some years later, Baird established a new enterprise, Henry Carey Baird and
Company, which, in 1849, became the first publishing house in America to make
a specialty of books on technical and industrial subjects. In the 1850's he was
a frequent correspondent of Simms.

[152] Abraham Hart.

packing up & might be looked for shortly to begin your task.[153]
— I trust you will succeed in *doing* the book of Laconics.[154] Bring
with you a copy of Godey's forthcoming number which is to
contain a little translation of my daughter from the French.[155]

Yours very truly &c

W. Gilmore Simms

R. W Griswold, Esq.

378: To BENJAMIN FRANKLIN PERRY

New York: May 20. [1847][156]

My dear Perry

In the hurry & confusion of preparing and packing for the
North, and in bestowing the last strokes & touches upon a new
work which has employed the best part of my winter, I am very
much afraid that I suffered your kind letter of March last to
escape my consideration. I have been puzzling my brain to determine whether I answered you or not. I have certainly brooded
over the matter for an answer, and lest I should have been remiss,
I snatch a moment from the troubles and daily annoyance of the
press to put myself *rectus in curia*. I am engaged in printing a Life
of the Chevalier Bayard. This will employ me some five or six

---

[153] Griswold was to start work on a biographical directory to be published
by Harper and Brothers. The project was abandoned in 1849. See Bayless,
Rufus Wilmot Griswold, pp. 201-202.

[154] For Simms' epigrams published in the *Southern Patriot* under the title of
"Wayside Laconics," see note 184, *c*. Oct. 1, 1846. Apparently Simms had
collected these and others and sent Griswold the manuscript in the hope that
he could find a publisher. Griswold probably returned the manuscript to Simms
when he came to New York in June (see letters to Griswold of May 29 and
c. June 8), for on July 25 it was in the hands of Duyckinck, who had been
asked by Simms to offer it to Wiley and Putnam and who apparently had had
as little success as Griswold. On that date Simms wrote to Duyckinck to give
the "Sybillane" (his new title for the volume) to Lawson, and to Lawson to
offer it to Appleton. The volume was finally published as *Egeria: or, Voices
of Thought and Counsel, for the Woods and Wayside* (Philadelphia: E. H.
Butler & Co., 1853). *Egeria* was also published anonymously in installments in
Richards' Weekly Gazette (see note 226, Nov. 24, 1849) during 1849-1850 (see
the review of *Egeria* in *S. L. M.*, XIX [Nov., 1853], 711, and clippings in
the Charles Carroll Simms Collection, South Caroliniana Library).

[155] Augusta's contribution, "translated from the French of Marc Perrin, by
Rose Ashley," is entitled "The Love Test; or, the Sequel of a Passionate
Attachment," XXXIV (June), 298-301.

[156] Dated by Simms' reference to Perry's articles, both unsigned, "The Election of Electors of President and Vice-President of the United States" and
"The Revolutionary History of South-Carolina," *S. Q. R.*, XI (April, 1847),
345-376, 468-485.

weeks. I visit the North this season somewhat in advance of the usual time, in order that I may get back in time for my contemplated trip in the back country. — I note what you say of the Mansion House.[157] My doubt is whether my family would relish remaining at a *public* house during my *absence*. My plan contemplated setting them down in a quiet & secure place under the sanction of some good Hostess, and wandering off on frequent excursions into the surrounding country, for a week perhaps, at a time. The charge of half price for all children, including infant at the breast, I suppose, would also greatly increase the expense of such a residence making it one third more at least than the usual cost at some of the best Georgia villages, Athens for example. My wife reminds me that we called to see a Lady friend who was lodging in Greenville with a private family — with a widow (I believe) whose accommodations were said to be good.[158] If, without too much trouble, you could ascertain something farther in regard to this subject, and let me know what is the best route to Greenville, whether by Columbia or Augusta, and what the expense in a public conveyance thither from Charleston, you will greatly add to previous kindnesses. I have read with pleasure and satisfaction your two contributions to the Southern Quarterly. The paper on the Election of the President, I regard as conclusive. You may remember that I expressed a similar conviction with your own, in a brief report which I made, from the minority of the Comt. on Fed. Relations in our House.[159] I am thinking of a new Edition of my History of South Carolina, in which I propose to incorporate all the matter that can be procured in regard to the up country history.[160] In this work I shall look to you for assistance. Your article on this subject will do good. I am glad that you so properly solved the case of the Cunninghams, and set them right in regard to the

---

[157] The Mansion House was a fashionable resort hotel at Greenville, S. C.

[158] Simms and his wife had visited the Perrys in 1842, and apparently this call was made at that time.

[159] See note 360, Dec. 12, 1845.

[160] The first and second editions of Simms' *History of South Carolina* were published in 1840 and 1842. A third edition did not appear until 1860, published in Charleston by Russell and Jones. Perhaps Perry's lament in "Revolutionary History of South Carolina," *S. Q. R.*, XI (April, 1847), 468, that "in all the histories which have been written of the Revolutionary War in South-Carolina, great injustice is done the upper country, by an entire omission of many a fierce and bloody battle, fought by her gallant sons, in defence of their country, against Indians, Tories, and British soldiers," suggested to Simms the need for a revision of his *History*.

necessity of insisting upon a total separation from Bill, whom they would in vain endeavour to rescue from public odium. Any farther attempt to do so will greatly endanger their own position. I have concluded to wait awhile upon Mr. Ward, before answering his first rude & feeble article. He promises more. Let him exhaust himself. I shall have no difficulty in showing him up as guilty of a wilful and deliberate perversion of my paragraphs.[161] — Do me the favor to present Mrs. S. and myself respectfully & affectionate[ly] to Mrs. P. and her family. Write me soon & believe me, though distant, Very faithfully.

> Your obliged friend & servt.
>
> W. Gilmore Simms

Hon. B. F. Perry.

379: To John Caldwell Calhoun

> New York: May 21. [1847][162]

dear Sir

Your kind & comprehensive letter reached me but a little while before my leaving Carolina for the North, and while I was busy in preparing & packing for the journey, to say nothing of the task of bestowing the last strokes & touches upon a biography of the Chevalier Bayard, the knight *sans peur sans reproche,* upon whom I have been engaged all the winter.[163] My purpose now is not so much to answer as to acknowledge your Letter, and to express the hope that I shall have an opportunity of seeing you at home this summer, and conferring with you in proper person, in regard to those great topices of national & local concern, upon which nobody can so properly or ably discourse as yourself. My visit to the North is some six weeks earlier this season than usual, in order that I may get back to Carolina in due time to give my family the benefit of a summer jaunt among our own mountains. Putting them down in quiet in some healthy neighbourhood, I shall probably ramble into yours, and contemplate a free & frequent conversation with you as one of the rewards of my wanderings. My purpose will be to pick up as much historical

---

161 See letters to Perry of Oct. 30, 1846, and March 10, 1847.
162 Dated by Simms' reference to completing *The Life of the Chevalier Bayard.*
163 We have been unable to locate Calhoun's letter to Simms, also mentioned in Simms' letter to Hammond of March 29, 1847.

material as possible in relation to the events of the revolution in the interior, so that I may make my History of the State more complete, and more satisfactory to the upper country. — My publishers, Harper & Brothers, have just addressed you a Letter in regard to the speeches which you have recently delivered & which they desire to incorporate with the volume already published.[164] I percieve that you are spoken of as engaged upon an analysis of the subject of Government and the Constitution. Such a work would be, indeed, at once the proper base & apex of your fame. In publishing your speeches, it will be well to class them according to their period; — and their applicability & value would be greatly increased to the younger generation, & those yet to follow, if a brief history of the events by which they were provoked, could be made to accompany & illustrate them. I throw out the suggestion with great deference, and simply as one accustomed to the manufacture of books, and not wholly ignorant of the many helps and appliances which our *hurrying* people require, in the attainment & appreciation of their histories. — I suppose that General Taylor, unless he experiences some unlooked for disaster, will be elected by acclamation. The successes of Scott, at Vera Cruz, and his victory at Cerro Gordo, have, in a measure, restored him to a front place among the Whigs, which, without securing their nomination of him, will prompt them to halt too long in regard to Taylor, with whom they have been coquetting. But they are very much bewildered.

> With great respect,
> Yr obt Servt &c

Hon. J. C. Calhoun.   W. Gilmore Simms

380: To Rufus Wilmot Griswold

New York: 29 May. [1847] [165]

My dear Sir

I wrote to you more than ten days ago to apprise you that the article on Greene was in progress and requesting to know

---

[164] In 1843 Harper & Brothers, New York, had published *Speeches of John C. Calhoun. Delivered in the Congress of the United States from 1811 to the Present Time.* Harper's plan to republish this volume with additional speeches was not carried out.

[165] Dated by Simms' reference to his article on Nathanael Greene for Griswold's *Washington and the Generals of the American Revolution.* For Simms' contributions to this volume see letter to Carey & Hart of Aug. 9, 1847.

by what medium I should send it so that no expense should be incurred. It is now ready and if you will just say how it shall be sent you shall have it with all promptitude. I have been looking for you in New York with some solicitude. Do you make any progress with the Laconics?[166] If not, be sure to bring them with you.

Yours truly, &c.

Simms.

R. W. Griswold. L.L.D.

P.S. Who does Moultrie, Sumter, Pickens &c. Can I do a second paper on any of these Southern subjects, in which I am at home?

381: To CAREY AND HART

[c. June 3, 1847][167]

Gent.

Enclosed you have the Biography of Greene, of which I must entreat proof sheets to correct all minor inaccuracies. Your understanding of the arrangement between us touching the work I am to prepare for you is perfectly correct. You will please send me by Mr. Griswold or any other opportunity, the portion of MS. which you have, in order that I may go on with it. I enclose you a little notice of Paulding's plays which I fancy will echo your own opinions.[168]

Yours truly &c

W. G. Simms

Messrs Carey & Hart.

---

166 See note 154, *c.* May 18, 1847.

167 The year is established by Simms' reference to his article on Nathanael Greene (see letter to Griswold of May 29, 1847). If Griswold replied promptly, this letter was probably written about June 3.

168 In his review of James Kirke Paulding's and William Irving Paulding's *American Comedies* (Philadelphia: Carey & Hart, 1847), published in the *Southern Patriot* of May 4, Simms writes: "James K. Paulding is one of our oldest living authors, who enjoys considerable American reputation as a humorist. We have never esteemed him greatly in this character, but have admired him more as a downright sensible writer, hearty, frank and unaffected, with a dash of gentlemanly pleasantry about him which was sometimes laborious and distressing. . . . These pieces may be read as sketches of miscellaneous life cut up into dialogue and unincumbered by description. They are nothing more."

382: To James Henry Hammond

New York: June 4, 1847

My dear Hammond

Since my arrival here I have been so completely overborne by business of several kinds that I have had no time even for the most necessary correspondence. As soon however, as I recieved your Letter I hurried to the store of Bartlett & Welford to secure the copy of Shakspeare which I commended to you, and arrived only a few days too late. The book was gone. I gave them your address with instructions to send you their catalogues. I was called upon by Mr. Allen, your agent's father, and looked in upon his office but without seeing himself.[169] I told the sire that I should be happy to cooperate with him, on your behalf, in any matter in which I might be useful to your interests while I remain in New York. It is scarcely possible that I shall be here beyond the present month as I am anxious to return and remove my family from Charleston to the back country. I shall greatly regret to miss you, as we should enjoy *here* a protracted conversation upon men & things in general, without provoking the peculiar suspicion of one's neighbours — a privilege which is scarcely to be enjoyed in Carolina, where one usually supposes his competitor to be likely to adopt just the sort of policy by which his own game is to be governed. Webster can do nothing for *himself* in the South; but it might very well become a question with some among us whether he might not, upon proper conditions, do something in the East for them.[170] Satisfactory considerations might bring such opposites easily together. The pliancy of Taylor, however, effectually settles the game. Let the old man but get back safe from Mexico (and I think it likely he will soon be on his way home) without any disaster in the meantime, and all the party organization, on both sides of the house, is pretty much knocked into a cocked hat. As for the Demo. Party, it has been doing its best with its subservience to Ritchie & Benton

---

169 On May 15 Hammond had written to Simms: "A. B. Allen of the American Agricultural now published by Harpers is my general agent in New York—buys me books—plows & pumpkin seed." (Original in the Hammond Papers, Library of Congress.)

170 Daniel Webster, at this time United States senator from Massachusetts, was on what Whig journals called his "electioneering journey" in the South. He visited, among other cities, Columbia, Charleston, Augusta, and Savannah. See Claude Moore Fuess, *Daniel Webster* (Boston: Little Brown, and Company, 1930), II, 174-178.

&c. to commit felo de se. Salt cannot save it, — and the simple object now for us — staving off the day of difficulty & gaining time, which is as much in politics as war, — is simply to elect a Southern president. A Southern Whig is a very different animal from the same sort of person in the North. You must not dilate against military glory. War is the greatest element of modern civilization, and our destiny is conquest. Indeed the moment a nation ceases to extend its sway it falls a prey to an inferior but more energetic neighbour. The Mexicans are in the condition of those whom God seeks to destroy having first made mad. They are doing their best to compel us to conquer them. It is now impossible that it should be otherwise. Mark my words — our people will never surrender an inch of soil they have won. They are too certainly of the Anglo Norman breed for that. We will pay for it, perhaps, but only out of the assessed expense & damage of the conquest to us. — I do not hear from Judge T. though I shall be happy to do so, and will cheerfully do all that I can to promote his objects.[171] Let him know that I shall be here in all probability till the 1st. of July. Say to him that prose is more in demand than verse, & historical material more than any other. Essay-writing out of the question, — and every book must be unique — single in its object — compact in arrangement and, if possible, picturesque or suggestive in treatment. I will read his drama [172] with pleasure, and if suitable for the stage & he wishes it, will get Forrest to examine it for that purpose. Still, the Constitutional History which you commend to him would be more likely to attract than any thing he could do. — Your billiard table is an attraction, but I fear I shall have little time next winter to be knocked over & pocketed. I must try on the contrary to do the pocketing myself — must work to make up the deficiency of one of my publishers, by whose failure I am the loser to an amount, which, though small was necessary to my cakes & ale. Besides, I am to deliver an oration before the Literary Societies of Oglethorpe in Novr. & be at Columbia to help Aldrich. For these *lapses* I must make up.— I heard of the arrangement by which Colcock was to succeed Rhett, & though I somehow kick at this mode of disposing of you me & our neighbours, yet I have a friendly feeling for Colcock, and, as I suppose it out of the

---

[171] See letters to Hammond of *c.* April 4 and May 1, 1847.

[172] The MS. of this play, "Viola," was finally sent to Simms in 1849. See letters to Tucker of Sept. 6 and Dec. 17, 1849.

question to think of taking the field myself, prefer him to any other than I can think of.[173] As for myself, I neither occupy such a position, nor am I such a man, as the professional politicians are likely to think of. The people will scarcely insist on me, and the wire-pullers will hardly find me malleable enough for their fingers — but you can advise me of what takes place or is conjectured in relation to this subject. — I am glad for Preston's sake, not to say your own, that he speaks a language you report.[174] I have been long satisfied that your *rôle* was *submission*. It is one of the highest forms of courage, implying moral endurance of the most difficult kind, and a calm resignation to penalties which we have thoughtlessly or wilfully incurred. The world will be the first to affirm the limit to this endurance, if we are not too eager in having it do so. — I met Aiken[175] in N. Y. the other day, and you & this affair were the subject. He resolutely disclaimed all knowledge of particulars, but heard that they were very bad &c. Had been told of letters &c. I said that your friends had earnestly challenged a sight of these letters, but that none had been shown — that you might have erred — must indeed, as your frank avowal had shown — but that your friends were not satisfied that the penalties of error should last till Doomsday. There must be some limit to the punishment. I need not report his talk which you may suppose was inconcievably idle & empty. Certainly, you should desire to heal the breach, but neither you nor your friends *now* can do more than *show* that you are not inaccessible. Patience and shuffle the cards, — make cotton, marl land, play billiards, prove yourself exemplary, — seek not and offend not — continue to write long letters to your friends, full of law & logic if not love, — and I can promise you that all will be hushed into repose and all will come right. You need not bestir yourself at all, and for a couple of years, at least, under present aspects, your friends need make no stir. Let Preston speak to Walker if he will, and the moment that he proposes to do so officially, let Walker be advised to smoke for you the calumet. I cannot say that I see what P's motives for activity may be. I must suppose that they are selfish ones — they can scarcely come from

---

[173] At this time William Ferguson Colcock was speaker of the South Carolina House of Representatives. In 1849 he succeeded Robert Barnwell Rhett as a member of Congress. In the following year Rhett was elected to Calhoun's seat in the United States Senate.

[174] See note 146, May 1, 1847.

[175] William Aiken. See note 326, "Christmas Day," 1846.

H.,[176] unless, discovering that his enormous anger has led to the most enormous & detrimental suspicions, he would now seek, by reconciliation, to satisfy the *outside* world, that if they thought the offense so grievous, they were greatly mistaken. To show that the offense is to be repaired, is to take away all imputation upon the damsel. Do not be too sure of the dislike of H. to M.[177] The very *bruit* of last winter creates a humiliating necessity which may make hate swallow her gorge & stomach the creature it most loathed beca[use] women's necessities, like their moods, are equally capricious & peculiar. — I congratulate you on the cotton prospect. I hear of nothing but trouble at our home. Negroes sick, dying and in the woods — no overseer &c. Give me shortly a long chapter of consolation.

Yours truly &c

Simms

J. H. H.

383: To RUFUS WILMOT GRISWOLD

[*c.* June 8, 1847][178]

dear Sir

I am glad to see that you are at length in New York. I trust to see you frequently in Twelfth St. and shall look in upon you in Bond. I return the sheets of Greene as far as I have recieved them; and will cheerfully undertake Moultrie, if you can provide me from your Library with the vol. of Gallery of National Portraits contg the biography as done by the Dr., — Garden's Octavo of Anecdotes and Moultrie's own history.[179] These will suffice. I

---

176 Col. Wade Hampton. See note 305, Dec. 11, 1846.

177 To Simms' report of a political alliance between Col. Wade Hampton and John Laurence Manning (see letter of May 1), Hammond had replied on May 15: "There is no truth I think in the report you mentioned of the engagement between M & H. They *all hated* him formerly & I doubt not do so still in a degree." (Original in the Hammond Papers, Library of Congress.)

178 Since this letter, addressed to Griswold at 16 Bond Street, New York, bears no postmark, it probably was delivered by hand. It was certainly written after the letter to Carey and Hart of *c.* June 3, which accompanied his manuscript of his article on Greene, and before the letter to Carey and Hart of June 19, which accompanied his article on Moultrie.

179 An unsigned biographical sketch of Moultrie appears in Volume I of James Herring's and J. B. Longacre's *The National Portrait Gallery of Distinguished Americans* (New York: Monson Bancroft, 1834). The volume does not have continuous pagination, but the sketch occupies eight pages and is the sixth in the volume. We have been unable to determine the authorship. The two other works requested by Simms are Alexander Garden, *Anecdotes of the American Revolution* [*Revolutionary War in America*], 2 Series (Charleston: Printed by A. E. Miller, 1822-1828), and William Moultrie, *Memoirs of the American Revolution*, 2 vols. (New York: Printed by D. Longworth, 1802).

have now some of your books which I will leave for you at Harper's or in Bond St. I looked for you at the former place yesterday & the day before, soon after recieving your card.

Yours truly &c

W. Gilmore Simms.

R. W. Griswold Esq.

384: To Rufus Wilmot Griswold

[*c.* June 9, 1847][180]

Dear Sir

When I mentioned that I should want the vol. of Portraits of Americans containing Moultrie, I did not know that it was contained in the vol. that I have. Still, as it is very imperfect, I shall need Garden's vol. & Moultrie's Memoirs, and will despatch the article as soon as I procure them.

Yours truly &c

Simms

385: To Carey and Hart

New York. June 19. 1847

Mess'rs Carey & Hart

Gentlemen.

Accompanying, I send you by mail this day a biographical sketch of the Life & services of General Moultrie, which Mr. Griswold requested me to prepare for your work. I did not see Mr. G. on his arrival in N. Y. and his absence from the city, somewhere up the river, has left it uncertain with me whether you immediately want the article or not. Thinking it highly probable that you do, I have not scrupled to send it by mail. — The next matter to which I invite your attention, you will suppose spoken *sub rosa.* Mr. G. contracted with me to prepare these papers at $25 each. I had supposed this a matter which would concern you, but for a casual remark of your Mr. H.[181] who said that he had expected Mr. G. to do them himself. Now, I

---

[180] This letter, which bears no postmark, was undoubtedly written shortly after that of *c.* June 8.

[181] Abraham Hart.

should be loth to say any thing to him (G) touching the money, unless I knew certainly that he alone was to pay for them. If this be the case let me know. If not, then let me frankly beg you to let me have it; — if not against your rule; — and without regard to the small account you have against me. Let that account lie over until I send you the MS. of the work we wot of. My reason for making this request is this: The failure of the Langleys, the Democratic Review & the Illustrated Magazine, to satisfy certain drafts which I had made upon them, has rendered it necessary that I should appropriate all the money I can conveniently lay hands upon for this purpose. Yours will help me to meet a momentary exigency, and if you can comply with my wishes, you will really oblige me.

> Very truly yours &c
>
> W. Gilmore Simms

386: To Rufus Wilmot Griswold

> June 24 [1847][182]

Dear Sir

The sooner you can procure me the material for the Lee memoir, the better. My candle's brief —

> Very truly Yours &c
>
> Simms

R.W. Griswold, Esq.

387: To Carey and Hart

> New York: July 3. 1847.

Mess'rs Carey & Hart,
    Philadelphia.

Gentlemen.

The Bearer of this, Mr. Montgomery,[183] is a worthy gentleman from Great Britain, whom it will give me great pleasure if you

---

[182] Dated by Simms' request for material for his memoir of Gen. Charles Lee, later published in Griswold's *Washington and the Generals of the American Revolution*. For Simms' contributions to this work, see letter to Carey and Hart of Aug. 9, 1847.

[183] Archibald Montgomery.

will recieve with favor. He has in hand the execution of a literary and publishing commission, which he will unfold to you, and to which he will invite your regards. If he can persuade you to take any interest in his project, it will be a gratification to

Your obt Servt. & friend

W. Gilmore Simms.

P.S. I am on the wing for the South, and shall leave for Charleston, by the Steamer this afternoon. You shall hear from me soon after I reach home.

W. G. S.

388: To James Lawson

Charleston, Tuesday Mg. [July 6, 1847][184]

dear Lawson

We made Charleston Light about midnight last night, and I got home to breakfast by eight this morning. I find all my little family in tolerable health & good spirits. My wife is still thin and feeble, but better than when I left her. Little Mary Lawson is a little palish, but is stout & heavy. Gilmore is a fifty pounder, always on the go — from daylight in the morning about the yard, without shoes, and only the half of a patched straw hat on his cranium. Mr. Roach & the girls are all well. Happy to find all things looking so well here, I look back with a sigh to the dear friends from whom I have just taken my departure. I feel for your family and self as if you were all my own, and the consolations of one home are somewhat dashed on the reflection that I have temporarily lost another. Tell your wife I shall not soon forget the affectionate kindness which on her part & yours has always made me feel that I have brother & sister, though nature has denied me both. We had quite a pleasant voyage, smooth sea & grateful temperature. I now see that the trip can be made from port to port in 48 hours. Another year will probably show this to all parties. Certainly, the thing can be done in smooth weather. If we can muster anything in the shape of

---

[184] The year is established by Simms' reference to his plan to start work on an edition of Shakespeare's apocryphal plays. The edition, entitled *A Supplement to the Plays of William Shakspeare*, was published in New York by George F. Cooledge and Brother in 1848. Simms sailed from Charleston on July 3 (see letter to Carey and Hart of that date), and July 6 is the first Tuesday thereafter.

Carolina vegetables which will be agreeable to you, we shall forward them by the return of the steamer. It may be well that you should enquire at all events, or get Rob. Donaldson to do so. I do not promise you for I know not what there is. —Kiss for me your wife and children. Request Duyckinck to read carefully the proof of the article furnished to Post.[185] —I shall go to work tomorrow on the Shakspeare & other matters without loss of time. But my hands are monstrous full. Once more God bless you & yours. I only write to show where I am & how we are.

Yours faithfully

Simms

J. Lawson Esq.
Beware of the night work.

My wife and Augusta send their love, — with many thanks for the beautiful present to dear little Mary Lawson, from dear little Mary Lawson Senr.

389 : To CAREY AND HART

[July 13, 1847][186]

Mess'rs Carey & Hart.

Gentlemen

Just before leaving New York, Mr. Griswold requested me to prepare & send you, by the earliest opportunity, a memoir of Major Gen. Charles Lee. You have it accordingly herewith. If read carefully by yourself or proofreader, it will not need my correction. I have gone over it carefully in M.S. and a careful printer can send it forth with all requisite corrections.

Yours truly &c

W. Gilmore Simms

Charleston, S. C. July 13.

------

185 "The Pilgrim of Love; or, the Biography of a Troubadour," *Union Magazine of Literature and Art*, I (Oct., 1847), 148-154. Israel Post was the publisher, Mrs. C. M. Kirkland the editor of the magazine. Earlier the tale had been published as "Geoffrey Rudel; the Pilgrim of Love" in *Southern and Western*, I (Jan., 1845), 26-33. It was later included in *Southward Ho!*, pp. 65-79.

186 Dated by Simms' reference to his memoir of Gen. Charles Lee, written for Griswold's *Washington and the Generals of the American Revolution*. For Simms' contributions to this volume, see letter to Carey and Hart of Aug. 9, 1847.

390: To Rufus Wilmot Griswold

Charleston July 15. [1847][187]

dear Sir

I have just forwarded as you requested the biography of Charles Lee to the Publishers, & have begun to institute some inquiries into the career of Gen. Huger and Gen. Pickens. These are the two, if I rightly recollect, to whom you addressed my attention. If others, let me know promptly. I have not the vol. of Washington papers which contains the List of names of Generals, so that if you will give me a list of such as remain undone, in the South, I will instantly detach from them such as lie in my way, and advise you touching the rest. I could wish that [you] would procure for me that number of Longacre's Gallery which contains the Life of Pickens [188] — if a single number can be procured at all. If not, let me know what will be the cost of the whole collection & whether it can be obtained in the unbound issues? — I have been drudging ever since I reached home. Shall drudge still until about the 10th August when I depart for the interior — the mountain country. Let me hear from you therefore with all despatch. Single numbers of the Gallery could be sent by mail. — Say to Saunders that I sent him on last week the proofs of Bayard with a dedication.[189] — Here, every thing is stagnant as usual, but there is a prospect of improvement. A little more infusion of popular energy will be the result of novel necessities which are beginning to press upon our people.

Yours &c. very truly

W. G. Simms.

---

[187] Dated by Simms' reference to his memoir of Gen. Charles Lee. See note 186, above.

[188] James B. Longacre and James Herring, *The National Portrait Gallery of Distinguished Americans,* III (New York: Herman Bancroft, 1836). Each sketch has separate pagination.

[189] The *Literary World,* I (July 31, 1847), 616, announces that *The Life of the Chevalier Bayard* "is rapidly passing through the press." It was, however, not published until much later. The *Literary World,* II (Dec. 11, 1847), 459-460, quotes excerpts from the biography and describes it as "now in press." It is dedicated to John Izard Middleton, of Charleston. For Frederick Saunders, see note 83, Feb. 11, 1845.

391: To James Henry Hammond

Charleston, July 15. 1847

My dear Hammond

I left New York on the 3rd. inst. and arrived here on the 6th; would have written you before, but have been drudging intensely ever since my return — 'closing rivets up' — in other words finishing off labors begun in N. Y. and needing to be finished before I left for the upper country. I shall be here most probably till the 10th or 12th Aug. when I propose to take my folk to the mountain region. My notion is to visit Spartanburg which I have never seen, &, leaving my family there, to push for King's Mountain & other places, gleaning scraps & glimpses for revolutionary & other illustration. I propose to make a book descriptive of Carolina — its history, manners of its people, scenery &c.[190] I looked anxiously while in N. Y. for communications from B. Tucker, and would most cheerfully have contributed to his objects — perhaps could have done much more, in consequence of my experience with publishers, than most of his friends. But, I fancy he has his morbid caprices, — that he is distrustful of new persons, — and probably shares in that prejudice, which, it has always seemed to me, that the Virginians entertain in respect to the Carolinians. I trust, at all events, that, in expressing on my behalf, my readiness to serve him, you did not omit to suggest that my time in New York would be limited. — I read with considerable interest, the sketch which you gave of the interview with Mess'rs Calhoun, McDuffie &c.[191] Of

---

[190] King's Mountain, York County, is the site of a battle fought on Oct. 7, 1780, between the Revolutionary forces under the command of Col. William Campbell and the Loyalists under the command of Col. Patrick Ferguson. This battle is considered the turning point of the Revolution in the South. The proposed volume containing the revolutionary traditions of the South Carolina Up Country was not written.

[191] On June 15 Hammond had written to Simms: "Since I wrote you I went up to see McDuffie & remained there three days on two of which I dined with Calhoun who happened to be in the neighborhood. He seems tamer than I ever saw him & *at the moment* in . . . despair of *ever* being President. He said he stood no chance. 'I don't think you do' said [John] Bones who went up with me. . . . Calhoun looked rather blank at this 'voice from Georgia.' I told him that in case he was not a candidate I preferred Taylor. He said we should not *at present* declare in favour of any man. I approved this & added that nothing would injure Taylor so much as for So Ca to take him up warmly at this time, which I believe. . . . His [McDuffie's] health is about the same as when you saw him. I told him you were to be his biographer & urged him to prepare materials. He seems to think it unnecessary, perhaps unbecoming —that if he had done anything worth recording it would be found out without his aid. I alarmed him on this point a little by hinting to him what you told

the election of Taylor there can be now no question. I almost doubt whether Whigs or Democrats will attempt a nomination. If they do hold a convention for this purpose, we may expect rare outbreaks. The more South Carolina delays in declaring herself in respect to this nomination, the less naturally will be her influence upon his administration. The wisest & best of men will naturally be shy of those who hold themselves aloof while there is a doubt, particularly should they happen to claim the exclusive keeping of the trophies after the triumph is achieved — and this has been very much the game which we have played for 20 years. The administration & Gen. Scott elected Taylor the moment they withdrew from him his regular troops, in the very face of a powerful & active enemy, — precisely as the vote of Mr. Calhoun, recalling Van Buren from England, carried that Gentleman into the Presidential fauteuil; which otherwise, all Gen. Jackson's popularity could never have done. Commend me to the people always for a most glorious sense of what is retributive justice! — I am pained to see what the papers say of McDuffie's situation.[192] Of course, no friend of his could desire to see his life greatly prolonged, when, according to his own acknowledge-ment, its uses are gone, and its sense of satisfaction waning or utterly subdued. But I was in the selfish hope to see him this summer, and to obtain something more from him which could be used as material. I hope still that such will be the case. — From Aldrich I have never a word since leaving home more than 10 weeks ago. He should have written me in regard to all local matters. I infer from some of the toasts in Colleton & Beaufort that Colcock is fairly in the field.[193] I like Colcock very much, and regard him as an amiable & honorable Gentleman; but

---

me Calhoun said to you—not mentioning your name. I did it to shew him how little reliance he could place upon *his friends* taking care of his reputation & to suggest that he would be *overshadowed* & forgotten if he did not give a clue to the chief events of his career. He spoke freely in *responses*—but no con-nected view of his course & acts. I sometimes fancy he may have the weakness to be ashamed of having his parentage brought forward. I never have heard him hint at any event of his life before he came to Augusta in 1806. . . . "
(Original in the Hammond Papers, Library of Congress.)

[192] The Charleston *Courier* of July 16 reports: "We regret to learn from the Abbeville Banner of the 7th instant, that the life of this distinguished statesman [George McDuffie] is at this time very low with a nervous affection, and fears are entertained for his recovery." McDuffie did not die until March 11, 1851.

[193] The Charleston *Mercury* of July 14 reports the Walterboro (Colleton District) celebration; the same paper of July 13 reports the St. Helena's Island (Beaufort District) celebration. But in neither instance are toasts to Colcock mentioned. Perhaps Simms heard of these toasts from some other source.

really, there is such a packing of juries and so much cutting and
drying, carving and apportioning in the politics of some of his
associates that I feel it would be better to have no friendly sympathies if we are to pay for them at the expense of our pride &
independence. There is after all, my dear H., a radical rottenness
in the old borough system, in comparison of which, all its supposed benefits are mere leather & prunella. The effect must always
be the success of the *creature* and in due proportion to his flexi-
bility and deficient character. I cannot but think that you will
before long come to view it with mine eyes. As yet you see it
only through that prescribed medium in which we were all trained,
but from which, our absolute safety seems to require that we
should shake ourselves free. — *You* are quite right to be quiet.
I have no doubt that such is your true policy since character is
always expressive, and will be sought, if stationary, when the
day of exigency arrives. My notion is that the whole policy of
our State must be revised before we can be successful — that our
feelings & opinions are destined to a rapid modification which
alone can save us. I look upon it now, that Mexico is necessary
to the Southern states — that a dissolution of the Union is inevitable —that for twenty years perhaps, Maryland will go with
the South; but that, after that period, she with Virginia and
the states south of her including the Carolinas & Georgia will
have incorporated among themselves new interests, which will
greatly change their characteristics. *At all events, the slave interest must be held intact without reference to the soil upon which
it happens to labor now.* Remember that! It is one inevitable
necessity with slavery that it must accommodate its habitation
to its profits — in other words that slave labor will only be continued where it yields an adequate profit. Slavery will be the
medium & great agent for rescuing and recovering to freedom
and civilization all the vast tracts of Texas, Mexico &c., and our
sons ought to be fitted out as fast as they are ready to take the
field, with an adequate provision in slaves, and find their way
in the yet unopened regions. The interest is one which must be
maintained without reference to places. In that is its hope. All
the Wilmot Provisos in the world will never keep us from the
possession of our Mexican conquests whenever we desire to use
them; and the necessity for the conquest which every politician
must now acknowledge declares the time at hand which Providence has appointed for their use. It is a coincidence of no small

signification, that these fields should be laid open to us, just at the time when our institutions, diminishing in their profits in the worn out states, are assailed by cupidity & fanaticism at home & abroad. The acquisition of Texas and Mexico secures the perpetuation of slavery for the next thousand years. But I began this letter only to say where I was, & to add that I was so wretchedly busy that you must not expect frequent or long letters from me. I have illustrated this necessity very happily. Write me soon & let me know the news. I have pretty well abandoned all notion of political life. Our people have shown me how well they can do without such poor help as mine, and I would not be intrusive. Let me hear from you at length. We may so arrange it as to meet this summer[.]

[*Signature cut.*]

J H Hammond Esq

392: To Benjamin Franklin Perry

Charleston July 15. [1847][194]

My dear Perry.

My wife has decided to take her course for Spartanburg during the present season, though I propose to visit Greenville, and she will probably do the same. I am not unwilling to give Spartanburg the preference for two reasons; — one is that I have never been there, and the other is that it lies more conveniently proximate to King's Mountain, Cowpens [195] and other places of historical interest which I propose to visit. I could wish to have you as a companion in some of those snatches of wandering which, at this moment, possess my mind with a vague idea of pleasure & instruction. You could greatly assist me with your knowledge of the country, the people & their traditions. At all events, I must put you in train for finding out the secrets of your mountain prison house, as I contemplate coining a volume out of my wanderings. — I left New York on the 3d. inst. and escaped the glorifications of the 4th. Mr. Polk provoked no enthusiasm. Gen. Taylor, I suspect, will sweep the East as certainly as the West. His successes in Mexico are exceedingly fortunate things for us,

---

[194] Dated by Simms' reference to Ward's second article attacking Simms, published in *S. L. M.*, XIII (July, 1847), 422-428. See letter to Hammond of Jan. 25, 1847, and following letters to Hammond.

[195] Cowpens is the site of a battle on Jan. 17, 1781, between the Revolutionary forces under Gen. Daniel Morgan and the British under Col. Banastre Tarleton.

in securing us a Southern President. This staves off the evil day
of abolitionism. Taylor is a fortunate event for us. — I suppose
you have seen the second and concluding portion of Mr. Ward's
answer to my strictures in the Messenger. I scarcely know
whether to answer it or not. It will be very easy to do so. His
certificates amount to nothing, and prove & disprove nothing
vital to the issue. His extracts from my papers are wretchedly
garbled & dishonest, and his flings and sneers at myself are such
really childish matters that I should be loth to have it thought
they provoked my consideration. Let me know what you think
of the matter. — As for the Messenger itself, I have resolved to
have nothing more to do with it. The Editor is scarcely wise
enough for his own interest. I sent him an article, the very sort
of thing for a magazine, embodying the tradition which, in the
South, insists upon identifying Ney & Rudolph. The foolish fellow
couples its publication with a sneering note, thus really crying
'stinking fish' to his own customers & in regard to his own com-
modities.[196] — I should like to add a few chapters to my history
of South Carolina so as to do justice to the upper country, but
the truth is that our people do not seem to care a straw whether
they had ancestors or not. The work will not pay for any labor
bestowed upon it, and has not paid me as much money as I have
realized in one weeks labour, writing stories! Nevertheless, if
you could give me a few heads of topics—note what were the
characteristics of the districts before & during the Revolution,
who were the leading men, what they did, what sides they took,
and what were the actions & events of importance, — I should
be greatly indebted to you. You must already have no small body
of material on hand. — I shall not be able to leave this city until
about the 12th August. I am now busy in editing the half dozen
plays which have been imputed to Shakspeare — tedious labour,
which with some others of more pleasurable performance, will keep
me occupied till that time. I have just finished running through
the press a memoir of the Chevalier Bayard, and should greatly
like, if the material could be procured to do one of Sumter &
Pickens.[197] — My wife joins me in affectionate respect to Mrs.
P. her mother & sisters. We shall be pleased to renew an acquaint-

---

[196] See note 65, March 2, 1847.

[197] Simms did not carry out his plans for biographies of Sumter and Pickens.

ance with them this summer. — Let me hear from you at your earliest leisure, & believe me

Very truly Your friend &c

W. Gilmore Simms.

Hon. B. F. Perry.

393 : To RICHARD YEADON

Wednesday Noon, [July, 1847?][198]

Dear Yeadon:

Assuming that your invitation is for 4 o'clock P. M. and not for 4 o'clock A. M., you may certainly expect me (D. V.) but, if you purpose any great moral or social reform, and you really desire to see your guests at the early hour which you name, I fear I must equally disappoint you and myself. I don't think I can be up and about at that early hour, and unless I take a lanthorn, doubt if I should find my way in the dark. There may be a moon at that hour, that morning, but I don't know; and I expect that the lamps of the economical Gas Company will all be blinking wofully. If then, you mean to compel your friends to adopt a new habit of early rising, let me know. In that event, pray let me know also, what order do you take for breakfast? When will you have supper? But, after all, it may be a slip of the pen and you really meant P. M. where you wrote A. M.; and have no design upon the peaceful slumbers of your friend, etc.

W. Gilmore Simms.

394: To EVERT AUGUSTUS DUYCKINCK

Charleston July 25. [1847][199]

My dear Duyckinck

I have been so exceedingly busy since reaching home that I have scarcely been able to think of friends & correspondents, and though busy, indeed, have certainly not been prepared with any

---

[198] We are unable to locate the original of this letter, published in the *News and Courier* (Charleston, S. C.) of March 28, 1937. At that time it was described as being in a "local library" at Pinopolis, S. C. We have dated it 1847, the earliest possible date, since the Gas Light Company was established early that year (see the *South Carolinian* [Columbia] of Feb. 17, 1847).

[199] Dated by Simms' reference to his work on editing the apocryphal plays of Shakespeare. See letter to Lawson of July 6, 1847, and following letters.

thing to say to them which would be worth their hearing. To you in especial, while I could have spoken much I have found nothing to write, and should scarcely trouble you now with a scrawl but that I have a word from Mr. Webber which I trust you will find it pleasant to communicate. The article which he sent to the Sou. Quarterly has been accepted & will appear in the Oct. No. when the publishers will pay him for it.[200] The Editor with whom I have spoken freely with regard to the abilities & necessities of W. is prepared to serve him as far as possible. He tells me in a note just recieved — "Whatever it is in my power to do for him through the Review I shall be most happy to do." The compensation is $1.00 a page. The publishers are sound but costive, sound perhaps, because they are costive. The Editor of the Review spoke of you very handsomely, and observed that there was a prodigious difference between the Lit World, since you left it.[201] Mr Russell, the Bookseller said the same thing, and remarked to me that this was the general sentiment. I do not hear anything from W & P. touching the scheme of the vol. of Poems, and in relation to the Sybillane. Will you oblige me by ascertaining their ultimatum, and, in the event of their declining, taking charge of the M.S. and pictures. The former you will place in the hands of Lawson to whom I will write in relation to it. The latter you will please retain for the present. I shall write also to Mr. Richards.[202] I have written two biographical sketches since reaching home and one story, each averaging 25 foolscap pages.[203] My correspondence has also called for some of my time if it has taxed little of my thought; and I have spent many tedious hours, — day & night in revising imputed plays of Shakspeare, a wearisome task which I am almost sorry to

---

[200] Charles W. Webber, "The Quadrupeds of North America," *S. Q. R.,* XII (Oct., 1847), 273-306. Charles Wilkins Webber (1819-1856), author, journalist, explorer, and naturalist, was a native of Kentucky. In 1847 he was living in New York City and was a frequent contributor to such periodicals as the *Literary World, Graham's,* the *Democratic Review,* and the *American [Whig] Review.*

[201] Duyckinck left the *Literary World* with the issue of April 24, 1847. See note 34, Feb. 2, 1847.

[202] The planned volume of poems is probably that described in the letter to Street of Jan. 15, 1847. For the "Sybillane," see note 154, *c.* May 18, 1847. Apparently Simms planned to have one or both of these volumes illustrated by his friend T. Addison Richards.

[203] The two biographies are those of Charles Cotesworth Pinckney and Isaac Huger for Griswold's *Washington and the Generals of the American Revolution* (see letters to Lawson and to Carey and Hart of July 25, 1847). The story is "Love's Last Supper" (see letter to Lawson of Sept. 5, 1847).

have undertaken. These and other labors will delay my departure to the interior until about the 10th. of August, leaving me ample time to hear from you & other friends in N. Y. if you write promptly. W & P. said nothing to me of a nature calculated to persuade me that they desired my book about the South.[204] Do they say any thing to you? Let me hear from you soon & give me a chart of the literary country. Here, you are aware, we have nothing. Present me to Mathews & the rest, & believe me very truly Yours &c.

W. Gilmore Simms

P. S. Remind W & P. when V & R's are ready, to forward two or three copies of both series done up together.[205] I wish one copy for the Quarterly and one or two more for newspapers, besides a copy for myself & one for the person to whom the work is inscribed.

Will you see Post touching pay for our 'Pilgrim', and when paid, pass the money into the hands of our friend Lawson. Ascertain from Post whether our letters from the South would suit him.[206] I have ordered the back reviews [207] to be sent you. Advise me if you have recieved them and what nos. are yet wanting.

395: To JAMES LAWSON

Charleston July 25. [1847][208]

dear Lawson

I unadvisedly wrote you to look out for certain good things on board the Southerner, without first being sure that I could send you such a rarity through that medium as would justify the very heavy charges of shipment; but I found our fruits of every kind so inferior, in consequence of heavy & daily rains, & the expense of freight by the Steamer so great, that I concluded

---

[204] See note 58, Feb. 25, 1847.

[205] *Views and Reviews*, Second Series, was issued separately as well as bound with the First Series. For its date of publication, see note 38, Feb. 2, 1847. The First Series is dedicated to Dr. Eli Geddings (see introductory sketch); the Second Series does not carry a dedication.

[206] Simms is here speaking of the series of letters from the South describing "our mountain scenery & . . . mountain traditions" which he had proposed writing to Duyckinck for publication in the *Literary World*. See letter to Duyckinck of March 25, 1847.

[207] Issues of the *Southern Quarterly Review*.

[208] Dated by Simms' reference to his work on an edition of the apocryphal plays of Shakespeare. See letter to Lawson of July 6, 1847, and following letters.

to abandon the purpose for the present. Besides, it has scarcely been possible for me to go forth since I have reached home. The rain storms are incessant — daily in fact, and the waters come down like an avalanche at the most unexpected moments. I have been very busy since reaching home, having succeeded, by incessant toil in doing *two* of the imputed plays for the Brothers Cooledge, and a few other small matters. I wish you would visit these Gentn. and ask to look at the condition of the MS. which I have sent them. You will then be better able to form a judgment of the labor it has cost me, and of the value of the service. I find that it takes me very nearly a week to do a play. I have in *two* days written two biographies, and in *two* more written a story which I will either send to Godey, or to the publishers of the Union Magazine, through your charge.[209] I shall certainly send you something which will enable you to secure the payment for the contribution sent through Duyckinck, and which ought to be paid for soon after being published.[210] I have written to D. to request that if W & P. do not desire my "Sybillane" or vol. of Laconics, that he will procure the MS. and place it in your hands.[211] This done, you will please alter the title to Sybillane &c and see if you can negotiate its publication with the Appletons. For $100 they can have an Edit. of 2000 copies — make any bargain you think proper but do not part with the copy right. The proof sheets to be sent to me. The next sheet is for your wife. Write me promptly & I shall recieve your answer before leaving for the interior.

Yours Ever as Ever

Simms

J. L.

396: To Carey and Hart

[July 25, 1847][212]

Messrs Carey & Hart.

Gentlemen

I cover to you a memoir of General Charles Cotesworth Pinckney — another of the subjects, in the South, which Mr. Griswold

---

209 See note 203, July 25, 1847.
210 "The Pilgrim of Love." See note 185, July 6, 1847.
211 See notes 154, *c.* May 18, 1847, and 202, July 25, 1847.
212 Dated by Simms' references to his memoirs of Pinckney, Huger, and Lee for Griswold's *Washington and the Generals of the American Revolution.* For Simms' contributions to this volume, see letter to Carey and Hart of Aug. 9, 1847.

desired that I should take charge of. In procuring materials for a life of Brigadier General Huger, I learn that there is an excellent portrait in the family, and would like to know whether it is desirable that you should have the use of it. I can procure it, and it will certainly contribute to the more unique & perfect character of your work. Perhaps, a daguerreotype made from it will answer all your purposes. Let me hear from you soon, and believe me

Very truly yours.

W. Gilmore Simms
July 25.

Have you recieved my biography of Charles Lee?

397: To JAMES LAWSON

Charleston July 31 [1847][213]

dear Lawson

Your letter fills me with all sorts of disquiet & vexation. That we should a second time swarm your house with searoaches, is certainly a most annoying conviction to us, as it will be a monstrous nuisance with you. My wife is greatly troubled at the intelligence and the concern spreads through the household. We can only hope that you will be enabled to put them to death, pursuing them and crushing them in all their crevices. — As for the rice, — do not let any dread of weavels afflict you. The rice is fresh, of the latest raising & just from the mill. All grain is more or less troubled with a small insect like that of which you may have seen something in the rice. Your cook could easily cleanse it at each washing, more easily than any other grain. Rice is less destructible than other grains by insects. It is the hardest & heaviest of grains, quite too flinty for the ordinary insect to penetrate. We can answer for what is sent you, that it is superior in freshness and, perhaps, quality, to any you can buy in New York market. — It is in the power of Stringer to get the money from Labree if he chooses, and he promised me that he would. B. & S. owe him money, and you have the proof in your hands that Labree acknowledges his indebtedness. With respects to the

---

[213] Dated by Simms' reference to his work on an edition of the apocryphal plays of Shakespeare. See letter to Lawson of July 6, 1847, and following letters.

Editor of the Democratic Review, pray see & assure him that he labors under some mistake. *While publishing the Sonnets, one by one,* the draft was frequently presented, and payment as frequently promised, — if we are to believe the assurances of Bartlett & Welford. Besides, it may be well to remind Mr. K. that the simple fact that they came to him with the office, does not impair my right of property. He continued to publish them while this right was brought to his frequent attention, and they served him in his publication, subsequently to Mr. O'Sullivan's departure from the work. Mr. O'S. never published any of them, and will tell him that he never paid for any of them.[214] Now, if Mr. K. used them, and I was unpaid, surely the simple fact that I communicated them just before he bought O'S. rather confirms my claim on the publication than disavows it. He cannot seriously assert the contrary. The brief state of the case, is that he alone has used my wares, and I have never been paid for them. Show him this, and I am persuaded he will see that he cannot with any propriety refuse to recognize the claim. But, to deal with him liberally, I left other things for him to be rendered him without charge, provided he satisfied the draft. An article I left with him when his clerk promised us the back volumes, has just appeared yet we hear nothing of the volumes.[215] They were to have been sent on nearly two months ago, while I was in N. Y. — I have been so busily engaged on the Shakspeare plays as not to have been able to do much, if any thing else. I have written a story, a biography rather, and a very romantic one — the work of a day only — which I designed to copy out for you to offer to Post,[216] provided he paid for the previous contribution.[217] Will you write & say whether the article appears, & whether he has paid it. The Mage. was to have been sent me, but has not been recieved. If he lacks an agent in Charleston, let him send to John Russell. At all events, send my copy to Russell's care. Duyckinck writes me that he has not been able from hot weather & press of engagements to get round to see you — and regrets it. He

---

[214] For Simms' sonnets published in the *Democratic Review* in 1846-1847, see note 23, Jan. 10, 1846, and note 48, Feb. 9, 1846. Thomas Prentice Kettell had succeeded J. L. O'Sullivan as editor of the *Democratic Review* early in 1846. He continued as editor until 1852.

[215] "Stanzas," signed "Werner," though indexed as by "the author of The Yemassee," appears in the *Dem. Rev.*, XX (July, 1847), 32.

[216] "Love's Last Supper" was eventually submitted to Robert T. Conrad of *Graham's.* See note 237, Sept. 5, 1847.

[217] "The Pilgrim of Love" was published by Post in the Oct. issue of the *Union Magazine.* See note 185, July 6, 1847.

speaks of you very kindly. Pray write to me immediately on the reciept of this, and I shall probably recieve it before I leave the city. It is impossible for me to get off before the 9th August. My engagements fetter me at least one week longer. I shall at the close of that week have finished all the plays but two. My anxiety to get them done arose from the fact that unless I had done so I should have been compelled to carry a squad of cumbrous volumes about with me. I hope as soon as I reach our point of destination to sit down to *the Tragedy*.[218] — But though drudging very hard, I have a renewal of domestic cares. Gilmore is quite puny, with loss of appetite & a cough; and little Mary Lawson is teething & very fretful, with occasional fever & looseness of bowels. We hope to get away from the city soon enough for their improvement. I trust you will see the Mess'rs Cooledge, and look at the revised plays I have sent them. You will see a toil which will frighten you. It has been pretty hard work with me to do an act a day, and one of the plays consumed a full week. — Your letter affords no news. I hear something of a strife between Mathews & Briggs in the Mirror.[219] Is this so? — Has Wetmore said anything to you anent our correspondence? Strange, that he should have gone out of town while in the reciept of my letter saying I should come & see him, without letting me know that he was going.[220] But, after I called, he was in town, — to meet Mr. Polk! — Yet he never looked in at 12th Street. Tell Mrs. Forrest that I have just opened *"Consuelo"* but shall read in the country.[221] What has Forrest to say touching the play. How comes on the house — the castle? — If you have got from W & P. the M.S. of "Sybillane" lay it up in lavender, till I see you or advise you further — i. e. assuming that you have done nothing with it as yet. — And how is our dear little Lady wife & mother. She has doubtless forgotten me, and all her regards for me long ere this. But, say to her that ten to one she sees

---

[218] *Norman Maurice; or, the Man of the People,* written for but never produced by Edwin Forrest, was published in *S. L. M.,* XVII (April, May, June, July, and Aug., 1851), 193-199, 281-289, 339-344, 410-415, 467-472. John R. Thompson, editor of the *Messenger,* also issued an edition in book form, dated 1851.

[219] We have not had access to a complete file of the New York *Evening Mirror* for this period. Nothing about the strife of Mathews and Briggs appears in the issues we have examined.

[220] We have been unable to locate Simms' letter to Prosper M. Wetmore, written during Simms' visit to New York City in May-July, 1847.

[221] Probably Catherine Sinclair Forrest had presented Simms with a copy of Francis G. Shaw's translation of George Sand's *Consuelo,* which had been published in Jan., 1847. See the *Literary World,* I (Feb. 13, 1847), 42.

me this winter when she least expects it, — and we will walk into the Bowery together, if she pleases. Kiss her on my account, and bestow a similar favor on the girls. As for Jim, say to him that Gilly sends him a hug, a genuine bruin's embrace, for which he will be properly grateful. But the night wanes to the short hours. The house is still, and I feel myself disposed to whisper as I write. God bless you & yours for Ever.

Yours Ever

W. G. S.

398: To CAREY AND HART

[August 5, 1847]

Mess'rs Carey & Hart

Gentn.

Yesterday I sent you a memoir of General Sumter for your biographical collection. Today I cover to you one of Kosciuszko for the same publication. If carefully read, there will be no need to send me any proofs of these sketches. If any thing doubtful occurs in the way of your usual proof reader, the sheet containing the difficulty may be sent to Mr. Griswold.

Yours truly &c

W. Gilmore Simms

5th. August 1847

399: To CAREY AND HART [222]

[August 9, 1847]

Messrs Carey & Hart

Gentlemen

Enclosed I send you a biographical sketch of the Life and Services of Brigadier General Isaac Huger of the Revolution. This is the last of the sketches which I promised Mr. Griswold to prepare. I have now sent you sketches of Genl. C. Lee, C. C. Pinckney, C. Gadsden, T. Sumter, Huger, and Kosciuszko, — since leaving New York; and, before that time, — of Greene &

---

[222] This letter is reproduced in facsimile in Alexander Cowie's edition of *The Yemassee* (New York: American Book Company, [1937]), facing p. 52.

Moultrie.[223] These papers will not need my revision, if the most ordinary attention is paid to the M.S. by the proof-reader. Should it be desirable to address me, during the next two months, I shall be heard of at "Spartanburgh (C. H.) South Carolina."

Very truly yours &c

W. Gilmore Simms.

Charleston, Augt. 9. 1847

400: To James Henry Hammond

Spartanburg C. H. August 21. [1847][224]

dear Hammond

Just as I was about to enter the cars on Wednesday morning, my boy brought me your letter apprising me that you would be in Charleston on Tuesday night. I presume you were there even then. Looking for you to reach town daily, & being exceedingly pressed with toils which I was anxious to dismiss from my hands before going into the Country, I suffered your preceding letter to lie unanswered. There was so much in it that could be scarcely answered in a letter that I felt disposed to wait for a personal opportunity. Your epistle is not now before me, & I can only glance at a few of its topics — that, too, very imperfectly. You were in one of your worst moods certainly when you wrote me. Despondency to a warm & impatient spirit, is as natural as the clouds which gather about & temporarily shroud the face of the sun in summer. It is the creature of the nature which it seems to oppress, but which it somewhat relieves and repairs. It is not often that I suffer myself to write to a friend when I suffer from this influence, nor would I have you do so. We seldom declare ourselves under such influences — we only show the depth, the dark & the dimensions of our cloud. In your case which has been one of a trial, of the severity of which I am fully sensible, I think the worst is over, and that the course is simply to continue as you have begun, bearing patiently and in silence the evil

---

[223] These sketches are included in Rufus W. Griswold's *Washington and the Generals of the American Revolution,* 2 vols. (Philadelphia: Carey & Hart, 1847).

[224] Dated by Hammond's letter to Simms of Aug. 7, 1847, in which he writes: "I expect to reach Charleston in the cars on Tuesday & shall put up at the Charleston Hotel. If you are still in Town do come round & see me. I propose to remain one day & go on the Wilmington Boat on Wednesday evening." (Original in the Hammond Papers, Library of Congress.)

which is difficult to say in what manner you should oppose. I
think it very probable that Beverley Tucker has heard something
to your disparagement — possibly, the worst story among the
many which have been told to your discredit.[225] You can scarcely
blame him if he has believed it, considering the many apparently
valid sources from which he may have derived it. What then?
Your patience is still the only remedy, and it is finally sovereign.
I am very sure that in a few years, less than two perhaps — the
progress of events will make all parties anxious to forget that
you have been a wrong doer. I saw Col. Lewis [226] on the cars
while on my way to Columbia. His language was to the same
effect. He spoke of you with great kindness. The Columbia influence is declining, according to his notions, and with a shrewd
political glance ahead, which I hardly looked for at his hands —
he predicted the demand for your services before long — a demand
which, more than anything else, would put you *rectus in curia*.
I have been speaking with Dawkins & Henry [227] in this place
with regard to you, and it is apparent to me that the only thing
that disturbs them, in regard to you, is a secret doubt how far
you are destined to interfere with Butler's reelection.[228] They did
not say this openly, but I could not forbear inferring it from
their *indirections*. It was clear to me that you did not suffer in
their regards from any excess of sympathy which they felt for
any Columbian. — In a few days I shall go over to Glenn's
Springs where I shall probably see many persons with whom I
may speak of the *future* of our State.[229] I will try to sound, as

225 On July 23 Hammond had written: "I don't know what has become of
Tucker. I have not heard from him since I wrote him that you were in N. Y.
& formally in your name offered him your services. I pressed him I fear
too far to write on our Constitution & publish *at my expense*. His proud
nature recoiled. Or it may be some of my enemies have poisoned his ear."
(Original in the Hammond Papers, Library of Congress.)
     226 William L. Lewis. See note 112, Feb. 25, 1845.
     227 Probably Thomas N. Dawkins (1806-1870), of Unionville (now Union),
and James Edward Henry (1796-1850), of Spartanburg. Earlier Henry had
contributed "Tales of the Packolette" to the *Magnolia,* and his work, together
with Simms' "Loves of the Driver," had been attacked by a correspondent
signing himself "A Puritan" (see note 76, Aug. 2, 1841). In 1847 Henry was
a member of the South Carolina House of Representatives. Simms and Henry
had served together in 1844 on the House Committee on Federal Relations.
     228 At this time A. P. Butler was in the United States Senate. He was
re-elected in 1848.
     229 In "Summer Travel in the South," *S. Q. R.,* N. S., II (Sept., 1850), 52,
Simms writes of Glenn's Springs (now Glenn Springs), located between Spartanburg and Unionville (now Union): "On your route, you pause at Glenn's
Springs, one of the most fashionable of the watering places of South-Carolina.
. . . At Glenn's Springs you will make the acquaintance of the gentry of the

a matter of course, in reference to yourself. I am deeply interested that your punishment should not be prolonged beyond the period of your atonement. You will have had far better voyaging to the North than we have had into the interior. Vexatious delays, petty pecuniary exactions, bad food, unclean beds, and the upsetting of the carriage in which were my women & children have fully sufficed to show me how impossible to hope, while this condition of things continues, to change the direction of our travel from the North to the South. Yet hundreds who go North would not prefer to do so. I am busy every day with certain tasks which I have brought with me. I write my Letters after being jaded with the labors of the morning. You must read them with indulgence. When I have anything to write you, I will not suffer delay. My scrawl now is simply to assure you that I am still your friend as ever

Simms.

401: To JAMES LAWSON

Spartanburg, S. C. Sep. 5. [1847][230]
dear Lawson

I am here at the foot of the mountains rusticating, and at my desk once more. For the last four weeks, I have been upon the road, idle or dissipating. We have had a pretty severe journey, the weather being bad, the roads in horrible condition, and we travelling in stages. One of our vehicles in which were my wife, Augusta, and a female relative of my wife (Mrs. Steele) [231] with the nurse & little Mary Lawson, was upset. I was ahead with Gilmore & Mr. Steele, in another stage, when we were apprised of the accident, but without being informed whether any one was hurt or not. You may judge of my feelings while I hurried back, nearly a mile, to the scene of disaster. There was some thing of a wreck. The whole top of our vehicle was smashed and dear little Mary Lawson had the narrowest escape. She was

---

middle and upper country generally, with a slight sprinkling of others from the seaboard. The former are here in considerable numbers throughout the season. You will find them equally courteous, intelligent and frank; easy in their manners, and prompt and graceful in their hospitalities."

[230] Dated by Simms' visit to the South Carolina Up Country in the summer of 1847.

[231] Eliza Russell Headly Steele, the English wife of William Govan Steele. Steele, uncle of Mary, Chevillette, and Washington Steele, was a cousin of Mrs. Simms.

thrown out of her mother's arms, completely through the window
of the stage, and lay just between the wheels. A single movement of the horses would have crushed her. Fortunately, they
were quite gentle, and the innocent thing got off with a few
slight bruises of the leg and arms. We were three days upon
the road, after leaving Columbia and the railway, and at length
reached the district (county) town of Spartanburg. Here we
remained a week while the family recruited. From this place we
set off to a fashionable watering place, called Glenn's Springs,
12 miles distant, where we have been wasting in idlesse the last
10 days. At this place, the mineral waters of which are very
popular, we found on an average some 200 persons, the most
fashionable & pleasant people of our interior & mountain
country.[232] Here we rode, and sang & danced, daily & nightly. I
wished sincerely that our good wife & mother, Lady Lyde, had
been with us to enjoy the frolicking a little. I promise her a
description some of these days. *You* would have been particularly
pleased with one of the party, Miss Martha Calhoun, a niece of
John C. Calhoun, who is a great musical genius. Her ear is
said to be exquisite. She composes waltzes & pieces, extempore,
some of which have been recently published. She has promised me
copies which I will send you. From Glenn's we returned to Spartanburg, from which place we have retired to a lovely farmhouse,
about four miles distant from the village, from which place I
now address you.[233] Here we propose to linger for a few weeks,
and here I hope to finish the play for Forrest, of which I have
sent him one act already.[234] — I have sent to Cooledge's all the
Dramas but one (Locrine) the analysis & correction of which I
shall have to delay — wanting certain books in my Library.[235] If
Post does not publish promptly, withdraw the article from him and
either send it to Godey, or sell it to any publisher who will give

---

[232] The Charleston *Courier* of Aug. 27, 1847, contains a letter from Richard
Yeadon, written from the resort: "Among the *distingues* now here are the
Hon. John M. Felder, the Hon. Wm T. Nuckolls and family, the Hon. F. W.
Pickens and family, the lady, two sons and niece of Hon. John C. Calhoun,
Hon. Jas. Gregg and family; Professor Twiss and family and Wm. G. Simms
and family. Gov. Johnson and Chancellor Harper with their families, are
expected . . . and the Hon. W. C. Preston and lady are expected to return. . . ."

[233] This house, still standing at what is known as Foster's Cross Roads, was
the home of Andrew Jackson Daniel, who later named a son for Simms.

[234] *Norman Maurice; or, the Man of the People.*

[235] For *A Supplement to the Plays of William Shakspeare,* see note 184,
July 6, 1847.

you $25 (cash) for it.[236] It is worth more. I had another paper of the same kind which I should have sent him, but Conrad tells me he will take it for Graham — to whom I will forward it in a few days.[237] Conrad will also take my dramatic poem of 'Arnold', & publish it in successive parts or chapters.[238] He writes me that the next number of Graham will contain my 'Ode to Time', which I sent him for $20.[239] The Cooledges write me that they are quite pleased with what I have done for them in regard to the Dramas. From Duyckinck I hear little — from Mathews nothing. It does not appear that the 2 Vol. of Views & Reviews has been published by W & P. and they decline the 'Illustrated Vol. of Poems.' [240] But this I do not regret. The time is coming when I shall make better terms for it. I suppose, though of this I hear nothing, that Bayard will shortly be forthcoming. I wish you would procure a draft on some Bank in Charleston, for the five hundred dollars, in favor of Mr. Nash Roach, or order, of Charleston, and write to him to the effect that you have done so. I will instruct him how to apply it. — As for Kettell, I fancy that he is not a person to rely upon. His work is too badly conducted ever to find the support of a party. I am as little prepared to believe that your friend, the Chevalier,[241] will prove more trustworthy. Neither you nor I will get a sixpence from them, and I at least, will trust the establishment no longer. I do not doubt that you can get the back volumes if you apply for them, & I hope you will not lose any opportunity of doing so. — Griswold wrote me that Briggs was down upon Mathews, & mentioned a paper which he had sent me; but I did not recieve it.[242] What's the matter now? — I see no reason why Stringer should not get the money from Labree. If he is positive about it, the

---

[236] "The Pilgrim of Love" was published by Post in the Oct. issue of the *Union Magazine*. See note 185, July 6, 1847.

[237] Though Mott in *A History of American Magazines, 1741-1850*, p. 544, lists Robert T. Conrad as an editor of *Graham's* only during 1848, apparently he held this position as early as Sept., 1847. The article here mentioned by Simms is "Love's Last Supper. Or the True Story of a Troubadour. A Provencal Biography," *Graham's*, XXXI (Dec., 1847), 277-286.

[238] "Benedict Arnold: The Traitor. A Drama, in an Essay" was published in the *Magnolia Weekly* (Richmond) during 1863.

[239] "Ode to Time," *Graham's*, XXXI (Oct., 1847), 202-203.

[240] See note 202, July 25, 1847.

[241] Henry Wikoff (1813-1884), publisher of the *Democratic Review* in 1846-1849, was commonly known as the "Chevalier," a title belonging to him as knight-commander of the Spanish Order of Ysabel la Catolica. For Simms' earlier remarks concerning his inability to collect payment for his contributions to the *Democratic Review*, see letter to Lawson of July 31, 1847.

[242] See note 219, July 31, 1847.

thing can be done. His letter, which I left with you, is an ample admission for the purposes of justice. But I must close. Tell Lady Lyde that I will urge Augusta to give her a chronicle of our doings. We are all improving, and so I trust are hers & yours. Give my best love to her, a kiss for the children and believe me Ever truly Yours

W. G. S.

402: To JAMES LAWSON

[September 6, 1847]²⁴³

dear Lawson

I wrote you by yesterday's mail to forward to Mr. Roach a draft for the five hundred dollars, but upon reflection, think it just as well to let the matter & money stay in abeyance, as I now think it probable I shall meet in the back country with the person to whom it should be paid. I enclose you certain literary notices which will furnish you with an occasion to call upon certain publishers — if you choose. Get, if possible, the money from Kettell & the Books. Do not let Stringer flag in pursuit of Labree, and be vigilant in extracting from Post, the $20., for the article. When sure of pay, from that quarter, more will be forthcoming. I look for a long budget of news from you. Write me to this place "Spartanburg, C. H. So. Carolina." Love to Lady Lyde & the little ones.

Yrs. in haste

Simms

J. L.

403: To CAREY AND HART

[*c.* September 6, 1847]²⁴⁴

Gentl.

Enclosed I send you a few notices of your & Lea & Blanchard's books, which I prepared for the Editorial department of the Charleston Courier.²⁴⁵ Others have appeared before, which were

---

²⁴³ Dated by Simms' reference to the draft for $500, which he had requested Lawson to forward to Nash Roach in his letter of Sept. 5. This letter is postmarked Sept. 7.
²⁴⁴ This letter is postmarked Spartanburg, S. C., Sept. 7. The year is established by Simms' being in Spartanburg at that time.
²⁴⁵ See, for example, the issues of Aug. 17 and Aug. 25.

forwarded you through Mr. John Russell. I write you from the foot of our Carolina mountains, and having been on the road for the last three weeks, I am sorry to say, I have made very little progress with the work of which you wot.[246] I hope, however, to have it ready early in the winter. — How comes on the biographical collection?[247] You should get it out as soon as possible, & particularly insist, in your advertisements, that it is a work to be relied on — the writers not concieving themselves justified in manufacturing their facts for the occasion. — Once more let me propose to you, my poetical writings for illustration next year.[248] You shall have the first thousand free of charge, 50 copies excepted for my private distribution. Address me, at any time during the next four weeks, at "Spartanburg, C. H. South Carolina." Has Master Baird [249] come back.

Yours truly &c

W. Gilmore Simms

Carey & Hart.

404: To James Lawson

Spartanburg, C. H. Sep. 23. [1847][250]

Dear Lawson

No word from you for the last hundred years. You are in debt to me fifty letters, more or less. I can only forgive it in the supposition that you are making averages and getting children with unusual expedition. I suppose it is the peculiar condition of Madame, and certain costly wrecks, that keep you from thinking of your friends. Here have I been vegetating, cogitating and rusticating for four weeks, meditating upon your silence, with grief, — and it is only by supposing the circumstances above mentioned, one or all, that I have concluded to forgive your sins of omission. Assuming that it is shipwrecks that have made you forget me, I congratulate you upon the ill wind that blows the average broker good. If our lady wife & mother be in the straw, take for granted that I only wait to know whether I shall rejoice on your account,

---

[246] Unidentified.

[247] Rufus W. Griswold's *Washington and the Generals of the American Revolution,* for which Simms had prepared various sketches. See earlier letters to Griswold and Carey and Hart.

[248] Carey and Hart refused to publish this edition of Simms' collected poetry. See letter to Carey and Hart of Dec. 13, 1847.

[249] Henry Carey Baird, of the firm of Carey and Hart.

[250] Dated by Simms' visit to Spartanburg in the summer of 1847.

for a son or a daughter. At all events write me soon that I may
forward my gratulations. — Tomorrow, I expect to set off on a
visit to the mountains of North Carolina. I shall be gone a week
or ten days when I begin my slow descent to the low country.
My purpose is to visit as much fine scenery, and to see & hear
as much as I can. I shall make a book of it. 'A chiel's among 'em
taking notes, & i' faith, he'll prent 'em!'[251]— While here, I
have been doing the tragedy.[252] It is finished. Four acts have
been sent to Forrest, and the fifth only needs to be copied out.
For the thing now that it is done, I can say nothing. I liked
it as I wrote, but have ceased to judge of it now. I leave that
for him & you to say. I presume he'll give you a glimpse of it,
and I trust 'twill like him. I have drawn the hero with F. himself
in my eye — a portrait which I hope will not displease him.
My notion is that if he likes it, it will tend very much to make
the audience identify him with it mentally & politically. *But, nous
verrons.* The fifth act, I shall probably copy out in another week.
I was in hopes to have heard from him touching the first acts
before I wrote the last three; but not a word. Had he written
his suggestions, I might have altered as I wrote. Now, he must
make his own amendments. If he don't like it, I will elaborate
& publish for the benefit of the fraternity. I confess myself very
anxious to hear from him. — My N. Y. correspondents have all
cut me. Out of sight, out of mind. From Duyckinck not a word,
I don't know the day when. — You must present me to the deserving — to Bryant, Forrest, and, if Wetmore says anything,
speak me regardfully to him. He has qualities which I always
liked, & I really regretted to suppose that he was indifferent to
my sympathies & good opinion. And how is our wife & mother.
Tell her that her little namesake is doing quite well now, though
she has had a severe attack of fever from teething, that gave us
no slight alarm. I sincerely trust that all are doing well with you.
Our folks improve. My wife weighs 112 pounds, Gilmore 38 &
myself 170. — The climate here is delicious. No hot weather.
Beautiful hills lie around us garnished with oak, hickory & chest-
nut, from clumps of which you see cottages gleaming white upon
the distant summits. We ride or walk at all times. Mineral Springs
bubble out on every hand — and the gold dust glimmers among

---

[251] This proposed volume never materialized. Simms' notes made on this
trip are in the Charles Carroll Simms Collection, South Caroliniana Library.
[252] *Norman Maurice; or, the Man of the People.*

the pebbles that pave the streams. There are several gold mines in this district, some worked by steam, and the mineral springs of Iron, Sulphur, Magnesia &c are frequent. One of the former is on the place where we remain. No healthier region in the world, few prettier, and a more persuasive climate, for August & Sept. could not be found. I shall buy here & you shall come & see me in the Summer. The trout streams are numerous. They are takes of 5 & 6 pounds. Come! — But they use live bait, not the fly. I shall take & eat one on your account. God bless you. Give my love to your wife and children. Kiss them all for me, & believe me Yours Ever truly &c.

Simms

J. L.

405 : To Robert Taylor Conrad

Charleston, Oct 19, 1847

My dear Judge

I am here again, on the seaboard, after a two months ramble among our mountains. I have been for some weeks the occupant of a camp among the hunters, beyond our remotest bounds of civilization. I have slept with the howling of the wolf & the sudden shriek of the panther in my ears,[253] and have eaten my steaks of venison, fresh from the haunches of the buck, eight hundred feet above the Atlantic levels. I could make you a series of descriptive sketches that might tell much better than most of our foreign travel, — and may do so. I regret that Mr. Russell, to whom I looked to bring on the MS. of 'Arnold', — did not succeed in seeing you, while in Philadelphia. Can you not contrive to send it to me, by some safe hand, as soon as possible. Address me in Charleston, to the 'Care of John Russell, Bookseller.' — The sooner I can get it, the better, though it will now scarcely be possible to prepare it in season to open with the New Year. Still, the 1st Act might be got in readiness for February, and the four remaining would just complete the volume. I see that the 'Ode to Time' is printed, & will thank you to send me a copy of the number in which it appears, as also of all those which may contain contributions of mine.[254] While in Spartanburg, I forwarded you a narrative, which

---

[253] Simms uses these very words in his notes of the experience, preserved in the Charles Carroll Simms Collection, South Caroliniana Library.

[254] "Ode to Time" is the only identifiable contribution by Simms in *Graham's* from Jan. through Oct., 1847.

I concieve a very remarkable one, being equally true & romantic.[255] Pray let me know if it suits you. — I have written the 'domestic Drama' for Forrest, of which I told you, but his opinion of the first act does not seem to be favorable.[256] Whether the remaining acts will better commend themselves to his regards, remains to be seen. At last advices he had not recieved them. I enclose you a couple of contributions in verse which Mr Graham will probably recieve at ten dollars each.[257] Should he not[,] keep them by you until you hear from me again. Pray write me, and let me know what matters in your literary world. I see that the N. Y. Literati are sparring as of old.

Yours very truly &c

W. Gilmore Simms

Hon. R. T. Conrad.

406: To James Henry Hammond

Charleston, Oct 20 1847

dear Hammond

I have but recently reached the city, and amid the variety of cares that distract my attention, I propose not so much to answer your letter, as to acknowledge its reciept, and report myself as considerate as ever of your kindness and remembrance. I am now quite as busy as I need be, in packing up & preparing to return to the plantation, which we do on the 1st prox. But in addition to this task of drudgery, I have in hand the further task of preparing an oration for the Literary Societies of Oglethorpe which I deliver on the 10th Nov.[258] Between these two antipathetic duties,

---

[255] "Love's Last Supper." See note 237, Sept. 5, 1847.

[256] We have been unable to locate Forrest's letter to Simms concerning the first act of *Norman Maurice; or, the Man of the People*.

[257] Most likely these are "The Memorial Tree," *Graham's* XXXII (Jan., 1848), 11-12, and "Ilenovar. From a Story of Palenque. A Fragment," *ibid.*, XXXII (April, 1848), 218-220. George Rex Graham (1813-1894) issued the first number of *Graham's* in Jan., 1841. In Aug., 1848, he assigned *Graham's* to Samuel D. Patterson and Co., though he continued as editor. He bought back the magazine in March, 1850, but sold it again in Dec., 1853. He was connected with various newspapers and magazines before and after his connection with *Graham's*.

[258] The oration, published as *Self-Development* (Milledgeville, Ga., 1847), is noticed in an editorial in the Charleston *Mercury* of Feb. 9, 1848: "He [Simms] takes a subject and gives himself up with all the warmth and strength of his genius . . . the author, not only by his advice, but by his life, presents a lesson of labor, of manly integrity, and honorable achievement most worthy of their respect and emulation."

my time at present is completely divided. — I am greatly obliged to you for your thoughtful friendship in the matter of the foreign mission. I have never sought to disguise from you & other friends, that such an appointment would be equally agreeable & serviceable to me. I need some respite, which the condition of my affairs, will not suffer me, unless under national appointment; and I flatter myself that I should be fully adequate to all the responsibilities of the station for which I sought. You did no more than right in saying that I approved generally of the proceedings of the administration. Indeed, it is scarcely to be accounted for — unless under a supposition that discredits the whole state — the hostility of S. C. to an administration which has succeeded in doing for us what we have most strenuously been fighting for & desiring for 20 years. I go further than you not only in seeing in the Mexican War an inevitable necessity, but in recognizing in our acquisitions of territory in that quarter an obvious advantage to the South, whether we go out of or remain in the Union. 'In the former event I should desire for the South the entire possession of all the regions tributary to the Gulf. I am not sure that the War has been urged judiciously; but the question is not with me the discretion of the administration in this or that *modus operandi,* — but simply its general policy. I conscientiously believe that to have been quite as Southern, as it was possible in the nature of things to have made it. — But I doubt if my opinions will at all avail in procuring me the appointment, and I am rather glad that your exertions & those of other friends have just stopped where they did. The Gentleman & man of honour must obtain his gifts by a simple suggestion of his claims, and not by any importunacy. I shall thank Rhett for his zeal, though *inter nos,* he is about the last man in the world to obtain any favor for himself or others.[259] — I have a long subject to discuss with you,

---

[259] On Sept. 21 Hammond had written Simms: "One day when in N. Y. I saw it announced that Polk's brother [William H.] had resigned his post at Naples & was appointed a Maj. of Dragoons. I instantly sat down & wrote to Rhett to apply for it for you. Fearing he might not be at Georgetown, I wrote the next day to the President myself & got Boyce who was there to write to him also. . . . I put in your claims on the grounds of your personal merit & being at the head of our Southern Literary Coopers among whom no appointments have been distributed. . . . I enclose you Rhett's answer to my letter. It is only proper that you shd. know how promptly & cordially he acted in the matter." In his letter to Polk of Sept. 4 Hammond speaks of Simms as "the most distinguished literary character of the South," a man who "promises as fairly as any man living who has not already done it, to achieve a reputation that shall go down to future ages." (Originals in the Hammond Papers, Library of Congress.)

but this can only properly be done when we meet. When shall it be? — When I was in the backcountry, I met Pickens. We conversed frequently together, and he appeared to unfold himself with exceeding freedom & always as a discontent. Among other things which he told me without reserve (though, as a matter of course such a matter is to be kept with ourselves) was this — that Elmore counselled to Butler the form of a communication to Calhoun, full of certain assurances of support — before it was resolved that Butler should be the nominee.[260] This, it appears, was a sort of stipulation — a prescribed faith, which E. himself, representing the *power,* exacted, and to which the other subscribed! Yet, we have been persuaded that E. held off wholly from this controversy. P. asked me what I thought of the movement on the subject of the Wilmot proviso. I answered that I thought the proposition to meet the evil (as described) by the establishment of a paper at Washington, — a wretched anticlimax — that I was unwilling to trust the question at all to a stipendiary in Washington — that such a paper must necessarily run into the Presidential question, and that such, in my opinion, was the true aim of some of those who were engaged in its establishment. It was my farther opinion that much of the outcry was meant to divert public attention from home concerns &c. Since my return to Charleston, I have found a confidential letter addressed to me, inviting me to a secret conference in Charleston. Elmore, also, spoke to me on the subject as I was leaving the city, and I told him I thought the establishment of a newspaper rather the belittling of the evil. Meeting Carew a few days ago, I spoke of the matter, and freely expressed these opinions. His answer was that *Mr. Calhoun would have it so.* — Pickens asked your opinion on the point. I told him that I could not answer for you precisely, but that I had every reason to think that you regarded nothing as more inauspicious & evil than that we should convert the slave question into political capital for any object. Pickens mentioned among other things — though this also *entre nous* — that Mr. Calhoun owed the Bank $20 or 21,000

---

[260] On Nov. 1, 1847, Hammond wrote in reply to Simms' letter: "He [Calhoun] is by the by *deeply offended* with Pickens. They have split entirely & forever. Pickens story of Butler & Elmore is probably true. Butler at least has truckled to Calhoun ever since his election in the most disgusting manner. He never concealed *before,* that he disliked him personally & never faild to sneer at him when he cd.—behind his back of course. B's sensational career thus far has I opine added no new laurels." (Original in the Hammond Papers, Library of Congress.)

dollars — debt incurred by his son &c in Mobile & elswhere —that this alone had keep him quiet when, at the last election, the Mercury had withdrawn his name wholly from the canvas. — Among the wanderers encountered at Glenn's was Felder. He asserts that Elmore is in the Bank, as principal & endorser to $400,000.[261] I counselled him not to urge the publication of *all* the debtors' & defaulters' names, but only those who had been *officers of the State,* — the Directors &c. To this no reasonable opposition could be urged. I also counselled that the taxes be cut off from all negroes under ten and over 60, and the Bank pay the deficiency. Another recommendation which I made was that the indebtedness of the candidate to the Bank, be insisted upon before the people, as a sufficient cause of objection to his fitness at the present moment. The several Rail Road projects are new instruments by which to secure the Bank a farther supply of *pablum.* The surplus fund (our share) will be collected by the Bank. Her paper will issue on the strength of it. She will take the promissory notes of subscribers to the several Roads, advance the money — build the roads — the notes being held as collateral security only, for which no call will be made until the charter becomes renewable. Then follows the coercion unless &c. The idea of a Rail Road in the mountain district silences all the scruples in that quarter, and the public men will every where [be] bought up, in this and other ways before the charter expires. The remedy is in the people, & in those bold few who, with more prudence & wisdom than Felder, shall take the bull by the horns at the popular elections. — But why should I fatigue you with speculations of which, in proportion to their truthfulness, you are already in full possession? It is only because, once set to thinking & seeing for myself, I fancy that I make discoveries. Let me hear from you soon. Address me at Woodlands as before. — I was very anxious to be with you in N. Y. but continued to be busy among our own mountains. For two weeks I was out with the hunters, camping among the wildest mtns of N. C. You shall hear anon of this expedition. My family has improved. How is it with yours? I see that Aldrich has been

---

[261] John M. Felder had long interested himself in the Bank of the State of South Carolina (see note 245, *c.* Nov. 19, 1846). In 1844 Simms, himself, had been placed on a committee to examine the Bank (see *House Journal,* Dec. 5, 1844). The committee examined the Bank on Nov. 17, 1845, and presented a somewhat favorable report to the legislature.

spouting fury against Wilmot & his Proviso. We must see that
A. does not lose his election against Graham.[262]

Yours truly &c

W. Gilmore Simms

J. H. Hammond Esq

407: To James Lawson

Charleston Oct 20. 1847

dear Lawson

We are again, as you see, safely delivered from our perils of
rocks & mountains, and once again upon the seaboard. I have
been among the mountaineers, in the very realm of wolf &
panther, bear, deer, and other small vermin, with a budget sufficiently stored for a volume. In all this time, more than two
months, not a syllable from my New York friends & bretheren.
Out of sight, out of mind. I have written you repeatedly, & fear, as
is usual & natural in such cases, that something matters you —
that you are in ailments & troubles from which I heartily wish I
could set you free. By this time, you too & yours should have got
back to the city. May you soon report yourselves as well and
happy as ever. We are all in good condition. Our little Mary
Lawson, after two attacks of fever from teething, is again quite
hearty, has grown much & is fatter than ever. The rest in due
proportion. — And now for business. I have, as you are no doubt
advised, succeeded in finishing my tragedy — the whole of which,
act by act, has been sent to Forrest. But I infer, from what he
writes me after perusal of the first act, that the thing does not
suit him. In his note he speaks of it as not being as 'carefully
elaborated' as it should be. It is not improbable that he draws
this inference from the fact that the style is not greatly elevated
above that of ordinary conversation. But this moderation of tone
was deliberately determined on, in consequence of my wish to
make the piece strictly a *domestic* drama. The style was just
sufficiently elevated to make it meet the exactions of rhythm. If
the piece has any dramatic susceptibilities — if, in other words —
it can be made a good *acting* piece, it will be quite easy to raise
the style where it is necessary, & to throw in those extraneous

---

[262] A. P. Aldrich was seeking re-election as commissioner in equity in Barnwell District. His opponent was Winchester Graham.

passages of poetry, which I rather suppressed in order that it should be strictly an acting drama. This you might say to Forrest, & under his suggestions, I would undertake to add or elevate a passage where he would designate the necessity of doing so. But do not let him suppose that I wish him to consider the piece for a single moment should he doubt its merit as a piece for the stage. Let him put it into your hands, and you can ascertain what chance there is of any of your managers, old or new, — or Mr. Murdoch, or Wallack,[263] holding it in better favor. My notion still is that it will act, and has in it the seeds of considerable American popularity. Of course, I may know nothing about it. Our friend, however, must not be unnecessarily troubled with it. — I could wish that you would propose my Laconics to the Messrs. Appleton, altering the title to "Voices from the Woods & Wayside." I am willing to let them have the publication for five years (the Copyright in my name) for half the profits. Should they consent to any arrangement, I propose to add to the collection & vary it with other matters. I see that the "Union" has published the "Pilgrim of Love." I will send you something for the publisher in a day or two — which, if he has paid you, you may dispose of to him.[264] It is also almost time for you to get the drft paid by Colton.[265] — Touching the $500 — pray send me and my order, a draft for it on any of the Banks of Charleston. Do this as soon as possible that I may get it before I leave town for the plantation which will be on the first prox. — I hear nothing from Duyckinck or Mathews — though I guess from various glimpses afforded by the newspapers that he is again in hot water! What is the affair?[266] — I learn that Forrest has made an offer

---

[263] James Edward Murdoch (1811-1893) and James William Wallack, Jr. (1818-1873), the actors.

[264] For "The Pilgrim of Love," see note 185, July 6, 1847. For Simms' later contributions to the *Union Magazine,* see note 15, Jan. 7, 1848.

[265] Payment for "A Sketch of the Life and Public Services of John Rutledge of South Carolina." See note 120, April 19, 1847.

[266] Mathews was involved in arguments concerning international copyright. A complete file of the New York *Evening Mirror* for this period has been inaccessible to us, but the issue for Jan. 4, 1848, reprints from a British magazine a letter from Mathews, dated Oct. 25, 1847, and concerned in part with his role in furthering the cause of international copyright. A portion of his letter, however, is devoted to an attack on American magazines and newspapers which, he claims, had attacked him in their opposition to international copyright. The *Mirror* prefaces the letter with the comment: "We give the letter out of justice to him because, we copied the anonymous letter to which he alludes, as a piece of literary gossip, never dreaming that we should be accused of doing it to 'gratify our spleen towards its writer.' . . . Mr. Mathews has unquestionably served the cause of copyright, but then he has served it very shabbily by

for a best tragedy? [267] If so, get and forward me a copy of his advertisement. I shall be quite sorry should I have failed utterly to suit him in my experiment. But I shall persevere in dramatic attempts. When you get my 'Man of the People' read it promptly, and with care, and tell me what you think of it, — though I take for granted that if it fails with F. it will not prove acceptable with you. Yet I should like to learn where the particular deficiency lies. — I sincerely trust that the Averages flow in freely, and that it is to their influx that I have to ascribe your silence for nearly three months. Let me hear from you soon. My wife sends love to yours, Augusta joins her, and if the parties most concerned will suffer it, I send mine also. Pray you it be acceptable to all. God bless & keep you

Yours &c.

Simms

J. L.

408: To James Lawson

Charleston, October 26, 1847

My dear Lawson

The seasons seem to have progressed with you with singular rapidity. Time has flown in the office of the Average Broker, far beyond the estimates of any almanac that we can boast, south of the Potomac. Here, for example, while our daily newspapers assure us that we only approximate the close of October, your letter, recieved today, is dated, "New York, 23d. Nov. 1847.["] I congratulate you on thus successfully stealing a march on time. I trust that your impulse here is measured by your fortunes, and that your earnings of October are so immense as to decieve you as to the time which you employed in effecting them. — Confound your apologies; they take up half your letter, and leave you no

---

endeavouring to identify his own name with it, and make the world believe he is the cause, and that anything said in his dispraise is an attack upon international copyright. . . . " The *Mirror* goes on to say that Mathews does not do the cause much good when he seeks "the medium of an English magazine for the purpose of venting ill natured and deprecatory remarks against American magazines. . . . "

[267] The *Knick.*, XXX (Sept., 1847), 277, says: "Edwin Forrest, the eminent American Tragedian, with his accustomed liberality has offered a *Prize of Three Thousand Dollars* for the best Tragedy by an American citizen, the prize to be awarded by a capable and distinguished committee. The amount offered is unprecedentedly large; and we hope Mr. Forrest will receive one worthy his great power of dramatic representation, and the generous remuneration he has tendered."

room for what you really have to say. I know that you are a rascally correspondent, & don't want your longwinded assurances to that effect. — I wrote you a few days ago to advise you of our arrival at the Seaboard. By this time, I trust, you are preparing to answer that letter. The answer to this, I shall look for in a week after reaching Woodlands, whither we set out, bag & baggage, on the 1st. proxo. I am up to my eyes in packing and preparation. Besides this task, I am awfully worried with the preparation of an oration which I have been appointed to deliver before the Literary Societies of Oglethorpe University at the Commencement on the 10th. Nov. 1847 — a period which *you* seem to have happily overpassed. I have just sketched an outline of my discourse, the subject of which is "Self Development." If you are charitable in the least, wish me well through with it. — I note what you say touching the Drama for Forrest. It will be very gratifying to me should it satisfy or suit him. His note, however, with regard to the 1st Act, however kindly expressed, was calculated greatly to depress any hopes which I might have felt on the subject. Should the main scheme & incidents suit him, it will be easy to expand and elaborate any portions which he may think wanting in force & finish. I am very sure that the story is fresh & truly national — more than that, the hero is drawn very much as an ideal which I fancy he would gladly realize. Pray urge him to an early examination & answer. Should it suit him, I should probably visit you this winter. His advertisement I have not seen, & I know nothing of his requisitions. Pray send me a paper containing his offer. My next conception *for him* would be *"Roscious, a Roman Tragedy."* [268] He knows my scheme. I have completed my correction of the imputed plays for Cooledge, all but the revision of the press, & the introduction to the play of Locrine, and to the whole body of the work. It has cost me immense labor, and I should be moderately recompensed with $500. At all events, I shall look to recieve $400. If I make a dedication for it, I shall probably inscribe to Forrest.[269] But of this — mum! — as soon as your annunciation was read of Jamie's weight, we rolled up Gilmore in purple gauze & sent him to the grocer. He weighs just 5 lb. more than your General — just 38 pounds, even as he weighed in Spartanburg. My wife weighs 118 and

---

[268] This play was not written.
[269] Perhaps Forrest's attitude toward *Norman Maurice* resulted in Simms' dedicating *A Supplement to the Plays of William Shakspeare* to the Rev. Alexander Dyce rather than to him.

yr hbl servt. 170. But say nothing of the dimensions of the latter person, to that critical woman, your wife, — or I may lose whatever small portions of her affections still remain to me. — We are sorry that Christina's health is at all fluctuating. You must not forget to try Woodlands if her disorder should increase. We wish for you all frequently. Mr. Roach, reading your letter today, & *your card,* remarked that now you have a partner, it would surely not be impossible to steal away for a month or two. He is anxious that you should take a few 10 lb. trout out of the Edisto. Confound Kettell & Wyckoff.[270] You need look for no money from either. The former is engaged to write many articles for the New Orleans Review at $20 each. How then can you expect that he should pay for ours. But you have his acceptance; and at all events, he cannot refuse you the vols. of the Review that were to be bound for us. Perhaps, he will pay you in *books?* See to it? If so: — accept my draft for your Library. — Duyckinck might easily get the money from Post. Let him ask if other contributions are desirable from the same source. My excursion will make a volume or two. I am full of material. Do not delay with Colton. Make him pay promptly, or you peril all. As for Labree, — Stringer told me that B. & S. owed him more money, and it could be done. In my last, I requested a draft for the $500 on one of our Charleston Banks. I have to pay it off very soon. I hear nothing from Duyckinck or Mathews. The latter, it is said, has fairly killed Yankee Doodle.[271] His humour will be the death of himself. — 'Views and Reviews' have not yet reached me; but I see a feeble notice in the Literary World.[272] —

---

[270] Thomas Prentice Kettell (see note 214, July 31, 1847), the editor, and Henry Wikoff (see note 241, Sept. 5, 1847), the publisher of the *Democratic Review.* Kettell was also a frequent contributor to the *Commercial Review of the South and West* (later called *De Bow's Review*), which Simms in this letter calls "the New Orleans Review."

[271] *Yankee Doodle* ceased publication with the issue of Oct. 2. In the *Southern Patriot* of Oct. 23 Simms comments: "The 'Yankee Doodle' newspaper, which when it started into existence in New York, was intended and promised to be quite a witty affair, has proved a failure both in the intellectual and pecuniary part, and its publication has ceased. The New York Despatch with bitter satire condoles with the proprietor, who has lost five thousand dollars, and congratulates the public that has lost Yankee Doodle. For our own part we never thought much of Yankee Doodle, but 'de mortuis nil nisi bonum.'"

[272] This review in II (Oct. 23, 1847), 282, is certainly far more favorable and somewhat longer than would be expected from Simms' characterization of it as "feeble." After considerable praise of Simms as a writer of fiction, the reviewer comments: "But it is in his character as critic and reviewer, that we are now to regard our author, who has *selected* a volume of his papers from magazines and reviews, Northern and Southern. The judgment and

What has become of Richards, and who has the pictures for the poems.[273] I am about to refer Carey & Hart to them. Love to Lady L. & a kiss all round for wife & little ones. My wife & Augusta join me in affectionate remembrance. Mary Lawson is much fatter than her namesake ever was or will be.

Yours Ever,

Simms.

409: To Carey and Hart
Confidential.

Charleston, Oct 26. 1847

Mess'rs Carey & Hart

Gentlemen

You will excuse my pertinacity in once more inviting your attention to the project of an illustrated edition of my complete poetical writings. I may be forgiven a certain degree of solicitude, in my own case, as I am so totally without that species of friends & supporters, who, in New England especially, never suffer a favorite to forfeit his chances, if a tenacious drumming in concert will sustain his pretensions. I trust that a few simple considerations will impress you favorably with this design. You are perhaps not unaware that I commenced my career as a poet. My first publications were commended by most of the critics of the day. I have the commendations of Brooks, Neal, Flint, Bucking-

---

literary art, the imaginative writer has displayed in his best fictions, he discovers in these critical essays.

"As a critic, the author is rather hearty and comprehensive, than fine and subtle; generally sound and just, he is always most sincere and honorable. We know not a more independent and honest critic, though we are inclined sometimes to dissent from his judgments. He is invariably clear and direct, frequently vigorous and at times eloquent. There is manliness and force in all he writes. He sins more in exuberance than in any other way. But this is one of the original sins of review writing.

"The fact that the critic discusses large and important questions, should excuse a tendency to dogmatism, and an occasional too rapid and too wide generalization.

"The critic is as national as the poet. Mr. Simms is truly American. The subjects of this collection from Americanism, the first paper, to the last, are purely American."

[273] See note 202, July 25, 1847.

ham and many others,[274] some of whom did not hesitate to place my name, as a beginner, among the first of our poets. I state these things, not egotistically, but as simple facts bearing on the question. My 'Atalantis' was a particularly successful poem, and recieved the favorable criticism of Thomas Campbell, then Editor of the "Metropolitan." [275] Several volumes of verse issued from my pen — a fact only important as you seemed to lay some stress on similarly frequent issues in the case of other poets whose writings you were publishing, and whose circulation, I am very sure, — the truth once known — was never greater than my own. Large numbers of my best pieces went the rounds of the press anonymously, repeatedly praised & quoted, some of which, to this day, are in circulation unclaimed. I am desirous to reclaim these, and to assert my pretensions as a poet, which the frequency and success of my prose reputation only have tended to obscure. I believe that the country will be prepared to recognize and acknowledge my claims, on the strength of such a selection, from my writings, as it is in my power to make. I believe that an

---

[274] See letter to Griswold of Dec. 6, 1846. Flint also reviewed Simms' *Lyrical and Other Poems* and *Early Lays* in the *Western Monthly Review*, I (Jan., 1828), 553-557, commenting (pp. 553-554): "We have read these two little volumes with a considerable degree of attention. We are impressed from the perusal, and the sparkling prose of the inscription and the notes, that the author possesses no stinted share of fancy and imagination; and that he is endowed with a mind, which is stored with the materials of poetry in no common degree. We certainly regret to find them, as it seems to us, a chaotic mass, 'void and without form.' To separate the elements by elective attraction, each to its kind; to discriminate, arrange, combine, and throw on the whole the due proportions of light and shade, so as to form them hereafter into the paintings of poetry, is a creation, that may be fairly expected from a mind so young, unformed, and yet of so much promise. He has evidently devoured poetry, as a northerner does tropical fruits, when he is first transported to the 'citrous groves.' We can not avoid seeing the images and the diction of Burns, Campbell, Byron and Moore, not to enumerate any American poets, that have indeed, passed through his mind; without, however, undergoing in the transit that complete assimilation, which destroys their identity and the evidence of their derivation, so as to constitute them, in their new form, entirely his own. He seems to write under the teeming sensation of a mind filled with such reading. . . . He has written too much, and too carelessly. . . . When years, and self-criticism and thought and labor and the pruning knife shall have been applied to his verses, we trust, he will not have cause to complain of the want of American patronage." The same periodical, II (Oct., 1828), 291, contains a notice of Simms' and Simmons' *Southern Literary Gazette*: "This is a respectable looking brother monthly, and we see an acquaintance of ours, as one of its editors. We wish him and his colleague and the work poetic visions of the paradise of fame, money and usefulness,—and hope, as the good Vicar of Wakefield used to say, that they and the region, where it circulates, may be the better for it at the end of the year."

[275] See note 268, Dec. 6, 1846.

illustrated volume from your house, will obtain a preference in a large portion of our country, particularly in the South & West. For such a volume, I have some illustrations already, painted by a clever young artist, which I will order to be sent you. These, with others which you might procure from other artists, would afford you a variety, and my portrait, which never yet has been published, might add something to the attractions of such a volume. Mr. Richards, the artist to whom I allude, has painted several pictures of Southern scenery, and one upon the river swamp at my residence at Woodlands, which might make a vignette at once novel & attractive.[276] I have only to refer you to the terms indicated in a previous letter. — The selection I would make from my writings would be conducted with a rigid regard to the highest standards in my judgment, and I should be careful, in polishing and perfecting the several pieces, with a due regard to the *setting* in which they were designed to appear. Let me beg that you will examine this scheme with a due consideration of the suggestions here stated. I can scarcely doubt that the *esprit de corps* of the South, will as heedfully foster the claims of such a volume, from my pen, as New England would those of Mr. Longfellow or New York those of Mr. Halleck. — I have recieved and written a notice of "Washington & *Your* Generals."[277] I do not see that your curtailments have hurt my biographies. I studiously made them ample; as my material, in some respects, was such as was possessed by few or no other persons. — Your publication must very soon assert its superiority,[278] on the score of integrity, fullness, good sense, and total freedom from all balderdash and gammon. The American people very soon detect the paste, though it did seem, at the first, a brilliant.

Yours truly &c.

W. Gilmore Simms

---

[276] An engraving of T. Addison Richards' "Turtle Cove" appears in the *Southern Literary Gazette* (W. C. Richards'), I (Dec. 16, 1848), 248, and N. S., I (Jan. 31, 1852), 54. See illustration (from the second of these) facing p. 291.

[277] The earliest review of Griswold's *Washington and the Generals of the American Revolution* that we have been able to locate in the Charleston newspapers is published in the *Courier* of Nov. 29.

[278] To J. T. Headley's *Washington and His Generals*, 2 vols. (New York: Baker and Scribner, 1847).

410: To James Lawson

Mr. Israel Post will pay to James Lawson Esq of New York, the sum of Twenty dollars due me for contribution to the Union Mage, entitled 'Pilgrim of Love' and oblige His obt servt

W. Gilmore Simms
Woodlands, S. C.
Nov. 3. 1847.

Dear Lawson. You see by the enclosed that our friend Post is in rather a hurry to pay.[279] He should be indulged by all means, and I send you order as above. I write him by the same mail with this to this effect, and to say that you are prepared to treat with him for other occasional contributions. My lowest price for an article is $20; or $20 for each division of an article that may run through successive numbers. You may say that if he will publish and pay promptly, other articles of the sort already contributed may be forthcoming from the same source. I am anxious to hear from you for various reasons. Of course, though I have little hopes in regard to the drama written for Forrest, I am anxious to hear the result.[280] I still think the play likely to make a hit. By this time, however, you are prepared to judge of it. Let me beg that you will in no respect whatever endeavour to influence F's judgment on the subject. I wish the play to have fair play only, and do not wish him to yield to friendship or friendly influence, what he would not otherwise concede. I trust you have put Colton's note [281] in Bank for collection. I wrote to you to forward the $500 to me in a dft, & was in hope to have recd it before leaving Charleston. If you have not already done so, get me a dft for the amt. on the Bank of Charleston (or any Bank in Charleston) & address me *here*. Love to wife & children.

Yours truly as Ever

J. Lawson Esq.   W. G. Simms

---

[279] In his letter, dated Oct. 28 (preserved with Simms' letter to Lawson), Post writes: "We are owing you Twenty Dollars for your Article entitled 'The Pilgrim of Love,' published in the Oct. No. of the Union Magazine. I am ready to pay it at once and would send it enclosed in this, but I understand it is uncertain about whether you are in Charleston or not. Please write me how & when I shall send it to you."

[280] Simms had sent Forrest the MS. of *Norman Maurice* and had also asked Lawson to read it. See letter to Lawson of Sept. 23, 1847, and following letters to Lawson.

[281] Payment for "A Sketch of the Life and Public Services of John Rutledge of South Carolina." See note 265, Oct. 20, 1847.

411: To James Henry Hammond

Woodlands, Nov. 7. 1847

Dear Hammond

I wrote you a week ago from Charleston, but a letter just recieved from R. De Treville (Senator)[282] suggests a reason for writing you again. He wishes to be made Attorney General, and even my poor assistance is solicited. Bailey,[283] it appears, is either to resign, or be made to do so. He has, *on dit,* been at worse pranks than ever. I have no objections that De T. should fill his place. Nay, I regard him with much more favor than I do some of the persons whom I hear spoken of. He is a good Lawyer, a shrewd sensible man, and though probably a selfish one, yet not wholly wanting in independence. I am of opinion too, that he, like ourselves, looks with some disquiet at the course of things among us. The whisper is that I. W. Hayne of Charleston is the nominee of the powers that be in that quarter.[284] This should be sufficient to cause him to be set aside by those who revolt at the damnable system of wire pulling which regulates everything now-a-days among us. Mr. Hayne has no claims. He has been absent from the State for many years, and failing elswhere has come back, it would seem, seeking office. The conspicuous position which is constantly assigned him in Charleston at all the petty explosions of the city, declares a purpose to thrust him forward for place, & to prepare the public mind for his claims. Now, as a general rule, one mode for breaking up the system is to break down the nominees. I do not know how you stand affected to De Treville, but if not unfavorable, pray bend yourself to the matter, small though it appear. It is really not a small matter. Every blow just now will tell, and the Attorney General, the creature of a clique has a large power for perpetuating its existence, particularly in Charleston, whence all your *systems* must henceforth arise. I have written to a few friends in the Legislature, & shall try to write to a few more; but just now I

---

[282] Richard DeTreville (1801-1874) was born in Beaufort, but moved to Charleston at an early age. In 1848 he was commissary-general of purchases, in 1854-1856 lieutenant governor. He was a signer of the Ordinance of Secession. Simms and DeTreville served together in 1844 on the Committee of Inspection of the Bank of the State of South Carolina at Charleston, DeTreville from the Senate and Simms from the House.

[283] Henry Bailey (1799-1849) had been elected attorney general of South Carolina in Nov., 1836. He held the position until Nov., 1848, when he declined to serve longer.

[284] Hayne did succeed Bailey in 1848.

am preparing to go to Georgia to deliver my oration before the literary societies of Oglethorpe — shall set off on Sunday next *via* Hamburg — deliver on the 10th & set off for home a day or so after. Perhaps, if you could stray to Hamburg on the 12th you would find me there, and I would spend a night with you — but no: It would be too much of a task to require you to send me to the Rail Road next day. If you could meet me there however on Tuesday night, a night together would enable us to disburthen. I wrote you a few heads of topics & might find more. I assume that you are writing Anti Debt.[285] The Surplus Revenue to which they now refer is an *undrawn* balance, still in the U. S. Treasury, i. e. if I rightly understand it. If not, — you are into them.[286] But a truce. I am weary of the pen, and my thoughts rise too slowly to be worth setting down. Let me hear from you soon & believe me

Very truly &c.
Yours

W. G. Simms.

Gen. Hammond.

P. S. Something cautionary to Aldrich may not be amiss. While his declamation is general about Wilmot & his proviso, it will do; but he should be warned to beware lest, under this pretext there lies other matters which he scarcely now concieves. Hint to him to save his money at all events — to speak freely, but

---

[285] Hammond wrote on Nov. 17: "I will own *to you* that I am the writer of 'Anti-Debt.' But I have kept it a secret from my Brother, from Walker, Aldrich &c. I don't want any of those supposed to know what I may be at, *& in the way of being quizzed* to know the author. . . . I found Carew willing & set out to handle the question & all its *collaterals* that might be pressed on me without gloves. . . . I shall have out another number on Friday or Saturday, cutting perhaps deeper. . . . Do if you can give me some facts & suggest some ideas & tell me where I have done well or where ill in reference to public sentiment. . . . " (Original in the Hammond Papers, Library of Congress.) Hammond's series of twenty-one essays, signed "Anti-Debt" and concerned with the "Railroad Mania" and the Bank of the State of South Carolina, was published in the *Mercury* during 1847-1848. The first is dated Oct. 21, 1847, the last Jan. 5, 1848. They were republished under the title of *The Railroad Mania: And Review of the Bank of the State of South-Carolina* ([Charleston], Burges, James & Paxton, Printers, 1848). Additional essays by Hammond, signed "Anti-Debt," were published during the summer of 1848.

[286] Hammond wrote on Nov. 17: "The money now at Washington to which you refer & have on your mind is an insignificant sum awarded to us a few years back under Clay's Bill for distributing the proceeds of the Public Lands, & which our State by a Legislative resolve *refused to receive*. It is probably much less than $50,000." (Original in the Hammond Papers, Library of Congress.)

subscribe costively. A paper *at home* is much more needed, and would be of much more effectual service.[287]

412: To JAMES LAWSON

Woodlands, Nov. 16. or 17. 1847.

dear Lawson:

Your letter covering draft on Bank of Charleston has *seasonably* reached me. I shall need the money on Monday next, so, you see, that the escape is a narrow one. You do not say that you recieved the dft on Post, nor whether he & Colton have paid you the monies. Do not allow these harpies to escape you. Delays, with such creatures, endanger everything. I am anxious, on *your* account, about the collection of the Colton dft, as it will nearly liquidate (I fancy) what I owe you. Pray let me know if he has done the needful. — I am but just returned from my visit to Milledgeville, Geo. whither I went to deliver the anniversary oration before the Literary Societies of Oglethorpe. My subject was "Self Development." It was written hastily, but appears to have given great satisfaction. I had a large & intelligent audience — all the great men of Georgia being present. The night before the anniversary, I went to a meeting of the Democratic Party, and was caught — was called out & made to speechify the assembly. They cheered me numerously, & those about me were quite warm & earnest in their congratulations. On Monday I go to Columbia, where our Legislature assembles, and where I have some business. After a week there, I return to Woodlands, to work or vegetate for the rest of the winter. — Passing through Augusta, I saw Forbes [288] — strolled to the theatre during the day and chatted with the men in buskin & buckram, and with the

---

[287] In his reply to Simms' letter of Oct. 20 Hammond had written on Nov. 1: "As to the Wilmot Proviso & the Paper I think of *both*, just as you do. From the first I took my stand agt. the Paper & wrote to them in Charleston, that 'I shuddered at the idea of the agitation of Slavery through a daily Press at Washington.' . . . Here again C. shews the cloven foot. Aldrich told me that Calhoun virtually wrote the Barnwell report. Read it. The Prospectus of the Paper says it is to have nothing to do with 'personal or party politics'— Mr. C. says in this Rep. that it must denounce caucus & convention nominations to the Presidency—thus going at once into the marrow of politics, & *driving off at a blow*, all the thorough Democrats *and* Whigs of the Slaveholding States. . . . My God, what asses the people are, & what scoundrels their Leaders." (Original in the Hammond Papers, Library of Congress.)

[288] William C. Forbes, the actor, who had an interest in the Augusta Theatre, and who had been the manager of the Charleston Theatre during the previous season.

women too. Tell your wife she need not be jealous, as none of the heroines of the drama there, were quite as handsome as herself. You may add that they did not find so much fault with me to my face either. Forbes proposes to make some alterations in my Michael Bonham & to bring it out there. Of course, I attach no importance now to the matter & let him do as he pleases. — I frankly confess to very different feelings in the case of the Man of the People, and shall feel quite anxious to hear what Forrest says on the subject. If he percieves any thing in the piece to warrant him in the belief that it will play, either in the whole or in some of the acts, — the alterations which you suggest may readily be made. It will be easy for me to impart more interest to the character of Clarice, and even to the Aunt, and it would not be difficult to afford to Maurice & Clarice an interview prior to their marriage and justifying that proceeding. Equally easy to introduce Warren while the marriage is in progress, and perhaps, at other places, to impose additional work upon the hero. I am free to recognize the legitimacy of some of your objections— that the situations are not sufficiently frequent in the 2 first acts — that Warren divides the interests too greatly with Maurice &c. These things may be amended somewhat. — But when you object that you are not suffered to know by what means Warren obtained his power over Osborne — the actual record of the misdoings of the latter not being declared, — I answer that this would not be necessary in narrative & is less so on the stage; — that some[thing] is properly left to the understandings of the audience — to their conjectures at least, particularly in the case of an inferior character in whom it is not intended to awaken their interest — that enough is shown when they understand (as they do) that Warren is in possession of a secret of Osborne's, which is fatal to his credit. Nor do I concur with you when you alledge want of motive for Warren's hostility to Maurice. There is motive enough. They are rivals in love — the inferior person has wronged the nobler — has robbed him, and hates his cousin for his superiority in every respect as well of character as talent. The love of Warren for Clarice *is* shown in the first act — and that of Clarice & Maurice for one another must be understood from their marriage which is also shown in the first act. That they were not married before the audience matters nothing, though still, should the audience doubt whether the ceremony was performed by a Parson in orders, we can have that matter amended, as I have said before. Whether it will help the interest much to make the Aunt a more important person is a question. She is the mere creature of Warren, and is necessarily feeble. I could omit her altogether. What you say of two master passions may be very just by way of generalization, but is not applicable here. Warren hates his cousin Maurice for several reasons. He has always proved his superior — has *proved* him a coward — has pardoned him a wrong, is his rival in love, and these rouse his *passion* for a vindictive triumph over him who has always triumphed hitherto. I can certainly love a woman, and hate a man, at the same moment, and these are the only master passions of Master Warren, — a man of loose morals, of bad feelings, mortified by defeats, by a sense of the scorn of another, and under the goad of conflicting emotions resolving desperately on the ruin of one whom he has wronged. I concur with much that you suggest touching the action of the piece for the stage, but look upon your philosophy as wholly wrong in respect to the characters. These may be heightened, strengthened, & more elaborately brought out. Should Forrest determine to take the piece, I would cheerfully come on to N. York this winter and amend it as he might suggest — always supposing that the compensation should be such as to justify me in doing so. But I fear that his advertisement for a drama will make him reluctant to recieve a piece separately from that offer. Now, I never write for prizes. I cannot afford to risk the time, and would prefer $1000 as a certainty to the chance only of $5000. Without annoying him on the subject. I could wish that you would persuade him to an early reading of the remaining acts. Do not you attempt to influence his judgment in any way. Be sure, he will know better what will suit him, than you can teach, with all your arguments. If he does not like it, I will make a volume of my Arnold, Michael Bonham, Locrine, Atalantis & adding this "man of the people", close my account with the Dramatic World in a single publication.[289] When does F. return from Phila., and when, think you, will he be able leisurely to read it? Write me soon, on this & all other matters. By the way, is not the closing scene of act the 2d. an effective one. — To this day, I have recieved no paper containing Forrest's offer for the prize. I should like to see his terms & requisitions, even though I engage not

---

[289] This volume was not published. For Forrest's contest, see note 267, Oct. 20, 1847.

in the contest. Pray send me a copy of his publication. — I see that Headley & Griswold are in conflict.[290] Where, in the meantime, are Duyckinck & Mathews., Have you made any inquiry touching the publication of my "Laconics" — my Voices from the Woods & Wayside? —

I have obtained for you the appointment of Commissioner for taking Deeds in New York for the State of South Carolina, from our Governor — and will send you the commission as it is made out by our Secretary of State. It may help to bring you more into note, & may add a few shillings per annum to the fund. Your situation and ability, as a man of business, may enable you to secure the best portion of it which is done in Charleston. — Our friend, Allen, is an invalid and looking badly.[291] *Inter nos,* I regard him as in a very bad way. His wife, too, is looking thin & feeble. We have invited them to Woodlands, & if they are wise they will come. You ask nothing about the children. Does your wife ever think of her little namesake. Gilmore is as broad as long, and may now be seen mounted barebacked on a horse, fifteen hands high, with his own hands only clutching the bridle. Mary Lawson likes no better fun than being on horseback, though in the lap of one of the girls. She thrives famously, and will weigh as much (nearly) as Kate. Kiss the children all round, and present us very lovingly to that woman, your wife, — i. e. if she be at all loveable at the moment you tell her of my letter.

Yours truly as ever

&c

W. Gilmore Simms

P. S. If you would only adopt the habit of answering a Letter, as I do, the moment that you recieve it, your correspondence would fall lightly upon your hands. — Procrastination increases your labors, and I am sorry, for your sake, to suspect that it grows upon you. But —. Is Duyckinck often to see you. What are his relations with W. & P.? — Should you be passing them, pray step in & request that they will send me a few copies of Views & Reviews, which they seem most strangely to have forgotten. I want *complete* setts — both vols.

---

[290] For this quarrel, occasioned by the rivalry between Headley's *Washington and His Generals* and Griswold's *Washington and the Generals of the American Revolution,* see Bayless, *Rufus Wilmot Griswold,* pp. 132-136.

[291] Probably Gilbert Allen. See note 231, June 17, 1845.

413 : To James Henry Hammond

Woodlands, Nov. 22, 1847.

My dear Hammond

Your letter, apprising me of your visit to the Court House, reached me when I was booted for my ride to Georgia and when there was no leisure left me to answer it. Another, just recieved, finds me about to start for Columbia, whither I go chiefly on Aldrich's account. He tells me he is to be hardly pushed. I can scarcely think it, but will do my little toward rendering his battle less arduous. — When I returned to Augusta (where I stayed a day) I learned from Mr. Wilson (your immediate representative) that your carriage had been seen in the streets of that city. I immediately went to Mr. Bones', where I was told that it had left some hours. I did not see Mr. B.[292] I was at the U. S. Hotel (I think they call it) one of the most public places, in the town, and my name was on the books. But, unless I could have got off next day, I could scarcely have got to your plantation. I too wish to converse with you, for letters are but wretched agents in the transmission of those collateral passages of thought which are so important to the right understanding of any subject. — I shall of course be very glad to hear from Judge Tucker,[293] & equally pleased to serve him in the matter we spoke of. — I have seen none of the Augusta papers of which you speak.[294] Their praise

---

[292] John Bones.

[293] On Oct. 13 Tucker had written to Hammond, apologizing for his long silence. (Original in the Hammond Papers, Library of Congress.)

[294] In his letter to Simms of Nov. 17 Hammond had written: "I was delighted to see the unqualified praise of your speech ['Self-Development'] in the Augusta papers. I can conceive that you would handle the subject you selected *con amore*, & I congratulate you sincerely on having won laurels in Georgia, where every thing Carolinian is viewed with such bitter prejudice. The Whig paper in Augusta, however, gave you the *devil* (literally) for proclaiming Christ as the Founder of Democracy. I am not so sure that I would dispute your view of the matter myself but I doubt very much the *prudence* of your publishing it in these days of cant. Men will not regard the matter historically or philosophically, but religiously & politically they will think you a 'scorner' & a run mad 'sans culotte.' But I suppose you *'don't* care.'" (Original in the Hammond Papers, Library of Congress.) The *South Carolinian* of Nov. 24 contains the following account of Simms' oration from "a correspondent of the Augusta Constitutionalist": "It has added, in the estimation of his auditors, to his reputation, and when published will be read with profit and pleasure by thousands of his admirers. It was chaste and pure in style, profound in thought, and in the main eminently practical and instructive. In some of its views and speculations it was somewhat strained and stilted — what might be called transcendental. . . . His theme may be expressed in a few words. Self-development is the great duty of man—his talents seem a trust for which he would be held to strict account, each man according to his endowment— *faith* to believe in his capacity to do his duty, *will* to determine that he *would*

& blame are equally new to me. I could wish, if you have them still, that you would scissorize all that concerns me specially, and cover to me in your next. I am not sure but that two very different things are confounded together. The night before I delivered my oration, I was told that I should hear Colquitt,[295] by attending a meeting of the Democratic party. There, to my surprise, I was called out, and specially designated by McAllister [296] in his speech. I was compelled to take the floor, — without being permitted to use the very topics which had brought the party together; and I was accordingly, at particular pains, in the opening of what I said, to disclaim, (as the guest of the community) any disposition or purpose to engage in the discussion of their domestic controversy. But I too was a democrat — not a partisan. That my democracy was in some degree the result of a religious conviction. That I regarded Jesus Christ as being the first exponent of a principle which recognized the man as superior to the caste or party, & first freed him from the shackles of an hereditary priesthood; & so on. I need not bore you with details upon a point which, I take for granted, your own studies must have led you to long ago. It is thus, I added, that I had come to regard the conservative principle as in the race — in the people — rather than in castes, professions or parties, which, however wise, were usually selfish, creatures of routine, and forever hostile to all novel forms of truth. Enough of this. The thing was a novelty to my hearers evidently. I passed from this to the defense of the Mexican war, on the very ground to which its opponents base their objections — viz: that it is & must be a war of conquest. So much for so much — and so little! The speech was applauded,

---

realize the destiny which Providence assigned him, were the requisites—the sole requisites, for Providence had created no dunces. Each man was endowed and fitted for his appropriate sphere. With *faith* and *will* he could be A MAN. Without them, NOTHING.

"It would give me pleasure to enter at large into an account of this fine oration, its style and imagery, the manner of its delivery and the evident admiration it excited. Though he commenced with a fatigued audience, who had already been listening to the speeches of the Graduating Class for more than two hours, he enchained their attention for nearly two hours longer."

295 Walter Terry Colquitt (1799-1855) was United States senator from Georgia at this time.

296 Matthew Hall McAllister (1800-1865), attorney from Savannah, Ga. The *Southern Patriot* of Nov. 12, 1845, quotes a sketch of McAllister from the "Weekly Portrait Gallery" of the New York *Morning News*. According to the *News'* account, McAllister was the unsuccessful candidate for governor in the last Georgia election, had been district attorney for Georgia under John Quincy Adams, and was known as the "War Horse of Chatham," Savannah being the county seat of Chatham county.

— and you now tell me — abused! Well! You are right! I am somewhat surprised with myself that I care so little about the canters. — My oration was on the subject of "Self development." I have heard it praised. Mr. Stevens [297] (the Geo. Randolph — *longo intervallo, indeed!*) did me the honor to like it very much. He was present. Petigru [298] was present also & paid me some high compliments upon its originality & eloquence. There were others, but my vanities must not distress you, particularly as the Philistines are upon me to rebuke them. Send me the scraps in your next. — I did not wish to '*waive* the subjects' of which you wrote me in your preceding. There was no foundation for the story of my pique or chagrin, except what was in the conscious hearts of some of our people.[299] Brown [300] for example, who months ago insisted that I must be the next man after Rhett, was the first to throw up his cap for Colcock. Poor fellow, he had only forgotten. He meant nothing ill, and I do not think the least unkindly of him. But you must know, it was a subject of consideration among certain of our friends in Orange & Barnwell, whether I should not be run after Rhett. Yet, when his resignation was announced, there was not a man to suggest my name, or to write to me on the subject. I should not have run agt. Colcock, but the least they could have done was to consult me. *Still, I have uttered no complaints, & feel no anger or mortification.* You will believe me. I am pretty well resigned to be laid on the shelf in so much good company. I see no hopes under present auspices for any of us. — You must not decieve yourself. Nobody doubts (I fancy) in Charleston that you are Anti debt. I am very sure that Elmore knows it. The 'Mercury' can never be a safe organ for you! That your shots tell is fairly to be concluded from the earnestness, the industry & the elaborateness of the replicants. As for your essays, they are better written than if you had more leisure. The want of documents is some-

---

[297] Alexander Hamilton Stephens (1812-1883) was a member of Congress from Georgia at this time. He was later vice-president of the Confederacy.

[298] James L. Petigru. See introductory sketch.

[299] On Oct. 31 Hammond had written that he had been mortified to hear it whispered in Barnwell that Simms was hurt that his friends, including Hammond, had not nominated him for Congress upon Robert Barnwell Rhett's announcement of his resignation. Hammond said that he did not know of Rhett's announcement until he saw it in the newspapers along with W. F. Colcock's announcement of his candidacy, that he knew Simms wanted the nomination, and that he expected to support him. (Original in the Hammond Papers, Library of Congress.)

[300] J. G. Brown and Simms had been members of the Barnwell Delegation to the South Carolina House of Representatives during 1844-1846.

thing as an embarrassment, but your memory is a sufficiently good one, & your mind is sufficiently clear & logical for the array of facts and arguments which are too true to be forgotten. I would say press on, and make your developments as thorough as you can, though, at present, you see no fruits. They are so much seed set to grow. The crisis is not yet. The logrollers will succeed in their object, and my only hope now, in the people regaining their liberties — in other words — in the overthrow of the machinery of politics by which we are at the mercy of some few men, will be in some terrible disaster, some blow-up, which will rend the wirepullers to pieces in the very act of working the engine. True, we shall be hurt? Are we less hurt now? As well lose a leg or arm, as die by inches, conscious of a death at every gripe. The error which these people are committing, consists in too rapidly urging the accouchement of the goose. There is but one remedy; and that is to bring the people into power at the expense of the politicians. You will dismiss the prejudices on this head which you have too fondly adhered to, rather with an affection than a thought, and will learn to feel & think with me, that there is no tyranny more lothsome, than that which labors always to stifle independence. You do not, I am sure, any longer decieve yourself with that wild impulse which filled your brain in 1830 — 2 — 4?[301] This tyranny not only keeps down mind & independence in individuals, but subdues the hopes, the energy & the enterprise of the man. The most sluggish states in the union are Virginia & South Carolina, — where the political pretension is greatest & where the great body of the people are least intelligent. — A word more as concerns myself. Nothing can be more idle than what Trotti says of our relations.[302] I never suspected his friendship, for I never decieved myself in the notion that I had it. It was he who suspected me, & you, and every body, from certain convictions in his own mind, that he was not the man to

---

[301] During this period Hammond edited the Nullification newspaper in Columbia, the *Southern Times,* while Simms edited the Unionist newspaper in Charleston, the *City Gazette.*

[302] In a letter to Simms of Oct. 31 Hammond reported that Col. S. W. Trotti had refused to support Simms for nomination for Congress: "I have been supporting Simms on all occasions up to this time. Yet for several years he has suspected my friendship. I can do nothing to remove his suspicions & will submit to them no longer." Hammond added, however, that Trotti had not yet committed himself to support Colcock. (Original in the Hammond Papers, Library of Congress.)

compel our adherence. I would have served him, *did* serve him, & in reference to this very election, a year ago, sent him word by his brother-in-law, that if he would run I should *not* oppose him. I can concieve of no reason in my conduct why he should speak in this fashion. He has been reserved to me a long time. I sought to conciliate him while it was proper for me to do so. But in a dozen particulars I could satisfy you, as I have been myself satisfied, that no matter who was the candidate opposed to me, the feeling of Trotti toward me has been such that such opponent of mine would always have commanded vote of his. — Should he ever allude to this matter again, pray ask him by what means, or in what circumstances, he discovered my doubt of his friendship. — By the way, a queer mode of convincing a man that he erred, to go against him tooth & nail. When he suspected me, what did I do? Showed the facts to his friends — to you & others, — and silenced his suspicions, at least, if I did not succeed, — as I feel sure I did not, — of reconciling him to me. — But, this is all idle talk, which, in your sleeve, hypocrite as you are, — you must smile at. Col. T. may be a very good fellow in his way — I have been willing to think so, — but his good fellowship will avail me nothing, and will scarcely do for you. I have always treated him kindly & respectfully — shall do so still, — but shall neither tax his friendship, nor seek his favor. I am not particularly good at the arts of conciliation, & only regret that he has not been willing to take me as he found me. I made him no pledges of friendship — we exchanged no guarantees. He may have served me, though I cannot say I know the fact, and I have certainly tried to serve him, and in so doing offended the jealousy of another friend, whom I had really tried. We are surely quits. — Write me soon. I shall be only a few days in Columbia — just long enough to see how the land lies with Aldrich, and do what I can for him. Shall be at home, God willing, on Saturday next.

Yours truly &c

W. Gilmore Simms

Gen. Hammond

414: To James Lawson

[c. November 30, 1847][303]

My dear Lawson.

I mentioned, in a previous letter, that I had procured for you, from our Governor, the appointment of Commissioner for New York, for taking the acknowledgment & proof of deeds &c. to be used in South Carolina. On a recent visit to Columbia, I made a copy, as above, of the form of the oath to be taken by you.[304] When you send me the oath, properly executed, the Commission issues; and I will then procure & send it you. I am of opinion that the appointment, giving you very little trouble, may yet be made to afford you a nice little addition to your sixpences. The intercourse between N. Y. & S. C. is greatly increasing and you are in the very way of business, accustomed to it, and very well known generally. — I have just recieved, under your address, a copy of the Evening Post, containing Forrest's offer.[305] Do write me as soon as you can in relation to the Man of the People. I now see where I can make sundry improvements in that piece. — It is not improbable — so I learn from my visit to Columbia, — that I may be called upon by the Legislature, to act as Commissioner or Intendant of Public Schools throughout the State.[306] An attempt will be made to reorganize the System, which is one of many crudities, — and the first object will be the election of a superintendent who is familiar with the subject & the people. I have been thought to answer these conditions in considerable degree, and have been applied to on two previous occasions by the Executive for my consent to serve. I have now signified my readiness to accept, provided they make the salary a good one. *Nous verrons.* — We are getting ready for Christmas, one way or another. This morning we killed a beef by way of beginning, & we are ransacking the country for geese & turkies. My wife is hanging curtains, & Augusta will soon leave us for a month with her relations in the parishes. I wish you & yours were here if for a month

---

[303] This letter is postmarked Dec. 1. The year is established by Simms' reference to Lawson's "appointment of Commissioner for New York, for taking the acknowledgment & proof of deeds &c. to be used in South Carolina." See letter to Lawson dated "Nov. 16. or 17. 1847."

[304] We have omitted the form, which Simms copied at the top of this letter.

[305] We have been unable to locate an account of Forrest's offer (see note 267, Oct. 20, 1847) in the New York *Evening Post* for this period.

[306] Simms did not receive this appointment.

only. Fine fishing until now — trout, pike, jack, perch, &c. Love to all.

Yours Ever &c

W. Gilmore Simms

J. L.

415: To JAMES HENRY HAMMOND

Woodlands, Tuesday Night [November 30, 1847][307]

dear Hammond.

I left Columbia on Sunday last. Up to that time, it was difficult to say what would be the success of the several rail road schemes.[308] Logrolling may do much, and where districts are greatly anxious for an object, it is not a moderate tenacity of principle, on the part of representatives, that will run counter to their wishes. Still, we have many stout & stubborn friends, and the very voracity of the applicants may defeat their objects. Besides, they are already at logger-heads anent the routes, & this may operate to baffle them in their cupidity. Anti Debt has undoubtedly done some good. He has alarmed fears which are not easily quieted, & there is some peril in going home at the close of a second session to constituents who have a proverbial terror of debt. We shall see, & may, in the meantime, be permitted to hope. — We were fortunate in Aldrich's election. He was narrowly beset. — I saw Walker just after his reciept of a letter from you. It is perhaps unfortunate that W. has his eye upon the Attorney Generalship. He tells me that Bailey will certainly resign or be removed. I doubt. The clique are putting forward Hayne. This outrages the Charleston Bar — in degree, I suppose. De Treville hopes to divide them. Walker has his hopes also. Entre nous, in his case I very much doubt. Clever & trusty, he is yet not sufficiently in the ring. One must either be loved or feared. He must be felt in some way. I certainly wish him successful & from the

---

[307] The year is established by Simms' reference to his dinner at R. F. W. Allston's, also discussed by Allston (see note 312, below). In his letter to Hammond of Nov. 22 Simms writes that he is going to Columbia to remain only a few days. He was there on Nov. 25 (see note 312, below), and he wrote to Lawson *c.* Nov. 30 after his return from Columbia (see letter of that date). This letter, therefore, has been dated Nov. 30, a Tuesday.

[308] The following railroad schemes were introduced in the 1847 session: Act to Incorporate Barnwell Rail Road Company, Act to Authorize Formation of the Spartanburg and Union Rail Road Company, Act to Authorize the Formation of the Colleton Rail Road Company, and Act to Incorporate the King's Mountain Rail Road Company

moment I heard of his wishes, I forbore to say a word in relation
to [De] Treville, whom I was rather disposed to help, quite as
much because of my hostility to cliquism, as in deference to his
particular merits. — Manning is the nominee of the same clique
that brings Hayne forward, that brought Colcock out in place of
Rhett, that puts up & pulls down at pleasure. Manning has his
nominees in town. One of these, James Simons,[309] is proposed to
succeed Colcock as Speaker. Whether Manning's nomination implies that of the party, I know not, but Simons is sufficiently feeble
for their purposes. Henry (J. E.) would have supported Manning
for Gov., but for this attempt in behalf of Simons. Elmore & his
friends are concieved to be bound to our up country friends. It is
very questionable whether the former so religiously esteemed the
obligation as the latter. We shall see. — I would you could be in
Columbia & traverse the House for a single day only. It would
do wonders for you. It is still an impression with many that you
dare not show yourself and this opinion is the only thing (almost)
that confirms the belief in the evil tales at your expense. Your
simple presence would undo the meshes. I could wish for this,
though I do not counsel it. I do not counsel it because a brawl
would be a very shocking thing in the case of one in your position,
& with regard to the positions you have held & may yet attain.
Otherwise, I should say, go to Columbia at all hazards. Still, I
am of no opinion that you would be molested by any body. The
game already played would seem to promise great personal forbearance in the future as in the past.[310] — I dined with Preston.
He is improving in health, & getting tired of the College.[311] He
is not enough of the phlegmatic for the situation; but had better
gnaw upon his heart than leave it now, in the hopes of a more

---

[309] James Simons (1813-1879), a lawyer at 77 Broad Street, Charleston, was
a member of the State House of Representatives from the combined parishes
of St. Philip's and St. Michael's. He was elected speaker of the House in 1850
and held this position for many years. He and Simms had served together in
the House during 1844-1846.

[310] In his reply of Dec. 6 Hammond writes: "As for going to Columbia,
the Hampton's are not there & therefore I ought *not* to go. . . . But if they
were there, would there not be something degrading to go there just to shew
I was not afraid? Can any body really believe I am? . . . If I take any step
to put down the calumnies afloat, where could I stop? I have never heard of
any thing from the opposite side against me. Is there any evidence that any
of them have said or intimated that I dare not go over to Columbia? . . . Some
day I will have a call to Columbia—then I will go. But so many ties have
been ruptured there that it will ever be an unpleasant visit. Indeed I am loth
to make it." (Original in the Hammond Papers, Library of Congress.)

[311] At this time William C. Preston (see introductory sketch) was president
of South Carolina College.

popular & grateful field. Still, Clay's election would send him to
France, & that I suspect is still a hope with him. — Butler & myself dined together at Gov. Johnson's. The Senator scarcely gains
ground in his new career. Aldrich will tell you of an amusing
scene, at Allston's, in which he was a party with our friend
Edwards.[312] By the way, King John [313] has been at me to run
against Colcock. He is cocked & primed with all sorts of arguments. He previously spent himself (I suspect) on McCord,[314] —
who was not unwilling, were his neighbors less so; — but he can
make no start anywhere. I told Edwards, that with me the thing
was out of the question — that I had no time for the canvass
and though, I thought it not unlikely that I could make a case
before the people, yet so fully were the leading men in all the
districts committed to Colcock that I felt reluctant to run counter
to their obvious preferences. Besides, I rather like Colcock, and
only revolt at his becoming a party to the wretched system of
management, by which we are kept in place or out of place, by
the presto — of this or that dextrous machinist. There it stands.
Aldrich speaks of a meeting at your house in Jany. Eh? Pickens,
I saw at Branchville. He is full of bile & overflow.

Yours truly &c.
W. G. Simms

J. H. Hammond Esq.

416: To CAREY AND HART

Woodlands Decr. 13. [1847][315]

Mess'rs Carey & Hart
Gentn.

I am in reciept of your letter declining the experiment of the
Illustrated volume.[316] I am not altogether sure that your conclu-

---

[312] On Nov. 25 Robert Francis Withers Allston wrote to Adele Petigru
Allston: "Judge [A. P.] Butler & W Gilmore Sims [sic] have left us. They
walk'd home one with [John D.] Edwards & the other with me from the
meeting of the Agl. Society, & sup'd with a great deal of pleasant and witty
colloquy. . . . " See J. H. Easterby, ed., *The South Carolina Rice Plantation*
(Chicago: University of Chicago Press, 1945), p. 98.

Allston (1801-1864) was a member of the South Carolina House of Representatives (1828-1832) and of the South Carolina Senate (1847-1856). During
1856-1858 he was governor of South Carolina. For John Edwards, see note
103, April 2, 1847.

[313] Edwards.

[314] David James McCord. See introductory sketch.

[315] Dated by Simms' reference to the payment for his contributions to
Griswold's *Washington and the Generals of the American Revolution*.

[316] See letter to Carey and Hart of Oct. 26.

sions are rightly drawn, but am willing to submit to them. I can
readily believe in the ordinary costiveness of the South as regards
such volumes, but flatter myself that it would relax greatly in
the particular case in question, & perhaps lead the way for more
future liberality. Still, you know the business best. Were I able
to appropriate the sum you mention, I should not scruple, and I
never trespass upon my friends in the way of loans. I must be
content, therefore, to wait my time; though there is one step
that may be taken towards it. It does not so much matter to me
that my poems should be illustrated as that they should be collected; and I am disposed to think that you might try the experiment with them in a neat pamphlet edition of 150 or 200 pages,
8 vo. double column, such as the cheap edition of Longfellow's.
If you will let me know how much it will cost to stereotype a
volume of this size, say 200 pages, I shall probably be willing to
incur half the expense of the plates in joint ownership — the
proceeds wholly accruing to you until you are paid, and my personal security being pledged to you for payment of all losses in
a reasonable time. The copyright of such a vol. remaining with
me. Let me hear from you on this point at your earliest convenience. — I confess myself somewhat surprised at the a/c which
you cover to me. In consenting to write the biographies,[317] it was
the distinct offer to me of our excellent friend, Griswold, that
I should recieve $25 for each biography that I furnished, and he
solicited me to prepare several others of the South, for which he
had not the materials. I certainly should never have attempted
them for the consideration given in your account. Several of the
short biographies were far more troublesome than the long, —
being the subject of various correspondence, frequent inquiries,
and a cross-examination of relatives & acquaintances which consumed a great deal of time. I could have written half a dozen tales
for each of which our friends Godey, or Graham would have
paid me 25 or $30 in the time employed in hashing up one of
these. But if $1.00 per page be the pay, why not apply it to the
long as well as the short articles. The sword should cut both ways.
If the one labour is one by which I must lose, the other should
surely be compensative. The life of Greene contains 44 pages —
that of Lee 32 — that of Moultrie 26, of Sumter 18, Gadsden 10,
Huger 9, Pinckney 8 & Kosciuszko 6. — In all 1953 pages
which, according to the rating of the short biographies should be

---

[317] For Griswold's *Washington and the Generals of the American Revolution.*

at least as many dollars. This is all for yourself. I submit to whatever you decided upon though by any other arrangement than that agreed upon with Mr. Griswold, I am greatly the loser. Still, let it be precisely as you determine. — I have not been an indifferent witness to your controversies with Mr. Headley.[318] His first error left him hopeless in the contest. Besides, his work is a wretched performance — wretched as a history, wretched as a work of art, and avowedly appealing only to a coarse & vulgar taste for its successes. I did not doubt that you would discredit him; and still less do I doubt that your publication will increase in permanent value while his goes out of sight. There are some errors in your edition — one or two in the sketch of Marion — which, when I have leisure I will designate. Meantime, I have only to congratulate you on your signal victory. — Will you do me the favor (through Mr. Hart or Mr Baird) to call on Judge R. T. Conrad, and obtain from him the M.S. Drama [319] which I lent him for perusal, and which it will be much more in your way than his, to forward to me here. Pray cover it in your first package to John Russell unless you have a private hand at your disposal. Will you oblige me also by asking Judge C. if my draft will be honored by Mr. Graham at sight for the two articles published,[320] of which, by the way, copies have never reached me. I cover to you a dft for the amount, in the event of his being prepared for its payment. — The volume [321] of which we conferred & about which we agreed last summer shall be ready for you in the spring when I propose to visit Philadelphia. I am so much discouraged by you Publishers that I scarcely feel venturous enough to say that I have a collection of Tales which I should like to publish [322] — such as the Wigwam & the Cabin, and for which I should be perfectly satisfied to take my pay out of the profits. What say you? The Tales might bear illustration admirably in the style of your ghost book. — Some of the titles are — 1. The Wager of Battle; 2. The Benefactress; 3. The Maroon; 4. The Lucumo of Etruria; &c.

---

[318] For this controversy, occasioned by the rivalry between Headley's *Washington and His Generals* and Griswold's *Washington and the Generals of the American Revolution,* see Bayless, *Rufus Wilmot Griswold,* pp. 132-136.

[319] "Benedict Arnold." See note 328, Sept. 5, 1847.

[320] "Ode to Time" and "Love's Last Supper." See notes 237 and 239, Sept. 5, 1847.

[321] Unidentified.

[322] The never published volume of tales of the imagination.

&c.[323] A bold woodcut to each of these would probably prove attractive, though I should think the Tales alone might answer. Thank you for the "Willis" [324]

Yours truly

W. Gilmore Simms

417: To CAREY AND HART

[December 14, 1847][325]

Mess'rs Carey & Hart

Gentl:

In writing to you yesterday, I omitted to enclose the dft on Mr. Graham of which I spoke in my Letter.[326] You have it above, and if not too troublesome a commission, I entreat you to attend to it. You will also be pleased to request Mr. Graham to send me his Magazine for the present year (1847) and to continue it hereafter. Say to Judge Conrad that I shall be happy to hear from him. — My solicitations are not ended. I am about to print here, at my own expense, a new edition of a wild witch drama which was first published in 1832 called "Atalantis." The thing was greatly praised in the day of its first publication, even by the Boston press which has usually been exceedingly costive where I was concerned. It was also honored with the praises of Tom Campbell in the "Metropolitan" which he then conducted.[327] My present desire is to employ your name in the imprint, and to get you to give your assistance in placing the work before your customers. Of course, I shall be responsible for all expenditures. Let me know as soon as possible whether the matter will be agreeable to you.[328] I could also wish that in the event of your getting up

---

[323] For the first two, see note 170, April 10, 1845. For "The Maroon," see note 198, Oct. 23, 1846. "The Last Feast of the Lucumo; or the Picture of the 'Grotta del Tifone'" was first published in *Southern and Western,* I (March, 1845), 166-181; republished as "The Picture of Judgment; or, the Grotta del Tifone. A Tale of the Etrurian" in *Graham's,* XXXIV (June, 1849), 337-345, and in *Southward Ho!,* pp. 221-224.

[324] Carey and Hart, Philadelphia, had recently issued Willis' *Poems of Early and After Years.* The volume is advertised as "nearly ready" in the *Literary World,* II (Oct. 9, 1847), 237. Subsequent issues contain further advertisements of the volume.

[325] Dated by Simms' reference to his letter to Carey and Hart of Dec. 13.

[326] See letter of Dec. 13.

[327] See note 268, Dec. 6, 1846.

[328] *Atalantis; A Story of the Sea* (see note 23, Jan. 15, 1847) was eventually published by Carey and Hart. Though dated 1848, it was not published until 1849 (see letter to Carey and Hart of Jan. 19, 1849).

publications, such as that of Washington & his Generals, or any [other] which may suit me as [well a]s any other person, that you will think of me; and give me an opportunity for employing myself profitably. Recent losses & disappointments almost persuade me to settle in the North with the view to active & constant literary occupation. I write to you, as you see, in confidence; having no reason, during our rather long acquaintance, to doubt that your interests in my successes should justify me in doing so.

Yours truly &c

W. Gilmore Simms

418: To JAMES HENRY HAMMOND

Woodlands. Decr. 24. [1847][329]

dear Hammond.

I am sorry for your poisoning, particularly as you will not allow me to cure you with umschlags and cold water. I trust you are recovered wholly, but these vegetable poisons are troublesome customers & require prompt tendance, and vigilant attention. Drink no wine while you are afflicted. — Your Anti Debt essays have done a great deal of good. I was in town a few days ago where I heard it said that they killed the Rail Road money seekers off. That they contributed to this end very considerably, along with the fact that it was the last session for the members of the lower house &c — I have no question. I have thought well of them from the first, and see no reason now to change my opinion when the subject has glided into the affiliate one of the Bank. I *know* that they have made considerable impression. I *feel* that they will occasion more. Could we go before the people, to whom alone I look for our safety & rescue, all would be right. *I* have no fear of the people. I only fear the cunning & the selfish who are *professionally* false to the country in their allegiance — which nothing can alter — to Self! Self! The people act wrong from impulse & ignorance. The professions from system & principle. Keep on. You cannot multiply these essays too frequently. When you have got through the whole question — repeat them if you can find the leisure, in other forms, and still farther simplify your examples. Take up the history of the Bank *ab ovo*. Make the numbers short,

---

[329] Dated by Simms' reference to Hammond's essays signed "Anti-Debt," which were appearing in the Charleston *Mercury* in the winter of 1847-1848.

and do not condense too much those portions which are likely to bother the simple. Half of your legislators are ignorant of your definitions. Make the history of a sinking fund clear to them — its laws, & the principle upon which it is founded — which is always false & pernicious unless there be an actual & ample capital as the basis. The vulgar notion really assumes the case to be quite different. A series of essays in a new character, as if auxiliary to Anti Debt, treating the subject historically and quietly, step by step, insinuating the argument, will help the public wondrously particularly in the country. The country is coming right & opening its eyes. It was that *they might see you* that I wished you in Columbia,[330] — & that they might not assume *a lack of moral courage to meet those whom it is thought you had greviously wronged.* That they question your physical courage is not thought of. But they assume with the pack that it is the conscience that makes cowards of us all. *The extent of the injury is necessarily magnified to those who fancy it keeps away a man notoriously intrepid.* You must not suppose tnat any such vulgar notion troubled my thought, that it was supposed you shrunk from personal, or physical encounter. Still, I deemed it only prudent, as you might have *vulgar* men to deal with that you were prepared for any issue. I repeat, that your essays have done & are doing good. Continue them if you can. Repeat them & still farther simplify them if you have the leisure. Do this through some friend, in a Columbia or Hamburg paper. What you have published are all well written, in an unaffected manly style, direct, full of purpose and force, & quite intelligible to the *intelligent*. But these are too frequently against you. If you could make them so to the people — if you can get these matters before the people your oligarchy — for we have been under such for twenty years — will be put down forever. If not, they will put you down & keep you down, and all the independence & talent of the State along with you. Their ramifications envelope us, as the sinuous spider web that winds around the halls of the Senate & the House, enmeshing all. The similitude will suit the case of these two bodies. But there is progress. There is a growing feeling with us, — but a man is wanted to embody it — to give it direction, to say the when, the where & the how, — and for this I would have you at Columbia. D — n the ties! Manhood must sunder these whenever they imply worse bonds. — No matter about the articles touching my

---

[330] See note 310, Nov. 30, 1847.

oration. I have seen some of them. The abusive ones were to be expected from the Whig Press. I did not remember the passage in Milton.[331] I have read most of his prose as well as verse, but have no recollection of it. My notion was founded on a course of original thinking which seperates me from all the Churches. I regard the penalty which was incurred by Adam & his race, as the forfeiture of the gift of immortality. The favorites of God from that period were translated in the flesh to Heaven. The Jews taught no such doctrine as the Immortality of the soul. The penalties followed to their generations. The Pharisees, or a portion of them, taught it as a speculative doctrine in philosophy. The moment this became the case, it showed the intellect prepared for the gift. Christ was vouchsafed, and his dying and resurrection was to establish a fact which could not otherwise have been believed, and which, indeed, was recieved with incredulity by the great body of the people. Immortality implies individuality of gift & character. Individuality seperates man from the mass, and lifts him into a responsible personality, crowning him with a will which is based on new considerations of his own importance &c. &c. I will not trouble you with my theology, which, if not orthodox, is without a shade of irreverance. I am glad you find anything in Milton which can assist me hereafter. I will con him anew. — I am afraid that I can't come to see you on the 5th. A week ago I thought differently & seeing your brother,[332] gave him to suppose that I should certainly be with you. But a recent searching examination into my affairs will place it out of my power. I am greatly behind hand with my publishers. I have numerous tasks before me which I cannot neglect. On the performance of these tasks depend my resources, which, to deal with you frankly, are small & diminishing. My residence in South Carolina, is unfavorable to me as an author. I lose $2000 per annum by it. Our planting interests barely pay expenses and my income from Literature which in 1835 was $6000 per annum, is scarce $1500 now, owing to the operation of cheap reprints which pay publishers & printers profits only & yield the author little or nothing. To earn this $1500 I

---

[331] On Dec. 6 Hammond had written to Simms: "Do you know that you have *good authority* for your argument about Christ's democracy? Milton, in his 'Ready & Easy way to establish a Free Commonwealth' enlarges upon Christ's having been an ardent 'Commonwealth's Man' who is the 'Democrat' of our day. Look over the article. It may serve you in a pinch." (Original in the Hammond Papers, Library of Congress.)

[332] Marcus Claudius Marcellus Hammond. See introductory sketch of the Hammonds.

have to labor constantly, and being absent from the field, I labor at a venture, not being able to seize upon the occasion. I think, accordingly, to remove from the State to New York. But this, for the present, *entre nous*. I shall determine by the Spring when I go North. Here I am nothing & can be & do nothing. The South don't care a d — n for literature or art. Your best neighbour & kindred never think to buy books. They will borrow from you & beg, but the same man who will always have his wine, has no idea of a library. You will write for & defend their institutions in vain. They will not pay the expense of printing your essays. I was desirous of having a collection of poems illustrated for a Christmas book — an expensive form of publication, & speaking of the South as being quite as likely to buy my illustrated book as that of Mr. Willis, the publisher assured me that of such books, the whole South & Southwest together did not buy one hundred copies! [333] At the North, the usual gift to a young lady is a book — in the South, a ring, a chain, or a bottle of Eau de Cologne! But I am at the bottom of my Sheet.

Yours

Simms

Try and find this scrawl intelligible. I do not know that I should find it so. But I shan't attempt it. I never read over a letter to one whom I can trust. — If you wish your secrets as a newspaper correspondent kept, beware how you write in your own hand & from your own postoffice. I was at Burges & James' a few days ago, when they showed me your *envelope* (of proof I believe) in your hand & fresh from Silverton. Send me a copy or two of the pamphlet.—W. G. S.

---

[333] See letter to Carey and Hart of Dec. 13.

1848

[c. January 2, 1848]¹

dear Hammond.

Just before the reciept of your letter of the 31. recd. this moment, I had deliberated with myself upon asking your notions upon a new & elaborate History of South Carolina, to contain a comprehensive analysis of all the transition periods, to comprise a careful review of the documentary matter & a selection from it, & to include all those portions of the history of the interior & hill country which are now scattered fragmentarily over numerous fields of publication, in pamphlets, periodicals &c. bringing down the narrative to the present period — giving the nullification history without discussing it. Such a work would be comprehensive & very valuable. It could not be compressed into less than two large octavos such as Prescott's Peru, and done up in similar style with maps & plates it would be somewhat costly. Now the question is what is the possibility of getting an adequate subscription to such a work by a circular among the gentry. The circular should contain these facts viz: that the work could have no circulation *out* of South Carolina — that its character is so perfectly local that no publisher would print it if you *gave* him the copyright — that it would be too heavy an expense for any single enterprise, and the hope of such a publication, *now,* — unless upon the plan proposed — would rest upon the rare union, in one person, of the requisite wealth, will, talents & industry. The cost of such a publication, according to the plan I propose, would not be short of five thousand dollars. A thousand subscribers at five dollars each would meet the absolute expense of the plates and printing of an edition of that number. The author would have to look for his profits to all sales beyond that number. Is it possible,

¹ This letter is in reply to one from Hammond dated Dec. 31, 1847. Since Simms replied immediately upon receipt of Hammond's, his must have been written c. Jan. 2.

think you, by a private circular to select individuals, to get this number of subscribers? There is yet another question, — could the State be got to subscribe under such a showing of the circumstances as I give you the clue to? Can she be persuaded to do what New York, Louisiana, Georgia and other states have done, make an appropriation for an Historiographer who shall go to Europe and ransack the Colonial Offices for documents relating to our Ante-revolutionary periods? Georgia has got some twenty huge folios relating to her own concerns. Albert Rhett [2] just before his death contemplated the appointment of such an officer by the Legislature, and applied to me to know if I would accept it. It appears to me that could we enlist leading men in all parts of the state by a circular, with reference to the preparation of such a history, it would greatly pave the way to a successful move, at a *first* session by the Legislature towards the creation of such an office. And the application would be quite as legitimate as the Geological Survey. A State never arrives at her true dignity until she is in possession of her own facts. But think the matter out for yourself, and let me know promptly how the thing strikes you, and how many names you can procure by private measures.[3] — I must think over much of your letter. This scheme, if successfully acted upon, would save me from a temporary necessity — for it would be temporary only — of going North. But you know nothing of the history of publication. I could get a great deal of employment which now I lose, were I at the North. *While there* I usually get as much as will employ all my leisure and I have great advantages over almost all the Northern authors. I write with ten times their rapidity — am more at home in a variety of departments — can meet exigencies better — think more rapidly, and have greater resources in historical material. You will understand & excuse the seeming egotism which is *inter nos*. The *puffing* (as you phrase it) would follow, — since it is the publisher's business to see that what he publishes finds its way to favorable hands. But I am not accessible for employment; and this is an important item when you remember that hack literature is not self suggestive but is prescribed to you. It is not what your genius prompts you to write, but what your publisher suddenly concieves will sell. There are several reasons why my

---

[2] Albert Moore Rhett (1810-1843) was a younger brother of Robert Barnwell Rhett. See introductory sketch of the Rhetts.

[3] This proposal never materialized.

works cannot be had entire without considerable painstaking. Some of them are out of print. You cannot get whole editions of any American writer, perhaps, but Cooper, and he, being a man of fortune stereotypes his works at his own expense & thus always has the plates when copies are called for. My works have been issued by various publishers. The Harpers can always furnish you with the following which are stereotyped — viz: 1. Martin Faber & other Tales 2 vols: 2. Guy Rivers 2 vols: — 3. The Yemassee 2 vols: 4. The Partisan 2 vols: 5. Mellichampe 2 vols: 6. Pelayo: 2 vols. In all 12 vols. These are really, with one exception, the feeblest as the least original of my writings. I was a mere beginner when I wrote them learning the use of my tools. To these succeeded 1. The Damsel of Darien 2 Vols: 2. The Kinsmen, 2 vols: 3. Confession, or The Blind Heart, 2 vols: 4. Beauchampe, the Kentucky Tragedy, 2 vols. These 8 volumes were published by Lea & Blanchard, but not stereotyped. It is possible that they may still be able to supply a few copies. Next are 1. Richard Hurdis, 2 vol: 2. Border Beagles, 2 vol. These 4 vols. were published by Carey & Hart. Carl Werner, 2 vol. Helen Halsey, 1. Castle Dismal, 1. Count Julian, 2 in 1; Views & Reviews; 2 vols; the Wigwam & Cabin 2 vols; Lives of Marion, Smith, Bayard, & History of South Carolina — in all 14 vols. may be obtained, I suspect from John Russell in Charleston. Indeed, I think it likely that Russell is as likely to procure a complete sett as anybody. Now, were I at the North, I could contrive to get up a uniform edition. But when I go there for a couple of months in summer, there is no time for anything, and at that season no business is doing. To write is idle. Out of sight out of mind. There is always a sufficient crowd present to thrust the absent & his schemes from the minds of a publisher. But a truce to these details which are innumerable, to be talked over, not scrawled on paper. — I will read your last letters carefully, & send to Burges for 20 copies of your pamphlet.[4] — I note what

---

[4] *The Railroad Mania: And Review of the Bank of the State of South-Carolina* (see note 285, Nov. 7, 1847). On Dec. 31, 1846, Hammond had written to Simms: "I have . . . ordered 1000 copies in pamphlet. I wish to give every reading *country* man a copy. Some will get to the marrow & explain to their neighbours. . . . Take as many of my copies from Burges & Co. as you wish & can dispose of to *advantage*. I think they might sell a few on their own account on the town." (Original in the Hammond Papers, Library of Congress.)

you say of H. & M.[5] What I suggest is always to be taken with respect to the condition of ignorance, with the regard to persons & things in which I am. Your informers, I suspect, are mistaken with respect to M's chances for Gov. See Aldrich. Richardson [6] & others I am told are quite industrious in his behalf. Better seize upon Major Eaves's Mexican fame (if he be not a fool) & make him the man to beat him.[7] Eh?

Yours

W. G. S.

420: To JAMES LAWSON

Woodlands Jany. 7. 1848

Dear Lawson

I had quite given you up. I had concluded that, after repeated letters without one answer in the whole space of two months, that you were rather wearied than interested in my letters, and certainly were not at all disposed to requite them or encourage the writer to farther trespasses, by any premature responses. In connection with this fear of your coldness and indifference was a farther apprehension that the capricious little woman your wife had found some other favorite & had discarded me entirely from her affections. Your letter relieves me in some degree from the

---

[5] On Dec. 31 Hammond had written to Simms: "Entre nous — I have received pretty direct propositions from [John Laurence] Manning's friends— no answer required from me & none given. They have only shown an *anxiety* to make up. . . . I will say *to you,* I would lick the dust from [Wade] Hampton's foot, before I would touch M's . . . shall not lose a chance to move against him. Hampton & [William C.] Preston will kill him of themselves — *if they can.* They are far from wishing to see him promoted." (Original in the Hammond Papers, Library of Congress.)

[6] John Peter Richardson (1801-1864) had been a member of Congress (1836-1839) and governor of South Carolina (1840-1842).

[7] Nathaniel R. Eaves, of Chester, a member of the South Carolina Senate in 1846, had been instrumental in organizing the Palmetto Regiment for service in the Mexican War. By Dec. 23, 1846, "*the father of the Palmetto Regiment*" (as he is called by the *South Carolinian* of that date) had himself volunteered and had been given the rank of color sergeant. Before his return from Mexico the *South Carolinian* reported on Oct. 29, 1847: "The numerous friends of the '*little warrior of Chester,*' will be delighted to learn, that although wounded, he is still numbered amongst the living . . . his name is amongst those who proudly and gallantly bore the Palmetto Flag into the City of the Montezumas, a memorable evidence of which we hope, he will bear home, as an *index* to the *honors which await him.*" Among the "honors" his friends hoped for was that of governor of South Carolina, and in the *South Carolinian* of Dec. 7, 1847, he is accordingly nominated for that position. See also the same newspaper of Dec. 10, 1847.

apprehensions I felt on your account, but not on hers; since if her heart were in the same place as formerly she would hardly have suffered you to remain so long in silence, the more particularly when she knows, as you ought to, how isolated I am here — how few correspondents I have or care to have — how few can be relied on to speak the truth, either to affection or to thought. From Duyckinck I get not a syllable, and have heard nothing since I left New York. Neither letter, nor paper, nor pamphlet reaches me from that source, and two of my letters to him remain unanswered. From Mathews I have no expectations. The Blackwood article I saw, but not D's notice of it.[8] It is evidently from an American, & I suspect a N. Y. hand — most probably from some friend of Mr. Ward, whose Curwen I cut up in the Messenger, and whose reply embodied much of the spirit & topic of the Blackwood article. Of course it must go for what it is worth. I have long since come to the conclusion that criticism at the present day, either for praise or blame (unless for temporary purposes) is not worth a straw, — and so long as I can make *out to live & put myself on record,* my highest present ambition is gratified. Remember this hereafter. It will afford your assigns and mine a key to much of my career. — I am quite disappointed to learn that Forrest has not even read my drama. I had hopes of this performance & if he was not pleased with it, my notion was to try Wallack or Vandenhoff,[9] after making such alterations in the first & second acts as would seem called for. The subject ought to be eminently popular with the American public. I inferred from what Forrest said after perusing the first act that it would not suit him, and was reminded instantly of what Forbes told me touching his playing of the Patrician's Daughter,[10] to which I hold my man of the people to be very far superior. In publishing it, I could

---

[8] "The American Library," LXII (Nov., 1847), 574-592. We have been unable to locate Duyckinck's notice of this article, a review of Simms' *Views and Reviews* and *The Wigwam and the Cabin,* Margaret Fuller's *Papers on Literature and Art,* Poe's *Tales,* and Hawthorne's *Mosses from an Old Manse.* The *Southern Patriot* of Jan. 11, 1848, says: "Maga's blade, which is always keen, has, we think, on this occasion, been wielded with unnecessary vigor. Miss Fuller, who is ungallantly spoken of as a married lady, and Mr. Simms, are abused with caustic sarcasm; and Mr. Poe and Mr. Hawthorne are 'damned with faint praise'. . . ." The *Knick.,* XXXI (Jan., 1848), 68-71, praises the article.

[9] James William Wallack, Jr. (1818-1873), and George Vandenhoff (1813-1885), the actors.

[10] In 1843 Forrest presented for the first time in New York Westland Marston's *The Patrician's Daughter.* See Odell, *Annals of the New York Stage,* IV, 643.

make it realize me $200 in the magazines. Do not suppose that I think at all amiss of Forrest, because of this seeming disinclination. *Au contraire,* my notion is & has been, when I published this & other plays in a volume to inscribe it to him. I am only unfortunate. — I have been engaged on my Don Carlos, of which two acts are finished — far superior I think to the man of the people. I should continue the piece but am discouraged.[11] I can't afford to work to keep my MSS in their pigeon holes. Up to this time you will scarce believe it, I have been more or less engaged upon my Ed. of Shakspeare, and am now writing the general Introduction. It has been a work of very great labor to me, taxing five times the time I had thought to give it, & vexing & wearying me by its tedious manipulations. I hope soon to send on the whole of the matter & wash my hands of it. On & off, it has kept me the whole summer & autumn until now — suffering me to engage in nothing elaborate to which I could be sure of giving my undivided attention. I hope to get a volume done by the first of May when I shall visit the North. It may be that I shall find my publisher this year in Phila.[12] In which event, I shall barely be able to look in upon you for a week, — for my purpose will be, if I can get through by the 1st June to return South again, and revisit the North in November. I have been thinking to reverse the period of my periodical visitations. There is a possibility that I shall be able to make better terms in Phil. hereafter than I have ever been able to make in N. Y. But of this anon & — *entre nous.* — You do not seem to read or refer to my letters when you undertake to answer them, and thus omit sundry matters which I keep in mind. Sometime ago, say Nov. 29, I wrote you from Columbia enclosing you the form of an affidavit which made secure [to] you the appointment which I promised you as Commissioner for this State in N. Y. I do not know whether you attach any importance to such an office, but in your hands it might be valuable. The intercourse between these states is important & increasing. The Gov.[13] instantly yielded to my application & gave me the appointment, but according to the Statute by which the office is just made, the Commission can only issue upon the making & reciept of the affidavit. This is simple & can offend no prejudices.

---

[11] See note 35, Jan. 15, 1845.

[12] Probably *Atalantis* (see note 328, Dec. 14, 1847) : possibly an unidentified work (see letters to Carey and Hart of *c.* Sept. 6 and Dec. 13, 1847).

[13] David Johnson (1782-1855) was unanimously elected governor in 1846. He served for one term.

Now, you say nothing of this Letter and its enclosure. If you
reluct at taking the oath, or if you would rather not be troubled
with the Commission, say so frankly, — though I really see no
reason why you should reject a means for putting at little cost or
painstaking a few hundred dollars annually into your pocket. Your
kinsman, Baker, in Charleston, by the way, gets his living entirely
from appointments of this nature.[14] Are you aware that his wife
is a lunatic & in the asylum? — I am confounded to hear that
Mr. Post should have said any thing impertinent to you. I can't
concieve or conjecture why. I have his letter soliciting the privilege to pay, and asking how & to whom to pay it. I have since
then another letter informing me of his having paid, and requesting other articles, which I have sent him to the amt. of forty
dollars. I enclose you a draft to be presented in two weeks after
they shall appear.[15] That you have got Colton's money relieves
me as it puts me in good credit with you again. Our accounts now
should stand pretty nearly square. Is it so? There are some forty
or fifty dollars to my credit in the hands of W. & P. — I am not
sure that either Duyckinck or Mathews are the persons to determine what the publisher may want. At all events, now that the
Holidays are over, I will get you to call upon Appletons & sound
them touching the volume of Laconics. There will be no harm,
at least, in making the experiment. Let it be at your convenience.
— I learn with great sympathy & sorrow that our Lady wife &
mother has been suffering so severely, as well as her little ones.
I am sure that a winter in the South would help them all, and
once more, though I trust unnecessarily, I say to you that our
house as our hearts, is always open & welcome to you & her,
and all in whom you take interest. Mary [16] is quite precocious.
The faculty is one which after some experience and much reflection, I should counsel you not to encourage. If it be a decided
gift, your discouragement will do nothing to suppress it — if only
a doubtful one your encouragement would give it a diseased

---

[14] Henry Harned Baker was commissioner for taking deeds for South Carolina, North Carolina, Florida, and Georgia.

[15] See letter to Lawson of Nov. 3, 1847. The *Union Magazine* for 1848
contains one tale and two poems by Simms: "The Voice of the Mute," II
(March), 97-102; "Sing Not of Fame. A Ballad," II (Feb.), 77; and "The
Captive of Perote. A Ballad," II (April), 183-184. "The Voice of the Mute"
is reprinted in the *South Carolinian* of April 14, 1848, and in *The Gem of the
Season: A Souvenir for MDCCCLI* (New York: Leavitt and Company, 1851),
pp. 103-119.

[16] Mary Lawson later became one of Simms' favorite correspondents.

activity which would only end in making life a disease, — leaving it an unprofitable struggle with no adequate results. Beware of this misdirection. Encourage her in diligence, study & all usefulness, & let the latent gifts of fancy & imagination develope themselves, if they will, in connection with these absolute virtues. Your climate is a terrible one for children in the winter, as ours is in the summer. I wish that we could all put on wings & go to & fro at pleasure. — Our boy and girl are thriving. Gilmore is forever in the woods & fields — now following wagon & horse, — now after the plough, — forever on the trot. Mary Lawson walks & talks — the latter after a fashion, — mimics cow & calf, & fowl, & cat and shows large musical tendencies. You have but to sing or whistle, or make any musical movement to see head & body keeping time. — I am glad to hear of Bryant's successes.[17] Noticing the Art Union the other day in one of our papers, I paid a compliment to its President,[18] — though it appears that, after regularly paying my sub. to the agent in Charleston I am suddenly stricken from the roll of membership. For a year or more I have had nothing from it, — no pictures, no demands on my purse, & looking over the list of members, I look for my name in vain. Have I been forging my neighbour's paper, saying 'Stand' to a true man on the highway, or what have I done? Love to wife & little ones.

God bless you & yours.

Simms

421: To EVERT AUGUSTUS DUYCKINCK

Woodlands, Feb. 11, 1848

Evert A. Duyckinck Esq

Dear Sir

Your letter found me at a moment when it was most acceptable. I have been suffering from one of the severest attacks of

---

[17] Carey and Hart, Philadelphia, had recently published Bryant's *Poems*. Though dated 1848, the volume is advertised in the *Literary World* during the latter part of 1847. Perhaps Simms is here referring to the success of the volume.

[18] The issues of the *Southern Patriot* for Jan. 1, 2, and 5 are missing from the file in the Charleston Library Society. Undoubtedly Simms' notice was published in one of these. Later, on Jan. 28, the *Southern Patriot* published a long article on the American Art-Union, of which Prosper M. Wetmore was president.

indisposition which has troubled me for twenty years. At such periods I am greatly the victim of despondency; as in all my illnesses, my brain is instantly & intensely affected. Your letter gave me a pleasurable sentiment, not so much by its contents, as because it assured me there was no real estrangement at the bottom of your silence, which I had reason to apprehend. You are one of those friends whom I should be sorry to lose, and I had fears that some sinister influence had been at work on you. The tone & spirit of your letter reassures me, and I lose no time in answering it. I shall be glad to see the copy of Count Julian to which you refer.[19] Get it from Lawson, and have it sent me, by Saunders, in some bundle of the Harpers, taking care to address it me specially under cover. If a second copy can be procured, get it for me, and I will pay the expense. Don't leave it to Lawson to do. He is so eager now after money making that he cares for nothing else. I have had but three letters from him since July last year, and he never answers any questions which I put. What with getting rich & Scotch Whiskey, his winter lapses without his consciousness. From Wiley & Putnam I get as little satisfaction. They apprised me of a balance of $60 or $70 in my favor. I drew in behalf of Bartlett & W. for $50; and they find an error which leaves me but $15. Of this I never hear until my dft is returned unhonored. Will you say to B & W., that I have written to W & P., and hope yet to find that they owe me something more than they fancy. I have required from them a detailed statement of our a/c from the beginning, since I have had to return most of their previous accounts because of their errors. They send me none of their books. A single copy of Views & Reviews came to me & not one for any of the Editors. My copy I accordingly gave up to the Editor of the Quarterly.[20] This book has been most shamefully treated. That it should sell is impossible. Even the notice in the Literary World could scarcely have issued from a friend or from one disposed to do me justice.[21] If you are in communion with them you should enforce the necessity of providing copies liberally to Editors. H. & B., Appleton's, C. & H. and others, supply nearly or quite every press in Charleston & Columbia, besides furnishing me with copies — which, indeed, bring

[19] An edition issued by Garrett and Company, 18 Ann Street, New York, n. d.
[20] *Views and Reviews* is favorably reviewed in *S. Q. R.*, XIII (April, 1848), 520-526. In the course of the article *The Life of Captain John Smith, The Life of the Chevalier Bayard,* and *Self-Development* are also praised.
[21] See note 272, Oct. 26, 1847.

them the best notices. Pray request W. & P. to send me a copy,
at least, of V & R. (complete) if they send me nothing more.
Oblige me also by enquiring of B & W. if they have a copy (and
the price of it) of Raynouard Poesies des Troubadours [22] — if
they know of any other works devoted to the same subject, —
their character & cost? I am glad you like Bayard. I was afraid
of it at this season of blood & thunder. The temptations to episo-
dical matter were numerous, but to indulge in them would have
impaired the continued interest of the biography — that *whole-
ness* which a biographer must no more lose sight of than a dramatist. In your Sidney, there is a difference.[23] Bayard's life was
wholly military — not so Sidney's, and a literary history implies
episode. You can make admirable groupings there. How, by the
way, do you get on with it? Do not weary, but stretch onward.
Devote three or four hours every morning to it in a warm sunny
attic. Your style & tastes fit you admirably for the subject. I shall
be glad to hear that you have not been idle. The Literary World
does not please any longer in S. C. That it should entirely fail
is a possible event. The coldness with which it treats me, and
the indifference, somewhat surprises me, as I have hitherto found
Hoffman a somewhat warm admirer.[24] The elaborate notices of
certain favorites can never work them into position. — Poe is a
very remarkable man. It is great pity that he should be wasted
and should waste himself, as he does. I should like to see him
succeed — still more gladly see him *deserve wholly* to succeed.
Present me respectfully to your brother [25] when you write. It may
require much more hard schooling before Mathews learns to feel
the importance of my counsel to appear hereafter *en masque* only.
He has contrived to provoke a world of enemies & prejudices
who will never otherwise do justice to his possessions. And, *inter
nos,* he has himself to thank for much of this hostility. My winter,
thus far, has past, leaving me few proofs either grateful to my

---

[22] François Juste Marie Raynouard, *Choix des Poésies Originales des
Troubadours,* 6 vols. (Paris, Didot, 1816-1821).

[23] For many years Simms urged Duyckinck in vain to write a biography of
Sir Philip Sidney.

[24] For Charles Fenno Hoffman's connection with the *Literary World,* see
note 34, Feb. 2, 1847. In spite of the fact that Simms speaks of the coldness
of the *Literary World,* the issue for Jan. 29 (III, 628-631) contains a review
of *The Life of the Chevalier Bayard,* which is far from cold. The reviewer
says (p. 629) : "This appears to have been a labor of love to Mr. Simms. . . .
His narrative is obviously arranged with judicious care, both in regard to the
authenticity of the facts, and the sequence of the events." For Hoffman's reviews of Simms' earlier works, see letter to Griswold of Dec. 6, 1846.

[25] George Long Duyckinck.

endowment or industry. I cannot well say that I have any thing. I have just finished reading the pro[of] of my Introduction to the Edition of the plays imputed to Shakspeare, which are now through my hands & may be published in the spring.[26] The job was a tedious & troublesome one. 'Self Development' was written late in Oct. A Review of Prescott in the So. Quarterly — in two articles from my pen, a Review of Stevens' Georgia,[27] some sketches & stories for the Magazines,[28] and some occasional verses touching the War in Mexico,[29] seem to complete my labors. And what to do next is doubtful. Write me soon again and stuff your budget more amply with the crumbs of interest & adventure. How do Mr. Jones & Mr. Webber?[30] If you can lay hands on the notices which have fallen from you in regard to V & R. & other of my writings send me them in your next. Present me respectfully to Mrs D. and believe me very truly as Ever,

Yours

W. Gilmore Simms

Have B & W.[31] any thing particularly in my way? Not that I mean to buy any thing more, until I have paid all my debts. I simply wish to meditate a good thing in anticipation of the taste & possession. Pray tell them that I hope to pay them on or before

---

[26] In the *Literary World,* III (April 8, 1848), 193, *A Supplement to the Plays of William Shakspeare* is advertised as "just published." It is favorably reviewed in the *Literary World,* III (April 15, 1848), 203, and in *S. L. M.,* XIV (May, 1848), 333.

[27] "Prescott's Conquest of Peru," *S. Q. R.,* XIII (Jan. and April, 1848), 136-187, 273-330; "A History of Georgia," *ibid.,* XIII (April, 1848), 470-501.

[28] For Simms' contributions to the *Union Magazine, Graham's,* the *Literary World,* and *Godey's* during 1848, see notes 15, Jan. 7, 1848; 115, Aug. 2, 1848; 206, Dec. 20, 1848; and 130, *c.* July 9, 1849. During 1848 he contributed "Summer Afternoon, in My Study" to the *American* [*Whig*] *Review,* VIII (Oct.), 346. To the *Southern Literary Gazette* for 1848 he contributed the following poems: "Exhortation," I (June 3), 25; "Stanzas: On the Banks of the Edisto," I (June 24), 49; "The Miniature," I (July 8), 65; Despondency of Ambition. In Two Sonnets," I (July 15), 73; "Oh! Bury Him Quickly," I (July 22), 81; "A Memorial," I (Aug. 5), 95; and "The Stars," I (Nov. 11), 209. Simms is listed among the contributors in the June, 1848, issue of the *Gentleman's Magazine* (Cincinnati, Ohio), inaccessible to us (see Charles F. Heartman and James R. Canny, *A Bibliography of First Printings of the Writings of Edgar Allan Poe* [Hattiesburg, Miss.: The Book Farm, 1943], pp. 197-198).

[29] *Lays of the Palmetto: A Tribute to the South Carolina Regiment, in the War with Mexico* (Charleston, S. C.: John Russell, 1848) was not published until July (see letter to Lawson of Aug. 2, 1848). Many of the poems in this volume originally appeared in the *Southern Patriot.*

[30] William Alfred Jones and Charles W. Webber. Webber (1819-1856) was associate editor of the *American* [*Whig*] *Review* during 1848-1849.

[31] Bartlett and Welford.

I visit New York, which will be in May next, God willing, **if** not before.

Yours again,

S.

422 : To James Henry Hammond

Woodlands Feb. 12. [1848][32]

dear Hammond

I have for some ten days past denied myself the privilege of pen & paper. The truth is I have been quite unwell, nay ill, and greatly suffering with that congestion of brain — that tendency of blood upward — which is now properly the subject of my fears. My usual remedy of cold water failed in some degree in consequence of the inveterate tenacity with which I continued the toils which I found were troubling me, and my suffering 'has been a caution,' employing the language of the West. I have been greatly busied beside, and have been to the city, since I last wrote you. These particulars are given that you may not suppose me ungrateful or indifferent in regard to the warmth & kindness with which you responded to my project of the history. The scheme has not ripened among my meditations, under the circumstances which have disquieted me, and whether it will mature is a question for the abundant hereafter. If there were twenty or even ten friends who, like yourself, would or could advance me at a stride so far on the progress to an ample subscription list, I should go to work with an eager spirit. But this is not to be hoped for. The task of getting a thousand subscribers, of soliciting Legislature & all that sort of thing — to say nothing of writing the book itself — is one at which a man of sensibility shudders. But we will see. I concur, at once, in your suggestion touching the era of Nullification, and if I prepare the work will bring it down only to the formation of the present Constitution or to the close of the War of 1812. Both of these epochs furnish adequate

---

[32] Dated by Simms' reference to his plan to publish an elaborate history of South Carolina. In his reply to Simms' letter of *c.* Jan. 2, Hammond had written on Jan. 14 : "I most cordially approve of your project of writing an elaborate history of South Carolina, & as the best evidence of my approval will undertake to get you fifty subscribers at $5 each on Savannah River. . . . As to any assistance from the Legislature—they ought to give it to you & it is worth your while to ask it." (Original in the Hammond Papers, Library of Congress.)

periods to such a history. The history of Nullification should be written *per se*. Why not you write it. There's a subject for you. But you respond in one of your morbid passages — 'Damn the people, — were pearl as plenty as persimmons, should I throw pearl to swine?' But write such a history for yourself — for your own exercise & gratification, in which you may honorably and, indeed, with peculiar nobleness recant your errors of opinion while proving your patriotism. Do justice then to your own as well as to the Union Party. I don't value a button what you say touching your repentance for having written the essays on Railroads & Bank. They have been of real & great service. They have saved the State in great part from a headlong expenditure. They have increased your reputation, — and if they have forfeited the friendship of any one man, they have been of great service personally in providing you with a touchstone of worth which relieves you from the dangers of one upon whom you could not safely have relied in the hour of trial or misfortune. They were well & admirably written essays which you have no reason to be ashamed of or to regret. (Burges, by the way, has neglected to send me the copies as he neglects every thing. Send me then a single one by mail.) You requested me to look out for *two* last essays which you had studiously simplified for popular reading. I saw but *one* in the Mercury, and that was eminently successful — the very thing — to be understood by all who could read at all.[33] You should more frequently engage in these performances, the better to prevent that feeling of exhaustion which must otherwise follow from the conclusion of a labor in which we have been excited. To concieve then a new subject is to refresh oneself from the fatigues of remeditating the old. Your style, by the way, is admirable for public writing. Neither too elevated nor too familiar — dignified without ceremony — frank without flippancy, and clear & transparent without baldness or coldness. A habit of close & searching analysis, great common sense, a cautious research and a confident conclusion, are your happiest essentials for discussion. That your temperament is distrustful somewhat, while hurtful socially, is helpful to a disputant politician. — Take up the Nullification subject — leave a volume of personal memorials —your table talk — pass, at least, to other exercises that you may as soon as possible forget the past. It is

---

[33] Hammond's last two essays had been published in the Charleston *Mercury* of Jan. 1 and Jan. 5. Evidently Simms did not see one of those issues.

the misfortune of amateur writing that its intervals of performance will not suffer it to forget what it has been doing.

Yours truly

Simms.

423: To James Lawson

Feb. [19, 1848][34] Woodlands. S. C.

Dear Lawson.

The first day of January you wrote me a letter full of profession for the future. I shall turn over a new leaf was your language — begin a new epoch of conduct with the New Year. Scarcely had I recieved your letter when I answered it, and here we are verging on the close of Feb. and we hear no more of you. You should be more generous. I am here in the solitude, and to you only do I look for *faithful* reports of men & things & progresses, in the wide and ample world where your lot is cast. A letter from you refreshes me. It comes from a family which, next to my own, possesses the best portion of my heart. All our family are taught to regard you & yours as the nearest kindred, and Mr. Roach who has never seen you, frequently expresses the wish that you and your wife could visit us before all people in the world. You should write often and report fully, the condition of your own household first, then of our friends, and then of your world of letters. But it is curious that your letters, speaking of your own household, almost invariably omit to say anything of your wife, Christina and Kate. You prattle only of Mary & the Boy. It is now our boy, — and now our poetess, — and we have only to guess that your wife & the other two Children are well as you say nothing about them. Your letters should be a chronicle, particularly crowded with details. — Of course, I am particularly anxious about the woman, as I half dread to hear that she has excluded me from her favor in giving the preference to some new and more youthful gallant. Not to have a message, or a hint from her, for more than six months contributes to my despondency. And I have had some most terrible fits lately, from which I am very far from relieved yet. You know but little how I suffer on these occasions; and it is then that your letters are particularly

---

[34] This letter is postmarked Feb. 20. The year is established by Simms' references to *Norman Maurice; or, the Man of the People,* "Don Carlos," and *A Supplement to the Plays of William Shakspeare.*

important to me, as showing me that there are those whom I
love still interested in my affections and fortunes. I want your
advice too, but I fear lest your answer will be deferred *ad Graecas
calendas.* The truth is, I am greatly thinking to reverse my usual
processes of life, — and going north in the winter, returning
south in the summer. I find your people averse to doing business
in the summer, which is there a season of respite and relaxation.
I feel, as I am, that I am burning daylight. — Next, I wish to
know frankly, whether you think that by certain available alterations in the first two acts, I can make the 'Man of the People,'
a successful *acting* play, and acceptable to Forrest. If I could
succeed in this, and get paid for it moderately well, I should be
freed from all embarrasments, and be able to concentrate myself
on the Drama, for a time at least. I have two acts of my Don
Carlos ready and have several dramatic schemes of which I entertain quite hopeful expectations. Write then to me at once,
touching the two points, my going North in the winter & returning South in summer, — and my dramatic prospects & expectations. My present calculation is to visit the North in May.
I have some business in Phil. which may detain me there a
couple of weeks. I have finished reading the last proofs of the
'Shakspeare' — doubtful plays — which has cost me a great deal
of labour & thought. The vol. will, I fancy, be quite a respectable
one. I suppose you have seen Bayard — I don't suppose you
have read it. Duyckinck wrote me a short time ago, the first letter
I have rec'd from him since I left New York. I like him, and
fear that the malign influence of C. M.[35] has made him cold &
indifferent, though he writes in very friendly manner. He speaks
well of Bayard. Did you get a copy of 'Self Development' and
did you read it? Do you know whether Forrest recd. a copy before he went West? Did he go west by way of Charleston? —
My wife mentioned having seen the arrival of a Mr. F. in Charleston, long after I had supposed him *en route* for N. O.? What
says he of the Tragedy? My last letter contained a copious budget
of matter some of which called for your answer. I refer you to it.
I enclose you an order on Israel Post which you may transfer
to Duyckinck to collect when the articles shall have appeared
in print.[36] Do let me have a vol. of news & say as much of the

[35] Cornelius Mathews.
[36] For Simms' contributions to the *Union Magazine* for 1848, see note 15,
Jan. 7, 1848.

domestic world as you can. My wife & Mr. R. send regards. Augusta is from home.

My love and remembrance, as usual, belong to you & your wife.

W. G. Simms.

424: To James Lawson

Woodlands, March 23 [1848][37]

dear Lawson

The moment I recieved your letter commending Mr. Taylor to my attentions, I wrote to him in Charleston (where I percieved that he had arrived the day before) and invited him to Woodlands.[38] I have not yet recieved his answer. If his complaint be pulmonary, Charleston is not the place for him. The climate is too salt & humid. I intimated to him that if health was at all his object he would be much more likely to find it in our middle country during a stay of a few weeks. I trust that this proceeding accords with your wishes. — I rejoice that your business is encouraging. The subject is one which I almost feared to bring up in my letters. I knew very well that you were doubtful and apprehensive, as was natural enough; and I well could concieve all the perils of exchanging a certain for a capricious income. But I have great faith in your fortunes, your known industry and intelligence in business, and in that providential assurance which seldom leaves occasion to doubt that the children of a good man will always find their bread. I am greatly a believer in prophecy & providence. For myself, never rich, always in debt, frequently harrassed by creditors and seldom permitted a day's respite from labor, I have yet every reason to be satisfied — when I think calmly, — with what the bounty of Heaven has done for me. It is my misfortune to recur only too seldom to this conviction, and source of consolation. — I have just got through one of my tasks for which I am to recieve a pitiful pair of hundreds;[39] and I feel momentarily easier till I begin another. That I expect to

---

[37] Dated by Simms' reference to the forthcoming publication of *A Supplement to the Plays of William Shakspeare.*

[38] The *Mercury* of March 15 lists J. J. Taylor among the passengers arriving on the *Northerner.* Perhaps he is Lawson's friend.

[39] Payment for several articles written for the *Southern Quarterly Review.* See letter to Lawson of April 30, 1848.

do next week, and hope to get through it by the first of May.[40]
It is my calculation then to set out for the North. I may stay a
week or even two in Philadelphia according to business, when
I hope to press forward and once more enjoy a cordial embrace
with you & yours. Tell your wife in the meanwhile that I hear
of her doings — that Augusta has recently got a long letter from
a lady of N. Y. who writes that Mrs. L. lately gave a most
magnificent & delightful party — that Mrs. L. was all smiles, and
animation — and that she certainly had the finest conception
of what a Ball should be of almost all her acquaintance. I can
fancy that I see her gliding & waltzing through your gas lighted
parlours, to the most light hearted music utterly forgetful of her
Carolina lover. — I can see C. M.,[41] dancing attendance — (*can*
he dance?) — and looking as impressive as a broken hearted
& broken headed oyster. I can fancy other swains in this brilliant
assembly, but shall reserve the list, with my chidings and com-
plainings until I see her. — I saw Mr. Allen [42] & the family not
long since in Charleston and found them cheerful & resigned.
They propose to go to Massachusetts where they have relatives.
Mrs. A. Mentioned that she had got a letter from you, or Mrs.
L. — I forget which, — and seemed to entertain the kindest
sense of your consideration. — I still cannot quite excuse you for
your letters. It does seem to me that you might say more than
you do about your friends & family. I still have a sincere feeling
of respect for Wetmore & regard which shall show itself when
he least expects it, and I should like you to include him in your
letters. Sometimes too when I ask you a question in literary
matters, a present answer is needed to determine some of my
projects. But your habit of never answering a letter soon after
recieving it, makes you wholly forgetful of its contents, and then
when in sheer shame & selfreproach you seize the pen, you
scribble off only the momentary emotions & feelings without regard to details at all. That phrase of Burns — The Prince of
Bad Correspondents (?)[43] is so grateful to your ear, that you
are neglectful in order to deserve it. — I have been doing a great
deal, and nothing! It is scarcely possible to show what I have
done since I left you. More than two months constant labour

---

[40] Probably "South Carolina in the Revolution," *S. Q. R.,* XIV (July, 1848),
37-77.
[41] Cornelius Mathews.
[42] Probably Gilbert Allen. See note 231, June 17, 1845.
[43] Unidentified.

was spent on the imputed Shakspeare — which by the way is soon to be published — to say nothing of a week or two at a time for months afterwards. I have written two or three tales for the Magazines — by the way, what of Post? — and a great deal of verse — chiefly versions from Scripture subjects in the shape of melodies. I may mention the Tragedy sent you, and a small volume which I have just finished. I have also finished the revised edition of Atalantis which I may publish — and you have probably, — though you say nothing about it — have recieved my oration. — This seems a good deal but it is comparatively little to what I have been in the habit of doing. But one month was spent in a mountain camp, in the midst of hunters where I gathered notes for a volume.[44] Love to wife & children, from ours. Little Mary Lawson is the fattest, fairest, funniest little thing you ever saw.

W. G. S.

425 : To James Lawson

Woodlands April 15, 1848

dear Lawson

I have had the pleasure recently of entertaining a sort of brother of your craft particularly, one Mr. Charles Lanman, a painter, an author, but in especial a trout fisherman who has written several volumes of sketches piscatorial, and is now on the search after new material among the lakes & rivers of the South.[45]

---

[44] Of these works only *Atalantis* (see note 23, Jan. 15, 1847), *Sabbath Lyrics* (see note 130, *c.* July 9, 1849, and *Norman Maurice* (see note 218, July 31, 1847) are not discussed in Simms' letter to Duyckinck of Feb. 11, 1848. The small volume "just finished" is *Lays of the Palmetto*.

[45] Lanman (1819-1895) was the author of *Letters from a Landscape Painter* (Boston: J. Munroe and Company, 1845), *A Summer in the Wilderness* (New York: D. Appleton & Company, 1847), and *A Tour to the River Sanguenay, in Lower Canada* (Philadelphia: Carey and Hart, 1848). Lanman's *Letters from the Alleghany Mountains* (New York: Geo. P. Putnam, 1849) is reviewed by Simms in "Summer Travel in the South," *S. Q. R.*, N. S., II (Sept., 1850), 24-65.

Among the newspaper clippings in the Charles Carroll Simms Collection, South Caroliniana Library, is an article entitled "A Novelist's Plantation," consisting of a letter dated "Woodlands, Barnwell District, S. C. April 10, '48," and signed "L[anman]." Lanman writes: "I now write you from the plantation of the novelist and poet William Gilmore Simms, Esq, where I am spending a few days as the guest, not only of that gentleman but of his father-in-law, an accomplished gentleman of the old school. It is a very beautiful and secluded retreat, within a mile or so of the railroad leading to Augusta, and seventy-two miles from Charleston. It contains about four thousand acres, and produces in great abundance cotton, rice, and almost every variety of the most delicious

He brought me letters from New York, and an ugly North
Easter along with him that kept me in discomfort for a week.
He left me yesterday on his way to Georgia but without having
shown me any proofs of his prowess, though I advised him that
our river was full of trout. I expect a friend day after tomorrow
to cruise with me a day in search of them. — I wrote to your
friend Mr. Taylor, in Charleston, the very day that I saw his

---

fruits. The family mansion is spacious, and surrounded with a brotherhood
of superb trees, and when viewed in connection with its out houses and an
occasional group of polite and happy slaves, (with the white and black
children frolicking under the trees,) produced a truly charming and comfortable effect upon my feelings. At the present time all nature is decked in
her summer garb, and a thousand birds, (chief amongst them the mocking
bird,) are filling the air with their sweet singing.

.   .   .   .

"On enquiring of Mr. Simms, yesterday morning, how he managed to take
the exercise usually required by the scholar, he led me through the winding
paths of an extensive forest, which he is gradually transforming into what he
designates a woodland. Every tree seemed to him a familiar friend, and the
grape vines which bound together many of his favorites, struck me as the
most luxuriant and beautiful that I had ever seen. The natural beauties of
everything I looked upon, even to the sparkling brooklet of the exquisite swamp
scenes, seemed to have been quietly enhanced by the hand of the Poet.

"On one side of Mr. Simms's plantation flow the clear waters of the Edisto,
a lovely and picturesque stream, which has already been made classic by the
productions of the Poet and Novelist of the South, *par excellence*. Mr. Simms
tells me that the Edisto abounds in fish, such as the bream, the trout, the black
perch, the sunfish and catfish. Alligators are also found here, but they are small
and harmless. Of game, such as deer, partridge, woodcock, rabbits and squirrels,
there is an abundance throughout the surrounding country; and in an 'aside,'
I was informed that there were few men in the lowlands of Georgia, who
could 'bark' a squirrel in a handsomer style than my host.

"The indoor attractions of Woodlands are fully equal to those of fields and
woods. This is not the place for me to speak of the delightful family with which
I am staying, but I may allude to Mr. Simms' Library. It must have cost, I
should suppose, from ten to twenty thousand dollars, and is made up of rare
and well selected works in almost every department of literature. Of the
productions given to the world by the proprietor himself, I counted no less
than 35, including histories, novels, poems, and miscellaneous matter. It is
not at all strange therefore, that Mr. Simms' reputation should be co-extensive
with the country, and even with the enlightened world. But in his native state,
and throughout the entire south, Mr. Simms is as highly esteemed as a man
and a quiet philosophic politician, as he is everywhere for his literary abilities.
— Among his more intimate friends he is also particularly celebrated for his
story-telling powers, and it does seem to me that he related more amusing
stories within the past two days, than I ever before heard in my life."

The *Knick.*, XXXII (Sept., 1848), 266, remarks of this letter: "Let us
hope that Mr. Lanman's '*Travels in the South*,' upon which he is now engaged,
will be somewhat more reliable than the work in question [*A Summer in the
Wilderness*]. But 'while we hope we fear;' for we heard two or three Southern
gentlemen, at the American Hotel, the other day, 'laughing consumedly' over a
portion of the book which had transpired in the columns of a daily journal,
descriptive of a visit which the writer had paid to the residence of a Southern
novelist, more voluminous than readable, and the wonderful things he saw
there. We doubt therefore but the Southern book must be taken something
more than 'cum *grano* salis.'"

arrival mentioned in the newspapers; but to this day have had
no answer to my letter.[46] I gave him a kind and cordial invitation to Woodlands avowedly in acknowledgment of your commendation. Tomorrow, my wife expects one of her aunts & three
cousins. The next day we look for another family of connexions,
and so, every three or four days until we remove to the city, we
anticipate the advent of one set of visitors after another. I would
rather have you & your flock than any one, or any whole, among
them. The misfortune is that all these visits are interruptions to
my labors. I have this spring lost an immense deal of time. I
commenced a new book on the 1st inst. and have got only five
chapters done when my calculation was to average a chapter a
day. It is a romance of Florida, the period, the invasion of De
Soto, and is entitled "Vasconselos, a Romance of Florida." [47]
It is contemplated for a single volume, and I fancy would be an
attractive one. Whether I shall be able to get it finished before
I go North, is now very questionable. These frequent interruptions throw me all aback, and put it entirely out of my power
how to calculate my progress. A desperate effort, night and day
may enable me to do something, but this effort, I am not now
disposed to make; the languid influences of the spring not disposing me to unnecessary tasks. For that matter, I have really
worked enough, as you will have conjectured from previous letters, and I now need relaxation. I am not sure that I have
suffered quite so much this season as usual from my usual complaint of low spirits, though I still have some occasional visits
that are quite distressing. Tell your wife that in all probability
I owe this degree of relief to the habit of segar smoking which
I began under *her auspices*. I ascribe to this habit the fact that
I am also considerably reduced in flesh. I fancy that I have lost
10 or 15 pds since I left N. Y. and I now regularly smoke at
least *one* segar *per diem* — and, when in company, two or more.
Augusta, I believe, wrote Lady Lyde a week or two ago. My
wife often speaks of *her*, — and Mr. Roach as frequently of *you*.
You are invariably a subject of reference whenever we have any
fine fish or game. Gilmore, you will say to Jimmy is spelling his

---

[46] See letter to Lawson of March 23, 1848.

[47] *Vasconselos a Romance of the New World* (New York: Redfield, 1853),
dedicated to Dr. John W. Francis, of New York, was published under the
pseudonym of "Frank Cooper." Perhaps it was begun at the suggestion of
Hammond, who wanted Simms to "immortalize Silver Bluff in a romance" (see
note 20, Jan. 7, 1847).

way through three or more letters, and beginning to read to his
Mama. He is a rough colt of a fellow — forever in the woods or
fields — now planting in the garden with his Grandpa, or now in
the cotton field with the negroes. He has a bed to himself in the
garden which is filled with salad, radishes &c. He is very strong
though not very active — shy and bashful *like his father,* but,
also like his father gentle and amiable. Mary Lawson is one
of the liveliest and most laughing things in the world — seldom
cries and is quite obedient *except when she wills* it otherwise,
and then, *like her namesake,* she is for having every thing her own
way. She prattles now a good many words. She is short and
stout, is full of life and health, & has never given us an hour's
uneasiness since she was weaned. All of us are doing well
physically. — I mention these details that you may learn how, in
like manner to inform us of your flock in turn. — I hear very
little from New York. A letter from Duyckinck prompted me
to an immediate answer, but I get nothing from him since. Mr.
Lanman mentions that Mathews has brought out through Murdoch in the West another Tragedy,[48] and that he M. now frankly
avows the authorship of Witchcraft — did so at least to L. L. said
among other things that I entertained a better opinion of M.
than any other man he had ever met. Do write me *instanter* if
Post has paid you any of the $40. I enclose you a draft for $20
upon him, if he has not accepted the first; — in as much as he had
not to the moment published the whole of the contributions, I
wish to know if he has paid any as until I know I shall keep back
another article which I have offered him.[49] I am told there has
been a flare up between Wiley & Putnam. I wrote to them to
complain of the constant errors in their a/c and to demand of
them a detailed a/c from the commencement of our intercourse.
Since then I have heard nothing from them, and have ceased
to recieve the "Literary World" — a most ungracious proceeding,
since I have paid for it in contributions for several years in ad-

---

[48] *Jacob Leisler.* The *Knick.,* XXXI (April, 1848), 373, in one of its attacks
on Mathews, gives an account of the author's complaints over the play being
"politely declined" for production in New York City. Murdoch finally brought
Jacob Leisler to New York City and presented it at the Bowery Theatre on
the night of May 8, 1848. It ran for nearly a week (see Odell, *Annals of the
New York Stage,* V, 351). The *Knick.,* XXXI (June, 1848), 557, reports that
the production "was a complete failure," and adds that Murdoch "will now
see that one who has utterly failed in every department of literature can
have no farther claim to add *him* to his list of victims."

[49] For Simms' contributions to the *Union Magazine* for 1848, see note 15,
Jan. 7, 1848.

vance. I fancy Hoffman knows nothing of the proceeding. — You see from these statements that unless I hear from you, I hear from nobody in New York. Mr. Richards [50] has written me a letter but he is chiefly among the painters. How is Bryant? — I see that Forrest has made his farewel bow in New Orleans. By the way when is he to decide upon the merits of the plays. My calculation is to reach New York between the 5th & 15th May, and I suppose I shall have time to re-dress & revise the Man of the People in season if I reach you then. Let me know on this point also. Write me soon. Present us all to Lady Lyde with the sincere affections of

Yours faithfully &c

Simms

J. L.

426: To JAMES LAWSON

Woodlands 30 April. [1848][51]

dear Lawson

It is Saturday night — we are on the eve of May, and my trunk is already packed for a journey. I leave home for Charleston on Monday next, God willing, and shall stay in that city till Saturday when I shall probably leave for Phil. should a steamer offer for that city. If not, I may go direct by land, though it is not improbable I shall prefer a N. Y. steamer. I write, therefore, as much to acknowlege yours of the 24th just recieved, as with any other object. In Charleston I am printing a new & revised edition of Atalantis, which the rascally printers who have had the copy in their hands for months, have deferred touching until the eve of my departure, and whether they will be able now to furnish me all the proofs before I leave is very doubtful. I have rewritten Atalantis & may fill up, with it, a volume of 100 or 120 pages which will bear the imprint of Carey & Hart. The thing is done at my own charges, an expense I should not willingly incur, but the printers, as proprietors of the South. Quarterly owe me very nearly $200 for contributions which I shall scarcely be able to get in any other way. That you

---

50 T. Addison Richards.

51 Simms erroneously dated this letter *30 May* (see the opening sentence). The year is established by his remarks about Charles Lanman, Cornelius Mathews' *Jacob Leisler,* and T. Addison Richards (see letter to Lawson of April 15).

have got the $40 from Post is grateful to my famished pockets. I have but slender resources now-a-days and the condition of the Cotton market adds to the necessity of our economy. We have about 50 bales to sell, which we propose to keep as long as we can. But the prospect must be bad for six months at least, and perhaps thrice as long. It will probably take two years to smooth the face of Christian Europe. — But *you* do not complain — *you* who live by *wrecks*. — You tell me of Bryant's notice of my Shakspeare.[52] You should have sent it. I seldom or never see the Post. Have you seen or got the Shakspeare itself. If not, wait til I come & I will get you one. It has been a work of far greater trouble & toil than I fancied when I commenced it, and I have demanded $400 for my Editorship — a sum which does not begin to pay [53] me for the time lost upon it. Still, I contemplate a new & revised edition of Shakspeare entire, for which my studies for years have been silently preparing me.[54] — But, God bless you, I am at the bottom of the page, meaning nothing more when I began than to send my love to you & Lady Lyde, with the fact of my movement. Yours

W. G. S.

P. S. I got a letter some time ago from Duyckinck — answered it & heard no more of it. From Mathews not a word. I had a visit from Mr. Charles Lanman, a fisherman, painter & bookmaker, who told me that Mathews had brought out a new play under the auspices of Murdoch, which was quite successful *at the West*. — Mr. Richards wrote me a few days ago & mentioned that he had spent an evening with Headley at Duyckinck's. In one of our Charleston papers, a few days ago, I saw mentioned the arrival of R. W. Griswold, D. D. from N. Y. What is he doing or saying. In my letter to Duyckinck, I hinted to [him] that my not hearing from him for so long, had almost persuaded me to ascribe it to some malign influence. — Wetmore I regard as a man of fine qualities in many respects, but I fear that he is tainted with a too great passion for distinguées. In this he does himself more hurt and injustice than he himself can possibly concieve. — I scrawl something on the other sheet for Madame.

---

[52] Bryant's brief notice was published in the *Evening Post* of April 19.
[53] Simms wrote *may*.
[54] This project was never carried out.

P. S. for Lady Lyde. We have lately had a lady visitor [55] who has quite turned the heads of our girls by *tableaux vivànt.* We have had several nights of scenic display at Woodlands which would have pleased you, and in which Augusta, Washington [56] &c distinguished themselves as Queens, Princesses, Sultanas, Sylphs, &c. There were Brides & Beauties without number. I too made a figure — a very fearful one, — as a Cumanché Indian, in three scenes which I planned myself, and had for an opponent in a hearty wrestle a fair & vigorous damsel who personated a Texan Hunter — and I let her — throw me! I suppose, Augusta, will include this history in her next letter, — unless she waits for an answer from you! But I will do something towards the telling when I get to Twelfth Street. — You should have seen our negroes. The whole plantation gathered to the Spectacle. Our piazza was crowded with them leaping over each other's heads & much more delighted than you & I have ever been at Niblo's.[57]

Yours faithfully.

W. G. S.

427: To JAMES HENRY HAMMOND

New York: May 20. [1848][58]

My dear Hammond.

You were good enough, on a previous occasion, to intimate a readiness to assist me in a pecuniary way, in the event of any necessity which might give me disquiet. I cannot say that such is the case at this moment, or indeed, will be likely to be for sometime, or at any time, but I owe about a thousand dollars for which I should like to escape dunning, which is my horror, — particularly when it needs that I shall solicit delay at the hands of a tradesman. The present condition of the book & cotton

---

55 Nancy Kellogg (see note 271, *c.* July 20, 1845). The Charleston *Courier* of March 8 lists among the passengers on the *Southerner* Miss Kellogg and Miss Bryant. Undoubtedly the latter is Julia, William Cullen Bryant's daughter, who probably accompanied Miss Kellogg to Woodlands.

56 Anna Washington Govan Steele (1831-1887), sister of Mary (see note 202, Oct. 23, 1846) and Chevillette Steele (see note 110, Aug. 2, 1848) and niece of Nash Roach.

57 Niblo's, in New York City, was a famous open-air amusement garden, where refreshments were served and entertainments given.

58 Dated by Simms' letter to Hammond of June 15, 1848, which contains further discussion of the loan here asked. For Hammond's previous offer of a loan, see note 329, Christmas Day, 1846.

market equally, as it delays and disappoints some of my calculations, will probably render this necessary; — unless I can,
by the help of some friend, substitute a Bonded debt for a book
debt. To be able to spread the payment of this sum over a couple
of years, instead of raising & appropriating it, in full, in as many
months, would agreeably relieve me, & if you have a thousand
dollars to spare in such a form of investment, you certainly may
find a customer. Of course, I make you no assurances — which
you will understand — of punctual interest; though I may be
permitted to say that I should claim the privilege, if at any moment able, of taking up the whole or a part of the bond within a
shorter period. I trust you will not regard it as an equivocal sort
of friendship, thus to give you a preference over all other of my
monied friends. I confess that I should have sought first a friend
of mine in Charleston, with whom I have had previous commerce
of this kind, but that he has been blundering at a speculation in
Rail Road Stock, by which he is denuded of his ready Cash, and
is forced to sell property to pay for a bal. on his scrip. But a
truce to this. Make me what answer you please, and I shall be
satisfied. — Here, at this moment, there is little to be done. I
have one or two schemes of publication afoot which are suspended
by the condition of things. The opinion, is, however, that the
difficulties are only temporary. England is thought by many to
have acquired a new lease of life & security by the failure of the
Chartist demonstration, but I am very doubtful. As for France &
the Continent, all will depend upon the advent of the proper man.
France does not so much require a ruler, as a leader — a hero-man
whose vocation implies equal rule and exercise. Something, too,
of her safety will depend upon the extent of the elective Fran-
chise, and upon a removal from Paris of the seat of Government.
At home, it strikes me that the necessity for Taylor's election
grows more & more apparent. He, only, can now be elected *from
the South,* and the vital matter is abolition. The Whig measures
are really all gone by the Board, & not even Clay himself, unless
an absolute fool, would attempt the restoration of the Protective
System or the Bank, or would be willing to risk his administration on the Int. Imp. System. So. Caro. should come out decidedly
for Taylor & secure, in this way, a claim upon his Govt. Will she?
What a glorious opportunity is afforded us of South. security
& progress, in the possession of Yucatan, — perhaps, next to Cuba
the best key to the Gulf. You know my policy. To use Uncle Sam

at large & all his resources, for those acquisitions, which in the event of a dissolution will enure wholly to the South. Let me hear from you while I am here — where I shall remain till the middle of June.

God bless you & Yours —

W. Gilmore Simms

J. H. H.

428: To James Lawson

Charleston, June 14. [1848][59]

Dear Lawson

I simply write to assure you & our blessed 'wife & mother' of our perfect safety & arrival at home. I got in yesterday, but a bad headache, the consequence of late hours, indigestion, and the usual sea congestion, kept me from pen & ink entirely. Here I find all tolerably well. Mary Lawson is peevish & a little puny, suffering from her gums and the advent of new teeth. My sudden arrival, finding the family yet in bed, put Augusta into hysterics, but otherwise provoked no unpleasant exhibition. Gilmore I found climbing & halfway up a peach tree. He's quite tall & slender — will go to school next week. As yet I have nothing to say, but will write you soon. Meanwhile, do not suffer that despotic woman your wife, to suppose that I am either unaffectionate or forgetful. Next to my own, your family is the dearest to me that I [have] ever known; and the affections which I have always found true in you & your wife, must necessarily command the best & most devoted recollections of my heart. Kiss your wife and children on my account, and hold me ever,

Dear Lawson,
Yours Ever truly &c.

W. Gilmore Simms

J. L.

429: To James Henry Hammond

Charleston, June 15. 1848

J. H. Hammond Esq.

Dear Hammond.

Enclosed I send you the Bond, leaving blank the name of payee, and the period at which payment is to be made. This I

---

[59] Dated by Simms' reference to the teething of Mary Lawson Simms, born Sept. 13, 1846.

leave in your hands, and should like it fixed at the opening of the year 1851 or at the close, if possible. This will afford me a better opportunity of ridding my skirts of all troubles. Two or three years will suffice me. — I have not been long enough here to obtain a *carte du pays* but will write you when I do. The opinion here among certain of the people, is that the *State* will not go the Taylor nomination, simply because it is Whig. The *people* are prepared for it, but it is thought that our *politicians* (?) will not find it to their interest to forego the pleasant privilege of throwing away our vote — certainly, at a time like this, when all that is valuable in our Institutions may depend upon it, — one of the most criminal as foolish of proceedings. I have been asked what you think in the premises. I answer that I *know* nothing, but that I have no reason to doubt that you prefer Taylor to the other nominee. I am disposed to choose Taylor with the Democratic Vice President, Butler. What say you. I write hurriedly at a Lawyer's office with a buz around me. Besides, I have truly nothing to say. I am told that Rice of Barnwell [60] comes out against the inquiry for the Bank facts &c. He is a traitor, probably in its meshes, and, it was whispered, when he was first a candidates for the Legislature, that his ultimate aim was a seat in the Direction. Let me hear from you on the subject of the Presidential Canvas & I will report whatever may occur to me. In haste, but very truly

Yours

W. Gilmore Simms.

430: To CAREY AND HART

Charleston, July 1. [1848][61]

Mess'rs Carey & Hart.

Gentlemen.

I have put up to be forwarded by private hand as soon as possible a copy of the sheets of my new Edition of "Atalantis." It comprises that poem and several beside, and makes 148 duodecimo pages, quite neatly printed, and with your imprint as

---

[60] Col. Henry B. Rice was a member of the South Carolina House of Representatives at this time. He had been elected in 1846.

[61] Dated by Simms' discussion of the revised edition of *Atalantis,* together with *The Eye and the Wing,* dated 1848, though not actually published until 1849.

publishers. The number of copies is 400. Now, as I do not wish
to be troubled with the dispersion of them, I propose that you
take the Edition, as it stands, *in sheets,* for the small sum of
fifty dollars — of course not a third of what the edition costs
me; but as I took the printing in lieu of a debt due me by the
printers, I *am able* to afford it on these very moderate terms.
Put up in boards, in the Boston style, it should readily sell at
50/100 per copy. — Should this proposal not meet with your
views, may I hope that when bound, you will consent to act as
the publisher in the distribution of the copies. Let me hear from
you soon & believe me, Very truly

Your obt servt & frnd

W. Gilmore Simms

431: To James Lawson

Charleston, July 12. [1848]

Dear Lawson

Enclosed I cover to you notes from Geo. R. Graham & Co.
and Bartlett & Welford. In answering Graham I have requested
him to forward you the money ($20) for the article published
and I trust that Conrad will publish with sufficient rapidity to
make the dft. available before I revisit you.[62] I suppose that I
must accept your kind offer made to B. & W. though I am
really sorry that you made it. He should have waited. I enclose
you, therefore, on this sheet a dft. in favor of B. & W. which,
if you can spare the money, you can present to them & honor,
as a substitute for the one in their hands; but you must not give
them a sixpence of interest, which from my knowledge of the
men, I am very sure they will desire to exact. I have had the
loan ($1000) and paid it out. It will relieve me from temporary
annoyances. My indebtedness, however, is something greater than
I thought it. I should have borrowed $1500 & squared off. But
I can do now and pay off gradually. I am busy on the Greene
which I will finish this month.[63] I am in hopes next month to
complete my Huguenots,[64] & at the close of September to look

---

[62] For Simms' contributions to *Graham's* in 1848, see note 115, Aug. 2, 1848.
[63] *The Life of Nathanael Greene, Major-General in the Army of the Revolution* (New York: George F. Cooledge & Brother, [1849]).
[64] *The Lily and the Totem, or, the Huguenots in Florida.* See note 171, April 10, 1845.

in upon you at 12th Street, and see how our lady wife & mother scolds & smiles in the same instant, — a sort of moral month of April. Here, I am likely to have *groaning* instead of smiling & scolding. I am just apprised that my wife is unequivocally "as women wish to be &c."[65] Our women, you are aware, do not love to be in this condition, and as a logical deduction, do not love their Lords. — Either the Poet or the wife is wrong. Our children are pretty well. Puny, but not sick. Gilmore is going to school daily. Mary Lawson has twelve teeth and is covered with prickly heat & boils. I took her in hand myself when she was really looking, as if sinking, like her sister on previous occasions. The doctor's drugs were already in the house, when I rejected their use, plunged her into the cold bath, which the mother had abandoned the moment the child's bowels were affected, and the change was almost magical. All the humors at once determined to the surface, and she has grown fattish again though fretful, full of life & energy. I am now in hopes to get over the summer without further tremors on this account. But Augusta is very thin & complaining as she did a few years ago when I sent her North. If she continues thin, I may send her to you, or possibly bring her on myself in Sept. and take her into the Berkshire country. There's no end to my domestic grievances & apprehensions — with you I trust things are otherwise. I suppose you are in the city still, with an occasional trip in stage & steamboat. And our excellent but imperious wife & mother! How does she carry herself? Sublimely, no doubt, meditating conquests and taking advantage of our absence. I shall try shortly to give her another scribble, when I hope to put myself in her good graces. — It is something difficult to find materials for a sheet, writing from this dull city, unless one scribble of himself. To this my native modesty relucts. Here, a Taylor meeting takes place shortly. I shall attend, & possibly, if there be much opposition, will take part in the struggle.[66] You shall hear anon. Has Forrest got back. Tho' without any expectations from the Tragedy,[67] I shall yet be glad to have my suspense at an end. I give you full discretion in the matter. Of course, should the *general* design & action suit, details may be hereafter amended; and the fact, once decided, that Forrest *will use it,* would persuade me certainly to come on early in Sep-

---

[65] "As women wish to be who love their lords." John Home, *Douglas,* I, i.

[66] See note 85, July 20, 1848.

[67] *Norman Maurice; or, the Man of the People.*

tember in order to do what I could to satisfy his judgment in the amendments. But nothing of this should be obtruded on him. In other words, he should be left unbiased to his decision, without our suffering the pleas of friendship to creep in. Present me to Wetmore, Duyckinck &c. Atalantis is ready, but I wait on Carey & Hart. You shall have an early copy.

Love to wife, and kisses for the children. My wife & Augusta declare themselves affectionately, & I, you know, am ever Yours &c.

W. Gilmore Simms

James Lawson Esq.

Ten days after sight pay to Mess'rs Bartlett & Welford one Hundred Dollars, & place to account of
$100.00

Your friend & servt.

W. Gilmore Simms
July 12. 1848

432: To Caroline Gilman [68]

[July? 1848][69]

My dear Mrs. Gilman

In utter despair of seeing you in proper person, — at least while this weather lasts — I have concluded to send you as well the trifles which I have on hand in relation to the poets, as some few that I have very hastily sketched for you, and which I have endeavoured to make properly characteristic. Enclosed, you will find a brief paragraph or two upon Chaucer, Spencer, Milton, Shakspeare, Byron, Scott, Burns, Moore, Campbell, Shelley, Wordsworth, Horne, Browning, Barrett, Tennyson, &c. I send you also a sonnet entitled "The Old Masters" in which you have a reference to Danté, Milton & Michael Angelo. Another sonnet which I enclose entitled "Poetry of the Forest" as it refers to Rosalind &

---

[68] See introductory sketch of the Gilmans.

[69] Mrs. Gilman published *The Sibyl, or, New Oracles from the Poets* (New York: Wiley and Putnam, 1848) around Dec., 1848 (reviewed in the *Southern Literary Gazette*, I [Dec. 16, 1848], 256). Of the poems Simms lists in this letter only that on Scott is included (p. 256); however, in her preface Mrs. Gilman promises (p. 6) another volume, *Thoughts of the Poets on the Poets* (no copy located by us), to include poems omitted from *The Sibyl* for lack of space. We have, therefore, dated this letter 1848. Simms' being in Charleston and his reference to the weather indicate July as a probable month.

Jaques, may answer your purpose. I have some things in my library at the plantation, — which I shall not be able to see until November — which I think are rare, will suit your volume, and which I think are not likely to have fallen in your way. These, if in season *then,* I will transcribe for you. — I am egotistically reminded, while thinking of your plan — of a very pretty sonnet, written by Mr. Bulfinch, and published in your Rose or Rosebud, in regard to my Poem of Atalantis.[70] This might serve as one of your paragraphs, but you must not so far defer to my wishes as to introduce it against your own judgment into companionship with subjects better chosen.

With great respect
Yr f'd & servt

W. Gilmore Simms

Mrs. Caroline Gilman.

433 : To Carey and Hart

Charleston, July 20. [1848][71]

Mess'rs Carey & Hart

Gentlemen

Enclosed you will find Bill Lading of box, per Paul Jones, containing the sheets of Atalantis, which I trust you will recieve in good order. Instead of 400 copies there are 450 or more. For the surplus 50 you will please send me a copy of Longfellow's Illustrated Vol. and if not too much above my equivalent, a copy of Thiers works on France.[72] — I shall avail myself of the privilege you allow me, of drawing upon you for $50. and shall do so, at a few days sight, in favor of Geo. Oates of this city.

Yours truly &c

W. Gilmore Simms

---

[70] See letter to Griswold of Dec. 6, 1846.

[71] Dated by Simms' reference to the sheets of *Atalantis.* See letter to Carey and Hart of July 1.

[72] Longfellow's *Poems* with illustrations by D. Huntington was published by Carey and Hart in 1845. Simms is requesting either Adolphe Thiers' *The History of the French Revolution,* 2 vols. (Philadelphia: Carey and Hart, 1840), or his *History of the Consulate and Empire of France under Napoleon,* which Carey and Hart started issuing in numbers in 1845.

P.S. You will find the sheets folded. For this service, the Binder tells me to intimate that he will expect such compensation as you pay in Phil. for the same work. The Printer here, who had it done without orders, will pay the difference.

434: To JAMES HENRY HAMMOND

Charleston, S. C. July 20. [1848][73]

dear Hammond.

I do not think it necessary to say to you, that, in reporting to you my own or the opinions of others in relation to yourself, I have no wanton or malicious motives. I take for granted that, like myself, you have often felt the want of someone who would frankly do so. On this subject I shall say nothing farther, but simply add, that, while I may err sometimes in my estimates of you, what I declare to you shall always be a frank utterance, the value of which must depend quite as much upon its honesty, as upon its felicity. Here we are all at the ears. There is confusion in the Wigwam, and, as you say, good will come of the uproar. Indeed that is the thing gained — uproar — agitation — in which the public mind now utterly paralyzed, will once more become active, and cast off in indignation those ancient Men of the Sea who have so long ridden upon its shoulders. I enclose you a couple of trifles which I wrote for the papers this morning. That ass of a fellow, King, who guides the Courier, has clipt & mutilated one of them so as greatly to impair its point; but on no other conditions would his insolence permit the article to appear.[74] We need greatly a newspaper, & indeed, cannot do without it. The Mercury is in the hands of the enemy. Rhett has too prevailing an influence. I feel sure that the mystic leader of this morning was written by Clapp.[75] Gadsden here is working hard for Taylor — for J. G.

---

[73] Dated by Simms' references to Taylor's campaign for president.

[74] William S. King, a native of Queenstown, N. Y., had acquired a half interest in the Charleston *Courier* in 1833 and was now senior editor. One of the "trifles" Simms here mentions is probably a pro-Taylor article entitled "The People Vs. Ancient Hunkerism" and signed "An Old Southern Democrat." It contains Simms' usual remarks about the Hunkers (see note 226, Nov. 17, 1846). Another article in this same issue of July 20, entitled "Democratic Meeting to Nominate Gen. Taylor" and signed *"Only the People's Democracy,"* may be the second "trifle."

[75] From 1831 until early in 1845 Robert Barnwell Rhett's brother-in-law, John A. Stuart, had been editor of the Charleston *Mercury*. John Milton Clapp (1810-1857), who had been junior editor for seven years and for two years practically sole editor, because of the illness of Stuart, had then taken it over. In 1847 John E. Carew had become proprietor and editor. For an account of

JOHN CALDWELL CALHOUN

"I concur with you in the fervent wish that Mr. C. should be made President, not only because he . . . would make one of the very best that we have had, but in order that there might be a resurrection of that independence among our people which can never be the case as long as his ambition remains ungratified. His shadow falls heavily upon our young men, and darkens all their pathways. . . ."

(From the picture collection of the South Caroliniana Library)

BENJAMIN FRANKLIN PERRY

"A good lawyer and an excellent Gentleman. . . . A great gatherer of revolutionary
lore. . . ."

(From the portrait by William G. Brown in the possession of Mrs. Sam Rice Baker, Montgomery,
Ala., as reproduced in Lillian A. Kibler, Benjamin F. Perry [Durham, N. C.: Duke University
Press, 1946])

Holmes,[76] rather perhaps.[77] — Elmore [78] is in Washington, for holding back — while Torré [79] has come out furiously for Taylor. The whole Charleston Deleg. is for Taylor except 3 or 4, including our unwise friend Walker, Hunt & Northrop.[80] So the great portion of the scribbling for Cass and Bat Carroll,[81] the talking at the corners. I still doubt that Carroll wrote 'Platoon'.[82] He is almost too costive to write anything. Besides, he is busy canvassing the County for the office of Laurens,[83] Com. in Equity. Pickens, it is understood, is at the bottom of the Cass movement in the interior. The report here is that all our Delega. in Congress go for Cass, except Holmes.[84] Yet Calhoun is said to have written, that he can't support Cass under any circumstances, and a northern paper announced Burt as being a Taylor man. The Mercury committed itself against Cass a month ago, too deeply to come out for him. So did Elmore in a most bitter speech. But the game is, to keep back the Taylorites, and suffer the Cassites to go ahead. The 'Mercury' prints all that it can against Taylor, suppressing all against Cass. Whether Taylor or Cass succeed in this State,

the newspaper, see White, *Robert Barnwell Rhett*: *Father of Secession*, pp. 22, 89n. The leading article in the *Mercury* of July 20 (which Simms here assigns to Clapp, at this time editor of the *Southern Quarterly Review*) is entitled "Presidential Candidates." It is so worded that the *Mercury*'s stand on the election is impossible to ascertain.

[76] In the *Mercury* of July 18 James Gadsden Holmes is commended for supporting Taylor at a meeting held on June 6. The article is signed "Many Hundred Democrats."

[77] James Gadsden was a director of the Bank of the State of South Carolina. He is listed as among the vice-presidents of Taylor meetings held on July 19 and Oct. 31 (see the *Mercury* of July 21 and Nov. 2).

[78] Franklin H. Elmore, president of the Bank of the State of South Carolina at this time, had recently declined Polk's appointment as minister to Great Britain because of the critical position of the Bank.

[79] Peter Della Torré was a member of the South Carolina House of Representatives during 1844-1848 and judge advocate general for many years. He and Simms served together on the House Committee of Inspection of the Bank of the State of South Carolina at Charleston.

[80] James M. Walker, B. F. Hunt, and Claudian B. Northrop. In 1848 Northrop was chairman of the executive committee of the Democratic Party.

[81] Bartholomew Rivers Carroll, brother of Charles R. Carroll (see introductory sketch of the Carrolls) and former editor of the *South Carolinian* (Columbia), was an ardent Cass supporter. Though Carroll was a near relative of Mrs. Simms, he and Simms were often at odds politically.

[82] An article entitled "The Bank of the State" and signed "Platoon"—a reply to Hammond's "Anti-Debt" papers—was published in the *Mercury* of June 12. In it the writer says: "If he ['Anti-Debt'] has any political aspirations in the way of which the political influence of the Bank officers may be supposed to stand, the fact must disqualify him totally from being a witness in the matter at all." Hammond replied in an article signed "File-Closer," published in the *Mercury* of June 20.

[83] Edward R. Laurens.

[84] Isaac E. Holmes.

it matters really little to the awakening of the people. I note that
the toasts from the Up Country, Chester & elswhere speak
broadly against Calhoun & his policy & opinion. Torré, yesterday, deplored to me the declining of a proper veneration in the
people. Thank God! was my inward response, but I smiled and
answered that I did not see symptoms sufficiently strong to call
for either regret or gratulation. The movement here is chiefly in
the hands of the young men. They will probably carry the State.
But the Cassites will die hard. The Whigs keep wholly aloof, but
their votes, probably 500, will certainly determine the scale. —
Last night at one of our informal meetings [85] — a few only —

[85] The *Mercury* of July 21 gives an account of this meeting at which Simms
was one of the vice-presidents. Simms is also listed as among the speakers of
the evening. In a letter to Hammond dated July 21 [20] James M. Walker
writes: "Our friend Simms, I am told, made a capital speech last night at the
Taylor meeting . . . they cheered Simms with delightful shouts when he thrust
his knife into the sides of Elmore." (Original in the Hammond Papers, Library
of Congress.) On July 28 the *South Carolinian,* which supported Cass, published two accounts of this meeting. Of Simms' speech one, signed "P. P.," says:
"Mr. Simms announced that he belonged to the school of 'young Carolina.'
That from his earliest youth—he meant his political youth, for he had always
been an obedient school-boy—he had been opposed to *hunkerism,* and that un-
reasoning submission to authority which had so long stifled the free voices of
the people of Carolina. He congratulated himself and the audience, that the
time had at length arrived, when the people rising like the strong man from
his sleep, had shaken off the bonds with which they had been bound. He then
proceeded to show the means by which this state of affairs had been produced
and perpetuated. And in order to illustrate his views, he told with great comic
power, a capital story of the best mode of cooking a plate of soup so as to
please those who like and those who do not like cayenne, and another, of the
manner in which Frenchmen *always* kill rattle snakes. He thus applied his
stories, and in a most playful manner, concluded by insinuating into the friends
of the Bank of the State, whom he confounded, in the heat of debate with the
old hunkers, a pretty considerable load of anti-debt grape shot — (at this
moment there was a good deal of restlessness exhibited by some of the officers
and orators.) Mr. Simms at length with a few eloquent remarks, elegantly
expressed, took his seat amidst shouts of applauding laughter." The other
account (unsigned) says: "Dr. Simms, of Barnwell — the novelist, historian,
and poet, was next called out. Judging from the applause with which it was
received, the Doctor's was evidently the speech of the evening. His denunciation of the party domination that had prevailed in South Carolina for the last
twenty years, was quite as severe as the Doctor is capable of. Broad hints
were thrown out that such political tyranny must no longer be submitted to—
that, those in authority must jump down from the top of the political ladder,
and the b'hoys be permitted to climb up *some.* In a word, that the old hunkers
must leave the Barn or have it burnt down over their heads. You would have
smiled to see how *droll* this last sentiment made some of the old hunkers look,
who, by the bye were the getters up of the meeting. Some rolled their tongues
into one side of their jaws, while others, with the 'how come you here' touch
of the thumb on the nose, seemed to say, the Doctor is making a *Ratification*
speech with a rush. The Doctor told an anecdote about making okra soup—
another about a rattle snake swallowing itself, and after a highly poetical
apostrophy or two to a chalk bust of Gen. Taylor, whom the boys took for
Jupiter or some other Heathen God—concluded amidst shouts of applause, and

a Gentleman from Georgetown mentioned that the Candidates for the Legis. in both Marion & Marlborough had unanimously come out for Taylor — that McQueen also, — and that he was to run for Congress against my namesake, a Dr. Sims,[86] who, with Hunt, was probably the originator of the name of Gen. Commander.[87] Commander is said to be declining on his own ground in popularity. A decisive demonstration will probably materially affect the country. Can't you set Bellinger,[88] Trotti, Aldrich & others to work in Barnwell. Of course, Hutson,[89] representing Colcock & Rhett will go for the regular party nominee. You see that the Bank men are carrionly identified — the leaders — with the Cass

---

beating of juvenile sticks, which left the Theatre damaged and bruised not a few."

[86] John McQueen (1804-1867), of Bennettsville, had been an unsuccessful candidate for Congress in 1844. He was again defeated by Alexander Dromgoole Sims (1803-1848), of Darlington, in 1848; but upon the death of Sims on Nov. 22, 1848, he was elected to fill the vacancy.

[87] On May 26 the *Mercury* quoted Gen. James M. Commander, of Georgetown, S. C., to the effect that at a meeting of members of the Democratic Party from all parts of the state he was elected a delegate to the National Convention in Baltimore, with the understanding that he should cast the state's nine votes. On May 29 the *Mercury* reported that South Carolina gave her nine votes to Calhoun on the first ballot, to Cass on the fourth. On May 30 the *Mercury* said: "With a population more unanimously democratic than that of any other State in the Union, there was but a single meeting for the purpose of sending a delegate to Baltimore. . . . Georgetown is a comparatively inaccessible little village of about five hundred white inhabitants. . . . In this place the meeting was called on the 10th of April. . . . The time was *changed*, however to the 17th of April . . . 54 persons [were] present. . . . Gen. J. M. Commander was nominated as the Delegate from this portion of the Congressional District. . . . Gen. Commander, then, knew well that he had not even the semblance or pretence of authority to represent the whole Congressional District. . . ." On June 9 the *Mercury* reported that it had received a "Pronunciemento from the distinguished individual [J. M. Commander] whose name graces the head of this paragraph" and that since it was so large it was being hung on the bulletin board in front of the office. For a brief summary of the *Mercury's* swing to the support of Cass, see White, *Robert Barnwell Rhett: Father of Secession*, pp. 97-98.

[88] Edmund Bellinger (1808-1859), born in Colleton District the year in which his father, Dr. John Skottowe Bellinger, moved from Colleton to the Springtown section of Barnwell District, was graduated from the South Carolina College in 1826. He was admitted to the bar in Charleston in 1829, practiced law at Barnwell Court House, and was a member of the State House of Representatives during 1838-1842. In 1854 he moved from Barnwell to Columbia, where he continued his practice of law and inaugurated a law school. In commenting on Bellinger's plan for the law school, Simms remarks in *S. Q. R.*, N. S., X (July, 1854), 260: "He [Bellinger] has had the benefit of a long and extensive practice in our courts, is a man of great research and erudition, and has long been esteemed one of the best lawyers in the State. He will bring to his task a rare industry, as well as a competent mastery of his subjects."

[89] Isaac McPherson Hutson (1819-1887), admitted to the bar in 1841, was Bellinger's partner. D. F. Jamison describes him in a letter to G. F. Holmes of March 12, 1847: "Hutson is somewhat starched I admit in exterior, but he buttons every day in his waistcoat a warm heart, and he is a high-toned, southern gentlemen." (Copy in Holmes' "Letter Book," Duke University Library.)

men. It will be quite satisfactory to us, if we continue to kick
up such pretty d——d fuss generally, as will clear the atmosphere.
'When rogues fall out', you know. — You will have seen what I
did with your article on Moultrie & what the Mercury says. It
will enable you to make a point, and show, as you note, that to
expose one of the patriarchs of the Rev. as a defaulter, & spare
the heroes of our day, is a monstrous outrage.[90] "Fair Play" seems
to be in no hurry.[91] Who is he? you ask. Who shall answer. If
Elmore, he is feeble & fretful. He has not followed up his first,
& this is against him. There is a publisher here who proposes to
start a Anti Bank paper, but one that gives *the Electoral Election
to the people,* which he calls the "Morning Star" at $5 per annum.
He will issue the first no. on the first of August, and will *fill* the
paper on that day with original articles from your hands & mine,
12 columns or more if you please — which urge these objects —
and sell these papers at $30 a thousand. Here then, if you think
proper you can have a fair field. The thing will only be valued
as a pamphlet, since such a paper has no circulation.[92] — Gadsden
wrote the first answer to you on the subject of Rail Roads. He
wishes to print them in pamphlet form, but has not the means
himself, and is waiting for authority *from the country,* before
he goes ahead.[93] — Nixon,[94] the man who projects the paper, has
gone North for a press. I freely told his *locum tenens* that 2000
subscribers, it was thought, could be got in the country for an

---

[90] In the *Mercury* of July 19 appears an article entitled "General Moultrie"
and signed "Seventy-Six," which defends the Revolutionary hero General
William Moultrie: "Whoever casts his eye upon her proud flag, whether it
be floating on the peaceful breezes of the parade ground, or waving amid the
smoke and flame of battle, must revert at once to the impregnable Palmetto
Fort and the Hero who, on the memorable 28th of June, 1776, won imperish-
able fame for himself and his native State. Yet in the last report of our Comptroller General, I find that 'William Moultrie, *former Treasurer,*' stands charged
with being indebted to the State to the amount of $583.67. . . . General Moultrie
was once wealthy. He died as most—I had nearly said as all great men who
were patriots have died—poor. To the error which he committed, it was 'his
poverty and not his will consented.' Let us throw over it the veil of endless
oblivion. . . ."

[91] Articles defending the Bank of the State of South Carolina and signed
"Fair Play" had been appearing in the *Mercury* since 1847.

[92] We have been unable to discover any information concerning this proposed newspaper.

[93] We have not determined which of the many answers to Hammond's
essays signed "Anti-Debt" (see note 285, Nov. 7, 1847) were written by Gadsden. The *Mercury* of Feb. 10 prints a report of the South Carolina Railroad,
signed James Gadsden, President.

[94] J. B. Nixon was at this time conducting a printing business at 48 Broad
Street, Charleston. He had just published a pamphlet *Oration* delivered before
the Charleston Library Society, June 13, 1848.

Anti Bank paper, — that you, myself & others, would cheerfully work to swell his sub. list. Whether he has the means or not, I can't say, — and then the worst difficulty occurs, — where shall we find the Editor? This inquiry & doubt are more important than either. — I wish you would write me an elaborate & carefully studied letter in favor of the Taylor movement, in reply to the many of mine to you, — so that we could bring it out. It would have great effect throughout this country. Ought you to withhold yourself? How is McDuffie? — We have a letter from Taylor, who distinctly asserts that he has not changed his position, — that he holds himself an Independent Candidate, and means not to ascend the Whig or any other platform. — My vol. of Poems I cannot now send you till Sept. The Publishers will not publish till then.[95] It will keep. The *exposé* of Jones [96] anent the Comp. Report & error, has not & will not appear in the Charleston prints unless cut out & newly phrased & forced upon the Newspapermen. Send me a copy of the paper which contains it & I will see what can be done. I have distributed all previously recd. I am weary, and know not well what I have written.

God bless you &c.

W. Gilmore Simms

Oh! Will you let me add your name to a Memorial to Congress for an Internal. Copyright Law? [97]

---

[95] *Atalantis*, though dated 1848, was not published until 1849 (see letter to Carey and Hart of Jan. 19, 1849). Simms did, however, send copies to his friends in the late summer and early autumn of 1848. Hammond had received his by Aug. 8, when he wrote Simms a critique of the poems included in the volume.

[96] On July 8 Hammond had written to Simms concerning A. D. Jones, a director of the Bank of the State of South Carolina: "Jones left out the Sinking Fund & the payment made last January,—not exactly comprehending them. Otherwise it would have appeared as I wrote before that the Bank *claims* to have paid over a million more than it *claims to have made*. Does it not follow that it has pilfered the State as Anti-Debt charges." (Original in the Hammond Papers, Library of Congress.)

[97] In his reply of July 26 Hammond writes: "I will cheerfully add my name to your Copy-right Memorial. I suppose you mean to give to foreigners the knowledge of copy-right. It is doubtful whether placing cheap foreign books in the hands of the masses has enlightened as much as it has corrupted—but it is certain that it [is] unjust to pilfer from foreigners & very injurious policy to break down home literature." (Original in the Hammond Papers, Library of Congress.)

435: To James Henry Hammond

Charleston, July 29, 1848.

My dear Hammond.

Your two letters have just reached me, at the same moment. It is highly important that you should be *correct* in your *details,* since figures are more easily converted into foes, whether necessary to the principle or not, in the comprehension of the vulgar. It is particularly necessary that you should take care of them in the present controversy since it is in this that the Bank will employ all its strength, intending that it shall bear on the approaching elections and with regard to the next Legislature. The *on dit* here is that "Fair Play" is the work of a committee, Furman [98] being the mouthpiece. I am not prepared to believe that the impression which he has thus far made is so decisive as you have heard. No doubt the boldness of his assertions has had its effect on some minds. Yeadon spoke to me the other night in respect to the assertion that the Bank had repaid all its capital & something over. I was not prepared to answer him except by saying that the *original* capital might have been repaid & probably was, but that the charge is that the State has been constantly engaged through various processes in adding to this capital, & that I had no doubt the statement of Fair Play was an evasion & a delusion, which *you* were prepared to expose. You will note that with a people so languid & uninquiring as ours, a broad & bold assertion goes a great way. For this reason, I would adopt some of the manner of the enemy. I would retort the imputation upon their motives, & in the opening sentences, would give them the lie in their throat, decently of course, assuming such a tone as indignant truth would justify, always preparing to prove my case. It might be well to reflect upon the game of brag & bully which 'Fair Play' plays. You are not, however, to believe all you hear in respect to the impression made. Tell me from whom you hear, — mention names to me as much as possible, — and perhaps, I may help you to some useful information. Of the *old* inhabitants, their position, authority &c. I know something, and can procure the necessary knowledge perhaps in respect to all. But, in truth, you can depend upon little that you hear in Charleston. Do not so much consider that as your progress in the country. Here there is so much

---

[98] Charles M. Furman was president of the Bank of the State of South Carolina during 1850-1865.

corruption, cowardice, dependence — so much to be concealed, so much to be feared, so much imbecility & so much ambition, that very few can be depended upon. Many *wish* that the answer of "Fair Play" may be conclusive, and toil to make this impression. Yet these are not in the Bank, nor desirous of being there. But the Bank is a political institution, and is important to those who do not seek its money. I do not sympathize with you in your groans at the necessity of the controversy. You know my notions on Self Development. The faculty is in you for the struggle, and I am sure the issue will benefit yourself no less than the country. I take for granted that you acknowledge the laws of duty as constituting the essential religion. What information I can afford shall not be withheld, but I go but little in the world's eye. Charleston has few resources & few attractions for me. My days are spent in drudgery, and a short ramble in the afternoon, which may bring me into contact with a prattler is the utmost of my mingling with society. I have little even to do with the Taylor men. The leaders I suspect no less than their opponents, and in speaking I spoke to the b'hoys — the rising youth, those who had precious & undiseased impulses, — and not to any others. The history of the speech will perhaps amuse you & show you what is the system here. I was asked to attend the meeting by some of the people.[99] I did so, and reported your opinions with my own. It was then proposed to me, by the managers that I should speak at the meeting. I said, regard me only as an auxiliar, to take the field in the event of any opposition. — This was anticipated from Hunt & others. They were pleased to say — 'No! No! You are our trump, and we must play you at the proper moment.' Do with me as you please, was my answer, and I asked to see their programme. Now note how prettily they were prepared to use me. The meeting was to take place at 8 o'clock. Pringle was to take the chair & make a speech. Keith was to succeed him with another speech, introducing a long preamble & resolution, Magrath to succeed Keith with a speech, Porter to succeed Magrath; Torre to succeed Porter, Simons to succeed Torré; Mitchell to succeed Simons; Richardson to succeed Mitchell; Tupper to succeed Richardson, and I was to bring up the rear & bestow the benediction. Here were nine speakers, to precede me, which allowing them 20 to 30 minutes each, — which the speakers mostly reached or exceeded, — would bring us nearly

---

[99] The Taylor meeting of July 19. See letter to Hammond of July 20.

to midnight, and I was pleasantly assygned an exhausted audience
or empty benches. I smiled in my sleeve, said nothing, but, of
course, gave up all idea of having to say a word. It so happened
that three of their appointed speakers were not forthcoming, and
I was called for when the bell was ringing, the vote taken, and
the crowd already on its feet for departure.[100] They tell me that
the speech has told & is still *telling*. I dealt freely in the language
of scorn, sarcasm & invective, using a two edged sword, and fighting as did Harry Smyth of the Wynd in Scott's novel of Fair
Maid of Perth on my own hook.[101] I was greatly cheered it is
true, but I was a novelty & my speech was a novelty, for I dared
to speak what was felt by half Charleston, but which none had
ever ventured to find breath for. Here all is selfishness & must be
regarded with suspicion. Magrath wants to recover position;
Gadsden to bolster up Holmes & perhaps delve out something for
himself. Porter [102] is timid but is to go to the Senate; Mitchell,
Simons & others are Candidates for Legislature, and Torré came
out for Taylor only a few days before the meeting. *What his
motives are none can say*. It is scarcely possible to suppose that
Elmore is not privy to every step he takes, & that he does not
sanction it. He goes, however, for making Manning Gov. Simons,
as you know, is Manning's nominee for the Speaker's Chair.
Both ought to be beaten.[103] Calhoun has (*on dit*) declared that
he can support neither Cass nor Taylor. In truth, the movements
throughout the country for Cass, declare nothing more than a
restive desire of the people to set up for themselves—a thing
sufficiently agreeable to me *per se* — and they thought it safer
to do so on the side of the Dem. nominee, thinking that Commander's proceedings would find sanction as those of Elmore &
Pickens had done on the previous occasion. The press naturally
took this course. You may have noted that a good many of the
4th July toasts contain broad & rude flings at Calhoun himself. I
don't doubt but that we have had something to do with the plant-

---

100 In the account of the meeting in the *Mercury* of July 21 William Bull
Pringle is listed as chairman. The following are reported to have made speeches:
Col. Matthew I. Keith, A. G. Magrath, William D. Porter, P. Della Torré,
James Tupper, and Simms. Thomas Y. Simons, F. D. Richardson, and Nelson
Mitchell did not speak. See note 85, July 20, 1848, for Simms' speech.

101 Chap. xxxiv.

102 William Dennison Porter (1810-1883) served as lieutenant governor of
South Carolina (1865-1868). He delivered the address at the unveiling of the
Simms monument on June 11, 1879, anniversary of Simms' death.

103 John Laurence Manning was defeated by Whitemarsh B. Seabrook, James
Simons by John Izard Middleton.

ing of the seed whose sudden growth somewhat surprises us. —
My letter must be scrappy. — Walker tells me that he goes for
Cass, for no other purpose than to divide the State. It is probable
that he decieves himself. I half suspect his sincerity, good fellow
as he is. He does not tell *me* a word of the elaborate letter from
Pickens, 6 sheets they say, which he has been reading about town;
and he is using the cudgels too earnestly for Cass, having simple
mischief in his eye. He has accepted, for example, an invitation to
visit Georgia electioneering for him. Walker, is, in brief, a discontent. He has lately been obliged to sell out, is humbled, does
no business or but little; is vain and ambitious, without an adequate degree of capital to build upon, and perhaps *feels* his defects
& disappointments. We did not seasonably open his eyes to the
proper case. Thus, for example: Suppose Elmore to return from
Washington & move for a general meeting of the Party in
Charleston with the hope of absorbing us, & undoing all that has
been done. How, with our own men divided, can we do battle
with him, — as otherwise we might, & take the cards out of his
hands. In Charleston, with proper boldness among the *managers*
this might be done. The b'hoys are true; but their guides are
selfish & will probably prove fruitless. They are now lying on
their oars, doing nothing, while the Cass men are moving. I have
been urging them to constant agitation & the establishment of
Ward Taylor Clubs. We may get them under way next week.
But I can do little for them. My days are devoted to drudgeries.
I have to work against time. I have been secretly applied to
run as well for Congress as the Legislature; but have declined.
To the latter I cannot afford to go; and I have no faith in the extent of the support which could be given me. I will risk nothing at
this moment. — What you say is very well about the paper. But
do not allow yourself to be deluded in the case of Carew.[104] I am
inclined to think that he is *un mauvais sujet*. His father in so far
as Boyce's connection with the father goes, may influence the son;
and regarding the aims of the latter as purely selfish, the question
will rest entirely upon the continued political strength & influence
of Elmore. The younger Carew has political aspirations which
his father probably encourages, and others stimulate, which will
show themselves in season. You will not get much out of him

---

[104] For the proposed paper, the *Morning Star,* see letter to Hammond of
July 20. John E. Carew, Jr., was the son of the editor and proprietor of the
Mercury.

except with a decided State influence in our hands. That you have got so much is entirely due to the necessities of himself and paper, both looking to the real strength which you possess in the country. 'Anti Debt' will not compel his echoes just yet, I fancy, though he may be willing that you may provoke your own. Don't listen to any of Felder's speculations on this subject. — I saw Chesnut [105] at Kershaw a day ago. He tells me that all Kershaw goes against the Bank — that there is but one voice on the subject. — Do not, for the world, say a word to provoke the apprehensions of the other Banks. You will unite them against you. They are now your allies. Awaken their suspicions, and you force them against the stomach of their senses to lend their succour to your enemy. — I will enquire anent your tutor. [106] Carew told me of one here on the 4th of July, who claimed to be your tutor, and wished to borrow money to get back to you. — Your young friend Boggs has presented your letter. [107] I took him with me to Fraser [108] who was quite pleased with his performances. He will write you about the boy. Fraser is a man who wants blood. His *forte* is delicacy of taste & excellence of finish. He has no courage as an artist, is consequently no genius. Genius frightens him. He has some *kinks,* and insists upon a classical education, though he admitted to me that Genius has a glorious outlawry which might dispense with it. — I have made up a package for young Boggs to take to you, but he has not for the last two days been to me as he promised. He took tea with me the night before. But I must stop. You must write the Taylor letter. McDuffie, I am *told,* declares himself for Taylor. Get him to write also. This is a wretched scrawl, but I write wearily, and you must make the most of it.

Yours truly

W. Gilmore Simms

The Political heads that are likely to prove most trouble over here are Elmore, Bailey, *Hayne,* Hunt &c. They have strength &

---

[105] James Chesnut. Simms and Chesnut (see introductory sketch of the Chesnuts) served in the House together in 1844.

[106] Hammond had asked Simms to find a tutor for his children.

[107] In this letter, dated July 20, Hammond writes: "This will be handed to you by Master Robert Boggs of Augusta. He has spent a few weeks latterly with me & made copies of some of my pictures; & considering his youth & the very little instruction he has had I think they exhibit a very high order of talent. I have suggested to his parents to send him to Charleston & endeavour to obtain the opinion of Mr. Fraser of his capacity. . . ." (Original in the Hammond Papers, Library of Congress.)

[108] Charles Fraser. See introductory sketch.

capacity, though *all* under suspicion of one sort or another. Could the people here be relied on they might be grappled with successfully since all of them are made of singularly penetrable stuff; but the people have been so habituate to the draft under yoke & lead, that like the personification of Fear in the Ode of Collins, they recoil, when most valiant —

'Even at the sounds themselves have made.' [109]

Were you here! But, enough! I shall only take part in the proceedings when I may indulge in a half sportive vein of indignation which will leave vinegar & salt in the smallest wounds. — By the way, your *gout* — you are to use the cold water by means of the compresses or wet bandages with dry ones about them. They will draw the heat from the foot. — Understand, — I never read my letters after writing. I leave that for the *reader*.

436: To James Lawson

Charleston 2d. August. [1848] [110]

dear Lawson

My anxieties are increasing about Augusta. She has been for some time growing sensibly thinner and feebler, exhibiting signs of exhaustion and prostration much more than usual, & resembling her condition when I sent her to the North a few years ago. Today, she fainted while taking a drawing lesson. Yesterday I consulted a physician who gave her medicine, & recommends that she be sent away. She has no appetite, and I have commenced giving her porter. It would be singularly inconvenient for me to leave home at this juncture, particular[ly] as my work is unfinished, but an opportunity to send her to you will probably occur next Saturday week, when some connexions of the family are going North. If you will at once ascertain & let me know whether she can get a room in the same family with your wife, and what will be the cost of board at the place, I may be able to make the necessary arrangements in season. If, therefore, on the reciept of this you will see your wife and let her ascertain if a cool & pleasant chamber can be got, *near her,* & the terms be moderate, and Lyde will consent to keep an eye to her, I should

---

[109] See William Collins, "The Passions," lines 17-20.

[110] Dated by Simms' reference to the death of Chevillette Eliza Steele (June 7, 1835—May 29, 1848), sister of Washington Steele (see note 56, April 30, 1848) and Mary Steele (see note 202, Oct. 23, 1846).

really be glad to send her on. It will require that you should not delay, as our friends will most certainly be on the move by Saturday week. I presume the board can scarcely exceed $5 per week. Let me know, & *frankly,* how far it will be agreeable to your wife, to take charge of a drooping damsel. I do not think that there is any organic or specific cause of complaint, but a general debility from which she always suffers more or less under the oppressive heats of our summer. I have no doubt that, as on the previous occasion, the more bracing atmosphere of the North will bring her up. In an extreme necessity, I should make sacrifices and go on with her myself. As she improves she may take advantage of any opportunity to run up into Berkshire. Her mind is somewhat unhinged besides, in consequence of the death of poor Chevillette to whom she was tenderly attached, and who was her bedfellow. I need not say how warmly I feel the cordial assurances contained in your letter. They serve but to confirm and strengthen my experience of your friendship for almost twenty years. — I am getting on slowly with the Life of Greene. It costs me more labor than I anticipated. Recently, on the celebration of the achievements of the Palmetto Regt. I put forth a pamphlet of lyrics written at various times in their honor, of which I shall send you copies for distribution in the course of next week — some 45 pages.[111] My Atalantis is printed and forwarded in sheets to Carey & Hart — I sold them the Edition. You shall have copies when published or before. It makes nearly 150 pages. Among my recent performances, I have been taking a dip into politics, and was called out to a mammoth public meeting in Charleston, in behalf of Taylor. I was greatly cheered & applauded, and my speech seems for a week to have been the talk of the city. All hands tell me I was singularly successful. Here we are all in an uproar. For the first time for 15 years, the State is loose from her moorings

---

[111] *Lays of the Palmetto* (see note 29, Feb. 11, 1848). The celebration in honor of the Palmetto Regiment took place on July 28. The *Courier* of July 31 gives a detailed account, remarking that "one of the principal attractions of the day was a Printing Press, placed on a Car, tastefully decorated," which "at intervals, during the march, . . . was put in operation, throwing off copies" of an ode by Simms, entitled "The Press; An Ode of the Charleston Typographical Society. At the Reception of the Palmetto Regiment in Charleston, July 28, 1848" (included in the account). The report continues: "The novelty of the Press at work, there being many in the city who had never before seen one in operation, attracted much observation, and there was great anxiety exhibited to obtain copies of the Ode, thus freshly thrown off, especially by the ladies, many of whom received them from the piazzas and windows, as the Car passed through the streets."

& public opinion divided. This is a great gain for the independence
of the people. — How prosper averages? And what are our
friends doing? Has Forrest returned, and is there to be a choice
among the dramatic candidates? You are aware how little I expect
or calculate on my venture.[112] Still I have my anxieties. Give my
best love to your wife, and kisses for her & the children. Tell
her that her little namesake continues to do well, is very talkative
& very imperious like herself. Gilmore goes to school, though I
believe his progress is not much beyond the usual sheep fold
lesson. He can *baa* equally well, I fancy, under the strap & over
the book. My wife, I think I told you, finds herself, strangely
enough, in the condition which Shakspeare says is grateful to
those women who love their husbands.[113] It is very certain that
my woman betrays no gratitude on the occasion.

God bless you & yours

W. G. S.

P. S. I omitted to say a word about the draft of Bartlett & Welford. I am quite mortified at their rapacity. Enclosed I send you a
draft on Graham & Co. for $55. This amount being actually due
for articles published. Their pretext for not paying the other was
that though they had the articles, they were not yet published.
By sending the dft. to your friend Coates [114] in Phila. with a
private letter to Conrad covering the items below, they will
probably suggest no objections to cashing the present.

Geo R. Graham & Co. to W. G. Simms Dr

To article entitled 'Antique oak or tree	. . . .	$ 10.00
" " "	Ilenovar	. . . .	10.00
" " "	Maid of Bogota	. . . .	35.00

$ 55.00

---

[112] Simms is here referring to *Norman Maurice; or, the Man of the People,*
written for Edwin Forrest, though not for submission in Forrest's contest
discussed in the letter to Lawson of Oct. 20, 1847, and following letters to
Lawson.

[113] Simms erred. John Home, not Shakespeare, was the author of the line
here paraphrased. See note 65, July 12, 1848.

[114] Unidentified. In an undated letter to Lawson of this period or later (to
be included in an appendix to this work) he is spoken of as "Mr. Coates."
Simms' addressing him as "Mr." rules out the possibility of his being Reynell
Coates (1802-1886), physician, author, and editor of gift annuals.

All of these are published. There are yet two other contributions —

Portraits of the Poets...................... 10.00
Bride of Fate............................. 35.00
                                          _____
                              $ 45.00 [115]

437: To James Lawson

Charleston Aug 7. 1848.

My dear Lawson

I have concluded without waiting for your answer to make my arrangements for sending Augusta on to you. An opportunity occurs with some friends of the family who go in the Southerner next Saturday. It is my present purpose that she shall go with them; so that you may expect (God willing) to see her on Tuesday morning after. Pray look out for her. She has had an invitation to go to Gt. Barrington with Miss Sherwood & join the Misses Kellogg, and perhaps it would be better for her that she should do so, *at once,* if it is found that Miss Sherwood is prepared *now* to make the visit. A conference will enable you & Augusta to time it. She might be with your wife for a week or two, & then go to Barrington; though, if things suit, I should prefer that she go first to the latter place. The climate is more invigorating, at present, and will late in the season, be too cold. But I leave the matter wholly in your hands. You must act as if Augusta were your own child. I feel that you will do so, and have no hesitation in leaving the decision with you. She is something better this week, and seems in better mood. I fancy the

---

[115] All of these were published in *Graham's* for 1848: "The Memorial Tree," XXXII (Jan.), 11-12; "Ilenovar. From a Story of Palenque. A Fragment," XXXII (April), 218-220; "The Maid of Bogota. A Tale from Colombian History," XXXIII (Aug.), 75-83; "Heads of the Poets," XXXIII (Sept.), 170-171; "The Bride of Fate. A Tale: Founded upon Events in the Early History of Venice," XXXIII (Nov.), 241-251. The first, second, and fourth of these are poems, and all are included in later collected editions of Simms' poetry. The others are tales. Under the title of "La Pola," "The Maid of Bogota" had earlier appeared in *The Cosmopolitan,* II, 169-181. It also was published in *S. L. J.,* IV (Dec., 1838), 464-470; *The Book of My Lady,* pp. 169-179; and *Southward Ho!,* pp. 36-58. As "Venetian Bridal," "The Bride of Fate" had been published earlier in *The Book of My Lady,* pp. 76-85. It was later included in *Southward Ho!,* pp. 138-165. During 1849 Simms published in *Graham's* "The Picture of Judgment; or the Grotta Del Tifone. A Tale of the Etrurian," XXXIV (June), 337-345, and "The Death of Cleopatra," XXXIV (Dec.), 363-364.

very idea of going north has something wholesome & healing in it. I write in haste. Love to wife & children.

Yours truly as ever

W. G. Simms

438: To JAMES HENRY HAMMOND

Charleston Aug. 10. [1848][116]

My dear Hammond.

Your last long article (too long) I read with pleasure, and supposed it to be conclusive, as summing up all your premises;[117] but closeted with Conner[118] the other day I questioned him on the subject. What he said struck me, and may be of service to you, since, if there be any force in his suggestions, it is not too late to employ them. He says, Hammond is a very powerful writer and thinker, but were he a mercantile man, he would have more conclusively illustrated his case (touching the profits or part of profits of the Bank) by taking the sums confided to the Bank, and showing what the profits must have been if in United States Stocks. He thought this the most likely method of compelling a popular recognition of your facts & reasonings. He says you do not sufficiently dwell upon the error in the inception of the Bank, i.e. its constitutionality, and the monstrous tyranny it employs in a thousand ways & particularly as a political engine. He admits that you touch these points, but thinks too passingly. He is of opinion that you are laying a snare for yourself, and that the call for a showing of the indebtedness of the Direction will, if complied with, strengthen the institution, by falsifying the assumption [of] their appropriations. He thinks the very warning you have given will have enabled them to prepare against it, and that the guilty persons, before the day of showing, will have, through other banks & other means, contrived to shift the responsibility, appearing on the back rather than the face of the papers, &c. Among

---

[116] Dated by Simms' references to Taylor's campaign.

[117] In the *Mercury* of Aug. 4 is printed a long article (nearly three columns) signed "Anti-Debt" and entitled "The Bank of the State." The issue of Aug. 6 is missing from the file of the Charleston Library Society, but from Hammond's letters to Simms of this period it appears that it too contains an essay on the Bank. Simms is referring to one of these.

[118] Henry W. Conner (1797-1861) was president of the Bank of Charleston during 1839-1840 and 1843-1850. He later was president of the South Carolina Railroad Company during 1850-1853.

other things, he suggested as a process which the State should employ for its own extrication, the propriety of winding up the Rail Road Bank & employing its assets for the liquidation of Rail Road indebtedness &c. These are all matters which it may be worth your while to consider. Frequent and *shorter* articles — articles something more confident in their tone — meant to over-bear the bullying of the opposition — confident in air — are of vast influence among our people *who are accustomed to be led and rely on the lead which promises most*. It might be well to write a paper speculating on the dextrous artifices which the friends of the Bank will employ in getting out of the scrape — anticipate the showing of hands — show how the thing may be evaded; and, *under* a different name, indicate the *inconclusiveness* of any such process in arriving at the truth. I asked Conner what was thought of "Fair Play", — he answered as I expected — that not much, as he could hear, was said about it — that "Fair Play" showed an acquaintance with figures, & with the figures in his own possession, could make them speak his own language. I do not believe that Fair Play has convinced any or many, who do not desire to be convinced. In fact I hear nothing said on the subject. This community takes little interest in anything which requires thought. It is essentially feeble — approximating the Italian & Spanish nobility — satisfied to pass the time indolently if not pleasantly — prepared to sell the shirt but keep the sword — full of assumption, conciet and ignorance, and, in majority of cases, scarcely capable of recieving the truth. In speaking on them the other night, I was careful to address the *youthful* & the people.[119] Mine was in fact an appeal to a new generation to whom I sedulously dwelt upon the imbecility (which I could make ap-parent) of the old. My object was to excite their self-esteem, and lessen their reverence. From what I can learn, something has been done; but the greater number are dreadfully *afraid to go alone*. Your writings must calculate only the interior. With Charleston & the Parishes little can be done. Shape your essays, therefore, with something of a scorn of this region — & throw out an oc-casional passage which shall awaken the dormant jealousies of the agricultural for the trading population. This indeed, is a legitimate consideration. — We are to have a Cass meeting here. It is headed by Northrop, Walker, Hunt, Carroll,[120] Sandy

---

[119] At the Taylor meeting on July 19. See letter to Hammond of July 20.
[120] Bartholomew Rivers Carroll.

Brown,[121] *et id omne genus* — mostly, in moral position, men of straw — having nothing to lose & every thing to gain. Such persons only live in regular venerations & in connection with party organization; in as much as they lack individuality. Bailey attended their Caucus, but declared that he went for a call of the party at large; but they gave him to understand that they meant to repudiate the 'Watch & Wait' meeting of June, and went for Cass decidedly.[122] Carew & Hayne were also present; the latter stopping as he found himself in danger of both stools; & Carew was asked abruptly by whom he had been invited. Bailey attempted to conciliate & was bullied. To *fix* him, they designated him to draft Preamble & Resolutions. He has accordingly cleared out for the North. Walker talks rather recklessly. He attaches no importance to the labors of the Abolitionists. Thinks nothing of Wilmot Provisos, nothing of our danger, and nothing of our resistance — thinks that the South will do nothing, let the Abolitionists do what they please. Certainly, our only danger on this score will result from the domination of a party which proves superior to sectional interest & feeling. — People talk of Van Buren's folly in suffering his name to be used in connection with the Abolitionists. He has never in his life shown more capacity or cunning. He foresees that if not this time, the very next Presid. Election, & the vote turns wholly on geographical boundaries, he is in the front rank to take advantage of it. But he will get (if he runs) no contemptible vote now. The true struggle in New York will be between Taylor & Van Buren. There, the former

---

[121] Alexander H. Brown, called "Sandy," was for many years sheriff of Charleston District. A Charleston *bon mot* records that Joseph J. Legaré and George Herbert Sass, while walking on the Battery, saw Brown ride past. Legaré said:
"There's old Sandy Brown
He rides up and down
On a cob."
And Sass replied:
"There's little Joe Legaré
Standing by the sea
He's a snob."

[122] The "Watch and Wait" meeting, as Simms terms the "Democratic Meeting" of June 6 (reported in the *Mercury* and the *Courier* of June 7), was presided over by Judge D. E. Huger. Isaac W. Hayne and Henry Bailey spoke, and William L. Yancey was present by invitation and addressed the assembly. Resolution 10 of the meeting reads as follows: "Resolved, that the Democratic party of Charleston District, had neither lot or part in the late Baltimore Convention, and that the resolutions of the Convention, the nomination of General Cass for the Presidency, and the proceedings generally are unsatisfactory and objectionable. . . ." The forthcoming Cass meeting, here mentioned by Simms, took place on Aug 21 (see letter to Hammond of Aug. 29).

will probably beat him, the vote of the democracy being divided between Cass & himself; but beyond, in the New England States, I am half sure that Van Buren will beat Taylor & Cass both. In fact, the instincts of the people satisfy them that the old party organization is at an end, and a new one is called for. They will now begin to make it. It is not impossible but that V. B. will go this very term with Taylor into the House. With his skill, cunning, knowledge of men, & unscrupulousness, — what may he not do? Let the vote of the South be equally divided between Cass & Taylor and what are his chances? — I am asked to entreat you to a conference here with the friends of Taylor. We also want you to speak for us at a great meeting to be held here when the Cass meeting takes place. Colcock is to be here to speak for them. We want you to speak for us. Will you not come? It may do you good. Something may come of it. What say you.[123] Write me soon.

Yours very truly &c

W. Gilmore Simms

P. S. Of course, what Conner says is *entre nous.*

439: To WILLIAM CULLEN BRYANT

Charleston Aug 22. [1848][124]

Dear Bryant.

I commend to you a young painter, Master Robt. Boggs, of Augusta, Geo. who is here considered a youth of remarkable natural endowments in art. His education is almost wholly self acquired, and his progress is astonishing. He goes to New York for the purpose of studying with the best models & masters. His family is one of the most respectable in Georgia, and his own morals are good, while a glance at his face would show you that he is amiable. You are in a position to speak for him & to him, when occasion needs & opportunities offer, & I feel sure that you

---

[123] Hammond declined to speak, though he openly supported Taylor. The *Courier* of Aug. 26 contains an extract from his letter: ". . . I have been anxious *not to share* in the responsibility of those Southern men who are opposing Gen. Taylor, and have never failed when a proper opportunity offered, distinctly and decidedly to avow myself to be in favor of his election." The *Mercury* of Aug. 31 gives the same account of Hammond's refusal.

[124] Dated by Simms' letter to Hammond of July 29, 1848, in which Robert Boggs is first discussed. For Hammond's remarks concerning Boggs, see note 107 of the same letter.

will not forbear to do so in respect to one who with rare gifts of mind lacks none of the necessary modesty. I commend him to your favoring countenance.

Very truly Yr friend &c

W. Gilmore Simms

Wm. Cullen Bryant, Esq.

440: To EVERT AUGUSTUS DUYCKINCK

Charleston, Aug 22. [1848][125]

Evert A Duyckinck Esq
Dear Sir

Master Robt. Boggs, of Augusta, Geo., by whom this will be handed you, is supposed by his friends, myself among them, to be possessed of remarkable talents in painting. He goes to New York for the purpose of advancing his studies in the art. Heretofore, he has had few of the advantages of education, — in the profession I mean. His general education has not been neglected, and his morals have been cared for. He comes from one of the most respectable families in Georgia, and your countenance may well be bestowed upon him as well in respect to his endowments as to his character. By facilitating his acquaintance with such masters in the art as it may be desirable that he should know, and giving him your own counsel on occasion, You will greatly oblige me, and serve him.

Yours Ever
Very truly &c

W. Gilmore Simms

441: To JAMES LAWSON

Charleston 27 Aug. [1848][126]

Dear Lawson

I wrote you briefly a few days ago; an open letter by a young lad who goes to N.Y. in order to become a painter.[127] I am in reciept of your kind note acknowledging Augusta's arrival and

---

[125] Dated by Simms' letter to Hammond of July 29, 1848, in which Robert Boggs is first discussed.
[126] Dated by Simms' references to Augusta's visit to the North, Taylor's campaign, and his work on *The Life of Nathanael Greene* and *The Lily and the Totem, or, the Huguenots in Florida.*
[127] Simms' letter to Lawson concerning Robert Boggs has not been located.

describing her condition. We have had two letters from her which report her own improvement, and the tenderness & affection which she enjoys at the hands of yourself & wife. I need not repeat, my dear Lawson, the acknowledgements which I feel always ready to make, for your own long tried attachment to myself & flock with that of the dear woman your wife. If there be any thing which annoys me, and has annoyed me, for years, in the relations between us, it is that I know no method of showing you both how deeply I feel your kindness and attachment, & how fondly I long for the opportunity to prove that my affections are not less plentiful than yours & hers. I must wait for the occasion, and, meanwhile, both of you, I trust, will take my feelings and desires for granted. Augusta writes a description of her present abode which seems to have been seen through the most rose coloured medium. I wish that we were all among you. Yet we are doing very well here. Gilmore, though as thin as he can well be, is always gay & elastic, forever on the bound. He goes to school & spells in four or five letters to the satisfaction of his schoolmistress. Mary Lawson has recently unscaled another tooth, so easily as to know nothing about it, & since the cold weather has resumed is doing excellently well. I am the only real sufferer here, drudging as I do, to get ready to visit you, if possible, between the 15th & 20th Sept. I have just got through the Greene (mum!) and am on my Huguenots in Florida. But I am writing 30 or 40 pages (letter sheet) per day, and feel perfectly prostrate by night. Still, I dash into the campaign for Taylor, & have made three or four flaming stump speeches, which seem to have been quite popular. I shall stop short, however, in order to attend more devotedly to the interests of No. 1. I have no news to give you, and am in no mood, as you may suppose, for long letters. Tell your wife that I shall have to go with her when I come on, to see this fine place Bergen, where she frolics so famously. According to Augusta's account, it is only another garden of Eden — an Elysium in which every third person is a beauty and every woman is an angel. Give my love to Lady Lyde, and as affectionate a kiss, as you can, all round, to herself & the little ones.

Yours Ever as Ever

W. Gilmore Simms

442 : To James Henry Hammond

My dear Hammond

Charleston Aug. 29 [1848][128]

I have been kept from writing you for some time by a variety of drudgeries & circumstances, some of which have only troubled me & others made me anxious. I have had to send my daughter North for her health, very reluctantly, as I could neither afford the money, nor spare the time to go with her. The thing was unavoidable however. To make up for lost time I have been concentrating myself on one of the jobs, in letters, which I have undertaken,[129] and which I am anxious to complete by the 15th prox. so as to enable me to leave at that time for the North myself. This will explain to you, & I trust excuse, my delay to answer some two or three of your letters. You must have misunderstood me in respect to Conner's opinions of your articles. I do not think he said or that I meant to write the word fanciful in their connexion. He spoke of them & of you with the greatest respect but suggested that the case might have been put, by a familiar example, in a way more likely to take with mercantile men. I thought it right to show you what he said; & not because I attached any importance to it; though I still think it will be well to dwell upon the general principles constantly in connexion with the details. I believe I said to you on one or more occcasions, to shape your statements & arguments for the country. The city don't care a copper about the matter. It is wholly selfish. In fact, the greater the indebtedness of the State, the better for Columbia & Charleston. The funds are drawn from the agricultural for the benefit of the trading population, let them be raised in what manner you please. Here, I verily believe, the controversy no longer provokes attention. Fair Play if read anywhere is only read in the country. Your essays at first took the popular mind here, and the time is gone by to remove the impression. If any thing was said to lead you to doubt this, it was meant simply as precautionary, & was the result of my anxiety that you should fortify at all points. — Your letter has given great satisfaction here.[130] Magrath, no doubt, has the arts of blarney, but I have

---

[128] Dated by Simms' reference to his letter to Hammond of Aug. 10, 1848, in which he discusses Henry W. Conner's criticisms of Hammond's articles.

[129] *The Lily and the Totem, or, the Huguenots in Florida.* See letter to Lawson of Aug. 27, 1848.

[130] Hammond's letter supporting Taylor. See note 123, Aug. 10, 1848.

every reason to suppose that in speaking of you, he is quite candid. We were together the other night till a late hour, awaiting the return of a committee, when he said to me that you unquestionably held the most enviable position of any man in the State, to take advantage of the mouvements which are in progress & which must be precipitated with the passing of Mr. C.[131] from the stage. Nobody but yourself supposes you to be a broken down politician. Your course has been wonderfully prudent, & will before long produce its fruits. *Par parenthese,* let me mention that a few nights ago I had a long private interview with Torré, the matter of which I suppose was intended for your ears. He spoke of you as one who could not be forgiven, but as one who could not yet be dispensed with &c. & added significantly, 'I have been as bitter an opponent as ever Hammond, but whoever shall predicate of my past opposition its continuance hereafter, will find himself greatly mistaken.' I at once began to scratch my head. What does all this mean. I arrived at two conclusions, which give me choice. His desire is probably to assist in discerning any opposition to Manning from your quarter, or he desires himself to go to Congress, and adopts this process for securing my support. Two days after, the whisper is current that he is in fact a candidate. His course is one which is somewhat mystified. What are his present relations to Elmore. Where is Elmore himself? There is no doubt that Rhett is at the bottom of the Cass movement in this State & that he will probably have office under Cass in the event of his election. The game played by the Mercury was necessary to convince Cass that Gen. Commander's nomination went for nothing.[132] He was accordingly denounced & Cass denounced & the Convention denounced, all very bitterly. Elmore at this time goes to Washington, Rhett paves the way to reconciliation in a speech in favor of Polk, which takes the South by surprise. Hart[133] (of the Mercury office) goes to Washington just after the meeting in June, & shortly after the Mercury pro-

---

131 John C. Calhoun.

132 See note 87, July 20, 1848.

133 John Heart, born in Philadelphia in 1806, was at the head of the *Spectator* and *Young Hickory,* organs of Calhoun Democracy in Washington, when he was appointed to a position on the Charleston *Mercury* about 1845. He soon became an editor, and on Sept. 1, 1849, joint proprietor, the firm being Carew and Heart. When Carew retired on Jan. 26, 1852, the firm became Heart and Taber, the other member being William Robinson Taber, Jr., nephew of Robert Barnwell Rhett. On July 1, 1858, Heart sold his interest to Rhett and returned to Washington.

ceeds to smoothe the way by apologetic articles for Cass, & articles against Taylor for the final movement. You have seen the follies played by Carew since. Now, *Carew & Furman are both secretly suspected of hostility to Elmore.* The pride of the former has been hurt, the ambition of the latter restrained, by him. His policy in keeping away is probably only that he may choose between parties when he returns, though Bailey who followed him to the North, insisted to the last moment that the State must not be committed to Cass. — Calhoun, Butler & Burt really incline to Taylor & go against Cass. Though very cautious & unwisely so, C & Burt evidently inclined to Taylor in their speeches. Butler if any thing inclined to Cass.[134] Yet in the morning he denounced him openly. But he dined that day with his brother in law Hayne with whom he stayed and Hayne is completely sold to Hunkerism. Simpson[135] told me that, though he preferred that the State should do nothing, yet if sides were to be taken he should go for Taylor. He repudiated with scorn the idea that the State should go for Cass. "In a month's time, Sir," said he to me, ["]no man in So. Ca. will dare to show his face for Cass." But all this could depend on Calhoun's speaking out manfully. Strange, that at the moment when it is important that he should speak he should be silent. Is it possible that he fails to see that a complete division of the State is fatal to his ascendancy. Any way, the results enure *pro bono publico.* Do not suspect me of writing the dramatic things you speak of.[136] How *could* you suspect me. They were shown to me in MS. and I suggested sundry graftings adding to the point, but I did so indifferently. I have written very little — made three or four speeches at the clubs, but not more, & shall do less. I am too busy. It is true there are some worn out politicians

---

[134] These speeches were made at a meeting held in Charleston on Aug. 19. See the *Mercury* of Aug. 21.

[135] Richard Franklin Simpson (1798-1882), of Pendleton, S. C., was a member of Congress during 1843-1849.

[136] On Aug. 13 Hammond had written: "I have read 2 nos of Palo Alto. . . . I was amused at the drama & recognized with your key most of the characters. But is not this going too far. It is a down right lampoon & I suspect you of the whole of it." (Original in the Hammond Papers, Library of Congress.) We have been unable to locate a copy of these pamphlets. Numerous satires were being published in Charleston at this time. Amos Head advertises in the *Courier* of Oct. 17: "The little pamphlets, touching Social, Religious, and Political Reform in the city, appear to be almost alone in request. A whole batch have been published—of Satire and Responses—and some have reached a third Edition! Any one wanting these 'documents' can get them at the 'Corner,' and at my Branch, 263 King Street."

in the Taylor ranks, but that party comprises the real substance of the city. The other side can offer no comparison. Their great meeting was almost an overthrow. The House was filled by their opponents who could have taken the vote out of their hands, and probably would have done so, but that Hayne appealed to their magnanimity not to vote. Northrop was hissed off the stage; Hunt had his share of hisses & totally failed. The cry at his appearance was — a Southern man, & no Yankee. Northrop, Hunt, Walker, Carroll, Brown, — all their active men — are notoriously unpopular — some of them odious.[137] Touching our friend Walker, indeed, a painful report is going about that he is yielding himself up to the most fatal habits & appearances seem to justify it.

Yours very truly

W. G. Simms

443 : To James Lawson

Charleston, Sep. 12. 1848

Dear Lawson

My present arrangement is to leave in the Northerner next Saturday for your city. This will certainly be the case if nothing happens to prevent. But just now our weather seems capricious. We have had a spell of North East, which looked stormy, and as we are to have an obscuration of the moon on Wednesday, there may be some repetition of the squall. I shall not take passage till after that event. Augusta had no reason to complain. Every body wanted, as a matter of course, to hear from her. Change was not probable with us who were stationary. I told her before she went, that she must not look to me to write, but

---

[137] On Aug. 22 James M. Walker had written to Hammond: "I delayed to answer your last, until our Cass meeting had been held and some idea of the state of the parties could be formed. It was held last night and I am sorry to say that the Taylor party exhibited a degree of rowdyism which I had thought belonged only to Tammany Hall. Col Hunt was hooted &c until they silenced him. Hayne was in addition to like treatment assailed with a glass tumbler which had it struck him would have inflicted a severe wound. . . . Our meeting has been held against the advice of Mr. Calhoun. The leaders of the 6 June meeting—Hayne &c—have been whipped into our ranks—Col. Elmore is nowhere . . . have often told Simms, my purpose when I originated the Cass movement was not to advance him [Cass], but to break up if possible the clique." (Original in the Hammond Papers, Library of Congress.) The meeting is reported in the *Courier* of Aug. 22.

to arrange with her mother and the girls. I believe I wrote first, and the mails must have delayed all our Letters. She has probably been consoled with a dozen by this time. We have heard from her since her arrival at Barington & have written to her twice or thrice. I counselled her to remain there until the cold weather should decidedly set in. I wish her to recieve all the benefit possible from the bracing air of the mountains. I suppose, we may look for her in N. Y. by the 10th of Oct. — Why did you return to the city so soon. One would think that the wilful woman, your wife, was in a sort of Elysium at Bergen Point. I was in hopes to have caught her there, and played gallant for her, among hosts of jealous candidates. — If Averages are dull, which were wont to make the Average maker dull, he is likely to have become brighter, — eh? Or is the fiend of avarice yet unexorcised. That with nothing to do, you should see nobody, hear nothing, and still write amazing short & infrequent letters, is surely a puzzle. Of old it was the hard work that kept you from scribbling. What is it now. Are you *yachting* too; or have you got any new passion? I half fear that, during the woman's absence at Bergen, you busied yourself in the Bowery. Don't tell her, but, those Bowery girls are not to be sneezed at. Ask Bob Donaldson.[138] — Gilly is rather pacific, you may say to Jimmy, but he can hit a hard thump. We measured his height a day or two ago, and found him exactly 3 feet 8 inches, which is a tall piece of a boy. He is spelling in two syllables, & brings home a very creditable report from school every Friday.

But why bore you with Epistles, when I hope to see you in a week more. Love to wife & a kiss for the children, from yours

Very truly as Ever

W. Gilmore Simms.

Tell your wife that she will have to get a clever creditable husband for Augusta in New York, that she may remove to a climate which better suits her than the South; or we will swap. — Give me Christina for the South and you take Augt. for the North. Eh?

---

[138] Mrs. Lawson's father.

444: To James Henry Hammond

Charleston, Sep. 14. [1848][139]

dear Hammond.

It is a very difficult matter to procure a *good* private tutor. When you wrote me before I made enquiries in several quarters but could hear of none. Since the reciept of your last letter I have renewed my enquiries with some little hope of success. Professor Bruns,[140] of the High School (its Principal) says he has in his eye a young man that will suit — a modest person, gentlemanly & capable. He will let me know. There is a young fellow about town, named Belcher, who is capable, but perhaps somewhat vain & presumptious. I am not sure. I may mistake his bearing. If unemployed, as I believe, I shall hear from him. He is said to be very capable, and is the son of one (Manning Belcher) who ranked very high as a classical teacher in Charleston. But *good* teachers, *who are known,* can always command a very large salary. Most of them, of this character, have made fortunes in ten years. Burns,[141] one of the best, has just retired, it is said on $50,000; and others flourish like green bay trees. From several quarters, I learn that $400.00 or $500 is not considered sufficient. Gregg [142] I am told, employs a private tutor and gives $1000. *But why not remove to Charleston. We want you here.* There is a favorable opportunity. Your wealth will tell a thousand times more in the city than in the country, and your talents will have free play, plenty of exercise, and will more certainly realize results. Be assured a revolution is in progress which renders necessary, here, on the scene of action, a leader like yourself. The public mind, in several quarters, is looking to

---

139 Dated by Simms' reference to his efforts to find a tutor for Hammond's children. See letter to Hammond of July 29, 1848.

140 Henry M. Bruns was the first principal of Charleston High School, serving from 1839 to 1871, when he received an appointment at the College of Charleston to succeed Simms' friend James W. Miles as professor of ancient languages.

141 Samuel A. Burns was tutor in the English School, College of Charleston, during 1833-1836.

142 William Gregg (1800-1867) was the leading Southern cotton manufacturer of his day. In 1846 he started construction of the plant of the Graniteville Manufacturing Company in Edgefield District. The Company began actual operation in 1848, Gregg acting as president. Gregg took a deep interest in the welfare of his workers and endeavored to give them comfortable working conditions and housing. During 1856-1857 he was a member of the South Carolina House of Representatives, and in 1860 a member of the convention that adopted the Ordinance of Secession. He was the author of a number of articles advocating industrial progress in the South.

you as a leader. The recent course of Mr. C. is suicidal.[143] He
shrinks from the Rubicon to which he has led his followers. The
more independent gladly avail themselves of the tacit permission
to set up for themselves. He has one hope; i.e. to operate in
Columbia upon unpledged members, & that I think he will do.
— You have, no doubt, seen with scorn the pitiful proceeding of
Burt, who denouncing Cass, here, *and privy to Cunningham's
proceedings before the Cass meeting,* approving his resolutions,
and writing to the Taylor men encouraging them in their work,
yet suffers himself to be driven from his property through apprehension of losing his seat.[144] The selfish cowardice of our public
men is cutting their throats. The struggle in which we are engaged leads to the direct result, — giving the Election of Electors to the people. To oppose it is not only weak, but a gross
& improvident surrender of so much good capital. Besides, by
this time, I trust you are satisfied that in no other way than
by appealing to the people, as the only conservative party, can

---

[143] On Sept. 5 the *Mercury* had printed a letter from Calhoun, dated Sept. 1,
in which he says: "If my friends, on both sides, would regard me as taking no
part between the two candidates, and as standing on independent ground, ready
to support or oppose the successful, as his measures may or may not accord
with the principles and views of policy which have long governed me, they
would avoid all misapprehension. I see much to condemn and little to approve
in either candidate." Concerning this letter Hammond had written to Simms
on Sept. 7: "I have been a little startled by Calhoun's letter to Carew. He is I
have reason to believe *furiously* opposed to Cass & will mark every prominent
Cass man here for future sacrifice . . . & his mortification will be great when
[or] if the State votes for Cass. He has been persuaded at Washington & here
that he cannot arrest the Cass movement & has been therefore afraid to attempt
it. His offended pride is manifest in this letter. He wanted the State to go
for Taylor without assuming the responsibility after the Whig nomination.
Hence his advice to vote but not agitate. He expected to manage an *unpledged*
legislature without being seen. . . . Every body has made himself ridiculous
that has talked out save the Whigs & the original still adhering Taylor men.
It is hard to say whether those who denounced Cass in June & now support
him or our *Great Men* who advise us to vote yet have no opinion themselves
have shewn the most contemptible folly. . . ." (Original in the Hammond
Papers, Library of Congress.)

[144] At the Cass meeting on Aug. 21 Col. John Cunningham offered resolutions that the Democrats of Charleston District support no one who "does not
amply satisfy us" and that Charleston District repudiate the Baltimore Convention (see the *Courier* of Aug. 22). Burt, also, denounced Cass at the Democratic
meeting on Aug. 19 (see the *Southern Patriot* of Aug. 21). On Sept. 14, however, the *Mercury* quoted a dispatch from the Abbeville *Banner,* commenting
on an address of Burt's at Abbeville: "With regard to the Presidential election,
he was also equally full and plain. He said when he considered the silence of
Gen. Taylor upon the main question, a question upon which every Southerner
should be bold and speak out, and that if elected his Cabinet would be made
up of staunch Whigs, he could not support him. Although he said but little in
favor of Gen. Cass, yet, from his remarks, it was clear he would support him
in preference to Gen. Taylor."

we beat down the oligarchy by which we are ruled. Their imbecility, just now, affords no help. Elmore keeps himself in reserve for the future, but does not sufficiently allow for the increased popular resistance which must arise from the very exercise which they have had in the struggle. What with his monetary affairs, the bad odour of the bank, and the present disruption of parties, all those who lived by *prescription,* will go by the board. So mote it be. — I am told there is little doubt that we shall carry the City & Neck. Our men are quite sanguine. Their active men are pretty much men of straw. We are working — I have done very little; made my last speech, and though we have a large meeting on Thursday night, shall endeavour to avoid it.[145] The truth is, I have acquired quite the favor of the people here as a stump speaker, and they sing out for me, on all occasions, to the exclusion no doubt of much better persons, — who, by the way were appointed to conjure by committee. My intrusions, I am inclined to suspect are looked upon as sometimes quite impertinent. They have spoken to me, numerously, to run for the House, and several persons have intimated a wish that I should strike in for Congress. Neither Holmes nor Rhett is popular.[146] But to all applications I have said 'no'. I have too

---

[145] In an account of this meeting held on Sept. 14 the *Mercury* of Sept. 16 remarks: "W. Gilmore Simms, Esq., at the close of Col. Cunningham's remarks, was loudly called for, and was received on his appearance in the most enthusiastic manner. Mr. Simms said, he would not regret that circumstances which had disappointed him in leaving the city, had so fully compensated him, by affording the opportunity he now enjoyed, of listening with them to the narrative Mr. [Isaac E.] Holmes had given. He rejoiced that he was permitted still to be here and to join hands with the true and bold spirits he saw gathered there, at a time when men at the South should stand shoulder to shoulder. If united at home, and elevated above the corrupting influences of party at the South, we had nothing to fear. Our own arms would be found an ample security for our rights. But the surrender of our position to the contest of any party, the unconditional abandonment of a proud self-reliance, would be indeed 'degrading and insulting' to us. Mr. Simms most strenuously urged on the friends of Gen. Taylor to be vigilant and bold. Do not trust, said he, the statements of those who are opposed to you. Their game is mere success. And if to keep you in the dark is to contribute to that end, never will you be enlightened. Read for yourselves. See the *virtues,* which at the North are paraded as recommending Gen. Cass, and then as men true to the South, tell if you can, how you can confide in him. Be true to your position and you will be true to the South. Mr. Simms' address was throughout received in the most flattering manner, and his bold strain of argument was, at times, happily relieved by strokes of wit which exhibited the position of our opponents, as equally devoid of the support of sound reason, and accessible to the shafts of an overwhelming ridicule."

[146] Isaac E. Holmes and Robert Barnwell Rhett.

much private toil before me. I can no longer afford to be a patriot; but think seriously of the necessity of going North to devote myself to the profession. I go to N. Y. on Saturday, and shall be gone till the middle of Oct. Write me accordingly & believe me

Yours truly &c

W. Gilmore Simms

445: To JAMES LAWSON

Charleston, Oct 17. [1848][147]

Dear Lawson.

I arrived home about an hour ago and found all well. We had head winds & heavy seas; the *debris* of a severe gale which has been prevailing in this quarter. We met two vessels in distress, one with her bulwarks stove in, the other with her main mast carried away, — one a brig & the other a schooner. On board we had a shocking time with the crowd, the confusion, want of space & want of cleanliness. Perhaps it will be well to secure a berth for Augusta before the vessel arrives, i.e. assuming that she may possibly stay a week longer. If she sails next Saturday, however, there is a friend of mine, Dr. Jos. Johnson,[148] an excellent & venerable Gentleman on board, with his daughter, whom you can easily find out & in whose care you can put her. Tell Lady Lyde that the grapes & pears came safely & in good condition. My head swims. I can only say to you & your wife, how deeply & tenderly I am yours & hers. Kiss Augusta & the rest for me.

Yours Ever

Simms

---

[147] On Sept. 14 Simms wrote to Hammond, "I go to N. Y. on Saturday, and shall be gone till the middle of Oct." This letter to Lawson, written on Oct. 17, immediately after Simms' return from New York to Charleston, undoubtedly should be dated 1848. Supporting evidence is Simms' reference to Augusta's being in the North.

[148] Joseph Johnson, Charleston physician and author. See note 17, March 15, 1843.

446: To James Lawson

Charleston, Nov. 1. [1848][149]

Dear Lawson

The Southerner, due yesterday morning at 6, did not reach the city until 6.p.m. I was in a great state of anxiety, as having very smooth weather here, we could not account for the detention. Head winds & high seas are the causes alledged for delay. Augusta & Miss Kellogg [150] reached us safely. The former looks worsted. I am afraid that tyrannical woman, *our mistress,* has been making her frolic at nights. But we shall soon go into the country when I trust she will recruit. The moment I recieved your note in regard to Murdoch, I called on him. I had purposed doing so before your letter was recieved. I have been trying to take care of him, but the wretched corps with which he has been associated has kept him almost wholly from his most favorite range of character. His houses have been small, *but the impression which he has made has been very favorable,* and is so much capital for the future. In this view of the subject he is satisfied. I have been writing all or nearly all the notices of him — two or three per diem. I enclose you a sample of them, which I procured Editorial places for. I had him to tea with us on Sunday night, and during the afternoon drove him out in the carriage along some of our favorite drives. He is a pleasing companion, & seems at once frank & highly intelligent. He speaks affectionately of you & Forrest, and is wholly disabused of the malign influence which haunted him, and made him seem forgetful of his friends. On these points he converses freely and frequently. It is probable he goes tomorrow when I may write you again briefly. — I made a speech an hour long at a public meeting last night — a scorer.[151] Today Augusta proposes to be confirmed, — recieved into the bosom of the Church & I must be present. Give my love, and hers, and my wife's to the cruel

---

[149] Dated by James E. Murdoch's engagement in Charleston from Oct. 25 through Nov. 1, 1848 (see Hoole, *The Ante-Bellum Charleston Theatre,* p. 127). Several of Simms' notices of Murdoch's performances are preserved with this letter in the South Caroliniana Library.

[150] Nancy Kellogg.

[151] The *Southern Patriot,* the *Mercury,* and the *Courier* of Nov. 2 give accounts of this meeting at which A. G. Magrath, Charles Macbeth, W. Alston Pringle, James Simons, and Simms spoke. None gives details of Simms' speech.

woman whose sway is so despotic over us, with a kiss on my account for her & the little flock.

Yours truly &c

W. Gilmore Simms

447: To JAMES LAWSON

Charleston Nov. 2. [1848][152]

dear Lawson

Having written to you by mail two days ago, I have no reason for writing now, but simply to avail myself of an opportunity by the hand of Mr. Murdoch. Of this Gentleman I spoke in my last. I enclose you some additional notices of his career among us, manufactured by my pen. His houses have been poor, but such as they were, they were drawn only by himself. The Company is the most wretched in the world, & no greater blunder could be made than when they opened with a star, since in this city, nobody attends the Theater (among the natives) during the first week. — I send for Lady Lyde, by Mr. M. some twelve or fifteen sweet oranges, gathered from our own trees. They are not yet ripened, but growing yellow slowly. The trees are loaded with fruit. They contain probably 300. — We go into the country on Monday next. Times very dull & hard, prospects gloomy. I made a furious political speech on Tuesday night,[153] the last that I shall make in all probability, for a long season. Some talk of my going into Editorial harness, but mum.[154] — Not a word from or of Duyckinck. Murdoch's eyes seem fairly opened in regard to the Centurion. Says he has lost in various ways more than $1500 by him.[155] God bless you all — all send love.

Yours Ever

W. Gilmore Simms

---

[152] Dated by Simms' reference to Murdoch's engagement in Charleston (see letter to Lawson of Nov. 1). The notices of Murdoch's performances enclosed in this letter are with the original in the South Caroliniana Library.

[153] See note 151, Nov. 1, 1848.

[154] Simms became editor of the *Southern Quarterly Review* with the issue of April, 1849.

[155] Murdoch had presented Cornelius Mathews' *Witchcraft* in Philadelphia, Cincinnati, St. Louis, and New York (see note 44, Feb. 2, 1847). He had recently performed in his *Jacob Leisler* (see note 48, April 15, 1848).

448: To James Edward Murdoch

Thursday Mg. [November 2, 1848][156]

dear Murdoch

I send you a small packet additional for James Lawson for which I beg that you will find space in your trunk. I shall make it a duty to be at the Wilmington Boat, this afternoon, between 2 & 3 to see you off. Shall be at home all the morning.

Yours truly &c

W. Gilmore Simms

J. Murdoch, Esq.

449: To James Lawson

Woodlands, Nov. 9. [1848][157]

Dear Lawson.

You see where I date from. We came up on Monday last. You will have seen, by previous letters, that Augusta came safely to hand, though not without occasioning us great anxiety. Due at 6 A.M. it was 6 P.M. before the Steamer made her appearance. Here, we are as yet scarcely seated. I have had hardly time to look about me. Our woods, at a glance, are now very beautiful. The leaves have not yet fallen, but are glorious in their autumn wear. The day after our arrival one of our fishermen brought us from the river half a dozen trout, the least of which was eighteen inches long. On such occasions Mr. Roach usually ejaculates — knowing your piscatorial infirmities, "I wish that Mr. Lawson were here." — Murdoch, you will have seen before this time. I found him a very pleasant fellow, and tried to do for him all that was possible in the brief space allowed me. I wrote, in fact, all the notices, in all the papers, in regard to his acting. He made a favorable impression upon all who saw him; — but was doubly unfortunate in two things — in having come to Charleston at the very opening of the Theatre when it is never attended here, & in his playing with as wretched a company, as ever disgraced the Boards any where — a company *chosen,* it is admitted, by your excellent friend Andrew Jackson Allen,

---

[156] Dated by Simms' reference to the packet for Lawson (oranges for Mrs. Lawson). See letters to Lawson of Nov. 2 and Nov. 9. Nov. 2 fell on Thursday.

[157] Dated by Simms' reference to Augusta's return from the North. See letter to Lawson of Nov. 1.

WILLIAM GILMORE SIMMS

"My portrait! will it serve when I am dead,
To bring me to thy memory, as beside
Thy cheerful fire thou sitt'st at eventide — "
— From Simms' "Sonnets. — With My Portrait."
(From the original painting, unsigned, in the possession of Mrs. John Rivers, Charleston, S. C.)

MARCUS CLAUDIUS MARCELLUS HAMMOND

"I behold you, towering like Saul, head and shoulders above the joyous circle, the silver drinking cup in hand, and all hands elevated and waiting for the pledge. . . . the words reach me as certainly as if I were present. I feel that I am remembered, and I requite you with like remembrance."
— From the dedication to *Mellichampe* (1854).
(From a photograph in the possession of Mr. James H. Hammond, Columbia, S. C.)

Costumier in Chief à la Excellence Edouin Forrest, Esq! By
Murdoch I sent for your wife a specimen of our garden oranges,
in return for your garden grapes which she did *not* send. I hope
they reached you in safety. Augusta has been giving rare accounts
of your doings with Mrs. Seba [158] and of her doings with you,
which have astounded all parties here. — Enclosed I send you a
poem entitled "Fonthill" which you will deliver to Mr. C. W.
Webber for his Magazine, whenever he shall call for it.[159] It is
one for which Forrest ought to send me a box of his best caba-
noes. I trust you will like it. We are just beginning to recieve
the Election Returns, by which it would appear that Taylor's
election is morally certain. If so, I ought to look out for my appointment.[160] I have no news. There are sundry satirical publications in regard to Charleston, in rhyme, of which I hope to obtain
copies which I shall send you.[161] They will afford some queer
pictures of our venerable city. Love to wife and a kiss for herself
& the young ones.

Yours & hers &c

Simms

See Stringer & ask him to send me the copy of Herbert's Book [162]
which he promised me for review.

---

[158] Elizabeth Oakes Prince Smith (1806-1893), author, lecturer, reformer,
and wife of Seba Smith (1792-1868), satirist and editor.

[159] Charles W. Webber was planning the establishment of a new monthly,
which never appeared (see letter to Lawson of Feb. 5, 1849, and the article
on Webber in the Duyckincks' *Cyclopaedia*). In his letter to Lawson of *c.* May
6, 1849, Simms writes that he has decided that "Fonthill" should not be published because of Forrest's domestic scandal. Fonthill, Forrest's estate on the
Hudson River, is described in detail in the Charleston *Courier* of Sept. 26, 1848.

[160] Having been disappointed in receiving a diplomatic post under Polk,
Simms hoped for one under Taylor, whom he had vigorously supported. Concerning Simms' campaigning for Taylor, James M. Walker facetiously wrote
to Hammond on Aug. 22: "Simms is supposed to have received from General
Taylor, that same 'old Whitey' which he wore at Buena Vista in complimentary
return for his services as a politician — Certainly the hat he wears, must
resemble it. . . ." (Original in the Hammond Papers, Library of Congress.)

[161] Undoubtedly one of the works Simms here refers to is *Charleston: A
Poem*, written (according to the preface) by a Northern lady and published
in Charleston in 1848. This work inspired Simms to write a reply, *Charleston,
and Her Satirists; A Scribblement*, published in two pamphlet numbers as "by
a City Bachelor" and printed in Charleston by James S. Burges in 1848. In
the preface to his first number Simms remarks (p. 3): "With many truths the
aim was too feeble, the shaft too dull, to prove otherwise than innocuous. I have
been tempted to a reply, — somewhat glad of the chance, indeed — to confirm the
justice of some of the satirist's points of censure, while dissenting from the
propriety of others. Charleston has many faults and foibles, — the whole State
indeed is open to criticism — vulnerable in its vanities, and particularly so in
its politics. It will do no harm to draw attention to these subjects."

[162] *Frank Forrester's Field Sports of the United States, and British Provinces, of North America*, 2 vols. (New York: Stringer & Townsend, 1848).
For Henry William Herbert, see introductory sketch.

450: To James Henry Hammond

Woodlands, Nov. 11. [1848][163]

dear Hammond.

I have foreborne writing you till the present moment in consequence of the pressure of tasks and troubles consequent upon
my return from the North and my removal to the plantation.
Small duties & petty cares have frittered away my time, until,
with most of my correspondence left undone, I am really incapable, while I look around me of saying or seeing what I have
done. I am scarcely yet at ease in my studio, and write now with
a conviction that many things I am anxious to say must be left
unuttered or barely referred to. The tidings of your affliction
reached me in N. Y., but I felt that I could say nothing, at that
moment, which would not be almost an impertinence.[164] I have
too frequently suffered in the same manner, not to be aware that
the best consolations of the sufferers are derived from thought
rather than from the expression of sympathies of the sincerest
friendship — thought which leads to God as the first and last
power, as it teaches our own incapacity & weakness, not only
tends to reconcile us to loss, but teaches us best where to look
for consolation. As an *earnest* man you are necessarily a religious one; though the world, judging wholly by externals,
would scarce look to either of us for the possession of the sentiment. That we believe, hope & struggle without ceasing, are the
satisfactory assurances to ourselves of the actual presence of a
religious and spiritual nature. This works out its own salvation
and its own sympathies. That you have mine you will readily
believe, as I have suffered like yourself, and am like yourself an
earnest and deeply feeling, though not very sentimental person.
These afflictions are perhaps necessary to natures such as ours, —
where the individual resource is great, and the will proportion-
ately strong. It is our misfortune that we do not sufficiently feel,
or sufficiently long; and thus it is that the watchful providence,
in which I firmly believe, finds it so frequently necessary —
as in my case — to repeat the punishment. I would not, as a
friend, spare you one tear, or one pang, accruing from the
chastisement; but will sincerely pray that they may work such

---

163 Dated by Simms' discussion of the campaign for Taylor.

164 Hammond's son Christopher FitzSimons, born June 28, 1833, had died on
October 4, 1848.

good results in your case (as they have not, I fear in mine) so that you will need no farther infliction of the scourge. — I sent you by yesterday's mail, a copy of a circular (prepared by myself) and a pamphlet copy of the last proceedings (political) in which I have been engaged in Charleston. The preamble was prepared by Magrath with small alterations of my own. Two of the resolutions are mine — three are Calhoun's (Congress) and the rest by Magrath & others of the Committee.[165] I trust that they will meet with your approbation. I think they embody your views generally. You will perhaps be better prepared to feel the importance of the course which we suggest, as already movements are in progress which have for their object an Independent State movement — a movement which places S. C. in the lead, from which & against which all our Sister States have revolted. Our only hope of successful resistance to abolition is by a concerted action of three or more States, and a resolved and earnest effort judiciously made, will, at this juncture, and particularly during the progress of the next session of Congress, will be likely to attain this object. It is, however, the selfish policy of certain of our politicians to move the State alone, thus keeping up a local organization purely, the only effect of which is to sacrifice rivals and maintain themselves in power. We can only defeat this by calling in the Sister States to council; and I am in great hopes that our people will rather second our aim than that of our Hunkers. Let me hear from you on this head. — You are perhaps hardly aware of the extent of the blow given to the enemy in the victory we gained in Charleston. Young Carolina, there, is in arms, and there is no ass so pitiful, who does not now kick at the dead lion. Elmore has been sorely prostrated by it; and a new affair about the Custom House has given him a new defeat.[166] The absquatulation of McDonald [167]

---

[165] We have been unable to locate copies of this circular and pamphlet. Undoubtedly the latter consists of the proceedings of the Taylor meeting of Oct. 31. The *Southern Patriot* of Nov. 2 prints the resolutions in its account of this meeting.

[166] A quarrel had arisen in Charleston over the site of a new Custom House. The *Mercury* of Nov. 2 reports the majority and minority decisions of the Board of Commissioners selected to choose the site.

[167] Alexander McDonald was a director of the Bank of the State of South Carolina for a number of years. According to information furnished by Professor J. M. Lesesne, in 1846 Franklin H. Elmore, President of the Bank, reported to the Legislature that $25,000 had been lost this year due to the fraudulent delinquency of McDonald, who had previously enjoyed the confidence of the city of Charleston and the State (see Greenville *Mountaineer*, Dec. 25, 1846).

& other losses, renders it necessary that the Bank should realize in some way some 80 or 100,000 dollars. It is the scheme accordingly to sell Stewart's Hotel, upon which the Bank has a lien, to govt. for the Custom H. by which the whole amt. of the mortgage may be realized. But in the Chamber of Commerce he was voted down 5 to 7 and got angry & became offensive. Were he now a candidate he could be beaten by anybody for anything. A very pretty affair is going on, the parties to which are Bailey (Atty. Gen.) DeTreville & Hayne. The latter has published a circular to the members of Legislature, showing why B. should go out, and he go in. Treville has also issued a circular which contains a letter of B. in which he says that "———— (supposed to be Hayne) is not only not fit for the Atty. Genl., but has not the stuff in him out of which a lawyer can be made." These I have not seen, but have the reports of those who have. A story of Elmore which has reached me runs to this effect, — Pres. Polk expressed a wish that E. should go to the Senate. E. apprised of this, said the thing could only be done by his getting beforehand a contract for supplies of iron for six years, — which he could not obtain as a member of Congress. A point was strained, and Polk secured him the contract. He did not go to the Senate, *but sold out the contract to a Mining Company in Penna.* Is it not monstrous. But I must see you to talk of these matters. The *Taylor* men in Charleston & the Legislature are mostly against the Bank. I am of opinion that *all* the latter are. This is so much clear gain. It was one of our points. Under the name of Taylor, we have done a great deal towards the disfranchisement of the city from Hunkerism. This was my text, and you can hardly guess my industry in its illustration. But enough for the present. I wrote to Dr. O'Bryan [168] the day that I recieved your letter. I suppose you will hear of or see him shortly, & think you will like him. Let me hear from you soon, particularly and at large on the subject of our proceedings. Let your friends be instructed to go for Richardson as Gov. [169] All will come right — the pure atmosphere from the storm. God bless you, and yours
                                        W. G. Simms

---

[168] Dr. O'Brien (misspelled here *O'Bryan*) was the tutor for Hammond's children. On Jan. 7, 1849, Hammond wrote to Simms: "Dr. O'Brien arrived here on the 30 Dec & we are so far much pleased with him." (Original in the Hammond Papers, Library of Congress.)

[169] John Peter Richardson had been governor of South Carolina during 1840-1842.

Should our pamphlet proceedings & circular please you, I can have a bundle of them forwarded you for distribution among friends in other States.

451: To James Lawson

Woodlands, Nov. 20. [1848][170]

Dear Lawson

Just before I left New York, I had a brief conference with one of the Brothers Appleton, in regard to an Illustrated volume of my poetry. It was a subject which he proposed to refer to his colleague & I saw neither of them after. As this matter is one that will need to be considered quickly, in order to secure all the time possible for bringing forth such a vol. in season for next years annual (should it be resolved on) I will beg you to call upon these Gentlemen, and resume the subject. I propose a careful selection from my published verse, making a volume of the size of Bryant, Willis, &c, and perhaps you might with propriety refer to Bryant as an authority for the assumption that no other American writer of verse, *as yet unillustrated,* remains, whose claims to popular favor can be opposed to mine. You may also indicate, as considerations especially in my favor, that I should exclusively command the preferences of the Southern people; that my poetry illustrates the country; that much of it is traditional & particularly suited to illustration, & that no portrait of me has yet been published. — In addition to these suggestions you are authorized to yield the most liberal terms, and indeed, for an edition of a thousand or fifteen hundred copies, I should be willing to recieve a compensation of 25 copies only, for friends; my chief purpose being to have my poetical claims put fairly before the public. In this matter, it appears that Bryant would not be unwilling or unprepared to urge my claims to *preference,* upon these Gentlemen. If you say so, I will write him upon the subject; but, in the meantime, you must take the Initiative in the affair, and see the Appleton's as soon as possible. I enclose you certain literary notices which I have made in our papers of their

---

[170] Dated by Simms' remark about sending Lawson "a couple of Charleston Satires just out." These may be the two numbers of his own *Charleston, and Her Satirists* (see note 161, Nov. 9, 1848), or they may be other pamphlets (see notes 136, Aug. 29, 1848, and 193, Dec. 15, 1848).

books, and which you will hand them.[171] — I have had a letter
from Israel Post of N. Y. who wants me to write at $5 per page
for a new magazine. Can you tell me anything of his proprietor
& prospects. I have written to him that I will send an article
probably next week, to be paid for when printed.[172] I shall give
you an order for the money. I hear nothing of Duyckinck & do
not now see his Journal.[173] I am afraid the old man sticks too fast
for his safety. I sent you an article for Webber.[174] Have you
recieved & read it? What of Forrest & Macready in Boston?[175]
What of the plays & play. I told Murdoch that in the event of
Forrest not liking or taking 'The Man of the People,' you were
to place it in his hands for examination. I am going on with my
Don Carlos. — My anxiety increases in regard to my wife. She
will go with me to the city in the ensuing month — when I can't
say — to be confined. The affair is altogether full of disquiets.
The last childbirth brought her almost to the grave. An inferior
cause of disquiet are my poor resources. I now seriously meditate,
when her confinement is well over — breaking away from home,
and establishing in the North professionally. I still think Phil.
the best opening. Will see. Write me soon and speak copiously.
I trust your business improves. But you must not suffer temporary
disappointment to distress you. Yours must always be temporary,
since shipwreck & suffering are inevitable. Love to wife & little

---

171 D. Appleton and Co. did not publish an edition of Simms' collected poetry.
Frequent notices of their books occur in the Charleston newspapers of this
period.

172 The *American Metropolitan Magazine,* edited by William Landon and
published by Israel Post, ran for only two numbers (Jan. and Feb., 1849). The
first installment of Simms' "The Egyptian Masque; A Tale of the Crescent
City" appears in the Feb. issue, 1, 69-73. The tale was later published as
"Marie De Berniere; A Tale of the Crescent City" in *Arthur's Home Gazette,*
II (Feb. 14, Feb. 21, Feb. 29, March 6, March 13, March 20, and March 27,
1852), and in *Marie De Berniere: A Tale of the Crescent City,* pp. 13-189.
Simms' first treatment of the story is "The Unknown Masque. A Sketch of the
Crescent City," *Southern and Western,* I (April, 1845), 262-269.

173 The *Literary World.* See note 34, Feb. 2, 1847.

174 "Fonthill." See letter to Lawson of Nov. 9, 1848.

175 Macready's New York and Boston engagements were successful and without violent incident. In Philadelphia, however, on Nov. 20, "Macready was met
by the most violent and disgraceful annoyances. His performance of Macbeth
was disturbed by constant noises throughout the evening; pennies were thrown
upon the stage, and an egg broken in front of his person." At the close of the
performance he made a speech concerning the "organized opposition" to him
and Forrest's part in it. Forrest replied with a "Card" published in the Philadelphia *Ledger.* For an account of the entire incident, see the *Literary World,* III
(Dec. 2, 1848), 877-878. For an account of the riot at the Astor Place Opera
House, New York City, on May 10, 1849, which terminated the feud that
season and resulted in the deaths of thirty people, see Alger, *Life of Edwin
Forrest,* I, 428-431.

ones in your best manner. Tell your wife we have had a week of sugar & molasses boiling — such a work. I send you a couple of Charleston Satires just out.

Yours truly &c

Simms

J. L.

452: To JAMES HENRY HAMMOND

Woodlands Nov. 24. [1848][176]

dear Hammond.

I am in reciept of your letter & greatly regret its tone of despondency. Doubtless the day at present is dark, but this is only, I trust, the forerunner of the dawn. I am in hopes that the fanatics in Congress will goad the Southern men out of their propriety, or into it this very session. What you suggest, touching the sources of our difficulty, is no doubt perfectly true; with this exception, that Calhoun, with all his selfish aspirations, has, through these, been made the instrument of other men. This particular instance — that of casting the vote of the state for Cass, is, I am sure, directly in hostility with his real desires; and has this advantage, that, if he be not utterly demented, he must see that the proceeding goes farther, & absolutely lays him on the shelf. The thing was worked through the Mercury & Carolinian, which are vulgarly supposed to be his organs but which have really been the organs of Mr. Rhett. He has been the mover of the wires in this instance, seconded by Elmore, Bailey & others below, and by Pickens & others above. The latter being governed directly by the wish to throw Calhoun aside, or give him a mortal stab. Their failure stabs themselves; since neither Rhett nor Pickens can possibly now realize their 30 pieces of silver. You must not despond. Above all you must not decieve yourself with the idea that you are no longer of use. I *know* that you are looked to, *as the future man* of S. C. if not of the South. Be true to yourself & you must be so. You have the faculties for a *public* leader. Your deficiencies are all *private*. I will explain this when we meet. You are in error, I think, about Virginia. She *cannot* lead & will not. She is already bought & sold through her politicians. The true state to lead, & to which we must ad-

---

[176] Dated by Simms' references to the election of 1848. This letter is printed in Odell, "Letters of William Gilmore Simms to James H. Hammond, 1847-1850," pp. 9-11.

dress ourselves is *Louisiana!* She has the deepest interest
(slavery &c. considered) of all of us in the contest. Her interest
in slavery cannot decline for the next 300 years. In Virginia,
N. C. &, I may add, S. C. it is visibly on the decline. In 15 years
Va. will be a free soil state, and will be instantly followed by N. C.
S. C. will be a frontier & where? Now *Louisiana* exports alone
85 millions. She holds the key of all the Valley of the West. *She*
can control Kentucky, Tennessee, &c, when we can't. Carry her
with us, at the head, and she closes the door upon Western exports
measurably. She has great talent, and a great ambition, & has
been too much neglected & oversloughed. We should put her in
the lead. We shall never be able to do so with Va. while her sons
are all in the market. Think of this. Touching Conner & the Bank,
I am doubtful. It may be true of Boyce. *He* is *jealous* of *Conner's
influence* in the city. A day or two before I left Charleston, I had
a talk with Conner. Among other things he told me this curious
story. The city of Charleston wanting money, sent a Circular
last summer to all the Banks to know upon what terms it might
be got. It held out the lure of doing business with the leading
Bank, making its tax deposits &c. The Bank of the State agreed
to let it have what was wanted at any time for 3 per ct! The
contract was made. But just as I was leaving, the City wanted
$6000, which the Bank *could not* provide! This, I fancy, accounts
for the preemptory sale of the Victoria & Charleston Hotels,
otherwise the City must have stopt payments! Rich, — eh?
Conner chuckles at all this, and, I am thinking, has come to feel
that he *must* wrestle with Elmore for life or death. I presume the
chief matter which has made him reluctant is the fact that both
Banks are to be rechartered during the same year. This afflicts
some others in the same category. — I will think of what you
suggest, touching your literary experiments. Without invention,
as you say, the drama is the last thing to be attempted; but you
are the very man for the subject you once suggested to me — viz.
the political History of the Country. Think of it. — For me, if
possible, the mission to Naples or Turin. There is this difficulty.
Holmes [177] has seen that he can scarcely hope again to be re-
elected from Charleston. But for the Taylor movement, he would
have been defeated. He must look out for employment. He will
be in the way, and Gadsden will support him. But, at all events,

---

[177] Isaac E. Holmes.

it is worth a trial & I will thank you to bestir yourself in it.
Holmes may get a Secretaryship. I need the mission. Literature
is in a wretched condition. I have a work ready which the publishers dare not publish.[178] They tell me it would be sacrificed to
do so now. And just now, my expenses are greatly increased. My
wife is as women wish to be &c,[179] and proposes to go to the city
to be confined. The thing could take place in the country just as
well [as] in the city & would save me considerable expense; but
she thinks differently, and the case is one which admits of no
discussion. It will take some $300 surplus out of my pocket, and
greatly abridge my chicken money. I think the Italian mission
could be got. It would save me, and place me free of the world.
The argument in my favor, ought to be of weight with Taylor. I
am almost the only professional author of the South, and have
done service. You could better show how than myself. I have
some claims to such a Court as that of Naples, where my literary
reputation might be felt. I once had a little Italian, which I shall
set myself to recover & improve. I should endeavor to go to that
court, speaking its dialect. But a truce to this. You know all. How
& through whom you will work I know not, but, as you say, the
sooner we move the better. I propose to go to the City by the
the 7 or 10 Decr. Is it possible for you to send or meet me at
Aiken or Hamburg, between this & then. I have none but the
carriage horses which I cannot take from my wife. My other
horses have gone the way of all flesh. If you can meet me at either
place, so as to let me return by the 10th Decr. I would run up
& spend a couple or three days with you. Let me know in season,
if the thing is possible. I scribble this the hour in which I have
read your letter. I send you a pamphlet of which you will give
me your opinion.[180] There is a sequel to it. But I am weary —
half desponding like yourself. But I go to work when I am dull
& expend my stupidity upon the public or my friends. God bless
you.

Yours

Simms

---

[178] Possibly Simms is here speaking of his collected poetry. See in this
connection Simms' letter to Hammond of Dec. 24, 1847.

[179] "As women wish to be who love their lords." This quotation from Home's
Douglas appears to have been a favorite with Simms. See letters to Lawson of
July 12 and Aug. 2, 1848.

[180] *Charleston, and Her Satirists.* See note 161, Nov. 9, 1848.

453: To James Lawson

Woodlands Nov. 28. [1848][181]

dear Lawson

I enclose you a brief note for the actor, Mr. W. C. Forbes to whom I confided the rude draught of my dramatic poem of Arnold, which he requested to see, and of which I desired his opinion. I wish you would ascertain his address (Forrest knows it) and send him the note. The M.S. when you recieve it, can be retained by you until an opportunity offers, or it can be sent by Harper & B. or Putnam, in some packet to the care of John Russell, Charleston. From Duyckinck I hear nothing and his paper has failed me several times. Will you ask him for the several papers in which the four poems appeared which I gave him.[182] I see that Lowell's satire devotes a few pages to himself & Mathews.[183] I hear nothing from you in answer to some half a dozen letters. Have you seen Murdoch. Have you recieved the poem (Fonthill) for Webber. What of this uproar between the friends of Forrest & Macready? I look to you for a budget of tidings, not omitting your own affairs which I trust are improving at the expense of the shipping interest. We shall go to the city next week, there to remain until my wife passes through her travail and is able to return to the country. Do let me hear from you there. Present me affectionately & gratefully to Lady Lyde, and kiss the children round on my account.

Yours Ever as Ever

W. G. Simms

---

181 Dated by Simms' reference to "Fonthill." See letters to Lawson of Nov. 9 and Nov. 20, 1848.

182 See note 206, c. Dec. 19, 1848.

183 James Russell Lowell, *A Fable for Critics* (New York: G. P. Putnam, 1848). In a notice of the volume in the Charleston *Courier* of Dec. 30, the reviewer (possibly Simms) writes: "It is to be regretted that he should have interspersed his pages with so many flings at the dear institutions of the South, since this will necessarily prejudice the chances of his circulation in our region. These, too, are mere impertinences, not called for by his subject, but lugged in by the head and shoulders, rather to indicate the settled mode of thinking in New England, than those of the poet himself." Simms later noticed the poem in *S. Q. R.*, XVI (Oct., 1849), 239-242.

454: To James Lawson

Woodlands, Nov. 29. [1848][184]

dear Lawson

I have rewritten the poem altering in compliance with most of your suggestions. But if I am too hasty as a Poet, you are ten times more so as a critic. Were I to suppress, as you counsel, the introductory verses, the poem would be a mere puff, as discreditable to Forrest as myself. The first verses describe the Landscape, *en route,* to Fonthill, and cannot be condensed. There are a succession of landscapes, to omit which, would be to make the whole thing abrupt and unsymmetrical. Some one or two of your detailed suggestions are wholly out of the question. Where, for example, was your ear (not in Apollo's keeping, surely) when you counselled me to alter the line —

"Each hidden motive home to trace—

to

Each hidden motive home*ward* to trace?"

Make music of the latter if you can. But you say not a word of any thing besides the poem. Have you seen Murdoch? What of Forrest & Macready. Write soon & fully.

Yours Ever

Simms

455: To James Lawson

Charleston, Decr. 15. [1848][185]

dear Lawson

We have just had the narrowest escape in the world. My wife and self left Woodlands for Charleston on Monday last, and she was taken with pains of labor in the car. She had miscalculated her time, and events were anticipated by something like three weeks. We sent for the Physician that night, and on the next the child was born — another girl — a fine fat hearty little fellow, with lungs of the most ample dimensions. Mother & child, I rejoice to say, are, thus far, both doing well, and I am relieved of the worst anxiety. I write as soon after the event as possible,

---

[184] Dated by Simms' discussion of "Fonthill." See letters to Lawson of Nov. 9, Nov. 20, and Nov. 28.

[185] Dated by the birth of Chevillette Eliza Simms on Dec. 13, 1848.

though I so seldom hear from you, that I almost question whether you care to hear from me. We left Augusta & Gilmore at Woodlands, where there are several visitors, young ladies, relations of the family. Today I learned that Wesley Harper [186] was in the city and went to see him. He was out, but I saw his son, Young Wesley, who, I think it probable, will pay a visit to Woodlands. There seems to be some apprehensions that a cough, with which he is troubled, might have serious results unless well guarded against. — Just before leaving the country I was on a Camp Hunt of three days; we killed some deer, caught a fox, and had a stag dance every night till daylight, — with plenty of liquors and segars. By the way, talking of segars, when you have helped yourself, send on the residue of Forrest's present, carefully put up and addressed to me in Charleston, care of John Russell. They will only come in season. — What of the plays? I see it now reported that the prize of $1000 has been awarded to a Gentleman of Baltimore.[187] What are the merits of the issue between Forrest & Macready. Has the former been doing anything rashly? I hope not. He *can afford* to be patient. — I trust the amendments of the poem [188] satisfy you. Should they not, do not give it to Webber, or publish it at all; but return it. At all events let me hear from you. — Times here are very gloomy. Short crops & poor prices make us all dull.[189] I am quite desponding. I sincerely hope that you, who live on your neighour's losses, have no reason to complain of deficient gains. I have sent you several commissions, attending to which may interfere with your occupation or your sleep. Do not let them do either. — I hear nothing from or of Duyckinck. Mathews, I percieve, is out with another book, which I knew to be his from the title & advertisement.[190] — I could wish that you would send me a budget of news. I am really stagnating. Consult with that capricious woman, your wife, & let her recal for you the numerous items of intelligence which, I doubt not, she possesses. At least give her my love, and a kiss all round for

---

[186] Joseph Wesley Harper (1801-1870), of the firm of Harper and Brothers.

[187] Unlocated. The *Knickerbocker* had reported that the prize was to be $3000 (see note 267, Oct. 20, 1847).

[188] "Fonthill." See letter to Lawson of Nov. 29.

[189] See Woodlands Plantation Book in appendix to this volume.

[190] We can discover no record of Mathews having published a book at this time. Probably Simms was mistaken in his attribution.

the young ones. I have now *four,* your number. May they love each other as their parents have done.

Yours truly

W. Gilmore Simms

456: To Augustin Louis Taveau [191]

Augustin Taveau Esq   Charleston, Decr. 15. [1848][192]
dear Sir

Let me thank you for the copy of the spirited little poem, entitled, "The Vindication" [193] which has been sent to my address, and which I am told is from your pen. The composition which provoked it, however, is scarcely worth the attention of its satirists. You have performed your voluntary task with animation, and exhibited higher proofs of your ability than have yet fallen from your pen. I do not doubt that you will persevere, and by a due use of the *labor limae,* attain, in proper season, that degree of perfection, which is requisite for triumphant verse. With sincerest wishes that you may realize this result, I am

Very truly Yours

&c

W. Gilmore Simms

---

[191] Augustin Louis Taveau (1828-1886) was born in Charleston, attended Mount Zion Academy under James Wilson Hudson, was graduated from the College of Charleston, and was admitted to the bar in Charleston in 1850. He then made a three years' tour of Europe, meeting and marrying at Gibraltar Delphine Sprague, daughter of Horatio Sprague, of Boston, Mass. Upon his return to the United States he became a rice planter on the Edisto River. At the outbreak of the Confederate War he sold his slaves and went to Richmond to join the Confederacy. After the war he settled in Maryland. He was a contributor to the Charleston newspapers, the *Southern Literary Messenger,* the *Knickerbocker, De Bow's Review,* the *Southern Literary Journal,* and the *Southern Literary Gazette.* In 1848 he published *The Vindication* (see note 193, below) and in 1855 a volume of poetry entitled *The Magic Word.* See David K. Jackson, "Some Unpublished Letters of John R. Thompson and Augustin Louis Taveau," *William and Mary College Quarterly,* 2nd. ser., XVI (April, 1936), 206-221, and a MS. sketch of Taveau (probably written by Taveau himself) in the Charles Carroll Simms Collection, South Caroliniana Library.

[192] This letter and Taveau's reply dated Dec. 18, 1848, are printed in Jackson, "Some Unpublished Letters of John R. Thompson and Augustin Louis Taveau," pp. 206-207.

[193] *The Vindication: A Satire, on 'Charleston: A Poem'* (Charleston, S. C.: Printed by Walker and Burke, 1848). *Charleston: A Poem* also inspired Simms' *Charleston, and Her Satirists* (see note 161, Nov. 9, 1848). The *Courier* of Nov. 21 contains a review of *The Vindication,* signed "Aristarchus": "The author has attempted, with no feeble pen, to defend his native city from the numerous accusations of the fair satirist. . . . In this harmless war of words many writers have engaged, but none has engaged in it with more spirit. . . ."

457: To James Henry Hammond

Charleston Decr. 15. 1848

Dear Hammond.

We had the most narrow escape in the world. Lingering too long in the country, my wife was taken in the cars with the pains of labor, and that night we called in the physician. Fortunately, no evil accrued from the journey, and another daughter [194] has been added to my flock. Mother & child are both doing very well, and in all probability, I shall be able to pay you the visit at an earlier day than was expected. I sincerely hope for it for several reasons. I know not that my budget contains much the clues to which have not already been put in your possession; but letters are such unsatisfactory matters to those who are wont to talk! I have seen Brisbane.[195] The difficulty is to bring him to any practical issues. I won't be imposed upon by his abstractions which are always vague & flighty. He is one of those who seldom make themselves understood. After long pallavering, — a whole morning — I reduced his matter to the simple scheme of diverting our capital & labor as much as possible to mechanic & manufacturing arts. To this we have long since given our assent, recognizing old Bacon's adage in regard to Agriculture, Manufacture & Vecture.[196] The immediate purpose of B. is a machine factory — no doubt a highly important matter. I told him to put aside, if possible, his abstractions about the rights & power of wealth, tho' in some degree correct, and address himself wholly to the *practical* matter. A company might be chartered with reference to the one project. I recommended him to make it popular, by so reducing the price of shares that the poorest mechanic might at least become

---

[194] Chevillette.

[195] Gen. Abbott H. Brisbane, born in 1804, was graduated from West Point in 1825 and served as an officer in the Seminole War. Later he was the president and general factotum of the Ocmulgee and Flint Railroad in Georgia, and after that professor of belles letters and ethics at the Citadel Academy, at Charleston, for five years. In 1848 he invited the mechanics of Charleston to form an association, but succeeded in assembling only about twenty. He thereupon solicited the aid of William Gregg, and in 1849 the association had about four hundred members from many parts of South Carolina. He was an intimate friend of Hammond, whom he frequently visited during the monthly meetings of the Beach Island Farmers Club at Redcliffe, Hammond's home.

[196] "It is likewise to be remembered that, forasmuch as the increase of any estate must be upon the foreigner (for whatsoever is somewhere gotten is somewhere lost), there be but three things which one nation selleth unto another: the commodity as nature yieldeth it; the manufacture; and the vecture or carriage. So that if these three wheels go, wealth will flow as in a spring tide." — Francis Bacon, "Of Seditions and Troubles."

the possessor of one. We talked a good deal about yourself. I
have no doubt that it would be politic & patriotic with you to
identify yourself, measurably, and not to risk much money, with
the people, in every domestic scheme having for its object, the
elevation to dignity of the industrial arts among us, & the diver-
sion of a part of our capital from the one pursuit. And here let
me say, that you mistake if you suppose that you are laid on the
shelf. Every step farther that we take into the mire, only compels
the popular voice to cry aloud — Ah! We want such men as
Hammond. We must have Hammond. Were you to be run for
example as Senator now, you would have 15 of 17 in the Charleston delegation; — if not all, — most of whom went against you
before. Here, you have risen wondrously in the last year; and I
am really persuaded that you ought to adopt the city as your
summer residence. Hunkerism here is dead. The young men are
full of ardor & only lack a leader; and all eyes are looking to
you. — For myself, I said to B. I see nothing that I can do. Indeed, I can't work any longer for nothing. I am poor. I have
been patriotic long enough. My expenses are increasing — my
resources diminishing, and if I am any longer to be worked, I
must be fed & stabled. I gave him my opinion fairly of his associates, most of whom are the d —— dest selfish & coldblooded
skunks in all creation. They would see you & me engage in their
fight & set us on, yet when the game was won, wouldn't suffer us
to pick the bones. I have worked for Carolina long enough, and
never had an office in her gift or a dollar at her hands. Few men
in the State have ever done more *pro bono publico*. By the way,
read an article in the *July* no. of the South Quarterly entitled
"South Carolina in the Revolution," if you would see, how I have
carried the war into Yankeedom, & furnished an argument, much
needed, to our politicians. Read it, & send me word.[197] I have
sent you the second no. of the Satire.[198] It is, of course, full of

---

[197] In his reply of Dec. 22 Hammond writes: "I read your article in the
Review. It is overwhelming. I don't think the North has ever received such a
mauling since Bunker Hill. The South should erect a statue to you for such
an article. I have heard it extravagantly praised. . . ." (Original in the
Hammond Papers, Library of Congress.)

[198] On Dec. 7 Hammond had written upon receipt of the first number of
Charleston, and Her Satirists: "It is very unequal & I can hardly think it all
yours, though parts undoubtedly are. There are touches equal to Pope &
passages that I could beat myself. It must touch the Hunkers sorely. . . . I
should like to hear it read out in the lobby of the State House about this
time." After reading the second number, he wrote on Dec. 22: "If you will let
me prune freely & then add & improve yourself here is a poem to carry you

inequalities, — the whole written *stans pede in uno,* — almost without alteration, — at some three sittings. You must take it *cum grano salis.* But it is doing good. It puts some things on record, in a portable form. — As to approaching Taylor, I really know not how the thing is to be done. I neither know him, nor any of his associates. Conner threatens to see him and will avail himself of any opportunity. But he is scarce the man. My claims, if I have any, are peculiar, and to be conveyed intelligibly only by a person like yourself; yet I do not see how you can get an opportunity. On all sides, my dear Hammond, I read the blanks only, and I have soothed and subdued all my hopes & expectations, whether from fortune or the public into that rational state of resignation, which, as it can promise itself nothing, will not be disgusted when nothing comes. Your last shot at the Bank makes a happy case of parallelism, which the vulgarest legislator may understand.[199] Now that de Treville has been baffled in his appetites, he has come out bravely against the Bank, — *by which influence he was defeated.*[200] Had he but taken his side fearlessly *before,* he must have been elected. The way has been so well paved for Memminger in the popular mind that he too has plucked up a degree of courage which will probably carry him through the contest.[201] Let the dogs harry each other. The conflict is all the better for us, since it was in the apathy of all class[es] that the State fell into the power of its enemies. — But to return, I will go some night with Brisbane to his Mechanical Conventicle, & see what it promises. There is a *truth* at the bottom of his fancies, but he needs men of ballast & surefootedness to help him extricate it from the well. — I have a letter from a friend who tells me that Dr. O'Brien craves a respite till Christmas or 1st of January, in order not to suffer a pecuniary loss where he is, by the non-completion of a term of tutorship.[202] Not unreasonable in him, though you suffer. — It has been, as you may suppose, something of an effort to write this letter, suffering as I do from domestic

---

down further than any poetry you have yet written." (Original in the Hammond Papers, Library of Congress.)

[199] Hammond's last article on the Bank of the State of South Carolina was published in the *Mercury* of Dec. 2. It is signed "Au Revoir."

[200] I. W. Hayne had defeated Richard DeTreville for the office of Attorney General of South Carolina.

[201] Christopher Gustavus Memminger was elected to the South Carolina House of Representatives.

[202] See note 168, Nov. 11, 1848.

excitements & scarcely fixed in my homestead. Let me hear from
you at length, and don't fling at me with my brevity.

Yours

W. G. S.

458: To EVERT AUGUSTUS AND GEORGE LONG DUYCKINCK

[*c.* December 19, 1848][203]

Mess'rs. E. & G. Duyckinck

Gentlemen

Speaking with Mr. E Duyckinck about contributions to the
World, he mentioned that he would pay at the rate of $5 per
page. I have accordingly thought of preparing a series of sketches
of Carolina life, of which the enclosed may be considered a specimen.[204] Should it suit you that I should continue them, write me
to that effect. Should they not suit you, you will oblige me by
placing the article in the hands of Mr. Lawson. It strikes me that
a series of South. papers would serve your purpose here. You
have done some things to annoy our bretheren. In quoting from
Whittier, for example, it is assumed that you extracted an offensive abolition poem only because it commended itself to your
opinions.[205] I have combated this notion but it seems to prevail.
I do not know whether you published all of the five poems which
I gave you before leaving. I have seen 'Eva', a 'Southern Areyto'
and 'Conquest', only. If the two remaining are published, one of
which was a Sunset at Sea, do send me the papers containing
them.[206] Some of your former friends here, express the opinion
that you have somewhat gone over to New England. Did you see

---

[203] This letter is postmarked Dec. 20. The year is established by Simms'
reference to his "South Carolina in the Revolution."

[204] These were not published until 1852, when they appeared under the title
of "Home Sketches, or Life Along the Highways and Byways of the South,"
Literary World, X (Jan. 3, Jan. 10, Jan. 24, and Feb. 7.), 1-3, 31-32, 63-65,
107-110; XI (July 31, Sept. 11, Nov. 20, and Dec. 11), 73-76, 163-166, 322-324,
378-379.

[205] In a review of John G. Whittier's *Poems* (Boston: B. B. Mussey & Co.,
1849) in the *Literary World,* III (Dec. 9), 894, is quoted a poem containing
the following lines:

"Back with the Southerner's
Padlocks and scourges!"

[206] The first three poems were published in the *Literary World,* III (Oct.
7, Oct. 21, and Oct. 28), 708, 773, 751. "Sunset at Sea" was published as "Evening at Sea," *ibid.,* IV (Jan. 27, 1849), 79. The fifth poem did not appear.

or recieve the South. Quarterly for July containing an article on the relative claims of S. Carolina & New England in the Revolution.

Yours truly &c.

W. Gilmore Simms

459: To JAMES LAWSON

Charleston Decr. 28. [1848][207]

Dear Lawson

The smiles & promises of the season upon you & yours. My best love to your wife and kisses for the children. The hearty shake of an old friend's hand for yourself. May this find you all prosperous, & may God keep you so. That you are doing well professionally, I infer from your long & eloquent expatiation upon your daily & nightly toils over wreck & disaster. It's an ill wind that blows nobody good, & if averages must thrive by the misfortunes of others, may your share of their profits be such as you desire & deserve. — We are all doing well. My wife is more vigorous than usual & the infant thrives. Mary Lawson chirps about the house with an ever restless foot & tongue, and in a visit to the plantation, where I ate my Christmas dinner, I found Augusta & Gilmore in good health & spirits.[208] I am drudging on as usual, with no leisure to be sick.

You are not severe as a critic — you are only unjust, and hypercritical.[209] Sonorous murmurs is legitimate. Sonorous is loud sounding. Loud is relative. The sounding of the waves upon the beach when all other sounds are still is loud, and sonorous murmurs admirably convey the idea of the billows of a river breaking against the rocky shores. I do not say that these murmurs *address* the Eye — I say they *persuade* the Eye. The Ear is the medium of communication. I may persuade Bryant or Forrest through you. The Ear is a conductor only to other senses. You are simply become *literal* in your criticism which in poetry is always apt to be untruth. Your *Ear* may be perfect, my dear fellow, but if *you* are

---

[207] Dated by Simms' reference to the review of Whittier's *Poems* published in the *Literary World*. See letter to Duyckinck of *c*. Dec. 19.

[208] A description of this trip from Charleston to Woodlands is the subject of the first article in Simms' "Home Sketches" (see note 204, *c*. Dec. 19, 1848).

[209] Apparently Lawson had written another letter criticising Simms' "Fonthill." See letters to Lawson of Nov. 29 and Dec. 15.

so, you are a monstrous exception to all humanity. My omissions
& alterations in the poem already, in compliance with your hasty
criticism, & Forrest's weaknesses, have impaired its merits. By
the way, as F. has given the prize, I suppose he has determined
upon the plays. In that event, what has been done with mine.[210]
Have you shown it or given it to Murdoch. It is in vain that I
enquire if you have seen M. since, while expending a page upon
the dangers of the sea, you have no space to answer a question
asked you in all the *four* letters. If you can get the play (assuming
it to be disposed of by F) let M. see it & answer. Did you have
the letter to Forbes sent to the P. O.[211] I trust you will say nothing
about the cigars to Forrest. — Not a word reaches me from
Duyckinck, and he is giving offense in the South by publishing
abolition matter. I have, just to sound him, sent him a first no.
of a series of South. papers. Before I see you again we shall probably have a rupture of the Union, for which the South is pretty
generally prepared. It shan't separate us, however. — I trust that
Christina will heed your injunctions to write to Augusta. We hear
from no family with half the satisfaction that we hear from yours.
Present me at home affectionately, and to Graham [212] with respect.
For yourself Believe me as Ever

Yours truly

W. Gilmore Simms

J. L.

---

[210] *Norman Maurice; or, the Man of the People.*

[211] Simms had written to W. C. Forbes concerning his play "Benedict Arnold"
and had asked Lawson to address the letter. See letter to Lawson of Nov. 28.

[212] George Rex Graham of *Graham's.*

1849

460: To [CORRESPONDENT UNKNOWN]

Woodlands Jan 16. [1849][1]

Dear Sir

Though somewhat slow in complying with, I have not been unmindful of your request to furnish you with a list of all publications. It has not been easy for me to procure the dates, as several of the volumes are not only out of print, but I have reserved no copies of them.[2]

Very truly &c

W. Gilmore Simms.

Writings of W. Gilmore Simms Esq.

1. Lyrical & other Poems By William G. Simms Jr. 1 vol. Charleston: Ellis & Neufville 1827. 18 mo. pp. 208 (*out of print*)

2. Early Lays. By William G. Simms Jr. Charleston: A. E. Miller. 1827 (*out of print*) — 1 vol. 12 mo.

---

[1] Since in the list of his works here given Simms has none dated after 1848, this letter has been dated 1849. Though the second edition of *Atalantis* had not been published at this time, it had been printed and copies distributed by Simms to his friends (see letter to Carey and Hart of Jan. 19, 1849). We are unable to identify the recipient of this letter.

[2] Simms omits from his list the following publications: *Monody on the Death of Gen. Charles Cotesworth Pinckney* (1825), *The Remains of Maynard Davis Richardson, with a Memoir of His Life* (1833), *The Cosmopolitan: An Occasional,* Nos. 1 and 2 (1833-1834), *Castle Dismal* (1844), *Helen Halsey* (1845), *The Charleston Book* (1845), and *Charleston, and Her Satirists* (1848). We have not located copies of Charleston editions of *The Social Principle, The Sources of American Independence,* or *Self-Development,* first published at Tuscaloosa, Aiken, and Milledgeville respectively in editions carrying the dates Simms here gives. We also have not located a copy of *Slavery in America* (Richmond: Thomas W. White, 1838) with the title *Slavery in the South.* The only copies of *Martin Faber . . . and Other Tales* which we have located are dated 1837. *Confession* was first published in 1841 instead of 1842, and *The Tri-Color* was first published by Wigfall and Davis, London, not at Charleston. Simms also occasionally errs in giving the sizes of the volumes. See Salley, *Catalogue of the Salley Collection of the Works of Wm. Gilmore Simms.*

3. The Vision of Cortes and other Poems. By W. Gilmore Simms. Charleston: J. S. Burges. 1829. 1 vol. 18mo. (*out of print.*[ )]

4. The Tri Color, or the Three Days of Blood in Paris. Charleston: 1830. 1 vol. 8 vo. (*out of print*)

5. Atalantis. A Story of the Sea. New York: J. & J. Harper 1832. 1 vol. 8 vo.

6. Martin Faber. A Tale. New York: Harper & Bro. 1833. 1 vol. 18 mo.

7. The Book of My Lady. A Melange. Phila. Key & Biddle. 1833 1 vol. 12 mo.

8. Guy Rivers: a Tale of Georgia. 2 vols 12 mo. New York: Harper & Brothers. 1834

9. The Yemassee: a Romance of Carolina. 2 vols. 12 mo. Harper & Brothers 1835

10. The Partisan: a Tale of the Revolution 2 vols 12 mo. Harper & Bro. 1835.

11. Mellichampe: a Legend of the Santee. 2 vols 12 mo. Harper & Bro. 1836.

12. Martin Faber & other Tales. A New Edition. 2 vols 12 mo. Harper & Bro. 1836.

13. Pelayo: a Story of the Goth. 2 vols. 12 mo. New York. Harper & Bro. 1838

14. Carl Werner; an Imaginative Story; with other Tales of Imagination. 2 vols 12 mo. New York: Geo Adlard. 1838.

15. Richard Hurdis; or the Avenger of Blood. A Tale of Alabama. 2 vols. 12 mo. Phil Carey & Hart. 1838.

16. Southern Passages & Pictures. 1 vol. 12 mo. New York. Geo. Adlard. 1839

17. The Damsel of Darien 2 vol 12 mo. Phil. Lea & Blanchard 1839.

18. The History of South Carolina, from its first European discovery to its Erection into a republic: with a Supplementary Chronicle &c. by W. Gilmore Simms. Charleston: S. Babcock & Co. 1840.

19. Border Beagles: a Tale of Mississippi. In two vols. 12 mo. Phil: Carey & Hart. 1840.

20. The Kinsmen: or the Black Riders of Congaree. In two vols. 12 mo. Phil: Lea & Blanchard. 1841.

21. Beauchampe: or the Kentucky Tragedy. A Tale of Passion. 2 vols. 12 mo. Phil: Lea & Blanchard. 1842.

22. Confession: or the Blind Heart. A Domestic Story. In 2 vols 12 mo. Phil: Lea & Blanchard. 1842.

23. The Geography of South Carolina; &c. by W. Gilmore Simms. 1 vol. 12 mo. Charleston: S Babcock & Co 1843.

24. Life of Francis Marion. By W. Gilmore Simms. New York: Henry G Langley. 1844. 1 vol. 12 mo.

25. Count Julian; or the Last Days of the Goth. (a sequel to Pelayo) 2 vols in 1 8 vo. Taylor & Co. 1845.

26. The Wigwam & the Cabin. 2 vols 12 mo. New York: Wiley & Putnam. 1845.

27. Views & Reviews in American Literature, History & Fiction. 2 vols. 12 mo. Wiley & Putnam. 1845

28. Life of Capt. John Smith, the Founder of Virginia. 1 vol 12 mo. New York: Cooledge & Bro. 1846.

29. Life of the Chevalier Bayard, the Good Knight, *sans peur sans reproche*. 1 vol. 12 mo. New York: Harper & Bro. 1847.

30. A Supplement to the Plays of Wm Shakspeare; comprising the seven dramas, which have been ascribed to his pen, but which are not included with his writings in modern editions &c. Edited, with notes & an Introduction to each play, by William Gilmore Simms Esq. 1 vol. 8 vo. New York: Geo. F. Cooledge & Bro. 1848.

(Omitted from above — to be placed according to date.)

1. Donna Florida. A Tale in Four Cantos. 1 vol. 18 mo. Charleston: Burges & James. 1843.

2. Grouped Thoughts & Scattered Fancies. A Collection of Sonnets. 1 vol. 18 mo. Richmond: Wm. Macfarlane. 1845

3. Areytos; or Songs of the South. 1 vol. 12 mo. Charleston: John Russell. 1846.

4. Lays of the Palmetto. 1 vol. 12 mo. Charleston: J. Russell 1848

5. Atalantis, a Story of the Sea. (New Edition) With the Eye & the Wing: Poems Chiefly Imaginative. 1 vol 12 mo Phil. Carey & Hart. 1848.

Pamphlets.

1. The Social Principle. The True Secret of National Permanence. Oration. 8 vo. Burges & James Charleston. 1842.

2. The Sources of American Independence. An Oration. 8 vo. Charleston: Burges & James 1844

3. Self-Development. Oration. 8 vo. Charleston: Burges & James. 1847.

4. Slavery in the South. 1 vol. 8 vo. Richmond: McFarlane. 1838.

5. The Prima Donna. A passage from City Life. Phil. L. A. Godey 1844

461: To Carey and Hart

Woodlands Jan 19. [1849][3]

Mess'rs Carey & Hart.

My dear Publishers

May I ask when you design putting forth 'Atalantis' and such other matter *as it may be interesting to me to see in print.* I do not wish to be importunate, but we *young* authors, you know, are necessarily impatient for a happy deliverance. As you mentioned your purpose of issuing Atalantis in Sept. last, I forwarded copies in that month to Bryant & other friends in New York, and the vol. has more than once been noticed accordingly. I enclose you Bryant's notice in the Evening Post.[4] I could send you others, similarly favorable, made when the original poem was published in 1832, one of which was from

---

[3] Dated by Simms' discussion of the publication of the second edition of *Atalantis.* See letters to Carey and Hart of July 1 and July 20, 1848.

[4] In the New York *Evening Post* of Oct. 6, 1848, Bryant writes: "The poem of Atalantis has been revised and amended by the author, who, we are glad to see, has pruned away nothing of the splendor of the imagery and wild adventures among the wastes and islets and in the depths of the ocean, which made this poem worthy to be placed among the most magnificent of the narratives of supernatural agency. The traces of a mature and vigorous mind are seen in the changes which have been made." The same issue contains a notice of *The Life of the Chevalier Bayard,* characterized as "deeply interesting from the first to the last." *Atalantis* is also listed among "new publications received" in *S. Q. R.,* XIV (Oct., 1848), 541.

the London Metropolitan, when that work was edited by Campbell &c.[5] I could wish, without desiring to counsel, that you could *deliver me entirely* as soon as possible. The truth is I am lamentably in want of money. I have been neither wiser nor more fortunate than the rest of my tribe. — Enclosed I send you some few book notices, among which is one of Mrs. Sigourney's vol. You did not favor me with a copy, but I borrowed one, in order to say some thing in behalf of Darley[6] whom I encountered in New York. Do you feel any more favorably disposed now to illustrate my select poems than you did two years ago. Let me hear from you soon & believe me very truly yrs

W. Gilmore Simms

462: To James Lawson

Woodlands, Feb. 5. 1849

dear Lawson.

Above you have a dft upon Israel Post for the first contribution to his magazine contained in the February number.[7] That number has not reached me, & you must get at it in order to fill up the hiatus above. Ascertain the number of pages at $5 each. I suppose there will be at least 7. I have sent him the second instalment & there will be a third. Say no more to him about the articles in your hand at present. As for submitting them to his Editor,[8] that is sheer impertinence. He can have the matter at $5. a page hereafter, when he is disposed to look for it. It is important that you should put the preceding dft. in requisition as soon as possible, since he already has the second article, & that I propose to draw for as soon as I send on the third, which will be before his March issue. I could wish that in employing the two articles left with you by Duyckinck, you should resolve them into one so as to render them more absolutely magazineish.[9]

---

[5] See note 268, Dec. 6, 1846.

[6] Felix Octavius Carr Darley (1822-1888) had drawn the designs for Lydia Howard Sigourney's recently published *Illustrated Poems* (Philadelphia: Carey and Hart, 1849). Simms' review of this volume appears in the Charleston *Evening News* of Jan. 13. Darley later designed illustrations for many of Simms' novels (see Salley, *Catalogue of the Salley Collection of the Works of Wm. Gilmore Simms*).

[7] "The Egyptian Masque; A Tale of the Crescent City." See note 172, Nov. 20, 1848.

[8] William Landon.

[9] See note 204, *c*. Dec. 19, 1848.

This is easily done. It only needs to remove the caption from the second & paste the parts together. If you were not the laziest man in the world, so far as literature is concerned, I should task you to read the two papers, so as to prepare an abridged statement of contents under the caption, but I can hardly expect you to read the matter, however much I may desire it. Let the criticism upon the poem, & the poem itself go to the devil.[10] I do not see that Webber's Mag. has been published at all. I hear nothing of it. I rejoice that you have so much work in averages, though greatly sorry that they keep you from slumber. This is a serious misfortune against which you should guard. Why should you bother your old head about the Union. At all events let us talk nothing of these matters. There is so much self complaisance & insolence in the speech of most Northern men when they address the South that the least said's the better. With us we have long since been satisfied that the North was the maggot in the brain of the Elk feeding on his vitals, yet destroying his benefactor. As for your random speech about the South & its institutions, it surely cannot be expected that you should be able to canvas them as thoroughly as you do the poetry on Fonthill. Such universality is not permitted to any man. Talk of Forrest, — did you send the note which I covered to you for Forbes? [11] — I have just accepted the Editorship of the Southern Review under circumstances of particular compliment. If you recieve the work, read the article in the July no. of last year, if you wish to be advised of the relations of South Carolina & the South & North to the Union.[12] That may teach you something which, at this juncture it is quite important for the North to know — how little the South owes to this connection. I rejoice to hear that you are all well. We are not so here. Mr. Roach has been quite ill for a few days, and there is an epidemic afloat of the Influenza sort, which has fretted all our girls. The baby[13] is troubled with it. Mary Lawson is doing well & is as mischievous as her namesake. Tell Jimmy that if he does not set off full start, that Gilmore will quite swallow him up. I fancy that Gil-

[10] For "Fonthill," submitted to Webber's proposed magazine, see letter to Lawson of Nov. 9, 1848, and following letters to Lawson.

[11] See letter to Lawson of Nov. 28, 1848.

[12] "South Carolina in the Revolution." See note 40, March 23, 1848.

[13] Chevillette.

more must be even taller than Kate & quite up to Mary. He grows like a briar, and is quite as thorny. Love to wife & a kiss for all the little ones. For yourself, hold me Ever as Ever.

Yours truly &c

W. Gilmore Simms

What of Richards,
Boggs & Co.[14]

463 : To BENJAMIN FRANKLIN PERRY

Woodlands, Feb 5. [1849][15]

Hon. B. F. Perry

My dear Perry

I have just consented to take Editorial charge of the Southern Quarterly Review, and my single purpose in writing you now (apart from the satisfaction of renewing correspondence with an old friend) is to request that you will resume your connection with the work as Contributor. We are at this moment in want of articles. The Publisher tells me that there is really but one paper on hand. Yet the work (due on the first of Jany) is to be issued on the first of April. My object in taking hold of it is with the view to place it on firm foundations. The South needs it, particularly now, and if our friends will help us to subscribers & writers we can make it permanent. I turn to you with confidence. Let me hear from you soon, and excuse the brevity of my epistle in the absorbing character of my tasks.

Yours truly as Ever

[*Signature cut.*]

---

14 T. Addison Richards and Robert Boggs, the artists.

15 Dated by Simms' reference to his taking "Editorial charge of the Southern Quarterly Review." He edited the periodical from the issue of April, 1849, through that of Oct., 1854. For the publishers of the periodical during his editorship, see note 56, March 15, 1849.

464: To WILLIAM ELLIOTT[16]

Woodlands Feb 7. [1849][17]

Hon Wm. Elliott
    Beaufort

dear Sir:

The charge of the Southern Review, — temporarily at least — has devolved upon me; and in casting about for contributors, your name naturally suggests itself to me as that of one whose writings would honor its pages, and be grateful to all its readers. I need not insist, with you, upon the importance of such an organ, at any time, for the mind & talent of the South: — still less, at this juncture, need I remind you of the uses of such a work for the defence of our Institutions, and the exhibition of our character. May I hope that you will not withhold yourself from an arena in which it behoves us properly to put forth all our strength. We are greatly in need of *Southern* contributors. We should not suffer our minds or fields to lie fallow. Your example will assist us in the effort to move others. I will not presume to suggest any topics to you for treatment. The choice of a subject is quite as much a matter for the individual mind, as its peculiar treatment. Yet, if you will allow me, there is one work, recently published, the pretensions of which are considerable, (and probably its value) which it seems to me might be peculiarly appropriate to your hands. I allude to the "Field Sports of America" by Herbert — a copious work in 2 octavos, which, if you signify any desire for examination our publishers will be glad to forward you.[18] — The first no. of the Review for this year will probably be put forth by the first of

---

[16] Elliott (1788-1863), of Beaufort, S. C., was a first cousin of Bishop Stephen Elliott (see introductory sketch), Simms' intimate friend. After attending Harvard from 1806 to 1809, he returned to South Carolina and served for a number of years in the State House of Representatives and Senate. Like Simms he was an opponent of Nullification, and in 1832 he resigned from the Senate rather than carry out the wishes of his constitutents to vote for Nullification. Also like Simms he later professed his belief in the institution of slavery and his dislike of Northern interference in Southern affairs, but unlike Simms he desired South Carolina to steer away from secession. He is best remembered for his *Carolina Sports, by Land and Water* (Charleston: Burges and James, 1846).

[17] Dated by Simms' reference to his becoming editor of the *Southern Quarterly Review*.

[18] Elliott did not review *Frank Forrester's Field Sports of the United States, and British Provinces, of North America* (see note 162, Nov. 9, 1848) for the *Southern Quarterly Review*.

April. Some delays in the publication have impaired its credit
& efficiency. Efforts are now making to place it on a firm foundation, and cause its future regular publication at the quarterly
periods. — Pray, Sir, let me hear from you at your earliest convenience, and hold me Ever

Very truly,

Yr friend & obt. Servt.

W. Gilmore Simms

P. S. Address through the Publisher, J. S. Burges, Charleston.

465 : To Brantz Mayer

Woodlands Feb 12. [1849][19]

Brantz Mayer Esq

dear Sir

The Editorial charge of The Southern Quarterly Review having devolved upon me, I am naturally desirous of securing
the favours of those contributors to whose aid it already owes its
character & position. With this view, I take leave to solicit a
continuance of your contributions. The work has been some what
carelessly conducted, on the part of the publishers, and its pecuniary resources are just now limited. For the present, the publisher begs me to say that he will pay at the rate of one dollar
per page of original matter. This inadequate compensation, he
adds, will be increased with the increasing means of the publication. I could wish to hear from you as soon as possible, particularly if it be in your power to contribute a paper for the forthcoming issue (forming the first of the present year) which will
be issued on the first of April. Address to the care of the publisher in Charleston.

Very respectfully

Yr obt Servt.

W. Gilmore Simms

P. S. It is highly desirable that the papers should not exceed,
on the average more than from 20 to 30 pages.

---

[19] Dated by Simms' reference to his taking "Editorial charge of The Southern Quarterly Review." Mayer acceded to Simms' request and contributed
"Origin of the War with Mexico" to the April issue (see note 80, April 27,
1849).

466: To John Pendleton Kennedy

Hon. J. P. Kennedy.   Woodlands, S. C. Feb 12. [1849][20]

My dear Sir

The Editorial duties of the Southern Quarterly Review have just devolved upon me; forced on me as much by the entreaties of its proprietors as by any desires of my own. Aware of the responsibilities of such a situation, and anxious that an organ so particularly belonging to the South, should gather to its support all the ability which can be found in our section, I naturally address myself to you, among others, for assistance. The contributors are already numerous, and many admirable articles have appeared in the work. Its circulation is comparatively extensive, ranging from Pennsylvania to the Mississippi & Texas: Upon the utility of such a periodical I need not enlarge to you. Still less, I hope, need I assure you that while in my hands I shall endeavour to make its utterances no less just and dignified than attractive. It will give me especial pleasure, if you will choose it for the vehicle of your opinions on any topics coming within the objects of such a periodical, and eschewing, as a matter of policy, all vexing questions which may more properly be left to other channels of publication. Let me add that, I am very sure, there is no contributor in the Southern Country, whom it would better please our people to see enter the lists among us. — I trust that in the repose of home, you enjoy its sweets as well as securities. Write me soon, and believe me, ever truly,

Yr friend & servt.

W. Gilmore Simms

---

[20] Dated by Simms' reference to his becoming editor of the *Southern Quarterly Review.* In his reply, dated March 11, Kennedy remarks: "I am glad to learn that the Review has fallen into your hands, as I am sure you will fully sustain its highest reputation. I cant promise you to become one of your auxiliaries,—but will say to you that I may sometimes send you an article. I dont *promise* because I would not have you rely upon me on any occasion, as I know how annoying it is to the conduct of such a work as yours, to have an *unpunctual and promising* friend. . . . Still . . . my respect for you, and the interest I take in your success, will be strong to enforce me to labor in your service. The South, it occurs to me, furnishes, just now, a special field for the good influences of a vigorous and sound periodical press. We have overheated zealots on our side of the line as they have in the North. He who teaches them moderation will earn a well deserved fame. Charleston is a very authoritative center of Southern opinion; and wholesome counsels coming from that point, through a channel so authentic as The Southern Review, will be listened to with more deference than from any other quarter. I predict for you, what I wish, an eminent success." (Copy in Kennedy's handwriting in the Peabody Institute Library.)

467 : To George Frederick Holmes

Woodlands, S. C. Feb 19, 1849

My dear Holmes.

I trust that you have not quite forgotten the lines of my hand in the long pause that has taken place in our Correspondence. I take for granted that your silence, like my own, has been the result of cares, anxieties & toils; transitions which kept us anxious about the moment, and troubles that left us nothing pleasant to communicate to friends. That you have been translated to a new situation and abode,[21] which, I believe, offers every encouragement to hope, is one reason why I should recal you to old memories; that new duties are imposed upon myself, in which I may claim your support and sympathy is another reason. Let me flatter myself that you will be no less pleased to hear from me, than I am in thus challenging your attention. — You have probably followed with some curiosity the fortunes of the Southern Quarterly Review. That work, after various vicissitudes, passed out of the hands of Mr. Whitaker, at a moment, I fancy, when he found himself no longer able to continue its publication. A number of Gentlemen of Carolina bought him out, & extricated the Journal, by a liberal subscription from most or all of its incumbrances. Mr. W., himself, was fairly lifted from its shoulders, and these Gentlemen with Burges became the entire owners. Mr. Clapp, Editor of [the] Mercury, on the sale of that paper passed into the Editorial fauteuil of the Review. He has conducted it for a year and better, and with considerable spirit and success. Some of his articles were particularly excellent. During this period I became a regular contributor, having been only an occasional one before, & furnished him with one or more papers for each number.[22] But Clapp retires upon an office under the Federal Government; and at the request of the proprietors, I have suffered myself to be persuaded to occupy his place. That I shall

---

[21] In 1848 Holmes had become the first president of the University of Mississippi.

[22] The following articles (all unsigned) can be ascribed to Simms: "Fanny Kemble," XII (July, 1847), 191-236; "Lives of the Lord Chancellors," XII (Oct., 1847), 375-408; "Prescott's Conquest of Peru," XIII (Jan. and April, 1848), 136-187, 273-330; "A History of Georgia," XIII (April, 1848), 470-501; "South Carolina in the Revolution," XIV (July, 1848), 37-77; "The Siege of Charleston in the American Revolution," XIV (Oct., 1848), 261-337; and "Headley's Life of Cromwell," XIV (Oct., 1848), 506-538.

do so very unworthily under any circumstances, I am ready to believe; and my only hope of doing well or tolerably even, is in organizing an able & efficient corps of contributors. This portion of the management of the Review has always been carelessly administered. I have accordingly been casting about for the proper men, and your name occurred to me among the first. I wrote immediately to Jamison to know where you are, and to request that he also will write to you. He has answered my request, tells me he has already written. I trust that this application will properly second mine, and that both will succeed in persuading you to a resumption of your intercourse with a journal whose pages afford so honorable a testimonial of your research & talent. Of course you pretty much understand the situation and resources of the Review. A part of my appeal must be to your patriotism, to your sympathies with Literature, & to your personal interest in myself. But Burges instructs me to say that he will be able to pay you one dollar a page for original matter, a sum which is deplorably inadequate as compensation, but which he will increase with the increasing resources of the journal. Even this pay he can afford only to a few contributors, so that you are requested not to give publicity to the fact that he pays at all. On this subject, I have only to add, that there is really no better organ for the exercise of your endowments. The reputation of the work has been rising, of late, considerably; and the circulation is large and increasing. With good management it may very soon be placed on the most permanent foundations. Pray let me hear from you at your earliest convenience. You will yourself readily find materials for reviewing, and if, among your associates & acquaintances in New Orleans you should happen upon any capable of contributing, I must entreat you to secure his assistance. The sooner you write the better, for in taking charge of the work, which is to be issued on the 1st of April, I find but a single contribution in the hands of the publishers. God bless you!

Very faithfully yours &c

W. Gilmore Simms

Prest. G. F. Holmes

468: To John Caldwell Calhoun [23]

Woodlands Feb 19. 1849

Hon. J. C. Calhoun

dear Sir

I am indebted to you for a pamphlet copy of your admirable address to the Southern States, for which you will please recieve my acknowledgments.[24] That it did not recieve the unanimous signature of the Southern Delegates, is, I apprehend to be ascribed only to the demoralizing influences of party organization, the very worst of the evils which, it appears to me, threatens our section. Still, its effects will be measurably beneficial. It will lessen the insolence of our enemies, in alarming their fears. It will put off the day of evil, and contribute considerably towards preparing our people for it. By the way, I am greatly disposed to think that our people of the Southern States are in advance, on this subject, of their halting representatives. I do not doubt that they will have to pay a heavy penalty yet to the popular feeling for the selfish coldness & indifference which baffled your efforts at unanimity — the only thing which is necessary towards the complete triumph of the South in regard to this vexing question. — While on this subject, permit me to draw your attention to another which may be made tributary to it. I have been honored by the patrons of the Southern Quarterly Review with its future Editorial conduct. Regarding periodical as an important vehicle for political writing, as well as that which belongs to General Literature, I am desirous of securing some contributors, who may be relied on, as much for their sympathy with us & good faith, as well as for their experience in political affairs. I should greatly like, for example, at this very juncture, to get from Washington an article reviewing the two addresses — yours &

---

[23] Part of this letter is published in Chauncey S. Boucher and Robert P. Brooks, eds., "Correspondence Addressed to John C. Calhoun 1837-1849," *Annual Report of the American Historical Association for the Year 1929* (Washington, 1930), pp. 498-499.

[24] The Charleston *Courier* of Feb. 2 reports: "From the Baltimore *American* we learn that both Mr. Calhoun's Address and Mr. Berrien's substitute are published. The latter is simply headed 'Address to the People of the United States,' while the first is entitled 'The Address of Southern Delegates in Congress to their Constituents.' Our Washington correspondent states that there are no names appended to the Address of Mr. Calhoun, published in the *Union*." Calhoun's was published in the *Courier* on Feb. 1, Berrien's on Feb. 3. John Macpherson Berrien (1781-1856) was United States senator from Georgia at this time.

Berrien's.[25] They would furnish an admirable text for the development of the whole subject, the encroachments of the North, the dangers of the South, the modes of combat, and the general prospects of the struggle, with a proper running accompaniment of warning notes, particularly in regard to the subsidizing influences of the National parties, in buying up our leading politicians. Articles of spirit and sense, of warmth and justice, could be written here; but not with that degree of intelligence which can only be derived from such a knowledge of details as belongs to you in the Federal City. Is it possible to get such a contributor or contributors? Are there not southern men in Washington, thus endowed, & having the leisure, who would be pleased to take up the cudgels through such a medium as the Southern Review? The work greatly needs assistance of this sort, and the results would amply repay it, from the circulation which it possesses among that class of independent and intelligent population in the South, who would prefer recieving their views from this organ, rather than through the usually doubtful & suspected medium of newspaper & speech. If your eye could single out such persons, as writers, a hint might secure their cooperation & industry. Your own views freely expressed in conversation would suggest all the necessary clues to the argument. — You will soon witness the change of administration. I feel sure that Taylor means well & will design and desire honestly. The question with him, as in the case of Queen Elizabeth — will he choose good counsellors? I trust, at all events, that in entering office, he will not allow himself to forget that he really owes his election to Democrats. The Whigs could not have elected him by themselves; and nothing but the revulsion which honest men of the Democratic Party necessarily felt, at the gross uses to which that party has been put, and the base hands into which it had fallen, could possibly have lost them the ascendancy.

With great respect
& very truly
Yr. obt servt &c.

W. Gilmore Simms.

---

[25] Calhoun's is reviewed in an unsigned article by David James McCord entitled "Slavery and the Abolitionists," XV (April, 1849), 165-223. James H. Hammond, in a letter to Simms of April 10, comments: "In the name of God how could McCord write 60 pages on the address. There must be a vast deal of twaddle." (Original in the Hammond Papers, Library of Congress.) For Berrien's address, see note 24, above.

469: To Marcus Claudius Marcellus Hammond[26]

Woodlands Feb 22. [1849][27]

[M]y d[ear M]ajor

[I than]k you for the promptness [an]d the frank[ness o]f
your letter. It embold[e]ns me to spe[ak w]ithout reserve. Do
not afflict yourself, as yo[ur bro]ther sometimes does, with im-
possibile st[andards.] A good writer is he whose style is f[ree
and un]altered like his ordinary conversation[, and at] the same
time expresses his ideas an[d suits his] material. Of course, the
ideas are [always to be] in possession. For my part I wr[ite
ver]y muc[h] as I converse. If the mind is in possession of facts
which it has digested for itself, all that is necessary is to let
it alone, and it will naturally utter itself rightly. A review is
necessarily more elaborate writing than a newspaper; but its
essentials are very much the same. He who can write decently
for the latter, w[i]thout an effort, may with moderate effort,
write well for the other. Your letters are well written, free, easy,
impulsive, and did you exhaust your subject in them, you would
write reviews instead of mere letters. Here, for example, speaking of California, in the one before me, you suggest all the topics
of a review article. You have only to follow out the idea. Fremont,
by the way, deserves reviewing in the South. I doubt if he has
been reviewed any where. Take up his & B[r]y[a]nt's Books
together.[28] Glance at the general events [of] the war in the
introduction — speak of th[e territory and] give its general
features, — ex[amine the country] physically — its influence,
pa[rticularly its] effects in opening new fields [for commerce
and] adventure — in building new [cities, and y]ou may indulge
in conjecture, [as to w]here they should be; — the rail Roads
the[n will] follow — & the probable march of politic[al and
soc]ial power Westward — the effect too of su[ch an] acquisition
upon the Pacific, as her co[ast compe]ting with the Atlantic &
Gulph Coast[s which] shall tend to furnish a new offi[cial

---

26 See introductory sketch of the Hammonds.
27 Dated by Simms' reference to his becoming editor of the *Southern Quarterly Review*. The MS. is badly mutilated.
28 Hammond's review of John Charles Fremont's *Geographical Memoir Upon
Upper California* (Washington: Wendell and Van Benthuysen, Printers, 1848),
Edwin Bryant's *What I Saw in California* (New York: D. Appleton & Company, 1848), and several other pamphlets and books was published as two
articles: "The Conquest of California, and the Case of Lieut. Col. Fremont,"
XV (July, 1849), 410-444; and "California," XVI (Oct., 1849), 82-115. The
first is unsigned; the second is signed "H."

b]alance of power to the overgrowth [& expansion] of the great
west. The fields for speculation are ample. The subordinate subjects are numerous. The mines, the deserts, the Indians, &c.
One thing must not be forgotten in a Review. Such writing is
chiefly suggestive. It contents itself with furnishing clues to the
subject which the reader may follow for himself. In details, the
most prominent are given, and those only which indicate & stand
for classes. — In another article I should like you to take up the
Indians, using for your text the Report of the Bureau in the
last publication of Congress. Documents. Here you can embody
your own experience — all that is impressive & picturesque. —
Another subject is the War in Florida. [Sp]rague's book is a
good one for rough hand[s.[29] H]e is grossly unjust to the volun-
teers. [In some] respects he is clumsy and bun[gling. The book
is re]ally only valuable for its [basic facts. Uti]lize its materials,
supply his [deficiences & illuminate] the whole with the running
[commentary of one w]ho knows his subject & has it r[ight
upon tap t]o make not only a good [r]eview, but a[lso a c]om-
pend of History. In this original anec[dotes] might be introduced,
and original biograp[hic not]es of distinguished chiefs, red &
white. Yo[urs i]s the very knowledge which is greatly va[lued.
The mo]st interesting of British writers are o[f the army] & navy.
— I entreat you to work un[sparingly, as] well in regard to
yourself as the Revie[w.] There is no life so really feeble and
wretched as that of a Southern Gentleman who does nothing. He
rusts always, and too frequently falls into bad habits. Write without regard to the opinions of the public. Keep your own secret
and write anonymously. I will keep your secret also. The audience
of the Reviewer is really little more exacting than that of the
newspaper writer. His effort is only a more prolonged one, and
the effects are all beneficial to himself. He becomes more cautious,
more industrious, more correct, more elevated. His mind is
rendered compact — not frittered away by small labours. — I
thank you for your information. If you can beg for me some

---

[29] John Titcomb Sprague, *The Origin, Progress. and Conclusion of the
Florida War* . . . (New York: D. Appleton & Co.; Philadelphia: G. S. Appleton, 1848). After his graduation from West Point in 1836 M. C. M. Hammond
served for about two years in the Seminole War. In 1838 he aided in the
removal to the West of the Cherokee Indians of Georgia and Tennessee. He
remained in the West for nearly three years, and on his return was a member
of the expedition into the Everglades in 1841. He resigned from the army in
1842, but during the Mexican War he again entered the army and served as
paymaster, resigning a second time in 1847.

specimens of Western bows & arrows, do so. I have w[ri]tten to the General.[30] Do not suppose, as he seems to have done, that in taking the review I have got m[yself enta]ngled so as to prevent my taking the mi[s]sion. [Do] let me hear from you soon. If you write for the Rev[iew, address to the] publisher in Charleston.

Very faithfully Yr fri[end]

[W. Gilmore] Simms.

P. S. Send me the Hamburg pa[per. Work on] your article. Do you not know [some of your friends] who could be persuaded, who are [equipped to write an] article [for the Review. I than]k you for what you are doing. [*Remainder of postcript missing or illegible.*]

470: To James Henry Hammond

[c. February 25, 1849][31]

My dear Hammond.

I take up the matters, *seriatim,* of your two Letters. I could have wished, as well as yourself, that we should have enjoyed better opportunities on the visit. But I am far from regretting the prolonged meeting with your brother whom I have learned to like. He, by the way, probably misunderstood me in one respect. It was in regard to Talcott, whose corns you trod upon so unscrupulously, that I held you erringly dogmatical: — But you know already that I thought you despotical enough.[32] I fancy I discriminated the cases of Hamilton & myself sufficiently; yet I am rather glad you refer to the matter as you do. I may feel

---

30 James H. Hammond. Hammond preferred his title of general of the South Carolina Militia to any that he ever held.

31 This letter, which bears no postmark, was written in answer to two from Hammond of Feb. 5 and Feb. 10, 1849. It is dated *c.* Feb. 25 (a Sunday) for the following reasons: Simms refers to his letter to M. C. M. Hammond of Feb. 22; he also speaks of "tonight (Sunday)."

32 In his letter of Feb. 10 Hammond had written: "As to dogmatizing with you & him [M. C. M. Hammond] & [?] Talcott who all more or less set yourselves up to be some pumpkins, you would not I know refuse such an indulgence to a man of few words like me to whom the chance occurs rarely. By the by I have a letter also from [William S.] King whom Talcott charged me with having treated roughly you remember. Well he writes about R. Road matters & after much *apparent deference,* takes occasion to say that he had heretofore said that Anti Debt was 'the best pamphlet ever written by any body on any subject.' So you see Talcott's charge was false, or if true my castigation has had only a salutary effect." (Original in the Hammond Papers, Library of Congress.)

much less disquieted, if not able to pay you when the time comes; though, even on this point, I presumed on a sufficient knowledge of you to believe that I need not annoy myself at your despotism as a creditor.[33] Confound your ill health. As old Abernethy [34] says — What right have you to suppose that you have a stomach at all. And pray who does *work really* more than four hours a day. The rest is usually the mere *show* of work — dawdling as you say. You are as healthy as you need be, and your condition was never less crippled than at this moment. — I have written to Wilson the Painter.[35] Shall hear probably very soon. — I have not had time to look up the passage in Gibbon, but am surprised that I should not have seen that element of the matter which you suggest.[36] — Memminger's speech is admirable. I had thought to write to him to get it into the City papers; but while I pored over the matter, the thing was done.[37] — Touching the Editorship. My engagement is by no means an entanglement. It depends upon myself when to sever it. The appointment should it offer, will always find me a free man.[38] I am not sure that I *considered* the question of Editorship with a due regard to the *pros & cons;*

---

[33] On Feb. 5 Hammond had written: "You heard me discourse so openly & freely of [James] Hamilton [see note 165, April 10, 1845] that I fear you may think I have little delicacy about such matters with my friends. But not so. Hamilton's affairs are notorious & my connection with them well known to most who know us. . . . I should be sorry if what you heard of Hamilton annoyed you for a moment, then or afterwards. I take great pleasure in these little accommodations to my friends . . . the pleasure is enhanced by the reflection that it is a secret between them & me." (Original in the Hammond Papers, Library of Congress.)

[34] John Abernethy (1764-1831), English surgeon, anatomist, physiologist, and teacher. Simms opens one of his unpublished orations, "The Choice of a Profession" (MS. in the Charles Carroll Simms Collection, South Caroliniana Library), with an anecdote about Abernethy.

[35] On Feb. 5 Hammond had written: "I intended to have written to Wilson the Painter by this mail but I have forgotten his name. . . . I beg you will . . . write to him for me & say that . . . I will pay him $150 (his price) for three portraits which I wish taken here." (Original in the Hammond Papers, Library of Congress.) The Gibbes Art Gallery, Charleston, S. C., has receipts for portraits of Mr. and Mrs. Thomas Porcher, both signed W. Wilson and dated 1850. Undoubtedly this is the painter to whom Simms refers.

[36] On Feb. 5 Hammond had written: "You mistook about Gibbon. He says in the 2nd sentence 5 ch. that 'no state can support more than 1 in 100 in arms & idleness.'" (Original in the Hammond Papers, Library of Congress.)

[37] Christopher Gustavus Memminger's speech against rechartering the Bank of the State of South Carolina, delivered in the House of Representatives on Dec. 9, 1848, was published in the *South Carolinian* (Columbia) of Feb. 2 and 6 and in the Charleston *Courier* of Feb. 15. It also appeared in pamphlet form, printed in Columbia "at the South Carolinian Office" and dated 1849.

[38] On Feb. 10 Hammond had written: ". . . I hope you have not so entangled yourself that you cannot take the foreign appointment if offered . . . I am ready to do anything I can do to sustain you in the matter." (Original in the Hammond Papers, Library of Congress.)

but I have made it a rule in life never to reject *certain* employment, when it promises compensation and is congenial to my tastes
& habits. My source of annoyance, in the present state of our
literature, is that its resources of employt. are so capricious. I
am conscious of many deficiencies as an Editor, and were I as
scrupulous a person as yourself, with such impossible standards,
I should have nothing to do with it. I am not a thoroughbred
scholar, and know precious little of science; but as the work
requires me to do nothing without my province, this does not
much trouble me. Some departments of History & Belles Lettres,
I feel as much as home in as any of my neighbours. Rashness,
you have long since discovered is something habitual with me.
As for hanging off as a Contributor, on the score of want of
reading, resource, books &c. that won't do at all. You disquiet
me in two ways when you talk in this fashion. You vex me
equally with myself & you. You rebuke my audacity, and decry
yourself. It requires a thoughtful & suggestive, rather than a
crammed mind for a reviewer. Any body may collect & compile
— few think. You will write, without books, a deuced sight
better than half the writers in the Edinburgh & Quarterly which
you entirely overrate. Half of these Reviews is merely Balaam.
For the other half I engage that you will think as justly & profoundly, and write as clearly & well as 7 in 8 of the Contributors.
If we had books, there are some subjects in which it would be
well to have them. But reviews are not treatises. We want suggestions & speculations, rather than details, & the man capable
like yourself of large & general, as well as original speculations,
is the very man for a reviewer. The *leading idea* of the subject
in your possession & you have the key note to the whole performance. But it is not required that we shall emulate a foreign
people. The question is have we the ability to teach our own.
If we waited for the endowments necessary to the first object,
our youth would acquire nothing; our people would grope in
absolute darkness. Do not question yourself so closely. Remember
Hamlet —

"Whose native hue of resolution
Was sicklied o'er by the pale cast of thought["]³⁹ (doubt)
— self disparagement. As the augur said to the Emperor — Cut
boldly. You must work for the Review, & you will do better

---

³⁹ III, i, 84-85.

things than you have yet done. Even you know not the extent
of your resources. Who even suspects them till he seeks & tries.
You *must* do something and soon. Review Seabrook's pamphlet.[40]
That is one topic upon which your mind is full. I will write to
Burges to send it you. There are others. Give me your help &
in 5 years, I can get as good a Corps of Reviewers as any review on the Continent — any & as half in Europe. Write to
Tucker & frame a Letter for me to Cumming.[41] I know too
little of, after your cautionary note, to attempt it. — I have written to your Brother and suggested to him several topics and
beg that you will not labor to discourage him by any of your
d——d impossible standards. — I am willing to let you into all
the secrets of the review as far as proper or possible. Where
the authors are willing I shall give their names. Hitherto, the
class has not been a very distinguished one. It is for that reason
that I want your help. I wish to exclude much of the matter that
is offered, and can only do so by the aid of a good corps of
contributors. By the way did you read my article on Cromwell in
the last.[42] It was written & sent sheet by sheet to Clapp, in all
haste, so that I never even revised, and had not read it, when
I got a letter from Grayson praising it highly, and giving the
like plaudit from Stewart.[43] This induced me to read it myself,
& bating some bungling sentences & some errors of the press,
I have come to think well of it myself. Clapp's art. on the French
Rev. is a good one.[44] I shall communicate to Burgess your wish
for the July no & Seabrook's Agricultural pamphlet. — I agree
with you about Brisbane, and if *he would let* us save him, the
thing might be done.[45] — I have written to make the inquiry

[40] Hammond did not review Whitemarsh B. Seabrook's *An Essay on the
Agricultural Capabilities of South Carolina* (Columbia, 1848).

[41] On Feb. 10 Hammond had written: "Do you know Col. Wm Cumming
of Augusta? I think if worked in a way not to ruffle his exorbitant & morbid
pride, he could give you something worth while. He could write something
racy on the Mexican War & many topics." (Original in the Hammond Papers,
Library of Congress.) Cumming had been a leader of the Union party in the
Nullification struggle. For his duels with George McDuffie, see note 177, April
23, 1845.

[42] "Headley's Life of Cromwell," XIV (Oct., 1848), 506-538.

[43] William John Grayson (see introductory sketch) at this time was collector of the Port of Charleston. John A. Stuart (here misspelled *Stewart*)
had formerly been editor of the Charleston *Mercury*.

[44] "The French Republic," XIV (July, 1848), 197-241. The article is signed
"C."

[45] On Feb. 10 Hammond had written of Abbott H. Brisbane (see note 195,
Dec. 15, 1848) : "I am sorry for Brisbane. Don't let them mortify him. He is
a good fellow. . . . Such men are the true advance guard of civilization &

about the oration.[46] — There! I believe I have dismissed & discussed all your topics. I have certainly written myself out. Be grateful for this long epistle. In truth, you owe me much for it, be it good or bad; for you must know that with the necessity before me of preparing the view for publication on the 1st April, I have recieved but a single article from without — have written but one myself, and unless supplies come in from some quarter, I have the agreeable prospect before me of writing the whole number. To write letters, under these circumstances, is scarcely possible, yet this is the sixth that I have written tonight (Sunday) and tomorrow I begin an article.[47] Talking of writing letters: Should your brother think to communicate (as he said was likely) to some persons in authority or influence touching myself in connection with the appt. would it not be well for you to frame the letter? You are more conversant with the true nature of my claims — if we may call them such — and perhaps know better how to approach persons in power in such matters. At all events you can suggest the points to be made. — While I think of it — you must disabuse Mrs. H. of the notion she appears to entertain that I am for forcing you into public life. I hope I need not assure you or her that I should never counsel you to any risks, or to any course not perfectly consistent, not only with an honourable ambition & your acknowledged claims.

Yours &c

WGS

P. S. I have written this without looking at a sentence after it was written. Overlook the blunderings & awkwardnesses.

---

in my opinion far more valuable than the mass of *'practical men.'*" (Original in the Hammond Papers, Library of Congress.)

[46] At the First Annual Fair of the South Carolina Institute (see note 195, Oct. 17, 1849). On Feb. 10 Hammond had written: "Do let me know the first moment you can whether I am to deliver an oration on *'Machinery'* & when it is to come off." (Original in the Hammond Papers, Library of Congress.)

[47] Simms' two articles (exclusive of the "Critical Notices") in the April, 1849, issue are the unsigned "Modern Prose Fiction" and "Guizot's Democracy in France" (XV, 41-83, 114-165). He acknowledged the authorship of the first, but not the second (see letter to Perry of April 27, 1849). James H. Hammond guessed the authorship of the second and wrote to Simms on April 30: "Guizot's Democracy is yours & very good — but not equal to Cromwell." (Original in the Hammond Papers, Library of Congress.)

471: To Thomas Caute Reynolds [48]

Woodlands Feb 27. [1849][49]

Hon. T. C. Reynolds.
Charleston, So Ca.

dear Sir

I have just seen your arrival in the newspapers, and write simply that you may not escape me. Having consented to take the Editorial Chair of the Southern Quarterly Review, I am anxious to enrol you among the contributors to that work. I trust you will have leisure to give us some of the fruits of your recent experience abroad. A paper on the Spanish Literature of the present day would be particularly acceptable — another on the Domestic Politics of Spain — so of the condition & character of the people; — or any of this, or such other class of subject, as may be most grateful to your tastes & studies.[50] Pray let me hear from you and believe me,

Very truly &c Yr friend

W. Gilmore Simms

472: To Thomas Caute Reynolds

Woodlands, March 5 [1849][51]

Hon. T. Caute Reynolds

dear Sir

In suggesting to you a subject, I did not by any means design to prescribe to you, but only aimed to indicate the class of topics which it seemed to me you might have been pleased yourself to prefer. Either of the topics which you suggest would no doubt afford sufficient scope to yourself, & interest to the reader. That in relation to Sir H. Bulwer, would, for the reason you give, naturally be desirable; though, it will necessarily require that you should digress into Spanish politics. The paper on the Jews

---

[48] See introductory sketch of the Reynolds brothers.

[49] At the top of this letter Reynolds wrote: "Rec'd Feb. 28th. in Charleston — Ans March. 1st 1849."

[50] Reynolds wrote on none of these subjects. His first contribution, published in two installments, each signed "T. C. R.," is entitled "History of Spanish Literature," N. S., II (Sept. and Nov., 1850), 85-123, 273-313.

[51] At the top of this letter Reynolds wrote: "Recd. March 23d. 1849 at Charleston S. C."

in Spain would be very acceptable; and none more so than that upon the newly discovered work of Cervantes, particularly if, as I suppose, you design to analyze its character. There is yet another subject which it appears to me, would be particularly available in your hands — a review of Howitt's Student Life in Germany.[52] Either of these subjects, or any that it would please you to take in hand, would greatly tend to give to our issues the variety which we desire. While in Barnwell, would it not be convenient to pay a visit to Woodlands? The Dr. (your brother)[53] who has already honored me with a visit, will, I doubt not, be ready to show you the way. Perhaps it would not conflict with other arrangements that you should bring your wife. Mine is a quiet little body who will be pleased to welcome her to our forest land, where we live in a seclusion which is quite simple, and very grateful to the student life. If you will intimate to me when it would please you to do us the honor of a visit, I shall meet you with the *caroche* at Midway, our Post town, which is but two miles from our plantation.

Yours very truly &c

W. Gilmore Simms.

473: To WILLIAM ELLIOTT

Woodlands, March 7. [1849][54]

W. Elliott Esq.

dear Sir:

We must take you on your terms, and will be happy to hear from you at any time and on any subject. The sooner, however, the better. Herbert's Book ought to be amply suggestive. He is a practical sportsman — too much of one, indeed, for his own

---

[52] Reynolds wrote on none of these subjects. Sir Henry Bulwer (later Baron Dalling and Bulwer), English ambassador to Spain (1843-1848), was ambassador to the United States at this time. James L. Reynolds (see introductory sketch of the Reynolds brothers), brother of Thomas Caute, published an article on *El Buscapié* in *S. Q. R.*, XVI (Oct., 1849), 205-223, signed "J. L. R." Earlier, in a letter dated Jan. 26, 1844, Simms had suggested to Reynolds that he review William Howitt's *Student-Life in Germany*.

[53] William Sims Reynolds. See introductory sketch of the Reynolds brothers.

[54] Dated by Simms' discussion of Henry William Herbert's *Frank Forrester's Field Sports of the United States, and British Provinces, of North America* as a subject for review, first suggested to Elliott in his letter of Feb. 7, 1849.

good, — and writes *con amore*. But of sporting in the South he knows nothing himself, and there may be such a difference between the practice of the North & South, as will afford room not only for discussion, but description — when a veteran like yourself may readily, and to the equal satisfaction of self & readers, fight his battles over again. But Herbert's book need not be the only subject in your hands. I am not to be taught, though it seems you yourself need to be reminded, that there are other fields with which your foolscap [?] is familiar. Did I not venture to hint to you that all that was necessary to make our Carolina Sports popular was such an incorporation with its details of the Social and Domestic Life of the Parishes, as would absolutely carry the reader to the scene, and supply the relief which is always essential in works whose chief object is exciting event and lively action? The impression with me is, that I particularly dwelt upon this particular. But what you omitted to do in your sketches, may be supplied in your reviews. A picture of the domestic history, and character of society in the parish settlements of Carolina — exhibiting its early graces, attractions & peculiarities, would be highly attractive & instructive to readers of the present day. Note the falling off in our social tone, indicate the causes of degeneracy — the evil influences of the Revolution — the abolition of the Rights of Primogeniture [55] — the suicidal practice of Intermarriages — in direct hostility with the practice — that of the aristocracy marrying the commoner — thus crossing the breed — by which the British nobility has been made the most splendid race of men in the world. — The subject is a pretty one & the study highly interesting. But *you* will not need for subjects. Let me hear from you on any, and believe me

Very sincerely
Yr frd & servt.

W. Gilmore Simms

---

[55] Nash Roach, Simms' father-in-law, clung to this practice and entailed his entire holdings (in the event of his daughter's death) to Simms for his lifetime, and after his death to his grandson William Gilmore Simms, Jr.

474: To George Frederick Holmes

Woodlands March 15 [1849][56]

George Fred Holmes Esq.

dear Holmes

Truly you have had a serious history of trouble and trial, of which I had not the most distant notion. I can well understand your sufferings. I have gone through just such a history; though I fancy one of extremer severity. If you be the man I take you to be, the benefit of such trials will be large. They will enure to you yet. Your misfortunes may have hurt your House, but they will equally benefit your head & heart. Pray convey to Mrs. H. my sympathies for her share of your mutual strifes and griefs. My right to make this offering accrues from my equal baptism in such sorrows.[57] — Your present situation is perhaps not the least of your troubles, though I trust it will be the last. It is to be hoped that there will soon be a change for the better in your moral atmosphere. It will be necessary above all things, whatever your trials now, that you should preserve your temper — keep cool, — be patient, forgiving, cautious — do not suffer yourself to be made angry, and make your wife your confidante in all your annoyances. Women, who are women at all and not children, have really cooler heads than men — are much less the creatures of passion & impulse. — I shall communicate your Letter to Burges, who is the present publisher — James having gone out, and exhort him to do what he can toward satisfying your claims. But he is wretchedly poor, and the Review has been so shockingly mismanaged that all I can hope to do at present is to keep it alive, until time shall enable us to recover & establish it permanently. It owes me probably quite as much money as it owes you; and my fear is that the debt is a hopeless one. If I succeed in getting pay for present & future performances, I shall be satisfied. And this is my experience of almost every Mag. & Review in the United States! I hope that my arguments

---

[56] Dated by Simms' reference to James S. Burges as the publisher of the *Southern Quarterly Review.* Burges and James published the periodical during Clapp's editorship, but with Simms' first issue for April, 1849, Burges became the sole publisher. He was succeeded by Walker and Richards, whose first issue is that for April, 1850. With the issue for July, 1853, Walker and Burke became the publisher, and that firm was succeeded in Jan., 1854, by C. Mortimer, with Trubner and Co., Paternoster Row, London, as an associate. Mortimer was the publisher throughout the remainder of Simms' editorship.

[57] Undoubtedly Holmes had just experienced the death of a child.

will find Burges able & prepared to remit you something on account; but whether he does or not, it is no reason why you should not obtain the quid for present labors. Send a single article to Jamison,[58] with a dft. for the money at three days, on James S. Burges, and I am disposed to think the money will be forthcoming. Do not let your anger for the past, prevent your accumulations for the future. Should you send the article to Burges direct in Charleston, I promise you it should not be used for the Review, while I am Editor, until the money was payed for it. An article of 25 or 30 pages in every number, for $25 or $30 would, I think, always be paid for promptly. But you should draw for each article, as you forward it, and never send but one. For my sake, I trust that you will review your decision and try the experiment, at least, with a single article. Jamison promises to contribute. I have secured numerous pledges of persons who were never sought before. I would have you meet in the field with them. Besides, the Review would tend to circulate your reputation & make your abilities better known to the country. This is so much capital hereafter. But I am hurried. Present me to Mrs. H. and Believe me Very Sincerely

Yr friend &c.

W. Gilmore Simms

475 : To Nathaniel Beverley Tucker [59]

Woodlands S. C. March 15. [1849][60]

Hon. B. Tucker.

dear Sir:

Though personally unknown to you, I trust that the nature of this communication will suggest a sufficient sanction for the present trespass upon your time and attention. Having lately been persuaded to take the editorial chair of the Southern Quarterly Review, published in Charleston, of this State, I am naturally anxious to strengthen myself in a position of so much responsibility, by calling around me an adequate and able corps of con-

---

[58] Holmes and David F. Jamison had become friends during the former's stay in Orangeburg, S. C.

[59] See introductory sketch.

[60] Dated by Simms' reference to his taking "the editorial chair of the Southern Quarterly Review."

tributors. As naturally, Sir — long familiar, as I have been, with your resources and performances — do I turn in your direction, with this object. I have been greatly encouraged in doing so, by my friend Gen. Hammond, who is of opinion that the argument which urges the importance, to the Southern States, of such a periodical, is one which you will be most ready to acknowledge and appreciate. In this present juncture of affairs in this country, with such a tangled web of federal politics, — and morality so equally loose and reckless among our politicians, — our recourse is really to the Southern *people;* and the more we enable them to recieve the truth — the more we elevate their standards of intellect as well as politics — the greater the prospect for refuge and security in the day of our difficulty. As an organ of opinion and education at home, and for all the Southern States — having for its objects in politics — the promotion of Free Trade, — the maintenance of State Rights — the arrest of centralism, — and the assertion of our Institutions, morally as well as socially — the Southern Quarterly is one of those agencies in a wholesome and necessary work, which those who entertain its objects, should not suffer to perish or to lose its influence. Its business department has been hitherto badly conducted. It has been issued irregularly, and but little pains have been taken to secure the right kind of contributors. Still, it has published many highly valuable articles, and it exercises a considerable influence among the men of thought and opinion in the South and Southwest. Its business will probably undergo improvement — a serious effort being now in progress to that effect; and the prospect is far from inconsiderable which promises a goodly increase of strength among the literary contributors. It is hoped that patriotism will supply the stimulus to our Statesmen and Men of Letters where other motives might be wanting. With improved resources, it is designed that the work shall adequately compensate contributors, since none is more aware than myself of the truth that Literature among us will never be properly valued, until it arrives at the dignity of a profession. In soliciting your Contributions, I am sensible that you will lack the incentive to labor, unless you find it in considerations of the Commonweal. Still, you have economic & political views to evolve — literary & other opinions: — and, as an organ for their diffusion — as an easy means of putting yourself on record — which is perhaps the highest literary ambition — the Southern Review is at least (regarded in the humblest point of view) as eligible a medium as any other. This periodical, I may add, has never been regarded by its proprietors as a means of profit. It has been sustained for a long time by private contributions, and it is rather with a sense of what is due to the South, than with any other consideration, that an effort is now making to give it permanence. May I hope, Sir, that you will contribute to this effort by giving us the succour of your mind, & the fruits of your tastes and studies — that you will represent the Old Dominion in our pages, where we hope to assemble in quarterly rë:unions the best intellects & virtues of all the Southern States.

With great respect, I am, Sir,
Yr. obt. & obliged Servt. &c

W. Gilmore Simms

476: To John Pendleton Kennedy

Woodlands March 17. [1849][61]

Hon. Jno P. Kennedy.

dear Sir

I write now simply to express my acknowledgments for your kind expressions, and to request that you will let me have early sheets of your Wirt. Give instructions to this effect to your publishers. I congratulate you that you are so nigh delivery.

Very faithfully
Yours &c

W. Gilmore Simms

---

[61] Dated by Kennedy's letter of March 11, 1849 (cited note 20, Feb. 12, 1849), in which he writes: "My daily task, all the winter, has been a biography of Wm Wirt, upon which I have been earnestly at work, with a hope of putting it to press in April. It is more voluminous than I had reason to suppose it would be, and it has kept me very much in my study." The biography was later published as *Memoirs of the Life of William Wirt, Attorney General of the United States,* 2 vols. (Philadelphia: Lea and Blanchard, 1849). Under the heading "Literary Intelligence" Simms says in *S. Q. R.,* XV (April, 1849), 271: "The admirers of Wirt, are aware, that the Hon. John P. Kennedy, of Maryland, has, for sometime, contemplated the preparation of a new biography of of [*sic*] that highly endowed lawyer and admirable orator. We are happy to learn that Mr. Kennedy has the work in a state of forwardness, and hopes shortly to be able to yield it to the press. It is one which considerably exceeds in bulk the original anticipations of the biographer, materially growing with the search after them, and with the study of the subject. From Mr. Kennedy's known habits of study, admirable judgment, keen research, and excellent style of composition, we may expect a work at once complete, truthful and eloquent."

477: To NATHANIEL BEVERLEY TUCKER

Woodlands, April 5. 1849.

My dear Sir.

My first impulse, on the reciept of your letter, was to sit down immediately and answer it. Its tone was so warm, its sentiment so frank and Southern, that it made its way at once to my heart. But I restrained the impulse in regard to a consideration of more selfish character. I was anxious to answer you about the Review of Macaulay. As you conjectured, the subject had been assigned to one of the old contributors of the Review — the Honorable Mr. Grayson — formerly in Congress from this State and now Collector of the Port of Charleston, — a very amiable and intelligent Gentleman. He consented to prepare the article, but proved dilatory; and, suspecting (what proved to be the truth) that he had done little or nothing towards it, instead of writing to you I wrote to him, frankly telling him that I was particularly anxious, if his own progress had not been so far as to interest him in the subject, that it should be yielded up to you. His answer has just been recieved and is such as I could wish. He, himself, is anxious that you should take Macaulay in hand for two reasons. He wishes to have your pen enlisted in behalf of the Review, and he is curious to see what are your objections to a writer, in whose work he has found everything to delight him. Opinions, even less indulgent to Macaulay than your own, have met his ears in Charleston. He writes — "I find that my enthusiasm in his favour is not shared by every body here. Some are so irreverent as to call him a Humbug." This Macaulay certainly is not. He may pretend to some things beyond his measure, but he is unquestionably a man of considerable research and sometimes forcible though perhaps not very profound reflection. His misfortune is, perhaps, to prefer a point to a truth, and his ambition at uniform brilliance is fatal to that *repose* which we desire mostly in the perusal of works which require patient and calm consideration. But I need not prate of him to you. I have read nothing of his present work but his introduction, which seems to me stiff and frigid, though comprehensive and perhaps complete, as regards the generalization which he intended. I shall be quite happy to recieve your article by the fifteenth of May. It will then be in season. Could I get it earlier, it should have, what I desire to give it, an earlier place in the number.[62] Hammond will probably furnish the initial article, which is devoted to Elwood Fisher['s] pamphlet comparing North & South.[63] Your opinion with regard to Hammond, is one to which I fully respond. He is one of the most remarkable men that the South has produced. We singularly agree on the subject of the Yankees. Their great deficiency is in the imaginative faculty. In argument, because of this deficiency, they are incapable of generalization & deal only in details. And this is the remarkable respect in which their Congressional speeches differ from those of Southern men. Did you ever see such a race of rhymers, men and women, without a thought or fancy of their own to go all fours upon? — The Southern Review up to a late period, *was* edited, as you conjecture, by a Yankee;[64] a consummate ass, who had not the slightest notion of the length of his own ears, and who was as obtrusive & impudent as the most indurated pedlar of his race. He was *bought* out by a certain number of our Gentlemen, not so much, I believe, with the view of making the Review successful, as to relieve the South of the discredit of such a representative. In taking charge of the work, I feel my own deficiencies sufficiently, and my policy is to arm myself with good contributors. In a little time we shall be able to shake off some of those who have been deluging us with stupidity & commonplace; but we shall, for a while, be burdened with some few of the Balaamites. Our forthcoming number is cumbered by heavy and I fear unattractive articles. But when I consented to take charge of the work, not an article was written, and the number already due. We had no alternative, but to take just such stuff as we could lay hands upon. To reform this altogether will depend upon the favour of a select body of Contributors which I trust we shall be able in season to secure. — Gradually, we may attempt some of the improvements which you counsel. At present it is perhaps better to forbear experiments. There is a vulgar notion that reviews are merely grave & learned things. To be witty or playful, or to employ other forms of Art than such as distinguish the grave essay upon a printed book, such as constitutes the common character of our reviews at present, would seem to such people

---

[62] "Macaulay's History of England," XV (July, 1849), 374-410. The article is unsigned.

[63] "The North and the South," *ibid.,* pp. 273-311. The article is unsigned.

[64] Daniel K. Whitaker.

exceedingly undignified. I am sure I could wish to be allowed
to go aside from the beaten track at times; since I should sometimes find it easier to put forth a story than a critique and by far
more pleasant. — I knew you to be a State rights man before I
wrote you. I was very far from wanting in the knowledge of
your various resources. I had read George Balcome when it was
first published with the greatest pleasure; and I felt sure that
I could rely upon you in any department, or in the treatment of
any subject which it would please you to adopt. Perhaps, the
better course, in choosing your subjects, would be to do so and
simply write me what you design. It shall then be my care to
reserve the topic & a place for you exclusively. With very great
respect & regard, I presume, as you permit me, to subscribe myself very faithfully

Your friend &c

W. Gilmore Simms

P. S. Compelled to write hurriedly, and after a day of exhausting labor at the desk, reading and revising *proof* & MS., I am
heartily ashamed of the rude & crude epistle I have scribbled
you. But you will make the necessary allowance. I trust we
shall have more leisure for correspondence hereafter. I was at
Hammond's a few weeks ago, where we both very much wished
for you. Have you ever visited Carolina? Don't let it be too late.
We should both rejoice to welcome you, — and it is so little
satisfactory to make a letter answer the purpose of conversation
— at least to Southern men. We occupy places in the same district though fifty miles apart. Had your town been less off the
route, I should have found my way to you years ago. I have
usually visited the North every summer, for the last 16 or 17
years, sometimes through Virginia, and I have greatly longed
to linger, when I did so. I do not yet despair that we shall find
our way to the same neighbourhood. Your 'life in Virginia'
would afford a good subject for the incidental & enlivening portions of a review article. There is something in Carolina life
which has struck me as deserving description. The rural attractions of both have a value but little understood & seldom dwelt
upon. But I am again at the bottom of my sheet.

Very sincerely Yours &:

W. Gilmore Simms

Please address me at this place, "Midway, P. O. S. C." I am 72 miles from Charleston at our country seat.

478: To CAREY AND HART

Woodlands April 12 1849

Mess'rs Carey & Hart.

Gentlemen:

I am greatly obliged for your Letter in spite of the discouraging character of the contents.[65] I have drawn upon you as advised, for One Hundred Dollars. The amount comes opportunely. You have perhaps been informed that I have consented to Edit the Southern Quarterly Review. The work has some 1700 subscribers, and an effort is now in progress among our leading politicians to extend its circulation. I will thank you to afford me the usual opportunity of discussing the merits of your publications. Early copies would be particularly useful. With the sincere desire that business in books will improve to our mutual relief & satisfaction, believe me Ever most truly

Yr friend & servt

W. Gilmore Simms

479: To MARCUS CLAUDIUS MARCELLUS HAMMOND

Woodlands, April 23. [1849][66]

My dear Major.

Your letter of the 21st just recieve[d. I] have accordingly written to Geddings,[67] a[nd the letter] will go by tomorrow's mail & be in the c[ity almost] as soon as Mr. Davis[68] himself. He is perf[e]c[tly safe] to try Geddings, who is probably one of the [leaders] of the profession in this country. Only, tell [him] not to hurry. Let him get good lodgings at some g[ood] house

---

65 Possibly Carey and Hart had again refused to publish Simms' collected poetry. See letter to Carey and Hart of Jan. 19, 1849.

66 Dated by Simms' reference to M. C. M. Hammond's article for the July number of the *Southern Quarterly Review*. For the article, "The Conquest of California, and the Case of Lieut. Col. Fremont," see note 28, Feb. 22, 1849. The MS. of this letter is badly mutilated.

67 Eli Geddings, Charleston physician. See introductory sketch.

68 Possibly the father of M. C. M. Hammond's wife, Harriet Pamela Davies, of Augusta, Ga., whom Hammond had married on July 12, 1842.

in Charleston, indulge his leisure, see all [the] sights, enjoy all
the amusements, and eat good things when he can get them. I
suspect a bottle of Champagne per diem would be his best medicine. Your previous letter was recieved while I was in the city,
whither I had gone to see after the Review, and where I was kept
four days. The Review is out of my hands, but not out of those of
the Printer. The steam press gave out & was in the founder's
shop for repair. I suppose the no. will appear next week. I hope
so. I have provided the publishers with most of the material for
the July issue, your article among them. I will send the note. I
am now busy with the Critical Notices — a tedious part of my
Quarter's drudgery. — I am sorry that you have not yet procured those documents. Why not write to Burt as well as Butler,
and request them, if they have not got them, to write for them
to the Department, with instructions to forward direct to your
address.[69] By all means keep your mind on the topic [unti]l you
have fairly despatched it. Revision [requir]es a *cool,* if not a
cold mind, — and [after th]e heat of conception & birth are
[over, you] can wash and clothe the infant [with muc]h more
taste than when you were [exhausted] from *accouchement.* I
would [prefer for] you, rather than to stop, to skip [for a]
moment those portions for which you [lack] the documents, and
pass to the prepara[tio]n of others. You can fill up the gaps
far more easily than you can rewarm yourself to the task of
composition after having suffered your metal entirely to cool.
At the same time let me counsel you to the course of reading,
bearing upon the large labor which I suggested to you for achievement. — I am glad that you relish 'Atalantis.' It is purely fanciful
& imaginative, & such writing is foreign to the desires or comprehension of the multitudes. I suspect that the odes which follow,
though superior as efforts of imagination, will be found too
obscure to delight you. They require a mood thoroughly ab-
stracted, & a long familiarity with the metaphysics of poetry. The
subjects I hold to be much nobler than those of Pindar; though
I suspect you never relished Pindar except [when] you were
grown [*one word illegible*]. Eh! We must talk of the [proposed]
trip hereafter. My daughter [70] would of course be delighted to

---

[69] On Feb. 22 Simms had written: "In another article I should like you to
take up the Indians, using for your text the report of the Bureau in the last
publication of Congress. Documents."

[70] Augusta.

participate in it[, but] the prospect before us is greatly un-
sett[led by my ab]sence at the North this summer. [My wife's]
indispositions, which are now freque[nt, and my] domestic matters, all render it advisa[ble that] she should stay at home to
assist my [wife as] her companion. It is barely possible [that I]
may be permitted a few weeks absence [from] home after my
return in September. [My wife sends] her best regards & remembrances to Mrs. H. and yourself. She greatly enjoyed her visit
to your House upon the Hill, and will always be glad to renew
it. — On Saturday I propose to run up to Clinton's,[71] meet Aldrich and ride out with him to his plantation, spend Sunday, &
be home again on Monday or Tuesday. — When Job was covered
with boils, had he any ale. Doubtful! Yet his ailing was greater
than yours. Be patient without ale, *mon ami,* and you will get
well. Purge & be decent. Do not write or dictate political articles.
'Sessa! Let the world slide.' [72] Neither you nor I was born to
mend it. — Try the wet sheet with your little boy, or give him
the cold bath, a single shock, rub him with coarse cloths, and
give him warm weak tea — no physic. God bless you and yours.

W. Gilmore Simms

480: To NATHANIEL BEVERLEY TUCKER

Woodlands S. C. April 23. [1849][73]

My dear Sir:

I sent you a batch of trifles in pamphlet form, such as could
be sent by mail, on the reciept of your letter. The daily arrival
of visitors, for a week, kept me from the desk, and consequently
prevented me writing at the same time. When I remove to the
city — which I usually do towards the last of May — I shall make
a collection of such of my volumes as are in my possession, and
gladly forward to your address. I am honored in your application for them. You will find them mostly crude and hasty performances — many of them the work of an inexperienced & un-
tutored youth — for I belong to the class of half-educated men,
and struggled into my acquisitions, such as they are, only by

---

[71] Now the town of Blackville, S. C.

[72] See *The Taming of the Shrew,* Ind., i, 6.

[73] Dated by Simms' references to Tucker's "Macaulay's History of England"
and Hammond's "The North and the South." See letter to Tucker of April 5.

actual labors in the field & without a leader. It is only now that
I begin to feel that I may effect something — time & opportunity
being afforded me — in an original & independent fashion. What
I have written has usually been the work of great haste and in
search of a present object. But I must not be apologetic. I am
only anxious to afford you the reason for my crudenesses without endeavouring to excuse them. If you shall discover that they
contain proofs of individuality, however rude, it is quite as much
as I can hope for. I believe I omitted to send you a fragment
which I cover to you by present mail. A local satire, in two nos.,[74]
will only interest you in parts. It was written at a couple of
sittings — standings rather — and at the request of some Gentlemen of Charleston; — the people of that goodly city being
greatly outraged at a spiteful pamphlet which purported to be
from the pen of a Yankee woman, who revenged herself on the
community by a lampoon, in resentment at the loss (it is said)
of a lover — a lad whom she chased from college. This is the
story. The portions of my scribblement that may interest you
will be such as compare characteristics of North & South. The
occasion was a good one for the utterance of some severities
which were more legitimately bestowed by a native pen, and
more appropriate to the deserts of our people. — A portion of
one of your letters makes me rather apprehensive in forwarding
to you one of my published vols. of verse. Your fling at productions purely fanciful — which relate to sylphs & fairies — the
'gay creatures of the element' — seems to hit one of my performances between wind & water. My "Atalantis" you have
probably never seen. I shall send it *now* with some misgivings.
It was written when I was but eighteen and published first in
1832. More recently, I rewrote & revised it and a new edition
has been just issued from the press. It is too cumbrous to go
by mail, and I frankly confess, since your anticipatory criticism,
I am scarcely anxious to send it; though thinking well enough
of it before. You will however recieve it with the rest. It will
be impossible to send you all that I have published, since I have
been reduced to single copies myself, and some of the volumes
are wholly out of print. In addition to the Poem of 'Atalantis'
and those which I have sent you, I have published a duodecimo
of 250 pages verse, entitled 'Southern Passages & Pictures.[']

---

[74] *Charleston, and Her Satirists.*

These complete my acknowledged dealings with the Muses. My prose writings extend to nearly 40 volumes, of which it is possible I shall be able to gather up only 15 or 20. What I can procure shall be put cheerfully at your service, and I shall rejoice to add your contributions to my collection — most proud to recieve them in exchange for my hurried achievements. — I shall look for your paper on Macaulay with anxiety. Hammond has just written me to say that his article on Fisher has been forwarded to the publishers in Charleston. By this time you will probably have recieved the review for April, which has been very badly got out by the publishers, clouded with errors of the press, and sadly lacking in variety and finish, because of haste, & the carelessness of politician contributors and my own absence from the city. You know how things are managed in the South. We shall amend in season, and you will make allowances *ad interim*. It is curious that a note in the review, speaking of your Geo. Balcombe, should express precisely the same opinions and make a like statement with one of Mr. Poe, in the S. L. Messenger, just recieved.[75] The critical notice to which this note is appended, is shockingly full of typographical errors; the proof never seeming to have been read. Do not be alarmed at these signs. We shall take better care of your contributions. All of our present annoyances spring from a necessity which demanded publication at all hazards. When I took charge of the review, it lacked [but five weeks][76] of publication, yet not an article had been recieved or written, and I could not so make my arrangements as to leave the plantation for my city residence, to attend to the work

---

[75] In a footnote to a notice of John Lothrop Motley's *Merry-Mount*, 2 vols. (Boston: James Munroe and Company, 1849), *S. Q. R.*, XV (April, 1849), 260, Simms writes: "The Hon. Beverly [*sic*] Tucker, of Virginia, is understood to be the author of George Balcombe, an American novel published by Harper and Brothers in 1836, and one of the most truly American, and one of the very best ever published in the country. It would be difficult, perhaps, to find a single New-England press which had ever accorded the slightest acknowledgment to this publication, or a single New-England citizen who had ever read it. It lacked the necessary *imprimatur* from the banks of the Charles. The saline flavor from the Plymouth rock, would have secured for it a thousand pæans." Similarly Poe says in "Marginalia," *S. L. M.*, XV (April, 1849), 220: "Had the 'George Balcombe' of Professor Beverley Tucker been the work of anyone born North of Mason and Dixon's line, it would have been long ago recognized as one of the very noblest fictions ever written by an American. It is almost as good as 'Caleb Williams.' The manner in which the cabal of the 'North American Review' first write of all our books and then review them, puts me in mind of the fable about the Lion and the Painter. It is high time that the literary South took its own interests into its own charge."

[76] Several words are cut. For this probable reading, see letter to Perry of April 27.

in person. — I shall certainly seek you out if I go north this summer. It is a mistake to suppose that nobody visits the South at this season. Charleston is perfectly secure for strangers at all seasons, & is now much visited during the summer. Besides, we have places of gathering and assemblage in the hot months, which are at once cool, healthy & attractive with society. If you are at any time disposed to run errant, I can give you all the needed information. I think I may venture to assure you that there are many Carolinians who would be at some pains to wander with you & guide you to our cities of refuge, showing you the pleasant vallies, and the delicious springs. — We shall discourse hereafter on the topics which you suggest in relation to the review. Were the work like Blackwood a monthly instead of a Quarterly Journal, I should unhesitatingly concur with you in the propriety of making the graftings which you counsel upon it. But its proprietors prefer the Quarterly form. This matter has been already under discussion. I should prefer the monthly, on the score of its greater susceptibili[ti]es, and more frequent utterance. In a quarterly, papers like the Caxtons[77] would lose their interest for the great body of readers unless completed in each number. All the advantages resulting from the continuous interest of the story would be forfeited; and how few would, like ourselves, value the narrative for its other qualities. But I am at the bottom of my sheet. You must take my letters, with many grains of allowance. I write only after long and dreary readings through vast tracts of dismal M. S. which, even to be discarded & rejected must yet necessarily be read. Hold me, I pray you, very faithfully & with great regard,

Your friend &c

[Signature cut.]

481 : To Benjamin Franklin Perry

Woodlands April 27. [1849][78]

My dear Sir

Your letter, though long delayed is welcome. I was a little afraid that you had forgotten me, though from my knowledge of

---

[77] Bulwer-Lytton's *The Caxtons* was appearing serially in *Blackwood's* at this time.

[78] Dated by Simms' reference to "my assumption of the duties of the Review."

your duties, I should have anticipated the causes of your delay. It gives me great satisfaction to find that my assumption of the duties of the Review is generally approved of. There is one exception as you will find, since the columns of the Courier have been used by Whittaker the former Editor for the purpose of vituperating one of the articles of the April issue which he knew to be mine.[79] The malignity of the creature betrays itself, however, too freely to do mischief. He is a miserable Yankee who failed with the work and had to sell out. He has lately been made angry that an application which he made to the proprietors to supersede me in the Editorship, was quietly rejected. The April number was prepared wholly in less than 5 weeks. When I consented to take charge of the work in March last, but a single article was written. This will account to you for the deficiency of variety, and the numberless errors of haste, and the inaccuracies which it contains. We shall do better hereafter, and have already secured such an array of good Southern Contributors & able men — real thinkers & good writers — that it will discredit no man to work for the journal. The first article in the April number, is by a Mr. Gwinn of Baltimore, the second by myself, the third by Brantz Mayer formerly Secy. of Legation to Mexico, the fifth, on Guizot, I am not allowed to mention, the sixth is by D. J. McCord, the 7 by Dr. W. H. Simmons of Florida.[80] I am

---

[79] The Charleston *Courier* of April 25 carries a long article (one and one-half columns), signed "Claverhouse," in which the April issue of the *Southern Quarterly Review* is discussed. Of "Modern Prose Fiction" "Claverhouse" (Whitaker) says: ". . . it would be well for his [Simms'] reputation as a reviewer . . . to prevent badly written articles from appearing in the pages of a work, which sets itself up as a standard of taste, and professes to give law to literary criticism . . . [There are] crudities, either style or sentiment, which disfigure almost every page of this highly lauded article." After a lengthy attack on Simms' grammar, rhetoric, and syntax, "Claverhouse" concludes: "It is unnecessary, however, to multiply examples of the numerous false, ridiculous and irrevelent [*sic*] opinions, and abuses of grammar, rhetoric and syntax, that disfigure the pages of this interminable article. It is affected and inflated in style almost beyond a parallel." Of this review Hammond comments in a letter to Simms of April 30: "I have just read the attack on you in the Courier. You laid yourself open by some of that careless writing I have scolded you so much about myself. But after that the attack has neither sense nor point & is purely malicious. I did not think you had an enemy who was violent enough & malignant enough to perpetrate such a thing. . . ." (Original in the Hammond Papers, Library of Congress.)

[80] By skipping "fourth" Simms indicates that there are seven articles exclusive of the critical notices. There are only six. The titles, signatures, and authors of the articles in the April issue of *S. Q. R.*, XV, are as follows:

1. "Political Economy," pp. 1-41. Unsigned, but by Charles John Morris Gwinn (1822-1894), a member of the Maryland State Legislature at this time.
2. "Modern Prose Fiction," pp. 41-83. Unsigned, but by Simms.

sorry to disappoint your wishes, but a review of Macaulay is in preparation for the July no. by Professor Beverley Tucker of Virginia.[81] I do not seè how you can make a paper out of the Pictorial History, the subjects are so numerous — unless you detach one of them — say for example, the social habits & history of the English from the beginning; but this would be a work of great painstaking and would probably preclude the paying exercise of original thought & suggestion. But you will probably find a sufficient variety of subjects. Our July number is already complete & ready for the press. But you can get an article ready for our October issue, which I trust you will do.[82] Our initial article for the next will be by Hammond — on Fisher's Pamphlet.[83] Macaulay will follow &c — all from first rate hands. Go to work industriously, take pains & do the thing handsomely. — It is doubtful whether I shall be able to visit the mountains this summer. I should rejoice to do so, but with three young children it is scarcely possible. Present me respectfully to Mrs. P. and believe me very truly

Yours as Ever

W. Gilmore Simms

Hon B. F. Perry.

---

3. "Origin of the War with Mexico," pp. 83-113. Signed "B. M." (Brantz Mayer).

4. "Guizot's Democracy in France," pp. 114-165. Unsigned, but by Simms. See note 47, *c.* Feb. 25, 1849.

5. "Slavery and the Abolitionists," pp. 165-223. Unsigned, but by David James McCord.

6. "Rail Road and Canal Routes to California," pp. 224-252. Unsigned, but by William Hayne Simmons (see introductory sketch of the Simmons brothers).

7. "Critical Notices," pp. 253-261. Unsigned, but by Simms.

8. "Quarterly List of New Publications," pp. 262-271. Unsigned, but by Simms.

9. "Literary Intelligence," p. 271. Unsigned, but by Simms.

[81] See letter to Tucker of April 5, 1849.

[82] Perry did not write an article on *The Pictorial History of England,* a series published by Harper and Brothers, of which Part 42 had recently appeared (see notice in *S. Q. R.,* XV [April, 1849], 269). No article which can be identified as Perry's appears in the Oct. issue. "Characteristics of Alabama," signed "B. F. P." (XVI [Oct., 1849], 178-205) is by Benjamin F. Porter, a frequent contributor.

[83] "The North and the South." See note 63, April 5, 1849.

482: To William Cullen Bryant

Woodlands May 5 [1849][84]

Dear Bryant

I got your Letter from Charleston at the same moment with the newspaper that announced your departure for the North. I greatly regret that your leisure did not enable you to repeat the visit to Woodlands, where the weather, though absolutely ruinous to the Crops, has been the very pleasantest that we have had this spring. Our nights are delightfully cool, and, out of the sun, the days are balmy and breezy in great degree. With your friend, Mr Leupp,[85] you might have passed a week with us to the gratification of most of your senses. Birds, blossoms, breezes, all in finest condition — acknowledging by play and scent, the acutest sense of life and enjoyment. I trust that future seasons will afford you better leisure, and "when you next do go abroad, may I be there to see." [86] I suppose I shall readily find the Book you left for me. You might have retained it. It was written at my instance, by Dr. Wurdemann, a very excellent and intelligent friend of mine, a most amiable man, who, for ten years or more, has been flying from death. I have just learned that he is suffering at this moment dangerously from a fresh attack of hemorrhage from which it is doubtful if he can ever recover. Poor fellow! I was just meditating to write him what you said of his book (which I knew would give him pleasure) when I got this painful intelligence.[87] — Miss Kellogg left us in a couple of

---

84 Simms erroneously wrote *April 5*. Bryant was at Woodlands on March 30 and 31 (see his unpublished "Diary," on microfilm in the New York Public Library). In the New York *Evening Post* of April 9 is published a letter from Bryant, dated March 31 and addressed from Barnwell District, later included as "Southern Cotton Mills" in *Letters of a Traveller; or Notes of Things Seen in Europe and America* (New York: George P. Putnam, 1850), pp. 345-350. Bryant left Woodlands for Charleston on March 31, Charleston for Havana on the following day, and returned to Charleston on April 25, leaving the same day for New York (see his "Diary" cited above). This letter was made available to us through the courtesy of Professor Herman E. Spivey, University of Kentucky.

85 Charles M. Leupp, a lover of art and literature and an active member of the Century Club, was Bryant's favorite travelling companion.

86 William Cowper, "The Diverting History of John Gilpin," lines 251-252.

87 Dr. J. G. F. Wurdemann, of Charleston, was a contributor to the *Magnolia* and *The Charleston Book*. His work here mentioned by Simms, *Notes on Cuba* (Boston: J. Munroe and Company, 1844), was first published as a serial in the *Magnolia* for Jan. through June, 1843 (see note 10, Feb. 25, 1843). In 1845 Simms reviewed the volume in the *Southern and Western* (see note 100, Feb. 12, 1845). A notice of Wurdemann's death in the Charleston *Courier* of May 7, 1849, concludes with this appraisal: "Dr. Wurdemann occupied a prominent position among the medical fraternity — and it is not only in this character

weeks after your departure. She is now in Charleston, unless she has taken her departure within the last two days. We have had a succession of visitors ever since you left us, which scarcely suffered me to steal away for a week — to Orangeburg. There I saw Gen. Jamison & others, who still entertain pleasant recollections of a visit which you made them years ago. I have often regretted that I could not accompany you on that occasion.[88] I could have so much better shown you where to look than any of those to whom I could refer you. — I hear nothing from Lawson. Have not recieved a Letter from him for four months, and have written him some 5 or 6 to which I have had no answer. His silence is particularly provoking at this moment when the newspapers advise us of the seperation of Forrest and his wife.[89] I confess to have long since apprehended something of this sort, and think I predicted it to Lawson if not to yourself. Pray write me what you learn of the particulars. My wife and daughter send love to Mrs. B and Julie. Present me also with affectionate respect to both, and believe me

Very truly Yours &c

W. Gilmore Simms

483 : To NATHANIEL BEVERLEY TUCKER

Woodlands S. C. May 6, 1849

Hon B. Tucker

Dear Sir:

The first instalment of your article [90] has been recieved and read with great pleasure. I am looking anxiously for the remainder. I certainly approve in high degree of your plan of balancing justly between the merits and demerits of your subject. No honest man has a right to complain of this process, & no wise man will. Macaulay would hardly desire other treatment, and if he be the man I think him, will find his advantage in it.

---

that his loss will be felt, but as a kind devoted son, and philanthropic gentleman, who never failed to seek and improve an opportunity to benefit his fellow man." MSS. of several of Wurdemann's letters to Simms are in the New York Public Library.

[88] Bryant's first visit to Woodlands was in March, 1843 (see Simms' letters of that date). Bryant notes in his "Diary" (cited note 84, above) that at Orangeburg he saw Jamison, George Frederick Holmes, and Thomas Worth Glover.

[89] The Forrests separated on May 1. See letter to Lawson of *c.* May 6, 1849.

[90] "Macaulay's History of England."

Yet in the vulgar, headlong and restlessly rude habits of our American Critics & criticism, how subtle will seem your refinements about Gentility! The idea, certainly, will be quite novel in New England, that the word involves duties to the dead, of the sort you indicate, and exacts a certain humane forbearance, in spite of justice, at the hands of the Historian who treats of the memory of an unfortunate subject. It is, perhaps, fortunate that you illustrate your point so happily by your own manner, and that Mr. Macaulay gives you occasion for it. The example, in your article keeps such even pace with the suggestion, that he will be at no loss to learn the lesson, if capable of the acquisition, — which I suppose he is, — though, as a Scotchman, Burly Sam Johnson would growl dissent.

Your excuse is an ingenious one, touching your anticipatory judgment upon 'Atalantis': Unfortunately, it fails both of us. True, the poem was originally written & printed when I was a boy; but I have lately been pottering at it, as if it were a favorite; — dressed it in new habiliments, and sent it forth on a new venture seeking approbation for it. But do not suppose me at all sensitive to a friendly criticism. I have survived that period of morbid egotism. In some degree, I have survived also those rose coloured fancies which first prompted the poem; and that I still value it somewhat is due perhaps, to the fact that I *have* survived them. Our delusions are not the less precious because we have found them out. They are perhaps even more valuable after the discovery that they are delusions. They have then lost all power of harm, and we cherish only what was innocent in the influence which at first was far from innocent. — By the way, a copy of this offender was not among the things I sent you. I reserved it to be forwarded from the city in a package. It was too massive for the mails. In less than three weeks we remove from the plantation to Charleston, where I trust our Correspondence will be continued. From that place I will forward you as many of my printed transgressions as I can gather, and more, in all probability, than you will care to read. Do you recieve the Review? Let me know. Have you seen the number for July last containing an article entitled "South Carolina in the Revolution?" I could wish you to read that. You will see how much of a Southron I am, & how little of a Yankee. You probably are not unaware that I am a proverbial object of hate & denunciation in N. E. You will see the reason for it when you read my books.

I do not ask you to excuse my egotism. It is a proof that I regard you as a friend

Believe me, very truly Yours &c

W. Gilmore Simms

484: To JAMES LAWSON

[*c.* May 6, 1849][91]

Dear Lawson

Nothing is usually more welcome to me than the sight of your well known scrawl. I confess that the extremely long silence which you have observed has given me a great deal of pain. Friendship is so precious at all times — particularly to those who are no longer youthful, and who find it not easy to make new friends in the decline of life, that the apparent falling off of old friends, is perhaps the source of our acutest and most enduring sorrows. We have now for so long a period been united by a confidence and sympathies which nothing has ever disturbed, that when you appear to fail me, I feel as if it were becoming necessary that I should begin the world anew, — struggling hopelessly for those affections which a past experience would seem to put beyond all hope. The interval consumed by your silence has frequently forced me to the endeavour to retrace my steps and to ask what fault or deficiency in me has led to a depreciation of my value as a friend. In this self-examination I do not know that I can reproach myself with anything. I certainly cannot think that I have erred in always counselling with you in good faith — in always preferring to speak frankly & sincerely, even at the risk of giving momentary annoyance. I know your nature to be warm & sincere, and could not suppose really that you would take offence at a course of conduct which always gave you the assurance of my truthfulness and fidelity. And so I always thought in respect to Lady Lyde. I know that I sometimes vexed & worried her by my advice, but I took for granted that she always did justice to my fondness for her & all that were precious in her eyes. In the end, I have usually come to the conclusion that you were suffering the *vis inertia* to get the better of your sympathies. In plain terms you were getting too fat and

---

[91] This letter is postmarked May 7. The year is established by Simms' reference to the marriage of Mary Steele (see note 95, below).

too lazy. Is this not quite as much the truth as your plea of toil and exhaustion? — But enough that you have spoken at last. I answer you the very day in which I recieve your letter. If you would adopt the same rule, which is always easy with a man of business, you would find your correspondence light, and would never fall so terribly in arrear with your friendly creditors. And now for details. If Post has failed and his magazine is stopt, it is highly important that I recover the portions of M.S. which remain unpublished, and which, as he printed it, would have furnished a chapter for each number.[92] Will you endeavor to see him for this purpose. Will you also write a note to C. W. Webber requesting the M.S. of the Poem on Fonthill. It ought *not* to be published now. To bring Forrest's name, at this moment before the public, unless in matters purely necessary, would be indelicate and perhaps offensive, even though the avowed object be complimentary. In such an affair as his, silence for a while is the best policy. Suppress the poem therefore, and be careful that you say no more about the segars. I have more than once regretted that you took up earnestly a playful suggestion. I am by no means suprised at the separation. You may not have forgotten that I predicted some such catastrophe. I do not see what friends can do, unless the subject is first broached by F. himself. The very fact that he deigns to give no reasons, is to me a very impressive one.[93] Be you careful not to burn your fingers by mixing in the affair, unless distinctly appealed to, and with a full knowledge of the facts before you. To work in the dark in such matters, and to work gratuitously, is only to do mischief. — Have you got the 'Man of the People?' Of course I do not wish that F. should be harrassed in regard to it just now; but as soon as you can properly bring his attention to it, procure the M.S. If you have it now, I wish it sent me, along with the two prose letters which I sent for Duyckinck, unless you can make an arrangement with the Democratic or Whig Review for publishing them

---

[92] "The Egyptian Masque; A Tale of the Crescent City." See note 172, Nov. 20, 1848.

[93] Edwin and Catherine Sinclair Forrest separated on May 1, 1849. Eventually he gave his reasons, charging her with adultery and naming nine corespondents. The trial for divorce started in New York on Dec. 18, 1851. The verdict, rendered on Jan. 24, 1852, accquitted Mrs. Forrest of the charges and awarded her $3,000.00 a year alimony. Forrest appealed a number of times, but in 1868 finally abandoned resistance and paid Mrs. Forrest $64,000.00. For an account of the separation and divorce, see Alger, *Life of Edwin Forrest*, II, 486-501, and Montrose Moses, *The Fabulous Forrest* (Boston: Little, Brown, and Company, 1929), pp. 265-294.

($20 for the two — to be published as one) and to be continued
monthly.[94] But perhaps better send them back to be remodelled.
Did you send a note to Forbes the actor, requesting the return
of a fragmentary drama which I lent him — & did he return it?
If not, will you address him through the post office making the
request. The piece is entitled "Arnold, The Traitor &c." This,
with the the two Letters, the M.S. from Post, and the 'Man of
the People' I should like forwarded as soon as you can get them
together, through one of the steamers, addressed to me in Charleston. To that place we go on the 25th inst. & I am beginning to
prepare for the transition. We are all quite well, and my wife
has just returned from a visit to the late Miss Mary Steele (now
Mrs. Rivers) who got married and left us a couple of months
ago.[95] I too have only recently got back from a visit to an ad-
joining District. Bryant passed a day & night with us on his
way to Cuba. I did not see the Letter from Barnwell & am
curious to do so.[96] Will you procure & send me a copy. Mary
Lawson grows plumply & prettily. Our boy is a rough colt forever in the woods. The Baby is said to be a beauty and you may
therefore readily infer that she looks like me. I am busy as man
can well be, & frequently overwhelmed with weariness seeking
repose. I had occasion to write to Wetmore in regard to Pictures
of the Art Union, and I found it easy to write him as an old
friend. — I believe now that I have emptied my budget. Present
me affectionately to Lady Lyde, and kiss the children for me.
We love them as part of our own. Let me hear from you soon
and believe me Ever as Ever Yours

W. Gilmore Simms

J. L.

485 : To LEWIS REEVE GIBBES [97]

Woodlands S. C. May 8 [1849][98]

Professor L. R. Gibbes

dear Sir

I fully concur with you that periodical Literature, to be valuable, must be paid for, & as soon as the South. Quarterly is able

---

[94] See note 204, *c.* Dec. 19, 1848.
[95] Mary Govan Steele (see note 202, Oct. 23, 1846) was married to Christopher M. Rivers on Feb. 25, 1849, by the Rev. Lucius Bellinger. At the time
of her marriage Mary was living at Woodlands.
[96] See note 84, May 5, 1849.
[97] See introductory sketch.
[98] Dated by Simms' reference to his "taking charge of the South. Rev."

to pay, I shall insist (if its conduct remains with me) upon giving ample remuneration for every published article. Even now, the Publishers authorize me to say that they will appropriate a certain amount for the payment of contributors, and will pay at the rate of $1. per printed page. This is a sorry trifle, it is true; but it is the same which is paid by the North American, and much more than *is paid* by 7 in 8 of the periodicals of the country. Few of them pay any thing, unless the Lady's magazines; and these, to a select corps of Contributors, pay much more. But most of them deal only in promises. I have lost $5000 by them, and know them all. — In taking charge of the South. Rev. I am doing so at loss — with the probability of losing all my labor. But it is the only organ of letters in the South, & I am willing to incur the same risk, in its behalf, to which I invite my neighbours. With great respect

Yr. Obt Servt. &c.

W. Gilmore Simms

486: To CHARLES L. WHELER [99]

[May 9, 1849]

Dear Sir

You are pleased to ask at my hands a leader for the first number of your contemplated periodical. I am scarcely in a condition to serve your purpose. Even were my abilities such as would fully justify your application, or permit me to suppose it anything more than the mere compliment, — the tribute rather of your personal good feeling than of my merit, — I have not just now the requisite leisure to attempt compliance with your wishes. My whole time is consumed in labors which are imperative, as they occur under the severest exactions of duty; and the constant exercise at the desk deprive pen, ink and paper of all those attractions which they would otherwise possess for a mind whose strongest passion is that of letters. But I have every disposition to promote your objects; and, if the brief and hurried considerations which are here set down will contribute in any degree to your design, they are cheerfully at your service.

---

[99] We have not located the original of this letter, published in *Wheler's Magazine* (Athens, Ga.), N. S., I (July, 1849), 1-6. For an account of *Wheler's Magazine,* see Bertram Holland Flanders, *Early Georgia Magazines* (Athens: The University of Georgia Press, 1944), pp. 110-118.

Of the advantages and importance of Periodical Literature there can be no question. It has been recognized in all countries that have made any progress in civilization, as contributing largely, first to the provocation to proper exercise of the domestic mind, and next, as enabling this mind to determine and mature the standards of a just judgment and a becoming taste. What has proved true of other countries must certainly prove true of ours. — What has been beneficent to the intellect of other communities, cannot fail of doing service in the South. In fact, there are special reasons why a Periodical Literature is more important and necessary to the South than to most other regions. The very sparseness of our population, which renders it so difficult a matter to sustain the Periodical, is the very fact that renders its existence and maintenance so necessary. — The great secret of mental activity, in most countries, is the denseness of their settlements, — the size and frequency of their great cities, and the constant attrition of rival minds, which can take place nowhere so constantly as in the commercial and populous marts. Wanting in these fields of attrition and collision, the mind of the Southern gentleman, residing on his plantation and secluded from the crowd, is apt to sink into languor or indifference. Why should he indulge in studies which seem unnecessary to his situation? Why pore over volumes, upon the merits of which he has no one to provoke him to discussion? We determine tacitly upon the importance of most exercises by their obvious uses. Of what use to him is that literary acquisition which has no connection with his daily toils, his pecuniary interests, and which invites neither the sympathy nor rivalry of his neighbor? Few persons would build fine houses if no one came to see them; and still fewer indulge in studies which seemingly conduct to no immediate profits, and which provoke none of the admiration of their fellows.

To persons, thus secluded by their modes of life, even where the taste for letters is innate, the very difficulty in procuring books, which cannot be transmitted by mail, opposes a barrier to that constant exercise which is necessary to keep up and to nourish the desire for literature. Periodicals, alone, appear calculated to supply these deficiencies, to counteract these discouraging influences, and to provide that gentle stimulus which keeps the mind true to its instincts and acquisitions, while furnishing new food for its progress as well as digestion. They bring us the reports of mind from other quarters; they tell us of the progress of letters and arts, philosophy and science, among other brethren, more fortunately placed, in other States and Cities. They not only show us what the race is doing elsewhere, but they goad us to exertion also. They give us clues for study and performance, while seeming to recreate and amuse us only; and, under the natural attrition, which accrues from the inevitable action of other intellects upon our own, they brighten us anew, and bestow that friction without which we should have been devoured by sloth and rust, not to speak of our danger from evil habits, which, in the absence of the nobler stimuli of thought, invariably seizes upon the souls of the idle and unperforming. We are not permitted to fold up our *one* talent, whatever it may be, in a napkin — heedless of its employment or profit — without paying for it in terrible penalties which it would be difficult to enumerate. Most of the vices, crimes, shames, and evil fortunes of men, are strictly the result of the *non-user,* or the perversion of their intellectual endowments. How shall we employ and counsel this intellect, in a region where the population seldom communes — where society lacks all the advantages which spring from frequent commerce with one's fellow — where books are scarce, and not to be had without great difficulty and expense? There are, really, for us in the South, but two great sources of popular tuition, apart from Schools and Colleges : one of these is the *stump,* during the political canvass; the other is a free circulation of a various literature, through the medium of the periodical. The former is efficient enough. The great body of the Southern people are better informed in political affairs — on the great questions which affect the interests of the Nation — in the absolute terms of the Constitution, and in many of the subtleties which belong to the various constructions put upon certain of its provisions — than any other people in the Union. They are as quick, keen, and discriminating, in regard to these subjects, and as jealously observant of their rights, as any people in the world — nay, beyond most; and all this is due to the habit — occasioned entirely by the sparseness of the population — of meeting their law-givers and statesmen at regular and frequent periods, and seeking at their hands the means of information.

I have often thought, that the same process should be employed in teaching the people on a variety of other subjects — law, literature, art, morals, and society. Popular lectures on all these topics would, in the case of minds nationally so quick, soon produce their proper effects; and we should rejoice in a people possessing an intelligence, acquired as well as natural, second to that of no other people in the world. I have more than once urged upon certain of my friends, whose political influence was such as to make it certain that they might readily command the popular ear for other than political topics; but regret to report that, though my suggestion usually met with a ready concurrence, it has not yet been subjected to the test of actual experiment.

Through this agency, and that of the periodical publication, most of our literary wants might be supplied. The monthly and weekly Journals not only afford much useful and interesting material, but are usually so various in their contents, and in the many writers whom they employ, that it is scarcely possible but that every mind in a family, however they might severally differ, must discover something in their pages which shall compel thought into activity, and gratify those tastes which are most necessary and grateful to the intellectual man. With the awakening of the tastes, and the activity of the thoughts, the desire grows for that food which has already been found so grateful. Knowledge begets knowledge, as surely as that the sparks fly upward. The appetite for study grows with its exercise; and, where the young student possesses original gifts of intellect, the result is, that in reading the writings of others, he is led gradually to seek in the right quarter for his own resources. He might read a hundred volumes in a library — as private libraries are ordinarily constructed — occupying but a single class in literature, without happening upon the clues which conduct him to his own endowments. The periodical, which is devoted to *all* the departments of art, letters and science, however superficial in each, is perhaps the most *suggestive* medium which Literature could employ for the benefit of the young beginner.

But it is surely unnecessary to dwell upon this subject. It is enough, that, in the peculiar situation of the Southern people, who are almost wholly agricultural in their pursuits, the periodical is at once the cheapest, the most eligible, and, perhaps, the most useful form, in which Literature may yield them its advantages. The mail brings it to the door of the farmer, to the cottage of the peasant, to the stately mansion, embosomed in deep forests, of the lordly and secluded planter. It is, along with the newspaper, the chief mode by which he communicates with the distant world without. It reports for him the progress of the race in Agriculture, as well as Literature; and from the discussion of the one subject, he passes by grateful transitions to an appreciation of all the rest. It supplies to him the deficiencies of society, the distant echoes of which, reaching him through this medium, and stript of all its petty present cares, envy, and rude collision, maintain in him those sympathies with his race, upon the activity of which depend his own humanity and the future fortunes of his children.

Assuming that Periodical Literature is so important to an agricultural people — to the people of the South in particular — a question occurs, arising from the immense variety of the publications of this class. — Great Britain and France send us weekly, monthly, and quarterly, an ample supply. The North floods us with all sorts of literature of this description, and in any quantity. "Shall we not take of these in preference to our own?" is the question. The answer to this question will depend upon the subscriber himself — upon his circumstances and objects. Take all, if you please, and can afford it. It would be well if the country gentleman of the South could take one or more British and French periodicals, and one from each great city in the Union. He should endeavor to possess himself of the means of information from every great centre of civilization and mental activity. But we must insist that he also takes his own — the periodical or periodicals of his own State and section of country. No doubt he will find the advantages mostly with the foreign periodical. — He will find there the proof of more deliberate thought, more thorough investigation, more profound attainment, more classical refinement. Old and large communities necessarily possess resources infinitely beyond any thing within the reach of our young and immature population. The Northern periodicals of our own country will also possess advantages, in these respects, beyond those of the South. They have men of greater wealth and leisure, libraries of greater extent and variety, opportunities for more immediate information, and a degree of mental activity greater than ours, in all those departments of art and science, which are more particularly fostered by the dense population and the trading city.

But, in taking the Southern, as well as the Northern periodical, your object is by no means comparison between them. You seek the proofs of local endowment. You seek to stimulate your own mental activity. Something is given to patriotism in what you do; and your complaints and reproaches, in respect to the deficiencies and inferiority of your own particular section, are restrained by the reflection that you yourself share these reproaches. If the performance is feeble, why is it no better? Is it the best that can be done by the mind of your section? Either it is, or it is not. If the best, it is your duty, as a citizen, to contribute to your best ability in improving the showing, by your own labors or your own patronage. If not the best, then the shame lies at the doors of those, inert, selfish, unpatriotic, who, able themselves to perform, prefer rather to sneer at the inferior performances of their neighbors, than to devote themselves generously, in order that their native clime should not be put to shame — should not suffer from the reproach of total deficiency. There is nothing honorable to be said of that talent which exercises itself only in petty sneer and criticism at the feeble efforts of others, which decries the attempts which it never seeks to surpass — discouraging the toil which it should rather promote and assist, as being, in fact, a toil undertaken for the country.

In all those respects of Literature which involve absolute possessions of learning and art, Europe must necessarily be greatly in advance of America. It is in the exhibition of *native* and *original* endowments alone, that American Literature can ever acquire or deserve reputation. Now, in this essential, the South occupies just as fair a position as the North. The development of individual genius demands no extensive libraries, nor any profound education; it needs but the stimulus arising from the sympathies of the community by which it is surrounded. Look at the effect of this sympathy, as shown by your statesmen and orators, in Congress and elsewhere. The politics of this whole country have been shaped by Southern men — brought up entirely in agricultural communities. In the conflict of rival minds in Congress, or at the Bar of the Supreme Court, wherever the men of the North and South have met in forensic or legislative conflict, the latter has had no reason to be ashamed of her representation; nor will she have any less reason for pride and self-gratulation, in the performance of her sons in the field of literature as well as politics, if her people will only yield to them a like degree of sympathy with that which they have been wont to show for their champions in the political arena. A large proportion of Southern writers are contributors to Northern periodicals. Why should not their performances be just as acceptable through a Southern medium? It needs not that patriotism should be appealed to, in answering this question. Let Justice answer. She will suggest that no ways inferior at this moment, in their contributions, to those of their neighbors, there is every reason to suppose that their writings would rise into still higher merit, written under the grateful consciousness that one's native region delights in the performance, and is eager and anxious in awaiting its publication. — There is no greater stimulus to literary effort, than to feel that your neighbors appreciate your toils, and are proud of them — a stimulus which has been but too commonly denied to the native of the South, where the popular mind has been too frequently taught to despise all intellectual exercise which is not political — and where Professors, Schoolmasters, Editors, and Critics, are but too generally Northern men, with their sympathies mostly elsewhere.

One objection which our people entertain to subscribing to the Southern periodical, arises from the so frequent failure of the enterprize. But this failure is scarcely more frequent here than in other regions, in proportion to the number of experiments. At the North, magazines are constantly rising to the surface, only to sink out of sight in the course of a single season. Hundreds, to my knowledge, have perished within the last twenty years, which scarcely survived the first. But two or three maintain more than a sickly existence, liable to be cut off in a moment by the smallest caprice of the popular mood — not fixed in the affections of the people by any sympathies of strength or character, and tolerated, rather because they amuse than for their supposed advantages or value. I suppose that Godey's and Graham's Magazines are the most firmly established of any, and the most profitable. Of periodicals of higher pretensions, there are very few that afford any profit to their proprietors — as few pay their contributors for articles, and most of them provide their contents by the contributions of amateurs, who, in their anxiety for print, disdain all vulgar consideration of the *money* value of what they write.

The history is precisely the same with the Southern periodicals. The experiments have been fewer, and they have failed in a like proportion with the Northern. But who shall venture to say that this failure was complete? Who shall deny that, in the brief period of their existence and career, they sowed fine seeds of thought, which have since ripened and grown into noble trees, promising goodly harvest? — How many truths and thoughts were scattered over the waste, to bring forth noble fruit hereafter? Truth is never wasted. Like the famous flower seeds which were found griped in the withered hands of the Egyptian mummy, having lain dormant three thousand years, the sacred gem may sleep till the proper moment of awakening. Though inert, it does not perish. The life is indestructible. The seed will spring at last into flower: and the boy who to-day pores over the pages of the frail periodical which stops to-morrow, may gather, as he reads, the sacred but unsuspected impulse which shall lay bare to him the path which he is required to pursue, and on which he is destined to obtain the highest triumphs, while conferring the greatest blessings on his race! How many more minds might have been led to like fortune, were the periodical to become a household book — one looked for at the regularly recurring period with anxiety, and read with faith and sympathy by all the family. How much would such a book appeal to the memories of the aged — how much would it convey to the minds and morals of the young! How admirably might it be made to minister to the guidance of many, and to the happiness of all!

But the periodical must be in good hands. This is one point of great importance, which is quite too little attended to. I have known some periodicals, particularly designed for women, under the conduct of some of the vilest and most unprincipled blackguards in the Union. An Editor should be a gentleman, as a matter of course — governed by a high sense of propriety — calm, firm, steady, unobtrusive, and studiously just and careful in his judgments. His principles must be fixed and certain — his taste refined and always vigilant, and his manners — the manners of a periodical are, by the way, quite as essential as its morals — such as would grace the best bred courtier in the best society. But I must not linger to dilate upon the essentials of an Editor. These will depend upon the requisitions of his readers. They can make him what they please; and, to do so, it only needs that they should take a deeper interest in his labors. I have attempted to shew that it is the *policy* of our Southern people to take this interest in Periodical Literature, as enabling them to supply many of the deficiencies, and to overcome many of the difficulties, of their peculiar situation. It is for you, sir, to afford them additional reasons for taking yours, by making it useful to their wants, necessary to their tastes, and of interest to society at large.

With a sincere hope that you will prove as successful as you desire and deserve, I must bring this hurried and rambling epistle to a close.

Very truly,
Your ob't. serv't., &c.,

W. Gilmore Simms.

Woodlands, May 9, 1849.

487: To WILLIAM BROWN HODGSON [100]

Woodlands, S. C. May 9. [1849][101]

dear Sir

It needs the enthusiasm of such writers and workers as yourself, to be busy for years in preparing the public mind for the due inception of your objects, before we can hope to realize any thing for Art & Science from the Govt. of the country. The worst feature in our condition is that our national Legislature is essentially illiterate as a body, having but one sort of knowledge only, and that of a kind which, as it constantly appeals to vulgar passions & prejudices, is likely to be more hurtful than helpful to Literature. Our Legislators consider no topic which is not already, or cannot be made, a popular topic; and this misfortune necessarily affects, in large degree, our scholastic institutions, which aim rather to rear politicians, than to send forth profound scholars and men devoted to the sublimer studies of the race. I do not know that the S. C. College is doing any thing in the way of Oriental Literature. Preston is *hors de combat,* or nearly so — the wreck (physically) of his former self. Lieber is a worker

---

[100] Hodgson (1801-1871), born at Georgetown, D. C., was a protegé of Henry Clay and held diplomatic posts in Algiers, Constantinople, Egypt, and Tunis. In May, 1842, he married Margaret Telfair, of Savannah, Ga., where he resided for the remainder of his life except for trips to Europe and New York. He is said to have been master of thirteen languages and to have spoken nine fluently, his favorite being the Berber of the Barbary States. He was the author of various books and articles on Africa and the Near East. For an account of his life see Leonard L. Mackall, "William Brown Hodgson," *Georgia Historical Quarterly,* XV (Dec., 1931), 324-345. Simms' letter to him is addressed to 19 Brevoort Place, New York City.

[101] Dated by Simms' suggestion of Sir Austen Henry Layard's *Nineveh and Its Remains,* 2 vols. (New York: G. P. Putnam, 1849), as a subject for review in the *Southern Quarterly Review.* The Rev. Patrick N. Lynch reviewed the work in the Oct., 1849, issue (see note 134, July 14, 1849).

& a thinker, but he does not seem to carry much patriotism into his toils, and seeks rather to perform his duties, than to go beyond them under the impulse of a generous enthusiasm.[102] It was one of my suggestions, several years ago, that our College should be elevated into an university. Preston, I learn, has this desire also. But some of the Professors object, even to the introduction of the Continental languages. A Professorship of Oriental Literature, might well take the place of that *nominally* devoted to Sacred Literature. *Our Review* may be made the instrument for urging the subject before the public mind. When we shall inform *that,* we compel the legislation of the country. But that's the initial process. — I doubt if the college has sent out a single other mind than that of Mr. Miles,[103] to whom Oriental Lit[erature] is any thing but an echo or a sound unmeaning, and of no sort of importance. Yet the subject is daily opening, more & more grandly upon us. A review of Layard's Nineveh would afford the proper provocation to an article, which, while treating of the resources of the East, — still open & newly opening to the scholar — would dwell sternly, and appeal earnestly on the subject of our educational deficiencies. I wish that you could be persuaded to an analysis of this interesting work, having a view to this two-fold object. It will give me great pleasure to hear from you always, as well *personally,* as in the character of Reviewer. I shall take leave to send your letter to Mr. Miles for perusal. As a young man, compliments, such as yours, will give him pleasure, & furnish encouragement.

With great respect &
very truly Yours &c

W. Gilmore Simms

---

[102] Francis Lieber was professor of history and political economy at the South Carolina College (see note 51, June 17, 1842). The *South Carolinian* (Columbia) of Feb. 2, 1849, reports: "The friends of . . . [William Campbell Preston] will be gratified to learn, that he is so far recovered from his recent illness, as to indulge the hope that he will be shortly able to start on a brief tour to the South-West for the restoration of his health. We understand that Professor Lieber has been appointed President *pro tempore* during his absence." Preston resigned the presidency of the College in May, 1850 (see the Charleston *Mercury* of May 15). This resignation was shortly withdrawn, but on Nov. 26, 1851, he again submitted his resignation, which was accepted.

[103] James Warley Miles. See introductory sketch of the Miles brothers.

488: To Nathaniel Beverley Tucker [104]

Woodlands, S. C. May 13. [1849][105]

My dear Sir:

I have just recieved and read the concluding portion of your paper on Macaulay. My only regret is that it is not something longer. You have probably touched upon all of the points of provocation which the historian has afforded you, but in writing for our farmer population of the South, it might be well also to embody a condensed view of the history itself. To Mr. Educated Gentleman of the country, you have said all that is necessary, and I have no doubt that a warm and grateful echo will everywhere be heard from among them. But our masses require something more, and a review in all countries now occupies a twofold position. It acts as a tribunal of criticism and as a summary of history. It embodies usually a general view of the whole subject. Your review I could not wish altered. It could hardly be improved, unless by extending it, and, with this object we could have given you a dozen more pages, which I feel sure you could have filled most happily. Do me the favor hereafter to remember this. We must not assume too much for our populations. It is one of the defects of the South that our people — even the professional men — read too little. This very history of Macaulay, though sent forth in the cheapest possible form, will very slowly find its way to our interior. Hundreds of our lawyers for example, take reviews in order to escape the necessity of going through the volumes which form their texts, and to secure ready made opinions upon their subjects. We have to provide for these, and make the review a sort of general library as well as Journal of Criticism. Wherever, therefore, the two objects can be compassed, it is always well to attempt it. This suggestion is thrown out respectfully for your consideration in future essays, but not with any desire of prescribing to you. On the contrary, — you must not suppose from what I have here said that I am not perfectly satisfied with what you have done. I am very sure that none of our friends to whom I could have entrusted the subject, would have handled it with half the ease, spirit and confidence, with

---

[104] The original of this letter, in the Archives of Colonial Williamsburg, has been misplaced. Our transcript is from a copy made by Professor Percy W. Turrentine, who is at work on a biography of Tucker.

[105] Dated by Simms' reference to his having received the concluding portion of Tucker's "Macaulay's History of England."

which you have reviewed it. To those, in the South, who have read, or who will read, Macaulay, your analysis is all that could be required. It is only in my desire to consider the wants of those who do not read him, and yet read us, that I could have wished some ten pages given to a close summary of the leading, or transition points, in the history. But the essential matter has been effected by your Review, that, namely, of suggesting the shortcomings of the Historian along with his merits, and of generalizing from his pages with regard to our claims and conditions. You have not kept my pace with my humble career as an author, or you would not have thought it necessary to attempt to persuade me that it is our duty to carry the attack into the enemy's country. The Yankee critics have long since denounced me as the bitter enemy of New England; and a review in the Southern Quarterly, to which in a late letter I requested your attention,[106] will satisfy you that so far as I am concerned, the Philistines may be smitten hip & thigh, without my interposition. Whether a greater degree of caution, on the part of the Review, as a mere question of policy, having in sight the petty whims of the Subscription List, would not be advisable, is a question rather for the publisher than the Editor. I see nothing in what you have written that I would not freely have written (as I feel the whole sentiment) myself. You refer to Bancroft. I was on the eve of indicating his history (under the provocation of the fourth volume, which is announced with the usual Yankee flourishes) as a subject which you would probably like to handle.[107] Hammond will be a famous bottle holder in every such conflict. General Jamison is an amiable gentleman who writes sensibly and is with us, heart & soul, in this very matter, but he is slow, and has numerous household cares which distract his mind. I have been trying to get a paper on Social Life in South Carolina prior to the Revolution. One such on Life in Virginia would enable you to discuss the relative merits of North & South, & thus supply that most important portion of a history which is usually left unwritten. Let me hear from you at your first leisure, and (with many thanks) believe me to be

                    Very faithfully your obliged friend &c.
                    W. Gilmore Simms.

---

[106] "South Carolina in the Revolution." See letter to Tucker of May 6, 1849.
[107] The fourth volume of George Bancroft's *A History of the United States, from the Discovery of the American Continent* was finally published by Little, Brown and Co., Boston, in 1852.

P. S. Much curiosity is usually manifested to know the authors of the several articles. Have you any objection that your article should close with your signature? It would certainly secure its being read by everybody here. It was one of the evil results of the former Yankee Editorship, that it gave admission to everything, of whatever character, by which the pages could be filled with little trouble to the Editor. This greatly disparaged the character of the work, & led to a disregard of all the papers which could not be traced to a creditable origin. Hammond, for example, writes me that he reads nothing in [it] unless assured by a knowledge of the writer. In referring to Macaulay's letter to the American publishers, I could wish that you would prepare a note to the comment in your text, embodying these suggestions: — that really it signifies nothing more than a somewhat too haughty indifference, on the part of this author, in respect to his American readers.[108] Recieving his pay from the publishers, he is careless of the rest; and in penning this note to them, he simply expresses himself in a manner quite too British, wherever America is the subject, and which, with a Briton, is rather habitual than intentional. The least that Mr. M. could have done was to declare his *preference*, with regard to the orthography of the American edition, while submitting to the American publishers to spell after their own fashion. His tone is only an additional proof of that low esteem to which the lack of personal character in our Yankee representatives, has so much reduced the national character. I submit this with all deference. You will act as you please in the matter, though I am of opinion that such a note will tend to strip the publishers of any advantages which they might have had, by the assumption that Macaulay's note was a sanction of the liberties which they have taken with his English.

489: To Nathaniel Beverley Tucker

Hon. B. Tucker.   Charleston May 29. [1849][109]
dear Sir

I have just put up a bundle for you — which shall be forwarded to the care of Mr. Crump [110] as soon as possible — con-

---

[108] See pp. 405ff. of Tucker's article.

[109] Dated by Simms' reference to reading Tucker's "Macaulay's History of England" in print.

[110] William W. Crump (1819-1897) studied law under Tucker at the College of William and Mary and became one of his most devoted disciples. He later practiced law in Richmond and was for a short time a judge.

taining as many of my volumes as I could lay hands on. There are several wanting, and some of these among the best of my performances. Among these are — Confession or the Blind Heart 2 vols — Richard Hurdis 2 vols; The Kinsmen 2 vols. and perhaps half a dozen others. As I succeed in supplying the deficiencies, it will gratify me to forward them to your address. I do not know that I should desire you to read the things which I have sent you. I feel all their feeblenesses and crudenesses. They were written most of them at an extremely early age, & under the pressure of necessities which left me too careless of any but present & momentary considerations. You will find them wanting in symmetry and finish, and grossly disfigured by errors of taste and judgment. If you discover in them proofs of original force, native character, and some imagination, it will be due chiefly perhaps to the industry with which you grope through much that is tedious, and offensive. But I must not fall into the folly of endeavouring to excuse in manhood the offenses which youth has had the hardihood to commit. I must only undergo the usual penalties of rashness, satisfied if a late repentance & the hope of better performances in future may tend to soften the severities of punishment. — I have just finished reading your article on Macaulay *in print*. I am happy to say it grows upon me. Though greatly pleased with it at first, I feel its points much more impresively upon a second perusal, reading it altogether. I was in error in my estimate of its length. It will fill at least 10 more pages of our work than I had expected.

> Very faithfully and
> respectfully.
> Yr. friend &c
>
> W. Gilmore Simms.

490: To Nathaniel Beverley Tucker

Charleston S. C. June 1, 1849.

Hon. Beverly Tucker

My dear Sir:

Is there any possibility of finding a text for a delineation of social life in Virginia prior to the Revolution, and how would you relish such a subject. The pleasant book of Col. Byrd, — the

Westover MS.S.[111] might afford you genial provocation to an article in which while delineating the domestic aspects of a community, you could elevate moral description, and discussion, by an occasional biography. Pray think over this. I was not aware that you had handled Bancroft before, & can readily understand the distaste which you would feel at the necessity of approaching him again.[112] Perhaps it might be well to suggest to me some of the topics which commend themselves to you, and I would advise you if any of them are already in hand. I do not see that you need any new work of Carlyle to make him a legitimate subject of review. The only misfortune, in our respect, is, that the previous Editor, Whitaker, has suffered the subject to be gnawed by some of his pups, and has made it stale accordingly.[113] The freshness of your treatment of it, would atone for all this, could the great body of readers undertake the Essay. With your initials they probably would; and the new Editions of Carlyle, from the presses of Harper & Brothers, and John Wiley, would give a sufficient caption. Be assured that I shall regard no topic as old, which you will undertake to discuss anew. — Vanity Fair would afford you exercise for 8 or 10 pages in print. You are safe there from interference.[114]

The Review shall be sent you, including the paper to which I referred you. — Care shall be taken to forward the copies to England as you direct, and with the autograph. In the single instance, the present number, I desire to use the full names of all the contributors (where they consent) — after that, the initials. We have to bring *authority* to bear in the endeavor to recover the lost credit of the work, which has but too frequently been filled with the most wretched drivel. — I put up a bundle of my literary offences for you & sent them to my agent to be forwarded. But he tells me that the Express is no longer in existence, and we have no direct business intercourse between the two cities. He proposes to send it via Baltimore. Have you any friend in that city to whose care it may be addressed. Or perhaps you may advise me of some more direct means of communica-

---

[111] William Byrd's *The Westover Manuscripts,* ed. Edmund Ruffin, was published by E. and J. C. Ruffin, Petersburg, Va., in 1841.

[112] Tucker reviewed the first volume of Bancroft's *History* somewhat savagely in *S. L. M.,* I (June, 1835), 587-591.

[113] An unsigned article entitled "Carlyle's Works" was published in XIV (July, 1848), 77-101.

[114] Tucker wrote on none of these subjects.

tion. — I find you closed your epistle nervously. I feel that I have written mine sleepily — much wearied & scarcely knowing what I am about. You percieve that I am now in Charleston. Please address me in that city.

Very faithfully Yours &c

W. Gilmore Simms

491: To Marcus Claudius Marcellus Hammond

[June, 1849][115]

My dear Major

Your brother knows nothing from me on the subject of the article. My only reason for suggesting that you should confide to him, arose from the notion that his attention would be drawn to the article when printed, from the knowledge that you had the subject in contemplation, and that he might then recognize. Besides, I could tell him the authorship of all else, and must evade in regard to this. So far from having told him anything, I have rather mystified him in respect to yourself, by expressing my regrets that your laziness would keep you from fulfilling your promises in respect to this very subject.[116] But in truth, your secret has been very carelessly guarded at home. I met Mr. Oates, your Augusta bookseller,[117] who coolly informed me that you had been or were writing for the Review! I treated the information slightly by saying you were too fond of your ease, I feared, to do anything in the shape of work! There! Do with your secret as you please but don't *suspicion* me. At all events, choose a nom de plume, upon which I can father the article. Take some dead soldier's name in vain. — And now for other matters. It is too late to strike off any extra copies for you. The article is already printed. You should have spoken sooner. It is struck off sheet by sheet, 12 pages at a time, and we should

---

[115] Since Simms here refers to six articles of the July, 1849, issue of the *Southern Quarterly Review* being printed, this letter (which bears no postmark) was probably written early in June. M. C. M. Hammond's article discussed herein is "The Conquest of California, and the Case of Lieut. Col. Fremont" (see letter to M. C. M. Hammond of Feb. 22, 1849).

[116] In a letter to Simms of June 4, 1849, James H. Hammond refers to two unlocated letters from Simms: "I have not answered the first of your two last letters. . . . Your second letter I received today." (Original in the Hammond Papers, Library of Congress.) It is doubtless one of these two letters that Simms here refers to.

[117] George A. Oates and Co., Broad Street, Augusta, Ga., dealt in music and musical instruments, books, and stationery.

know what is wanted, in the way of extras, before a single sheet is printed. Again, it is quite too late to make alterations or additions to an article when reading the proofs. If a word is to be put in, another word must come out to give it place, or the whole of the *form,* 12 pages, must be overrun. This increases fearfully the expense of printing. I have read the proof very carefully. I think the article will satisfy you. I have freely altered passages, in respect to mere style, and so as to avoid *involutions,* which is the great defect in your composition. I have changed neither the order nor the ideas of your argument & statement. I have gone over the article as if it were my own, & trust that you will find no reason to regret that it is yours. I hope you are going on with the sequel.[118] Do that carefully. Draw out your argument, arrange your facts in sequence, and then amplify & put it into narrative. We have now six articles printed — viz. 1 North & South. J.H.H. 2. Tract on Church & state by J. W. Miles. 3. Fine Arts in America by T. S. Piggott of Balto. 5 Macaulay's England, by B. Tucker; 4. Justice & Fraternity, by Mrs. McCord. 6 Conquest of California & Case of Fremont, by M.C.M.H. 7. Study of Botany. 8. Capt. Blakely & the U. S. Sloop of War Wasp. 9. — So for our list.[119] I thank you for your efforts in my

[118] "California." See note 28, Feb. 22, 1849.

[119] The titles, signatures, and authors of the articles in the July, 1849, issue of *S. Q. R.,* XV, are as follows:
1. "The North and the South," pp. 273-311. Unsigned, but by James H. Hammond.
2. "The Union of Church and State," pp. 311-333. Signed "J. W. M." (James Warley Miles).
3. "The Fine Arts in America," pp. 333-355. Unsigned, but by Thomas S. Piggott. Piggott (1829-1868) was a journalist and later, during 1860-1862, editor of the Baltimore daily newspaper, the *South.*
4. "Justice and Fraternity," pp. 356-374. Signed "L. S. M." (Louisa S. Cheves McCord).
5. "Macaulay's History of England," pp. 374-410. Unsigned, but by Nathaniel Beverley Tucker.
6. "The Conquest of California, and the Case of Lieut. Col. Fremont," pp. 410-444. Unsigned, but by M. C. M. Hammond.
7. "Genera Florae Americae Boreali — Orientalis Illustrata," pp. 444-448. Signed "C. W." (possibly the Rev. C. Wallace, listed among the contributors in *S. Q. R.,* N. S., VIII [July, 1853]).
8. "The Fate of the Wasp Sloop-of-War," pp. 449-460. Signed "J. J." (Joseph Johnson?).
9. "Barhydt's Industrial Exchanges," pp. 460-483. Signed "D. J. M." (David James McCord).
10. "Later Poems of Henry Taylor," pp. 484-526. Signed "S." (Simms).
11. "Monograph of the Fossil Squalidae of the United States," pp. 526-531. Signed "L." (Oscar Montgomery Lieber). Lieber (1830-1862) was the son of Francis Lieber and a promising geologist.
12. "Critical Notices," pp. 532-544. Unsigned, but by Simms. In a letter to Simms of July 9 J. H. Hammond says: "Your review of Taylor is evidently

favor. If I am not sanguine, I do not despond. That is not in my
nature. I am a patient waiter upon Providence, and one who
seldom grumbles even though he waits in vain. *Can* Toombs do
much? [120] If Taylor means to do any thing for his Taylor Democrats, I suppose I am as little objectionable as anybody that could
be mentioned. Excuse the hurry of th[is scrawl. I] have scarcely
got [*remainder of letter cut.*]

492: To Robert Wilson Gibbes [121]

[July? 1849][122]

dear Sir

I am in reciept of your paper on Tuomey for which I am obliged
to you. It will appear in the October issue. Is there any friend in
Charleston to whom you would wish the proofsheets sent for
revision?

Very respectfully
Yr obliged Sert. &c

W. Gilmore Simms

Professor R. W. Gibbes.

---

not an effort & was written I suspect for the last number, to fill up. It is
perhaps more in the genuine style of a review than is common nowadays,
being a mere criticism of the author illustrated by quotations & a synopsis of
the works. The fashionable style of writing Essays for a Review is in truth
a fraud upon the Magazines to which they ought to be sent. The article is
agreeable & interesting & good in its line — which is a good line, but you have
not said much on your own hook. I thought better of Tucker's article than you
did. It is full of good things & to be sure no body wields so keen a pen as he
does. I have written him in a very complimentary manner & you should do so
to the extent you can to retain him as a Contributor. You will have none better.
McCord's article is full of common-place trash & is enough to make a man
disgorge who has waded through the tomes we have on Free Trade. . . . His
wife's article has one good idea — tho' not a new one — & perhaps not a true
one, that a civilized world cannot fall back. . . . I am sorry to be so un-
gallant to so fine [a] lady & to differ so much from you as to think the balance
of the article that is hers is mere stuff — puerile declamation not above common
stump oratory." (Original in the Hammond Papers, Library of Congress.)

[120] Robert Toombs (1810-1885) was later secretary of state of the Confederacy and a brigadier general in the Confederate Army. At this time he was
a member of Congress from Georgia, and had promised M. C. M. Hammond
to aid Simms in securing a diplomatic post. James H. Hammond was
skeptical, and on June 4 wrote to Simms: "Toombs might do much for you
but I doubt whether he will tho' he promised the Major. I have no faith in
any politicians." (Original in the Hammond Papers, Library of Congress.)

[121] See introductory sketch.

[122] Dated by Simms' reference to Gibbes' article on Michael Tuomey's *Report on the Geology of South Carolina* (Columbia, S. C.: A. S. Johnston,
1848), published in *S. Q. R.*, XVI (Oct., 1849), 161-178.

493 : To James Lawson

Charleston July 3. 1849

My dear Lawson

My wife has been for some two months at me to forward to yours some of her petty handiwork, wrought by herself for the use of your little Mary; but I have been telling her that I have no reason to suppose that James Lawson cares to hear from me again. However, really standing in need of the play of "The Man of the People" and desiring that you should cover and send to Louis A. Godey Esq. in Phila. the two MS. Letters descriptive of the South, which I had sent to Duyckinck,[123] I once more send you a scribblement, doubtful of its fate. I suppose you have procured from Forrest the M.S. Play. There can be no reason why you should not, and with the delay to do so, there is necessarily some danger of its loss. This, if you have procured, I will thank you to seal up carefully to my address, call or send to J. W. Harper, and ask him to forward it carefully, under wax & twine, in the next package forwarded to me (care of J. Russell, Charleston) by his House. I do not know whether you have heard any tidings of W. C. Forbes and of the dramatic MS. I lent him.[124] If that has been recieved, cover it in with the other MS. I am almost cut off from all my sources of information in New York. You have failed me as a correspondent, Richards [125] has failed me, Duyckinck has failed me &c. The latter has not only failed me, as a Correspondent, but seems to have failed me entirely as a friend. His notice of Atalantis seems to have been a painstaking effort to say as little & speak as coldly as possible.[126] But I can readily detect the source & secret of his position. I sincerely hope that during this cholera prevalence, you keep your family out of the city. Tell your wife that if she had not failed me also, you would probably not have forgotten me. Where are you all now? I presume at Bergen Point. Here we are still in the enjoyment of the most singular health. With the exception of a few days, our weather has been cool and pleasant. It is now breezy in high degree after some grateful showers, — cool enough,

---

[123] See note 204, c. Dec. 19, 1848.

[124] "Benedict Arnold." See letter to Lawson of Nov. 28, 1848.

[125] T. Addison Richards.

[126] Duyckinck's review of *Atalantis* in the *Literary World,* IV (May 19, 1849), 434, is short, though complimentary.

were it night, to be sleeping with a blanket. I am busy with the Review — have just published our July number which is thought a very good one, — and am preparing that for October as rapidly as possible. It keeps me busy. Even the correspondence of the work is the business of an ordinary man. I have written to H. & B. touching a Book I desire to publish, but am doubtful whether the times will justify the attempt.[127] Business in N. Y. must suffer greatly under the present dispensation. I am curious & anxious touching the affair of Forrest & his wife. Is there no reconciliation — any prospect of it. Has any thing transpired to account for it. Surely, F. cannot, through mere whim & caprice, have discarded her? He is required to account to Society for such a proceeding. And what does she say? Is it a mutual willingness? — Do you see young Boggs. I am told that he has improved wonderfully, and certainly has it in him. Bryant, I see, has gone to Europe again. A fortunate man. What of him & Wetmore? — Tell your wife that her namesake is fat, forward & flourishing, considered quite a surprising fellow; glib of tongue and full of consequence, like herself; very fair, with light brown, almost auburn hair, big blue eyes, and fair fresh cheeks — a mouth & chin like mine, and a nose like Augusta's, rather too small for character. Say to Jimmy that Gilly has just brought home a great medal about his neck, one of his school trophies. He is a great wild boy, always racing about the yard when not in school, and tall with little flesh upon his bones. A rough, hardy dog. The baby is doing well — now nearly seven months old, with, probably the best head & face of all my children. Give my love to your wife & a kiss for her & the children; and believe though you all forget me, you are all unforgotten.

W. G. S.

---

[127] Possibly this is a volume of poetry.

494: To Joseph Lemuel Chester [128]

[*c.* July 9, 1849][129]

Jos L. Chester Esq.

dear Sir:

I have suffered your friendly letter to lie by me for some time in consequence of the rather heavy duties which I have recently undertaken in the assumption of the Editorial duties of the Southern Quarterly Review; but I have not been forgetful of your courtesy. I greatly thank you for the interest you have in the Scripture poems, & do not suffer any annoyance from the failure of your attempt to serve me in respect to them.[130] I am not sure that you are wrong in your notion of the difficulties in the way of poetical publications, but I still doubt whether you are right. The great difficulty in the way of Am. publishers — or one of the great difficulties, — seems to lie in the fact they themselves are incapable of judgment upon the books they publish. They are thus in the hands of selfish little individuals, or of little cliques just as selfish, and never know where they are until they pay the penalties. Our literary reputations depend so much upon the same causes (which are continually fluctuating) that few of them last a year. — I shall be very glad to hear from you — more glad to see you — & if I go North this year, taking Phil. *en route,*

---

[128] Chester (1821-1882) was at this time living in Philadelphia, where he spent the business hours in a counting room on Market Street, his spare time with literature and music. Since 1843 he had been publishing poems in the *Knickerbocker* and in *Godey's* under the pseudonym of "Julian Cramer." He later worked on the Philadelphia *Inquirer* and the *Daily Sun,* and after 1858 resided in England, where he gained the reputation of one of the leading genealogists of his day. Perhaps "Alice" of this letter is a pseudonym for (or of?) his wife, Catherine Hendrickson Hubbard Chester, whom he had married in 1839.

[129] On the back of this letter Chester wrote: "W. Gilmore Simms Charleston, S. C. July 12/49." If this is the date on which Chester received Simms' letter, it was probably written *c.* July 9.

[130] *Sabbath Lyrics; or, Songs from Scripture. A Christmas Gift of Love* (Charleston: From the Press of Walker and James, 1849) was published in Dec. (see note 252, Dec. 24, 1849). It is dedicated to "My Wife and the Mother of my Children." Several of the poems included appeared in *Godey's* during 1848 and 1849 under the heading of "Sabbath Lyrics": XXXVII (Oct., Nov., and Dec., 1848), 200, 307, 346; XXXVIII (June, 1849), 376; XXXIX (Aug., Oct., and Dec., 1849), 127, 240, 375. Other poems published by Simms in *Godey's* during this same period are "The Prophecy of Napoleon," XXXVII (July, 1848), 5; "Apostrophe to the Sea," XXXVIII (Jan., 1849), 41-42; "Saul's Last Battle," XXXVIII (Feb., 1849), 83-84; "The Rebellion of Absalom," XXXVIII (March, 1849), 191-192; "Francesca da Rimini," XXXVIII (April, 1849), 243-244; and "Saul at Endor," XXXIX (Nov., 1849), 311-312.

I shall most probably enjoy that pleasure. My best respects to
our fair friend 'Alice', whom I should gladly know more nearly.

Very truly Yours,

W. Gilmore Simms.

495: To Nathaniel Beverley Tucker

Charleston July 13. 1849.

Hon. Beverly Tucker.

dear Sir

I do not hear from you. I trust that you have not tired of
the toils in which you have begun so admirably. Your paper on
Macaulay has given great satisfaction in our quarter. Hammond
writes to me of it with great zest, and I find that nobody feels the
lack of that analysis of the whole history, to which I was perhaps
disposed to attach too much importance. In fact, the book, from
the number & cheapness of the editions, has passed so generally
into the hands of the public, that an analysis seems unnecessary.
I still think that, under ordinary circumstances, and in regard to
the greater number of works published, such a general review
of the materials of the work is advisable. With respect to Macaulay, however, you did all that was important in seizing upon, &
applying yourself to those points which were most important in
application to our own society. You, perhaps, have seen that some
of the English Reviews are down upon M. for alledged unfaith-
fulnesses in his record. Party, doubtless, has some thing to do
with this. Personal grudges (as in the case of Croker's Review)[131]
were also at work in the melancholy work of marshalling &
dwelling upon defects — but still, I suppose we must allow that
M. himself is a partisan — unavoidably — and has had his social
& political bias to sustain. He is doubtless more likely to have
erred in his *atmosphere,* than in the absolute statement of details;
and it is in the essayical portions of his history, and seeing
through a certain medium, that he has, I take for granted, unconsciously — wandered something wide of the truth in his social
delineations. I am still disposed to think his portrait of the
planting aristocracy of Engd. an exaggerated one. But, the reader

---

131 For an account of this review and its composition, see Myron F. Bright-
field, *John Wilson Croker* (Berkeley, California: University of California
Press, 1940), pp. 368-377.

of history, — at all familiar with it — will probably know, in stinctively, w[h]ere to interpose his doubts, — and to qualify the offensive traits of the picture. — I have had the copies — with your autograph put up for Europe. It will give me pleasure to address in other quarters, any other copies, should you desire them. — I greatly regret that as yet no opportunity has offered for sending the packet with my own small wares to your address. It has been for some time in the hands of the publisher for transmission. No express now runs between Richmond & Charleston. Can you give me the name of any person in Baltimore, to whom I may forward the bundle & from whom you might recieve it promptly? It is such a mass that one scruples about placing it in the hands of the private traveller — even where such is to be found bound to the Old Dominion. — Let me repeat that it will give me great pleasure to hear from you, whether as a Correspondent of the Review or of

Yours very faithfully &c.

W. Gilmore Simms

496: To William Porcher Miles [132]

Charleston July 14. 1849.

My dear Professor.

You are busy *orationing* I hear.[133] I pity you. I have declined no less than three such honorable tasks this year, for as many colleges & societies. But it is more in your way, and you have to go through a certain probation. It will do you no harm. Touching the article, I am so anxious to have you in our October issue, that I will strive to keep a space for you, but hardly of 40 pages print. I trust you mean MS. when you mention this number. I like your subject and am glad that it grows upon you. That is the true secret of all good thinking. If you can be ready for me

---

[132] See introductory sketch of the Miles brothers.

[133] Miles had delivered an oration before the Fourth of July Association in Charleston. Published by James S. Burges, it is reviewed by Simms in *S. Q. R.,* XVI (Oct., 1849), 257-258: "His oration, with a full knowledge of history, was marked by a parallel between the principles governing our revolutionary action, and the history which is most pressing upon us in the progress of present times. He speaks the sentiment of a large portion of the South . . . when he declares the indignant conviction that we have no longer any constitutional securities upon which to rely."

by the 15th August, I shall prefer it greatly.[134] To tell you the truth, I am already full of matter from various hands, but I desire something more of a choice, and am anxious to bring out as many Charlestonians as I can. You will be pleased to learn that I have brought into the field many whom it will not discredit our best writers to commune with. If the work were only on a good pecuniary footing so that it might pay contributors, I should be able to make it whatever we desired. — Atalantis, you will see, is rewritten entirely.[135] You might be interested to compare it with the old Edition.

Yours faithfully &c

W. Gilmore Simms

Professor Miles.

[134] The titles, signatures, and authors of the articles in the Oct., 1849, issue of *S. Q. R.*, XVI, are as follows:

1. "Nineveh and Its Remains," pp. 1-31. Signed "L." (Patrick N. Lynch).
2. "Free School System in South Carolina," pp. 31-53. Signed "P." (Frederick Adolphus Porcher). For Porcher, see note 213, c. Nov. 1, 1849.
3. "Histoire des Girondins: par A. DeLamartine," pp. 53-76. Signed "J." (David F. Jamison).
4. "Œuvres des Spinoza," pp. 76-81. Signed "M." (William Porcher Miles).
5. "California," pp. 82-115. Signed "H." (M. C. M. Hammond).
6. "The Philosophy of the Beautiful," pp. 115-138. Unsigned, but by James Warley Miles.
7. "The Right to Labor," pp. 138-160. Signed "L. S. M." (Louisa S. Cheves McCord).
8. "Report on the Geology of South-Carolina," pp. 161-178. Signed "R. W. G." (Robert Wilson Gibbes).
9. "Characteristics of Alabama," pp. 178-205. Signed "B. F. P." (Benjamin Fanueil Porter). Porter (1808-1868), born in Charleston, was admitted to the bar at Charleston in 1825. In 1828 he moved to Chesterville (now Chester), S. C., and in 1830 to Monroe County, Ala. He later settled in Tuscaloosa, was a member of the legislature, and was elected a judge. He returned to South Carolina in 1850. He died in Greenville, Ala., in 1868.
10. "El Buscapié" pp. 205-223. Signed "J. L. R." (James L. Reynolds).
11. "Recent American Poets," pp. 224-232. Unsigned, but by Simms.
12. "Critical Notices," pp. 233-272. Fifty-four unsigned notices by Simms. Of this number Hammond wrote to Simms on Oct. 28: "The last Review is a fine no. — great variety & many excellent articles. Porcher's & Reynolds I think the best in style. Both the Miles write well (by the by *I* can define the 'beautiful'). The major's article is a decided improvement on the last & very fair. Nineveh is beneath the subject. I wish Tucker had handled it. It has glorious points which he would have brought out with unction. Jamison is respectable — like himself. I don't compare yours with the rest — you alone shew the veteran. But by the Lord, if you touch off 54 subjects every quarter, what will you leave for your correspondents?" (Original in the Hammond Papers, Library of Congress.)

[135] The Charleston *Courier* of April 10 carries a review of *Atalantis*, signed "G. E. W.": "Indefatigable Simms! we hail thee with pleasure. Again thine active and busy imagination has given to us more beautiful thoughts. Thou standst ever at Apollo's lathe, and turnest there unwearingly. . . .

"Mr. Simms is not fully appreciated, we believe, particularly in our Southern land. . . . [His] poems ought to be in every library . . . he ranks almost as high as any living American poet."

497: To NATHANIEL BEVERLEY TUCKER

Charleston July 14. 1849.

My dear Sir

Growing impatient to hear from you again, it was only yesterday that I despatched to you a hurried scrawl, — and the next mail brought me your letter, which, addressed to me at my country Post town, necessarily took a circuitous route in reaching me here, where I am quartered for the summer. I am exceedingly mortified to see the Errata you furnish. I may mention that the Review has been badly managed & that we are now by degrees endeavouring to correct past mistakes. The publisher, a worthy man, is in feeble health, liable to sudden caprices of condition which make him almost incapable of those tasks which belong properly to him. Among these were proofreading. My own eyes have made me reluctant to undertake this duty. It will be my care to do something toward ensuring you a correct press hereafter. I am not sure that the copies have been yet forwarded to Europe. They were sent to an agent in the city for the purpose of transmission. If not already forwarded, I will make the corrections which you indicate. — Nobody regrets more than myself that you should ever be anticipated in your choice of subjects, when writing for the Review. Successful reviewing really depends so much upon writing *con amore,* that it were desirable always to be able to assert a preference in one's topics. I beg that you will not suspect me of any unbecoming or unreal profession when I assure you that I should gladly give you a first choice of subjects, writing for the Review, over all other contributors. It is therefore with a peculiar feeling of annoyance that I find you disposed to Layard's Nineveh. That subject is in the hands of the Rev. Dr. Lynch, of this City, a very clever priest of the Catholic Church, from whom I expect the article every day.[136] I know that he has it in progress. — What remains? Can any thing be done with Lynch's expedition? [137] — Will not this

---

[136] Patrick Neilson Lynch (1817-1882) was made vicar-general in 1850, bishop of Charleston in 1858. In 1863 he went to Rome bearing a letter from Jefferson Davis to Pope Pius IX, expressing the desire of the Confederacy for peace. His contribution to the *Southern Quarterly Review,* here mentioned, is signed "L." and is entitled "Nineveh and Its Remains," XVI (Oct., 1849), 1-31. The subject had originally been offered to William Brown Hodgson (see letter to Hodgson of May 9, 1849).

[137] Of William Francis Lynch's *Narrative of the United States Expedition to the River Jordan and the Dead Sea* (Philadelphia: Lea and Blanchard, 1849) Simms says in *S. Q. R.,* XVI (Oct., 1849), 233: "We are far from

suffice, as a text for enabling you to dilate in the same strain of reflection which you suggest as appropriate to the case of Nineveh — nay, will it not enable you to refer to Nineveh incidentally? You will not find it difficult to effect the necessary transitions from topic to topic, justifying these general conditions which illustrate human society equally in each. — It is not very easy, — not knowing the course of one's reading or reflection, — to suggest subjects for review. I spoke of Bancroft.[138] Have you seen Ingersoll's very strange medley miscalled a History of the Late War.[139] Is that in your way at all? Hotch pot as it is, it yet contains much that is provocative. There is a good text, in the details which he gives (with some unction too) of the malignant & miserably selfish course of New England during the War of 1812, for such a picture of the sectional character, as will almost make them turn in loathing from the presentment. — Pray give me a list of the topics to which you incline, that I may always interpose to prevent others from undertaking them. This might be done, on the mere annunciation of a Book, even before its publication be undertaken, or the work recieved in the country.

> Very faithfully though hurriedly,
> Yr obliged friend &c

> W. Gilmore Simms.

Hon B. Tucker.

P. S. Thinking that you may desire to use it elswhere, I return to you the fragment of the article on Guizot, repeating my sincere regret that you have been forestalled in our pages by one who has taken a different view of the subject from that to which you evidently incline.[140] There is no doubt of the truth of the distinction which you make between Guizot as the statesman & the political philosopher.

---

satisfied with the narrative of Lieutenant Lynch. He . . . has been unwisely ambitious of authorship, and has made his volume unnecessarily cumbrous and heavy. . . ."

138 See letters to Tucker of May 13 and June 1, 1849.

139 Of Charles J. Ingersoll's *Historical Sketch of the Second War Between the United States of America, and Great Britain,* 2 vols. (Philadelphia: Lea and Blanchard, 1845-1849), Simms says in *S. Q. R.,* XVI (Oct., 1849), 255-256: "Mr. Ingersoll was held a very good writer when he published his Inchiquin Letters. Nobody will impute this merit to him now. His career in Congress has spoiled all his grace as a writer . . . in spite of bad style, and a crude arrangement of materials, these volumes are essential additions to our historical collections. . . ."

140 Simms, himself, was the author of "Guizot's Democracy in France." See note 47, *c.* Feb. 25, 1849.

498: To Nathaniel Beverley Tucker

Charleston July 27. [1849][141]

dear Sir.

Do not be confounded if I some day put your letters into print. They are quite too racy to be locked up selfishly in any single keeping. I shall certainly put them away in the conviction that my executors will find them when I shall be unable to estop them in their progress to the press. [Let me thank yo]u for your com[p]liment[ary remarks upon my pa]per on Tay[lor.[142] It] was a h[astily written ma]tter, as I usually write *stan*[*s pe*]*de* [*in un*]*o,* and disfigure[d] by numerous defects & errors, the equal result of my own carelessness and of the blunders of the printers. By some mischance, it happens to be most carelessly printed of all the articles in the number. At present I am doing little in my proper person towards filling our pages. My object is to secure a steady and sterling corps of contributors upon whom we can always rely, and this desire imposes on me an extensive correspondence. Are you able to give me any names of persons in Virginia to whom I might refer? — I esteem Hammond very much as you do, and deem it unfortunate that I shall have nothing from him in our next. He is now engaged in preparing orations for the anniversaries of two Societies, one Literary & the other ind[us]trial.[143] This keeps him bu[s]y, and I dare not complain [s]in[ce m]y pe[r]sua[sion] chiefly did [result in his] taking up these tas[ks. He will p]robably furnish a paper fo[r Ja]ny[.[144] I] happened to meet with the Rev. Mr. Miles just after recieving your Letter & did not scruple to read him the passage which relates to himself. The mixed draught of praise and censure was drunk as a pleasant medicine, for which he is grateful. — The article on the Fine Arts [145] was by a Dr. Piggott of Balto, of whom I know nothing. I found him one of the contributors under the old regime. I hope that you will seize an early occasion to give your views in relation to the fine

---

[141] Dated by Simms' reference to the contents of the Oct., 1849, issue of the *Southern Quarterly Review* (see note 134, July 14, 1849). The MS. of the letter is badly mutilated. On the back of this letter is written (not in Simms' handwriting) : "Letter dated July 23, 1849, sent to Mrs. Judge R. H. Hughes, Norfolk, Va." Presumably this is an unlocated letter from Simms to Tucker.

[142] "Later Poems of Henry Taylor." See note 119, June, 1849.

[143] See notes 195, Oct. 17, 1849, and 237, Dec. 17, 1849.

[144] Hammond did not contribute to the Jan., 1850, issue.

[145] "The Fine Arts in America." See note 119, June, 1849.

arts. Have you seen the volumes entitled "Modern Painters" &
"The Seven Lamps of Architecture?' These volumes are novelties, are suggestive and deal largely in the *moral* of the subjects.
They might afford you the proper text and provocation.[146] I do
not suppose that you will find any difficulty in procuring one for
th[e t]hough[ts] which you would have employe[d in review-
in]g Layard. *En[tre no]u[s]* I am [b]y [no means sa]t[is]fied
with th[e review] of Dr. Ly[nch which app]ears in our next[.]
He has *review[ed]* the b[oo]k, but I fear n[ot] *grasped* the
subject. It is in the moral, and not the fact merely, that the
material for such a review should be found. Of Fremont I know
nothing personally. The article upon him was written by Major
Hammond, a brother of our friend.[147] It is Fremont's misfortune
that he is coupled with *Bully* Benton[148] (Brigand is a somewhat
ennobling epithet). Were he alone he might be saved, and he has
talents worthy of protection. Have you read his reports, &c?
Our next number is more than full, *but there will always be a
place for you,* if your article can be recieved a month before
publication. If you can send me a short paper, such as I wrote to
you anent, a day or two ago, I should like to have it by the 15th
of August so as to give it an early place among the contents which
are rather grave in character, rather long, and needing variety.
The first article will be Layard's Nineveh — I have a paper from
Dr. Miles on Morell's Philosophy of Religion; a paper from
General Jamison on Lamartine's Girondins, one from McCord on
the Nav[i]gation Laws; another from Professor Porcher on t[he]
Free School System of S. C: — a[no]ther from Dr. G[ibbes]
of Col. S. C., on the G[eology of South Carolina] — to say
no[thing o]f a dozen more [articles on] not greatly di[ssi]milar
topics. Thr[ee or more of] our papers [h]ave been kept in
[waiting for] four months, as I prefer to bring as m[an]y of
our young men into the harness as possible, and we have a smart
corps who need nothing but training to become clever writers.
A paper of 10 pages from you for Oct. and one of 25 or more for
Jany. will be sure of a place, — the first if recieved by the 15
or 20th Augt., the latter by the 20th of October. I should like,
if recieved in season, to make this last the leading article for

---

146 Tucker did not write this suggested article on Ruskin.
147 See note 28, Feb. 22, 1849.
148 Thomas Hart Benton.

the Oct. issue.[149] That you do not now read verse does not prevent me from sending you with this, a few first sheets of a little vol. which I have in press.[150]

Very faithfully &c

W. Gilmore Simms

499: To JAMES HENRY HAMMOND

Charleston July 31. [1849][151]

dear Hammond

In a Letter just received from B. Tucker, he uses this language — "If I may be allowed to speak of my colaborers, I would say that Hammond is your *Interim Sidus*. His manly sense, his clear vigorous style, his deep insight into human nature, his shrewd wit, & his directness in approaching, stating & treating his subject, make him one of the best writers of the day." —[152]

There! you should be satisfied. Will it help the matter at all that I should say I fully concur with Tucker? And now, am I, after this concession & this conviction, to lose the help of that pen whose power it pleaseth us thus to acknowledge? No! By the Powers of Pen! No! I look to you for a leader for the January number, following up North & South and devoted to a kindred topic.[153] And, by the way, Grayson, in a conversation with him the other day, reminds me that you give a partial promise to this effect in your last. Do not dodge it or me! Your orations are now I suppose pretty nearly finished. Had Gregg given himself a little more time, he would have effected the post-

---

[149] For the contents of the Oct., 1849, issue of the *Southern Quarterly Review,* see note 134, July 14, 1849. James Warley Miles' article is "The Philosophy of the Beautiful." Tucker did not contribute. In the Jan., 1850, issue Tucker published "The Present State of Europe" (see note 155, Aug. 16, 1849).

[150] *The Cassique of Accabee.* See note 185, Sept. 19, 1849.

[151] Dated by Simms' reference to his proposed trip to the mountains of Georgia. See letter to Tucker of Aug. 16.

[152] Tucker's letters to Simms have not been located. Hammond, in his letters to Simms in the Hammond Papers, Library of Congress, refers to a number of Simms' letters of this period which we have also been unable to locate. On April 6 Hammond wrote, "I recd your letter at Barnwell"; on April 22, "You ask me who Dr. Ford is"; on June 4, "I have not answered the first of your two last letters"; on July 9, "I am glad to hear that you are coming this way."

[153] Hammond did not contribute. For the titles and authors of the articles in the Jan., 1850, issue of the *Southern Quarterly Review,* see letter to Holmes of April 13, 1850.

ponement desired for the Anniversary of the Industrial. But both
orations, in the case of a man of your temperament must be
dismissed from your thoughts long before delivery.[154] I wrote
to your brother to advise you that I should be at Hamburg tomorrow night, on my way to Georgia — a hurried trip which
I have promised myself for years — to be 8 or 10 days gone.
It is my hope to meet you there since I can't come down to you.
And I should like greatly to read your oration, for the City.

I shall bring with me a complete sett of my writings (with the
exception of one vol. which Russell can procure) and which you
will do me the grace to accept at my hands. It is not possible
to procure a set. The one I send you, is one of two copies reserved
for myself & contains one or more publications of youth which
I have since suppressed — The Book of My Lady for example.
You will also find my Review of Martineau on Slavery. In reading any of these books, take up first, "Richard Hurdis." It is
from that book that I first date my self emancipation from certain
Conventional Laws among novelists. But — I am weary & sick
& have no more to say but that I am as Ever Yours

&c

W. Gilmore Simms

500: To NATHANIEL BEVERLEY TUCKER

Charleston Augt. 16, 1849.

My dear Sir

I have just got back from a two weeks visit to the mountains
of Geo. which must account to you for my delay in answering
your Letter of the 6th. The enclosure interests me. I have no
quarrel with your opinions though possessed of a stronger faith
than yourself in our securities & progress. I do not hesitate to
assure you that I will cheerfully publish any thing that you may
offer for our pages, satisfied of the equal justness of your mind
& its resources. But you will probably conjecture from my previous letters that, for so long an article, I shall be able to find
no room in our forthcoming issue. I propose to make it our
Leader for the next ensuing — Jany.[155] And yet I am greatly

---

[154] For Hammond's orations before the Industrial Institute and the South
Carolina College, see notes 195, Oct. 17, 1849, and 237, Dec. 17, 1849.

[155] "The Present State of Europe," XVI, 277-323. The article is signed
"B. T."

anxious to have something from you for the present. I could wish a brief paper of 5 or 10 pages, in your liveliest vein. We have for the number in hand a list of long & grave papers, some of which have been lying over and must needs have delivery with speed, if not for their own, for the sakes of their proprietors. With some half dozen papers of my own on hand (such as they are) I am compelled to yield our whole space to contributors, particularly as we desire to give them all possible practice after having once got them into the harness. Unless we keep them at their speed — amateur writers in the South being as restive as young colts not yet bridle-wise, — we shall have them taking the studs, and using their heels rather than their heads. I wish to conciliate them as much as possible, and find that prompt publication of their performances is the first requisite for the attainment of this object. — I regret that you should describe yourself as an invalid. Men of letters usually keep well, so long as they are suffered to pursue the vocations which they love. I could wish, and have wished, that you could have been with us on our recent excursion to our mountains, where, clambering hills — and scaling almost inaccessible crags, you might have realized some of that physical provocation the effect of which appears so grateful to the intellectual energies of old Kit North.[156] Had you been one of our party, I could have secured the two Hammonds for the road, and we should have raised such echos among the hills of Georgia, as the said hills would not have been willing to let die in a hurry.[157] — May this scrawl find you in improved condition. Do not fail to send me the sequel of the article, and that too while you are i' the vein. But let me renew my entreaty for the lively little essay, — a sort of moral flying serpent, such as the pyroballists manufacture, which darts about in the most playful caprices, now winding its way among the feet of the boyish multitude, and now flinging its fiery tail into the faces of graver people. Believe me, at the bottom of the sheet, still very faithfully Yours &c

W. Gilmore Simms

Hon B. Tucker

---

[156] Pseudonym for John Wilson (1785-1854). James Grant Wilson says in *Bryant and His Friends* (New York: Fords, Howard, & Hulbert, 1886), p. 260: "There was at the period of my first meeting with Mr. Simms, about 1850, something in his strong, earnest, clean-shaven face, blue eye, and stalwart figure singularly suggestive of Christopher North."

[157] Writing as "The Wanderer," Simms described this trip in letters to an unidentified newspaper (Scrapbook in the South Caroliniana Library).

501: To Evert Augustus Duyckinck

Charleston, Sep 3, 1849

E. A. Duyckinck Esq

My dear Sir:

This will bring you to a personal knowledge of my friend, Mr. John Russell, of this city, whom you perhaps already know as a bookseller of great worth & intelligence. Mr. R. has in charge the publication of a pamphlet on the Foreign Relations of this Country, well argued & properly suggestive, by W. H. Trescott of Charleston — an able and excellent friend of mine, to whose work let me persuade your friendly attention.[158] He (Mr. R) has also in charge certain exquisite paintings of Mr. Charles Fraser,[159] — of whose reputation as an honored contemporary of W. Allston & Thos Sully — as a painter of fine taste and elaborate finish — you are probably aware. — Mr. Russell is desirous of putting these pictures into the Gallery of the Art Union, and of having the public eye drawn upon them, through the medium of the press. May I hope that you will assist him in these objects. — Mr. Fraser is one of the time honored & accomplished Gentlemen of our city — equally esteemed as a citizen and as an artist. He is one of those men whom *you* would particularly love — mild, calm, gentle, persuasive — graceful & correct in thought & sweet in expression. His favorable treatment as an artist in N. Y. will be grateful to all of us in Charleston.

Yrs truly as Ever

W. Gilmore Simms

---

[158] For William Henry Trescot, see introductory sketch. In reviewing Trescot's *A Few Thoughts on the Foreign Policy of the United States* (Charleston: J. Russell, 1849) in *S. Q. R.*, XVI (Oct., 1849), 252-253, Simms summarizes (p. 253) Trescot's somewhat prophetic ideas: "Mr. Trescot reasons against the narrow policy which has hitherto prevented the United States from taking a just rank among the nations. He feels that she is a first rate, instead of a third rate power, and that her politics and opinions must assert themselves in all regions in which we may have a future interest. His views are not so much pitched to the survey of the present as the probable. It is true that the relations of France, Russia and Great Britain are of a sort to leave the latter in no apprehension of any immediate alliance by the two former against her; but is this to be so, when Russia fairly steps forth upon the sea as a great maritime power? It is true that, at this juncture, there has been no rupture, and no cause of quarrel between Russia and the United States. But will the harmony continue, when Russia, becoming a great maritime power, shall penetrate the Pacific and plant her cities on the northwest coast?

"Mr. Trescot's argument goes to insist on the natural and inevitable affinities between the United States and Great Britain. . . ."

[159] See introductory sketch.

502: To James Henry Hammond

Charleston Sep. 5. [1849][160]

dear Hammond.

I have just got back from a week's visit to Sullivan's Island, where my life has been rather that of a locomotive system than of a moral & responsible being. My nervous system has scarcely got in balance yet, and I write to you simply that you may know where I am & that I am still as ever yours. The Review keeps me busy though it makes but little progress. Its correspondence has become a sufficient duty, by itself, for an ordinary man, and the accumulation of letters during the week, keeps me scrawling & scribbling through the day, in vain seeking to lessen the pile before me. Our publisher is behindhand. The want of means is the secret of his shortcomings. He is now on a tour into the interior canvassing for subscribers. Two were recd. indirectly from you, a day or two ago; and if all our professing friends would *give the law* to their several neighbourhoods, however small, after your fashion, the work might be rendered safe from all caprice of fortune. It tries my temper greatly the slowness of the printers.[161] The material is ample. I have matter enow for two numbers on hand. — Just recd. one from Campbell of Ala. on the Brit. West. Ind. a day or two ago,[162] one from Tucker

---

[160] Dated by Simms' reference to his "week's visit to Sullivan's Island" (see letter to Tucker of Sept. 6). In a letter dated Sept. 2, 1849, Hammond refers to an unlocated letter from Simms: "I have recd one letter from you since your return to Charleston." (Original in the Hammond Papers, Library of Congress.)

[161] On Sept. 18, 1849, James H. Hammond wrote to M. C. M. Hammond: "You must not be too hard on Simms. I judge from his last to me that he is much out of sorts — probable [*sic*] in pecuniary trouble. He has a very hard time of it I know. You are a prompt correspondent & expect others to be so. [Simms had, however, written to M. C. M. Hammond on Sept. 5.] You forget that very few have your leisure, & most, many more correspondents. Simms is much oppressed in this line & probably on an average does more writing every day (& *has it to do*) than you do in twenty. I feel greatly for him, condemned to drudge, when he is qualified to soar, & feeling time fly by without any improvement of his prospects. He is not popular, because he looks as I do with utter contempt on most men whom he meets & has got something of an overbearing habit, partly because he can't help treading on the pigmies in his way — partly because his is a proud spirit, which has had to fight its way against great odds — *without help*. He is a true hearted fellow & far — very far less selfish than most men, with far more talent than he has ever shown or had a chance to shew. As to the Review, I think one article a year from each of us as much as we should claim room for or shall have time to write *creditably*." (Original in the Hammond Papers, Library of Congress.)

[162] "British West India Islands," XVI (Jan., 1850), 342-377. The article is signed "J. A. C." (John Archibald Campbell). Campbell (1811-1889) was later associate justice of the Supreme Court (1853-1861) and assistant secretary of war of the Confederate States.

on the present state of Europe, and I have succeeded in forcing
into the harness several very clever young men of Charleston.
This very moment the mail brings me an article from Alex.
Mazyck (in Va.) on the opinions of the Judges of the Supreme
Court in relation to the Passenger Laws of New York & Massachusetts.[163] McCord writes me anxiously asking after you & your
farther contributions.[164] The language of Tucker is to the same
effect. I have replied that I look for you in our *April* number.[165]
— I can tell you nothing anent my Georgia wanderings. My head
is all in commotion and confusion. I am in no mood to quarrel
with your critique on Hurdis.[166] I give him up to you. You
will find a similar subject in "Confession" although, in some
respects, that work is one of my best. You will there find a
curious prophecy touching the Conquest of Mexico.[167] The
Yemassee is the work of most invention, although it is disfigured
by numerous faults of inexperience. It was in writing the most of
these works that *I acquired my education,* such as it is. Read
'Beauchampe' & 'Border Beagles' immediately after the Yemassee — i. e. if you are in the mood to read at all, which, from
your letter, I somehow question. You need a frolic — some excitement — a regular breaking up of the waters. Contrive it. — I
saw Hatch & Jones[168] recently & urged upon them the deferring

---

[163] "Opinions of the Judges of the Supreme Court of the United States, in
the Cases of 'Smith *v.* Turner,' and 'Norris *v.* the City of Boston,'" XV (Jan.,
1850), 444-502. Alexander Mazyck (born in 1801) was admitted to the bar
in 1822 and represented St. James's Parish in the State Senate for many years
prior to the Confederate War.

[164] Hammond was certainly not "anxiously asking" for McCord's or his
wife's further contributions. See his comments on their articles in the July,
1849, issue, quoted in note 119, June, 1849.

[165] Hammond did not contribute to the April, 1850, issue of the *Southern
Quarterly Review.* For the contents of this issue, see note 104, April 13, 1850.

[166] In his letter to Simms of Aug. 17 (a reply to Simms' of July 31)
Hammond writes: "I . . . read Richard Hurdis, but altho' I am a great de-
vourer of novels I am too poor a critic to perceive wherever you have violated
or departed from the essential rules of modern novelists. John Hurdis is the
Hero of your story, for with him rests the moral. I do not like Richard, whom
you have made as silly as he was surly. . . . I don't think even a novelist
should allow any success to such perverse — coarse — sour tempered & jealous
minded rascals as Richard Hurdis . . . the story is admirably told & the
interest thrilling . . . But my dear Simms, History & Biography are your
departments." (Original in the Hammond Papers, Library of Congress.)

[167] See chapter xxviii.

[168] Lewis Melvin Hatch (1815-1897) and James Jones (1805-1865). Hatch
born in Salem, N. H., was in the insurance business at 120 Meeting Street,
Charleston, and was a director of the South Carolina Institute (see the
Southern Literary Gazette, III [Dec. 14, 1850]). According to David Duncan
Wallace (MS. sketch of Jones attached to Jones' "Letter Book," South Caro-
liniana Library) Jones, born in Edgefield District, was editor of the Edgefield

of the anniversary of the Institute to November. They will probably make another, and I have no doubt a successful effort. I cannot consider now, & will not attempt to review that part of your letter which is devoted to yourself. I am not in the vein. Yet there is a significance in one part the full force of which does not escape me. Your infirmity, is in truth, *old age.* That is, you are prematurely old. You were never altogether young. Your judgment & reason were too rapid developments, and they have impaired your physique & perhaps somewhat affected other qualities of mind & temper. It is the misfortune of such persons that they too quickly exhaust the usual resources of mental excitement. The legitimate provocation fails them. Their policy is, accordingly, to economize their materiel, — not pour it out in a full & exhausting shower. Your only hope is in constant employment. I am afraid you don't think so. But when you cease to struggle and work, you will die. It is your misfortune that you too much underrate the value of public opinion even when it takes the form of admiration. In fact your love of approbation bears no sort of proportion to your self esteem. You have not vanity enough to seek for applause. — But I am weary and weak. — Let me once again entreat you to fling yourself into the arena — into any arena, — nay show some eagerness & anxiety for success. Do not mock your neighbors with an exhibition of contempt for those honors which make them madden. Read, write, speak *pro bono publico,* and I honestly believe that better health will be the result, happier moods, and a daily increase of reputation. You have powers of such variety as might justify your efforts in almost any field. — Your brother has probably advised you that Bliss writes him that the share of South Carolina has been already accorded to Clemson as her

---

Advertiser in 1836, a captain in the Seminole War, and inspector general of South Carolina in 1837. In 1840 or 1841 he began his long connection with Vaucluse Cotton Factory as manager, part owner, or owner. In 1845 he was closely associated with his brother-in-law, William Gregg (Gregg had married Marina Jones), in founding the Graniteville Manufacturing Company, of which Jones was a director and the first secretary of the board of directors. In 1855 he received the appointment of commissioner of the new State House in charge of its construction, sold Vaucluse, and moved to Columbia. He served as colonel in the Confederate War and in 1862 was appointed quartermaster general of South Carolina, with the rank of colonel. In May, 1865, he was elected treasurer of the Graniteville Manufacturing Company and served until his death in October.

representative.[169] Is not this excellent. There is a pitiful effort to bribe Calhoun into silence, and through him control the State. Perhaps nothing more conclusively proves the feebleness of the Cabinet as politicians simply. But a truce. Present me respectfully to Mrs. H. and Believe me Very faithfully Yours &c

W. Gilmore Simms

503: To JAMES LAWSON

Charleston Sep. 5. [1849][170]

Dear Lawson

I have just returned to the City after a week's loitering at Sullivan's Island, one of *our* watering places. The baby who was puny, has improved. We are all tolerably well, though we labor under a change of weather, in consequence of the prevalence of Easterly winds which are usually injurious, like Eastern politics, to Southern constitutions. I read the Queen of Sheba's [171] letter with interest & pleasure, and shall answer it as soon as I get comfortably adjusted in my fauteuil once more. How does the world go now with her Highness. And how goes the world with her Ladyship of Lawson. She has cut me I fear. She never directs me the least remembrance in your Letters, and I apprehend that she has transferred her affections entirely to new courtiers. But she will find me her *true* knight long after she has proved the falsehood of all other followers. Pray tell her this. — I am disquieted to hear of the indisposition of the children. Let me entreat you if Christina or any of the little ones continue to suffer, to compel yourself & persuade your wife, to give them & herself

---

169 Thomas G. Clemson (1804-1888), son-in-law of Calhoun, was chargé d'affaires to Belgium (1844-1852). On March 9 Hammond wrote to Simms, reporting his own and his brother's efforts to obtain an appointment for him: "[George Washington] Crawford [(1798-1871), of Augusta, Ga., at this time secretary of war] & myself are on the best terms & I think I can do something with him for you — but he must get warm in his place first. He is a hard, sagacious man educated solely by the newspapers." On March 15 he reported that he had written to Crawford "expatiating on your merits in such a style as must touch him," but Crawford had not replied by the time Hammond wrote Simms on June 21. In this last letter Hammond mentions having received a public letter from Charleston urging Simms' appointment to a foreign mission, and remarks, "My brother might send it to [William Wallace Smith] Bliss [son-in-law and secretary to President Taylor] but Bliss has not replied to his letter about you & he might pocket it." (Originals in the Hammond Papers, Library of Congress.)

170 Dated by Simms' reference to his "week's loitering at Sullivan's Island." See letter to Tucker of Sept. 6.

171 Possibly Christina, Lawson's daughter.

a winter at Woodlands. I need not repeat former protestations. You & she both I trust need no assurance of the delight which we should all feel to have you all with us for any length of time. For your own part, I know not the visit of any living man which would give me half the pleasure that I should enjoy in yours — you, my old friend, as full of faults as an egg's full of meat, but abounding also in virtues which make you as grateful to those who know you, as if you had never a fault at all. — I wished a thousand times that you could have shared some of our recent fishing expeditions. The coast & harbor of Charleston furnish the best fishing in the world. I went out the other day with a small party in a small boat, and in less than half an hour, more than fifty fish were taken, although the weather was against us. — A party the day before of six, caught 700 in less than two hours, — trout, sheepshead, whiting, cavalli, blackfish &c. and these are frequent performances. You would luxuriate in such employment, I am sure. — That you are so overwhelmed with business, I rather rejoice, but you should not undertake too much to keep you always at the desk. Remember your eyes. You are no longer a boy and should not presume upon the vigor of youth always. Take an hour or two of exercise out of doors every day at least. — Have you forwarded me the packets of MS. — the Tragedy & the two Letters.[172] This requires only 2 minutes of your time, as you have the MS.S. in possession, can easily bundle them up to my address, and your boy can send them, *as freight,* by the Southerner or Northerner. Pray let it be done. I have *contracts* for the Letters. — It is *possible* that I may visit you in the winter — barely possible, — for except to see you all, I have no motive. I have pretty much arranged to do my business without making it necessary that I should go on. I have partly agreed with Godey for a novel in *Series*.[173] Present me to Darley & other friends. — My best devotion to our Lady Wife & Mother, with a kiss for herself (if she will have it) and any number for the flock. — Tell Jimmy that Gilly has been wearing the medal for a month.

Yours as Ever &c.

W. Gilmore Simms

---

[172] "Benedict Arnold" and the two letters later published as part of "Home Sketches." See Simms' letters to Lawson during the first part of 1849.

[173] Simms first submitted *Vasconselos,* then *Katharine Walton.* See letter to Mrs. Sara J. Hale of Oct. 15, 1849.

504: To Marcus Claudius Marcellus Hammond

Charleston S. C. Sep. 5 [1849][174]

Dear Major:

I have space to say a few words only — have just got back from a week's loiterings on Sullivans Island, where I went for the benefit of a puny infant. My labors — particularly my Correspondence — great[ly] in arrear. Do not concern yourself about yo[ur] article.[175] I will see to it. Can't send you the proofs, but will be careful. I enclose you the Letter of Bliss. It disappoints no expectations. I was quite prepared for the result. Don't let it concern you, and take no farther trouble in regard to it. The Cabinet is evidently not one to rise to the appreciation of a generous idea. They have no conceptions whic[h] are not narrowly selfish, and based upo[n] the most humble party calculations. — There is one point however. Bliss's letter especially & unnecessarily names certain places vacant or about to be vacant, in other parts than these for which you put in.[176] Was this designed you as a hint. It is barely possible. But I repeat, let the matter trouble us no longer. It only nurses an anxiety which, in my case, has at no period, risen to the dignity of a hope. Best respects to Mrs. H.

Yours Ever truly,

W. Gilmore Simms

[P.]S. I have been too much hurried & on the go, to tell you of any thing. I did not see Gen. Taylor.[177] I sent the Letter to his house. I staid but a couple of days in Athens, going & returning — was on the road most of the time. What is this article that is to be a crusher of Crawford — and where published?[178] — I shall be glad for the Review's sake of all the subscribers you can send. It needs them all. Burges i[s] now on a tour canvassing in the interior. But the only secret of success is when our leading

---

[174] Dated by Simms' references to his "week's loiterings on Sullivans Island" (see letter to Tucker of Sept. 6) and to his trip to Georgia (see letter to Tucker of Aug. 16).

[175] "California," *S. Q. R.*, XVI (Oct., 1849), 82-115.

[176] William Wallace Smith Bliss had finally replied to M. C. M. Hammond's letter recommending Simms for a foreign appointment. See note 169, Sept. 5, 1849.

[177] Robert Taylor, militia general, born in Savannah, Ga. Taylor built several of the famous ante-bellum homes of Athens.

[178] We have been unable to locate any information about this article about (or by?) George W. Crawford. For Crawford, see note 169, Sept. 5, 1849.

men give the word to those around them — make it a point, — and compel public opinion.

505: To WILLIAM GOWANS [179]

Mr. Gowans,   Charleston S. C. Sep. 6. 1849.
   Publisher.

Dear Sir:

I find in your Catalogue, No 8. the names of a few books which I shall be obliged if you will send me. I have no means of sending you the money at this moment, but you may draw upon me, through any of the booksellers here, or wait until I visit New York, which may be in October or November. At all events I can contrive your payment by the last named period in N. Y. — The books are as follow[s]:

page 16. Jones's Memorials of N. Carolina		$1.00.
" 11. Drayton's View of South Carolina		3.50.
" 18 Lee's Campaign of 1781 (Phil. 1824)		1.50
" 20 McClung's Sketches of West. Adventure		1.00
" 24 Reed's Life & Correspondence 2 vols.		3.00
" 29 Thickness' Memoirs		1.50.
" 18 Life of Rich. H. Lee	2 vols	2.50
		$14.00

Should you see Mr. John Russell, Bookseller of this city, now in New York, he will honor your dft upon me for the above amount. Send the books to his care & oblige

Yr obt. Sert.

W. Gilmore Simms

506: To NATHANIEL BEVERLEY TUCKER

Charleston Sep. 6. 1849.

dear Sir

I have been absent from the city for a week or more, carried by a sick infant to one of *our* watering places. This has pre-

---

[179] Gowans (1803-1870), a native of Scotland, was a bibliophile, bookseller, and publisher of 178 Fulton Street, New York City. Simms erroneously addressed the envelope which covers this letter to "J. Gowans" at the above address.

vented me from taking due care of my correspondents, and led
me seemingly to neglect them. But I have in that period carefully
read your article and the portions of the drama you were so
good as to send for my perusal.[180] The former pleases me very
much. There is no substantial difference in our ways of thinking. I am a democrat, but rather upon our South Carolina platform than that of the nation's, and my democracy really has
nothing at all to do with party. Regarding democracy as the principle which lifts man into *responsibility* & trust, mine is rather a
religious sentiment than a principle in politics. It consequently
renders me conservative and not destructive — intent on that
progress which leads to natural transitions and a regular advance, rather than that which is forever in the fashion of children, throwing down that it may reconstruct. But, I flatter myself
we understand each other without many words.— Your article
is already a long one, but a few more pages would not be objectionable, and would enable you to render your work unique
— always a great object in periodical writings. Permit me to
say that I still hope that you may be able to send us a brief &
lively essay for our present number. As this, by reason of slug-
gishness of the publisher, is destined to be some what delayed,
any thing in moderate space which may be sent me by the first
of October, would be in season.[181] — I have gone through your
drama with care, and have enjoyed the perusal very much. I
should deem it unsuited for representation, & take for granted
that you designed it only for perusal. I suspect that the Editor of
the Messenger [182] was governed in his opinions by certain false
notions of decency & virtue. He disliked your staple — having
nice notions which suggested to him nasty thoughts. Still, the
scene being in N. Y. he may have had some pecuniary misgivings, as I well know that in former years the proprietor of that
work was very solicitous of Northern patronage, made great
efforts to obtain it, and published freely the mutual puffings &
laudations of Northern Hacks. Of the present Editor I know
nothing. I am curious to see how you bring about the catastrophe.

---

180 The article is "The Present State of Europe" (see note 155, Aug. 16,
1849) ; the play is "Viola" (see letters to Tucker of Dec. 17, 1849, Dec. 24, 1849,
and Jan. 30, 1850). Professor Percy Turrentine, who is at work on a biography
of Tucker, informs us that the MS. of this unpublished play is not extant.

181 Tucker did not contribute. For the contents of this issue, see note 134,
July 14, 1849.

182 John Reuben Thompson. See introductory sketch.

The scene which terminates the portion sent me, opens with Viola's full discovery of the villainy of Alfred. Ought she not to have discovered this before. Have you not rendered her a little too obtuse, and is not her meekness & modesty inconsistent with that vulgar thirst for fashionable display, upon which you found measurably her dependence upon Alfred, & her sacrifice of the worthy lover? Love, or passion, we well know, blinds the best judgment, and something must be allowed on this score, — but I still think that in the case of Viola, the degree of interest which she felt in Alfred has always been combated by a sense of the superior virtues of Henry &c. Many of your passages are very fine & forcible, particularly when you pass from dialogue into reflection; but it lessens the *realness* of the performance, that the speeches are too long, not sufficiently broken, and needing more frequent interruption. Is it not an oversight, which might turn the tables upon you in the event of publication that your names of persons, are so frequently those of good old Virginian families — Singleton, Conway, Harrison. In the dialogue, referring to persons in society, you speak of Randolph &c. Your names are either Virginian or English, — not Yorker or Yankee. — These are as peculiar to themselves almost as their *virtues* or their *patois.* It seems to me that this little point deserves your attention. I am disposed to think that, by a slight remodeling of the piece, you could admirably adapt it to the present state of society in N. Y. City, where the women are regularly engaged in organized cliques & bodies, in procuring converts to Fourierism — the absolute gratification of their passion being the chief motive. *They* are found to be most successful in procuring converts to a doctrine which begins with the most grateful indulgence. You can scarcely conjecture the extent of their organization, their numbers, and the progress which attends their efforts. By making your drama illustrate the pernicious doctrines of communism, as well as mere fashionable life, you can popularize your subject, and impart to it an additional element of novelty. Were ours a Magazine I should not scruple to find a place for it. — When you have copied out the residue, I should like to complete the perusal of it. I am curious to see your process for working out the conclusion, as, to my present thinking, you have been premature in the full exhibition of the hoof of your villain. — I have written a long and cheerless scribble which you must read with due allowance. The tasks of the Review — the merely mechanical duties

— are alone a sufficient labor. The correspondence grows daily, and returning after a week's absence, I have a mountain of letters before me to answer, from which I shrink with feelings akin to despondency. As for work of a literary kind, that is next to impossible. All that I can undertake is to furnish up for the Magazines, occasionally, old matters, embryos of verse or tale, or pen a brief notice of the current publications. — I am interrupted & have time only to assure you of my respect & friendship.

Very faithfully Yours &c.

W. Gilmore Simms

Hon. B. Tucker

P. S. I reopen to say that had my trip to Georgia been *premeditated* sufficiently long, you certainly should have had an opportunity of being with us. God willing, we shall secure you in any future indulgences of the same sort. — I long to devote a summer to ramble in your state, & shall do so as soon as I can.

507: To Evert Augustus Duyckinck

Charleston Sep. 19. [1849][183]

My dear Sir.

It recals pleasantly old times the reciept of a Letter from your hand. I know not how far your moods may sympathize with mine, but I confess to a frequent pleasure in the reference to those periods when our scribbles were as freely exchanged as if there was a virtue in the currency equally appealing to the avarice of both parties. I will not ask why it is otherwise now, satisfied that I cannot reproach myself, and equally satisfied with the hope of the resumption of ancient intimacies. I see your world with pleasure — not weekly exactly, for it reaches me with some occasional interruptions; but when I do see it I usually find in

---

[183] Dated by Simms' reference to having "just run through the press" *The Cassique of Accabee* (see note 185, below). On Aug. 25 Duyckinck's *Literary World*, V, 159, commented that the volume was in press and printed (from the *Chronotype*) an account of Simms' "conversational resources": "As a storyteller, I have never met his equal. He has travelled through all the Southern and South-western States, has been among the 'up country' farmers, the turpentine manufacturers, the backwoods hunters, and the Indians, and has laid up an apparently inexhaustible supply of stories and anecdotes for the amusement of his friends. These anecdotes and stories he tells with the greatest zest, and with the skill of an accomplished actor imitating to perfection the dialect, tones, and action, of the various characters introduced."

it much that is refreshing, and something that may be considered
new. I fancy I am not often mistaken in your especial ear marks,
though more than once I have been struck with a tone, particularly in regard to certain of the Boston literati for which, in your
respect, I was not altogether prepared. There have been instances
also, when it seemed to me that your Journal was paying a little
too much heed to the local press — aiming to conciliate a power
which it should be your rôle rather to compel into respect &
decency. But I am too far removed from you to be always a
proper judge in such matters, and I can very well understand
that considerations of a peculiar & exigent character may arise in
the progress of every man, as well as Editor, to move him to
forbearance, and even a waver of his special mood, in regard to
persons & parties whom at another period he would prefer to
avoid or crush. Let me entreat you, if my opinions may have
any influence to look as much as you possibly can *beyond* the
claims and considerations of the moment, whenever these shall
seem to come in conflict with the permanent and the true. You
have resources of taste, thought, judgment, &c sufficient to sustain
you in the long run, against any unreasonable or unjust opponent
however temporarily powerful. But these generalizations may
well be spared, particularly as it is not possible for me now to
recal the special topics which induced me to think as I have
done in connection with your labors. I gladly repeat that I have
found little but satisfaction in the perusal of the 'World.' The exceptions are such, I doubt not, as were of too light a sort to
weigh any thing against the general estimate of your labours.
I take for granted that your paper must supersede & drive all
competitors from the field. It has merits which should do so. —
I have had the wanting nos. of the South Quarterly sent to your
address, care of Putnam. I shall look over my numbers of the
World & let you know what are deficient. You promised me a
bound vol. to the close of Hoffman's administration. At present
address the copy to the Rev. here as well as to myself. When I
remove to the plantation I will advise you when the one for
myself may be sent thither. — I hear little from N. Y. My friends
have pretty generally cut me. Lawson no longer writes me, and
all my sources of information seem dried up in that quarter.
I wrote to Putnam some time ago touching an Edition of Castle
Dismal & Helen Halsey from *my* stereotype plates, to be sent
forth with broad margin & fine paper as 50 cent books, but he

never answered me. I am compelled therefore to exercise what philosophy I can in respect to your city. I trust that your present is a harbinger of future favors.

Regards to Mrs. D, your brother, Mr. Panton [184] & other friends

Yours truly &c

W. Gilmore Simms

P. S.

I have just run through the press here a little brochure of verse, entitled the Cassique of Accabee & Other Poems, of which Putnam will publish a small Edit. with you.[185] Copies shall be sent you. It puts the Indian in a new and not unnatural light. The scene is one under our city's eye. You will probably remark among the accompanying pieces the one entitled "The Traveller's Rest." [186] The vein, I think, is not a common one, yet distinguished by its simplicity. — By the way Mathews has put forth I learn a couple of volumes.[187] They have never reached this city, and I have asked for them in vain. What are they & what has been their success. He is so wilful & has been so unjust to me, that I cannot put the question to himself. I still flatter myself that the day will come when he will be pleased to remember, and perhaps adopt my counsels. Till then! — Yours again &c.

W. G. Simms.

How does Darley prosper.

508: To Evert Augustus Duyckinck

Charleston 27 Sep. 1849.

E. A. Duyckinck Esq.
dear Sir.

I have been looking over the numbers of the Literary World, and find the following to be wanting for the completion of my

---

[184] Henry or John Albert Panton, brothers of Mrs. Duyckinck (Margaret Wolfe Panton).

[185] *The Cassique of Accabee. A Tale. With Other Poems* (Charleston: J. Russell, 1849). Some copies of this edition bear the imprint "New-York: Geo. P. Putnam, 1849," and some "New-York: Harper & Brothers, 1849." Oscar Wegelin records (*A Bibliography of the Separate Writings of William Gilmore Simms,* 3rd ed. [Hattiesburg, Miss.: The Book Farm, 1941], p. 15) an edition issued by John Russell, Charleston, and dated 1848. Apparently Wegelin errs, since the copies he lists bear the date 1849.

[186] Pp. 53-69. "The Traveller's Rest" had appeared earlier in the *Magnolia.* See note 114, Nov. 22, 1842.

[187] Probably *Moneypenny.* See note 56, Feb. 16, 1850.

sett — viz: Nos. 21. 23. 24. 26. 30. 31. 32. 33. 34. 35. 46.
50. 54 to 64 inclusive — from 66 to 87 inclusive — 90. 101.
107. 112. 116. 117. 120. 122. 128. 132. The last number recieved
is 137. These, if you have them, may be forwarded at your
leisure. In the meantime I should be greatly obliged if you would
execute for me the following commissions. There was a work
published, I think in Boston, by an Englishman — originally put
forth serially in one of the Boston papers, — entitled, I think,
Pen & Pencil Sketches. They closed with a Life of Chatterton, or
sketches of him. The leading feature of the volume was its
portraits of contemporaries. I saw the book when first published
in a 25 or 50 cent vol. but did not value it, and now that I desire
it, I can find it in none of our bookstores.[188] If you can pick it
up for me in N. Y. without inconveniencing yourself, I will thank
you. Again, our friend Lawson has in his hands a MS. play of
mine (which was designed for Mr. Forrest) — with other
MSS.[189] I have been writing to him for sometime to forward
them, but he is so lazy at home, and so busy at the office, that
what he hasn't leisure to do at the one place, he hasn't wakeful-
ness enough to attempt at the other. The consequence is that I
write to him in vain. I wish you to visit him & say that you will
see to forwarding them to me, through Putnam. — Ascertain for
me also, if in your way, if Mr. Wm. C. Forbes, the actor is in
New York, or where? I had hopes to have sent you the Cassique
of Accabee before this, but the atrocious binder has disappointed
me, and the few copies which were ready were distributed among
friends, before I had any notion of the delay that was to follow.
I trust you have seen Mr. Russell of our city. He is a very
worthy Gent. and a first rate Bookseller. He can do much toward
promoting your circulation in the South. — Pray let me hear the
on dit among your authors of Gotham. I feel that I implore a
charity for there is nothing here with which I can compensate
your intelligence. I am already beginning my preparations for the
country, whither a portion of the family will go sometime in

---

[188] John Rosa Dix, *Pen and Ink Sketches: By a Cosmopolitan* (Boston:
William Hayden & Thos. M. Brewer, Atlas Office, 1845). In the "Introduction"
(p. 7), dated "Boston, *August*, 1845," the author says that his sketches "first
appeared in the *Boston Atlas*, and that from the columns of that journal, they
have been transferred to those of the leading journals of the United States."
The book contains "Pen and Ink Sketches," pp. 9-164, and "Chatterton: A
Romance of Literary Life" (in six chapters), pp. 165-198. Price 50 cents.

[189] *Norman Maurice*, "Benedict Arnold," "The Egyptian Masque," and the
letters later published as "Home Sketches." See letter to Lawson of *c.* May 6,
1849, and following letters to Lawson.

October — if the weather become cold — freezing — the whole of us. Let me remind you of your quasi promise to visit the South in general, and myself in particular. I shall rejoice to welcome you at Woodlands

Yours truly &c

W. Gilmore Simms

509: To Sarah Josepha Buell Hale [190]

Charleston Oct. 15. 1849.

My dear Mrs. Hale

I trust you do not think so lightly, either of my good sense, or of my philosophy, as to suppose that I could feel offended at objections so gently, dispassionately and amicably expressed as those in your letter. I can readily concieve, in your situation, and with such responsibilities upon you, the propriety of your objections. In fact, I sent you on the first five chapters of "Vasconselos" promptly, in order that you might seasonably determine upon their suitableness for your pages. Of an intense and passionate temperament myself, delighting in deep tragedy, and the sternest provocations to the passions, I have learned to distrust my own judgment in such matters, and gladly give ear to the suggestions of a more deliberate method and a calmer mood. I do not think that Vasconselos would ever be considered an immoral story. It is one of dark & terrible imaginings & will, I think, prove one of the wildest interest and the most intense powers. It is a tale of crime, but not of voluptuousness, & none of the scenes would have embodied an argument for, or an inducement to sensuality. On the contrary, crime, as in the Holy Scriptures, would be shown, almost entirely, in its griefs, its glooms, and its terrible penalties. So much for my defence of my story *per se*. But I do not argue for its appropriateness to a publication which, like yours, appeals so intensively to the more delicate sensibilities of your sex. I cheerfully accept your decision, and will endeavour to supply its place, with another to which, I pledge you, no exception can possibly be taken. With this I write to Mr. Godey, and beg to refer you to him for the plan

---

[190] Mrs. Hale (1788-1879), novelist, poet, and editor, founded the *Ladies' Magazine* (Boston) in 1828. When Godey purchased the periodical and combined it with his *Lady's Book* in 1837, she continued as one of the editors. Her final issue of *Godey's* is that for Dec., 1877.

of a work which I only wait his answer to begin.[191] — I owe you a Letter, and must apologize for my delay in answering your previous communication. My labors on the Review have been very considerable of late, in order that I might enjoy an unembarrassed respite in which to proceed with my novel. I am greatly obliged to you for the copy of the "Opal." Pray remember that when you desire assistance for any similar work, I shall be glad to be summoned to your service.[192]

Very respectfully, Yr frd & Servt

W. Gilmore Simms

510: To James Henry Hammond

Charleston, Oct. 17. 1849.

My dear Hammond.

You seem in a bad humour. I hope not with me. I shall take this for granted as I am not conscious of having given you any provocation. I may be mistaken in regard to what is needful to your health & happiness; but I think not. At all events the

---

[191] After the rejection of *Vasconselos* (eventually published under the pseudonym of "Frank Cooper" by Redfield, New York, in 1853), Simms submitted *Katharine Walton: or, the Rebel's [Partisan's] Daughter. A Tale of the Revolution.* The novel appears in *Godey's,* XL (Feb.-June, 1850), 107-118, 161-169, 243-251, 320-326, 397-411; XLI (July-Dec., 1850), 13-27, 89-100, 162-179, 205-219, 286-298, 332-352. In 1851 A. Hart, Philadelphia, republished the novel as *Katharine Walton: or, the Rebel of Dorchester. An Historical Romance of the Revolution in Carolina.* There were many later editions (see Salley, *Catalogue of the Salley Collection of the Works of Wm. Gilmore Simms,* pp. 74-78). *Godey's,* XLVIII (March, 1854), 274, later remarks of *Vasconselos:* "This is a powerfully written romance, founded on the adventures of De Soto, which we think deserving of more than the usual attention paid to works of fiction. The style is energetic, and the incidents and the plot, though the latter is not altogether agreeable to our taste, are full of the spirit of the age and of the characters represented."

[192] Mrs. Hale edited *The Opal* (an annual published in New York by J. C. Riker) for 1845, 1848, and 1849 (see Ralph Thompson, *American Literary Annuals & Gift Books, 1825-1865* [New York: The H. W. Wilson Company, 1936], p. 100). *The Opal* for 1848 contains (pp. 27-29) a poem by Simms: "A Sunset Piece." Simms' other contributions to annuals during 1845-1850 include "Pocahontas," *The Missionary Memorial: A Literary and Religious Souvenir* (New York: E. Walker, 1846), pp. 199-220; "Children's Evening Gambols," *The Rainbow. 1847* (Albany: A. L. Harrison; New York: Bell and Gould, 1847), pp. 98-99; "Could I Weep As I Have Wept," "Meet Me by Moonlight Alone," and "Mynha," *The Floral Offering* (Philadelphia: Carey and Hart, 1847), pp. 12, 21, 56; "Sonnet.—The Good Brother," *The Odd-Fellows' Offering, for 1849* (New York: Edward Walker, 1849), p. 52. *The Rainbow* was reissued in 1848, and *The Missionary Memorial* was reissued as *The Evergreen* (see note 239, June 25, 1845). No contributions by Simms appear in *The Opal* for 1846 or 1847, in *The Odd-Fellows' Offering* for 1848 or 1850, or in *The Gem of the Season* for 1846, 1849, or 1850.

opinion ought not to ruffle you. Without any reference to your doubtful health, I do not well see how you should be in ill humour with any body or the world. Seeing you as I do, and knowing how steadily you have been advancing in the estimation of our little world, I think you should find many causes of genuine satisfaction. You are not superior to the sympathies of men, however indifferent to their awards. I have daily opportunities for knowing that hundreds regard you as the chief hope of the State hereafter. Do not, I beg you, do or say any thing to discourage this hope. It is one upon which your friends build, and I believe with a warmth of regard which ought to gratify you. Besides, at a moment when Providence smiles upon you in one grateful respect, you must not prove ungracious, for that is to be ungrateful. I congratulate you on the birth of your daughter, and hope that Mrs. H. is in good condition as well as the young one.[193] The crops worry you, but you are not alone. If it be any consolation your friends are in no better condition. We shall probably make little over 1/3 of a crop. For myself, I fear that my labors on Edisto will be unproductive.[194] I find it difficult to get any thing from Burges. Must see the year out [at] all events. Your orations will be looked for with great anxiety.[195] Your worst enemy will be your reputation. I do not fear that you will write up to it. That you should feel sick & disgusted with a labor that has tired you, is a thing that I can well understand. *Experientia docet.* It is probable that I shall remove to the country about the 1st prox. In that event, I shall seize an early moment, after it, to run up to your brother, who has promised to drive me down to your habitation. We will read the essays together. An hour & a half will not be too long for either oration, though better *nipping,* in delivery to 1¼ hours, and *restore* in print. The oration of 28th. June might be ac-

---

[193] Elizabeth Hammond (called Betty) was born on Oct. 4. Hammond reported her birth in his letter to Simms of Oct. 12 (original in the Hammond Papers, Library of Congress). Betty married Dr. William Raiford Eve on Dec. 7, 1871. She died in 1939.

[194] See APPENDIX.

[195] Hammond's address before the South Carolina Institute was delivered on Nov. 20. The Charleston *Mercury* of Nov. 21 reports: "The large and spacious hall of the Hibernian Society, was filled to overflowing last night by a highly intellectual and fashionable audience. The address of Gov. Hammond was a chaste and elegant production, worthy of the subject, and of his high reputation as an orator and as a statesman." The address was published the same year by Walker and James under the title of *An Address Delivered before the South-Carolina Institute, at Its First Annual Fair, on the 20th November, 1849.*

cepted.[196] You will have 6 months. Half an hour will do for
that. A lively, bold picture, with a few suggestive points on
politics & government. *Soon or late,* the Senate vacancy will occur.
I am inclined to think that you will be looked to by the great
majority, and no need of canvassing.[197] To be seen at Columbia
implies something more, but any thing, than canvassing. We shall
make you a young man again, if you are not predestined to be
an old one. How would you like to be in Congress, with me
in the lower House? This *inter nos.* A caucus has recently been
held in Charleston among *our* friends. In plain terms the movement is made by the solely powerful party, and I have been applied to to succeed or to supersede Holmes, as their nominee.
I have consented promptly & frankly, telling them that the place
would please me.[198] As the matter as yet is secret keep it to
yourself. — I have only to say that next to the pleasure I should
find in such election would be the gratification I should feel, at
enjoying your counsels from the other wing of the Capitol. —
I wrote your brother but yesterday, but neglected to mention to
him a matter which may affect himself. I saw Col. Summer in
town a few days ago. He tells me that Burt is about to abdicate.[199]
That he is in the field as his successor. — That Yancey & J. P.
Carroll are also out.[200] He mentioned one or two more. Why
should not the Major [201] put in? Has he no ambition that way?
Let him know, if he has not heard already. — When you consulted me anent Legaré, I was studious to say nothing that might
disparage his claims. But now, I may mention that I think lightly

---

196 On Oct. 12 Hammond had written: "They have written me to deliver
the Fort Moultrie Oration next 28 June. How can I undertake it?" On Oct. 28
he wrote: "I am glad to see you have a whole number [of the *Review*] on hand.
You don't want help in the writing way & I am glad to see it for I have
accepted the Moultrieville oration & that is enough for me next year." (Originals
in the Hammond Papers, Library of Congress.)

197 On Oct. 12 Hammond had written: "As to the Senate I never had the
least idea of a vacancy. Should there be one, I should be proud & grateful if
the State would call me to the position, tho' I have no idea I should hold it
long. . . ." (Original in the Hammond Papers, Library of Congress.)

198 In his reply of Oct. 28 Hammond remarks: "I entirely approve of your
going to Congress. I wish Holmes would decline in your favour." (Original
in the Hammond Papers, Library of Congress.) Simms was publicly nominated
in Oct., 1850, but he declined (see letter to Lawson of Oct. 14, 1850).

199 A. G. Summer, of Newberry, former editor of the *South Carolinian*
(Columbia), was misinformed: Burt continued to serve in Congress until
March 3, 1853.

200 Benjamin Cudworth Yancey (see note 215, Oct. 30, 1846) and James
Parsons Carroll (1809-1883), of Edgefield.

201 M. C. M. Hammond.

alike of father & son.[202] The former, Burges claims to have been ruined by. B. says that he got his endorsement a week or so before his declared bankruptcy and when his condition was fully known to himself. The son (B. tells me) is keeping school at Augusta, & he has no reason to suppose him more an invalid than usual. He is vain & ambitious, & is the author of an article in the Mercury a few days ago, disparaging all the Northern Magazines but the Knickerbocker, the Editor of which he knows I denounced in print as a liar &c.[203] The fact is that every petty poetaster of Charleston looks upon me as an enemy. Yet scarcely a Southron has ever recieved a kind word in the South, unless from my pen; and even Legare is indebted to me for a genial notice in the present issue of the Review.[204] Tucker's play I will probably bring with me to you.[205] I will express no opinion upon it. I do not know that he wishes it published, but infer so. Should

---

[202] Early in September in an unlocated letter to Hammond, Simms offered to aid James Mathewes Legaré (1823-1859), son of James D. Legaré, the founder of the *Southern Agriculturist* (1828-1846), in the publication of a projected work. Hammond replied on Sept. 20: "It is very kind to me & generous to Legaré to offer to serve him in getting out his work. You evidently do not fear him & this detracts somewhat from your generosity, though not from your kindness. . . . You were right. He has fancy but no imagination or genius—What a curse to have the one & not the others." On Oct. 12 Hammond again wrote of Legaré: "I returned Legaré's MSS. & condemned it. He was greatly hurt & I equally so to have had any thing to do with it." Later on Oct. 28 he wrote: "In the meantime, Legaré also came & went. The impression he has—entre nous—been any thing but favourable. His talents are slender & he is utterly wanting I fear in straightforward honesty. . . . I have agreed to advance him funds to visit Cambridge next Summer & look for materials in that Library. Some $200. . . . Unless the work is really worth something, when done, I will not aid in foisting it on the world. . . . Legaré's ambition is awful." (Originals in the Hammond Papers, Library of Congress.)

[203] In an unsigned article entitled "Magazines of the Day," published in the *Mercury* of Oct. 11, Legaré says: "I know of but two (original) magazines of a manly tone in America, and of these the Knickerbocker stands undeniably foremost; indeed I have no scruple in claiming for it a higher merit, apart from political address, than even its Edinburgh prototype!" In his letter to Simms of Oct. 28 Hammond remarks: "You must excuse his puff of the Knickerbocker—*he did it for bread.*" (Original in the Hammond Papers, Library of Congress.)

[204] In "Recent American Poets," XVI (Oct., 1849), 224-232, Simms writes (p. 228) of Legaré's *Orta-Undis, and Other Poems* (Boston: William D. Ticknor & Co., 1848): "The poems before us are full of instances of rare felicity of phrase, happy turns of thought, analogies equally sweet and curious, and fine moralities that crown the verse, at its close, with a sudden surprise and beauty. His fancy is very delicate; his command of language considerable; and his tastes find provocation, to life and utterance, from the casual encounter with wood, lake or forest scene."

[205] In his letter to Simms of Sept. 20 Hammond offered to finance the publication of "Viola" (see Simms' letter to Tucker of Sept. 6, 1849): "How much did you intend to assess me on Tucker's play?—Money is *scarce* with me, but I think I would divide with him as soon as with any one. Name the sum at least." (Original in the Hammond Papers, Library of Congress.)

he, I will see that you are not assessed more than half the sum you mentioned, if that. — But I am disposed to assess you myself to the tune of $20. *perhaps.* The articles to the Mercury had an object beyond what was apparent on the surface. It is not improbable that they contributed to the nomination to Congress. I have been applied to to put them in pamphlet or book form, and with $20. or $30 help from without will be enabled to do so.[206] — You misconstrue the suggestion touching the acquisition of agriculture. I specially encourage the idea of gaining knowledge on the subject from every quarter. — But enough. I hope soon to see you in the country & console you. I trust not in vain to make the effort. There is still a good deal of fever in the City, though they tell me, it abates. It is chiefly confined to the very poor, the very dissipated among foreigners, chiefly

---

[206] Of Simms' "The Home Tourist," a series which was appearing anonymously in the *Mercury* (Sept. 18, 19, 20, 21, 22, 27, 29; Oct. 1, 3, 6, 10, 13, 16, 23, 27; Nov. 3, 5), Hammond wrote on Oct. 12: "I have not read your lucubrations in the Mercury. I did not dream they were yours & I never attempt any thing so long in a newspaper without some special motive. Two passages struck my eye in the middle of two articles. One when you speak of my suggestion about Moultrie's debts & I think rightly—the other where you speak of a man's learning agriculture solely by experience, which won't do altogether." (Original in the Hammond Papers, Library of Congress.) In Dec., 1849, the collected numbers were republished (as by Simms) under the title of *Father Abbot, or, the Home Tourist, a Medley* (Charleston, S. C.: Printed by Miller & Browne, 1849). The *Mercury* of Dec. 20 comments: "We are glad to see these sketches, which appeared originally in the *Mercury,* republished in a very handsome little volume. . . . Mr. Simms has dedicated it 'to the Hopeful, the Believing and the Working Spirits among us, as designed, in part to inoculate a faith in *place,* as necessary to a just performance of appointed duties.' . . . It contains 235 pages and is placed at the very low price of 25 cents." The *Courier* of Dec. 21 also carries a notice of the volume: "These entertaining and well written essays, with which the pen of Simms graced our Mercurial neighbor's columns, during the past summer and autumn, have assumed the shape of a neat little volume, from the press of Mr. A. E. Miller, Broad St."

On Feb. 1 Hammond wrote Simms: "I have read Father Abbot & charge you flatly with stealing a great deal of my thunder. How & where I cant specify & in fact much of it I don't think I had ever given light (or lightening) to—but I had made it for myself in various times past. . . . On the whole it is a capital thing & among your best productions. . . . It will be read with pleasure fifty years or more hence. I am not sure the Abbot with all his affectations of paternal kindness was not a devil of a bore. . . . He was dreadful long winded & dogmatical, & talked with such a fervor! One runs out of breath in trying to keep up with him. . . . I cannot help thinking that all this turbulence of yours is put on. Your western experience, at a critical period of life, fascinated you with energy, & you very unwisely set up as your beau ideal, a dashing, impetuous, booted & spurred, break neck crusader, & have carried him through in peace as well as war through the whole circle of your performances. . . . I fancy that when you come abroad out of your den, it is with pretty much the feelings of a silent boy at recess. To make the most of your play time like him you jostle every one that crosses your track & run a muck all round the ring." (Original in the Hammond Papers, Library of Congress.)

Irish & Dutch. Others have been taken but recovered. — **Once** more let me make my congratulations in respect to your daughter. We are to live in our children.

God bless you & Yours

Simms

511: To Marcus Claudius Marcellus Hammond

Woodlands, [*c.* November 1, 1849][207]

Dear Ma[jor]

I have leisure only f[o]r a very bri[ef l]etter[,] being just as busy as one can well be, preparing the desks for next number, and doing a hundred things besides. I have not yet recieved your Mines,[208] but shall be into them as soon as I do. Don't mistake about style. Don't let them praise you into a compact diction which shall be obscurity. Let me keep you from extremes. Your mind is a clear one — that is one thing; but your style has yet to work up against your habit of letter writin[g] in which you have acquired certain [manneri]sms [whic]h injure the tone and [*several words missing*] impose [*several words missing*] and these are [*several words missing*] essen[tial]s of style. When [you have] written half a dozen articles [for the] Review, with an occasional dig [from me] into your small ribs, you will [probab]ly be an admirable style monger — if you consent to have but little faith in yourself during your probation and *believe every word* which *I* tell you on [the s]ubject of you[r w]ritings. — I did not see Cooper[?][209] about the books after recieving your Letter. It came just as I was leaving town, so I sent it to Russell. At the worst, we can only pay for the books between us, and if you will credit me for awhile, I will take the Seneca, Callimachus & some others, including Raleigh, off your hands. If the General has not Rushworth's Hist. Collections,[210] *he ought* to have it. Don't suppose me angry or peevish in the

---

[207] Nov. 1 is a probable date for this letter, written after Simms' return to Woodlands on Oct. 28 (see letter to Lawson of Nov. 24) and before Nov. 19, when Simms says he plans to go to Charleston to attend the Fair of the South Carolina Institute, which opened on Nov. 20 and closed on Nov. 23 (see the Charleston *Mercury* of Nov. 12). The MS. is badly mutilated.

[208] "The Mines of California," published in the April, 1850, issue of the *Southern Quarterly Review.* See note 104, April 13, 1850.

[209] Possibly Col. William Cooper, a State senator from Williamsburg at this time.

[210] John Rushworth, *Historical Collections* . . . . 8 vols. (London, 1659-1701).

matter. Give me none of your d —— n irony at the [expense of] my etheriality. I [know] ten [or twenty more] practical, matter of fact me[n than you.] You are, with all your asserti[ons full of et]heriality. Get out! — We will ta[ke] the sub. to Father Abbot; [211] herea[fter] should we need your $5, I will [ask for it.] Don't be too sure about Burt & Summer but keep your eyes open in the matter.[212] Let me [instruc]t you. Porcher is not a beginner [n]ow. He commenced under my auspices in 1842 when I edited the Magnolia.[213] I claim to have first forced him into the field. So I brought out Wurdemann. He wrote his Notes of Cuba under my instigation. They were first published in the Magnolia.[214] You are right. Poverty is the word for Gibbes. He is a poor devil & a devilish poor writer.[215] I don't see Moragne's paper.[216] You percieve that I pepper Yankeedom somewhat in my n[oti]ces.[217] [I] can't come to see you till af[ter the] Fair. [I g]o down [the] day before the [Fair a]nd retur[n] the day after. Will [try to arr]ange to come up — not before [*part of word missing*]ay. Dont consume all the [*several words missing or illegible*] before you see me. [I will] look for an article from you by the 1st. Feb. for the April number, 15 pages.[218] — Keep working until you are home in it.

Yours Ever

Simms

---

[211] The publication of Simms' series in book form. See note 206, Oct. 17, 1849.

[212] See letter to James H. Hammond of Oct. 17, 1849.

[213] Frederick Adolphus Porcher's "Free School System in South-Carolina" had been published in the Oct., 1849, issue of the *Southern Quarterly Review* (see note 134, July 14, 1849). Porcher (1809-1888), professor of history and belles lettres at the College of Charleston (1848-1888), wrote to Simms in an undated letter (1855) : "I have lived an idle person all my life, dreaming on the plantation, and have hardly written a line but at your suggestion or that of our Charleston Club." (Original in the Duyckinck Collection, New York Public Library.) We are unable to identify his contributions to the *Magnolia*.

[214] See note 87, May 5, 1849.

[215] Robert W. Gibbes' "Report on the Geology of South-Carolina" had appeared in the Oct., 1849, issue of the *Southern Quarterly Review*. See note 134, July 14, 1849.

[216] William Caine Moragné (1818-1862), brother of the novelist, poetess, and diarist, Mary Elizabeth Moragné (1816-1903), was a lawyer in Edgefield, S. C. and editor of the Edgefield *Advertiser*. He was a graduate of the South Carolina College in 1837, studied in Heidelberg and Berlin, and served as first lieutenant in the Mexican War and as colonel in the Confederate service.

[217] See, for example, Simms' notice of Lowell's *A Fable for Critics* (see note 183, Nov. 28, 1848), *S. Q. R.*, XVI (Oct., 1849), 239-242.

[218] "The Mines of California" (see note 208, above) appears to have been promised for the Jan., 1850, issue.

512: To John Pendleton Kennedy

Woodlands, Nov. 2. 1849.

Hon. J. P. Kennedy.

My dear Kennedy.

I forebore answering your letter till I had recieved and read your book. This I have done with real pleasure & satisfaction. You have made not only a satisfactory, but an interesting volume. I do not know but you have greatly raised my estimate of Wirt's endowments by your details & summaries. His domestic letters will do much towards that knowledge of his character, which was perhaps essential to the appreciation of his endowments; while your own estimates, thus sustained, will find ready faith with every dispassionate reader. I will endeavour to find a place for a review of you & him, in the next, or January issue of The Southern Quarterly. Meanwhile, I enclose you a hasty notice of the work, which I penned Editorially for the Charleston Mercury, — the daily journal of most character in our State.[219] You will note some small fault-finding, with which I trust you will not be disposed to quarrel. In haste, but very truly Yours &c.

W. Gilmore Simms.

513: To James Lawson

Woodlands Nov. 24 [1849][220]

My dear Lawson

Your letter postmarked 3 Nov. never reached me till yesterday, delayed by the oversight & carelessness of the Clerk in the office of the Review, where it was kept until I visitd the city last week. We returned to the plantation on the 28th ult. & I have been quite busy there ever since until last week when I went to Charleston to attend the Fair of the Industrial Institute, of which I

---

[219] This notice of *Memoirs of the Life of William Wirt* appears in the issue for Oct. 20. In reply to this letter Kennedy wrote on Dec. 20: "I owe you an apology for this delay in acknowledging the pleasure I received from your letter of the 2nd. of November. At that date I was in Boston. . . . I read the notice in the Charleston Mercury whilst I was in Boston, and was greatly gratified by its friendly tone, which led me to ascribe it to you before I was positively informed upon the point. . . . I am quite willing, my dear Simms, to trust myself to your hands, and I shall take your dissection like a polite and well-bred body which has a proper respect for the cause of science." (Copy in Kennedy's handwriting in the Peabody Institute Library.)

[220] Dated by Simms' reference to his contract "with Godey for a novel in his magazine to commence with January." The first installment of *Katharine Walton* was published, however, in the February issue.

am a member.[221] I need not assure you that though always a great gratification to hear from you & of yours, this gratification was enhanced when I discovered that my long failure to do so was due to no neglect of yours. If I understand the somewhat mysterious opening of your letter, you are of opinion that we knew or conjectured beforehand, the great recent event in your household. This is a mistake, and Miss K.[222] is perfectly innocent. We had no sort of notion that you & your wife ever seriously meditated so pleasant a surprise. Our first inkling of the affair was in your own exulting revelation of it. — We all rejoice that affairs have gone on so well with you, and that our fair wife, and the famous boy — the last Edition — thrives so wondrously, and unfolds such admirable promise. Let me implore you & Lady Lyde, not to conflict with nature by petting the urchin too greatly; for whatever his chosen name may be, it is one that we must require him to distinguish. On the subject of this name, I see all your difficulties. It is one upon which I must not permit myself a suggestion, however, I may allow myself a hope. The combination of W. G. S. L. would, as you say, be quite too long & unwieldy, and looking to the agreeable possibility to which you refer, it would surely be unadvisable to employ the S. The W. G. L. may be well enough, and has quite a poetical & euphonious sound upon the ear.[223] We shall feel honored — nay, feel that we are beloved — a more gratifying consciousness still, should this latter combination prevail; but we must forbear to say more in this connection; contenting ourselves with the hope that the infant stranger will realize all his father's expectations, requite all his mother's affections, and confer honor upon the friend, no matter who, upon whom it shall fall to provide the future name of one who is so grateful an object of interest. In all these wishes my wife & daughter join with the warm feeling of persons who feel from our long & precious ties, that we already constitute a portion of your family, as well as of your affections. Tell Lyde, I look forward to our conference with great anxiety. It is so long

221 William Gregg was president of the South Carolina Institute for the Promotion of Art, Mechanical Ingenuity, and Industry, which in 1849 numbered 160 members (see the Charleston *Courier* of May 8, 1849). The first annual fair was held in Hibernian Hall. Prizes were awarded for many sorts of inventions, among them cotton mill machinery, rice-harvesting devices, and silk machinery. For James H. Hammond's address delivered on the occasion, see note 195, Oct. 17, 1849.

222 Nancy Kellogg, of Great Barrington, Mass.

223 Lawson's son was named William Gilmore Simms.

—- it seems an age — since I have seen her. Has she forgiven my manifold offences. As for coming North this winter, I am afraid the thing is an impossibility. In addition to the Review, I have contracted with Godey for a novel in his magazine to commence with January. I have sent him seven chapters already. The tasks of the Review keep me busy, and its correspondence seems interminable. But my hope is to visit you next summer. And here, by the way, I must give you a matter which must be a strict secret between your wife and yourself. I have been applied to by the leaders of a party in our State to go to Congress, and have partially consented. The Election takes place next Oct. In a measure I am committed to them; though it is still possible that nothing may come of it. Something depends on our present secrecy. As the matter advances, you shall hear. — I am greatly touched at the brief account which you give of Forrest. Can I do any thing in the matter. Would a Letter from me to him be of any service, or is the unhappy topic *tabooed* entirely. Will you ask Bryant if he has recd. the Cassique? If not — let him ask for his copy at Putnam's, (see Panton) to whom I sent one with my compliments, addressed to B. as well as several others. I have reason to think that none have been delivered. Ask the same question of Duyckinck. To what do you allude when you tell me of your being such a good critic of verse — more than a verbal critic — and that I am an ungrateful fellow in not making due acknowledgements. If you have been writing any thing of late, *I have not seen it.* I have read "Frontenac" which I mean to speak kindly of; but it will not bear comparison with much that Street has already done.[224] The story is full of improbabilities, and the 'red paint' is in the most monstrous excess; but for your sake, and Street's own (whom I much like) I will be as kindly as possible. You see in the last number of the Review, I have been using the tomahawk & scalping knife, myself, with some freedom.[225] — Richards spent yesterday with me, at the plantation. We came from the city together. He is about to remove his paper to Charleston, having made engagements in that city of an auspicious nature.[226] — I see that Wetmore is in a whirl of

---

[224] A notice of Alfred Billings Street's *Frontenac: Or the Atotarho of the Iroquois* (New York: Baker and Scribner, 1849) appears in *S. Q. R.*, N. S., I, (April, 1850), 241-242.

[225] Of the forty-nine works reviewed in "Critical Notices," many are severely damned.

[226] *Richards' Weekly Gazette,* edited by William Carey Richards and published by C. L. Wheler in Athens, Ga., was first issued on May 13, 1848, as the

art conflicts. I get a paper occasionally (I think) from him; showing the progress of the conflict.[227] Give him my respects. Say to your wife that our children get on very well. Gilmore is a strapping urchin, and Mary Lawson quite an interesting sunny-haired, blue eyed Lassie. The baby walks, but has only three teeth. Augusta is well, and, with my wife, sends love in abundance, which you will please bestow in kisses as from me. I am truly anxious to see you all once more. I fancy it is because of the long interval of denial that I have grown thin. I am as slender now as at 24. — The Cigars will be acceptable, but you must say nothing about them. Forrest promised to send me a dog. I want it. Let him send it by Northerner or Southerner to the care of William Roach, Charleston.[228] God bless you all.

W. Gilmore Simms

514: To Francis Peyre Porcher [229]

Woodlands, S. C. Nov. 28. [1849][230]

Francis Peyre Porcher M D.
dear Sir:

I have read with pleasure the graceful notice by Mr. Ravenel

Southern Literary Gazette. The title was changed with the beginning of the second volume (May 5, 1849), and was again altered to the original title with the issue of May 4, 1850. After the issue of Dec. 22, 1849, the periodical was moved to Charleston. It was there first published by Walker and Richards (Richards having sold a half-interest to Joseph Walker), then by Walker, Richards and Co. (Walker and Richards having sold an interest in their firm to Edwin Heriot on Oct. 1, 1851). During 1850 and part of 1851 Richards was assisted in the editorship by D. H. Jacques. Heriot, also, served in an editorial capacity after he entered the firm. In Dec., 1852, Richards severed his connection with the *Southern Literary Gazette* and moved to New York City, and early the following year the periodical was merged with the *Weekly News*, edited by Paul Hamilton Hayne. For an account of the magazine, see Flanders, *Early Georgia Magazines,* pp. 95-105, and William Stanley Hoole, *A Check-List and Finding-List of Charleston Periodicals, 1732-1864* (Durham, N. C.: Duke University Press, 1936), pp. 55-56. Since no complete file of Richards' periodical is known to us, we have been unable to ascertain the extent of Simms' frequent contributions.

[227] N. P. Willis in the *Home Journal* charged Wetmore with mismanagement of the Art-Union. The New York *Evening Mirror* of Nov. 21 contains a defence of Wetmore, signed "Truth": "How contemptible in the 'Home Journal' are its flings at the gentleman whom the subscribers to the Art Union elect as the President—a man of fine taste, a scholar, passionately fond of the arts. . . ."

[228] Roach, half-nephew of Nash Roach, was a Charleston factor, operating a large shipping concern. His brother Edward later married Augusta Simms.

[229] See introductory sketch.

[230] Dated by Simms' reference to Henry William Ravenel's review of James Kearsley Mitchell's *On the Cryptogamous Origin of Malarious and Epidemic Fevers* (Philadelphia: Lea and Blanchard, 1849), *S. Q. R.*, N. S., I (April, 1850), 146-159. The article is signed "R." Ravenel (1814-1887) was an authority on fungi.

of the vol. of Dr. Mitchell on the cryptogamous origin of malarious & epidemic fevers, and shall endeavour to give it a place in the January number of the Review. As the contents of this number, however, had all been provided & were partly in the press before the receipt of Mr. Ravenel's article, it is possible that I may be compelled to defer its publication till the ensuing number; in which event I will hope that the author will be satisfied to submit to the temporary delay. — I gladly avail myself of your friendly offer to revise the proofs, which I shall instruct the printers to send to your address.

Yours very truly &c

W. Gilmore Simms

P. S. I trust that Mr. Ravenel will be persuaded to suffer the use of his initials in connection with his article.

515: To NATHANIEL BEVERLEY TUCKER

Woodlands S. C. Dec. 17 [1849][231]

Hon. Beverley Tucker.

dear Sir:

Your letters have quite spoiled me; and in your protracted silence I feel that I have reason for complaint: — for regret, certainly, as I had found a pleasure in their perusal very far superior to that which I draw from most similar sources. I trust that you suffer from no personal discomforts of health or association. Your last advices announced you as *en route* to Warrenton (?) Springs.[232] To that place I addressed you, and have been looking to hear from you ever since, in vain. I am the more solicitous to hear from a cause apart from the satisfaction which I derive from your correspondence. In my last (I think it was) I ventured some suggestions in respect to the social drama which you confided (in part) to my keeping; and almost apprehend from your long silence that I may have said something which was liable to misconstruction. May I hope that you will relieve

---

[231] Dated by Simms' reference to Tucker's "paper on the Present State of Europe . . . the initial article of the next number of the South. Quarterly." See note 155, Aug. 16, 1849.

[232] On Aug. 20 Tucker had written to Hammond: "I go, day after tomorrow to the Warrenton Springs (address me there). . . . " (Original in the Hammond Papers, Library of Congress.)

my doubts on this score. The closing portions of the Drama, I think I mentioned, never reached me. Have you any design of publishing it, — or have you any desire that I should find employment for it? — Your paper on the Present State of Europe forms the initial article of the next number of the South. Quarterly. I instructed the Printer, before I left the city, to send the proof sheets to yourself, if he could possibly allow of the delays unavoidable from doing so. He has not advised me whether this has been done or not. I should be pleased, if you design following up the subject, as you intimate, that your sequel should reach me in season for our April number.[233] We have material enough, and to spare, for that quarter, but I should prefer making some of my correspondents, here, give way to you; and should always forbear my own stuff, having before me contributions so much valued as are yours. — I have faltered over this clumsy sentence from a desire to avoid a seeming flattery, — of which I trust you will not suppose me guilty. I frankly assure you that I only consult the wishes of our readers, and the interest of the work, when I yield to you always a first place in our pages. — Hammond has been recently preparing & delivering a couple of orations very different in object from each other, — one before a Manufacturing & Industrial Institute, — and a manly capital performance; — the other before the Literary Societies of the S. C. College, — in which he shows an equal & just appreciation of polite letters and true philosophy. You will recieve them both when published. I have recently been relieving the *secretions* of some months by writing an Indian Tale in the octo syllabic, of some 1200 lines.[234] I like the thing — probably because it cost me so little effort — and may publish it. I sent you, by the way, a little volume of verse during the Summer, & by mail.[235] Did it reach you, — and have you yet recieved the mortal packet of my literary sins, done up for you & I hope despatched, more than six months ago? Have you seen Hildreth's History of the U. S.[236] The man seems to design to be just; but the justice of the historian implies the necessity of being the Philosopher also, — which Hildreth is evidently not.

---

[233] Tucker did not publish a sequel to his article.

[234] *Tselica.* See note 60, Feb. 16, 1850.

[235] *The Cassique of Accabee.* See letter to Tucker of July 27.

[236] Richard Hildreth, *The History of the United States of America, from the Discovery of the Continent to the Organization of Government under the Federal Constitution,* 3 vols. (New York: Harper & Brothers, 1849). The first two volumes are noticed in *S. Q. R.,* XVI (Oct., 1849), 258-259.

His pert preface is almost conclusive against him. But I have glanced only at a few pages, just enough to satisfy me that if the U. S. have heretofore wanted a Historian, the deficiency is not repaired by the new pretender. — Are we at the close of our experiment? You are of course, closely watchful of the proceedings in Congress. I frankly confess the difficulty about the Speaker is to my mind a grateful augury. It makes the issue in anticipation of the issue, and will afford an opportunity to our Yankee enemies to appreciate the future. The pretaste is evidently not palatable. I hardly care how long this state of things may continue. Let them sicken of it first. — And yet, after all, would it not be better to let the abolitionists precipitate the struggle, madly eager as they are — by suffering them to do their worst, so that there should be no patching up of the rents, which must soon again open. We in the South have really far less to apprehend from dissolution than the East or West. Our interests are almost single — unique. But what will be the bond of Union between New York, Phil. and Massachusetts. They clash in interest, in character, in almost every thing. But what need we care what becomes of them? They are our *fungi,* drawing the substance from our strength, and without either the gratitude to acknowledge, or the sense to know the fact. — Pray let me hear from you. I write this scrawl, without stopping to measure its meaning, after a day of toil, and with fingers stiff from the unbroken exercise of the pen. I do not even read what I have written, relying on my own intentions & your indulgence.

Very faithfully yr friend &c

W. Gilmore Simms

516: To James Henry Hammond

Woodlands Dec. 17. [1849][237]

Gen. J. H. Hammond

Dear Hammond.

You have every reason to rejoice in your triumph, which, so far as I can learn, has been complete in every respect which im-

---

[237] Dated by Simms' reference to Hammond's "triumph"—the oration delivered at the South Carolina College on Dec. 4, 1849. On Dec. 13 Hammond had written to Simms: "My address in Columbia was satisfactory to the boys & my friends generally—at least they all said so. I recd many compliments tho' I think few comprehended it. The Society has not asked for its publication

mediately concerns yourself. I had no doubts of your oration being perfectly successful, and just as few concerning your own reception. Your election with Cheves, Barnwell & Elmore, is another most conclusive triumph.[238] I should really like to be with you in the Southern Convention, and hope that our friend Conner will think of the matter, as properly initiatory of that which lies beyond. The business of the Bank, you percieve, is unfavorably disposed of in the House. The miserable absurdity of State faith to the foreign creditor, is a pretext of which the Coons of the House readily availed themselves. My warning to Memminger that he had foreborne to strike while the iron was

---

& I presume will not. . . . Preston (Wm) & his interesting wife, made every possible effort to keep every one they could from attending the chapel & P. openly vented his indignation & mortification when he heard there was a crammed audience of both sexes. The social cordon was drawn stringently in Columbia. No one but [James L.] Clark [teller at the branch at Columbia of the Bank of the State of South Carolina and formerly a director of the Bank] & Maxcy Gregg of the Columbians *dared* to call on me & I called on no one.— Yes [Maximilian] Laborde & [Francis] Lieber called. I have no reason to complain of others. On the whole Aldrich thought my visit did me good. To me it was damned dull & I never wish to repeat it. Harry [Hammond's son] entered College & is there—how long to remain I can't tell. There is no baseness to which Preston & others of my enemies there would not descend to wound & injure me." (Original in the Hammond Papers, Library of Congress.) Hammond's oration was printed under the title of *An Oration, Delivered before the Two Societies of the South-Carolina College, on the 4th of December, 1849* (Charleston: Walker and James, 1850). It is reviewed by Tucker in *S. Q. R.*, N. S., I (April, 1850), 37-48.

238 Langdon Cheves (1776-1857), of Charleston, was a member of the South Carolina House of Representatives (1802-1808), attorney-general of South Carolina (1809), a member of Congress (1810-1815), and president of the Bank of the United States (1819-1822). In 1850 he declined the appointment as successor to Calhoun in the United States Senate.

Cheves, Robert W. Barnwell, Franklin H. Elmore, and Hammond had been elected to be the delegates from South Carolina at the Southern Convention to be held in Nashville, Tenn. The Charleston *Mercury* of Dec. 13 reports: "The selection of Delegates . . . made by the Legislative caucus, has been received, as far as we can judge, with great satisfaction. It is said, on all sides, that a better choice could not be made. Messers. Elmore and Hammond are among the strong men identified with the stirring scenes of present politics. . . . " Hammond wrote to Simms on Dec. 20: "As to my success in Columbia *dubito*. I have seen the balloting for the Convention & will confess to you that it is truly mortifying. It is as follows: 1 bal—Cheves 91—Elmore 57—Barnwell 49— Hammond—47. 113 votes. 2 bal—Barnwell 82 Hammond 55—99 votes. Thus I got on after a scramble & on less than *one third* of the votes of the whole Legislature. Can I feel that I represent the State? . . . You see the Mercury put me down with Elmore as among the *active* politicians, *pushing* forward. Of all positions this is one I least desire to occupy. . . . In dead earnest I wish my friends to drop me forever rather than keep up the fighting, to their own disadvantage & my mortification.

"I wish very much you may be sent to the Convention & Jamison & I will try to give hints in the proper quarters." (Original in the Hammond Papers, Library of Congress.)

hot, has been realized.[239] I felt sure that he had only scotched, not killed the snake. Elmore was in the condition of the despot described by Byron —

> 'The tyrant waked to sudden strife,
> By graze of ill directed knife." [240]

Under such circumstances he adds the audacity of desperation to the use of the ordinary skills and weapons. There was another matter which a veteran like Memminger should not have over-looked — viz: that the members of the House, at the closing Session & about to return to their constituents, are the most timid race in the world — frightened easily by their own shadows, — who will then never do any thing of a decisive character. All measures involving change, new appropriations &c. must be con-summated in the opening Session of a new House. This point it will be well to look at hereafter. — Your brother writes me that the Gubernatorial contest is to lie between Pickens & Means, and that as Pickens is Anti Bank & Means neutral, we must go for the former.[241] But this is a matter which needs a little more policy. If Means be neutral, may he not be made to come out — *pour ou contre*? Better be defeated on the question fairly made, than beaten apart from the question with the probability, not only of yielding the Gov. to the enemy, but of impressing the vulgar with the idea of their superior strength. Now, my notion is that, if the contest rest only on the issues of their rival popularity, Means is the strongest man. He seems to me a good fellow also, upon whom if we could get him with us, I should cheerfully rely. Might he not be managed, so as to adopt a decisive resolution, running against Pickens upon com-

---

[239] For Christopher Gustavus Memminger's speech against rechartering the Bank of the State of South Carolina, delivered before the House of Repre-sentatives on Dec. 9, 1848, see note 37, c. Feb. 25, 1849. Hammond had written to Simms on Dec. 13: "The Bank I think will escape this time & Memminger & [Alexander] Mazyck are such miserable managers that if it can be done, our party will be defeated before the people. I merely spoke to Mem. once in the street—not a word of Bank. I attempted once to talk of it with Mazyck & found him an ass. If the present Bill is carried, it will be about the worst plan that could have been adopted to get rid of the institution." After the post-ponement of the Bill (see the Charleston *Mercury* of Dec. 15), Hammond wrote to Simms on Dec. 20: " . . . I discovered that his Bill which was a weak—half way measure—just not worse than the Bank if properly carried out & *much worse* in *bad hands*—would not pass." (Originals in the Hammond Papers, Library of Congress.)

[240] See *The Bride of Abydos,* Canto I, 11. 342-343.

[241] Francis W. Pickens did not enter the race for governor. John Hugh Means (1812-1862) defeated John H. Buchanan in Dec., 1850, and served for one term.

mon ground? The thing is worth the inquiry. — I wrote to you in Columbia, but as appears, too late. I waited on Miles.[242] You have my letter by this time, & I wait on you for an answer. I look also for a long letter in regard to your Columbia experiences. I have had some hints in regard to them, — some of which are amusing enough. I almost regret that I did not go; but I had such a world of work! — I see that DeLeon's paper [243] has come out for the Bank. I suspected something, as I found him fight shy of both of us in the city. — What are those revelations of Marshall [244] — have they any signification, — or is he only blundering to the detriment of his own skull. Mazyck seemed to think light of him, & it appears doubtful that the Bank officers should yield him any real hold upon their secret operations. If he fails, the recoil will hurt the assailants. — Let me hear from you soon. — By the way I have written to Jamison to propose the first week in Jan. as the time for our onslaught upon you.[245]

Yours Truly &c

W. G. Simms

P. S. I have also counselled Jamison to run as the delegate from this Congressional District, for the Southern Convention. We owe J. something, and this distinction, I fancy, will prove grateful. Besides, he is a true fellow, and will keep the right position. Should *we* all go, we shall carry some strength which may be quite important to the issue. If you concur with me, in regard to J., set the Ball in motion in your quarter.

517: To NATHANIEL BEVERLEY TUCKER

Woodlands, S. C. Decr. 24. [1849][246]

My dear Sir:

It is only two or three days ago since I sent you a scribble deploring your silence. The last mail brings me your letter ad-

---

[242] Probably William Porcher Miles.

[243] The Columbia *Daily Telegraph.*

[244] J. Foster Marshall, a graduate of the South Carolina College in 1837, was a captain in the Palmetto Regiment during the Mexican War. He was State senator from Abbeville from the meeting of the General Assembly in December, 1848, to his death at Second Manassas, August 30, 1862, where he was serving as colonel of the South Carolina Regiment.

[245] See letters to M. C. M. Hammond of *c.* Jan. 10, 1850, and to Tucker of Jan. 30, 1850.

[246] Dated by Simms' references to Tucker's "paper on the Present State of England [Europe]," published in the Jan., 1850, issue of the *Southern Quarterly Review,* and to Tucker's play, "Viola," discussed earlier in Simms' letter to Tucker of Sept. 6.

dressed to me at Charleston. We are now at the plantation, and
I have just quaffed to your health in a bowl of eggnog. I wish
you were with us to share the draught. We do not forego our
cakes and ale, even though virtue is in such great increase
throughout the land; and I hope shortly to make a tour among
certain friends, Hammond among them, in full expectation of
mixing Pope & Cardinal, the good old English beverages, in
honour of what was genial in Old England. We shall not forget
you when the bumper goes round. I should have greatly relished your mountain progress. I trust we shall not always be
denied. Let us hope. — I think I may venture to say that Campbell's Lords Chancellors has not been anticipated, and that you
may undertake it. I suggested it to Chancellor Lessesne, a clever
man of this State, now of Alabama, who promised to put himself
in harness, but he has not responded.[247] Should he do so, you
will scarcely come in conflict, particularly, if I understand you as
designing a special notice of one portion only of the work. His
would be general, if he wrote at all, taking up certain points &
principles chiefly, — certain decisions & perhaps sprinkling the
article with biographical sketches of certain of our local authorities in past times. I hope that you will deliver yourself of the
matter which you find so provocative. It is perhaps important,
regarding it as you do, that you should put forth your opinions,
and insist upon your objections. But does not your paper on the
Present State of England, promise a continuation? I find that the
Publishers, pleading want of time, have not sent it to you. — I
am not sure that you are right in assuming your first scene in
the drama to be the best or most animated. I think the most
forcible writing, the best thought, and most lively dialogue occurs
nearly at the close of the portion sent me. I was aware that you
mentioned in a previous letter that the plan was based upon a
fact occurring within your experience; but that if you will permit
me to say does not wholly render it an art — probability — particularly in a form of composition which admits of no preliminary

---

[247] Joseph W. Lesesne (1811-1856), born at Georgetown, S. C., moved to
Alabama as a young man, where, in 1847, he became chancellor. During the
heated controversies of 1855-1856 Lesesne acquired considerable reputation as a
political writer. His wife was the daughter of Dr. Thomas Cooper (see note
84, Dec. 1, 1840). Simms had earlier reviewed the First Series of John, Lord
Campbell's *The Lives of the Lord Chancellors and Keepers of the Great Seal
of England*, 3 vols. (Philadelphia: Lea & Blanchard, 1847), in *S. Q. R.*, XII
(Oct., 1847), 375-408. No further review of the work was published in the
Southern Quarterly Review.

explanations. I have no doubt that if you were to employ the same subject in the form of the narrative — make it a novel, — all difficulties of this sort could be reconciled & it rendered easy. In such a work you could have frequent opportunities for that detailed progress of events which would enable you to harmonize all the inequalities and smooth over all the objections to the leading fact, as an improbable, or at least so unfrequent a one, as *per se,* must rather startle & offend, than persuade the faith of the reader. — I have written to my agent in the city to forward the bundle to the care of Mr. Kennedy.[248] I do not now remember what volumes I have sent you. They will probably rather represent the unequal & irregular progress of my mind, than its power. Many of them are productions of a very immature and rudely tutored youth. You will make allowances for these. Looking back over the long tract of a busily employed life in letters, I am constrained to feel that I have done myself no justice. I need not say to you how discouraging to an independent mind is the field in which the literary American has to work, at least when he is compelled to combine with his hope of fame, the necessity of procuring the means of subsistence. My hope now is in what remains to me to perform, not in what is already on the record. But I must not fall into egotism. — I note what you say of the last number of the Review. I have no doubt that the printers have sadly mischieved several of the articles. I am myself unwilling to examine the proof except of my own writings, and we have no competent persons in Charleston who can be got for this purpose. Indeed, the work is not in a condition to procure their services. You allude to the impressive reflection with which the Reviewer of Layard, closes his article.[249] You are yourself the source of that reflection. I read to Dr. Lynch your letter which contained it, and counselled the use of it as a sort of a keynote for the Review; but he had already made some progress in the paper and could not remodel. Indeed, though a very clever man, he is by no means capable of rising from his immediate topic to the great governing moral, of the subject, and could not have expanded the idea, or done more than he has done with

---

[248] John P. Kennedy. See letter to Tucker of July 13, 1849.

[249] "In that after life the individual receives the chief award due to his virtues or his sins. Nations and cities receive theirs *in this world.* We need but look at the social misery of our own times, the wild spirit of anarchy and excess that has seized the minds of men, and contemplate the yet darker abyss into which sinful nations are even now plunging, to know the HAND that laid Nineveh waste can yet punish."—XVI (Oct., 1849), 31.

it. Let me hope that you will seize upon some text which will enable you to do so, and to develope that fine strain of reflection which fills the letter now before me. The happy union of the moral & the contemplative, with the historical, which is a distinguishing feature in your writings, constitutes the leading charm in Review literature, and I earnestly entreat you to work out the vein while the daylight lasts. — Hammond has recently written an oration of a literary character, delivered before the Societies of Columbia College. When published, I could wish that you would review it.[250] I fancy you will find it copiously suggestive of considerations which could rise in no mind more successfully than yours, and be illustrated by no pen more gratefully or gracefully. — I think I mentioned to you in my last that I had recently written an Indian Story of some 1200 lines,[251] which I shall publish after a season. I have just given to a couple of printers in Charleston for their own benefit, a couple of slight volumes. One consists of versions from & paraphrases of various passages in Scripture, chiefly from Isaiah, & some original things of serious character. I call it Sabbath Lyrics, a *brochure* of 72 pages.[252] I shall send this to you soon. The other volume is entitled "Father Abbot" or the Home Tourist, a series of dialogues — essays in that form, which were published last summer in one of our city papers, were liked, and have been gathered into a little pocket volume of 240 pages. This will also reach you soon after I recieve my copies. — I have written you a long & wretched scrawl, with numbed fingers and weary eyelids. I should rather read your letters than write my own. Do not spare yours because mine are short & valueless. Remember my toils.

Yours very faithfully &c.

W. Gilmore Simms

---

[250] Tucker's review of Hammond's *Oration . . . before . . . the South-Carolina College* was published in *S. Q. R.*, N. S., I (April, 1850), 37-48. See note 68, Feb. 26, 1850.

[251] "Tselica." See note 60, Feb. 16, 1850.

[252] See note 130, *c.* July 9, 1849. The Charleston *Courier* of Dec. 31 says: "It is hardly necessary to speak of the contents of the work, rather than to say it contains short Poems, on religious subjects, from the pen of W. Gilmore Simms, to insure its general perusal. The dedication of the unpretending, yet very elegant little holyday present is touching, and characteristic of one devoted to the Muses. . . . "

518: To James Lawson

Woodlands, Decr. 24. 1849.

Dear Lawson.

On the Eve of Christmas, I sit down to send you our affectionate remembrance in a hurried scribblement. We hear from you at such intolerable fits & starts, that during the long intervals which settle down between your letters, we are always kept in some anxiety, as to your safety, health, good fortune & other matters. We write accordingly in some doubt lest during the pause you may have had sorrows and losses, and exposing our fears in the very utterance of our hopes that such may not be the case. How is the last new domestic publication?[253] That is the first question. We pray that mother and child both maintain their places, healthfully & happily in your sight, and that the elder children, with their noses (as a matter of course) somewhat out of joint, are yet free from any annoyance in any other of their joints. All of my household unite with me in the expression of a warm solicitude in respect to yours, and we give you a 'Merry Christmas' with hearts as fond as you desire, and I fear much more fond than such a woful (if not wilful) correspondent deserves. Bestow a kiss for me on the lips of the fair woman whom you have for wife, and request her to bestow the same on my behalf, upon each of her many little ones. I could wish to do this duty in pro. per. but the Gods who deny in my case, more than *half* the prayer of the mortal, have set their veto upon every desire of this sort that I may entertain. — We are all as well as could be expected, or almost wished. Our babe flourishes with five teeth, and promises, it is thought, to be a beauty. Our boy is as sturdy as a sapling, and growing famously like one. He can outrun, outjump, outclimb, Master Jemmy any day — tell him that — though I some what doubt if he can stand a tug with him at syllables & syntax. In writing, he is now deep in sticks, Hooks, Pothooks, and other hieroglyphics which do not call for a Champollion, *la jeune.*[254] — As for Mary Lawson, she is a tender, talkative thing, very much like her amiable namesake. She is as plump as a partridge, as fat and round as Christina. But a truce! We owe thanks to God for his favors to us, and faithfully implore le bon Dieu that he will bless yours. — I am

---

[253] William Gilmore Simms Lawson. See letter to Lawson of Nov. 24, 1849.
[254] Jean François Champollion (1790-1832), Egyptologist.

now engaged in getting out the Review for January. This keeps me busy. If this were not enough, — I am busy with a novel to be furnished in parts to Godey's Book. Ten chapters are already written. It is entitled "Katharine Walton, or the Rebel's Daughter." It is to run through Godey's Year, or 12 Nos. During the last summer, I wrote a series of Essays in one of the Charleston papers entitled "The Home Tourist, a medley". These were liked & have been gathered into a 16 mo of 240 pages. I will send you a copy soon. Another little brochure of mine entitled "Sabbath Lyrics" has also been given to the press, some 72 pages, — which I will also send you; and some two weeks ago, under a full blast of the divine afflatus, and at a single bound, I wrote an Indian Poem of 1200 lines [255] — the work (the rough draft) of 4 days. So, you see what occasions I have had to be busy. — Have you recieved for me from Forbes a bundle of MS?[256] If so (and he writes me to this effect) forward it to the care of "John Russell, Bookseller, Charleston." Any of the publishers will forward for you. — You have all my news. I have none, at least, that can much concern you out of my family. Did you ask Bryant if he got the Cassique? I see that miserable skunk of the Knickerbocker has been indulging in some flings at you.[257]

---

[255] "Tselica." See note 60, Feb. 16, 1850.

[256] "Benedict Arnold."

[257] The *Knick.*, XXXIV (Sept., 1849), 279, speaks of "a conceited Scotch littérateur, of the smallest calibre, who once brought in a 'critique' on Halleck's *'Marco Bozzaris*,['] of which noble poem he had a very poor opinion indeed! —*he*, who, as his first American employer informed us the other day, could not, on his arrival in America, write a common newspaper paragraph of three lines without a grammatical error!"

Simms also had not escaped the *Knickerbocker's* attacks. In XXXIII (June, 1849), 553, is the following comment: "There is nothing about which there are more unmeaning twaddle and pure cant than in the dissertations of certain of our small uneducated *littérateurs* upon the necessity of a *'National Literature.'* A sectional novelist, let us suppose, who has survived a shortlived reputation for cleverness at elaborating 'things in books' clothing,' when informed by one of our first publishers, in declining his MSS., that his works *do n't sell,* whether published in New-York, Philadelphia, or Charleston, shall reply, with mortification 'in 's aspect,' 'It is because we have no encouragement for a National Literature!' National fiddlestick! Do Irving, Cooper, Prescott, Bryant, Halleck, Longfellow, and kindred men of mark and genius, complain that there is no encouragement for *their* 'national literature?' No; and for the best of good reasons; their repeated editions find a ready market, instead of being tied up in sheets, and crowded upon the highest shelves of our popular book-stores, labelled with names which repeat to every visitor, *'No Sale!'"* The *Knick.*, XXXIV (Nov., 1849), 442, further remarks: "Time was, when even Mr. Simms' 'novels' were read; but now few publish, and fewer read, elaborations of that class."

What is the affair between him & Mathews.[258] What of Duyckinck, Mathews & the rest. How does Forrest come on in his lonely castle. I sorrow for him truly. Pray make me up a budget of items that may rejoice me on the New Year. — Once more my love to your wife — who I fear forgets me (or you would not) — and believe me

Ever faithfully as Ever
Your friend &c

W. Gilmore Simms

---

[258] The New York *Evening Mirror* of Nov. 27, 1849, reprints from the New York *Tribune* a letter by Mathews, dated Nov. 26, 1849, in which he accuses Lewis Gaylord Clark of "malignant malice" in reviews of his books.

APPENDIX

Of the plantation books kept at Woodlands only one, now in the South Caroliniana Library, appears to be extant. It was started in 1845 and contains regular entries through 1850. A few lines only are devoted to 1851, when this book was evidently discarded as the regular register of plantation events, though miscellaneous entries dating from the mid-1850's through 1874 are included in the latter part of the volume. Those covering the period 1845-1850, printed below, were entered for the most part by Nash Roach, though some entries were made by Simms, and others (those relating to the churning) appear to have been made by Mrs. Simms. At this time Simms was not the sole manager of the plantation, as he later became; yet this book is important in presenting a phase of his career not revealed elsewhere.

WOODLANDS PLANTATION BOOK, 1845-1850

1845 April 22. Isaac sheared the sheep which he reports in number as follows

> 18 old Ewes.
> 5 young Ewes
> 3 old Rams
> 5 old wethers
> 9 young wethers

---

    40 now in the Yard—and he reports *three* in the pasture, & some yet to be hunted for by Antony. This memorandum drawn from Isaac's Tally, he being present.

W. G. S.

April 22 Planted Potatoes during a spell of dry weather which has lasted three months or more: The beds dry as dust: Weather cloudy but cool, morning and evening, and very hot at noon in the sun.

April 22, 1845

Weighed 70 lbs. wool, sheared this day from 26 head sheep.

[585]

Sent to Mrs. Dewitt, a few months ago—35—lbs Woolen and 26 lbs. Cotton spun into thread: in return for which she sent us 44 yards Cloth, yard wide, and returned 16 lbs Woolen and 2 lbs Cotton yarn.

April 23. A slight shower this day, just to sprinkle the ground. The weather cloudy and cool.

Mem: On the 11th. 12 & 13 April (this month) Corn killed by the frost.

May, 6 a fine shower —
May, 12 *a fine rain*
May, 13 a do shower. This day put a piece of *cloth in the* loom, of 52 yrds.
May 17. A very cool and clear morning—Some of the negroes reported a frost
May 18, 1845. Churned this day one pound nine ounces

$$
\begin{array}{r}
\text{and a half.} \quad 9\frac{1}{2} \\
9 \\
9 \\
\hline
16)27(\frac{1}{2} \\
16 \\
\hline
1
\end{array}
$$

May 24 — Several tassels are seen this day in the pine-land field, planted the 12th of March.

Carolina seed ⎱
October 21   planted wheat in Ginhouse field ⎰

"   22d planted do in negro house do ⎱   ⎧gathered
New York seed ⎰   16 bushels to
the acre
New York seed,
31   planted do in wheat patch ⎱   and 12 bushels
over the branch ⎰   Carolina seed

Gathered from Devils Cut Swamp field . .   14 loads Corn

from Bickley* "   " **11**

* This field is now called "Beckley."

" Fish trap & sand ridge... 8

" Piney Island 4

" Over the Lake 4

" House field 5

" Pine Land do 32

There is besides
about 24 loads,
or 600 bushels
of old corn,
remaining, from
Last Year.

total 78 Loads

Novr 5th *Ice* & white frost first time

Nov 23 (Sunday) churned 2 lbs 5½ oz of butter

Nov 25 ('Tuesday) churned 2 lbs of butter

Nov 28 (Friday) churned 2 lbs 5½ do

Nov 30 (Sunday) churned 2 lbs 8 oz of butter

Dec 21 ('Tuesday) churned 2 lbs 11 oz of butter

Dec 5 (Friday) churned 3 lbs 5½ oz of butter

Dec 7 (Sunday) .... 3 lb 11½ oz ....

Dec 10 (Wednesday) .... 3 lbs 13½ oz ....

Dec 12 Friday .... 3 lbs 9½

Dec 14 Sunday .... 3 lbs 5½

Dec 16 Taken from the Loom this day 46 yards cloth—wool—&
cotton—

pr Centage of State Tax 1845

800 acres @ $3 — $2400

1806 " @ 20 361.20

Taxes

Tax Collector appears
about the 27 February

100   2761.20 @ 30 Cts is $8.28
62 Barnwell Negroes @ 55 .... 34.10

100    $42.38

Robt Roskill, Liverpool,

500 acres tendable swamp @ $4 pr acre

9140 No of my [Roach's] watch

300 do unprofitable @.... $1

1806 poor pine land @ 20 cents

[1846]

March 13th finished planting potatoes this day, 10 acres
    "   14th commenced dropping manure in pine land field,
             finished on the 17th.
        18th commenced planting corn today in pine land and potatoe
             patch fields, finished on 20th 90 acres.

March 20 — 28 yrds woollen up stairs and 66¼ yrds of cotton —
domestic manufacture. *2 pieces* of kersey, and a small roll — *bought*

    "   21st ⎰Commenced planting corn in the swamp Devil's **Cut**
          ⎱60 acres—finished 25th. two lost days from **rain**—
           no manure
    "   26th. Began planting the lowermost rail road field in **corn**
           (40 acres) 20 of which manured, ground cut.
           finished 28th.
        28th. Planting today Bickleys lower swamp in corn 40 **acres**
           finished 4 April ground too wet
        31   Commenced planting corn in Lower Swamp field 40 **acres**
        31st Rain all day and night. Corn pretty well up; first **plant**,
           C.
April 1st. Rain—a constant drizzly rain with occasional **heavy**
           showers day & night
        2d   Rain till 10 oClock A. M
        3d   Clear and cool this morning the wind still east
           finished planting corn over the Lake 20 acres flint
        4th. Planted Piney Island field flint Corn 16 acres
           Drizzly weather for some days. ground wet and **some**
           time lost in planting Cotton
        8th. Planted Cotton on the river field, and will continue **to**
           plant out all of the cotton until done
        10   Replanting corn in pine land field —
        13   Stella had a male mule colt
        15   Cowslip — a female mule colt
        21   Commenced plowing Corn upland
        "   Planting Rice & hoeing scalp-off potatoes
        "   First mess green peas
      a great deal of rain all of this month. much time lost
April 25 — Churned 2 lbs 12 oz½ of butter
April 29 — Churned 3 lbs 6 oz½ of butter & commenced a **piece**
    of cloth —

May 1st   Finished ploughing upland running only 3 ploughs most
           of the time: the last two days 6 ploughs — the rest
           were throwing up cotton beds — time lost by a good
           deal of rain —
           Put in the vat today, 18 Hides and 5 skins for tanning,
           after liming and soaking 20 days —

May 6   Sheared the Sheep this day   viz 40 old ones & 10 lambs
           20 old Ewes and 6 Young ones   26
           14 old wethers and 4 do   18
           6 Rams   &½   6
                                                 —
           (Amount of wool 84 lbs)   50 head
           Turned in the pasture and several remain in the woods
           not yet found —

"   13th   Commenced ploughing the pine land field a second time
    14th & 15th Rain — a great deal of rain this month also.
"   first mess of snap-beans to day —
"   17.   Counted young poultry — 85 chickens & 28 ducks
    18th   Rain — 20th Rain.
"   20th   101 chickens and 45 young ducks

                           1846

Octr 1st   planted bearded wheat in Gin house Lot
    20th   "   Carolina do in Negro do   "
           thin ice reported on the 21st

Gathered from Devils Cut of Corn this Year   12 loads Corn
           from Bickleys lower swamp   4
           from   "   & Estes' line field 11
           from Piney Island   2
           from Over the Lake   3
           from Pine land field   22
           from Potatoe Patch do   4
                                            ——
           bushels 28½.61.64.40   58 loads
     Rice made this Year ....   ⎫
           42.52.60.53½   save away   ⎬
                          7 bushels   ⎭   341 bushels
     Potatoes ....   38 stacks
Shoemakers Last No 1 will make two pair

Viz   Stewart and
     Abraham   Yards of Cloth Decr 1846 to 1847
_____

Last No 2 will make   1 piece 24—Yards Colored Wool & Cotton
12 pair
     Viz   1 piece 17½ Yards Cotton
     Willm. Carpenter   "   17—   "   "
     Antony
     Bob   "   34¾   Stripes   "
     Tom   "   18   dark striped
     Jacob
     Oliver   "   47¾   Yellow   "
     Jim   "   50 Yards Wool & Cotton by Rose
     Bourdeaux
     Jim (Young)   Jany   50 Yards   do   do
     Landy   28th. 50 Yards   do   do
     Moses
     John   April 23. 50 Yards   Do   Do

_____

Last No 3 will make 11 for
     Viz
     Robert
     Champion
     Willm. (fat)
     Delia
     Amelia
     Aaron
     Cassandra
     Albert
     Flora
     Jenny O
     Jenny S

_____

Last No. 4 will make 11 pair
     Viz
     Diana
     Abbey
     Tyrah (little)
     Ned
     Albert (big)

Betty
Billy
Tyrah O
Sylvia
Mary
Peggy

Last No 5 will make 9 pair
    Viz
        Charlotte
        Maria
        Doll
        Sancho
        Laurence
        Harriet
        Cynthia
        Emma
        Emily

Mrs Clayton 12 small chickens
    1 doz & 9 eggs 14 more " 6 of which grown
Mrs Sanders 1 Doz eggs
List of Young Calves from 1st Octr 1846
    Browning has a bull calf red & marked like old Bull
    Old Blue Cow a Hieffer   do   do   do   do —
  Big White Cow with black head do   do   " and speckled
    Young black & mottled cow from the old blue a Bull do red &
    white
    Young black   do   (Crow) a Bull dark brown by Young bull
Jany 8th Killed hogs (first killing) 12 head
1847
Jany 16 Turned the Sheep on the Rye this day.
  "   22d Killed 14 head hogs
March 4 planted sugar cane
March 10th. Planted Corn at Jenning's this day 40 acres
        15 commenced planting Corn pine land 90 acres (manur'd)
        finished in 4 days: weather cold and icy
March 17 Made 10 dozen candles
        19th Commenced planting Corn in Swamp this side Rail road
        finished 23d 11 oClock 80 acres (manured)

23d Commenced planting Corn swamp at Devils line 60 acres
finished at 2 oClock 24th no manure

24th   planting lower swamp field 40 acres Corn
not manured will finish tomorrow 25th. when all
of the Corn Crop will have been planted.

26   planted potatoes (two days) some other bedding in the
field for Cotton (10 acres potatoes & 2 acres for Cotton

April 7th   Planted Mastodon Cotton in Rye patch
Replanting Corn Pine land & every where

12 plows {

12th. Commenced plowing Corn upland Jenning's 40 acres
and pine land 90 acres, finished 18th (7 days)

20th. Commenced plowing Corn Morris field swamp over
the Rail Road 40 acres finished 21st—2 days

22d Commenced the field this side Rail road and the horse
pen opposite 40 acres finished 23d at nooning time
ground broke in the winter, which was not the case
with Morris field lower down and opposite

23d   Commenced plowing corn Lower Swamp 40 acres
finished 26th   Sunday intervening—2½ days

27   Commenced plowing corn next Devils 60 acres
finished 29. Got over the first plowing 16½
days—2 day & ½

" Sheared the Sheep this day Viz 47 old ones 20 lambs

28 old Ewes and 6 Young ones	28	
20 old Wethers " 14	"	34
6 Rams		6
		———
	68 head	

Amount Wool 116 lbs
21st. Put the hides to soak
25th   first mess green peas
28th and 29th   planted Rice
29th noon — Commenced plowing 2d time Corn at Pine
land & Jennings' 12 plows finished 7 oClock 7
days ¼ Rain

May 1   Put the hides in lime
7th   Commenced 2d time plowing Morris field 40 acres this
morning 10 oClock finished Monday at 10 oClock 2 days
10th   Commenced the field this side Rail road & horse pen
opposite 40 acres finished 11th 2 days

12   Commenced plowing lower swamp field 40 acres
        finished 15th 13 & 14 ploughs stop — rain.

"   Took the hides out of lime haired them and put them to
        soak or bail [?] for ten days

13   Plows stop today on a/c of a heavy rain last night.
        We have had several heavy showers during the last 8
        or 10 days—

20th   Finished ploughing Devil Cut Corn 60 acres
        Got round 2d ploughing of all the Corn in 22 days,
        plowed potatoes & some Cotton up to 21st

22d   plowed out the potatoes today preparatory to hauling
        them up

Monday 24 Commenced today plowing Corn 3d time beginning with
        pine land field, Jenning's

26   Rain stop the ploughs

27   send the ploughs in the swamp to
        plough Cotton

28th & 29th ploughs at home, too wet.

Monday May 31

        Plows 9 in number begin today at Jenning's. Corn looks
uncommonly well. three plows in Cotton Bickleys near the
big lake

Result last Year, or Crop of 1847 too much Rain for Cotton

Novr 1

        Gathered from Devils Cut this Year Corn

		say	9 loads
over the Rail Road			13
This side	do		9
Lower Swamp			10
Jennings			8
Potatoe patch —			5
Pine Land field			29
			83 Loads

Cotton .... 40 Bales
Rice .... 90 bushels
Sugar ....

Novr 23d.   Planted wheat this day, the first Rain since 1 Sept
        last. The first patch of wheat planted 1st October
        not up yet on account of the long drought

[1848]

March 9	Bought 1 doz & ½ weeding hoes
13	planted Corn at Jenning's 50 acres
18th	Commenced planting Corn in pine land and will go through until all is planted
30th	finished planting all of the Corn 200 acres of which is manured
April 10th	Commenced planting Cotton
11th	Commenced plowing Corn today at Jenning's
15	do do pine land on Saturday
29th	Finished plowing all of the Corn First time today
May 20	finished plowing all corn 2d time today.
" "	Best Mule killed today by a rattlesnake in 10 minutes
22	Commenced plowing Corn third time today

May 24 — 1848   Negro cloth wove from 1st January 1848
Sept 12 pieces of soap   Jan
and 16 candles

     1 piece 51 Yards Cotton & Wool
    22-1 piece 51 Yards Cotton & Wool
    Feb-1 piece 51 Yards Cotton & Wool
   May—18-1 piece 51 Yards Cotton & Wool

1849

   March 19½ Yrds left from 1848
  21st " 1 piece 49 Yrds woollen cloth

Result of Crop of 1848 *Dry Year, no Rain,* Burnt up.

Novr 1	Gathered from Bickleys Corn	15 loads
	Over Swamp field	14
	Fish trap	2
	Over the Lake	5
	Potatoe patch field	3
	Pine land	26
	Jenning's	12

              77 Loads
    new wagon body larger than last Year
Cotton
Rice .... 85 bushels
Sugar ....
Wheat planted middle October

Nov 4   planted sugar cane
             Commenced planting Corn on the 1st March
             finished planting all on the 15th.
             Dry, warm and pleasant weather
          All of the Rice planted also

                        [1849]

March 26th. All of the corn cut down by frost about one plant
             in 20 killed—the Green peas not injured!
     30th.   Commenced plowing Corn this day, first rounds
Apl   15   first mess of green peas; the ground and house tops
             covered with snow!
      16   finished plowing all the Corn 1st round
             We have had scarcely any rain at all thus far
             Winter & Spring
May 6th.   the drought still continues   No rain. the upland corn
             has recovered from the snow and successive 5 days
             of black frost; all of the swamp corn nearly killed
             with frost & dry weather: it has all been replanted
             not more than 1 hill in 20 standing, the Cotton planted
             the 6th of April is still in the ground, and the seed
             as dry as when put in   very little is up in the swamp,
             and the upland cotton cannot come up at all unless we
             have rain
             Prospects gloomy enough
             every vegetable in the garden burned up, the whole
             earth a bed of hot sand, and the cattle suffering for
             water
             Isaac sheared this year the following sheep
                 25 old ewes and 10 Young Ones   35
                 23 old wethers & 4   do   27
                  3 Rams   3
                                                    ————
                                        head   65
May 7   a heavy rain
     13th   the Cotton which has been in the ground since the 6 Apl
             is nearly all up: it does not look well.
Novr 2   planted wheat
  " 10   finished gathering Corn, Result
                 Over the Lake . . . .   9 loads
                 Fish trap   4

Pasture of Bickley . . . .　4

House Lots . . . .　4

Jennings barn . . . .　8

"　　House . . . .　9

"　　Long . . . .　16

Rail Road . . . .　10

Bickley, R R . . . .　6

　do　this side . . . .　5

　　　　　　　　　　　　　　——————

　　　　　　　　　　　　　　75 Loads

Peas (wagon loads) 24

Rice . . . . 72 bushels

Potatoes　　　　　　　　　　　　　46 Banks

Cotton . . . . 49 Bales

　　　　　　　　Sugar　　　　½ barrel

24th　planted Rye

[1850]

March 9　Commenced planting Corn

23d　We had to stop today on account of incessant rains the swamp inundated, and no cotton beds lapped yet planting Potatoes

The seasons have been so wet and rainy and [not] having an overseer there seems to have been nothing done at the usual time, I have not therefore kept any regular Register

Apl 30th　The first mess of green peas this day —

May 8　the two upland fields of Cotton on the Road were hauled up and finished this day.

Commenced at first with 3 or 4 hands and one skimmer — cotton looks well. weather dry —

" 28th.　The two fields upland on the main road were a second time hauled up and thinned to one, Bickleys is as fine or finer than any in the State. Johnsons field is run away with, with the Lice, most persons say it will survive and shake them off, as the weather becomes hot, my own opinion is that the Cotton will be injured 50 pr cent, and a great deal of it killed—time will shew — There are no persons can say what will be the result; they all talk nonsense on the subject ————*The Lice quit the cotton by the 10th June but the dry weather

& the stunt given by the lice made the cotton turn out not more than a half crop.

Wheat has the rust badly but the grains are large and look well, and will be ripe in one week. No body can say what will be its fate—it is folly to ask experienced neighbors riding by—their opinions are worthless— turned out Two barrels flour to 15 acres

May 30th Forms are to be seen in the Cotton at Bickleys
A Tassel on the Corn behind Anteleys house

This has been a most disastrous Year, no rain of consequence but twice, and those light showers —

Result of the Year 1850

Corn

Lot back of Antellys	1 & ½ Loads
Over the big Lake	4
Next to Pine[y] Island	2
Over the Rail Road	10½
Next Murphys	14
Morris Cut	9
Long field	14½
Jennings house field	7½
" Barn do	10½

Loads	73½
Peas		10
Rice	"	10
Potatoes		15 banks
Cotton		65 bales
Sugar		1 Barrel

ACCOUNT BOOK & RECEIPTS

1847

Decem 6th	50 lb Bacon, From G. H. Walter & Co	
Jany 21st	18 yards Bagging 30 lb Rope " "	
Feby 22	154 lb Bacon @ 12¢	$18.48
"	1 Barrell Flour	11.00
"	Freight & Drayage	1.75
		$31.23

March 7th	4 Bags Corn 10.B @ 1.40 $14.00	
"	6 Bags Oats—24 Bushels @ 90	21.60
"	Freight & Drayage	3.65
		$39.25
March 25	11 Bags Corn 22 Bushels @ 1.38	30.36
"	1 One sack Salt	2.00
"	Freight & Drayage	3.05
		$35.41
April 9th	(504) lb Bacon 11¾¢	59.22
"	Freight & Drayage	4.25
		$63.47

Mar 18   Sale 3 B'/C By G. H. W & Co
By Geo A Hopley & Co   For 2 B'/C
R 2 347,365   739 lb @ 30. $221.70

" 21   By P. Fogarty 1 B'/C
R 1   144   144 lbs @ 25. $36.00

$257.70

Charges
Freight & Drayage 75   825
Weigh 8   30 Storage 1.50   180
Ins. ct 1.28 Rev Tax 25.84   27.12
   Commission 2½%   1.44   43.64

214.09
Less 75th on a/c W. G. Simms at 25¢   14.29

$799.80

INDEX

Since the final volume of the *Letters* will contain an index of all volumes, this index is designed for temporary use only. It consists merely of two types of entries: the titles of Simms' published volumes, and the names of people and firms mentioned by Simms in his letters. All references to these, both in the letters and in footnotes, are listed. The titles of books by writers other than Simms are not given, though in each case an entry is made under the name of the author or editor. Women are indexed under their married names, with their maiden names given if possible. There are no analyses of entries, and there is no entry under William Gilmore Simms.

When the most complete identification of a person is not on the first page referred to after his name, that page which does contain it is given first parenthetically; frequently this reference is to the first volume of the *Letters*.